INTERNATIONAL RELATIONS THEORY

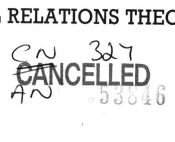

D0413633

International Relations Theory

Realism, Pluralism, Globalism

Second Edition

Paul R. Viotti
Mark V. Kauppi

MACMILLAN PUBLISHING COMPANY
New York

MAXWELL MACMILLAN CANADA
Toronto

Editor: Robert Miller and Bruce Nichols
Production Supervisor: Sharon Lee
Production Manager: Sandra E. Moore
Text Designer: Tash Sylvester
Cover Designer: Proof Positive/Farrowlyne Associates, Inc.

This book was set in Century Expanded and Rockwell Light by Digitype, Inc. and was printed and bound by Book Press, Inc. The cover was printed by New England Book Components, Inc.

Macmillan Publishing Company
866 Third Avenue, New York, New York 10022

Macmillan Publishing Company is part of the Maxwell Communication Group of Companies.

Maxwell Macmillan Canada, Inc.
1200 Eglinton Avenue East
Suite 200
Don Mills, Ontario M3C 3N1

Library of Congress Cataloging-in-Publication Data

Viotti, Paul R.
    International relations theory : realism, pluralism, globalism /
Paul R. Viotti, Mark V. Kauppi. — 2nd ed.
        p.   cm.
    Includes bibliographical references and index.
    ISBN 0-02-423021-9 (pbk.)
    1. International relations.   I. Kauppi, Mark V.   II. Title.
JX1391.V57   1993
327 — dc20   92-14320
                                                                  CIP

Printing: 2 3 4 5 6 7   Year: 3 4 5 6 7 8 9

Preface to the First Edition

Numerous works are designed to introduce the student to international relations and world politics.* Some are thematic, with chapters devoted to such topics as diplomacy, the making and implementation of foreign policy, the arms race, international organization, transnationalism, interdependence, and the management of global resources. Other works are encyclopedic in nature, a veritable "who's who" in the field, providing brief summaries of writers and approaches from ancient times to the present. Each approach has its place, and both serve important purposes.

This book takes a different approach. We make no claim to have covered every topic in the field, much less every writer or scholarly contributor. We do have four major purposes: (1) to discuss the underlying assumptions and images that influence scholarly work in the international relations field — images that we label *realism, pluralism,* and *globalism;* (2) to provide in the chapters and readings representative samples of theoretical works; (3) to introduce to the upper-division and graduate student key concepts used by scholars in their study of international relations; and (4) to encourage the student to scrutinize critically works dealing with international politics.

The fourth purpose is of particular importance. If a student leaves the classroom better equipped to analyze everyday events, to ask the right questions, to recognize underlying assumptions of written works by academics, government officials, and journalists, this would transcend any achievements made in memorizing which author is associated with what theory. Although we have attempted to avoid overwhelming the reader with names, particular authors are mentioned when it is necessary to highlight a critical concept, debate, trend, or theory. Important concepts in each chapter are highlighted in boldface type and are found in the glossary.

We fully recognize the problem of generalizing about a particular image of international relations when very often there are varying perspectives within any one image. Where such schisms exist, we attempt to point them out. Given the length of this book, it is impossible to cover every shade of opinion, every theoretical variation, or every point of contention, let alone every well-known scholar of international relations. Some readers may object because we have not discussed certain theorists, whereas other may disagree with our interpretation of a particular work. This is to be expected in an enterprise of this nature. We provide a broad overview of the field by presenting the three basic images, allowing pro-

---

*Although distinctions can be drawn between the terms *international relations* and *world politics* (or international *relations* and international *politics*) and different scholars do have different preferences in this regard, we use the terms interchangeably throughout this book.

fessors to concentrate on an area of the discipline they find to be of particular interest and importance.

It is appropriate at the outset to comment on our own biases. We believe in the possibility and necessity of explaining the world around us and that a rigorous social science should be the goal of scholars of international relations. Although different methods may be used, the goal of scholarly research should be to increase our understanding of how the world functions and is interpreted by human beings. To deny the possibility of explanation is to deny the relevancy of the works discussed in this book. We also contend, as do E. H. Carr and others, that values are relevant to the study of international relations. In our view there is a need for normative theory that can be a guide for policy choice. Empirical theory and normative theory operate in separate domains, but each has a role to play.

The idea for this book resulted from a conversation between the authors in 1982 as they strolled through the grounds of Schloss Solitud, located outside Stuttgart, Germany. The topic of discussion was the perennial problem of presenting to our students — in a relatively coherent manner — a significant portion of the vast amount of literature that comprises the international relations discipline. After several years of classroom experimentation and numerous other conversations between the authors, the result is this textbook. We would therefore like to thank our former students and colleagues who provided important feedback, insights, and criticisms.

We would also like to thank a number of individuals who commented on earlier drafts of various chapters: James Caporaso, James Dixon, Michael Dziedzic, Karen Feste, Schuyler Foerster, Kenneth Kemp, George Modelski, R. Craig Nation, Joseph Rallo, J. David Singer, Douglas T. Stuart, William Tow, Malham Wakin, Kenneth Wenker, and David Wessels. Thanks also to those individuals who reviewed sections of the manuscript that deal with their work: Graham Allison, Ernst Haas, Robert Jervis, Henry Kissinger, James Rosenau, and Kenneth Waltz. We would also like to acknowledge James L. Busey and Douglas J. Murray for their suggestions and encouragement. As for any errors of fact, interpretation, or conceptualization, the authors of this textbook accept full responsibility.

Preface to the Second Edition

In the five years since the first edition of this book was published, stunning changes have occurred in the world. The same cannot be said for international relations theory, a field of inquiry in which there have not been comparable advances in our understanding of world politics. One can argue that this lack of theoretical breakthroughs is oddly reassuring — perhaps works from the 1970s and 1980s dealing with topics such as balance of power, regimes, and the world-capitalist system have provided a sufficient number of conceptual frameworks and hypotheses to allow scholars to make sense of what has happened and engage in informed speculation. On the other hand, it can be argued that one recent trend in world politics — the proliferation of new states in Europe — runs counter to earlier expectations. There continues to be a tremendous and growing diversity with respect to what should be studied and how it should be studied. For some this is a cause of despair, for others celebration.

Whatever the case may be, such diversity encourages the delineation of various images, paradigms, perspectives, or other meta-theoretical frameworks in an attempt to help the student make some sense of the literature. Such delineation was one of the initial reasons we felt a book such as this would be useful. In the words of a former professor of ours, the field suffers from excessive differentiation and a lack of integration. In writing this textbook and selecting articles, we were also guided by the aphorism of not mistaking obscurity for profundity. Any book should aim for clarity of presentation, which does not mean simplifying difficult concepts and ideas to the point of distortion, but rather attempting to make them intelligible. Finally, we heeded the advice of a number of friends and colleagues who cautioned us against making sweeping changes in the text, or attempting to turn it into an encyclopedia of international relations theory. We wish to thank, in particular, Joseph Lepgold, Georgetown University; Timothy Lomperis, Duke University; and Dale Smith, Florida State University.

CONTENTS

3   PLURALISM: DECISION MAKING, TRANSNATIONALISM, AND INTERDEPENDENCE   228

To Linda and Kathleen

Theory, Images, and International Relations: An Introduction

Why do wars occur? Is nationalism the primary cause? Or ideology? Or the lack of world government? Or misperception? Or are people innately aggressive? How can stability (if not peace) be achieved? Why is there such tremendous social and economic inequality between different regions of the world? These are the sorts of questions that have preoccupied scholars and statesmen at various times over the millenia, whether the political entity in question were an ancient city-state or a modern nation-state, a centralized empire or a decentralized feudal system, a socialist or a liberal democratic society. Nor are these questions the private preserve of intellectuals, diplomatic practitioners, and assorted political pundits and commentators. At one time or another, most citizens reflect on one or more of these important queries.

The discipline of **international relations** addresses such questions. Despite the adjective *international*, the field is concerned with much more than relations between or among states. Other actors, such as international organizations, multinational corporations, and terrorist groups, are now all part of what could more correctly be termed **world politics**. Studies have also focused on factors internal to a state, such as bureaucratic governmental coalitions, interest groups, presidents, and politburos. The discipline ranges from balance of power politics and economic structures at the international level to the ideological and perceptual predispositions of individual leaders.

Given the tremendous diversity and complexity of *what* is studied, it is not too surprising that there is a multiplicity of views concerning *how* one studies international relations. The possible avenues go well beyond the realms of history and political science. They now include economics, psychology, social psychology, sociology, and anthropology. All this may seem rather intimidating to the student. If it is any consolation, it can also be intimidating to the professional in the field. As a result, many professionals tend to focus on one particular aspect of international relations, perhaps the foreign policy of the United States, the functioning of the United Nations and other international organizations, or decision making in crisis situations.

No matter how ambitious or modest an international relations research project may be, however, every scholar approaches it from a particular point of view. Although some would argue that values ought to be central, most academics strive (or at least claim to strive) to reduce the impact of personal values when it comes to **empirical** research. Nevertheless, personal background and the nature of academic training inevitably influence the manner in which scholars interpret and examine international relations. As the German scholar Max Weber once argued: "All knowledge of cultural reality is always knowledge from particular points of view." How research is conducted will be "determined by the evaluative ideas that dominate the investigator and his age."[1] In other words, each individual's work will be influenced by a particular doctrine, image of the world, ideology, paradigm, or perspective. One may strive to be value free and objective, but at best these goals can be achieved only imperfectly.

Different perspectives on international relations naturally generate debates. In the 1930s **realists** and **idealists** argued over the nature of international politics and the possibility of peaceful change. In the 1960s the so-called second great debate between **traditionalists** and **behavioralists** dealt with the question of appropriate **methodology**. Traditionalists emphasized the relative utility of history, law, philosophy, and other traditional methods of inquiry. Behavioralists argued in favor of social science conceptualization, quantification of variables, formal hypothesis testing, and causal model building. **Dialectical** approaches drawing on history and Marxist insights have been the subject of much discussion in certain journals in the field, although this debate is not widely reflected in the textbook literature. More recently, **critical theory** perspectives have raised doubts about the **epistemological** and **ontological** assumptions underlying much of the social science work on international relations, generating what could be termed another great debate.

In this book we deal with three alternative images or perspectives of international relations we label **realism, pluralism,** and **globalism.** Our depiction of the international relations field in terms of these three images compares in some respects to a categorization devised by James N. Rosenau: state-centric, multicentric, and global-centric approaches to international politics.[2] We argue that these images have provided the basis for the development of theoretical works that attempt to explain various aspects of international relations. The image that one has of international relations is of critical importance. Each image contains certain assumptions about world politics — whether or not explicitly recognized by the researcher — concerning critical actors, issues, and processes in world politics. These images lead one to ask certain questions, seek certain types of answers, and use certain methodological tools in the construction and testing of hypotheses and theories. The advantage is that such images bring order to the analytical effort and make it more manageable. A potential disadvantage, however, is that alternative perspectives and insights may be ignored or overlooked. Although the realist, pluralist, and globalist images are not mutually exclusive in all respects, the differences in point of view and emphasis are much greater than any apparent similarities. The resultant attempts at theory building, therefore, also vary considerably.

In this chapter we first address the question of what is meant by the term *theory*. We then briefly discuss the three images as alternative perspectives that influence the construction of international relations **theory**.

WHAT IS THEORY?

The word *theory* means different things to different people. It may even mean different things to the same person. In common parlance, for example, something may be true "in theory" but not in fact or in a particular case or set of circumstances. In this rather loose usage, "in theory" equates to "in principle" or "in the abstract."

Another meaning, somewhat more consistent with usage in this volume, is theory as the task of making the world or some part of it more intelligible or better understood. Theories dealing with international relations usually aspire to achieve this goal. Making things more intelligible may, of course, amount to nothing more than better or more precise *description* of the things we observe. Although accurate description is essential, theory is something more.

For many people, theory is *explaining* or *predicting*. One goes beyond mere description of phenomena observed and engages in **causal** explanation or prediction based on certain prior occurrences or conditions. Thus, whenever A is present, then B can be expected to follow. "If A, then B" as hypothesis may be subject to empirical test—that is, tested against real-world or factual data. "If states engage in arms races, then the likelihood of war increases" is an example of such a hypothesis. Indeed, formal statement and testing of hypotheses through the use of a statistical methodology is seen by many as central to the theory-building process. Others prefer to rely on nonquantitative case and comparative case studies, historical methods, and reasoned argument—the so-called traditional methods of theory building.

War is an example of a topic of considerable theoretical concern among international relations theorists using a wide variety of methodological approaches to developing better causal theory. Quincy Wright's *A Study of War* was a pioneering effort. Kenneth Waltz's *Man, the State and War* examined causes in the context of three **levels of analysis**. Since the 1960s, J. David Singer and others sharing his preference for formal hypothesis testing through the use of statistical methods have been engaged extensively in studying the phenomenon of war. Bruce Bueno de Mesquita's *The War Trap* is an example of another work in this continuing effort to gain a better understanding of war by building better theory.[3]

One view is that the underlying cause of war is the absence of any world government or central authority vested with the capability to enforce rules, settle disputes, and maintain peace among states. It is this **anarchy** or lack of common government that poses no obstacle and thus permits war to occur. As such, anarchy is the *permissive* cause of war.[4] Misperception may be the immediate or direct cause of a given war. Or, by contrast, war may break out not so much as the result of misperception or misunderstanding but because of the hardheaded, rational calculation that the benefits of going to war appear to outweigh the costs.

Theory in a stronger or more formal sense will go beyond proposing the cause of war in such broad terms and will insist that the relations among variables be clearly specified and weighted with the precision one finds in an algebraic equation or set of related equations.[5] Such fully developed theory is not common to the social sciences, which are often said to be at a lesser level of progress than are the natural sciences.

General theories that would provide a complete account of the causes of war are less common than *partial,* or *middle-range* theories that are more modest in the scope of what is to be explained or predicted. Part of the war puzzle addressed by such middle-range theorists, for example, involves crises and decision making in crises. Are partial theories about such things as crisis decision making like building blocks that can at some future date be assembled into a fully developed, general theory of war? Some theorists would say yes and that the most productive enterprise for the present is the development of better middle-range theories. Not everyone would agree; some would argue that formulating general theory comes first, with partial theories being deduced or flowing from it. What virtually everyone would agree upon, however, is that the best theories are parsimonious —meaning they explain a great deal utilizing only a few basic assumptions and variables. Furthermore, the best theories are also progressive — meaning they lead researchers to ask new and interesting questions.

The world of theory is an abstract one. Theories may exist apart from facts. Mathematical theorists, for example, deal entirely in the realm of abstraction, whether or not their work has direct relevance to problems of the world in which we live. Practical application for the work of mathematical theorists is sometimes found years later, if ever. Empirical theories in the social or natural sciences, by contrast, relate to facts and provide explanation or prediction for observed phenomena. Hypotheses associated with these theories are subject to test against real-world data or facts. The theorist need not have any purpose in developing such empirical theories other than satisfying his or her intellectual curiosity, although many will seek to make their work "policy relevant."[6]

An important point to keep in mind, however, is that attempts at theory building are focused on explaining and predicting *general* trends or phenomena, such as the conditions under which war is most likely to occur. The theoretical enterprise is *not* devoted to attempting to predict on what day Country *X* will attack Country *Y*. To state it in simple language, theorists are interested in the forest, not in particular trees. As Thomas Aquinas wrote in the 13th century, "the slenderest knowledge that may be obtained of the highest things is more desirable than the most certain knowledge obtained of lesser things."[7]

Policy-relevant theories may have explicit purposes that stem from the value preferences of the theorist, such as reducing the likelihood of war or curbing the arms race. Acting on such theories, of course, is the domain of the policymaker, a task separate from that of the empirical theorist. Theorists who become policymakers may well make choices informed by what theories say will be the likely outcomes of implementing one or another alternative. Their choices may be informed by empirical theory or understanding of world events, but the decisions they make are still based on value preferences.

Normative theory deals precisely with values and value preferences. Unlike empirical theory, however, propositions in normative theory are not subject to empirical test as a means of establishing their truth or falsehood. Normative theory deals not with what *is*, the domain of empirical theory. Rather, normative theory deals explicitly with what *ought* to be — the way the world should be ordered and the value choices decision makers *should* make. Although the bulk of the effort in this volume is allocated to empirical theory within the context of separate images of world politics, we consider normative theory to be an important and policy-relevant, if often neglected, enterprise. Chapter Five deals explicitly with normative theories relevant to international relations and foreign policy choices. We also identify normative preferences often associated with the three images of international relations theory that are at the core of our effort.

ALTERNATIVE IMAGES

This section provides an overview of the two most striking or immediately apparent distinctions among the three images of international relations under consideration: (1) the key *actors*, or *units*, and (2) the *assumptions* made about them. In the succeeding chapters we go well beyond this brief examination of actors and underlying assumptions. The discussion of realism, for example, focuses on the concepts of power and the balance of power, the chapter on pluralism emphasizes decision making and transnationalism, and the treatment of globalism stresses the concept of dependency in a world capitalist context. We also discuss the intellectual precursors of these images, and philosophical and conceptual issues such as **determinism, voluntarism, system,** and system change. Although normative assumptions and implications of the three images are treated explicitly in Chapter Five, they are also woven throughout the discussion in earlier chapters.

We begin this introductory overview with a discussion of *realism*. As will become apparent, proponents of the other two perspectives have to a certain degree been forced to come to terms with this long-established tradition. Indeed, many of their arguments are addressed directly to the strengths and weaknesses of work by realists.

Realism — Major Actors and Assumptions

Realism is based on four key assumptions. First, *states are the principal or most important actors*. States represent the key **unit of analysis**, whether one is dealing with ancient Greek city-states or modern nation-states. The study of international relations is the study of relations among these units. Realists who use the concept of system defined in terms of interrelated parts usually refer to an international system of states. What of nonstate actors? International organizations such as the United Nations may aspire to the status of independent actor, but from the realist perspective this aspiration in fact has not been achieved to any significant degree. Multinational corporations, terrorist groups, and other transnational and international organizations are frequently acknowledged by realists, but the position of these nonstate actors is always one of lesser importance. States are the dominant actors.

Second, the state is viewed as a *unitary actor*. For purposes of analysis, realists view the state as being encapsulated by a metaphorical hard shell. A country faces the outside world as an integrated unit. A common assumption associated with realist thought is that political differences within the state are ultimately resolved authoritatively such that the government of the state speaks with one voice for the state as a whole. The state is a unitary actor in that it is usually assumed by realists to have one policy at any given time on any particular issue. To be sure, exceptions occur from time to time, but to the realists these are exceptions that demonstrate the rule and that actually support the general notion of the state as an integrated, unitary actor.

Even in those exceptional cases in which, for example, a foreign ministry expresses policies different from policy statements of the same country's defense ministry, corrective action is taken in an attempt to bring these alternative views to a common and authoritative statement of policy. "End running" of state authorities by bureaucratic and nongovernmental, domestic, and transnational actors is also possible, but it occurs unchecked by state authorities in only those issues in which the stakes are low. From the realist perspective, if the issues are important enough, higher authorities will intervene to preclude bureaucratic end running or action by nongovernmental actors that are contrary to centrally directed policy.

Third, given this emphasis on the unitary state-as-actor, realists usually make the further assumption that *the state is essentially a rational actor*. A rational foreign policy decision-making process would include a statement of objectives, consideration of all feasible alternatives in terms of existing capabilities available to the state, the relative likelihood of attaining these objectives by the various alternatives under consideration, and the benefits or costs associated with each alternative. Following this rational process, governmental decision makers evaluate each alternative, selecting the one that maximizes utility (maximizing benefit or minimizing cost associated with attaining the objectives sought).

As a practical matter, the realist is aware of the difficulties in viewing the state as a rational actor. Governmental decision makers may not have all the factual information or knowledge of cause and effect they need to make value-maximizing decisions. The process may well be clouded by considerable uncertainty as decision makers grope for the best solution. They also have to deal with the problem of human bias and misperception that may lead them astray. In any event, the choice made — if not always the *best* or value-maximizing choice in fact — is at least perceived to be a satisfactory one. It is a **satisficing** or suboptimal choice — less than a value-maximizing choice, but still good enough in terms of the objectives sought. The assumption of the unitary, rational actor is particularly important in **game theory** and many works on **deterrence** theory.

Fourth, realists assume that within the hierarchy of international issues, *national security* usually tops the list. Military and related political issues dominate world politics. A realist focuses on actual or potential conflict between state actors, examining how international stability is attained or maintained, how it breaks down, the utility of force as a means to resolve disputes, and the prevention of the violation of territorial integrity. **Power**, therefore, is a key concept. To the realist, military security or strategic issues are sometimes referred to as **high politics**, whereas economic and social issues are viewed as less important or **low politics**. Indeed, the former is often understood to dominate or set the environment within which the latter occurs.

Pluralism — Major Actors and Assumptions

The pluralist image consists of a different set of assumptions. First, *nonstate actors* are important entities in international relations that cannot be ignored. International organizations, for example, can be independent actors in their own right. The organization's own decision makers, bureaucrats, and other associated groups have considerable influence in areas such as agenda setting — determining which issues are most important politically. International organizations are more than simply arenas within which sovereign states compete. Organizational power and autonomy are neither absolute nor nonexistent but something in between, varying from organization to organization. Similarly, other nongovernmental actors, such as multinational corporations (MNCs), cannot be dismissed merely as being of only marginal importance, given an increasingly **interdependent** world economy. Indeed, in some cases they are even capable of circumventing the authority of the state.

Second, for the pluralist, *the state is not a unitary actor*. Indeed, the realist view of the state as unitary actor is an abstraction that masks the essence of politics that is found principally within the state. The state is not some **reified** entity — an abstraction to be treated as if it were a physical being that acts with single-minded determination, always in a coherent manner. It is, rather, composed of individual bureaucracies, interest groups, and individuals that attempt to formulate or influence foreign policy. Competition, coalition building, conflict, and compromise among these actors are the stuff of politics. To speak of "U.S. foreign policy" is really to speak of a number of foreign policy decisions determined by competition among a number of actors. Pluralists disaggregate the state — break it into its component parts. They reject the notion of the state as an integrated entity, impermeable to outside forces. Both governmental and nongovernmental actors pass through this soft outer shell, sometimes taking actions with policy implications contrary to preferences of central state authorities. These are not just exceptional cases from the pluralist perspective. In fact, focusing on the state as if it were a unitary actor again misses the essence of politics. This is not only in terms of interactions *within* the state; equally important, it is the **trans-**

national dimension of state and nonstate actors that operates *across* national borders. The pluralist image thus offers greater complexity than the relatively simpler image of states as unitary actors interacting with one another.

Third, pluralists *challenge* the utility of the realist assumption of *the state as rational actor*. This follows logically from the pluralist image of the disaggregated state in which the foreign policy decision-making process is the result of clashes, bargaining, and compromise between and among different actors. In some cases, a particular policy may be suggested in order to enhance the bureaucratic power, prestige, and standing of one organization at the expense of others. Although this may seem rational from the perspective of an individual bureaucracy, it can lead to poor, if not disastrous, foreign policies. The pursuit of individual, value-maximizing strategies at the organization level can lead to collective disaster at the nation-state level. Moreover, the decision-making process is typically one of coalition and countercoalition building, bargaining, and compromising that may not yield a best or optimal decision. Attempting to establish a consensus or at least a **minimum winning coalition** is a process far different in kind from the earlier simple description of what is usually meant by the term **rational**. Misperception on the part of decision makers as a result of incomplete information, bias, stress, and uncertainty about cause and effect is also a key focus of attention for some pluralist scholars. All such factors undercut the idea of a rational decision-making process.

Finally, for the pluralist, *the agenda of international politics is extensive*. The pluralist rejects the notion that the agenda of international politics is dominated primarily by military-security issues. Foreign affairs agendas have expanded and diversified over recent decades such that economic and social issues are often at the forefront of foreign policy debates. Former Secretary of State Henry Kissinger, himself a realist, noted in 1975 that

> progress in dealing with the traditional agenda is no longer enough. A new and unprecedented kind of issue has emerged. The problems of energy, resources, environment, pollution, the uses of space and the seas now rank with questions of military security, ideology, and territorial rivalry which have traditionally made up the diplomatic agenda.[8]

Not surprisingly, such a statement was made at a time of détente or relatively relaxed tensions between East and West. It may be that as international tensions decrease, economic and social, or **welfare**, issues tend to come to the forefront of international debate.

Globalism — Major Actors and Assumptions

Globalism, as we use the term, is a third perspective, fundamentally different from both the realist and the pluralist images. In the 1970s, debate within the international relations discipline tended to focus on the realists and pluralists. Only recently has attention been paid to the globalist perspective. Globalists typically assume that the starting point of analysis for international relations is *the global context within which states and other entities interact*. Globalists emphasize the overall structure of the international system or, more colloquially, the "big picture." To explain behavior, one must first grasp the essence of the global environment within which such behavior takes place. This is a dominant theme within the globalist image, although some realists and pluralists also share this perspective. To understand the external behavior of states requires more than merely examining factors internal to a state. One must first grasp how the structure of the system conditions and predisposes certain actors to act in certain ways.

Second, globalists assume that it is not only useful but also imperative to *view international relations from a historical perspective*. It is only through an examination of history that one can understand the current environment within which world politics takes place. For many globalists, Marxists as well as non-Marxists, the defining characteristic of the international system is that it is **capitalist**. This requires the study of the rise of capitalism as it emerged in sixteenth-century Western Europe, its development, changes, and expansion to the point at which today we can speak of a **world capitalist system** that conditions and constrains the behavior of all states and societies. Some states and societies benefit from this capitalist system; others do not. Furthermore, the evolution of the world capitalist system supposedly accounts for the creation of states, not just their behavior. While realists and pluralists tend to see states as a given, utilizing them as *independent variables*, some globalists view states as *dependent* variables—that which is to be explained.

Third, although globalists recognize the importance of states-as-actors, international organizations, and transnational actors and coalitions, the particular focus of their analysis is on how these and other factors act as *mechanisms of domination* by which some states, classes, or elites manage to benefit from this capitalist system at the expense of others. More specifically, globalists are typically concerned with the development and maintenance of **dependency** relations among northern, industrialized states (in North America, Europe, Japan) and the poor, underdeveloped, or industrially backward Third World or less developed countries (LDCs) of Latin America, Africa, and Asia. The basic argument is that these latter states and societies are underdeveloped not because they have failed to develop capitalist economic systems or because they are poorly integrated into the world capitalist system. On the contrary, it is not a matter of too little capitalism but too much. Far from being placed outside the mainstream of the world capitalist system, LDCs have become an integral part of it. The structure of the global political economy has developed in such a manner—intentionally and unintentionally—as to keep the Third World countries underdeveloped and dependent on the rich northern states. The LDCs play a crucial role in the economic well-being of such countries as the United States by providing cheap labor, raw materials necessary to fuel the American economy, and markets for American manufactured goods. As part of the world capitalist system, LDCs cannot choose their own path toward economic and political development. Autonomous development in these circumstances is not possible.

Finally, as should now be apparent, globalists emphasize to a greater extent than either realists or pluralists the critical *importance of economic factors* when

TABLE 1.1   Alternative Images of International Relations:
Underlying Assumptions

	Realism	Pluralism	Globalism
Analytic Unit(s)	1. State is the principal actor	1. State and nonstate actors are important	1. Classes, states, and societies, and nonstate actors operate as part of world capitalist system
View of Actor(s)	2. State is unitary actor	2. State disaggregated into components, some of which may operate transnationally	2. International relations viewed from historical perspective, especially the continuous development of world capitalism
Behavioral Dynamic	3. State is rational actor seeking to maximize its own interest or national objectives in foreign policy	3. Foreign policymaking and transnational processes involve conflict, bargaining, coalition, and compromise — not necessarily resulting in optimal outcomes	3. Focus is on patterns of dominance within and among societies
Issues	4. National security issues are most important	4. Multiple agenda with socioeconomic or welfare issues as, or more, important than national security questions	4. Economic factors are most important

it comes to explaining the dynamics of the international system. Realists, you will
recall, subordinate economic factors to those of a political-military nature. Pluralists argue that this is an open question; they typically reject this high versus
low politics dichotomy. Social and economic issues to pluralists are at least as important as the security concerns of the realists. Globalists, however, start with
the assumption that economics is the key to understanding the creation, evolution, and functioning of the contemporary world system. Although the pluralist
and globalist would seem to share common ground because both place importance on economic and social questions, they differ fundamentally in the ways in
which they deal with them. The more fragmented pluralist image of multiple

actors bargaining, compromising, and building coalitions within and across national borders contrasts sharply with the structural image of the globalist. The globalist would tell a pluralist that the outcome of bargaining among various actors is in most cases predetermined if it involves a **North – South** issue. Such interactions take place within the context of an exploitative and dependent relation that works, at the most general level, to the benefit of maintaining the world capitalist system and, more specifically, to the benefit of particular groups or classes.

Images of International Relations: Some Qualifications

We find the threefold division of realism, pluralism, and globalism to be a useful way to view the diverse images on which theoretical efforts are based in the field of international relations. We are the first to admit that this classification scheme also has its limitations. Accordingly, we offer several qualifications and clarifications.

First, each image should be viewed as an **ideal** or **pure type** in that each image emphasizes what a number of seemingly diverse theoretical approaches have in common.[9] For example, there are substantial differences in the works of Kenneth Waltz, Stanley Hoffmann, and the late Hans J. Morgenthau, but all three scholars share core assumptions of the realist perspective. What unites them as international relations theorists is more important for our purposes than what divides them.

Second, the overview of key assumptions of each of the three perspectives might give the impression that the three images are mutually exclusive in all respects. This is not the case. Realists such as Robert Gilpin, for example, do not deny the importance of economic factors in international relations; they simply differ with many pluralists and globalists as to the relative importance of political-military considerations compared to economic factors. Such globalists as Immanuel Wallerstein also recognize the significance of the state in international relations but prefer to emphasize economic trends and class relations. Similarly, many interdependence theorists of pluralist orientation do not deny the importance of the state as a key international actor, but they prefer to examine nonstate actors as well as transnational, socioeconomic factors that they see as having reduced the autonomy of the state-as-actor. Even if the three images are not mutually exclusive in every respect, and even if every observer of international relations can agree that sensitivity to alternative perspectives on world politics is commendable, the reader may want to keep in mind how difficult it is to combine three images with so very different underlying assumptions from which all subsequent analyses, hypotheses, and theories derive.

Third, we readily confess that not all international relations specialists can be assigned conveniently to one particular image. Bruce Russett, for example, has written on dependency, international integration, and conflict between states-as-actors — each subject associated, respectively, with globalist, pluralist, and realist images. Robert Jervis has bridged two camps in his pluralist examination of psychological factors in foreign policy decision making and in his realist focus on national security questions associated with deterrence, arms races, and how the anarchical international system provides the environment within which wars occur. Works by Robert O. Keohane and Joseph S. Nye recognize the importance of insights from realism as well as insights derived from the pluralist perspective with which both were earlier identified.

Although we believe that the vast majority of writers within the international relations discipline tends to be associated with one of the three perspectives, notable exceptions do not, in our estimation, undermine the utility of the tripartite division of the field that we employ in this volume. We acknowledge a certain amount of conceptual eclecticism by scholars in the study of international relations, perhaps reflecting the absence of a single, dominant perspective. For some, conceptual diversity is to be applauded; for others it is a source of despair. Be that as it may, our focus is primarily on ideas, trends, and generalized images of international relations and only secondarily on the work of particular authors. Indeed, our references to work in the international relations field are meant to be representative of the images we discuss, not encyclopedic in scope. Just as it is hoped that the reader will come to appreciate the strengths and weaknesses of each of the three perspectives, so too do many specialists in the field weigh the relative utility of these alternative images in generating insights helpful in answering particular theoretical questions they may be asking.[10] Moreover, it is not surprising to find a certain amount of conceptual eclecticism in the work of a number of theorists whose interests have changed over the years.[11]

Fourth, the images tend to focus more on *what* is studied than on *how* to conduct such studies. A central argument we make is that quantitative and nonquantitative approaches to the study of international politics are methods that transcend the three images we have identified. Statistical methods, formal hypothesis testing, and **causal modeling** find their adherents within each of the perspectives, as do the more traditional, nonquantitative, historical, philosophical, legal, case study, and comparative case study methods. Our point remains that these are *methods*, not images of international relations or world politics. Images may influence the choice of methods, but images and methods are not one and the same.

Although it has been the subject of endless debates and much bloodletting in academic circles, the behavioralist–traditionalist (or the "science"—traditionalist) dichotomy is not particularly useful for our purposes. One can argue over the relative merits of particular methods for answering political questions, but a more fundamental concern is the conceptual framework within which those methods are used. Are these methods informed by realist, pluralist, or globalist images of international politics, and how useful are these alternative images by which we order or make some sense of what we observe?[12]

Efforts to predict global futures through complex modeling, for example, reflect one or another of the three images we identify.[13] An image of international or world politics influences the selection of units or processes examined and **variables** identified and operationalized. Thus, for realists, states and state interactions are of key importance; for pluralists, transnational interactions to include communications flows across national borders may well be the central focus; and for globalists, patterns of class or North–South relations of dominance or dependence are perhaps most important.

Similarly, methods associated with the literature on **decision-making** and **public choice theory** — economic models applied to political decision making — transcend the three world images we identify.[14] Assumptions made about actors and processes are informed by realist, pluralist, and globalist images and color the use a particular method is given. Thus, **public or collective goods theory, game theory, econometrics**, and other approaches identified with the rapidly growing interdisciplinary field of **political economy** find their adherents among scholars holding diverse images and thus are not the exclusive preserve of realists, pluralists, or globalists.

Finally, we wish to state explicitly that the three images we identify are not *theories* of international relations.[15] Rather, they represent general perspectives on international relations out of which particular theories *may* develop. Assumptions of an image may become part of a theory (such as the realist assumptions of a unified, rational, state-as-actor in some realist works), but more often than not, they simply help to orient a scholar's research by highlighting certain units of analysis for investigation in the construction of a theory and help to determine what constitutes evidence in the testing of hypotheses.

THE LEVELS OF ANALYSIS

It is necessary to address further the question every scholar of international relations must first ask no matter what image or perspective one holds: Where should one focus his or her research efforts? Let us assume that we are rather ambitious and wish to explain the causes of war between states. Does one deal with individual decision makers or small groups of individuals engaged in the policy process? How important, for example, are such factors as the correctness of individual perceptions or bargaining skill in determining the decision to go to war? On the other hand, if one looks outside the individual or small decision-making group to the entire state apparatus, society as a whole, or the international political system of states, one is acknowledging the importance of external or environmental factors as well.

Work by Kenneth N. Waltz in the 1950s on the causes of war represented a path-breaking effort due to his identification of distinct **levels of analysis** and his attempt to specify the relations among these levels.[16] Was the cause of war to be found in the nature of individuals? (Are humans innately aggressive?) Or in the nature of states and societies? (Are some types of states more aggressive than others?) Or in the nature of the international system of states? Each answer reflects a different level of analysis — individual, state and society, or international (see Figure 1.1). Waltz's conclusion was that the *permissive* cause of war is the condition of anarchy in the international political system of states, whereas the *efficient* causes of any given war can be found as well at the other levels of analysis (individual or state and societal levels). Whether or not one agrees with his conclusion, the important point is that his analysis of the problem of war was at

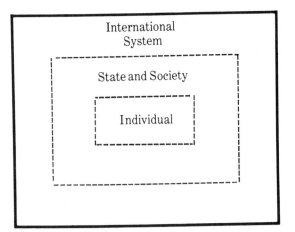

Figure 1.1 Levels of analysis

different levels. In 1961, the importance of the question of levels of analysis to the study of international relations was further discussed in detail in an often-cited article by J. David Singer. Singer argued that one's choice of a particular level of analysis determines what one will and will not see. Different levels tend to emphasize different actors and processes.[17]

For example, it is quite common for the levels of analysis to include (1) the international system (distribution of power among states, geography, technology, and other factors); (2) the state (often treated as a unified actor) and society (democratic, authoritarian, etc.); (3) bureaucratic politics; (4) individual psychology and social psychology. It is also quite typical for these various levels to be used to explain the foreign policy behavior of states — the **dependent** variable. The state, in other words, is often the **unit of analysis**, and explaining its behavior could entail taking into account factors at all of these levels of analysis.

But *which* level of analysis, one may ask, is most important? To take a specific example, let us assume that the foreign policies of most states exhibit relative constancy, or slowness to change. How is this constancy to be explained? Some scholars point to external factors such as the balance of power among states that is relatively slow to change in any major way. Others emphasize relatively constant factors within the state — the same decision makers or decision-making processes, with incremental or small changes being the rule.

Another example: How are arms races explained? Some scholars point to international factors such as the military expenditures and hostility of other states that lead to an increase in the production of weapons. Other researchers emphasize the importance of domestic factors such as bureaucratic competition between branches of the military services and budgetary processes that encourage a steady increase in expenditures.[18]

The easy answer to the question of which level of analysis should be emphasized is that all levels of analysis should be considered. Such a response is not particularly useful because it suggests that we have to study everything under the sun. Few scholars would even attempt such a task,[19] and the resulting theory would hardly be parsimonious. Hence, a great deal of the literature on international relations is constantly posing the questions of *what* should be examined *within* each level of analysis, and *how* actors, structures, and variables relate to one another across levels of analysis and over time.

This issue of levels of analysis also subtly pervades the three images. What have been termed **neorealists**, for example, emphasize how the overall structure of the international system influences the behavior of states or the perception of decision makers. Hence, neorealist analysis begins with the systems level. Similarly, certain globalists, as we have noted, examine how the historical development of the capitalist world economy generates state actors. Despite their differences, both neorealists and *world-system theorists* emphasize the systems level. Those authors associated with the pluralist image, however, who examine bureaucracies, interest groups, and individuals tend to emphasize the state-societal and individual levels of analysis.

There is a final important issue that should be mentioned in conjunction with the levels of analysis, but that goes well beyond the latter as it raises basic philosophy-of-science questions concerning the so-called *agent – structure* problem. As summarized by one author, the problem

> emerges from two uncontentious truths about social life: first, that human agency is the only moving force behind the actions, events, and outcomes of the social world; and second, that human agency can be realized only in concrete historical circumstances that condition the possibilities for action and influence its course. "People make history," observed Marx in an often-quoted aphorism, "but not in conditions of their own choosing." These truths impose two demands on our scientific explanations: first, that they acknowledge and account for the powers of agents; and second, that they recognize the causal relevance of "structural factors," that is, the conditions of action. The "agent – structure problem" refers to the difficulties of developing theory that successfully meets both demands."[20]

This problem is usually viewed as a matter of **ontology**, the branch of metaphysics concerned with the nature of being. In this case the ontological issue deals with the nature of both agents (very often viewed as the state) and structures (such as the international system), and relations between them. As we will see in the following chapters, a constant theme is how authors deal with the relative importance of human agents and "structural factors" or what we call the issue of **voluntarism** and **determinism**. Very often unstated, one's position on this issue heavily influences how one goes about explaining international politics as well as assessing the possibilities and means of peaceful change.

SUMMATION

For the realist, states are the principal or most important actors on the international political stage and represent the key unit of analysis. States are viewed as unitary actors that behave in a generally rational manner. National security issues dominate the hierarchy of the international agenda. For the pluralist, by contrast, nonstate actors are also important entities. The state is disaggregated into its component parts and is continually subjected to outside elements, including state as well as nonstate actors. The hierarchy of world issues is also subject to change and is not always dominated by matters of military security. For the globalist, all actors must be viewed within the context of an overarching global structure. The defining characteristic of this structure is its capitalist nature; it must be viewed in a historical context with a particular emphasis on the role of dominant classes that transcend the particular confines of any one state. To understand the mechanisms of dependency whereby rich, industrialized states maintain poor LDCs in a subordinate position within this world capitalist system requires an appreciation of the paramount role played by economic factors.

We now turn to a more comprehensive discussion of the three images of international relations, giving in subsequent chapters summaries of major actors and assumptions, intellectual precursors and influences, key concepts and representative theoretical works, and criticisms.

NOTES

1. Max Weber, *Methodology of the Social Sciences*, trans. and ed. E. A. Shils and H. A. Finch (New York: Free Press, 1949), pp. 81, 84.
2. James N. Rosenau, "Order and Disorder in the Study of World Politics," in *Globalism Versus Realism: International Relations' Third Debate*, ed. Ray Maghroori and Bennett Ramberg (Boulder, CO: Westview Press, 1982), pp. 1–7. Such categorizations are increasingly popular, in part reflecting a desire to bring some degree of order to the theoretical chaos of the field.
3. Quincy Wright, *A Study of War* (Chicago: University of Chicago Press, 1942); Kenneth N. Waltz, *Man, the State and War* (New York: Columbia University Press, 1959); Bruce Bueno de Mesquita, *The War Trap* (New Haven, CT: Yale University Press, 1981).
4. Waltz, *Man, State, War*, pp. 232–38. Consistent with this view, anarchy is also a *necessary* condition for war to occur, but it is by no means *sufficient* as a sole cause of the phenomenon. The distinction between underlying and immediate causes of war can be traced back to Thucydides, a 5th century B.C. Greek historian.
5. For a discussion on how to approach the study of international conflict, see the articles by Bruce Bueno de Mesquita, Stephen Krasner, and Robert Jervis in *International Studies Quarterly* 29, no. 2 (June 1985): 121–54. Bueno de Mesquita in particular calls for the development of rigorous, deductive, axiomatic theory.
6. For arguments challenging the supposed ability to determine in an objective manner what constitutes "facts," let alone "the real world," see Richard J. Bernstein, *The Restructuring of Social and Political Theory* (New York: Harcourt Brace Jovanovich, 1976).
7. As cited by John Mueller, *Retreat From Doomsday: The Obsolescence of Major War* (New York: Basic Books, 1989), p. xx. For one argument on the importance of developing "generic knowledge" about international relations, see Alexander L. George, "Is Research on Crisis Management Needed?" in *Avoiding War: Problems of Crisis Management*, ed. Alexander L. George (Boulder, CO.: Westview Press, 1991), p. 5. Cf. Kenneth N. Waltz, "Realist Thought and Neorealist Theory," *Journal of International Affairs*, 44, 1 (Spring/Summer 1990): 21–37.

8. Henry A. Kissinger, "A New National Partnership," *Department of State Bulletin*, 72 (17 February 1975): 199, cited in Robert O. Keohane and Joseph S. Nye, *Power and Interdependence: World Politics in Transition* (Boston: Little, Brown, 1977), p. 3.

9. On ideal types, see Weber, *Methodology*, pp. 90–93. Cf. Max Weber, *Basic Concepts in Sociology*, trans. H. P. Secher (Westport, CT: Greenwood Press, 1962, 1969), pp. 52–55.

10. Whether different images of the world lead to the formulation of different questions or whether the questions themselves have resulted in these different mental constructs for dealing with them is arguable and may depend on the particular theorist.

11. See, for example, articles in W. Ladd Hollist and James N. Rosenau, eds., *World System Structure: Continuity and Change* (Beverly Hills, CA: Sage Publications, 1981). It is one thing to produce a work that is purposely eclectic, drawing on insights from a wide variety of sources, but this is different from attempting to reconcile underlying assumptions reflecting fundamentally divergent perspectives on world politics without relaxing one or more of these critical assumptions. For attempts at reconciliation, see Joseph S. Nye, Jr., "Neorealism and Neoliberalism, *World Politics* 40, 2 (January 1988): 235–51; Richard K. Ashley, *The Political Economy of War and Peace* (London: Frances Pinter, 1980); Nazli Choucri and Robert C. North, *Nations in Conflict: National Growth and International Violence* (San Francisco: W. H. Freeman, 1975); Richard W. Mansbach and John A. Vasquez, *In Search of Theory: A New Paradigm for Global Politics* (New York: Columbia University Press, 1981). See also John Gerard Ruggie, "Continuity and Transformation in the World Polity: Toward a Neorealist Synthesis," *World Politics* 35, no. 2 (January 1983): 261–85; and Robert O. Keohane, "Theory of World Politics: Structural Realism and Beyond," paper presented at the 1982 meeting of the APSA, Denver, September 1982; reprinted in *Political Science: The State of the Discipline*, ed. Ada W. Finifter (Washington, DC: American Political Science Association, 1983), pp 503–40.

12. See the articles in Klaus Knorr and James N. Rosenau, eds., *Contending Approaches to International Politics* (Princeton, NJ: Princeton University Press, 1969). See also G. David Garson, "Marxism as Methodology," in his *Handbook of Political Science Methods*, 2d ed. (Boston: Holbrook Press, 1976), pp 9–20.

13. The dominant image among most world modelers, however, is a pluralist one informed by what Ashley calls "liberal positivist commitments." See Richard K. Ashley, "The Eye of Power: The Politics of World Modeling," *International Organization* 37, no. 3 (Summer 1983): 500.

14. See, for example, Bruno S. Frey, "The Public Choice View of International Political Economy," *International Organization* 38, no. 1 (Winter 1984): 199–223; Mancur Olson, *The Rise and Decline of Nations* (New Haven, CT: Yale University Press, 1982) and *The Logic of Collective Action* (Cambridge, MA: Harvard University Press, 1965). See also "Symposium: Mancur Olson on the Rise and Decline of Nations," *International Studies Quarterly* 27, no. 1 (March 1983): 3–37; and John A. C. Conybeare, "Public Goods, Prisoners' Dilemmas, and the International Political-Economy," *International Studies Quarterly* 28, no. 1 (March 1984): 5–22.

15. Nor are the images equivalent to the research program discussed by Imre Lakatos. Such a research program, if formulated for international relations, would be more specific than the images discussed in this book but more general than any particular theory we mention. See Imre Lakatos, "Falsification and the Methodology of Scientific Research Programmes," in *Criticism and the Growth of Knowledge*, ed. Imre Lakatos and Alan Musgrave (Cambridge: Cambridge University Press, 1970).

Lakatos is attempting to refute what he sees as the relativism of Thomas Kuhn's influential *The Structure of Scientific Revolutions* (Chicago: University of Chicago Press, 1962).

16. Kenneth N. Waltz, *Man, the State and War* (New York: Columbia University Press, 1959).

17. J. David Singer, "The Level-of-Analysis Problem in International Relations," in *International Politics and Foreign Policy*, ed. James N. Rosenau (New York: Free Press, 1969), pp. 20–29.

18. The literature of arms races is extensive. For reviews, see Urs Luterbacher, "Arms Race Models: Where Do We Stand?" *European Journal of Political Research*, 3, no. 2 (June 1975): 199–217, and Kendall D. Moll and Gregory M. Luebbert, "Arms Races and Military Expenditure Models: A Review," *Journal of Conflict Resolution* 24, no. 1 (March 1980): 153–85. A preliminary test of an external model of arms races is Thomas R. Cusack and Michael D. Ward, "Military Spending in the United States, Soviet Union, and the People's Republic of China," *Journal of Conflict Resolution*, 25, no. 3 (Septbember 1981): 429–69. See also Matthew Evangelista, *Innovation and the Arms Race* (Ithaca, N.Y.: Cornell University Press, 1988).

19. See, however, the series of books by Rudolph J. Rummel under the title *Understanding Conflict and War*. The first of the series is subtitled *The Dynamic Psychological Field* (Beverly Hills, CA: Sage Publications, 1975).

20. David Dessler, "What's at Stake in the Agent–Structure Debate?" *International Organization*, 43, 3 (Summer 1989): 443. See also Alexander E. Wendt, "The Agent–Structure Problem in International Relations Theory," *International Organization*, 41, 3 (Summer 1987): 335–70; John S. Dryzek, Margaret L. Clark, and Garry McKenzie, "Subject and System in International Interaction," *International Organization*, 43, 3 (Summer 1989): 475–504.

SUGGESTED READINGS

Newly added to this edition. Suggested readings from earlier works follow this more recent list.

Art, Robert, and Robert Jervis. *International Politics: Enduring Concepts and Contemporary Issues.* 3d ed. New York: Harper Collins, 1992.

Ashley, Richard K. "The Geopolitics of Geopolitical Space: Toward a Critical Social Theory of International Politics." *Alternatives* 12,4 (October 1987): 403–34.

Ashley, Richard K., and R. B. J. Walker, eds. *Speaking the Language of Exile: Dissidence in International Studies.* Special Issue of *International Studies Quarterly* 34,3 (September 1990): 259–417.

Bhaskar, Roy. *Scientific Realism and Human Emancipation.* London: Verso (New Left Books), 1986.

Biersteker, Thomas J. "Critical Reflections on Post-Positivism in International Relations." *International Studies Quarterly* 33,3 (September 1989): 263–67.

Carr, E. H. *What is History?* Harmondsworth, England: Penguin Books, 1964.

Coleman, James S. *Foundations of Social Theory.* Cambridge, MA: Harvard University Press, 1990.

Collin, Finn. *Theory and Understanding: A Critique of Interpretive Social Science.* Oxford, England: Blackwell, 1985.

Czempiel, Ernst-Otto and James N. Rosenau, eds. *Global Changes and Theoretical Challenges.* Lexington, Mass.: Lexington Books, 1989.

Derian, James, and Michael J. Shapiro, eds. *International/Intertextual Relations: Postmodern Readings of World Politics*. Lexington, MA: Lexington Books, 1989.

Dyer, Hugh C., and Leon Mangasarian, eds. *The Study of International Relations: The State of the Art*. New York: St. Martin's, 1989.

Ferguson, Yale H. and Richard W. Mansbach. "Between Celebration and Despair: Constructive Suggestions for Future International Theory." *International Studies Quarterly* 35,4 (December 1991): 363–496.

————. *The Elusive Quest: Theory and International Politics*. Columbia: University of South Carolina Press, 1988.

————. "The State, Conceptual Chaos, and the Future of International Relations Theory." Graduate School of International Studies Monograph Series, University of Denver. Boulder, CO: Lynne Rienner Publishers, 1989.

Elster, Jon. *The Cement of Society: A Study of Social Order*. New York: Cambridge University Press, 1989.

————. *Solomonic Judgements: Studies in the Limitations of Rationality*. New York: Cambridge University Press, 1989.

George, Jim. "International Relations and the Search for Thinking Space: Another View of the Third Debate." *International Studies Quarterly* 33,3 (September 1989): 269–79.

Giddens, Anthony. *Central Problems in Social Theory: Action, Structure and Contradiction*. Berkeley: University of California Press, 1979.

————. *Profiles and Critiques in Social Theory*. Berkeley: University of California Press, 1982.

Hindess, Barry. *Political Choice and Social Structure: An Analysis of Actors, Interests, and Rationality*. Brookfield, VT: Edward Elgar, 1989.

Hoffmann, Stanley. *Janus and Minerva: Essays in the Theory and Practice of International Politics*. Boulder, CO: Westview Press, 1987.

Holsti, K. J. "Mirror, Mirror on the Wall, Which are the Fairest Theories of All?" *International Studies Quarterly* 33,3 (September 1989): 255–61.

Karns, Margaret P., ed. *Persistent Patterns and Emergent Structures in a Waning Century*. New York: Praeger, 1986.

Kauppi, Mark V., and Paul R. Viotti. *The Global Philosophers: World Politics in Western Thought*. New York: Lexington/Macmillan, 1992.

Lapid, Yosef. "The Third Debate: On the Prospects of International Theory in a Post-Positivist Era." *International Studies Quarterly* 33,3 (September 1989): 235–54.

Laudan, Larry. *Science and Values: An Essay on the Aims of Science and Their Role in Scientific Debate*. Berkeley: University of California Press, 1982.

Leplin, Jarett, ed. *Scientific Realism*. Berkeley: University of California Press, 1984.

Light, Margot, and A. J. R. Groom, eds. *International Relations: A Handbook of Current Theory*. Boulder, CO: Lynne Rienner Publishers, 1985.

Linklater, Andrew. *Beyond Realism and Marxism: Critical Theory and International Relations*. New York: St. Martin's, 1990.

————. *Men and Citizens in the Theory of International Relations*. New York: St. Martin's Press, 1982.

Modelski, George. "Is World Politics Evolutionary Learning?" *International Organization* 44,1 (Winter 1990): 1–24.

Most, Benjamin A., and Harvey Starr. *Inquiry, Logic and International Politics*. Columbia: University of South Carolina Press, 1988.

Onuf, Nicholas G. *World of Our Making: Rules and Rule in Social Theory and International Relations*. Columbia: University of South Carolina Press, 1989.

Ordeshook, Peter C. *Game Theory and Political Theory.* Cambridge, England: Cambridge University Press, 1986.

Rothstein, Robert L. *The Evolution of Theory in International Relations.* Columbia: University of South Carolina Press, 1991.

Singer, J. David. *Models, Methods, and Progress in World Politics.* Boulder, CO: Westview Press, 1990.

Smith, Steve, ed. *International Relations: British and American Perspectives.* Oxford, England, and New York: Basil Blackwell, 1985.

Tsebelis, George. *Nested Games: Rational Choice in Comparative Politics.* Berkeley: University of California Press, 1989.

Wendt, Alexander E. "The Agent–Structure Problem in International Relations Theory." *International Organization* 41,3 (Summer 1987): 335–70.

SUGGESTED READINGS FROM THE FIRST EDITION

Agnew, Neil M., and Sandra W. Pyke. *The Science Game: An Introduction to Research in the Behavioral Sciences.* Englewood Cliffs, NJ: Prentice Hall, 1982.

Alker, Hayward R., Jr., and Thomas J. Biersteker. "The Dialectics of World Order: Notes for a Future Archeologist of International Savoir Faire." *International Studies Quarterly* 28, 2 (June 1984): 121–42.

Almond, Gabriel A., and Stephen J. Genco. "Clouds, Clocks, and the Study of Politics." *World Politics* 29, 4 (July 1977): 489–522.

Art, Robert J., and Robert Jervis, eds. *International Politics: Anarchy, Force, Political Economy, and Decision Making.* 2d ed. Boston: Little Brown, 1984.

Ashley, Richard K. "The Eye of Power: The Politics of World Modeling." *International Organization* 37,3 (Summer 1983): 495–535. A review essay.

Axelrod, Robert and Robert O. Keohane. "Achieving Cooperation Under Anarchy." *World Politics* 31,1 (October 1985): 226–54.

Banks, Michael. "Two Meanings of Theory in the Study of International Relations." *The Yearbook of World Affairs* 20 (1966): 220–40.

———. "Ways of Analyzing the World Society." In *International Relations: A Bibliography,* ed. A. J. R. Groom and Christopher R. Mitchell. London: Frances Pinter, 1978.

Bernstein, Richard. *The Restructuring of Social and Political Theory.* New York: Harcourt Brace Jovanovich, 1976.

Bronowski, Jacob. *The Origins of Knowledge and Imagination.* New Haven, CT: Yale University Press, 1978.

Bueno de Mesquita, Bruce, Stephen D. Krasner, and Robert Jervis. Articles in *International Studies Quarterly* 29,2 (June 1985): 121–49.

Connolly, William E. "Theoretical Self-Consciousness." *Polity* 2,1 (1973): 5–35.

Conybeare, John A. C. "Public Goods, Prisoners' Dilemmas and the International Political Economy." *International Studies Quarterly* 28, 1 (March 1984): 5–22.

Dougherty, James E., and Robert L. Pfaltzgraff, Jr. *Contending Theories of International Relations.* 3d ed. New York: Harper & Row, 1989.

Eulau, Heinz. "Multilevel Methods in Comparative Politics." *American Behavioral Scientist* 21, 1 (September/October 1977): 39–62.

Frey, Bruno S. "The Public Choice View of International Political Economy." *International Organization* 38, 1, (Winter 1984): 199–223.

Garson, G. David. *Handbook of Political Science Methods.* 2d ed. Boston: Holbrook Press, 1976.

Guetzkow, Harold, and Joseph J. Valadez, eds. *Simulated International Processes: Theories and Research in Global Modeling*. Beverly Hills, CA: Sage Publications, 1981.

Habermas, Jürgen. "Technology and Science as Ideology." In *Towards a Rational Society*. Translated by Jeremy Shapiro. London: Heinemann, 1970.

Heath, Anthony. *Rational Choice and Social Exchange*. Cambridge: Cambridge University Press, 1976.

Hettne, Bjorn. "Conceptions of the Present World Order in the Social Sciences." *Cooperation and Conflict* 16 (1981): 109–18.

Hoffmann, Stanley. *Contemporary Theory in International Relations*. Englewood Cliffs, NJ: Prentice Hall, 1960.

Holsti, K. J. *The Dividing Discipline*. Winchester, MA: Allen & Unwin, 1985.

Kaplan, Abraham. *The Conduct of Inquiry: Methodology for Behavioral Sciences*. New York: Harper & Row, 1964.

Keohane, Robert O., and Joseph S. Nye. *Power and Interdependence: World Politics in Transition*, Boston: Little, Brown, 1977.

Kindleberger, Charles P. "Dominance and Leadership in the International Economy: Exploitation, Public Goods, and Free Rides." *International Studies Quarterly* 25, 2 (June 1981):242–54.

———. "On the Rise and Decline of Nations." *International Studies Quarterly* 27, 1 (March 1983): 5–10. A review essay on Mancur Olson, *The Rise and Decline of Nations*.

Knorr, Klaus, and James N. Rosenau, eds. *Contending Approaches to International Politics*. Princeton, NJ: Princeton University Press, 1969.

Knorr, Klaus, and Sidney Verba, eds. *The International System: Theoretical Essays*. Princeton, NJ: Princeton University Press, 1969.

Kubalkova, Vendulka, and A. A. Cruickshank. *Marxism–Leninism and Theory of International Relations*. London: Routledge & Kegan Paul, 1980.

Kuhn, Thomas S. *The Structure of Scientific Revolutions*. Chicago: University of Chicago Press, 1962.

Lakatos, Imre. "Falsification and the Methodology of Scientific Research Programmes." In *Criticism and the Growth of Knowledge*, ed. Imre Lakatos and Alan Musgrave. Cambridge: Cambridge University Press, 1970.

Lauren, Paul Gordon. *Diplomacy: New Approaches in History, Theory, and Policy*. New York: Free Press, 1979.

Lieber, Robert J. *Theory and World Politics*. Cambridge, MA: Winthrop, 1972.

Light, Margot, and A. J. R. Groom, eds. *International Relations: A Handbook of Current Theory*. Boulder, CO: Lynne Rienner Publishers, 1985.

McClelland, Charles A. "On the Fourth Wave: Past and Future in the Study of International Systems." In *The Analysis of International Politics*, ed. James N. Rosenau. New York: Free Press, 1972.

———. *Theory and the International System*. New York: Macmillan, 1966.

Maghroori, Ray, and Bennett Ramberg, eds. *Globalism Versus Realism: International Relations' Third Debate*. Boulder, CO: Westview Press, 1982.

Moon, J. Donald. "The Logic of Inquiry: A Synthesis of Opposed Perspectives," In *Handbook of Political Science*, Vol. 1, ed. Fred I. Greenstein and Nelson W. Polsby. Reading, MA: Addison-Wesley, 1975.

Morgan, Patrick M. *Theories and Approaches to International Politics*. 4th ed. New Brunswick, NJ: Transaction Books, 1986.

Mueller, John E. *Approaches to Measurement in International Relations: A Non-Evangelical Survey*. New York: Appleton-Century-Crofts, 1969.

Olson, Mancur. *The Logic of Collective Action*. Cambridge, MA: Harvard University Press, 1965.

———. *The Rise and Decline of Nations*. New Haven, CT: Yale University Press, 1982.

———. "Towards a Mature Social Science." *International Studies Quarterly* 27, 1 (March 1983): 29–37.

Nagel, Ernest. *The Structure of Scientific Explanation*. New York: Harcourt Brace Jovanovich, 1961.

Palmer, Norman D. "The Study of International Relations in the United States: Perspectives of Half a Century." *International Studies Quarterly* 24, 3 (September 1980): 343–64.

Parkinson, F. *The Philosophy of International Relations*. Beverly Hills, CA: Sage Publications, 1977.

Rapoport, Anatol. "Various Meanings of Theory." *American Political Science Review* 52, 4 (December 1958): 972–88.

Rogowski, Ronald. "Rationalist Theories of Politics: A Midterm Report." *World Politics* 30, 2 (January 1978): 296–323. A review article.

Rosenau, James N., ed. *International Politics and Foreign Policy: A Reader in Research and Theory*. 2d ed., rev. New York: Free Press, 1969.

Ruggie, John Gerard. "Collective Goods and Future International Collaboration." *American Political Science Review* 66 (1972): 874–93.

Simon, Herbert A. *Models of Thought*. New Haven, CT: Yale University Press, 1979.

Singer, J. David. *A General Systems Taxonomy for Political Science*. New York: General Learning Press, 1971.

———. *The Scientific Study of Politics: An Approach to Foreign Policy Analysis*. Morristown, NJ: General Learning Press, 1972.

Smith, Michael, Richard Little, and Michael Shackleton, eds. *Perspectives on World Politics*. London: Croom Helm, 1981.

Stinchcombe, Arthur L. *Constructing Social Theories*. New York: Harcourt Brace Jovanovich, 1968.

Sullivan, Michael P. *International Relations: Theories and Evidence*. Englewood Cliffs, NJ: Prentice Hall, 1976.

Thompson, Kenneth W. *Masters of International Thought: Major Twentieth-Century Theorists and the World Crisis*. Baton Rouge: Louisiana State University Press, 1980.

———. "Toward a Theory of International Politics." *American Political Science Review* 49, 3 (September 1955): 733–46.

Toulmin, Stephen. *Foresight and Understanding: An Inquiry Into the Aims of Science*. New York: Harper & Row, 1963.

Waltz, Kenneth N. *Theory of International Politics*. Reading, MA: Addison-Wesley, 1979.

———. "Theory of International Relations." In *Handbook of Political Science*, Vol. 8, *International Politics*, ed. Nelson W. Polsby and Fred I. Greenstein. Reading, MA: Addison-Wesley, 1975.

Zinnes, Dina A. "A Consumer's Guide to Texts on Mathematical Modeling." *World Politics* 31, 3 (April 1979): 434–56. A review article.

———. "Three Puzzles in Search of a Researcher." *International Studies Quarterly* 24, 3 (September 1980): 315–42.

Thinking Theory Thoroughly

James N. Rosenau

James Rosenau addresses creative theorizing and develops nine principles to guide those who would engage in this enterprise.

It rarely happens, but now and again in academic life one is jolted into returning to fundamentals, into ascertaining whether one has unknowingly strayed from one's organizing premises. This happened to me recently when a graduate student inquired whether she should take an "independent reading" course under my direction. Noting that my competence was limited, I responded by asking what topics or problems she planned to investigate. Her answer startled me, perhaps partly because it was ungrammatical but mainly because I found it pedagogically challenging. Her answer was simple: "I would like you to teach me to think theory!" I agreed to take on the role of advisor.

At this writing, some eleven weeks, many conversations and much reflection later, I still find the assignment challenging, though now I am beginning to wonder whether the capacity to think theoretically, the inclination to perceive and assess the course of events as suggestive or expressive of larger forces, is a talent that can be taught. It may be, instead, a cast of mind, a personality trait, or a philosophical perspective that some acquire early in life and others do not.

If this is so, there is not much that a professor can do to teach students how to think theoretically. They can be introduced to the nature of theories, taught the various purposes theories can serve, exposed to the controversies over the relative worth of different theories, and instructed on the steps required for the construction of viable theories. And, to solidify the learning of these lessons, they can then be given assignments in which they have to formulate concrete hypotheses and tie them together into an actual theoretical framework. The learning of these skills underlying the design of theories is not, however, the equivalent of learning

From James N. Rosenau. *The Scientific Study of Foreign Policy*, rev. ed. London; Frances Pinter, 1980, pages 19-31. Reprinted by permission.

how to think theoretically. Or, more accurately, it is not the equivalent of what I understood my student as wanting me to teach her. In fact, she may only have been asking instruction on the dos and don'ts of theoretical design. But because of the way she worded her request I interpreted her as seeking more than an introduction to the procedures and techniques essential to creative theorizing. It seemed to me she was looking to acquire not a set of skills, but rather a set of predispositions, a cluster of habits, a way of thinking, a mental lifestyle — or whatever may be the appropriate label for that level of intellectual existence that governs the use of skills and the application of values — that she did not possess and that she thought she valued enough to want to make part of her orientation toward international phenomena. It is this more fundamental dimension of the life of the mind that I now suspect may not be teachable or learnable, a caveat that needs emphasis at the outset because the ensuing analysis amounts to nothing less than a pronouncement on how to think theoretically.

NINE PRE-CONDITIONS FOR CREATIVE THEORIZING

It follows that the task of disciplining ourselves and our students to think theoretically consists, first, of identifying the cognitive inclinations and perceptual impulses from which creative theory springs and, second, of then forming intellectual habits which assure the prevalence of these inclinations and impulses whenever we turn to theory-building endeavors. The central question examined in this paper follows: what are the mental qualities that best enable one to "think theory" and how can their acquisition be best assured? Nine such qualities strike me as especially conducive to the development of good theorists. Each of the nine seems equally important and there is some overlap among them. Accordingly, the sequence of their elaboration here should not be interpreted as implying a rank ordering.

> To think theoretically one has to avoid treating the task as that of formulating an appropriate definition of theory.

So as to clarify what is involved in thinking theoretically, let me start with the proposition that the task is not one of developing a clear-cut definition of theory. On balance, it is probably preferable to have a precise conception of the nature of theory rather than a vague one, but definitional exactness is not the only criterion of thinking theoretically and it may not even be a necessary requirement for such thought. I can readily imagine a young student thinking theoretically about international phenomena well before his or her first course on the subject turns to the question of what constitutes theory and the various uses to which it can be put. Indeed, I have had the good fortune of encountering a few students who were, so to speak, born theoreticians. From their very first comments in class as freshmen it was clear that they thought theoretically even though they have never had any methodological training or any exposure to the history of international relations.

Most of us are not so lucky. Most of us have to be trained to think theoretically and then we have to engage in the activity continuously in order to achieve and sustain a genuinely theoretical perspective. Hence, the fact that a few among us can maintain such a perspective without training and practice is a useful reminder that definitional clarity is not a prerequisite to creative theorizing.

The reminder is important because many of us tend to exaggerate the importance of exact definitions. To be clear about the nature of theory is not to guarantee the formulation of meaningful theory. Such clarity can be misleading. It can provide a false sense of security, a misguided confidence that one needs only to organize one's empirical materials in the proper way if one is equipped with a clear-cut definition of theory. It is my impression that much of the writing in our field derives from this premise that good definitions automatically yield good theories, as if the definitions somehow relieve the observer of the need to apply imagination and maintain philosophical discipline.

To be sure, much of the writing also suffers from loose and ambiguous conceptions of theory or from a confusion between theory and method. Such research would, obviously, be more valuable if it proceeded from a tighter and clearer notion of what the theoretical enterprise entails. So, to repeat, I am not arguing against definitional clarity. On the contrary, I believe it is highly appropriate to help students achieve such clarity by introducing them to the vast array of articles and books now available on the dynamics, boundaries, uses, and abuses of theory in the international field. But I am arguing for more than definitional clarity. I am arguing for caution and restraint in the use of definitions: in digesting the literature on theory and building a more elaborate conception of what it involves, one has to be careful not to lean too heavily on definitions and guidance. Also needed is a cast of mind, a mental set that focuses application of the definitions and facilitates creative theorizing.

> To think theoretically one has to be clear as to whether one aspires to empirical theory or value theory.

Progress in the study of international affairs depends on advances in both empirical and value theory. But the two are not the same. They may overlap; they can focus on the same problem; and values always underlie the selection of the problems to which empirical theories are addressed. Yet they differ in one overriding way: empirical theory deals essentially with the "is" of international phenomena, with things as they are if and when they are subjected to observation, while value theory deals essentially with the "ought" of international phenomena, with things as they should be if and when they could be subjected to manipulation. This distinction underlies, in turn, entirely different modes of reasoning, a different rhetoric, and different types of evidence.

The habit of making the necessary analytic, rhetorical, and evidential distinctions between empirical and value theory can be difficult for young students to develop. Indeed, it can be weak and elusive for any of us who have strong value commitments and a deep concern for certain moral questions. The more intensive are our values, the more are we tempted to allow our empirical inquiries to be guided by our beliefs rather than by our concern for observation. For this reason I have found that helping students become habituated to the is – ought distinction is among the most difficult pedagogical tasks. They can understand the distinction intellectually and they can even explain and defend it when pressed; but practicing it is another matter and often their empirical analyses slip into moral judgments without their being aware of it. It is as if they somehow fear that their values and the policy goals they want to promote will be undermined if they allow themselves to focus on observable phenomena. Such, of course, is not the case. On the contrary, moral values and policy goals can be well served, even best served, by putting them aside and proceeding detachedly long enough to enlarge empirical understanding of the obstacles that hinder realization of the values and progress toward the goals.

This is the one line of reasoning on behalf of thinking theoretically that my most value-committed students find persuasive. If empirical theory is posited as a tool of moral theory, they can approach it instrumentally and see virtue in habituating themselves to distinguishing between the two. It takes a while, however, before the perceived virtues of habituation are translated into actual habits and, in fact, some never manage to make the transition, hard as they may try. Impatient with the need for change, convinced that time is too scarce to afford the slow pace of empirical inquiry, many simply give up and dismiss the is – ought distinction as one of those picayune obsessions to which some academics fall prey.

It is my impression that impatience with empirical theorizing is likely to be especially intense among Third World students of international relations. The newly developed consciousness of the long-standing injustices built into First World – Third World relationships, the lure of dependency theory, and perhaps a frustration over the central tendencies of social science in the First World have made Third World theorists particularly resistant to detached empirical theorizing. Their resistance gives a First World scholar pause: is his insistence on habituating oneself to the is – ought distinction yet another instance of false superiority, of projecting onto the developing world practices that have worked in industrial societies? It could be. Of late I have become keenly aware of the biases that may underlie my intellectual endeavors and thus I am not prepared merely to brush aside the idea that the is – ought distinction may be inappropriate to theorizing in much of the world. In this particular instance, however, I cannot even begin to break the habit. The relevance of the distinction strikes me as global, as independent of any national biases, as necessary to thinking theoretically wherever and whenever enlarged comprehension is sought. Empirical theory is not superior to moral theory; it is simply preferable for certain purposes, and one of these is the end of deepening our grasp of why international processes unfold as they do.

Aware that my own expertise, such as it may be, lies in the realm of empirical theory, the ensuing discussion makes no pretense of being relevant to thinking theoretically in the moral context. All the precepts that follow are concerned only with those mental qualities that may render us more thoroughgoing in our empirical theorizing.

> To think theoretically one must be able to assume that human affairs are founded on an underlying order.

A prime task of empirical theory is to explain why international phenomena are structured as they are and/or behave as they do. To perform this task one must assume that each and every international phenomenon is theoretically explicable, that deeper understanding of its dynamics could be achieved if appropriate instruments for measuring it were available. To assume that everything is potentially explicable is to presume that nothing happens by chance, capriciously, at random, that for every effect there must be a cause. That is, there must be an underlying order out of which international relations springs. If this were not the case, if events could occur for no reason, there would be little point in theorizing. If some events are inherently inexplicable, efforts to build creative theory are bound to fall short to the extent that they embrace phenomena that may occur at random. Indeed, in the absence of the assumption of an underlying order, attempts to fashion theory are futile, pointless exercises, a waste of time that could be better spent writing poetry, playing tennis, or tending the garden.

This is *not* to say that thought only acquires the status of theory when it purports to account for every event. As indicated below, theory is also founded on the laws of probability. Hence it only purports to account for central tendencies, but this claim is unwarranted if an assumption of underlying order is not made. That is, to think theoretically one must presume that there is a cause for every effect even though one does not seek to explain every effect.

I have found that most students have a difficult time becoming habituated to the assumption of an underlying order. They see it as a denial of their own freedom. To presume there is a cause for everything, they reason, is to deprive people of free will, perhaps even to relieve them of responsibility for their actions. The assumption of an underlying order does not, of course, have such implications. One's freedom of choice is not lessened by the fact that the choices made are not random and, instead, derive from some source. Yet, fearful about compromising their own integrity, many students cannot accept this subtlety and insist on the premise that people have the capacity to cut themselves off from all prior experience and to act as they please for no reason whatsoever. To support their resistance to the assumption of an underlying order, they will often cite instances of international history when the unexpected occurred or when a highly deviant, impetuous, and irrational action was undertaken, as if somehow irrationality and impetuosity are capricious and do not stem from any sources.

Besides patiently reassuring dubious students that there are no insidious threats in the assumption of an underlying order, resistance to the idea can be lessened, even broken in some instances, by pointing out how the assumption offers hope for greater understanding and deeper comprehension. To presume that there is a cause of every effect is to assume that everything is potentially knowable, that inquiry can pay off, that one is not necessarily destined to go down an intellectual path that dead ends, leads nowhere. The assumption of an underlying order, in other words, is pervaded with hope. We do not make it to allow ourselves to be hopeful, but it has that consequence. It enables us to view ourselves as totally in charge of our own investigations, limited only by our imaginations and the resources at our disposal. It allows us to approach the chaos we perceive in the world around us as a challenge, as an orderliness that has yet to be identified and traced. It permits us to dare to think theory thoroughly because the affairs of people are patterned and the patterns are susceptible to being uncovered.

> To think theoretically one must be predisposed to ask about every event, every situation, or every observed phenomenon, "Of what is it an instance?"

Of all the habits one must develop to think theoretically, perhaps none is more central than the inclination to ask this question at every opportunity. It must be a constant refrain, a melody that haunts every lurch forward in the process of moving from observations to conclusions. For to see every event as an instance of a more encompassing class of phenomena is to sustain the search for patterns and to avoid treating any phenomenon as inherently unique. To think theoretically is to be at home with abstractions, to generalize, to discern the underlying order that links otherwise discrete incidents, and such a mode of thinking cannot be achieved and maintained unless every observed phenomenon is approached as merely one instance of a recurring sequence.

Again students appear to have a hard time building up this habit. They are inclined to probe for the special meaning of an event, to explore it for what sets it apart from all other events, rather than to treat it as an instance of a larger pattern. They want to understand the Iranian revolution, not revolutions as a social process, and to the extent this is their preference, to that extent do they resist building up the impulse to always reach for more general theoretical insights. Indeed, I have had many students who simply do not know where to begin when asked to indicate of what pattern some event they regard as important is an instance. Their faces turn blank and their tongues turn silent. They are paralyzed. They do not know what it means to treat the event as merely an instance of something, as just part of a larger category. And so they stumble, mumble, or otherwise resist thinking in those elementary terms out of which theorizing springs.

My response here is twofold. First, I try to portray the pleasure, the sheer joy, to be had from taking steps up the ladder of abstraction. Fitting pieces into larger wholes offers, I believe, a special sense of satisfaction, a feeling of accomplishment not unlike that which accompanies solving a puzzle or resolving a mystery. Indeed, theory building can readily be viewed as puzzle solving, as uncovering the dynamics embedded deep in the interstices of human relationships, and there are few students who are not intrigued by the challenge of solving puzzles.

If appealing thus to the curiosity of students does not succeed in getting them to ask habitually "Of what is this an instance?" (and often it is not a sufficient incentive), I revert to a second line of reasoning which, in effect, amounts to an attempt to shame them into the habit. This involves pointing out the implications of stumbling and mumbling, of not being able to discern any larger class of phenomena of which the observed phenomenon is an instance. The implications are unmistakable: to be paralyzed by the question "Of what is this an instance?" is not to know what one is interested in, to be lacking questions that generate and guide one's inquiry, to be confused by the phenomena one claims to be worthy of investigation. Based on the presumption of an underlying order, I believe that no phenomenon exists in isolation, unique only unto itself, and thus I believe that we always have an answer to the of-what-is-this-an-instance question, whether we know it or not. Accordingly, the task is not one of figuring out an answer presently unknown to us; it is rather that of explicating an answer that we have already acquired but have yet to surface. I am arguing, in other words, that we do not get interested in an international phenomenon for no reason, that our interest in it stems from a concern about a more encompassing set of phenomena, and that there is therefore no need to be paralyzed by the question if we press ourselves to move up the ladder of abstraction on which our intellectuality is founded. Once shamed into acknowledging that their concerns are not confined to the lowest rung on the ladder, most students are willing to begin to venture forth and approach the phenomena they observe as mere instances of something else.

> To think theoretically one must be ready to appreciate and accept the need to sacrifice detailed descriptions for broad observations.

One cannot begin to mount the rungs of the ladder of abstraction if one is unable to forgo the detailed account, the elaborated event, the specific minutia. As indicated, the theoretical enterprise is committed to the teasing out of central tendencies, to encompassing ever greater numbers of phenomena, to moving up the ladder of abstraction as parsimoniously as possible. Thus theory involves generalizing rather than particularizing and, in so doing, it requires relinquishing, subordinating, and/or not demonstrating much of one's impulse to expound everything one knows. It means, in effect, that one must discipline one's self to accept simple explanations over complex ones.

These are not easy tasks. Most of us find comfort in detail. The more details we know, the more are we likely to feel we have mastered our subject. To forgo much of the detail, on the other hand, is to opt for uncertainties, to expose ourselves to the criticisms of those who would pick away at our generalizations with exceptions. The temptations to fall back on details are thus considerable and much concentration on the upper rungs of the ladder of abstraction is required if the temptations are to be resisted.

Happily this is less of a problem for beginning students than more mature ones who are introduced late to the theoretical enterprise. The former have yet to acquire extensive familiarity with details and they are therefore not likely to feel threatened by the loss of their knowledge base. They want to focus on the unique, to be sure, but at least it is possible to expose them to the case of theorizing before they find security in endless minutiae. Exactly how more mature scholars accustomed to the comforts of detail can be persuaded to be theoretically venturesome is, I confess, a problem for which I have yet to find anything resembling a solution.

> To think theoretically one must be tolerant of ambiguity, concerned about probabilities, and distrustful of absolutes.

To be concerned about central tendencies one needs to be accepting of exceptions, deviations, anomalies, and other phenomena that, taken by themselves, run counter to the anticipated or prevailing pattern. Anomalies ought not be ignored and often explorations of them can lead to valuable, path-breaking insights; but neither can anomalies be allowed to undermine one's focus on central tendencies. Empirical theories deal only with probabilities and not with absolutes, with how most phenomena are likely to respond to a stimulus and not with how each and every phenomenon responds. Theorists simply do not aspire to account for every phenomenon. They know there will be anomalies and exceptions; indeed, they are suspicious on those unlikely occasions when no exceptions are manifest. Rather their goal is to build theories in which the central tendencies encompass the highest possible degree of probability, with certainties and absolutes being left for ideologues and zealots to expound.

Although they engage in it continuously in their daily lives, students tend to be resistant to the necessity of thinking probabilistically when they turn to theorizing. More accurately, they tend to be reluctant to ignore the ambiguity, to be restless with anything less than perfect certainty, as if any exception to the anticipated central tendencies constitutes a negation of their reasoning. I have found this low tolerance of ambiguity difficult to contest. Many students, fearful of uncertainty, seem to get fixated on the exception, and it is very hard at that point to recapture their interest in central tendencies. The very rhetoric of their every-day language — that things are "completely" the case or that an observation is "absolutely" accurate — reinforces their inclinations to be intolerant of deviations. In this mood they recognize only the "whole truth" as valid and regard central tendencies as a partial rather than a legitimate form of knowledge.

I confess to perplexity over how to handle this obstacle to theorizing on the part of students. I have tried elaborating on the many ways in which probabilistic thinking underlies their daily lives. I have tried making analogies between the physicist and the political scientist, pointing out that the former does not aspire to account for the behavior of every atom any more than the latter aspires to accounting for every voter. I have tried sarcasm, stressing the noxious values that derive from a concern with absolutes. Neither alone nor in combination, however, do such techniques seem to have any effect on many students. Whatever its sources, their intolerance of ambiguity is apparently too deep-seated to yield to reasoning or persuasion. So, reluctantly, I have concluded that students with a low tolerance of ambiguity and a high need for certainty are unlikely to ever think theory thoroughly and that it is probably wasted energy to try to teach them to do so.

To think theoretically one must be playful about international phenomena.

At the core of the theorizing process is a creative imagination. The underlying order of world affairs is too obscure and too complex to yield to pedestrian, constricted, or conventional minds. Only deep penetration into a problem, discerning relationships that are not self-evident and might even be the opposite of what seems readily apparent, can produce incisive and creative theory. Thus to think theoretically one must allow one's mind to run freely, to be playful, to toy around with what might seem absurd, to posit seemingly unrealistic circumstances and speculate what would follow if they were ever to come to pass. Stated differently, one must develop the habit of playing and enjoying the game of "as if" — that is, specifying unlikely conditions and analyzing them *as if* they prevailed.

Put in still another way, it has always seemed to me that good theory ought never be embarrassed by surprises, by unanticipated events that have major consequences for the system on which the theory focuses. A Hitler – Stalin pact, a Nixon resignation, or a Sadat peace initiative should not catch the creative theorist unawares because part of his or her creativity involves imagining the unimaginable. One images the unimaginable by allowing one's variables to vary across the entire range of a continuum even if some of its extreme points seem so unlikely as to be absurd. To push one's thinking beyond previously imagined extremes of a continuum is to play the game of "as if," and it involves a playfulness of mind that mitigates against surprises as well as facilitates incisive theorizing.

How one teaches playfulness is, of course, another matter. In some important sense it is an intellectual quality that cannot be taught. One acquires — or perhaps inherits — creativity early in life and no amount of subsequent training can greatly enhance the imaginative powers of those with tunnel vision and inhibited mentalities. On the other hand, encouragement to playfulness can bring out previously untapped talents in some students. Many have become so used to being told what to think that their creative impulses have never been legitimated and, accordingly, they have never even heard of the existence of the "as if" game. So no harm can be done by pressing our students (not to mention ourselves) to be playful and flexible in their thinking, and just conceivably such an emphasis may produce some unexpected results.

> To think theoretically one must be genuinely puzzled by international phenomena.

Creative use of the imagination requires humility toward international phenomena. One must be as concerned about asking the right questions about the order underlying world affairs as finding the right answers. To focus only on answers is to be sure about the questions one wants to probe and this, in turn, is to impose unnecessary limits on one's capacity to discern and integrate the deeper structures of global politics. If, on the other hand, one is genuinely puzzled by why events unfold as they do, one is committed to always asking why they occur in one way rather than another and, in so doing, pressing one's theoretical impulses as far as possible.

I do not use the notion of "genuine puzzles" casually. They are not simply open-ended questions but refer, rather, to perplexity over specific and patterned outcomes. To be genuinely puzzled about the declining capacity of governments to govern effectively, for example, one does not ask, "Why do governments do what they do?" Rather, one asks, say, "Why are most governments unable to control inflation?" or "Why do they alter their alliance commitments under specified conditions?" Genuine puzzles, in other words, are not idle, ill-framed, or impetuous speculations. They encompass specified dependent variables for which adequate explanations are lacking. I do not see how one can begin to think theoretically if one does not discern recurrent outcomes that evoke one's curiosity and puzzlement. Some analysts believe they are starting down the road to theory when they start asking what the outcomes are, but such a line of inquiry leads only to deadends, or worse, to endless mazes, because one never knows when one has come upon a relevant outcome. Genuine puzzles can lead us down creative paths, however, because they discipline us to focus on particular patterns.

One cannot teach others to be puzzled. Again it is very much a matter of whether curiosity has been repressed or allowed to flourish at an early age. It is possible, however, to keep after students and colleagues with the simple question, "What genuinely puzzles you about international affairs?" Hopefully repetition of the question will prove to be sufficiently challenging to facilitate a maximum expression of whatever may be the curiosity potential students may possess.

To think theoretically one must be constantly ready to be proven wrong.

Perhaps nothing inhibits the ability to be intellectually puzzled and playful more than the fear of being embarrassed by the inaccuracies of one's theorizing. Many of us have fragile egos that are so sensitive to error as to lead us to prefer sticking close to conventional wisdom rather than risking speculation that may be erroneous. It is as if our stature as students depends upon the soundness of our observations.

Fragile egos are not readily bolstered and some students may never be capable of venturing forth. In my experience, however, there is one line of reasoning that some students find sufficiently persuasive to lessen their fears of appearing ridiculous. It involves the thought that our comprehension of international phenomena can be substantially advanced even if our theories about them prove to be woefully wrong. Such progress can occur in two ways. One is that falsified theory has the virtue of indicating avenues of inquiry which no longer need be traversed. Doubtless egos are best served by theoretical breakthroughs but if one presumes that knowledge is at least partly developed through a process of elimination, there is some satisfaction to be gained from having narrowed the range of inquiry through theory that subsequently proves fallacious.

Secondly, unsound theory can facilitate progress by provoking others into demonstrating its falsity and attempting to show how and why it went astray. Indeed, assuming that the erroneous theory focuses on significant matters, often the more outrageous the theory is, the more it is likely to provoke further investigation. Thus even if one cannot negotiate a theoretical breakthrough on one's own, one can serve one's ego by the possibility that one's errors may sustain the knowledge-building process. This is surely what one astute analyst had in mind when he observed, "it is important to err importantly."[1]

CONCLUSION: BRINGING IT ALL TOGETHER

Plainly, there is no easy way to evolve the habit of thinking theoretically. Indeed, if the foregoing nine precepts are well founded, it can be readily argued that theorizing is the hardest of intellectual tasks. Clearing away the confusion of day-to-day events and teasing out their underlying patterns is not merely a matter of applying one's mental skills. Sustained, disciplined, and uninhibited work is required, and even then theory can be elusive, puzzles difficult to identify, details hard to ignore, and probabilities tough to estimate. And the lures and practices of non-theoretical thinking are always present, tempting us to forgo the insecurities and ambiguities of high levels of abstraction in favor of the comfortable precision available at low levels.

Yet the payoffs for not yielding to the temptations and persisting to think theoretically are considerable. There is an exhilaration, an exquisiteness, to be enjoyed in the theoretical enterprise that virtually defies description. Stimulated by the rarified atmosphere, energized by the freedom to roam uninhibitedly across diverse realms of human experience, one gets giddy at high levels of abstraction. It is that special kind of giddiness that comes from the feeling that one is employing all the resources and talents at one's command, moving beyond anything one has done before. And if one should be so fortunate as actually to achieve a theoretical breakthrough, then the exhilaration, the excitement, and the sense of accomplishment can approach the thrill of discovery that Darwin, Einstein, Freud, and the other great explorers of underlying order must have experienced at their moments of breakthrough.

For all the difficulties it entails, then, thinking theoretically is, on balance, worth the effort. And so, therefore, is the effort to teach others to think thoroughly in this way. The habits of theoretical thinking may not always be teachable, and they may not even be teachable at all; but if our efforts successfully manage to reach only a few students, they are worth undertaking. And it is even conceivable that in trying to teach others to think theoretically, we may refine and enlarge our own capacities for comprehending the underlying order that sustains and alters the human condition.

NOTE

1. Marion J. Levy, " 'Does It Matter If He's Naked?' Bawled the Child," in Klaus Knorr and James N. Rosenau (eds.), *Contending Approaches to International Relations* (Princeton, NJ: Princeton University Press, 1969), p. 93.

2

Realism: The State, Power, and the Balance of Power

MAJOR ACTORS AND ASSUMPTIONS: A SUMMARY

In the previous chapter we stated that realism is an image of international relations that is based on four assumptions. Scholars or policymakers who identify themselves as realists, however, do not all perfectly match the realism ideal type. We find, however, that the four assumptions identified with this perspective are useful as a general statement of the main lines of realist thought and the basis on which hypotheses and theories are developed.

To recapitulate, for the realist *states are the principal actors*, and the study of international relations focuses on these units. Nonstate actors, such as multinational corporations and other **transnational** organizations are decidedly less important. International organizations, such as the United Nations or the NATO alliance (North Atlantic Treaty Organization), do not have independent standing because they are composed of sovereign, independent, or autonomous states that determine what these international organizations will do. In short, for the realist the focus is on states and interstate (or international) relations.

What, then, is the nature of this actor that is at the core of international relations? For purposes of analysis, the realist views the state as both *unitary* and *rational*. The state is said to be unitary because any differences of view among political leaders or bureaucracies within the state are ultimately resolved so that the state speaks with one voice. If there are exceptions in practice (as when one agency of government adopts a foreign policy line different from that of another agency of the same government), these cases either deal with trivial issues or are corrected in due course by the leadership. In any event, exceptions are precisely that — exceptions or marginal cases that in effect demonstrate the general rule that unitary states are the principal actors in world politics.

Realists also assume that states are rational actors. Given particular goals, states consider feasible alternatives to achieve these goals in the light of their existing capabilities. Realists recognize problems of lack of information, uncertainty, bias, and misperception, but it is assumed by realists that decision makers strive to achieve the best possible decision even with these constraints.

One may well ask if this characterization of the formulation of foreign policy is accurate. Could one not just as easily argue that history is better characterized as a "march of folly?"[1] Was it wise, for example, for Germany to invade Poland in 1939? Was it in Japan's interest to attack Pearl Harbor in 1941? Was the American conduct of the Vietnam war an example of rationality at work?

From the standpoint of **methodology**, the image of a unified, rational state is a realist *assumption*, not a description of the actual world. Assumptions, it is sometimes argued, should be viewed not in terms of descriptive accuracy but, rather, in terms of how fruitful they are in generating insights and valid generalizations about international politics. From this point of view, assumptions are neither true nor false; they are more or less useful in helping the theorist derive testable propositions or hypotheses about international relations. Once hypotheses are developed, they are tested against the real world. The image of the unified, rational state is, therefore, the starting point for realist analysis, not a concluding statement. Hans J. Morgenthau has explained the utility of the rational, unitary actor assumption as follows:

> We put ourselves in the position of a statesman who must meet a certain problem of foreign policy under certain circumstances, and we ask ourselves what the rational alternatives are from which a statesman may choose . . . and which of these rational alternatives this particular statesman, acting under these circumstances, is likely to choose. It is the testing of this rational hypothesis against the actual facts and their consequences that gives meaning to the facts of international politics and makes a theory of politics possible.[2]

Game theory involves the use of such simplifying assumptions as an aid to developing hypotheses and theories about the causes of various international political phenomena including war, arms races, the formation and maintenance of international organizations, and so on. Many works on **deterrence** also use the rational, unitary actor assumptions.[3]

Finally, realists typically assume that among the array of world issues, *national security* tops the list for states. Military and political issues dominate the agenda and are referred to as high politics. States act to maximize what is often called the **national interest**. Put another way, states try to maximize the likelihood that they will achieve whatever objectives they have set. These objectives include high-political concerns of assuring state survival — security matters — as well as the more mundane or low-political objectives in such fields as trade, finance, monetary exchange, and health. States use the power they have to serve their interests or achieve their objectives. To most realists, the struggle for (or use of) power among states is at the core of international relations. In the words of Morgenthau, "International politics, like all politics, is a struggle for power. Whatever the ultimate aims of international politics, power is always the immediate aim."[4]

As an image of politics, therefore, realism is concerned with power and power politics among states, but as will become clear in subsequent discussion, many realists (including Morgenthau) have also been concerned with values and norms and the role they play in ordering international politics. In our view, realism is not the opposite of an idealism preoccupied with values to the exclusion of power considerations, although the degree of emphasis placed on power and values among realists varies widely. Indeed, some realists place a greater emphasis on values, norms, and formal rules agreed on by states than other realists who see relations of power and the balance of power as the dominant factors. This is true whether the theorist approaches the subject matter of international relations through historical case studies or through the use of quantifiable data in the pursuit of understanding such topics as the causes of war. The common denominator is a conceptual emphasis on a unitary, rational state and problems of national security.

Where did these assumptions of contemporary realist thought come from? They obviously did not appear out of thin air following World War II. Rather, they represent the culmination of thinking about international relations over the centuries. We now turn to some of the more notable intellectual precursors who have had a significant impact on the writings of contemporary realists.

INTELLECTUAL PRECURSORS AND INFLUENCES

Thucydides

Thucydides (471 – 400 B.C.) is usually credited with being the first writer in the realist tradition as well as the founding father of the international relations discipline.[5] Anyone who has taken a class in political philosophy would probably agree that the profound insights of many ancient Greek writers are not easily grasped on first reading. One might initially find this less a problem with Thucydides' *The Peloponnesian War* because this famous work chronicles twenty-one of the twenty-eight years of war between Athens and Sparta (and their respective allies) in the fifth century B.C. Taken simply as history, it is a masterful account of this era, filled with tales of heroism and brutality, victory and defeat, brilliance and stupidity, honor and deceit. These human traits are certainly exhibited not only in one particular war but in all wars throughout the ages. This is what makes *The Peloponnesian War* such a classic.

The task Thucydides set for himself, however, was much more ambitious than simply describing what was occurring. Particular events were dealt with in great and vivid detail, but his goal was to say something significant not only about the events of his own time but also about the nature of war and why it continually recurs. For Thucydides, the past was the guide for the future. He was less interested in the immediate causes of the Peloponnesian War than he was in the underlying forces at work. Leaders might point to a particular event to justify a policy, but for Thucydides this simply obscured more profound factors that operate throughout history. At heart, *The Peloponnesian War* is a study of the struggle for military and political power.

Thucydides was younger than Socrates and Sophocles and older than Aristophanes. In 424 B.C., during the eighth year of the Peloponnesian War, he was elected an Athenian general. While stationed in Thrace, he failed to prevent the

Spartan capture of a city and was punished with twenty years of exile. Athens might have lost a general, but the world gained a historian.

As a member of one of the more notable Athenian families, Thucydides spent the rest of the war observing events, traveling, and interviewing participants. As an exile, he was detached yet obsessed with politics. Although concerned with accuracy, he gave precedence to understanding the motives and policies of the leaders on all sides of the conflict and used the technique of liberally reconstructing speeches and episodes. His purpose was to draw historical lessons for future statesmen who might read his work.[6] By analyzing the particular, he hoped to illuminate the general.

Why did war break out between Athens and Sparta? Thucydides states:

> I propose first to give an account of the causes of complaint which they had against each other and of the specific instances where their interests clashed [i.e., the immediate causes of the war]: this is in order that there should be no doubt in anyone's mind about what led to this great war falling upon the Hellenes. But the real reason for the war is, in my opinion, most likely to be disguised by such argument. What made war inevitable was the growth of Athenian power and the fear which this caused in Sparta [i.e., the underlying cause of the war].[7]

Thus, the real or underlying cause of the war was *fear* associated with a shift in the balance of power. Sparta was afraid of losing its preeminent role in the Hellenic world and therefore took countermeasures to build up its military strength and enlist the support of allies. Athens responded in kind. In the ensuing analysis, the situations, events, and policies Thucydides described lend themselves to comparison with such familiar notions as arms races, deterrence, balance of power, alliances, diplomacy, strategy, concern for honor, and perceptions of strengths and weaknesses.

Thucydides' emphasis on fear as a cause of the Peloponnesian War, fear that resulted from the increase in Athenian power relative to that of Sparta, is echoed throughout history. As statesmen perceive the balance of power to be shifting in their disfavor, they make efforts to rectify the situation that in turn cause fear, suspicion, and distrust on the part of their rivals. One could quite easily substitute for Athens and Sparta other historical examples such as France and Britain in the seventeenth and eighteenth centuries, Napoleonic France and the rest of Europe in the early nineteenth century, Germany and Britain after the Franco-Prussian War of 1870, and the Soviet Union and the United States in the four decades following World War II. In all such historical examples, a good case can be made that fear is a dominant characteristic and a motivating factor for arms races and war itself.

One reason Thucydides is deemed a scholar of international relations, however, is that the cause of fear he identifies is not so much man's innate or basic nature as it is the nature of interstate politics. In a world in which no superordinate or central authority exists to impose order on all states — whether ancient city-states or modern states often encompassing large expanses of territory — "the strong do what they have the power to do and the weak accept what they have to accept."[8] Although fear may lead to war, power and capabilities relative to that of others determine the outcome.

Thucydides is sometimes unfairly criticized as an advocate of harsh and brutal wartime policies, one who rationalized such events as he described in the famous Melian dialogue. Thucydides, however, favored the democracy of the Golden Age of Pericles. In fact, the second half of *The Peloponnesian War* is a description of the degeneration of Athenian democracy and the resulting fanaticism that turned the war from a defensive effort to a war of conquest. The Melian dialogue reflects the latter phase of the war and should not be viewed as a personal preference on the part of Thucydides.

Machiavelli

By his own admission, the Italian political philosopher Niccolo Machiavelli (1469–1527) drew heavily from his study of ancient Greek and Roman writings. In some respects, the situation in sixteenth-century Italy, divided as the peninsula was into separate city-states, was similar to the Hellenic world of Thucydides. Machiavelli worked as a civil servant and diplomat until the Republic of Florence fell in 1512. During his enforced idleness, he put his time to good use by reflecting on the chaos and political instability of Italy.

Like Thucydides, Machiavelli wrote of power, balance of power, formation of alliances and counteralliances, and the causes of conflict between different city-states. His primary focus, however, was on what contemporary writers refer to as national security. For Machiavelli, survival of the state (identified with the ruling prince) was paramount. The prince could lose his state by not coping effectively with both internal and external threats to his rule. The German term **Realpolitik**, so central to realist thought, refers to power and power politics among states. Machiavelli's most famous work, *The Prince*, is a practical manual on how to gain, maintain, and expand power.[9] It is dedicated to the ruler of Florence at that time, Lorenzo di Medici.

One of the more controversial parts of Machiavelli's thesis is the notion that the security of the state is so important that it may justify certain acts by the prince that would be forbidden to other individuals not burdened by the princely responsibility of assuring that security. The end — security of the state — is understood to justify any means necessary to achieve that end. **Machiavellianism** (or **Machiavellism**) has been condemned by many who consider such a view to be immoral. Others have argued, however, that the actions of statesmen do (and should) follow a code of conduct different from that of the average citizen. Thus, it has been observed that there are two separate and distinct ethics: first, conventional religious morality concerned with such matters as individual salvation (the ethics of ultimate ends) and, second, by contrast, the moral obligations of rulers who must take actions to provide for national security (the ethics of responsibility).[10] Following this interpretation, one can understand Machiavelli's view that rulers should be good if they can (good in the conventional sense) but be willing to practice evil *if necessary* (consistent with their obligations as rulers).

Another point of view is that Machiavelli wrote of the world as it *is*, not the world as it *should* or *ought* to be. Ethics and politics are divorced from each other. His advice to the prince, following this interpretation, was based on an analysis of history, and of what actually occurs in the political realm, not on abstract ethical principles:

> Many have imagined republics and principalities which have never been seen or known to exist in reality; for how we live is so far removed from how we ought to live, that he who abandons what is done for what ought to be done, will rather learn to bring about his own ruin than his preservation. A man who wishes to make a profession of goodness in everything must necessarily come to grief among so many who are not good.[11]

For Machiavelli, in an amoral (if not immoral) world, what meaning does the preaching of conventional morality have? Indeed, an extreme statement of realist thinking is that considerations of power and power politics are the *only* relevant factors.

In the modern world, a convenient way to discredit an opponent is to accuse him or her of being Machiavellian. Nevertheless, it must be emphasized that Machiavelli did not encourage rulers to use violence for its own sake. In numerous passages he advises the prince not to be needlessly cruel because this may eventually undermine his rule.[12] The yardstick one should use is how a particular policy contributes to the security and stability of the state.

Hobbes

The political philosophy of the Englishman Thomas Hobbes (1588–1679) was developed during the first fifty turbulent years of the seventeenth century. After attending university in Oxford, Hobbes became a tutor to the son of a nobleman, and throughout his life he remained associated with the family. A Royalist, Hobbes left for France in 1641 at a time when Parliament was asserting its power against the monarchy. For three years he tutored the son of Charles I, the latter eventually being executed in 1649 during the English civil war. Hobbes returned to England in 1652, pledging loyalty to the republican regime.

Hobbes's famous work *Leviathan*, which was the first general theory of politics in English, was published that same year.[13] Like Machiavelli, Hobbes had a pessimistic view of human nature. His primary focus was domestic politics, and his goal was to make the strongest case possible for the necessity for a powerful, centralized political authority. To illustrate his philosophical points, Hobbes posited that prior to the creation of society, men would live in a "state of nature" that would be a condition of war of "every one against every one." There would be "a continual fear and danger of violent death; and the life of man, solitary, poor, nasty, brutish, and short."[14]

Hobbes did not argue that such a state of nature had ever really existed. To him, the state of nature was the result of a thought experiment — imagining what the world would be like without governmental authority or any other social structure. Accordingly, he was interested in showing how people could escape from this hypothetical situation by agreeing to place all power in the hands of a Leviathan (a state authority, or supreme ruler) that would maintain order and end the anarchy of the state of nature. If governmental authority did not already exist, it would have to be created. In his words: "There must be some coercive power to compel men equally to the performance of their covenants, by the terror of some punishment, greater than the benefit they expect by the breach of their covenant."[15] Without order, he argued, civilization and all its benefits are impossible — no economic development, art, knowledge, or anything else of value.

Hobbes's impact on the realist view of international relations stems from this image of individuals in a mythical state of nature. His description is equally applicable to relations among states because in the state of nature as well as in international politics, there is no Leviathan or superordinate power to impose order. It is a condition of **anarchy** — the absence of central or superordinate authority over states that claim to be **sovereign** with a *right* to be independent or autonomous with respect to one another. In Hobbes's words:

> In all times, kings, and persons of sovereign authority, because of their independency, are in continual jealousies, and in the state and posture of gladiators; having their weapons pointing, and their eyes fixed on one another; that is, their forts, garrisons, and guns upon the frontiers of their kingdoms; and continual spies upon their neighbours; which is a posture of war.[16]

As anarchy prevails in the state of nature, so too is anarchy a dominant characteristic of international politics. Without a Leviathan (or, in the language of contemporary international relations literature, a **hegemonic** power or world state), suspicion, distrust, conflict, and war are seemingly inevitable. In the absence of any **social contract** among (or authority over) them, there are no moral obligations to govern the relations of states.

Grotius

Hugo Grotius (1583 – 1645), a Dutch contemporary of Thomas Hobbes, offered a different view of international relations from that associated with Hobbes and Machiavelli. Grotius dealt with the essential anarchy of international relations by calling for the establishment (or acknowledging the existence) of laws or rules accepted by states as binding. That the relations of states *ought* to conform to such rules is a central tenet of the Grotian tradition in international relations. To Grotians, values or norms, particularly when recognized as international law, are important in maintaining order among states.

Grotius dealt with the problems of international relations (including commercial transactions) from a very practical point of view. Given the importance of trade to his native Holland as a seafaring nation, he addressed this subject in his *Law of Prize and Booty* (1604 – 1605) and questions of freedom of navigation and territorial seas in his *Freedom of the Seas* (1609). Probably his most important work was his *Law of War and Peace* (1625), three volumes that dealt with war and questions of national security — central themes in much realist writing then and now.

What are the sources of international law? Grotius looked to the use of reason and to the "natural law" for general principles. He also looked to customary practice and to rules agreed on by governments that would be binding on states.

Such treaties or formal covenants would be binding (in Latin, *pacta sunt servanda*) in the sense that states are obligated to follow them even in the absence of central authority to enforce their adherence. Changing circumstances might lead to the alteration of rules, but the important point is that to Grotians order in international relations and matters of war and peace involve both power *and* values. In this regard, some contemporary realists owe as much to Grotius and the Grotian tradition as they do to Thucydides, Machiavelli, and Hobbes.[17]

Clausewitz

Carl von Clausewitz (1780–1831), a Prussian officer who rose to the rank of general and who served in the Napoleonic wars, thought the military element of a state's power to be extremely important but subordinate always to the political. Consistent with the writings of Machiavelli on war, Clausewitz argued in an oft-quoted phrase that war is "a continuation of political activity by other means."[18]

Much of Clausewitz's writing took place in the interwar period between the defeat of Napoleon in 1815 and Clausewitz's recall to duty in 1830 for service in East Prussia. Clausewitz died in 1831, never having completed his magnum opus *On War*. His legacy, nevertheless, remains a central contribution to the realist school. As significant as his view that the military is properly a political means was his exposition of societal (including social and economic) dimensions of national capabilities. At the same time, his focus on national security problems places him in the mainstream of realist thought.

Carr

Many students of international relations consider Edward Hallett Carr's *The Twenty Years' Crisis, 1919–1939* already a classic. Although Carr can be viewed as an intellectual precursor for realists, his work transcends narrow classification in that he has also been influential, as has Grotius, on the thinking of certain authors whom we would label pluralist.

The writings of Thucydides, Machiavelli, Hobbes, Grotius, and Clausewitz illustrate how great works are often written during the most difficult times. *The Twenty Years' Crisis* is no exception in that it was completed in the summer of 1939 with the shadow of war looming over Europe. As with other authors we have discussed, Carr was less interested in apportioning blame to particular leaders for the imminent onset of World War II than he was in attempting "to analyse the underlying and significant, rather than the immediate and personal, causes of the disaster."[19] Unless this were done, he argued, we would fail to understand how war could break out twenty short years after the signing of the Versailles Treaty in 1919. He dedicated his book "to the makers of the coming peace."

In attempting to understand "the more profound causes of the contemporary international crisis," echoes of Thucydides can be discerned. Carr, for example, placed a great deal of emphasis on the role of fear in explaining World War I.[20] Similarly, he also argued (and quoted Machiavelli and Hobbes to this effect) that "the exercise of power always appears to beget the appetite for more power. . . . Wars, begun for motives of security, quickly become wars of aggression and self-seeking."[21] Just as Thucydides saw Athens at the outset of the Peloponnesian War claim "self-defense" and then turn into a more ambitious, aggressive power, so too Carr noted that during the course of World War I

> nearly every country participating . . . regarded it initially as a war of self-defense; and this belief was particularly strong on the Allied side. Yet during the course of the war, every Allied government in Europe announced war aims which included the acquisition of territory from the enemy powers. In modern conditions, wars of limited objective have become almost as impossible as wars of limited liability.[22]

Throughout *The Twenty Years' Crisis* Carr refers to the impact of Machiavelli and Hobbes on realist thinking. Although his work is best known as a critique of **utopian** or **idealist** thought, Carr also evaluates the more extreme versions of realism that posit the divorce of morality from politics in international relations. He argues that

> any sound political thought must be based on elements of both utopia [i.e., values] and reality [i.e., power]. Where utopianism has become a hollow and intolerable sham, which serves merely as a disguise for the interests of the privileged, the realist performs an indispensable service in unmasking it. But pure realism can offer nothing but a naked struggle for power which makes any kind of international society impossible.[23]

Hence, for Carr, politics is made up of two elements, inextricably intertwined: utopia and reality, values and power.

More than a third of the book is devoted to such Grotian topics as the role of morality in international relations, the foundations of law, the sanctity of treaties, the judicial settlement of international disputes, peaceful change, and the prospects for a new international order. Because Carr critically estimated the strengths and weaknesses of utopianism as well as realism, he can be viewed as an important influence on many contemporary international relations theorists, both realists and nonrealists.

This brief overview of the intellectual precursors of realism illustrates a distinct realist preoccupation with war. A concern with the causes and consequences of conflict helps to explain why the realist perspective is held by statesmen throughout the world; over the centuries leaders have engaged in the very battles and struggles described by authors from Thucydides to Carr. Realism, from the statesman's point of view, is indeed realistic because it tends to correspond to personal experiences.

Among realists there are two basic concepts that traditionally have been the foci of analysis at the state and international levels: **power** and **system**. In the following pages, we discuss how realists have attempted to define these terms. We then give examples of how theorists have used these concepts in generating insights and explanations of the causes of war. This is followed by a discussion of how realists deal with the concepts of **interdependence** and *change*. We conclude with a critique of the realist image of international relations.

POWER

Definitions

In discussing several of the more important intellectual precursors of realism, the concept of power was mentioned time and again. Any attempt to give the reader a more complete understanding of the realist image of international relations starts with a discussion of this crucial term. Power is the core concept for realists.

Having said this, it is rather ironic that even among realists there is no clear consensus on how to define the term *power*. Some realists understand power to be the sum of military, economic, technological, diplomatic, and other *capabilities* at the disposal of the state. Others see power not as some absolute value determined for each state as if it were in a vacuum but, rather, as capabilities *relative* to the capabilities of other states. Thus, the power of the United States is evaluated in terms of its capabilities relative to the capabilities of other states.

Both of these definitions — whether treating capabilities of a state in isolation or relative to the capabilities of other states — assume a *static* view of power. Power is an attribute of the state that is the sum of its capabilities whether considered alone or relative to other states. An alternative, *dynamic* definition of power focuses on the interactions of states. A state's influence (or capacity to influence or coerce) is not only determined by its capabilities (or relative capabilities) but also by (1) its willingness (and perceptions by other states of its willingness) to use these capabilities and (2) its control or influence over other states. Power can thus be inferred by observing the behavior of states as they interact. The relative power of states is most clearly revealed by the *outcomes* of their interactions.

Examples of diverse views of power are the following definitions drawn from the literature: power as the capacity of an individual, group, or nation "to influence the behavior of others in accordance with one's own ends," power as "man's control over the minds and actions of other men," and power as "the ability to prevail in conflict and overcome obstacles."[24]

Measurement

Given these definitional and conceptual disputes, it follows that attempts to measure power will also be divergent. If one understands power as being equivalent to capabilities, one looks for some way to measure military, economic, and other component elements. If one views power as actual control or influence, some measurement of capabilities may still be a useful "first cut" if one is engaged in predicting the outcome of interactions between or among states.

Even if one assumes that it is possible to measure these capabilities adequately through such indicators as defense expenditures or gross national product, the further problems of weighting and aggregating or adding up such diverse capabilities into a common measure of power remains. How should one weight different component capabilities? Which, for example, is the more important — military or economic capabilities — and how much more important? How does one measure geographic, technological, or diplomatic factors with any degree of precision? What about the unity and strength of a society, which one scholar claims is the "forgotten dimension of strategy"?[25] And, if capabilities are difficult to measure, are not *relative* capabilities between and among states even more difficult to specify?

Scholars who focus on power in the international system are well aware of these difficulties. Nevertheless, in order to use power as an analytical concept, certain measurements have been suggested. A. F. K. Organski, for example, has argued that gross national product, or national income, is perhaps the best yardstick of national capability. J. David Singer and his associates emphasize military, industrial, and demographic capacities as the critical variables required to indicate overall national capabilities.[26]

We must remember that the purpose in devising such formulas is not trivial. Measuring the power or capabilities of states is a critical step in attempts to explain the behavior of states and the functioning of the international system with regard to matters of war and peace. Such concerns are evident in the Correlates of War project headed by Singer, in which state power is a key variable. Similarly, Bruce Bueno de Mesquita uses Singer's national capabilities scores as key elements of his expected utility theory that seeks to explain the causes and outcomes of wars. The theory logically assumes that decision makers attempt to calculate the power capabilities of a rival before initiating armed conflict. The probability of success is a function of each state's relative power adjusted for such factors as alliance commitments. Bueno de Mesquita found, for example, that between 1816 and 1974, states with a positive expected utility score who initiated a war won 83 percent of the conflicts.[27]

Some would say that the view of power as a unitary concept calculated by aggregating component capabilities or relative capabilities misses the key point, which is that the power of a state is dependent on the *issue* involved. Consider, for example, the argument that some states, such as Japan, have substantial economic power but are militarily weak. Hence, in a particular area, the Japanese are powerful. Opponents of this disaggregation of power into its component capabilities note that persuasive as it may be on the surface, it is misleading because it overlooks the relations among the various power components. Thus, the *economic* capabilities of Japan as a global trader are said to be related to its *military* ties with the United States that assure Japan's freedom to engage in commerce. From this perspective, whether addressing the power of Japan, Europe, or Third World countries, one cannot understand economic, military, political, or other component capabilities of power as if they were factors independent of one another. Much as military ties and divisions among states may define the framework within which economic relations take place, so military capabilities of states are bolstered (or weakened) by the strength or relative strength of their economies.

SYSTEM

In the preceding section we discussed the concept of power and attempts to measure state power. Using that discussion as a basis, we now move on to a discussion of the concept of system.

When applied to international relations, the term *system* has currency within each of the three images we have identified—realism, pluralism, and globalism. As one might expect, however, there is considerable diversity among theorists on both the *definition* of the term and the *uses* to which it should be put in the construction of international relations theory.

Thus, some theorists define a system in terms of various distributions of power or capabilities and other attributes. Others understand system to be the set of interactions among states and other nonstate actors, a behavioral definition. Hence, we find a certain symmetry between definitions of power and definitions of system: static and dynamic.

However system may be defined, the uses to which the concept is put vary considerably. Some theorists are content to use systems as mere **taxonomies**, frameworks for organizing knowledge about international relations. Others are more ambitious. Beyond **heuristic** purposes—that is, contributing to common understanding of the subject—they may see utility in actually using the system concept to explain and predict outcomes of international relations.[28]

Some scholars view the concept of system as an abstraction. Systems are mental images that may help to describe, explain, or predict international phenomena. They are, in effect, superimposed on the real world by a scholar in order to make the real world more intelligible and easier to understand. Other theorists go beyond this and ascribe such properties to systems as **equilibrium**, or balance, or their component parts (such as among states). Critics, however, find little use in such notions as "equilibrating tendencies." Treating a system as if it were a concrete or tangible entity and ascribing properties to it is of questionable validity from this point of view. To do so, according to critics, is to be guilty of the methodological error of **reification**—treating abstractions as if they were real and had a life of their own.[29]

A response by some system theorists to this line of criticism is that dealing in abstractions is useful in the generation of propositions or **hypotheses** about international relations. These, in turn, can be tested **empirically** to determine whether or not they have factual support. To the extent, then, that use of the systems concept enables the theorist to describe, explain, or predict international phenomena, the use of the concept is justified.

The reader may or may not wish to visualize international relations or world politics as a system that is defined in terms of patterns of interactions, a particular structure, equilibrating tendencies, or some other characteristics. We do note, however, that the systems concept as an approximation to the nature of world politics is present within the mainstream of contemporary realist thought, even if some realists avoid its use.

Speaking of abstractions, this discussion has been rather abstract. To lend substance to the concept of system, we next examine two ways in which the concept of system has been used by realists: *system* as patterns of interactions, and *system* as anarchy plus the distribution of capabilities. In each case the intention of scholars has been to explain some aspect of international relations concerning such matters as instability, conflict, and war. In each case the state and state power have been a key focus of analysis and investigation.

System As Interactions

Two examples of viewing the international system as sets or patterns of interactions are to be found in the works of Rudolph J. Rummel and Charles A. McClelland. In his Dimensionality of Nations (DON) Project, Rummel attempts to explain and predict the behavior of states. In doing so he identifies recurrent patterns of behavior by using **factor analysis**, a statistical tool designed to identify patterns of variation in the data being analyzed. In one study, ninety-four **variables** falling into such categories as military, international conflict, international collaboration, colonialism, communication, and international organization were selected for factor analysis. The analysis involved eighty-two countries. According to Rummel, tentative findings included first, that conflict is not a necessary consequence of a nation's increased involvement in foreign affairs (which would seem to be counterintuitive, or contrary to what one might expect); and second, that the genesis of foreign conflict behavior lies outside the state, not internal to it (one answer to the questions raised in the discussion of the problem of levels of analysis). Such conflict behavior "is a *relational* phenomenon depending on the degree of economic, social, and political similarity between nations, the geographic distance between them, and their power parity." This latter point — that conflict is primarily relational — is the basis for Rummel's extensive work in what is termed *field theory*.[30]

Charles McClelland focused on international transactions and interactions between states in his World Event/Interaction Survey (WEIS) project. The data base consists of the actions and responses of states over a number of years as reported in the press since 1966. Events are coded and placed in specific categories. Quantitative analyses of the data are meant to reveal patterns of behavior between and among states, the basis for prediction. Although the major focus is on conflict behavior and periods of high tension (particularly international crises), the data are not limited to this type of state action. The underlying assumption is that the past behavior of a state is a source for the prediction of its current and future behavior. The major results of the WEIS project have been reported in a number of articles.[31]

System As Anarchy and the Distribution of Capabilities

Many realist writers have emphasized anarchy and the distribution of capabilities, or power, among states as critical components of the international system. These so-called system-level, or **structural**, attributes are viewed as crucial because they act as constraints on decisionmakers. As we will see, the condition of international anarchy is seen by realists as contributing to the amount of distrust and conflict among states. Realists have also been concerned whether particular distributions of capabilities involving various balances of power make war between states more or less likely. We will first take up the concept of anarchy and related terms.

Anarchy. The word *anarchy* brings forth images of violence, destruction, and chaos. For realists, however, anarchy simply refers to the absence of any authority above states. States are **sovereign**. They claim a right to be independent or autonomous from other states, and they claim a right to exercise complete authority over their own territories. Although states differ in terms of the power they possess or are able to exercise, none may claim the *right* to dominate another sovereign state.[32]

We wish to be clear on the term *anarchy* and the difference between **authority** and **power**. When we use the term *anarchy*, we are referring to the absence of any hierarchy of authority. There *is* hierarchy of power in international politics, but there is not a hierarchy of authority. Some states are clearly more powerful than others, but there is no recognized authority higher than that of any state.

Anarchy, so understood, is the defining characteristic of the environment within which sovereign states interact. Violence and war may be evident but so too are periods of relative peace and stability. This absence of any superordinate or central authority over states (such as a world government with authority to enforce rules and to maintain order) is fundamentally different from domestic societies, where an authority exists to maintain order and act as an arbiter of disputes.[33]

Realists argue that the absence of a central and overriding authority helps to explain why states come to rely on power, seeking to maintain or increase their power positions relative to other states. For one thing, the condition of anarchy is usually accompanied by a lack of trust among states in this environment. Each state faces a **self-help** situation in which it is dangerous to place the security of one's own country in the hands of another. What guarantee is there against betrayal, however solemn another state's promises may be to an ally? Consistent with the world described by Hobbes, there is really nothing to keep a supposed ally from reneging on a security agreement or any other international pact. There is no world governmental authority to enforce covenants or agreements among states. In such a world it is logical, rational, and prudent to look out for number one. Indeed, this was the same counsel reported by Thucydides when he noted Athenian advice to the Melians not to place their hope for survival in the hands of the Spartans and their allies.

Given international anarchy and the lack of trust in such a situation, states find themselves in what has been called a **security dilemma**.[34] The more one state arms to protect itself from other states, the more threatened these states become and the more prone they are to resort to arming themselves to protect their own national security interests. The dilemma is that even if a state is sincerely arming only for defensive purposes, it is rational in a self-help system to assume the worst in an adversary's intentions and keep pace in any arms buildup. How can one know for certain that a rival is arming strictly for defensive purposes? This is the stuff of arms races. Isn't it best to hedge one's bets by devoting more resources to match a potential adversary's arms buildup? Because a state may not have sufficient resources to be completely self-reliant, it may join an alliance in an attempt to deter aggression by any would-be adversaries.

Given an understanding of the anarchic condition of international politics, one can more easily grasp certain dynamics of arms races. All sides involved may sincerely desire peace, but the anarchical nature of international politics leads states to be suspicious of one another and engage in worst-case analyses of one another's intentions. This realist insight, it is argued, is just as applicable to understanding the ancient competition between Sparta and Athens as it is to understanding contemporary international relations. It is a system-level explanation in that the emphasis is placed on the anarchic structure of international politics as a whole, not on the *internal* nature of a particular state. An example of an explanation that relies on internal factors is the claim that a given country keeps building more and more weapons because of demands from its own military-industrial complex or because of the nature of a national mentality that reflects its regional or global ambitions. *External* factors such as the anarchic structure of the system or the reactions of other states are ignored.

Finally, an anarchical, self-help system obviously makes cooperation among states difficult to achieve. How are states to act in such a world? Is it inevitable that they will be self-seeking, attempting to maximize their short-term individual or self-interests? Or is it possible that states can upgrade their common (perhaps enlightened) self-interests over both the short and long term? What is the rational thing to do? The informing image for some realists is provided by the allegory of the stag hunt, taken from the writings of the Geneva-born eighteenth-century philosopher Jean Jacques Rousseau.[35]

Each of five individuals in the state of nature — a world without government or any other form of social structure — has to decide (1) whether to collaborate in the hunting of a stag necessary to meet the hunger needs of all five or (2) to defect from the group to capture a hare. To choose the latter course of action would be to serve one's own self-interest at the expense of the group (see Figure 2.1).

If the individual prefers to serve the common interest (go after the stag), can he trust the others to do so? And if he can't trust the others, is it not rational for

	Individual interests: pursue the hare	Group/collective interests: pursue the stag
Short run	Serve immediate self-interest	May provide basis for possible future collaboration
Long run	No apparent basis for collaborative behavior	Serve long-term common interest

Figure 2.1 The stag hunt fable: a dilemma of rational choice

him to go for the hare and defect from the group before any of the others do? Or is it possible to develop the basis for collaboration on a continuing basis by all five? [36] Scholars who deal with **game theory** attempt to answer such questions. Game theory is an approach to determining rational choice or optimum strategy under conditions of uncertainty. As such, game theory has direct relevance to the study of foreign policy choice and to much scholarly work on deterrence as a means of avoiding war.

How one understands Rousseau's stag hunt fable has a great deal to do with how one sees states interacting in world politics. Some tend to see the state as serving only narrow self-interest. Pessimists point to the number, duration, and intensity of wars. Those of a more optimistic bent note that in many cases states live in peace and harmony for years, and there is, indeed, great potential for collaboration among states.

The Distribution of Capabilities: Balance of Power.   Unless one state or some sort of superordinate international authority comes to dominate the world, anarchy will continue to be a defining characteristic of the international system. Within this anarchical environment, however, various distributions of capabilities or power among states are possible. Anarchy plus the distribution of capabilities define for many realists the international system at any one time.

As we have seen, many realists begin with the security dilemma in an anarchic world. Where does order come from under such conditions? What keeps states from continually attacking one another? One answer — associated with the thought of Hugo Grotius — is the development of international norms as codified in international law. Another answer offered by realists is that states find it expedient to band together and pool their capabilities whenever one state or group of states appears to be gathering a disproportionate amount of power, thus threatening to dominate the world, or even a portion of it.

This reasoning — the need to maintain a **balance of power** to avoid the triumph of a dominant power — is a realist concern dating back to the works of Thucydides. It is also found in a report of the British Foreign Office written before World War I:

> History shows that the danger threatening the independence of this or that nation has generally arisen, at least in part, out of the momentary predominance of a neighboring State at once military powerful, economically efficient, and ambitious to extend its frontiers or spread its influence. . . . The only check on the abuse of political predominance derived from such a position has always consisted in the opposition of an equally formidable rival, or a combination of several countries forming leagues of defense. The equilibrium established by such a grouping of forces is technically known as the balance of power, and it has become almost an historical truism to identify England's secular policy with the maintenance of this balance by throwing her weight now in this scale and now in that, but ever on the side opposed to the political dictatorship of the strongest single State or group at a given time.[37]

A **bipolar** balance of power (two states with relatively equal power) or a **multipolar** balance of power (three or more states engaging in checks and balances) are two realist categorizations of particular distributions of capabilities.

Such power configurations have occurred in the aftermath of major European wars—the Peace of Westphalia in 1648 following the Thirty Years' War, the Congress of Vienna in 1815 following the defeat of Napoleon, and the settlements following both twentieth-century world wars. Although the post-World War I arrangements bought only twenty years of peace, the Congress of Vienna was more successful in establishing a basis for maintaining a balance of power without general or major war for almost a century. Assessing the efforts of the diplomats at Vienna and subsequent meetings, Henry Kissinger concluded: "Their goal was stability, not perfection, and the balance of power is the classic expression of the lesson of history that no order is safe without physical safeguards against aggression." In short, according to Kissinger, a "new international order came to be created with a sufficient awareness of the connection between power and morality; between security and legitimacy."[38]

Two questions are subject to debate among realist scholars: (1) Do balances of power automatically occur, or are they created by statesmen? and (2) Which balance of power—bipolar or multipolar—is more likely to maintain international stability?

As to the first question, Kissinger's view emphasizes **voluntarism**—the balance of power is a foreign policy creation of statesmen; it doesn't just occur automatically. Makers of foreign policy do not act as automatons, prisoners of the balance of power and severely constrained by it. Rather, they are its creators and those charged with maintaining it. They are free to exercise their judgment and their will as agents for their states in the conduct of foreign policy with the expectation that they can have some effect on outcomes.

In contrast to this voluntarist conception is that of Kenneth Waltz, who sees the balance of power as an attribute of the system of states that will occur whether it is willed or not.[39] Given the assumptions that the state is a rational and a unitary actor that will use its capabilities to accomplish its objectives, states inevitably interact and conflict in the competitive environment of international politics. The outcome of state actions and interactions is a tendency toward equilibrium, or balance of power. Balance of power from this point of view, then, is a systemic tendency that occurs whether or not states seek to establish such a balance. Indeed, states may be motivated to improve their own positions so as to dominate others, but such attempts will likely be countered by other states similarly motivated. Thus, a balance of power more often than not occurs as states tend to balance against a rising power as opposed to joining its bandwagon. Balance-of-power theory so viewed can be used to account for arms races, alliances and counteralliances, and other forms of competitive behavior among states.

This image of the balance of power, therefore, refers to a recurrent phenomenon characteristic of international relations. It seems to matter little whether the states are democratic or authoritarian; the systemic tendency toward balance, or equilibrium, is always the same. It is as if states were billiard balls colliding with one another.[40] The faster and larger balls (the major powers) knock the smaller balls (the lesser powers) out of the way, although their own paths may also be deflected slightly by these collisions. These interactions, it is argued, tend toward international equilibrium or stability just as billiard balls eventually come to rest, at least until the balance is upset once again. But then the same tendency toward equilibrium repeats itself, only to be upset again. And so forth. The actors involved in this timeless drama remain the same: states. Actor combinations involving two or more states can be observed as the mechanical workings of the balance of power: multipolar prior to World War II, bipolar (the United States and the Soviet Union) in the years following the war.

Thus, Kenneth Waltz observes that in international relations "the freedom of choice of any one state is limited by the actions of all the others." Moreover, he argues that "the balance of power is not so much imposed by statesmen on events as it is imposed by events on statesmen."[41] For Waltz, the statesman has much less freedom to maneuver, much less capability to affect the workings of international politics, than Kissinger would allow. In a sense, then, Kissinger and Waltz represent alternative ends of a spectrum of contemporary realists conversant with balance-of-power thinking. Realists such as Waltz who emphasize balance of power as a system tendency have been labelled as "structural realists" or "nonrealists" because they have allegedly departed from a realist tradition that granted the statesman or policymaker greater freedom from constraint and thus greater ability to affect international events.[42]

Some critics of balance of power as a system tendency reject this mode of thinking precisely because of its mechanistic quality. One such critic, Ernst B. Haas, who finds little if any use in realist notions of balance of power, rejects "this formulation" because of its "system-dominant automaticity."[43] In other words, this mode of balance-of-power theory is too **deterministic**; individual policymakers can do little to affect events. Haas is even more explicit in later writings, criticizing determinists who

> see the components [of systems, i.e. states] as relatively unchangeable and arrange them in an eternal preprogrammed dance; the rules of the dance may be unknown to the actors and are specified by the theorist. The recurrent patterns discovered by him constitute a super-logic which predicts the future state of the system.[44]

The voluntarism–determinism debate is comparable in some ways to theological dispute over determinism and free will. As we use the term, *voluntarism* does not refer to freedom of choice only but to the ability of human beings to influence the course of events. How free are individuals to determine their own fates? How much effective choice do they have? How much are events *determined* by factors independent of human will exercised by statesmen? In the context of international relations, the question is whether states or their decision makers can affect their environment or whether their actions are severely constrained by other states interacting in a system of states. How much is free? How much is determined?

Kissinger's position is closer to the voluntarist pole, but he definitely would not argue that foreign policymakers are totally free of external constraints. Indeed, their ability to maneuver within these constraints is at least partly a function of their diplomatic skill. Similarly, Waltz would reject the idea that he is in any way a determinist. Nevertheless, his views are far removed from the purely voluntarist pole. The implication of his view of the balance of power is that individual decision makers and their states have much less freedom or capability to affect the course of events than others such as Kissinger would assert.

In some respects, the writings of Hans J. Morgenthau are an attempt to combine the two perspectives, thus inviting wrath by proponents of both. Morgenthau acknowledged the balance of power as a tendency within international politics while, at the same time, prescribing what statesmen should do to maintain the balance. He argued that "the balance of power and policies aiming at its preservation are not only inevitable but are an essential stabilizing factor in a society of sovereign nations."[45] Quite apart from the apparent determinism in this statement, Morgenthau assigned to diplomats not just the task of maintaining the balance of power; he also charged them to "create the conditions under which it will not be impossible from the outset to establish a world state."[46]

In short, for Morgenthau, escape from the balance of power and the voluntarist creation of a new world order remained possibilities worthy of pursuit. At the same time, his detractors have noted that, on the one hand, to argue that the balance of power is an inevitable system tendency and, on the other hand, to prescribe what should be done to maintain a balance or transform the system itself is to argue in contradictory terms. Be that as it may, Morgenthau's thinking represents a middle ground between realists who tend toward voluntarist or determinist poles.

Balance of Power and System Stability

We conclude this discussion of the realist's use of the system concept with reference to a long-standing realist debate: Is a bipolar or a multipolar balance of power more conducive to the stability of the international system? Stated another way, is war more likely to occur in a bipolar or a multipolar world?

The best-known statements on this matter are by Kenneth Waltz on the one hand and J. David Singer and Karl Deutsch on the other.[47] All three agree that the amount of uncertainty about the consequences of a particular action taken by a decision maker increases as the number of international actors increases. The logic of this assumption is that as the number increases, a decision maker has to deal with a greater quantity of information; more international actors mean more information is generated that has to be taken into account in the formulation of foreign policy. Therefore, all three authors agree that as an international system moves from being bipolar to being multipolar, the amount of overall uncertainty in the system increases. So far, so good.

Where they part company is on the matter of whether an increase in the number of actors (and hence uncertainty) makes war more or less likely. Waltz argues that greater uncertainty makes it *more* likely that a decision maker will misjudge the intentions and actions of a potential foe. Hence, a multipolar system, given its association with higher levels of uncertainty, is less desirable than a bipolar system because multipolarity makes uncertainty and thus the probability of war greater. Singer and Deutsch, however, make the opposite argument. They believe a multipolar system is more conducive to stability because uncertainty breeds caution on the part of decision makers. Caution means following tried and true policies of the past, avoiding deviations. Furthermore, they argue that "the increase in number of independent actors diminishes the share [of attention] that any nation can allocate to any other single actor."[48] This, it is argued, also reduces the probability of war because a state's attention is allocated to a larger number of actors.

Both arguments seem logical. But if *both* cannot be correct, it is still possible that *neither* one is correct. This is a proposition put forth by Bruce Beuno de Mesquita. For example, he challenges the assumption that uncertainty is greater in a multipolar world, arguing that "if the system's structure — be it bipolar or multipolar — does not change, there will be little uncertainty" because "learned patterns from prior behavior will aid decision makers to anticipate the likely consequences of similar behaviors under similar circumstances." Hence, "the level of systemic uncertainty, by itself, neither increases nor decreases the likelihood of war. Consequently, neither the number of blocs, nor the magnitude of change in the number of blocs in the system is expected to be associated with the likelihood of war."[49] Bueno de Mesquita goes on to discuss a number of other propositions dealing with such matters as the relation between the increase in overlapping interests of states (détente) and war, and the relation between the tightening and loosening of alliances and the probability of war. He found, for example, that since the early nineteenth century the amount of war tended to rise as commitments within a bloc became more tight-knit. This was particularly true for the twentieth century. Bueno de Mesquita's work is an example of explicitly stating commonly held and sometimes conflicting assumptions and hypotheses about the causes of war and then subjecting them to formal empirical tests. Though working separately, J. David Singer, Manus Midlarsky, Jack Levy, and others have continued this quantitative work on the causes of war and on the phenomenon of militarized disputes.[50]

Leaving aside the question of uncertainty, other arguments have been advanced concerning the relative stability of bipolar and multipolar worlds. This is of more than passing interest, given the fact that with the demise of the Soviet Union and the economic rise of Japan and Germany there is a consensus that the world will become increasingly multipolar. Waltz now concurs with those who see a shift taking place in the distribution of capabilities among states. Since the 1960s, Waltz had argued that the international system was still bipolar — counter to what was a commonplace view that the world already had become (or was becoming) multipolar. While agreeing that the relative power position of the United States had changed from the late 1940s and early 1950s, when European states and Japan were still suffering the devastation wrought by World War II, Waltz pointed to both economic and military indicators that put the United States and the Soviet Union as superpowers so far above Germany, Japan, or any other state as to make the world still very much bipolar. Responding to changes he has observed in the 1980s and 1990s, Waltz now sees the structure of the international system as becoming multipolar, perhaps by the end of the decade. Although the decline and breakup of the Soviet Union leaves the United States for the short term as the single most powerful global actor, Waltz contends that the principal poles in the new multipolar world that is emerging likely will be the

United States, Germany (or "Europe" if it unites), Japan, and Russia (which likely will reassume its historical position as a defensive great power).[51]

For Waltz, this change in systemic structure is not without significant behavioral consequences. Relations in a bipolar system between superpowers were relatively simple and predictable, resulting in a relatively stable world order in which direct conflicts between superpowers usually were avoided, thus reducing the likelihood of general war. By contrast, Waltz still contends that the uncertainties attendant to calculations in a more complex, multipolar world make relations somewhat less predictable. From Waltz's view, we may come to regret the passing of what was a stable, bipolar world. Based upon Waltz's logic, one scholar has deduced a sobering scenario for Europe.[52]

The gradual emergence of multipolarity has spurred other scholars to examine earlier periods of multipolarity, such as those occurring prior to the two world wars. On the encouraging side, work on alliance formation has concluded that (1) while democratic polities are not particularly less inclined to go to war than other forms of government, they are (2) disinclined to go to war against each other and, (3) except for the late 1930s, democracies tend to ally with one another at a higher rate than random probability would indicate.[53] Given the rapid expansion in the number of democratic regimes during the 1980s, such work is particularly relevant. Other works examine different factors at the state-societal levels of analysis, such as the economy and concern for domestic political stability that may influence foreign policy choices. Such a focus is a welcome corrective to traditional work on alliances that tends to assume that external threats virtually alone determine a state's international alignment.[54] More ambitious attempts, however, have been made to integrate societal and system-level variables (such as polarity, technology, and geography) in the hope of gaining insight on how to explain and predict alliance strategies.[55]

INTERDEPENDENCE

To this point we have discussed some of the intellectual precursors of realism and have then examined two concepts important to the realist analysis of world politics: power and system. In the next two sections, we discuss the realist view on two current concerns within the international relations discipline: interdependence and accounting for system change. As will become apparent in Chapter Three, the concept of interdependence is an important one to many scholars whom we would classify as pluralists. It is useful, therefore, to present the realist view of this concept, a view that is derived from the realist emphasis on power in the international system.

Interdependence and Vulnerability

To realists, interdependence is not necessarily such a good thing. Rather than being a symmetric relation between coequal parties—which is how many people view the term—interdependence is, realists argue, usually dominance–

dependence, with the dependent party particularly vulnerable to the choices of the dominant party. Interdependence does not mean equality. Interdependence connotes some degree of vulnerability by one party to another. Indeed, interdependence as vulnerability is a source of power of one state over another. To reduce this vulnerability, realists have argued that it is better for the state to be independent or, at least, to minimize its dependency. For example, the state needing to import oil is vulnerable to an embargo or price rise engineered by the state or states exporting the commodity. To reduce this vulnerability would require reducing oil imports — by finding an alternative source, for example.

To realists, interdependence does not affect all states equally. Although the economies of most oil-importing countries were affected by the quadrupling of oil prices in 1973–1974, they were not all equally vulnerable. Vulnerability is in part a question of what alternatives are available. For example, as a matter of policy the United States has tried to increase domestic production, create a strategic oil reserve to be drawn from only in emergencies, find other foreign sources of oil, and substitute alternative forms of energy whenever feasible. Given these measures, the United States has been able to reduce somewhat its vulnerability to a new oil embargo. Not all oil-importing countries have been able to develop even this degree of protection against the oil embargo risk. In short, in any given issue area, not all states are equally vulnerable. Therefore, the realist is suspicious of such blanket statements as "the entire world is interdependent" to the extent that such claims are supposedly *equally* applicable to all states.

Realists thus tend to see interdependence as being between or among states. Therefore, the balance of power is a kind of interdependence. To be sure, some realists of a more eclectic sort acknowledge interdependence involving nonstate actors such as multinational corporations and try to take them into account. But at the core of realist thought is the image of states interacting like billiard balls. This captures the essential meaning of interdependence for the realist, which is a fundamentally different view of interdependence from that held by either pluralists or globalists.

Interdependence and Economics

Economic factors, as we noted earlier, are important to realists to the extent that they reflect or affect national power or capabilities. Industrial countries that effectively combine technology with capital, skilled labor, and raw materials not only enjoy a higher standard of living but also tend to have more leverage in their relations with other states. In addition to trade, financial, and monetary influence that flows from a strong economy, military capabilities are usually greatest in states with advanced industrial economies. This is particularly true in modern military establishments that rely so heavily on technology and on a relatively large pool of skilled labor.

As is clear from reading Machiavelli, the relation between socioeconomic and military capabilities was also acknowledged in earlier, preindustrial times. But the realist has tended to see the economy as subordinate to political choice. If grand strategy, alliance theory, and national and international security are the stuff of high politics, then trade, finance, monetary exchange, fishing rights, and other socioeconomic issues have traditionally been viewed by the realist as somewhat less important — low politics.

On the other hand, realists do understand that maintenance of access to oil and other natural resources is essential to national security. Some economic issues, for example, have been elevated to the status of high politics, as was true following the 1973 oil embargo and the subsequent rise in the real price of petroleum. Maintaining access to oil supplies was a core objective of the multistate coalition that forced Iraq to withdraw from Kuwait in 1991.

Conceiving of world politics in terms of separate issue areas or, in the words of one realist, alternative "chessboards," is one example of awareness among realists of the importance to the state of socioeconomic and other nonmilitary issues.[56] If a state wants to be more powerful, however, it avoids or minimizes economic dependency on other states just as it avoids political or military dependency on other states if this amounts to a reduction of its relative power position. Dependency on others is to be minimized, whereas dependency of others on one's own state may be desirable to the extent that it increases one's leverage over those other states.

Interdependence, Peace, and Hegemony

Interdependence, according to realists, may or may not enhance prospects for peace. Conflict, not cooperation, could just as easily result. Just as in households or community conflicts, one way to establish peace is to eliminate or minimize contact among opponents or potential adversaries. Separation from other units, if that were possible, would mean less contact and thus less conflict.[57]

Some realists, however, do have something to say about the conditions under which international cooperation in nonmilitary issues may be enhanced. In the 1970s, several scholars argued that leadership exercised by one state or another is conducive to stability even if this "leadership" becomes hegemonic. According to the theory of **hegemonic stability**, the hegemon, or dominant power, assumes leadership, perhaps for the entire globe, in dealing with a particular issue. Thus, Britain was seen as offering leadership in international monetary matters in the nineteenth and early twentieth centuries. The gold standard associated with the international exchange of money was managed from London by the Bank of England. After World War II, the leadership role was finally assumed by the United States.[58]

The absence of hegemony, or leadership, may result in chaos and instability, as happened in the 1930s when the United States was unwilling to assume leadership of the world economy and Britain, given its weakened position, was unable to do so.[59] Competitive depreciation of currencies, erection of trade barriers, and a drastic reduction in the volume of trade were the outcome.

Although not all realists would subscribe to the view, stability is therefore seen by some as enhanced by a concentration of power in international politics; there is virtue in inequality among states. The hegemonic state or states benefit, but so too do other, less powerful states. By contrast, the decline of hegemony and the consequent fragmentation of power in international politics is said to produce disorder — a breakdown or unraveling of previously constructed international agreements. Leadership provided by hegemonic states is understood as facilitating achievement of collaboration among states.

Theoretical and empirical controversy in the 1980s and 1990s over whether the United States was a hegemon in decline was sparked primarily by the work of the historian Paul Kennedy, who examined the rise and fall of great powers over some five hundred years.[60] The debate influenced (and was influenced by) discussion already under way mainly among neorealists on the stabilizing role performed by global hegemons, a view originally set forth by the economic historian Charles Kindleberger and developed by others. Thus, Joseph Lepgold examined American adaptation to hegemonic decline.[61] Other writers challenged the whole notion of U.S. decline in any absolute sense.[62] After all, U.S. "decline" was *relative* only to the rise of other actors such as Germany and Japan. Notwithstanding all of America's economic problems, this gradual "leveling" of relative standings still left the United States effectively in first position. Moreover, the breakup of the Soviet Union resulted in the United States, at least for a short term, being the only global superpower — a "unipolar" structure, however multipolar the world might eventually become.

Perhaps because of its intuitive plausibility — not to mention the issue of the relative "decline" of American power and the problem of international cooperation "after hegemony"[63] — the theory of hegemonic stability has been applied to a wide range of issue areas during various historical periods. The hegemon influences states to cohere and establish the rules by which international relations are to be conducted in various issue areas such as the exchange of money, trade, finance, health, environment, communications, air transportation, and fishing and navigation on the high seas. Using the concept of hegemonic stability is one approach among several dealing with the emergence and functioning of **international regimes** governing these issue areas, regimes having become a major empirical and theoretical focus in recent years. Regimes have been defined as "implicit or explicit principles, norms, rules and decision-making procedures around which actors' expectations converge in a given area of international relations."[64] Hence, an international regime can be viewed as a **dependent variable** — something to be explained — and an **independent variable** — a possible influence on the behavior of states. Those realists who apply the theory of hegemonic stability to the question of regime development begin with the assumption that the structure of the international system — particularly the distribution of capabilities — defines the possibilities of cooperation. Other realists, using game theory and its attendant assumptions of unified, rational state actors, try to explain how cooperation in an anarchic international system can be achieved.[65]

In sum, the realist view of interdependence challenges many conventional ideas of the concept: (1) Interdependence is not necessarily a good thing for any one particular state if interdependence is defined in terms of vulnerability; (2) increasing interdependence may produce conflict as opposed to peace; and (3) in an interdependent world, there are certain virtues in having a hegemonic power capable of enforcing stability in a number of different issue areas.

CHANGE

Realists stress the continuity of international relations. Many of the insights of Thucydides are deemed to be as relevant today as they were 2,500 years ago. Balance of power involving states, whether viewed as a policy or a recurrent outcome, has existed at least since the fifteenth and sixteenth centuries. Although continuity is the watchword for realists, this does not mean that they are uninterested in change. For many theorists of international relations, understanding the evolution of the international system and predicting its future should be the preeminent research goals. The methods for discovering global patterns may vary. Some scholars have applied quantitative measures to historical data, as in the Correlates of War project.[66] Others have approached the issue of international political change by attempting to discern cycles of national power and their relation to the outbreak of war.

To illustrate how realists have dealt with the issue of change, we will briefly discuss the works of Robert Gilpin and George Modelski. As the title of his book suggests, Gilpin is interested in developing a framework for thinking about *War and Change in World Politics*. He believes "it is possible to identify recurrent patterns, common elements, and general tendencies in the major turning points in international history." International political change is the result of efforts of political actors "to change the international system in order to advance their own interests," however these interests may be defined (security, economic gain, ideological goals, etc.).[67] Gilpin lists five assumptions concerning the behavior of states that will guide his analysis. For example, the realist emphasis on the unified, rational actor state is revealed in the second assumption: "A state will attempt to change the international system if the expected benefits exceed the expected costs (i.e., if there is an expected net gain)."[68]

Various periods of history are marked by equilibrium (such as after the Congress of Vienna in 1815) or disequilibrium. As long as the system can adjust to the demands of its constituent states, stability is maintained. What accounts for change and the undermining of the status quo? The key factor, originally identified by Thucydides, "is the tendency in an international system for the powers of member states to change at different rates because of political, economic, and technological developments. In time, the differential growth in power of the various states in the system causes a fundamental redistribution of power in the system."[69] A state with ever-increasing power may determine that the costs involved in attempting to change the nature of the system are outweighed by the benefits if such an endeavor is successful. What has been the principal mechanism of change throughout history? War, because wars determine which states will govern the system. The peace settlement after the war codifies the new status quo. This equilibrium reflects the new distribution of power in the international system until eventually the differential growth in the power of states leads to another attempt to change the system.

George Modelski has argued that the global political system goes through distinct and identifiable historical cycles or recurrent patterns of behavior.[70] The global political system dates from about A.D. 1500, and over the years various world powers have helped to shape and maintain the system. According to Modelski, since A.D. 1500 four states have played dominant roles, each one corresponding to a "long cycle": Portugal (1500 to the end of the sixteenth century), the Netherlands (the seventeenth century), Great Britain (early eighteenth century to the Napoleonic Wars, and a second cycle from 1815 to 1945), and the United States (1945 to the present). As in the case of Gilpin's analysis, war tends to mark the end of one cycle and the beginning of another.

What produces these cycles? Two conditions are critical: (1) the urge of a power to create a global order, and (2) particular properties and weaknesses of the global system. Modelski notes that, as with long-term business cycles, world order is also subject to decay. The dominant power is inevitably faced with the growth of rival power centers, and attempts to maintain territorial control around the globe prove to be a costly task that drains the vitality and energy of the home country. Each cycle, therefore, exhibits a particular nation-state in an ascending and then a descending phase. As Modelski notes, following a major war one world power

> emerges from that conflict in an advantageous position and organizes the world even as the struggle still goes on and then formalizes its position in the global layer in the peace settlement. For the space of another generation that new power maintains basic order and is the mainspring of world institutions, often taking transnational forms. But the time comes when the energy that built this order begins to run down. . . . The prominent role of world power attracts competitors (other great powers) . . . ; the system moves into multipolarity. Rivalries among the major powers grow fiercer and assume the characteristics of oligopolistic competition. Gradually, as order dissolves, the system moves toward its original point of departure, that of minimal order and a Babel of conflicting and mutually unintelligible voices.[71]

Modelski and Gilpin, therefore, both present a dynamic view of the international system. Patterns of behavior are evident throughout history. Periods of rapid change alternate with periods of relative stability. Given the emphasis on the importance of war in changing the structure of the system, are we currently experiencing a lull before some sort of global cataclysm? Both Gilpin and Modelski would undoubtedly find such a question too pessimistic. As Modelski notes, it is possible that the international system may be "propelled in a new direction. We have no means of predicting what that new direction might be except that it could be moved away from the present system that relies too heavily on the steady, if long-spaced-out, progression of global wars."[72] Work continues by Modelski and his associates on the "rhythm of global politics." To those using this mode of analysis, long cycles "organize international relations in the past and they clarify the future."[73]

There is a growing body of literature emphasizing how changes in the power positions of states — some of which are in an ascending phase and some in a descending trend relative to other states — contribute to the outbreak of war.[74] This "power transition" work on war has been criticized on historical, empirical, and conceptual grounds.[75] Nevertheless, given the ongoing shifts in the distribution of world power and the increase in the number of democracies, it can be expected that scholars will devote even more attention to specifying the links between the international and domestic levels of analysis in order to understand better the dynamics of peace and stability.[76]

REALISTS AND THEIR CRITICS: AN OVERVIEW

Realism: The Term Itself

What is perhaps most impressive about the realist image of international politics is its longevity. Although modifications, clarifications, additions, and methodological innovations have been made down through the years, the core elements have remained basically intact.

If realism represents a "realistic" image of international politics, what does that say about competing images? Are they by definition "unrealistic"? In debate and discourse, labels are important. A good example of this involves the interwar years during which realists were challenged by advocates of the League of Nations, world federalism, or peace through international law. Many of these individuals came to be known as "idealists" or "utopians."

The very labels attached to these competing images of world order obviously put the so-called idealists at a disadvantage. Realists could claim that they were dealing with the world as it actually functioned. The idealists, on the other hand, were supposedly more concerned with what *ought* to be. "Yes," a realist might say, "I too wish the world were a more harmonious place, but that unfortunately is not the case." Those persons who were placed in the idealist camp certainly did not choose this particular label for themselves. Who did? The realists. By so doing, the opposition was stripped of a certain amount of legitimacy. Idealism conjured up images of wooly-headed professors, unsophisticated peace advocates, and impractical, utopian schemes.

Realists would respond that *realism* should be taken at face value; it is an appropriate term precisely because its basic tenets in fact closely approximate the world as it is. This is nothing of which to be ashamed. The longevity of the realist tradition is not simply a function of the expropriation of a particular label but a result of realism's inherent descriptive, explanatory, and predictive strengths.

Another reason for the longevity of realism is that this particular image of the world most closely approximates the image held by practitioners of statecraft. Realism has always had a strong policy-prescriptive component, as we have already noted. Machiavelli's *The Prince*, for example, was expressly presented as a guide for the ruler. Nor is it mere coincidence that two of the best known American academics who held high positions in the U.S. foreign policy establishment in the 1970s, Henry A. Kissinger and Zbigniew Brzezinski, are both self-professed realists. The realist as academic speaks much the same language as the realist as statesman: power, force, national interest, and diplomacy.

It has been argued, however, that some realist writers help to perpetuate the very world they analyze. By describing the world in terms of violence, duplicity, and war, and then providing advice to statesmen as to how statesmen should act, such realists are justifying one particular conception of international relations. Realism becomes a self-fulfilling prophecy. Even more recent efforts to place realism on a stronger theoretical foundation (referred to as "structural realism" or "neorealism") that favor explanation over policy prescription have the same effect. Critics contend that such realists suffer from a lack of imagination and an inability to consider seriously alternative conceptions of world politics and how these might be achieved.

The realist response is that there is nothing inherently wrong with being policy relevant and helping leaders navigate through dangerous waters. Advice based on wishful thinking and questionable assessments of international forces and trends could lead to disastrous policies, particularly if one is the lone "idealist" leader in a world of realists. Moreover, most criticism is understood to be based on a selective reading of realists, ignoring their genuine concern not only with the causes of war but also with how peace can be achieved or maintained. Finally, not all realists would claim to be particularly interested in providing advice to statesmen. They would rather use realist assumptions and insights to develop better theories of international politics. Being policy relevant or ingratiating oneself with political leaders is not the goal for these realists who entertain the scholarly goal of explaining how the world functions.

The System and Determinism

As we have seen, the concept of system is critical to many realist writers. Whether the rather simple notion of anarchy or the more elaborate formulations devised by contemporary realist authors, the system is deemed important for its impact on international actors. It is charged, however, that recent realist writers portray the system as having a life of its own, seemingly independent of the wishes and actions of states. Statesmen are granted too little autonomy and too little room to maneuver, and the decision-making process is seemingly devoid of human volition. Human agents are pawns of a bloodless system that looms over them, a structure whose functioning they do not understand and the mechanics of which they only dimly perceive. Statesmen are faced with an endless array of constraints and few opportunities. It is as if they are engaged in a global game, a game called power politics, and they are unable to change the rules even if they so desire. In sum, critics claim there is a fatalistic, deterministic, and pessimistic undercurrent to much of the realist work. As a result, some of these critics have turned to the sociology discipline in search of more dynamic conceptions of structure that emphasize the reciprocal influence of structure and human agents.[77]

Realists differ among themselves as to how much explanatory emphasis is to be given the international system. There is disagreement as to what extent the system functions as an independent variable in influencing state behavior. For some realists, the system is more than the aggregation of state interactions. Rather, it represents a structure that does indeed influence the behavior of states that are part of the system. It is these scholars who have drawn the most criticism, but they reject the charge that they are structural determinists who ignore actors operating at the unit, or state, level of analysis. One realist who argues that a systemic theory of international politics is composed of "the structure of the system and its interacting units," notes that if structure influences without determining, then one must ask how and to what extent the structure of a realm accounts for outcomes and how and to what extent the units [i.e., states] account for outcomes. Structure has to be studied in its own right as do units.[78]

Another realist categorically states that "no new realist that I have read argues that political structure determines all behavior."[79] Realists therefore differ on the extent to which statesmen impose themselves on events, or vice versa. No realist is completely determinist or voluntarist. It is not a matter of either-or but varying assessments as to how strong are the constraints placed on statesmen and how much room leaders have to maneuver.[80]

Realists and the State

The state is the centerpiece of realist work. Few persons would disagree as to the importance of the state in international affairs. The criticism, however, is that realists are so obsessed with the state that they ignore other actors and other issues not directly related to the maintenance of state security. Other nonstate actors —multinational corporations, banks, terrorists, and international organizations —are either excluded, downplayed, or trivialized in the realist perspective. Furthermore, given the national security prism through which realists view the world, other concerns such as the socioeconomic gap between rich and poor societies or international pollution rarely make the realist agenda. At best, such issues are dealt with in a derivative manner. A preoccupation with national security and the state by definition relegates other issues to secondary importance or bans them entirely from the realist agenda.

Realists counter that simply because nonstate actors are not dealt with in depth does not mean that they are considered irrelevant. Political scientists, one realist notes, should avoid slipping "into thinking that what an author fails to concentrate his attention upon, he takes to be inconsequential."[81] Similarly, another realist has stated that to argue "that the state . . . is the principal actor in international relations does not deny the existence of other individual and collective actors."[82]

Second, realists contend that theories are constructed to answer certain questions and to explain certain types of international behavior and outcomes. As a result, they purposely limit the type of actors analyzed. A theory concerned with explaining state behavior naturally focuses on states, not multinational corporations or terrorist groups. Similarly, a concern with national security issues by definition makes it unlikely that global welfare issues will receive the same degree of attention.

Finally, it can be argued that focusing on the state is justified on normative grounds. Many scholars, for example, are concerned with how unbridled arms races and military spending (a trillion dollars worldwide) contribute to international tension, devastating regional wars, and socioeconomic deprivation.[83] Because it is almost exclusively states that spend this money to buy or produce military hardware, it makes sense to focus on them as the unit of analysis. Hence, far from being enamored of states, many realists are critical of these political entities that are deemed too important to be ignored.

Realists and the Balance of Power

Given the emphasis on the state and the concern with national security issues, we have seen how the concept of balance of power has played a dominant role in realist thought and theory. Although balance of power has been a constant theme in realist writings down through the centuries, it has also come in for a great deal of abuse. Balance of power has been criticized for creating definitional confusion. Hans Morgenthau, a realist himself, discerned at least four definitions: (1) a policy aimed at a certain state of affairs; (2) an objective or actual state of affairs; (3) an approximately equal distribution of power, as when a balance of power exists between the United States and the Soviet Union; and (4) any distribution of power including a preponderance of power, as when the balance of power shifts in favor of either superpower. One critic has found eight meanings of the term.[84] If the balance of power means so many different things, does it mean anything?

Balance of power has also been criticized for leading to war as opposed to preventing it, serving as a poor guide for statesmen, and functioning as a propaganda tool to justify defense spending and foreign adventures. Despite these constant attacks and continual reformulations of the meaning of the term, balance of power remains a crucial concept in the realist vocabulary.

At times it has appeared that the harshest critics of balance of power as a concept have been the realists themselves. All of these criticisms have been acknowledged and some deemed valid. Attempts have been made, however, to clear up misconceptions and misinterpretations of balance of power, placing it on a more solid conceptual footing. One such effort has been made by Kenneth Waltz.[85] Even these more recent formulations, however, are not without their critics.

Realism and Change

Given the realist view of the international system, the role of the state, and balance of power politics, critics suggest that very little possibility for the fundamental and peaceful transformation of international politics is left. Realists, claim the critics, at best offer analysis aimed at understanding how international stability is achieved but nothing approaching true peace. Realist stability reflects a world bristling with weapons, forever on the verge of violent conflict and war. Alternative world futures—scenarios representing a real alternative to the dismal Hobbesian world—are rarely discussed or taken seriously. The timeless quality of international politics, its repetitious nature and cycles of war, and a world in which the strong do as they will and the weak as they must dominate the realist image. We are given little information, let alone any hope, say the critics, as to how meaningful and peaceful change can occur and help us escape from the security dilemma. Realists, it is argued, simply assume state interests, but tell us little about how states come to define their interests, or the processes by which those interests are redefined.

The issue of change, of course, is intimately connected to that of determinism and to what was referred to in Chapter One as the *agent-structure* problem. Although power politics and the state are central to all realist analyses, this does not mean that fundamental change is impossible, or that change is limited to war and the cyclical rise and fall of states. Robert Gilpin argues that

> the state is the principal actor in that the nature of the state and the patterns of relations among states are the most important determinants of the character of international relations at any given moment. This argument does not presume that states need always be the principal actors, nor does it presume that the nature of the state need always be the same and that the contemporary nation-state is the ultimate form of political organization.[86]

Another realist has held out the possibility of diplomacy leading to a world state.[87] What separates realists from some other writers on the question of system change, however, is a belief that "if the nation-state is to disappear . . . it will do so through age-old political processes and not as idealists would wish through a transcendence of politics itself."[88] Hence, realists claim that fundamental change *is* possible and is taken into consideration in their work. Once again, however, the strength of this view varies depending on the author under consideration.

Realism: The Entire Enterprise

Critics of realism have always felt that they have been faced with a difficult task because the image comes close to approaching an impregnable edifice seemingly unscathed by years of criticism. Indeed, scholars who at one time in their careers struggled to devise alternative approaches based on alternative images of international politics have in some instances given up the quest, become converts, or resigned themselves to modifying existing realist explanatory frameworks.

Critics are faced with several problems. First, as noted earlier, given realism's affinity to the real world of policy making, this particular image of the world is automatically imbued with a certain degree of attractiveness and legitimacy. It represents the world out there, not some ivory tower perspective on human events. Not only is the realist perspective the accepted wisdom of the Western foreign policy establishments, but even in the Third World leaders more often than not speak the language of realism as a result of concern over the survival of their regimes and states. Within the halls of academe, realism also has great attractiveness; "peace studies" programs sometimes find it advantageous to change the title to "security and conflict studies" in order to generate student interest. Realism can be as seductive to the academic professional as it can be to the student.

Second, realism is also seductive in that it has been given an increasingly scientific face. Earlier criticisms of the realist literature were very often based on the contention that such concepts as balance of power had less to do with theory building and more to do with ideology and self-justification of one particular approach to conducting international relations. Much of the realist work was, therefore, considered "unscientific." But at least some realists have cast their hunches and insights in the form of hypotheses, testable either quantitatively or with nonquantitative indicators.[89] The work is better grounded scientifically and placed within the context of the **positivist** view of how we comprehend reality. The positivist approach to knowledge still reigns in the natural and social sciences. As a result, any image of international politics that can be presented in the cloak of positivism is immediately granted a certain stature.

Realism has a lot going for it: It has a venerable tradition, is often policy relevant, addresses the big issues of war and peace, is intuitively plausible, and has more recently aspired to truly scientific status.

More recent formulations of realism, however, have actually been criticized for violating the realist tradition, particularly by ignoring the value sensitivity of the realist legacy as represented by E. H. Carr and Hans J. Morgenthau. In a sweeping attack on those he calls *neorealists*, Richard Ashley argues that their work presents a "self-enclosed, self-affirming" view of the world biased toward the existing state-centric order, subordinates all issues to a concern for control and survival of this state system, presents a historically homogeneous view of world history, trivializes alternative conceptions of world order, and dismisses the possibilities of fundamental change and peaceful transformation of the international system.[90] Neorealism, it is claimed, represents the new orthodoxy of the international relations discipline, and hence "students must prepare themselves to retell and carry forward yet another lore."[91] Neorealists reject these charges.

In conclusion, a comment is in order on criticism in general. One may wish to be wary of sweeping criticisms concerning an entire image, whether it be realist, pluralist, or globalist. It is not particularly difficult to find fault with the work of individual theorists, compile a list of their shortcomings, and then present the results as criticisms of the image as a whole. Such selectivity can be misleading. As this chapter illustrates, although realists may find common ground in terms of basic assumptions and key international actors, they also differ in a number of important respects such as methods they use, levels of analysis they choose, and what they assume about the ability of decision makers to influence international outcomes. That is why it is imperative for the serious student of the international relations literature to go to the original sources, evaluate the validity of such criticisms, and assess the value of each image as the basis for a mode of thinking about international relations.

NOTES

1. See Barbara W. Tuchman, *The March of Folly* (New York: Knopf, 1984).
2. Hans J. Morgenthau, *Politics Among Nations*, 4th ed. (New York: Knopf, 1966), p. 5.
3. Some works assume *procedural* rationality or omniscience on the part of actors. Other works simply assume *instrumental* rationality or choice, meaning given two or more alternatives, the actor will choose the one likely to yield the preferred outcome. Logically consistent preference orders can exist despite incomplete and erroneous in-

formation. See Frank C. Zagare, "Rationality and Deterrence," *World Politics* 42, no. 2 (January 1990): 238–60.

4. Morgenthau, *Politics Among Nations*, p. 25.

5. For a discussion of what type of realist Thucydides may have been, see Michael W. Doyle, "Thucydides: A Realist?" in *Hegemonic Rivalry: From Thucydides to the Nuclear Age*, eds. Richard Ned Lebow and Barry S. Strauss (Boulder, CO.: Westview Press, 1991), pp. 169–88. On Thucydides' importance to current theory, see Mark V. Kauppi, "Contemporary International Relations Theory and the Peloponnesian War," in Lebow and Strauss, pp. 101–24. See also George Modelski, "Kautilya: Foreign Policy and International System in the Ancient Hindu World," *American Political Science Review* 58 (September 1964): 549–60.

6. See John H. Finley's introduction to *The Complete Writings of Thucydides* (New York: Modern Library, 1951), pp. ix–x.

7. See Thucydides, *History of the Peloponnesian War*, trans. Rex Warner (Harmondsworth, England, and New York: Penguin Books, 1982), p. 49. Cf. Finley, *Complete Writings*, p. 15.

8. See "The Melian Dialogue" in Thucydides, *History*, p. 402. The idea that "it has always been a rule that the weak should be subject to the strong" is discussed earlier in the same work in "The Debate at Sparta and Declaration of War 432," pp. 80–81.

9. In his lengthier work, *The Discourses*, Machiavelli's republican preferences are apparent. Given the audience for which he wrote *The Prince* (the Medicis), Machiavelli does not emphasize there this republican orientation as he does in *The Discourses*. For a discussion of Machiavelli's thought, see the introduction by Max Lerner in Niccolo Machiavelli, *The Prince* and *The Discourses* (New York: Modern Library, 1950), pp. xxv–xxvi.

10. The distinction between the ethics of "responsibility" and "ultimate ends" is drawn by Max Weber, "Politics As a Vocation," in *From Max Weber: Essays in Sociology*, eds. H. H. Gerth and C. Wright Mills (New York: Oxford University Press, 1946, 1978), p. 120.

11. See Machiavelli, *The Prince*, Chapter XV, p. 56.

12. For example, Machiavelli argues in Chapter XVIII that the prince "should not deviate from what is good, if possible, but be able to do evil if constrained." Indeed, "it is well" for the prince "to seem merciful, faithful, humane, sincere, religious, and also to be so." *The Prince*, p. 65.

13. See William Ebenstein, *Great Political Thinkers: Plato to the Present*, 4th ed. (New York: Holt, Rinehart and Winston, 1969), p. 364.

14. Thomas Hobbes, *Leviathan*, edited by Michael Oakeshott (New York and London: Collier Macmillan, 1974). These classic citations are drawn from Book 1, Chapter 13.

15. Ibid., Book 1, Chapter 15, p. 113.

16. Ibid., Book 1, Chapter 13, p. 101.

17. One such realist is Hedley Bull. See his *The Anarchical Society: A Study of Order in World Politics* (New York: Columbia University Press, 1977).

18. Carl von Clausewitz, *On War*, ed. and trans. Michael Howard and Peter Paret (Princeton, NJ: Princeton University Press, 1976), p. 87. See also Peter Paret, "The Genesis of *On War*," Michael Howard, "The Influence of Clausewitz"; and Bernard Brodie, "The Continuing Relevance of *On War*" and "A Guide to the Reading of *On War*," all in *On War*, pp. 3–58 and 641–711. For an extension of Clausewitzian ideas on the importance of societal factors, see Michael Howard, "The Forgotten Dimensions of Strategy," *Foreign Affairs* 57, no. 5 (Summer 1979): 975–86.

19. Edward Hallett Carr, *The Twenty Years Crisis, 1919–1939* (London: Macmillan and Co., 1962), p. ix.
20. Ibid., pp. 111–12.
21. Ibid., p. 112.
22. Ibid., p. 112–13.
23. Ibid., p. 93.
24. A. F. K. Organski, *World Politics*, 2d ed. (New York: Knopf, 1968), p. 104; Morgenthau, *Politics Among Nations*, p. 26; Karl Deutsch, *The Analysis of International Relations* (Englewood Cliffs, NJ: Prentice Hall, 1967), p. 22.
25. Howard, "The Forgotten Dimensions of Strategy."
26. Organski, *World Politics*, p. 358; and J. David Singer, Stuart Bremer, and John Stuckey, "Capability Distribution, Uncertainty, and Major Power War, 1820–1965," in *Peace, War, and Numbers*, ed. Bruce Russett (Beverly Hills, CA: Sage Publications, 1972), pp. 21–27. See also Klaus Knorr, *Military Power and Potential* (Cambridge, MA: D. C. Heath, 1970).
27. Bruce Bueno de Mesquita, *The War Trap* (New Haven, CT: Yale University Press, 1981), p. 153. J. David Singer and associates, *Explaining War: Selected Papers from the Correlates of War Project* (Beverly Hills, CA: Sage Publications, 1979).
28. See the discussion in Ernst B. Haas, "On Systems and International Regimes," *World Politics* 27, no. 2 (January 1975), especially pp. 149–55. For examples of the use of the concept of system, see Morton Kaplan, *System and Process in International Politics* (New York: Wiley, 1957), and Richard Rosecrance, *Action and Reaction in World Politics* (Boston: Little, Brown, 1962).
29. For a discussion of a number of supposed fallacies, including reification, see Marion J. Levy, Jr., " 'Does it Matter If He's Naked?' Bawled the Child," in *Contending Approaches to International Politics*, ed. Klaus Knorr and James N. Rosenau (Princeton, NJ: Princeton University Press, 1969), pp. 87–106.
30. Rudolph J. Rummel, "Some Dimensions in the Foreign Behavior of States," in *International Politics and Foreign Policy*, ed. James N. Rosenau, p. 612. A pioneering work on field theory is Quincy Wright, *The Study of International Relations* (New York: Appleton-Century-Crofts, 1955).
31. Charles A. McClelland and Gary D. Hoggard, "Conflict Patterns in the Interactions Among Nations," in *International Politics and Foreign Policy*, ed. James N. Rosenau, pp. 711–24. Also Charles A. McClelland, "Warnings in the International Events Flow: EFI and Roz as Threat Indicators," *International Interactions* 5, nos. 2 and 3 (1978): 135–204; "The Acute International Crisis," in *The International System: Theoretical Essays*, ed. Klaus Knorr and Sidney Verba (Princeton, NJ: Princeton University Press, 1961), pp. 77–92; "The Anticipation of International Crises: Prospects for Theory and Research," *International Studies Quarterly* 21, no. 1 (March 1977): 15–30. For another example of system as interaction, see K. J. Holsti, *International Politics: A Framework for Analysis*, 4th ed. (Englewood Cliffs, NJ: Prentice Hall, 1983), p. 27.
32. See. J. L. Brierly, *The Law of Nations: An Introduction to the International Law of Peace* (New York: Oxford University Press, 1963), p. 47.
33. For an excellent critique of the concept of anarchy and the argument that the dichotomy between domestic and international politics is overdrawn by neorealists, see Helen Milner, "The Assumption of Anarchy in International Relations Theory: A Critique," *Review of International Studies* 17, no. 1 (January 1991): 67–85.
34. See John H. Herz, "Idealist Internationalism and the Security Dilemma," *World Politics* 5, no. 2 (January 1950): 157–80.

35. Kenneth N. Waltz develops the stag hunt allegory in his *Man, the State and War*, pp. 165–71. For a critique of Waltz's interpretation of Rousseau, see Stanley Hoffmann, "Rousseau on War and Peace," *American Political Science Review* 57, no. 2 (June 1963): 317–33. Cf. J. J. Rousseau, "A Discussion on the Origins of Inequality," in *The Social Contract and Discourses*, trans. G. D. H. Cole (New York: E. P. Dutton and Co., 1950), pp. 235–38.

36. A nonrealist, Ernst B. Haas, argues that such collaboration is indeed possible. Although collaboration is not an inevitable outcome, even "if the cooperative hunting of the stag is demonstrated to be impossible" a likely possibility would be for the hunters to "make informal rules regulating the separate or cooperative hunting of hares." See Haas, *Beyond the Nation-State* (Stanford, CA: Stanford University Press, 1964), pp. 69–71. An important work that has influenced the use of game theory in international relations is John von Neumann and Oskar Morgenstern, *Theory of Games and Economic Behavior* (Princeton: NJ: Princeton University Press, 1944, 1953). See also Martin Shubik, *Games for Society, Business, and War: Towards a Theory of Gaming* (New York: Elsevier, 1975); Barry R. Schlenker and Thomas V. Bonoma, "Fun and Games: The Validity of Games for the Study of Conflict," *Journal of Conflict Resolution* 22, no. 1 (March 1978): 1–28; Anatol Rapoport and A. M. Ghammah, *Prisoner's Dilemma* (Ann Arbor: University of Michigan Press, 1965). On bargaining, see Thomas C. Schelling, *The Strategy of Conflict* (Cambridge, MA: Harvard University Press, 1960). For a discussion of games such as stag hunt, prisoner's dilemma, deadlock, and chicken, see Robert Axelrod and Robert O. Keohane, "Achieving Cooperation Under Anarchy," *World Politics* 38, no. 1 (October 1985): 226–54.

37. See "Memorandum by Sir Eyre Crowe on the Present State of British Relations with France and Germany, January 1, 1907" in G. P. Gooch and H. Temperly, eds., *British Documents on the Origin of the War, 1898–1914* (London: H. M. Stationery Office, 1928), 5, no. 3, pp. 402–7 and 414–20. Reprinted in Fred A. Sondermann, David S. McClellan, and William C. Olson, eds., *The Theory and Practice of International Relations*, 5th ed. (Englewood Cliffs, NJ: Prentice Hall, 1979), p. 120.

38. See Henry A. Kissinger, *A World Restored: The Politics of Conservatism in a Revolutionary Age* (New York: Grosset & Dunlap, 1964), pp. 317–18.

39. Kenneth Waltz, *Theory of International Politics* (Reading, MA: Addison-Wesley, 1979). The use of the term *voluntarism* differs somewhat from the technical use of the term by many philosophers. See Paul Edwards, ed., *Encyclopedia of Philosophy* 5, nos. 7 and 8 (New York: Free Press, 1972), pp. 270–72.

40. The billiard ball metaphor for the balance of power is generally attributed to Arnold Wolfers, "The Actors in International Politics," in *Theoretical Aspects of International Relations*, ed. William T. R. Fox, (Notre Dame, IN: Notre Dame University Press, 1959), pp. 83–106.

41. See Waltz, *Man, the State and War*, pp. 204, 209.

42. Richard K. Ashley, "The Poverty of Neorealism," *International Organization* 38, no. 2 (Spring 1984): 225–86.

43. See nonrealist Ernst B. Haas, *Beyond the Nation–State*, p. 70.

44. See Ernst B. Haas, "On Systems and International Regimes," *World Politics* 27, no. 2 (January 1975), p. 151.

45. Morgenthau, *Politics Among Nations*, p. 161.

46. Ibid., p. 519.

47. Kenneth N. Waltz, "The Stability of a Bipolar World," *Daedalus* 93 (Summer 1964): 881–909; Karl W. Deutsch and J. David Singer, "Multipolar Power Systems and International Stability," *World Politics* 16, no. 3 (April 1964): 390–406.

48. Deutsch and Singer, "Multipolar Power Systems," p. 400.
49. Bruce Bueno de Mesquita, "Systemic Polarization and the Occurrence and Duration of War," *Journal of Conflict Resolution* 22, no. 2 (June 1978): 245, 246. See also Michael D. Wallace, *War and Rank Among Nations* (Lexington, MA: D. C. Heath, 1973).
50. See, for example, Melvin Small and J. David Singer, eds., *International War: An Anthology and Study Guide* (Homewood, IL: Dorsey Press, 1985); John A. Vasquez, "The Steps to War: Toward a Scientific Explanation of the Correlates of War Findings," *World Politics* 40, no. 1 (October 1987): 108–45; Manus I. Midlarsky, ed., *Handbook of War Studies* (Boston: Unwin Hyman, 1989); Midlarsky, *The Onset of War* (Boston: Unwin Hyman, 1988); and Jack S. Levy, "Theories of General War," 37, no. 3 (April 1985): 344–74.
51. Discussions with Kenneth Waltz, November 1991 and January 1992.
52. Waltz, *Theory of International Politics*, pp. 165–70; John J. Mearsheimer, "Back to the Future: Instability in Europe After the Cold War," *International Security* 15, no. 1 (Summer 1990): 5–56. See also Glenn Snyder, "The Security Dilemma in Alliance Politics," *World Politics* 36, no. 4 (July 1984): 461–95.
53. Steven Chan, "Mirror, Mirror on the Wall. . . . Are Freer Countries More Pacific?" *Journal of Conflict Resolution* 28, no. 4 (1984): 617–48; Melvin Small and J. D. Singer, "The War-Proneness of Democratic Regimes, 1816–1965," *Jerusalem Journal of International Relations* 1 (1976): 50–69; Erich Weede, "Democracy and War Involvement," *Journal of Conflict Resolution* 28, no. 4 (1984): 649–64; Zeev Maoz and Nasrin Abdolali, "Regime Types and International Conflict," *Journal of Conflict Resolution* 33, no. 1 (1989): 3–35; Randolph M. Siverson and Juliann Emmons, "Birds of a Feather: Democratic Political Systems and Alliance Choices in the Twentieth Century," *Journal of Conflict Resolution* 35, no. 2 (1991): 285–306.
54. See, for example, Michael N. Barnett and Jack S. Levy, "Domestic Sources of Alliances and Alignments: The Case of Egypt, 1962–73," *International Organization* 45, no. 3 (Summer 1991): 369–95; Steven R. David, "Explaining Third World Alignment," *World Politics* 43, no. 2 (January 1991): 233–55.
55. See, for example, Thomas J. Christensen and Jack Snyder, "Chain Gangs and Passed Bucks: Predicting Alliance Patterns in Multipolarity," *International Organization* 44, no. 2 (Spring 1990): 137–68; Stephen M. Walt, *The Origins of Alliances* (Ithaca, NY: Cornell University Press, 1987).
56. Stanley Hoffmann, "Weighing the Balance of Power," *Foreign Affairs* 50, no. 4 (July 1972): 618–43.
57. Steven L. Spiegel and Kenneth N. Waltz, eds. *Conflict in World Politics* (Cambridge, MA: Winthrop, 1971), pp. 454–74.
58. Robert O. Keohane, "The Theory of Hegemonic Stability and Changes in International Economic Regimes, 1967–1977," in Ole R. Holsti, Randolph M. Siverson, and Alexander L. George, eds., *Change in the International System* (Boulder, CO: Westview Press, 1980), pp. 131–62. For a critique and citations of the literature, see Arthur A. Stein, "The Hegemon's Dilemma: Great Britain, the United States, and the International Economic Order," *International Organization* 38, no. 2 (Spring 1984): 355–86; Susan Strange, "The Persistent Myth of Lost Hegemony," *International Organization* 41, no. 4 (Autumn 1987): 551–74; Isabelle Grunberg, "Exploring the 'Myth' of Hegemonic Stability," *International Organization* 44, no. 4 (Autumn 1990): 431–77.

59. Charles P. Kindleberger, *The World in Depression, 1929–1939* (Berkeley: University of California Press, 1973); Robert Gilpin, *U.S. Power and the Multinational Corporation* (New York: Basic Books, 1975); and Stephen Krasner, "State Power and the Structure of International Trade," *World Politics* 28, no. 3 (April 1976): 317–47.

60. Paul Kennedy, *The Rise and Fall of the Great Powers* (New York: Random House, 1987). Cf. the earlier work of the economist Mancur Olson, *The Rise and Decline of Nations* (New Haven: Yale University Press, 1982).

61. Kindleberger, *The World in Depression*; Joseph Lepgold, *The Declining Hegemon: The United States and European Defense, 1960–1990* (New York: Praeger, 1990).

62. For example, see Henry R. Nau, *The Myth of America's Decline* (New York: Oxford University Press, 1990); Joseph S. Nye, Jr., *Bound to Lead: The Changing Nature of American Power* (New York: Basic Books, 1990); and Samuel P. Huntington, "The U.S.—Decline or Renewal?" *Foreign Affairs* 67, 2 (Winter 1988/89): 76–96.

63. Robert Keohane, *After Hegemony: Cooperation and Discord in the World Political Economy* (Princeton: Princeton University Press, 1984).

64. Stephen Krasner, "Structural Causes and Regime Consequences: Regimes as Intervening Variables," in Krasner, ed., *International Regimes* (Ithaca: Cornell University Press, 1983), pp. 1–21.

65. See the special issue of *World Politics* 38, no. 1 (October 1985), edited by Kenneth Oye; R. Harrison Wagner, "The Theory of Games and the Problem of International Cooperation," *American Political Science Review* 70, no. 2 (June 1983): 330–46; Robert Jervis, "Realism, Game Theory, and Cooperation," *World Politics* 40, no. 3 (April 1988): 317–49; Robert Axelrod, *The Evolution of Cooperation* (New York: Basic Books, 1984); Michael Taylor, *Anarchy and Cooperation* (New York: Wiley, 1976). For an overview of the various approaches to regimes, see Stephen Haggard and Beth A. Simmons, "Theories of International Regimes," *International Organization* 41, no. 3 (Summer 1987): 491–517.

66. For works associated with the Correlates of War project, see "Suggested Readings" for this chapter under Singer's name.

67. Robert Gilpin, *War and Change in World Politics* (New York: Cambridge University Press, 1981), pp. 3, 10.

68. Ibid., p. 10.

69. Ibid., p. 13. The implications of the uneven growth of power were also addressed in Lenin's concept of "uneven development."

70. George Modelski, "The Long Cycle of Global Politics and the Nation-State," *Comparative Studies in Society and History* 20, no. 2 (April 1978): 214–35. Notice that Modelski does not describe the international system as being anarchic. Although a central authority is lacking, order and authority do exist. See his comments in "Long Cycles and the Strategy of the U.S. International Economic Policy," in *America in a Changing World Political Economy*, ed. William P. Avery and David P. Rapkin (White Plains, NY: Longman, 1982), p. 99.

71. Modelski, "The Long Cycle of Global Politics," p. 217. It is Modelski's emphasis on the primacy of political factors that places him within the context of the realist as opposed to globalist image.

72. Ibid., p. 235.

73. George Modelski, ed., *Exploring Long Cycles* (Boulder, CO: Lynne Rienner Publishers, 1987), p. ix. See also George Modelski and William R. Thompson, *Seapower*

in Global Politics, 1494–1993 (Seattle: University of Washington Press, 1988). Cf. Nathaniel Beck, "The Illusion of Cycles in International Relations," and Joshua S. Goldstein, "The Possibility of Cycles in International Relations," *International Studies Quarterly* 35, no. 4 (December 1991): 455–80.

74. Aside from Robert Gilpin and George Modelski, other authors who deal with power cycles include Charles F. Doran, *The Politics of Assimilation* (Baltimore: Johns Hopkins University Press, 1971); Charles F. Doran and Wes Parsons, "War and the Cycle of Relative Power," *American Political Science Review* 74, no. 4 (December 1980): 947–65; Mancur Olson, *The Rise and Decline of Nations* (New Haven, CT: Yale University Press, 1982); A. F. K. Organski and Jacek Kugler, *The War Ledger* (Chicago: University of Chicago Press, 1980); William Thompson, *Multiple Perspectives on the World System* (Beverly Hills, CA: Sage Publications, 1983).

75. See, for example, Jack S. Levy, "Theories of General War," *World Politics* 37, no. 3 (April 1985): 344–74.

76. For example, see Randall L. Schweller, "Domestic Structure and Preventive War: Are Democracies More Pacific?" *World Politics* 44, no. 2 (January 1992): 235–69.

77. Anthony Giddens' theory of structuration has been particularly influential. See, among other works, *A Contemporary Critique of Historical Materialism* (Berkeley: University of California Press, 1981); Giddens, *Central Problems in Social Theory* (Berkeley: University of California Press, 1979).

78. See Kenneth N. Waltz, "Letter to the Editor," *International Organization* 36, no. 3 (Summer 1982): 680, which cites his *Theory of International Politics*, p. 78.

79. Robert G. Gilpin, "The Richness of the Tradition of Political Realism," *International Organization* 38, no. 2 (Spring 1984): 302.

80. In a review of Kenneth Waltz's *Theory of International Politics*, Richard Rosecrance suggests Waltz's work is heavily determinist. Rosecrance, "International Relations Theory Revisited," *International Organization* 35, no. 4 (Autumn 1981): 691–713. Waltz rejects this charge in his "Letter to the Editor," p. 680.

81. Waltz, "Letter to the Editor," p. 680.

82. Gilpin, "Richness of Political Realism," p. 300.

83. U.S. Arms Control and Disarmament Agency, *World Military Expenditures and Arms Transfers 1989* (Washington, DC: Government Printing Office, 1990), p. 1.

84. Morgenthau, *Politics Among Nations*, p. 161; and Ernst B. Haas, "The Balance of Power: Prescription, Concept or Propaganda?" *World Politics* 5, no. 2 (July 1953): 442–77.

85. Waltz, *Theory of International Politics*.

86. Gilpin, "Richness of Political Realism," p. 300.

87. Morgenthau, *Politics Among Nations*, p. 548.

88. Gilpin, "Richness of Political Realism," p. 299; Morgenthau, *Politics Among Nations*, p. 9.

89. See, for example, P. Terrence Hopmann, Dina A. Zinnes, and J. David Singer, *Cumulation in International Relations Research* (Denver, CO: University of Denver, Graduate School of International Studies, 1981).

90. Richard K. Ashley is criticizing such authors as Kenneth Waltz, Robert Gilpin, Stephen Krasner, George Modelski, Robert Tucker, and Charles Kindleberger. See Ashley's "The Poverty of Neorealism," *International Organization* 38, no. 2 (Spring 1984): 225–86, p. 228. Also see Ashley, "Political Realism and Human Interests," *International Studies Quarterly* 25, no. 2 (June 1984): 204–35; Ashley, "Three Modes of Economism," *International Studies Quarterly* 27, no. 4 (December 1983): 463–96.

91. Ashley, "Poverty of Neorealism," p. 230. See also Robert Keohane, *Neorealism and Its Critics* (New York: Columbia University Press, 1986).

SUGGESTED READINGS

Newly added to this edition. Suggested readings from earlier works follow this more recent list.

Achen, Christopher H., and Duncan Snidal. "Rational Deterrence Theory and Comparative Case Studies." *World Politics* XLI, 2 (January 1989): 143–69. (Responding to this article in the same journal issue are Alexander L. George and Richard Smoke, Robert Jervis, Richard Ned Lebow and Janice Gross Stein, and George W. Downs.)

Axelrod, Robert. *The Evolution of Cooperation.* New York: Basic Books, 1984.

Baldwin, David A. *Economic Statecraft.* Princeton, NJ: Princeton University Press, 1985.

Beck, Nathaniel. "The Illusion of Cycles in International Relations." *International Studies Quarterly* 35, 4 (December 1991): 455–76.

Boswell, Terry, and Mike Sweat, "Hegemony, Long Waves, and Major Wars." *International Studies Quarterly* 35, 2 (June 1991): 123–49.

Brams, Steven J. *Superpower Games: Applying Game Theory to Superpower Conflict.* New Haven: Yale University Press, 1985.

Brams, Steven J., and D. Marc Kilgour. *Game Theory and National Security.* New York: Basil Blackwell, 1988.

———. "Threat Escalation and Crisis Stability: A Game-theoretic Analysis." *American Political Science Review* 81, 3 (September 1987): 833–50.

Brown, Seyom. *The Causes and Prevention of War.* New York: St. Martin's, 1987.

———. *New Forces, Old Forces and the Future of World Politics.* Glenview, IL: Scott, Foresman, 1988.

Bueno de Mesquita, Bruce. *Forecasting Political Events: The Future of Hong Kong.* New Haven, CT: Yale University Press, 1985.

Bueno de Mesquita, Bruce, and David Lalman. "Domestic Opposition and Foreign War." *American Political Science Review* 84, 3 (September 1990): 747–65.

———. "Empirical Support for Systemic and Dyadic Explanations of International Conflict." *World Politics* XLI, 1 (October 1988): 1–20.

———. "Reason and War." *American Political Science Review* 80, 4 (December 1986): 1113–29 and the subsequent debate in "Modeling War and Peace." *American Political Science Review* 81, 1 (March 1987): 221–30.

Calleo, David. *Beyond American Hegemony.* New York: Basic Books, 1987.

Caporaso, James A., ed. *The Elusive State: International and Comparative Perspectives.* Newbury Park, CA: Sage Publications, 1989.

Catudal, Honore. *Nuclear Deterrence — Does it Deter?* Berlin: Verlag Arno Spitz, 1985.

Christensen, Thomas J., and Jack Snyder. "Chain Gangs and Passed Bucks: Predicting Alliance Patterns in Multipolarity." *International Organization* 44, 2 (Spring 1990): 137–68.

Cimbala, Stephen J. *Nuclear Strategizing: Deterrence and Reality.* New York: Praeger, 1988.

Clegg, Stewart R. *Frameworks of Power.* London: Sage Publications, 1989.

Conybeare, John A. C. *Trade Wars: The Theory and Practice of International Commercial Rivalry.* New York: Columbia University Press, 1987.

Conybeare, John A. C. and Todd Sandler. "The Triple Entente and the Triple Alliance

1880–1914: A Collective Goods Approach." *American Political Science Review* 84, 4 (December 1990): 1197–1206.

Craig, Gordon A. and Alexander L. George. *Force and Statecraft: Diplomatic Problems of Our Time.* New York and Oxford: Oxford University Press, 1983.

David, Steven R. "Exploring Third World Alignment." *World Politics* 43, 2 (January 1991): 233–56.

Dell, Edmund. *The Politics of Economic Interdependence.* New York: St. Martin's, 1987.

Dessler, David. "Beyond Correlations: Toward a Causal Theory of War." *International Studies Quarterly* 35, 3 (September 1991): 337–55.

———. "What's at Stake in the Agent-Structure Debate?" *International Organization* 43, 3 (Summer 1989): 441–74.

Doran, Charles. *Systems in Crisis: New Imperatives of High Politics at Century's End.* New York: Cambridge University Press, 1991.

Doxey, Margaret P. *International Sanctions in Contemporary Perspective.* New York: St. Martin's, 1987.

Doyle, Michael W. *Empires.* Ithaca, NY: Cornell University Press, 1986.

Duchacek, Ivo D. *The Territorial Dimension of Politics: Within, Among, and Across Nations.* Boulder, CO: Westview Press, 1986.

Etcheson, Craig. *Arms Race Theory: Strategy and Structure of Behavior.* New York: Greenwood, 1989.

Evangelista, Matthew. *Innovation and the Arms Race.* Ithaca, NY: Cornell University Press, 1988.

Friedberg, Aaron L. *The Weary Titan: Britain and the Experience of Relative Decline.* Princeton, NJ: Princeton University Press, 1988.

Gaddis, John Lewis. "The Long Peace: Elements of Stability in the Postwar International System." *International Security* 10, 4 (Spring 1986): 99–142.

Garthoff, Raymond L. *Reflections on the Cuban Missile Crisis.* Washington, DC: Brookings Institution, 1987, 1989.

Gilpin, Robert. *The Political Economy of International Relations.* Princeton, NJ: Princeton University Press, 1987.

Gochman, Charles S., and Alan Ned Sabrosky, eds. *Prisoners of War? Nation-States in the Modern Era.* Lexington, MA: D. C. Heath, 1990.

Goldstein, Joshua S. *Long Cycles: Prosperity and War in the Modern Age.* New Haven: Yale University Press, 1988.

———. "The Possibility of Cycles in International Relations." *International Studies Quarterly* 35, 4 (December 1991): 477–80.

Gowa, Joanne. "Rational Hegemons, Excludable Goods, and Small Groups: An Epitaph for Hegemonic Stability Theory?" *World Politics* XLI, 3 (April 1989): 307–24.

Gray, Colin S. *The Geopolitics of Super Power.* Lexington: University Press of Kentucky, 1988.

Grieco, Joseph M. "Anarchy and the Limits of Cooperation: A Realist Critique of the Newest Liberal Institutionalism." *International Organization* 42, 3 (Summer 1988): 485–507.

———. *Cooperation Among Nations.* Ithaca, NY: Cornell University Press, 1990.

Grunberg, Isabelle. "Exploring the 'Myth' of Hegemonic Stability." *International Organization* 44, 4 (Autumn 1990): 431–77.

Haftendorn, Helga. "The Security Puzzle: Theory-Building and Discipline-Building in International Security." *International Studies Quarterly* 35, 1 (March 1991): 3–17.

Hicks, Alexander. "National Collective Action and Economic Performance: A Review Article." *International Studies Quarterly* 32, 2 (June 1988): 131–53.

Hirschman, Albert. *National Power and the Structure of Foreign Trade.* Berkeley: University of California Press, 1980.

Hollis, Martin, and Steve Smith. *Explaining and Understanding International Relations.* Oxford, England: Clarendon Press, 1990.

Holsti, K. J. "The Horsemen of the Apocalypse: At the Gate, Detoured, or Retreating." *International Studies Quarterly* 30, 4 (December 1986): 355–72.

Houweling, Henk, and Jan G. Siccama. *Studies of War.* Dordrecht, Holland: Martinus Nijhoff, 1988.

Howard, Michael. *The Lessons of History.* New Haven, CT: Yale University Press, 1991.

Huntington, Samuel P. "The U.S.—Decline or Renewal?" *Foreign Affairs* 67, 2 (Winter 1988/89): 76–96.

Huth, Paul K. *Extended Deterrence and the Prevention of War.* New Haven, CT: Yale University Press, 1988.

Huth, Paul, and Bruce Russett. "Testing Deterrence Theory: Rigor Makes a Difference." *World Politics* XLII, 4 (July 1990): 466–501.

Ikenberry, G. John, and Charles A. Kupchan. "Socialization and Hegemonic Power." *International Organization* 44, 3 (Summer 1990): 283–315.

James, Alan. *Sovereign Statehood: The Basis of International Society.* London: Allen & Unwin, 1986.

James, Patrick. *Crisis and War.* Montreal: McGill Queen's University Press, 1988.

Jervis, Robert. *The Meaning of the Nuclear Revolution: Statecraft and the Prospect of Armageddon.* Ithaca, NY: Cornell University Press, 1989.

———. "Realism, Game Theory, and Cooperation." *World Politics* XL, 3 (April 1988): 317–49.

Katzenstein, Peter J. *Corporatism and Change: Austria, Switzerland and the Politics of Industry.* Ithaca, NY: Cornell University Press, 1984.

———. *Small States in World Markets: Industrial Policy in Europe.* Ithaca, NY: Cornell University Press, 1985.

Kegley, Charles W., Jr., and Gregory A. Raymond. *When Trust Breaks Down: Alliance Norms and World Politics.* Columbia: University of South Carolina Press, 1990.

Kennedy, Paul. *The Rise and Fall of the Great Powers.* New York: Random House, 1987.

Keohane, Robert O. *International Institutions and State Power: Essays in International Relations Theory.* Boulder, CO: Westview Press, 1989.

———, ed. *Neorealism and Its Critics.* New York: Columbia University Press, 1986.

———. "Reciprocity in International Relations." *International Organization* 40, 1 (Winter 1986): 1–27.

Krasner, Stephen D. "Sovereignty: An Institutional Perspective" in James A. Caporaso, ed. *The Elusive State.* Newbury Park, CA: Sage Publications, 1989: 69–96.

Kratchowil, Friedrich. "Of Systems, Boundaries, and Territoriality: An Inquiry into the Formation of the State System." *World Politics* XXXIX, 1 (October 1986): 27–52.

Krugman, Paul R. *The Age of Diminished Expectations.* Washington, DC.: Washington Post Co., 1990.

———. *Rethinking International Trade.* Cambridge, MA: MIT Press, 1990.

———, ed. *Strategic Trade Policy and the New International Economics.* Cambridge, MA: MIT Press, 1986.

Lake, David. "Power and the Third World: Toward a Realist Political Economy of North–South Relations." *International Studies Quarterly* 31, 2 (June 1987): 217–34.

———. *Power, Protection and Free Trade.* Ithaca, NY: Cornell University Press, 1988.

Lebow, Richard Ned, and Janice Gross Stein. "Deterrence: The Elusive Dependent Variable." *World Politics* XLII, 3 (April 1990): 336–69.

Lebow, Richard Ned, and Barry S. Strauss, eds. *Hegemonic Rivalry: From Thucydides to the Nuclear Age.* Boulder, CO: Westview Press, 1991.

Leng, Russell J., and J. David Singer. "Militarized Interactive Crises." *International Studies Quarterly* 32, 2 (June 1988): 155–73.

Lepgold, Joseph. *The Declining Hegemon.* New York: Praeger, 1990.

Levy, Jack. "Declining Power and the Preventive Motivation for War." *World Politics* XL, 1 (October 1987): 82–107.

Liska, George. *The Ways of Power.* Cambridge, England: Basil Blackwell, 1990.

Luard, Evan. *War in International Society.* New Haven, CT: Yale University Press, 1987.

Luterbacher, Urs, and Michael D. Ward, eds. *Dynamic Models of International Conflict.* Boulder, CO: Lynne Rienner Publishers, 1985.

Mandelbaum, Michael. *The Fate of Nations: The Search for National Security in the Nineteenth and Twentieth Centuries.* Cambridge, England: Cambridge University Press, 1988.

Mastanduno, Michael, David A. Lake, and G. John Ikenberry. "Toward a Realist Theory of State Action." *International Studies Quarterly* 33, 4 (December 1989): 457–74.

McKeown, Timothy J. "The Foreign Policy of a Declining Power." *International Organization* 45, 2 (Spring 1991): 257–79.

———. "The Limitations of 'Structural' Theories of Commercial Policy." *International Organization* 40, 1 (Winter 1986): 43–64.

McLennan, Gregor, David Held, and Stuart Hall, eds. *The Idea of the Modern State.* Philadelphia: Open University Press, 1984.

Midlarsky, Manus I. *The Disintegration of Political Systems: War and Revolution in Comparative Perspective.* Columbia: University of South Carolina Press, 1986.

———, ed. *Handbook of War Studies.* Boston: Unwin Hyman, 1989.

———. "A Hierarchical Equilibrium Theory of Systemic War." *International Studies Quarterly* 30, 1 (March 1986): 77–105.

———. *The Onset of World War.* Boston: Unwin Hyman, 1988.

Miller, J. D. H. "E. H. Carr: The Realist's Realist." *The National Interest* 25 (Fall 1991): 65–71.

Milner, Helen V. "The Assumption of Anarchy in International Relations Theory: A Critique." *Review of International Studies* 17, 1 (January 1991): 67–85.

———. *Resisting Protectionism: Global Industries and the Politics of International Trade.* Princeton, NJ: Princeton University Press, 1988.

Mitchell, Timothy. "The Limits of the State: Beyond Statist Approaches and Their Critics." *American Political Science Review* 85, 1 (March 1991): 77–96.

Modelski, George, ed. *Exploring Long Cycles.* Boulder, CO: Lynne Rienner Publishers, 1987.

Modelski, George and William R. Thompson. *Seapower in Global Politics, 1494–1993.* Seattle: University of Washington Press, 1988.

Morrow, James D. "Social Choice and System Structure in World Politics." *World Politics* XLI, 1 (October 1988): 75–97.

Morrow, James D., Barry L. Price, and Roslyn Simowitz. "Conceptual Problems in Theorizing About International Conflict." *American Political Science Review* 85, 3 (September 1991): 923–40.

Mueller, John. *Retreat from Doomsday: The Obsolescence of Major War.* New York: Basic Books, 1989.

Nau, Henry R. *The Myth of America's Decline.* New York: Oxford University Press, 1990.

Niou, Emerson M.S., and Peter C. Ordeshook. "Stability in Anarchic International Systems." *American Political Science Review* 84, 4 (December 1990): 1207–34.

Niou, Emerson M.S., Peter C. Ordeshook, and Gregory F. Rose. *The Balance of Power: Stability in International Systems.* New York: Cambridge University Press, 1989.

Nye, Joseph S., Jr. *Bound to Lead: The Changing Nature of American Power.* New York: Basic Books, 1990.

———. "Neorealism and Neoliberalism." *World Politics* 40, 2 (January 1988): 235–51.

Nye, Joseph S., and Sean M. Lynn-Jones. "International Security Studies: A Report of a Conference on the State of the Field." *International Security* 12, 4 (Spring 1988): 5–27.

Olson, Mancur. *The Rise and Decline of Nations.* New Haven, CT: Yale University Press, 1982.

Oye, Kenneth A., ed. *Cooperation Under Anarchy.* Princeton, NJ: Princeton University Press, 1986.

Posen, Barry R. *The Sources of Military Doctrine: France, Britain, and Germany Between the World Wars.* Ithaca, NY: Cornell University Press, 1984.

Powell, Robert. "Absolute and Relative Gains in International Relations Theory." *American Political Science Review* 85, 4 (December 1991): 1303–20.

Quester, George H. *The Future of Nuclear Deterrence.* Lexington, MA: Lexington Books, 1986.

Rock, Stephen R. *Why Peace Breaks Out: Great Power Rapprochement in Historical Perspective.* Chapel Hill: University of North Carolina Press, 1989.

Rogowski, Ronald. *Commerce and Coalitions: How Trade Affects Domestic Political Alignments.* Princeton, NJ: Princeton University Press, 1989.

Rosecrance, Richard. "Long Cycle Theory and International Relations." *International Organization* 41, 2 (Spring 1987): 283–301.

———. *The Rise of the Trading State: Commerce and Conquest in the Modern World.* New York: Basic Books, 1986.

Rotberg, Robert I., and Theodore K. Rabb. *The Origin and Prevention of Major Wars.* Cambridge, England: Cambridge University Press, 1988.

Sabrosky, Alan Ned, ed. *Polarity and War: The Changing Structure of International Conflict.* Boulder, CO: Westview Press, 1985.

Sagan, Scott D. *Moving Targets: Nuclear Strategy and National Security.* Princeton, NJ: Princeton University Press, 1989.

Schweller, Randall L. "Domestic Structure and Preventive War: Are Democracies More Pacific?" *World Politics* 44, 2 (January 1992): 235–69.

Simowitz, Roslyn. "The Expected Utility Theory of Conflict: Measuring Theoretical Progress." *American Political Science Review* 84, 2 (June 1990): 439–60.

Siverson, Randolph M., and Harvey Starr. "Opportunity, Willingness, and the Diffusion of War." *American Political Science Review* 84, 1 (March 1990): 47–67.

Sloan, Geoffrey R. *Geopolitics in United States Strategic Policy, 1890–1987.* New York: St. Martin's Press, 1988.

Small, Melvin and J. David Singer, eds. *International War: An Anthology and Study Guide.* Homewood, IL: Dorsey Press, 1985.

Snidal, Duncan. "Relative Gains and the Pattern of International Cooperation." *American Political Science Review* 85, 3 (September 1991): 701–26.

Snyder, Glenn H. "Alliances, Balance, and Stability." *International Organization* 45, 1 (Winter 1991): 121–42.

Strang, David. "Global Patterns of Decolonization, 1500–1987." *International Studies Quarterly* 35, 4 (December 1991): 429–54.

Strange, Susan. "The Persistent Myth of Lost Hegemony." *International Organization* 41, 4 (Autumn 1987): 551–74.

Sullivan, Michael P. *Power in Contemporary International Politics*. Columbia: University of South Carolina Press, 1990.

Thompson, Kenneth W. *Toynbee's Philosophy of World History and Politics*. Baton Rouge: Louisiana State University Press, 1985.

Thompson, William R. "Long Waves, Technological Innovation, and Relative Decline." *International Organization* 44, 2 (Spring 1990): 201–33.

———. *On Global War: Historical-Structural Approaches to World Politics*. Columbia: University of South Carolina Press, 1990.

Vasquez, John A. "The Steps to War: Toward a Scientific Explanation of the Correlates of War Findings." *World Politics* XL, 1 (October 1987): 108–45.

Vincent, Jack. "Freedom and International Conflict." *International Studies Quarterly* 31, 1 (March 1987): 103–12.

Wagner, R. Harrison. "Nuclear Deterrence, Counterforce Strategies, and the Incentive to Strike First." *American Political Science Review* 85, 3 (September 1991): 727–49.

———. "The Theory of Games and the Balance of Power." *World Politics* XXXVIII, 4 (July 1986): 546–76.

Walker, R. B. J. "Realism, Change, and International Political Theory." *International Studies Quarterly* 31, 1 (March 1987): 65–86.

———. *State Sovereignty, Global Civilization, and the Rearticulation of Political Space*. World Order Studies Program Occasional Paper No. 18. Princeton, N.J.: Center of International Studies.

Walt, Stephen M. *The Origins of Alliances*. Ithaca, NY: Cornell University Press, 1987.

———. "The Renaissance of Security Studies." *International Studies Quarterly* 35, 2 (June 1991): 211–39.

———. "Testing Theories of Alliance Formation." *International Organization* 42, 2 (Spring 1988): 275–316.

Waltz, Kenneth N. "The Emerging Structure of International Politics" in *Relations in a Multipolar World*. U.S. Senate. 101st Congress, 2nd Session. November 26, 28, and 30, 1990. Part I.

———. "Nuclear Myths and Political Realities." *American Political Science Review* 84, 3 (September 1990): 731–45.

———. "Realist Thought and Neorealist Theory." *Journal of International Affairs* XLIV, 1 (Spring/Summer 1990): 21–37.

Zagare, Frank. *The Dynamics of Deterrence*. Chicago: University of Chicago Press, 1987.

———. "Rationality and Deterrence." *World Politics* 42, 2 (January 1990): 238–60.

Zysman, John. *Governments, Markets and Growth: Financial Systems and the Politics of Industrial Change*. Ithaca, NY: Cornell University Press, 1983.

SUGGESTED READINGS FROM THE FIRST EDITION

Aron, Raymond. *On War: Atomic Weapons and Global Diplomacy*. London: Secker and Warburg, 1958.

———. *Peace and War*. Garden City, NY: Doubleday, 1966.

Ashley, Richard K. "Political Realism and Human Interests." *International Studies Quarterly* 25, 2 (June 1981): 204–36.

———. "The Poverty of Neorealism." *International Organization* 38, 2 (Spring 1984): 225–86.

Baldwin, David A. "Power Analysis and World Politics." *World Politics* 31, 2 (January 1979): 161–194.

Brams, Steven J., Morton D. Davis, Philip D. Straffin, Jr. "The Geometry of the Arms Race." *International Studies Quarterly* 23, 4 (December 1979): 567–88.

Brodie, Bernard. *War and Politics.* New York: Macmillan, 1973.

Bueno de Mesquita, Bruce. "The Costs of War: A Rational Expectations Approach." *American Political Science Review* 77, 2 (June 1983): 347–57.

———. "Risk, Power Distributions, and the Likelihood of War." *International Studies Quarterly* 25, 4 (December 1981): 541–68.

———. *The War Trap.* New Haven, CT: Yale University Press, 1981.

———. "The War Trap Revisited: A Revised Expected Utility Model." *American Political Science Review* 79, 1 (March 1985): 156–173.

———. "Theories of International Conflict: An Analysis and an Appraisal." In *Handbook of Political Conflict*, edited by Ted R. Gurr. New York: Free Press, 1980.

Bull, Hedley. *The Anarchical Society: A Study of Order in World Politics.* New York: Columbia University Press, 1977.

Buzan, Barry, and R. J. Barry Jones, eds. *Change and the Study of International Relations.* London: Frances Pinter, 1981.

Claude, Inis, Jr. *Power and International Relations.* New York: Random House, 1962.

Doran, Charles F., and Wes Parsons. "War and the Cycle of Relative Power." *American Political Science Review* 74, 4 (December 1980): 946–65.

Duncan, George T., and Randolph M. Siverson. "Flexibility of Alliance Partner Choice in a Multipolar System." *International Studies Quarterly* 26, 4 (December 1982): 511–38.

Ferris, Wayne H. *The Power Capabilities of Nation-States: International Conflict and War.* Lexington, MA: D. C. Heath, 1973.

George, Alexander, David K. Hall, and William R. Simons. *The Limits of Coercive Diplomacy.* Boston, MA: Little, Brown, 1971.

George, Alexander, and Richard Smoke. *Deterrence in American Foreign Policy: Theory and Practice,* New York: Columbia University Press, 1974.

Gilpin, Robert G. "The Richness of the Tradition of Political Realism." *International Organization* 38, 2 (Spring 1984): 287–304.

———. *U.S. Power and the Multinational Corporation.* New York: Basic Books, 1975.

———. *War and Change in World Politics.* Cambridge: Cambridge University Press, 1981.

Haas, Ernst B. "The Balance of Power: Prescription, Concept or Propaganda?" *World Politics* 5, 4 (July 1953): 442–77.

Haas, Michael, ed. *International Systems: A Behavioral Approach.* New York: Chandler, 1974.

Hart, Jeffrey. "Three Approaches to the Measurement of Power in International Relations." *International Organization* 30, 2 (Spring 1976): 289–305.

Herz, John H. *International Politics in the Atomic Age.* New York: Columbia University Press, 1959.

———. *The Nation-State and the Crisis of World Politics.* New York: David McKay, 1976.

———. *Political Realism and Political Idealism.* Chicago: University of Chicago Press, 1951.

———. "Political Realism Revisited." *International Studies Quarterly* 25, 2 (June 1981): 182–241.

Hoffmann, Stanley. *Contemporary Theory of International Relations.* Englewood Cliffs, NJ: Prentice Hall, 1960.

———. "Obstinate or Obsolete? The Fate of the Nation-State and the Case of Western Europe." *Daedalus* 95 (Summer 1966): 862–915.

———. *Primacy or World Order*. New York: McGraw-Hill, 1978.

———. "Raymond Aron and the Theory of International Relations." *International Studies Quarterly* 29, 1 (March 1985): 13–27.

———. *The State of War*. New York: Praeger, 1965.

Howard, Michael E. *The Causes of War and Other Essays*. Cambridge, MA: Harvard University Press, 1983.

———. *War and the Liberal Conscience*. New Brunswick, NJ: Rutgers University Press, 1978.

Iklé, Fred C. *How Nations Negotiate*. New York: Harper & Row, 1964.

Jervis, Robert. "Cooperation Under the Security Dilemma." *World Politics* 30 (January 1978): 167–86.

———. "Deterrence Theory Revisited." *World Politics* 31, 2 (January 1979): 289–324.

———. *The Illogic of American Nuclear Strategy*. Ithaca, NY: Cornell University Press, 1984.

Kaplan, Morton, ed. *New Approaches to International Relations*. New York: St. Martin's, 1968.

———. *System and Process in International Politics*. New York: John Wiley, 1957.

———. *Towards Professionalism in International Theory: Macrosystem Analysis*. New York: Free Press, 1979.

Kegley, Charles, W., Jr., and Gregory A. Raymond. "Alliance Norms and War." *International Studies Quarterly* 26, 4 (December 1982): 572–95.

Kennedy, Paul. *Strategy and Diplomacy, 1870–1945*. Winchester, MA: Allen & Unwin, 1984.

Keohane, Robert O. *After Hegemony: Cooperation and Discord in the World Political Economy*. Princeton, NJ: Princeton University Press, 1984.

———. ed. *Neorealism and Its Critics*. New York: Columbia University Press, 1986.

———. "The Theory of Hegemonic Stability and Changes in International Economic Regimes." In *Change in the International System*, edited by Ole Hosti, Randolph M. Siverson, and Alexander L. George. Boulder, CO: Westview Press, 1980.

———. "Theory of World Politics: Structural Realism and Beyond." In *Political Science: The State of the Discipline*, ed. Ada W. Finifter. Washington, DC: American Political Science Association, 1983.

Keohane, Robert O., and Joseph S. Nye. *Power and Interdependence: World Politics in Transition*. Boston, MA: Little, Brown, 1977.

Kissinger, Henry A. *A World Restored*. New York: Grosset & Dunlap, 1964.

———. *The Necessity for Choice*. New York: Harper & Row, 1961.

———. *Nuclear Weapons and Foreign Policy*. New York: Harper & Row, 1957.

Knorr, Klaus. *Military Power and Potential*. Lexington, MA: Lexington Books, 1970.

———. *On the Uses of Military Power*. Princeton, NJ: Princeton University Press, 1966.

———. *The Power of Nations: The Political Economy of International Relations*. New York: Basic Books, 1975.

Krasner, Stephen D. *Defending the National Interest*. Princeton, NJ: Princeton University Press, 1978.

———, ed. *International Regimes*, Ithaca, N.Y.: Cornell University Press, 1983.

———. "State Power and the Structure of International Trade." *World Politics* 28, 3 (April 1976): 317–48.

———. *Structural Conflict: The Third World Against Global Liberalism*. Berkeley: University of California Press, 1985.

Kratchowil, Friedrich. "On the Notion of Interest in International Relations." *International Organization* 36, 1 (Winter 1982): 278–300.

Levy, Jack S. "Historical Trends in Great Power War, 1495–1975." *International Studies Quarterly* 26, 2 (June 1982): 278–300.

———. "Misperception and the Causes of War." *World Politics* 36, 1 (October 1983): 76–99.

———. "Theories of General War." *World Politics* 37, 3 (April 1985): 344–74.

Liska, George. *Beyond Kissinger: Ways of Conservative Statecraft.* Baltimore: Johns Hopkins University Press, 1975.

———. *Nations in Alliance: The Limits of Interdependence.* Baltimore: Johns Hopkins University Press, 1968.

Mackinder, Sir Halford J. "The Round World and the Winning of the Peace." *Foreign Affairs* 21, 4 (July 1943): 595–605.

Majeski, Stephen J., and David J. Sylvan. "Simple Choices and Complex Calculations: A Critique of The War Trap." *Journal of Conflict Resolution* 28, 2 (June 1984): 316–40, and rejoinder by Bruce Bueno de Mesquita.

March, James G. "Bounded Rationality, Ambiguity, and the Engineering of Choice." *Bell Journal of Economics* 9, 2 (Autumn 1978): 587–608.

Modelski, George. *A Theory of Foreign Policy.* New York: Praeger, 1962.

———. "The Long Cycle of Global Politics and the Nation-State." *Comparative Studies in Society and History* 20, 2 (April 1978): 214–35.

———. "Long Cycles and the Strategy of U.S. Economic Policy." In *America in a Changing World Political Economy,* ed. William P. Avery and David P. Rapkin. New York: Longman, 1982.

———. *Principles of World Politics.* New York: Free Press, 1972.

Modelski, George, and Patrick M. Morgan. "Understanding Global War." *Journal of Conflict Resolution* 29, 2 (September 1985): 391–417.

Morgenthau, Hans J. *In Defense of the National Interest.* New York: Knopf, 1951.

———. *Politics Among Nations: The Struggle for Power and Peace,* 5th ed. New York: Knopf, 1978.

———. *Scientific Man vs. Power Politics.* Chicago: University of Chicago Press, 1946.

Moul, William B. "The Level of Analysis Problem Revisited." *Canadian Journal of Political Science* 6, 3 (September 1973): 494–513.

Osgood, Robert E. *Alliances and American Foreign Policy.* Baltimore: Johns Hopkins University Press, 1967.

Osgood, Robert E., and Robert W. Tucker. *Force, Order and Justice.* Baltimore: Johns Hopkins University Press, 1967.

Rapoport, Anatol. *Strategy and Conscience.* New York: Schocken Books, 1969.

Rapoport, Anatol, and A. M. Ghammah. *Prisoner's Dilemma.* Ann Arbor: University of Michigan Press, 1965.

Ray, James Lee. "Understanding Rummel." *Journal of Conflict Resolution* 26, 1 (March 1982): 161–87.

Richardson, Lewis F. *Arms and Insecurity.* Pittsburg, PA.: Boxwood, 1960.

Riker, William H. *A Theory of Political Coalitions.* New Haven, CT: Yale University Press, 1962.

Rogowski, Ronald. "Structure, Growth and Power: Three Rationalist Accounts." *International Organization* 37, 4 (Autumn 1983): 713–38.

Rosecrance, Richard. *Action and Reaction in World Politics.* Boston: Little, Brown, 1963.

———. *International Relations: Peace or War?* New York: McGraw-Hill, 1973.

————. "International Relations Theory Revisited." *International Organization* 35, 4 (Autumn 1981): 691–713. A review of Waltz, *Theory of International Politics* and Bull, *The Anarchical Society*. See also the Waltz–Rosecrance exchange in *International Organization* 36, 3 (Summer 1982): 679–85.

Ruggie, John Gerard. "Continuity and Transformation in the World Polity: Toward a Neorealist Synthesis." *World Politics* 35, 2 (January 1983): 261–85. A review of Waltz, *Theory of International Politics*.

Rummel, Rudolph. *Dimensions of Nations*. Beverly Hills, CA: Sage Publications, 1972.

————. *Field Theory Evolving*. Beverly Hills, CA: Sage Publications, 1977.

————. *Understanding Conflict and War*. Five volumes. Beverly Hills, CA: Sage Publications, 1975–1981.

Russett, Bruce M. *International Regions and the International System*. Chicago: Rand McNally, 1967.

————. "The Mysterious Case of Vanishing Hegemony." *International Organization* 39, 2 (Spring 1985): 207–31.

————, ed. *Peace, War, and Numbers*. Beverly Hills, CA: Sage Publications, 1972.

Schelling, Thomas S. *Arms and Influence*. New Haven, CT: Yale University Press, 1966.

————. *The Strategy of Conflict*. New York: Oxford University Press, 1960.

Schlenker, Barry R., and Thomas V. Bonoma. "Fun and Games: The Validity of Games for the Study of Conflict." *Journal of Conflict Resolution* 22 (March 1978): 9–13.

Sigal, Leon V. "The Logic of Deterrence in Theory and Practice." *International Organization* 33, 4 (Autumn 1979): 567–79.

Singer, J. David. "Accounting for International War: The State of the Discipline." *Journal of Peace Research* 18, 1 (1981): 1–18.

————, ed. *Correlates of War I: Research Origins and Rationale*, New York: Free Press, 1979.

————, ed. *Correlates of War II: Testing Some Balance-of-Power Models*. New York: Free Press, 1980.

————. "Confrontational Behavior and Escalation to War 1816–1980: A Research Plan." *Journal of Peace Research* 19, 1 (1982): 37–48.

————, ed. *Quantitative International Politics: Insights and Evidence*. New York: Free Press, 1968.

Singer, J. David, and Michael D. Wallace, eds. *To Augur Well: Early Warning Indicators in World Politics*. Beverly Hills, CA: Sage Publications, 1979.

Singer J. David, and Melvin Small. *The Wages of War 1816–1965: A Statistical Handbook*. New York: John Wiley, 1972.

Singer, J. David, and associates. *Explaining War: Selected Papers From the Correlates of War Project*. Beverly Hills, CA: Sage Publications, 1979.

Siverson, Randolph M., and Michael R. Tennefoss. "Power, Alliance and the Escalation of International Conflict, 1815–1965." *American Political Science Review* 78, 4 (December 1984): 1057–69.

Snidal, Duncan. "The Limits of Hegemonic Stability Theory." *International Organization* 39, 4 (Autumn 1985): 579–614.

Stoessinger, John. G. *Why Nations Go to War*. New York: St. Martin's, 1978.

Sylvan, David J. "The Newest Mercantilism." *International Organization* 35, 2 (Spring 1981): 375–93. A review article.

Tucker, Robert W. *The Inequality of Nations*. New York: Basic Books, 1977.

Wagner, R. Harrison. "War and Expected Utility Theory." *World Politics* 36, 3 (April 1984): 407–23. A review of Bueno de Mesquita, *The War Trap*.

———. "The Theory of Games and the Problem of International Cooperation." *American Political Science Review* 77, 2 (June 1983): 330–46.

Wallace, Michael P. "Arms Races and Escalation." *Journal of Conflict Resolution* 23, 1 (March 1979): 3–16.

Waltz, Kenneth N. *Foreign Policy and Democratic Politics*. Boston: Little, Brown, 1967.

———. *Man, the State and War*. New York: Columbia University Press, 1959.

———. *Theory of International Politics*. Reading, MA: Addison-Wesley, 1979.

Wayman, Frank W., J. David Singer, and Gary Goertz. "Capabilities, Allocations, and Success in Militarized Disputes and Wars, 1816–1976." *International Studies Quarterly* 27, 4 (December 1983): 497–515.

Wight, Martin. *Power Politics*. New York: Holmes and Meier, 1978.

———. *Systems of States*. Edited by Hedley Bull. Leicester, England: Leicester University Press, 1977.

Wolfers, Arnold. *Discord and Collaboration*. Baltimore: Johns Hopkins University Press, 1962.

Wright, Quincy. *A Study of War*. Chicago: University of Chicago Press, 1964.

———. *The Study of International Relations*. New York: Appleton-Century-Crofts, 1955.

Zinnes, Dina. "Empirical Evidence on the Outbreak of International Conflict." In *Handbook of Political Conflict*, ed. Ted R. Gurr. New York: Free Press, 1980.

Zinnes, Dina, and Francis W. Hoole, eds. *Quantitative International Politics: An Appraisal*. New York: Praeger, 1976.

The Melian Dialogue

Thucydides

This classic contains the essential ingredients of the realist perspective stated in perhaps its boldest and most extreme form. The Athenians have no interest in whether the demands they make on the Melians are just or moral. In a classic statement, the Athenians emphasize the overriding importance of power: "The strong do what they have the power to do, and the weak accept what they have to accept." Other important concepts and notions such as honor, perception, neutrality, self-interest, alliances, balance of power, capabilities, and the uncertainty of power calculations are also discussed.

Next summer Alcibiades sailed to Argos with twenty ships and seized 300 Argive citizens who were still suspected of being pro-Spartan. These were put by the Athenians into the nearby islands under Athenian control.

The Athenians also made an expedition against the island of Melos. They had thirty of their own ships, six from Chios, and two from Lesbos; 1,200 hoplites, 300 archers, and twenty mounted archers, all from Athens; and about 1,500 hoplites from the allies and the islanders.

The Melians are a colony from Sparta. They had refused to join the Athenian empire like the other islanders, and at first had remained neutral without helping either side; but afterwards, when the Athenians had brought force to bear on them by laying waste their land, they had become open enemies of Athens.

Now the generals Cleomedes, the son of Lycomedes, and Tisias, the son of Tisimachus, encamped with the above force in Melian territory and, before doing any harm to the land, first of all sent representatives to negotiate. The Melians did not invite these representatives to speak before the people, but asked them to make the statement for which they had come in front of the governing body and the few. The Athenian representatives then spoke as follows:

From Thucydides, *History of the Peloponnesian War*, translated by Rex Warner. Penguin Classics, 1954, pages 400–408. Reprinted by permission of Penguin Books Ltd.

"So we are not to speak before the people, no doubt in case the mass of the people should hear once and for all and without interruption an argument from us which is both persuasive and incontrovertible, and should so be led astray. This, we realize, is your motive in bringing us here to speak before the few. Now suppose that you who sit here should make assurance doubly sure. Suppose that you, too, should refrain from dealing with every point in detail in a set speech, and should instead interrupt us whenever we say something controversial and deal with that before going on to the next point? Tell us first whether you approve of this suggestion of ours."

The Council of the Melians replied as follows:

"No one can object to each of us putting forward our own views in a calm atmosphere. That is perfectly reasonable. What is scarcely consistent with such a proposal is the present threat, indeed the certainty, of your making war on us. We see that you have come prepared to judge the argument yourselves, and that the likely end of it all will be either war, if we prove that we are in the right, and so refuse to surrender, or else slavery."

Athenians: If you are going to spend the time in enumerating your suspicions about the future, or if you have met here for any other reason except to look the facts in the face and on the basis of these facts to consider how you can save your city from destruction, there is no point in our going on with this discussion. If, however, you will do as we suggest, then we will speak on.

Melians: It is natural and understandable that people who are placed as we are should have recourse to all kinds of arguments and different points of view. However, you are right in saying that we are met together here to discuss the safety of our country and, if you will have it so, the discussion shall proceed on the lines that you have laid down.

Athenians: Then we on our side will use no fine phrases saying, for example, that we have a right to our empire because we defeated the Persians, or that we have come against you now because of the injuries you have done us — a great mass of words that nobody would believe. And we ask you on your side not to imagine that you will influence us by saying that you, though a colony of Sparta, have not joined Sparta in the war, or that you have never done us any harm. Instead we recommend that you should try to get what it is possible for you to get, taking into consideration what we both really do think; since you know as well as we do that, when these matters are discussed by practical people, the standard of justice depends on the equality of power to compel and that in fact the strong do what they have the power to do and the weak accept what they have to accept.

Melians: Then in our view (since you force us to leave justice out of account and to confine ourselves to self-interest) — in our view it is at any rate useful that you should not destroy a principle that is to the general good of all men — namely, that in the case of all who fall into danger there should be such a thing as fair play and just dealing, and that such people should be allowed to use and to profit by arguments that fall short of a mathematical accuracy. And this is a principle which affects you as much as anybody, since your own fall would be visited by the most terrible vengeance and would be an example to the world.

Athenians: As for us, even assuming that our empire does come to an end, we are not despondent about what would happen next. One is not so much frightened of being conquered by a power which rules over others, as Sparta does (not that we are concerned with Sparta now), as of what would happen if a ruling power is attacked and defeated by its own subjects. So far as this point is concerned, you can leave it to us to face the risks involved. What we shall do now is to show you that it is for the good of our own empire that we are here and that it is for the preservation of your city that we shall say what we are going to say. We do not want any trouble in bringing you into our empire, and we want you to be spared for the good both of yourselves and of ourselves.

Melians: And how could it be just as good for us to be the slaves as for you to be the masters?

Athenians: You, by giving in, would save yourselves from disaster; we, by not destroying you, would be able to profit from you.

Melians: So you would not agree to our being neutral, friends instead of enemies, but allies of neither side?

Athenians: No, because it is not so much your hostility that injures us; it is rather the case that, if we were on friendly terms with you, our subjects would regard that as a sign of weakness in us, whereas your hatred is evidence of our power.

Melians: Is that your subjects' idea of fair play — that no distinction should be made between people who are quite unconnected with you and people who are mostly your own colonists or else rebels whom you have conquered?

Athenians: So far as right and wrong are concerned they think that there is no difference between the two, that those who still preserve their independence do so because they are strong, and that if we fail to attack them it is because we are afraid. So that by conquering you we shall increase not only the size but the security of our empire. We rule the sea and you are islanders, and weaker islanders too than the others; it is therefore particularly important that you should not escape.

Melians: But do you think there is no security for you in what we suggest? For here again, since you will not let us mention justice, but tell us to give in to your interests, we, too, must tell you what our interests are and, if yours and ours happen to coincide, we must try to persuade you of the fact. Is it not certain that you will make enemies of all states who are at present neutral, when they see what is happening here and naturally conclude that in course of time you will attack them too? Does not this mean that you are strengthening the enemies you have already and are forcing others to become your enemies even against their intentions and their inclinations?

Athenians: As a matter of fact we are not so much frightened of states on the continent. They have their liberty, and this means that it will be a long time before they begin to take precautions against us. We are more concerned about islanders like yourselves, who are still unsubdued, or subjects who have already become embittered by the constraint which our empire imposes on them. These are the people who are most likely to act in a reckless manner and to bring themselves and us, too, into the most obvious danger.

Melians: Then surely, if such hazards are taken by you to keep your empire and by your subjects to escape from it, we who are still free would show ourselves great cowards and weaklings if we failed to face everything that comes rather than submit to slavery.

Athenians: No, not if you are sensible. This is no fair fight, with honour on one side and shame on the other. It is rather a question of saving your lives and not resisting those who are far too strong for you.

Melians: Yet we know that in war fortune sometimes makes the odds more level than could be expected from the difference in numbers of the two sides. And if we surrender, then all our hope is lost at once, whereas, so long as we remain in action, there is still a hope that we may yet stand upright.

Athenians: Hope, that comforter in danger! If one already has solid advantages to fall back upon, one can indulge in hope. It may do harm, but will not destroy one. But hope is by nature an expensive commodity, and those who are risking their all on one cast find out what it means only when they are already ruined; it never fails them in the period when such a knowledge would enable them to take precautions. Do not let this happen to you, you who are weak and whose fate depends on a single movement of the scale. And do not be like those people who, as so commonly happens, miss the chance of saving themselves in a human and practical way, and, when every clear and distinct hope has left them in their adversity, turn to what is blind and vague, to prophecies and oracles and such things which by encouraging hope lead men to ruin.

Melians: It is difficult, and you may be sure that we know it, for us to oppose your power and fortune, unless the terms be equal. Nevertheless we trust that the gods will give us fortune as good as yours, because we are standing for what is right against what is wrong; and as for what we lack in power, we trust that it will be made up for by our alliance with the Spartans, who are bound, if for no other reason, then for honour's sake, and because we are their kinsmen, to come to our help. Our confidence, therefore, is not so entirely irrational as you think.

Athenians: So far as the favour of the gods is concerned, we think we have as much right to that as you have. Our aims and our actions are perfectly consistent with the beliefs men hold about the gods and with the principles which govern their own conduct. Our opinion of the gods and our knowledge of men lead us to conclude that it is a general and necessary law of nature to rule whatever one can. This is not a law that we made ourselves, nor were we the first to act upon it when it was made. We found it already in existence, and we shall leave it to exist forever among those who come after us. We are merely acting in accordance with it, and we know that you or anybody else with the same power as ours would be acting in precisely the same way. And therefore, so far as the gods are concerned, we see no good reason why we should fear to be at a disadvantage. But with regard to your views about Sparta and your confidence that she, out of a sense of honour, will come to your aid, we must say that we congratulate you on your simplicity but do not envy you your folly. In matters that concern themselves for their own constitution the Spartans are quite remarkably good; as for their relations with others, that is a long story, but it can be expressed shortly and clearly by saying that of all people we know the Spartans are most conspicuous for believing that what they like doing is honourable and what suits their interests is just. And this kind of attitude is not going to be of much help to you in your absurd quest for safety at the moment.

Melians: But this is the very point where we can feel most sure. Their own self-interest will make them refuse to betray their own colonists, the Melians, for that would mean losing the confidence of their friends among the Hellenes and doing good to their enemies.

Athenians: You seem to forget that if one follows one's self-interest one wants to be safe, whereas the path of justice and honour involves one in danger. And, where danger is concerned, the Spartans are not, as a rule, very venturesome.

Melians: But we think that they would even endanger themselves for our sake and count the risk more worth taking than in the case of others, because we are so close to the Peloponnese that they could operate more easily, and because they can depend on us more than on others, since we are of the same race and share the same feelings.

Athenians: Good will shown by the party that is asking for help does not mean security for the prospective ally. What is looked for is a positive preponderance of power in action. And the Spartans pay attention to this point even more than others do. Certainly they distrust their own native resources so much that when they attack a neighbour they bring a great army of allies with them. It is hardly likely therefore that, while we are in control of the sea, they will cross over to an island.

Melians: But they still might send others. The Cretan sea is a wide one, and it is harder for those who control it to intercept others than for those who want to slip through to do so safely. And even if they were to fail in this, they would turn against your own land and against those of your allies left unvisited by Brasidas. So, instead of troubling about a country which has nothing to do with you, you will find trouble nearer home, among your allies, and in your own country.

Athenians: It is a possibility, something that has in fact happened before. It may happen in your case, but you are well aware that the Athenians have never yet relinquished a single siege operation through fear of others. But we are somewhat shocked to find that, though you announced your intention of discussing how you could preserve yourselves, in all this talk you have said absolutely nothing which could justify a man in thinking that he could be preserved. Your chief points are concerned with what you hope may happen in the future, while your actual resources are too scanty to give you a chance of survival against the forces that are opposed to you at this moment. You will therefore be showing an extraordinary lack of common sense if, after you have asked us to retire from this meeting, you still fail to reach a conclusion wiser than anything you have mentioned so far. Do not be led astray by a false sense of honour — a thing which often brings men to ruin when they are faced with an obvious danger that somehow affects their pride. For in many cases men have still been able to see the dangers ahead of them, but this thing called dishonour, this word, by its own force of seduction, has drawn them into a state where they have surrendered to an idea, while in fact they have fallen voluntarily into irrevocable disaster, in dishonour that is all the more dishonourable because it has come to them from their own folly rather than their misfortune. You, if you take the right view, will be careful to avoid this. You will see that there is nothing disgraceful in giving way to the greatest city in Hellas when she is offering you such reasonable terms — alliance on a tribute-paying basis and liberty to enjoy your own property. And, when you are allowed to choose between war and safety, you will not be so insensitively arrogant as to make the wrong choice. This is the safe rule — to stand up to one's equals, to behave with deference towards one's superiors, and to treat one's inferiors with moderation. Think it over again, then, when we have withdrawn from the meeting, and let this be a point that constantly recurs to your minds — that you are discussing the fate of your country, that you have only one country, and that its future for good or ill depends on this one single decision which you are going to make.

The Athenians then withdrew from the discussion. The Melians, left to themselves, reached a conclusion which was much the same as they had indicated in their previous replies. Their answer was as follows:

"Our decision, Athenians, is just the same as it was at first. We are not prepared to give up in a short moment the liberty which our city has enjoyed from its foundation for 700 years. We put our trust in the fortune that the gods will send and which has saved us up to now, and in the help of men — that is, of the Spartans; and so we shall try to save ourselves. But we invited you to allow us to be friends of yours and enemies to neither side, to make a treaty which shall be agreeable to both you and us, and so to leave our country."

The Melians made this reply, and the Athenians, just as they were breaking off the discussion, said:

"Well, at any rate, judging from this decision of yours, you seem to us quite unique in your ability to consider the future as something more certain than what is before your eyes, and to see uncertainties as realities, simply because you would like them to be so. As you have staked most on and trusted most in Spartans, luck, and hopes, so in all these you will find yourselves most completely deluded."

The Athenian representatives then went back to the army, and the Athenian generals, finding that the Melians would not submit, immediately commenced hostilities and built a wall completely round the city of Melos, dividing the work out among the various states. Later they left behind a garrison of some of their own and some allied troops to blockade the place by land and sea, and with the greater part of their army returned home. The force left behind stayed on and continued with the siege.

About the same time the Argives invaded Phliasia and were ambushed by the Phliasians and the exiles from Argos, losing about eighty men.

Then, too, the Athenians at Pylos captured a great quantity of plunder from Spartan territory. Not even after this did the Spartans renounce the treaty and make war, but they issued a proclamation saying that any of their people who wished to do so were free to make raids on the Athenians. The Corinthians also made some attacks on the Athenians because of private quarrels of their own, but the rest of the Peloponnesians stayed quiet.

Meanwhile the Melians made a night attack and captured the part of the Athenian lines opposite the market-place. They killed some of the troops, and then, after bringing in corn and everything else useful that they could lay their hands on, retired again and made no further move, while the Athenians took measures to make their blockade more efficient in the future. So the summer came to an end.

In the following winter the Spartans planned to invade the territory of Argos, but when the sacrifices for crossing the frontier turned out unfavourably, they gave up the expedition. The fact that they had intended to invade made the Argives suspect certain people in their city, some of whom they arrested, though others succeeded in escaping.

About this same time the Melians again captured another part of the Athenian lines where there were only a few of the garrison on guard. As a result of this, another force came out afterwards from Athens under the command of Philocrates, the son of Demeas. Siege operations were now carried on vigorously and, as there was also some treachery from inside, the Melians surrendered unconditionally to the Athenians, who put to death all the men of military age whom they took, and sold the women and children as slaves. Melos itself they took over for themselves, sending out later a colony of 500 men.

On Princes and the Security of Their States

Niccolo Machiavelli

In this selection from The Prince, *Machiavelli makes a number of his famous observations on how a prince should rule. Although a prince may not wish to be hated, Machiavelli argues "it is much safer to be feared than to be loved, if one must choose." Although the prince may be criticized for being cruel, this is acceptable to Machiavelli so long as the prince keeps his subjects united and loyal. These are the sorts of argument that have given Machiavellianism a negative connotation, but followers of Machiavelli would respond that the ultimate goal meant to justify particular policies is the security of the state, not just the security of an individual ruler.*

ON THINGS FOR WHICH MEN, AND PARTICULARLY PRINCES, ARE PRAISED OR BLAMED

We now have left to consider what should be the manners and attitudes of a prince toward his subjects and his friends. As I know that many have written on this subject I feel that I may be held presumptuous in what I have to say, if in my comments I do not follow the lines laid down by others. Since, however, it has been my intention to write something which may be of use to the understanding reader, it has seemed wiser to me to follow the real truth of the matter rather than what we imagine it to be. For imagination has created many principalities and republics that have never been seen or known to have any real existence, for how we live is so different from how we ought to live that he who studies what ought to be done rather than what is done will learn the way to his downfall rather than to his preservation. A man striving in every way to be good will meet his ruin among the great number who are not good. Hence it is necessary for a prince, if he wishes to remain in power, to learn how not to be good and to use his knowledge or refrain from using it as he may need.

Putting aside then the things imagined as pertaining to a prince and considering those that really do, I will say that all men, and particularly princes because of their prominence, when comment is made of them, are noted as having some characteristics deserving either praise or blame. One is accounted liberal, another stingy, to use a Tuscan term — for in our speech avaricious (*avaro*) is applied to such as are desirous of acquiring by rapine whereas stingy (*misero*) is the term used for those who are reluctant to part with their own — one is considered bountiful,

From Niccolo Machiavelli, *The Prince*, translated and edited by Thomas G. Bergin. Reprinted by permission.

another rapacious; one cruel, another tenderhearted; one false to his word, another trustworthy; one effeminate and pusillanimous, another wild and spirited; one humane, another haughty; one lascivious, another chaste; one a man of integrity and another sly; one tough and another pliant; one serious and another frivolous; one religious and another skeptical, and so on. Everyone will agree, I know, that it would be a most praiseworthy thing if all the qualities accounted as good in the above enumeration were found in a Prince. But since they cannot be so possessed nor observed because of human conditions which do not allow of it, what is necessary for the prince is to be prudent enough to escape the infamy of such vices as would result in the loss of his state; as for the others which would not have that effect, he must guard himself from them as far as possible but if he cannot, he may overlook them as being of less importance. Further, he should have no concern about incurring the infamy of such vices without which the preservation of his state would be difficult. For, if the matter be well considered, it will be seen that some habits which appear virtuous, if adopted would signify ruin, and others that seem vices lead to security and the well-being of the prince.

CRUELTY AND CLEMENCY AND WHETHER IT IS BETTER TO BE LOVED OR FEARED

Now to continue with the list of characteristics. It should be the desire of every prince to be considered merciful and not cruel, yet he should take care not to make poor use of his clemency. Cesare Borgia was regarded as cruel, yet his cruelty reorganized Romagna and united it in peace and loyalty. Indeed, if we reflect, we shall see that this man was more merciful than the Florentines who, to avoid the charge of cruelty, allowed Pistoia to be destroyed.[1] A prince should care nothing for the accusation of cruelty so long as he keeps his subjects united and loyal; by making a very few examples he can be more truly merciful than those who through too much tender-heartedness allow disorders to arise whence come killings and rapine. For these offend an entire community, while the few executions ordered by the prince affect only a few individuals. For a new prince above all it is impossible not to earn a reputation for cruelty since new states are full of dangers. Virgil indeed has Dido apologize for the inhumanity of her rule because it is new, in the words:

> Res dura et regni novitas me talia cogunt Moliri et late fines custode tueri.

Nevertheless a prince should not be too ready to listen to talebearers nor to act on suspicion, nor should he allow himself to be easily frightened. He should proceed with a mixture of prudence and humanity in such a way as not to be made incautious by overconfidence nor yet intolerable by excessive mistrust.

Here the question arises; whether it is better to be loved than feared or feared than loved. The answer is that it would be desirable to be both but, since that is difficult, it is much safer to be feared than to be loved, if one must choose. For on men in general this observation may be made: they are ungrateful, fickle, and deceitful, eager to avoid dangers, and avid for gain, and while you are useful to them they are all with you, offering you their blood, their property, their lives, and their sons so long as danger is remote, as we noted above, but when it approaches they turn on you. Any prince, trusting only in their words and having no other preparations made, will fall to his ruin, for friendships that are bought at a price and not by greatness and nobility of soul are paid for indeed, but they are not owned and cannot be called upon in time of need. Men have less hesitation in offending a man who is loved than one who is feared, for love is held by a bond of obligation which, as men are wicked, is broken whenever personal advantage suggests it, but fear is accompanied by the dread of punishment which never relaxes.

Yet a prince should make himself feared in such a way that, if he does not thereby merit love, at least he may escape odium, for being feared and not hated may well go together. And indeed the prince may attain this end if he but respect the property and the women of his subjects and citizens. And if it should become necessary to seek the death of someone, he should find a proper justification and a public cause, and above all he should keep his hands off another's property, for men forget more readily the death of their father than the loss of their patrimony. Besides, pretexts for seizing property are never lacking, and when a prince begins to live by means of rapine he will always find some excuse for plundering others, and conversely pretexts for execution are rarer and are more quickly exhausted.

A prince at the head of his armies and with a vast number of soldiers under his command should give not the slightest heed if he is esteemed cruel, for without such a reputation he will not be able to keep his army united and ready for action. Among the marvelous things told of Hannibal is that, having a vast army under his command made up of all kinds and races of men and waging war far from his own country, he never allowed any dissension to arise either as between the troops and their leaders or among the troops themselves, and this both in times of good fortune and bad. This could only have come about through his most inhuman cruelty which, taken in conjunction with his great valor, kept him always an object of respect and terror in the eyes of his soldiers. And without the cruelty his other characteristics would not have achieved this effect. Thoughtless writers have admired his actions and at the same time deplored the cruelty which was the basis of them. As evidence of the truth of our statement that his other virtues would have been insufficient let us examine the case of Scipio, an extraordinary leader not only in his own day but for all recorded history. His army in Spain revolted and for no other reason than because of his kind-heartedness, which had allowed more license to his soldiery than military discipline properly permits. His policy was attacked in the Senate by Fabius Maximus, who called him a corrupter of the Roman arms. When the Locrians had been mishandled by one of his lieutenants, his easy-going nature prevented him from avenging them or disciplining his officer, and it was à propos of this incident that one of the senators remarked, wishing to find an excuse for him, that there were many men who knew better how to avoid error themselves than to correct it in others. This characteristic of Scipio would have clouded his fame and glory had he continued in authority, but as he lived under the government of the Senate, its harmful aspect was hidden and it reflected credit on him.

Hence, on the subject of being loved or feared I will conclude that since love depends on the subjects, but the prince has it in his own hands to create fear, a wise prince will rely on what is his own, remembering at the same time that he must avoid arousing hatred, as we have said.

NOTE

1. By unchecked rioting between opposing factions (1502).

Of the Natural Condition of Mankind

Thomas Hobbes

Hobbes analyzes why conflict and violence between individuals or states is to be expected. Although his focus in The Leviathan *is on domestic societies, his observations are also relevant to international politics and have had a major impact on realism. In the absence of a sovereign or central, superordinate authority, the world described by Hobbes is a rather dismal one in which the life of the individual is "solitary, poor, nasty, brutish, and short" and "kings . . . because of their independency, are in continual jealousies, and in the state and posture of gladiators."*

Men by Nature Equal.   Nature hath made men so equal, in the faculties of the body, and mind; as that though there be found one man sometimes manifestly stronger in body, or of quicker mind than another; yet when all is reckoned together, the difference between man, and man, is not so con-

From Thomas Hobbes, *Leviathan*, introduction by Richard S. Peters. New York: Macmillan/Collier Books, 1962.

siderable, as that one man can thereupon claim to himself any benefit, to which another may not pretend, as well as he. For as to the strength of body, the weakest has strength enough to kill the strongest, either by secret machination, or by confederacy with others, that are in the same danger with himself.

And as to the faculties of the mind, setting aside the arts grounded upon words, and especially that skill of proceeding upon general, and infallible rules, called science; which very few have, and but in few things; as being not a native faculty, born with us; nor attained, as prudence, while we look after somewhat else, I find yet a greater equality amongst men, than that of strength. For prudence, is but experience; which equal time, equally bestows on all men, in those things they equally apply themselves unto. That which may perhaps make such equality incredible, is but a vain conceit of one's own wisdom, which almost all men think they have in a greater degree, than the vulgar; that is, than all men but themselves, and a few others, whom by fame, or for concurring with themselves, they approve. For such is the nature of men, that howsoever they may acknowledge many others to be more witty, or more eloquent, or more learned; yet they will hardly believe there be many so wise as themselves; for they see their own wit at hand, and other men's at a distance. But this proveth rather that men are in that point equal, than unequal. For there is not ordinarily a greater sign of the equal distribution of any thing, than that every man is contented with his share.

From Equality Proceeds Diffidence.   From this equality of ability, ariseth equality of hope in the attaining of our ends. And therefore if any two men desire the same thing, which nevertheless they cannot both enjoy, they become enemies; and in the way to their end, which is principally their own conservation, and sometimes their delectation only, endeavour to destroy, or subdue one another. And from hence it comes to pass, that where an invader hath no more to fear, than another man's single power; if one plant, sow, build, or possess a convenient seat, others may probably be expected to come prepared with forces united, to dispossess, and deprive him, not only of the fruit of his labour, but also of his life, or liberty. And the invader again is in the like danger of another.

From Diffidence War.   And from this diffidence of one another, there is no way for any man to secure himself, so reasonable, as anticipation; that is, by force, or wiles, to master the persons of all men he can, so long, till he see no other power great enough to endanger him: and this is no more than his own conservation requireth, and is generally allowed. Also because there be some, that taking pleasure in contemplating their own power in the acts of conquest, which they pursue farther than their security requires; if others, that otherwise would be glad to be at ease within modest bounds, should not by invasion increase their power, they would not be able, long time, by standing only on their defence, to subsist. And by consequence, such augmentation of dominion over men being necessary to a man's conservation, it ought to be allowed him.

Again, men have no pleasure, but on the contrary a great deal of grief, in keeping company, where there is no power able to overawe them all. For every man looketh that his companion should value him, at the same rate he sets upon himself: and upon all signs of contempt, or undervaluing, naturally endeavours, as far as he dares, (which amongst them that have no common power to keep them in quiet, is far enough to make them destroy each other), to extort a greater value from his contemners, by damage; and from others, by the example.

So that in the nature of man, we find three principal causes of quarrel. First, competition; secondly, diffidence; thirdly, glory.

The first, maketh men invade for gain; the second, for safety; and the third, for reputation. The first use violence, to make themselves masters of other men's persons, wives, children, and cattle; the second, to defend them; the third, for trifles, as a word, a smile, a different opinion, and any other sign of undervalue, either direct in their persons, or by reflection in their kindred, their friends, their nation, their profession, or their name.

Out of Civil States, There Is Always War of Every One Against Every One.   Hereby it is manifest, that during the time men live without a common power to keep them all in awe, they are in that condition which is called war; and such a war, as is of every man, against every man. For WAR, consisteth not in battle only, or the act of fighting; but in a tract of time, wherein the will to contend by battle is sufficiently known: and therefore the notion of *time*, is to be considered in the nature of war; as it is in the nature of weather. For as the nature of foul weather, lieth not in a shower or two of rain; but in an inclination thereto of many days together: so the nature of war, consisteth not in actual fighting; but in the known disposition thereto, during all the time there is no assurance to the contrary. All other time is PEACE.

The Incommodities of Such a War.   Whatsoever therefore is consequent to a time of war, where every man is enemy to every man; the same is consequent to the time, wherein men live without other security, than what their own strength, and their own invention shall furnish them withal. In such condition, there is no place for industry; because the fruit thereof is uncertain: and consequently no culture of the earth; no navigation, nor use of the commodities that may be imported by sea; no commodious building; no instruments of moving, and removing, such things as require much force; no knowledge of the face of the earth; no account of time; no arts; no letters; no society; and which is worst of all, continual fear, and danger of violent death; and the life of man, solitary, poor, nasty, brutish, and short.

It may seem strange to some man, that has not well weighed these things; that nature should thus dissociate, and render men apt to invade, and destroy one another: and he may therefore, not trusting to this inference, made from the passions, desire perhaps to have the same confirmed by experience. Let him therefore consider with himself, when taking a journey, he arms himself, and seeks to go well accompanied; when going to sleep, he locks his doors; when even in his house he locks his chests; and this when he knows there be laws, and public officers, armed, to revenge all injuries shall be done him; what opinion he has of his fellow-subjects, when he rides armed; of his fellow citizens, when he locks his doors; and of his children, and servants, when he locks his chests. Does he not there as much accuse mankind by his actions, as I do by my words? But neither of us accuse man's nature in it. The desires, and other passions of man, are in themselves no sin. No more are the actions, that proceed from those passions, till they know a law that forbids them: which till laws be made they cannot know: nor can any law be made, till they have agreed upon the person that shall make it.

It may peradventure be thought, there was never such a time, nor condition of war as this; and I believe it was never generally so, over all the world: but there are many places, where they live so now. For the savage people in many places of America, except the government of small families, the concord whereof dependeth on natural lust, have no government at all; and live at this day in the brutish manner, as I said before. Howsoever, it may be perceived what manner of life there would be, where there were no common power to fear, by the manner of life, which men that have formerly lived under a peaceful government, use to degenerate into, in a civil war.

But though there had never been any time, wherein particular men were in a condition of war one against another; yet in all times, kings, and persons of sovereign authority, because of their independency, are in continual jealousies, and in the state and posture of gladiators; having their weapons pointing, and their eyes fixed on one another; that is, their forts, garrisons, and guns upon the frontiers of their kingdoms; and continual spies upon their neighbours; which is a posture of war. But because they uphold thereby, the industry of their subjects; there does not follow from it, that misery, which accompanies the liberty of particular men.

In Such a War Nothing Is Unjust. To this war of every man, against every man, this also is consequent; that nothing can be unjust. The notions of right and wrong, justice and injustice have there no place. Where there is no common power, there is no law: where no law, no injustice. Force, and fraud, are in war the two cardinal virtues. Justice, and injustice are none of the faculties neither of the body, nor mind. If they were, they might be in a man that were alone in the world, as well as his senses, and passions. They are qualities, that relate to men in society, not in solitude. It is consequent also to the same condition, there there be no propriety, no dominion, no *mine* and *thine* distinct; but only that to be every man's, that he can get: and for so long, as he can keep it. And thus much for the ill condition, which man by mere nature is actually placed in; though with a possibility to come out of it, consisting partly in the passions, partly in his reason.

The Passions that Incline Men to Peace. The passions that incline men to peace, are fear of death; desire of such things as are necessary to commodious living; and a hope by their industry to obtain them. And reason suggesteth convenient articles of peace, upon which men may be drawn to agreement.

The State of War: Confederation as Means to Peace in Europe

Jean Jacques Rousseau

Rousseau observes that "man is naturally peaceful and shy." He takes issue with the Hobbesean view of man's nature, contesting the idea that it could be so negative. At the same time, it is the "liberty" that states have in relation to one another that results in "accidental and specific wars." He portrays states as unitary and rational (purposive) actors that may come into conflict, engaging in warfare with one another. War does not depend upon the nature of man. No, to Rousseau war is the product of a social context within which the state (or body politic) finds itself — one in which there is no authority higher than the state itself. Rousseau does not reject the view that a European confederation could produce peace, but considers it unlikely that such a restructuring of politics will be achieved. This selection is key to understanding realist and neo-realist views.

I open my books about rights and morals, I listen to scholars and legal experts, and inspired by their suggestive discourses, I deplore the miseries of nature, admire the peace and justice established by the civil order, bless the wisdom of public institutions, and find consolation for being a man by seeing myself as a citizen. Well instructed as to my duties and my happiness, I close the books, leave the lecture room, and look around me. There I see a miserable people groaning under an iron yoke, the whole human race crushed by a handful of oppressors, and an enraged mob overwhelmed by pain and hunger whose blood and tears the rich drink in peace. And everywhere the strong are armed against the weak with the formidable power of the law.

All of this happens peacefully and without resistance. With a tranquility like that of Odysseus's imprisoned companions waiting to be devoured by the Cyclops, we can only groan and be quiet. But I must draw a veil over these horrors. I lift my eyes and look into the distance. There I see fires and flames, deserted countrysides, pillaged villages. Monstrous men, where are you dragging these poor creatures? I hear a terrible noise, an uproar, screams! I draw near. Before me is a panorama of murder — ten thousand slaughtered men, the dead piled up in heaps, the dying trampled by horses — and everywhere the sight of death and agony. And yet all of this is the fruit of peaceful institutions. Pity and indignation rise up from the depths of my heart. Barbarous philosopher, come read us your book on a battlefield!

What human soul would not be sickened by such painful scenes? But one is no longer a man if one pleads the cause of humanity. Justice and truth must be twisted in the interest of the strongest. That is now the rule. The poor cannot provide pensions or employment, they do not grant academic honors or endow university chairs, so why should we protect them? Magnanimous princes, I speak in the name of the literary class: oppress the people in sound conscience. It is from you alone that we expect everything; the people can give us nothing.

How then will a feeble voice make itself heard above so many selfish clamors? Must I simply keep quiet? Cannot a voice from the heart break through these oppressive silences? No. Without entering into horrifying details that would be considered satirical if only because they are true, I will limit myself, as I have always done, to examining human institutions by means of their principles; to correcting, if it is possible, the false ideas given about them by self-interested authors; and, at the very least, to ensuring that injustice and violence do not shamelessly take on the names of right and equity.

When I reflect upon the condition of the human race, the first thing that I notice is a manifest contradiction in its constitution. As individuals we live in a civil state and are subject to laws, but as nations each enjoys the liberty of nature. The resulting continual vacillation makes our situation worse than if these distinctions were unknown. For living simultaneously in the social order and in the state of nature, we are subjected to the evils of both without gaining the security of either. The perfection of the social order consists, it is true, in the conjunction of force and law. But for this it is necessary that law direct force. According to the notion that princes must be absolutely independent, however, force alone, which appears as law to its own citizens and "raison d'état" to foreigners, deprives the latter of the power and the former of the will to resist, so that in the end the vain name of justice serves only to safeguard violence.

As for what is called the law of nations, it is clear that without any real sanction these laws are only illusions that are more tenuous even than the notion of natural law. The latter at least addresses itself to the heart of individuals, whereas decisions based on the law of nations, having no other guarantee than the utility of the one who submits to them, are respected only as long as those decisions confirm one's own self-interest. In the double condition in which we find ourselves, by doing too much or too little for whichever of the two systems we happen to prefer, we in fact have done nothing at all, and thereby have put ourselves in the worst possible position. This, it seems to me, is the true origin of public calamities.

For a moment let us put these ideas in opposition to the horrible system of Hobbes. We will find, contrary to his absurd doctrine, that far from the state of war being natural to man, war is born out of peace, or at least out of the precautions men have taken to assure themselves of peace. . . .

Who could imagine without shuddering the insane system of a natural war of every man against every man? What a strange animal this man must be who believes that his own well-being depends upon the destruction of his species! And how could anyone think that this species, so monstrous and detestable, could last even two generations? But it is to extremes such as these that the desire, or rather the fury, to establish despotism and passive obedience has led one of the greatest geniuses that ever lived. Such an insidious theory was surely worthy of its underlying purpose.

The social state that governs all our natural inclinations cannot, however, eliminate them. In spite of our prejudices and in spite of ourselves, our natural inclinations speak to us from the depths of our hearts and often lead us back to the truth that we have abandoned as fantasy. If a destructive and mutual enmity were essential to our constitution, it would make itself felt even more and would burst forth, unopposed, from within every social bond. The fierce hatred of humanity would eat away at the heart of man. He would mourn at the birth of his children, rejoice at the death of his brothers, and kill every sleeping man he happened to come across.

The benevolence that enables us to share in the happiness of our fellow men, the compassion that identifies us with those who suffer and that touches us with their pain, would be unknown sentiments and contrary to nature. A sensitive and sympathetic man would be considered a monster, and we would be naturally that which we have taken great pains to become in the midst of the corruption that surrounds us.

In vain could our sophist argue that this mutual enmity might not be innate and immediate but that it is founded on an inevitable competition resulting from the right of each for all things. For the sentiment of this alleged right is no more natural to man than the war that it gives birth to.

I have said before and cannot repeat too often that the error of Hobbes and the *philosophes* is to confuse natural man with the man that they have before their eyes, and to transport into one system a being which could only exist in another. Man wishes for his own well-being and for all that can contribute to it — this is incontestable. But by nature the well-being of man is limited to physical necessity. For when he has a healthy soul and his body is not in pain, what does his natural constitution lack to make him happy? He who has nothing desires few things; he who commands no one has few ambitions. But surplus awakens greed: The more one accumulates, the more one desires. Those who have much want to have all, and the mad passion for universal monarchy has only tormented the hearts of great kings. This is in the nature of things — this is how the passions expand. A superficial philosopher observes souls that are endlessly kneaded and allowed to ferment in the yeast of society and believes he has observed man. But in order to know man well, he must know how to separate out the natural growth of the sentiments. And it is not among city dwellers that he must search to find nature's first imprint on the human heart.

Thus, this analytic method offers only mystery and abyss where those who are most wise understand the least. Let someone ask the *philosophes* why morals are corrupted in proportion to the enlightenment of minds. Being unable to find the cause, they will have the audacity to deny the fact. Let someone ask them why primitive people brought among us share neither our passions nor our pleasures and do not worry about the things that we desire with so much fervor. Either the *philosophes* will never explain this or they will explain it with the principles put forth by me. They know only what they see, and they have never seen nature. They may very well know a bourgeois from Paris or London, but they will never know man.

But even if it were true that this unlimited and uncontrollable greed had developed in every man to the extent that Hobbes presumes, still it would not bring on that state of universal war of each against all that he has described in such odious terms. For the frenzied desire to appropriate everything for oneself is incompatible with the desire to destroy one's fellow men. The victor in such a war would face the world alone, and having gained everything he would enjoy nothing. What good are riches if they cannot be exchanged? What good would it be to possess the whole universe if one were its only survivor? Can one man's belly devour all the earth's fruit? Who would harvest for him all the world's crops? Who would carry the word of his empire to the vast wastelands where he himself could never live? What would he do with his treasures, who would consume his commodities, before whose eyes would he display his power? I know: Instead of massacring everyone, he would put them all in chains and then he at least would own some slaves. And this of course would immediately change things, for as soon as destruction itself is no longer the issue, the state of war as such disappears. May the reader here suspend his judgment; I will return to this point.

Man is naturally peaceful and shy; at the slightest danger his first movement is to flee. He only becomes emboldened by force of habit and experience. Honor, self-interest, prejudice, vengeance — all the passions that can make him brave the perils of death — are far from him in the state of nature. It is only after having associated with one man that he determines to kill another. He only becomes soldier after having been citizen. It is not in natural man that one finds the great propensities for war. But I need not dwell on a system that is as revolting as it is absurd, and that has been refuted a thousand times.

In the state of nature there is thus no general war of every man against every man; the human race was not created simply to destroy itself. But it still remains for us to consider those accidental and specific wars that might arise between two or several individuals.

If natural law were inscribed only on human reason, it would hardly be capable of directing most of our actions. But it is also indelibly engraved in the human heart. It is from the heart that natural law speaks to man more powerfully than all the precepts of philosophers. It is from there that it cries out to him that he may not sacrifice the life of his fellow man except to save his own, and that even when he sees himself obliged to do so, he cannot but feel a sense of horror at the idea of killing in cold blood. . . .

CONCERNING CIVIL SOCIETY

We now enter into a new order of things where we see men united by an artificial accord coming together to cut one another's throats, and where all the horrors of war arise from the efforts that were taken to prevent it. But first of all it is important to formulate more exact notions than we have up until now about the essence of this body politic. . . .

The state . . . since it is an artificial body, has no fixed measure and is never sure of its proper size. It can always expand, and yet it always feels weak as long as there are other states that are stronger than itself. Its security, its defense, demand that it try to appear more powerful than its neighbors; and it can only grow, feed itself, and test its strength at their expense. Even if it does not actually need to seek its subsistence beyond its own borders, it is ceaselessly on the lookout for new members who might give it a more stable base. For the inequality of men has limits put in place by the hands of nature, but the inequalities of states can grow incessantly, until one alone absorbs all the others.

Its power thus being purely relative, the political body is forced ceaselessly to compare itself in order to know itself. It depends on its surroundings, and must take an interest in all that happens there. For in vain might it wish simply to keep to itself without risking gain or loss; whether a state becomes small or great, weak or strong, depends on whether its neighbor expands or pulls back, adds to its forces or reduces them. Finally even political stability, insofar as it results in a more systematic foreign policy, can give an added forcefulness to a state's actions and thus make its conflicts more severe. . . .

For the state to survive it is thus necessary that the intensity of its passions supplement the intensity of its actions, and that its will become animated to the extent that its strength becomes slack. This is the law of self-preservation that nature herself established among the species and which sustains them all in spite of their inequality. It is also, I must say in passing, the reason why smaller states have in proportion more vigor than larger ones. For public vitality does not increase with territory. The further a society extends itself, the weaker grows its will, and the great body that is overburdened with its own weight soon sinks down, falls into decline, and perishes.

After having seen the earth become covered with new states, after having discovered among them a general relationship which tends toward their mutual destruction, it remains for us to see what exactly it is that constitutes their existence, their well-being, and their life, in order then to identify the kinds of hostilities by which they are able to attack and harm one another.

It is from the social pact that the body politic receives its unity and its "*moi commun.*" The government and the laws determine the robustness of its constitution, the hearts of its citizens give it its life, their courage and their customs determine its durability, and the only actions that it undertakes freely and that it can be accountable for are those dictated by the general will. It is by these actions that we can judge whether the being that produced them is well or poorly constituted.

Thus as long as there exists a common will to observe the social pact and its laws, the social pact will continue to survive; and as long as this will manifests itself as external acts, the state is not destroyed. But without ceasing to exist, the state can find itself at a point of vigor or decline from which — weak, healthy, or ill, and tending either to destroy itself or to assert itself — its power can grow or alter in an infinite number of ways, almost all of which are contingent upon its well-being. . . .

THE GENERAL IDEA OF WAR BETWEEN STATE AND STATE

The life principle of the body politic, and, if I may say so, the heart of the state, is the social pact, which, if harmed in any way, immediately dies, falls apart, and dissolves. But this pact is not a charter made out of parchment that can simply be torn apart into shreds. It is written into the general will, where it is not at all easy to get rid of.

Unable at first to be broken up all at once, the social pact can be attacked part by part. If the body is invulnerable, its separate members can be struck at one by one. If its life cannot be taken, at least its health can be altered. If the source of its life cannot be reached, that which maintains it — the government, laws, customs, holdings, possessions, men — can still be destroyed. When everything that preserves it is annihilated, the state will finally die.

All these means are used or can be used in a war of one power against another, and they are also often the conditions imposed by the conquerors as a way further to harm a disarmed and defeated state. For the objective of all the harm inflicted on one's enemy at war is to force him to accept those things that he will have to suffer even more from when at peace. . . .

WHAT THE STATE OF WAR IS

Although these two words *war* and *peace* appear to be exactly correlative, the second contains a broader significance, since peace can be troubled or interrupted in many different ways without leading to war. Repose, unity, concord, and all the notions of benevolence and mutual affection seem contained in the sweet name of peace. It brings to one's soul a fullness of sentiment that makes us love simultaneously our own existence and that of others; it represents the tie among beings that unites them into a universal system. Its full meaning is to be found in the spirit of God, whom nothing can harm and who desires the preservation of all the beings that he has created.

The constitution of this universe does not permit all the sensible beings that compose it to concur at the same time in their mutual happiness. Instead, the happiness of one is the misfortune of another, and thus according to the law of nature each gives himself preference, both when he works to his own advantage and when he works to the disadvantage of others. As soon as peace is upset on the side of the one who suffers, then not only is it natural to rebuff the hurt that is directed at us, but, in cases when an intelligent being sees that this hurt comes from the ill will of someone else, it is natural to get angry and seek to counter it. From this arises discord, quarrels, sometimes conflicts, but still not war.

Finally, when things have arrived at the point where a rational being is convinced that the care for its own preservation is incompatible not only with the well-being of another but with that other's existence, then this being takes up arms and seeks to destroy the other with the same ardor with which it seeks to preserve itself, and for the same reason. The one that is attacked, sensing that the security of its existence is incompatible with the existence of the aggressor, attacks in turn with all its strength the life of the one who is after him. This manifest will to destroy each other and all the actions that it gives rise to produce between the two enemies a relation that is called war.

From the above it follows that war does not consist of one or a few unpremeditated conflicts, or even of homicide or murder as long as they are committed in a brief fit of anger. Instead, war consists in the constant, reflected, and manifest will to destroy one's enemy. For in order to judge that the existence of this enemy is incompatible with our well-being, one needs coolness and reason—both of which produce a lasting resolve; and in order for the relationship to be mutual, the enemy in turn, knowing that its life is in jeopardy, must have the intention to defend its own life at the risk of ours. All these ideas are contained in the word war.

The public effects of this will reduced into acts are called hostilities. But whether or not there are hostilities, the relation of war, once established, can only cease by means of a formal peace. Otherwise, each of the two enemies, having no proof that the other has ceased resenting its existence, cannot or should not cease defending its own life at the cost of the other's.

These differences lead to a certain distinction in terminology. When both sides continue to engage in acts of hostility, there is what is properly called the *waging of war*. On the other hand, when two self-declared enemies remain stationary and take no offensive actions against each other, the relationship has not in any way changed, but so long as there are no actual effects there is what is called only *a state of war*. Long wars that people get tired of but that they cannot end ordinarily produce this state. Sometimes, far from being lulled into inaction, the animosity needs only to wait for a favorable moment to surprise the enemy, and then often the state of war that produces this release is more dangerous than war itself.

It has been argued whether a truce, a suspension of arms, a "Peace of God" are a state of war or peace. It is clear from the preceding notions that they all constitute a modified state of war in which the two enemies tie their own hands without losing or disguising the will to harm each other. They make preparations, pile up weapons and materials for a siege, and all the nonspecified military operations continue apace. . . .

I thus define *war* between one power and another the effect of a mutual, constant, and manifest intention to destroy the enemy state, or at least to weaken it by all possible means. This intention carried into action is *war* properly so called; but as long as it does not come into effect it is only the *state of war*. . . .

ON THE PERPETUAL PEACE PROJECT

Just as there is no greater nor more beautiful and useful project for the human spirit to reflect upon than one which aims at a perpetual and universal peace among all the peoples of Europe, so there is no author who better deserves the attention of the public than one who proposes the means for putting this project into effect. It is even difficult for a sane and virtuous person not to become enthusiastic about such a project, for in this case I am not sure whether the dreams of a truly human heart whose own zeal makes everything seem easy are not to be preferred to that cold and calculating reason which always finds in its indifference to the public good the first obstacle to everything that might benefit it.

I do not doubt that many readers are armed in advance skeptically to resist persuasion in these matters, and I pity them for so stubbornly mistaking hard-headedness as realism. But I hope that at least a few good souls will share the gratifying feelings with which I take up my pen on a subject so vital to humanity. I am about to see, at least in my mind, men coming together and loving each other; I am about to imagine a sweet and peaceful society of brothers, living in an eternal concord, all led by the same beliefs, all content with common pleasures; and, realizing in myself such a touching scene, the image of a happiness which does not exist will allow me to enjoy a few moments of one that does.

I could not withhold my sentiments from these first lines, but now let us reason realistically. Determined to put forth nothing that I cannot prove, I believe I can ask the reader in turn to deny nothing that he cannot refute. For it is not the true polemicists whom I fear so much as those who, while refusing to accept any proofs, yet have no objections to bring to them.

It is not necessary to have thought long about the means of perfecting any government to perceive the difficulties and obstacles that arise less from its constitution than from its foreign policy — to the extent that we are forced to give over to our defense most of the attention that should be devoted to enforcing the law and to think more about being in a state of readiness to resist others than about perfecting the government itself. Indeed, if our social order were, as it is claimed to be, the work of reason rather than of the passions, would we have taken so long to see that as far as our well-being is concerned we have accomplished either too much or too little; that each one of us being both in the civil state with his fellow citizens and in the state of nature with the whole rest of the world, we have prevented private wars only so as to set off public wars, which are a thousand times worse; and that by uniting with a few men we have really become the enemies of mankind?

If there is any means of removing these dangerous contradictions it can only be by a form of confederative government, which, by uniting nations with ties similar to those which unite individuals, submits each of them equally to the authority of laws. This form of government, moreover, appears preferable to any other in that it combines at the same time the advantages of both large and small states. It is externally secure because of its power, internally sound because of its laws, and it is the only form which is able to include subjects, leaders, and foreigners on an equal basis. . . .

All the powers of Europe constitute among themselves a sort of system in which they are united by a common religion, by a common sense of the customary laws governing the relations among states [*droit des gens*], by manners, literature, and commerce, and by a sort of equilibrium which is the necessary effect of all that, and which, without anyone consciously maintaining it, would nevertheless not be as easy to disturb as many people might think. This society of European peoples has not always existed, but the particular causes that gave birth to it serve to maintain it still. Indeed, before the conquests of the Romans all the peoples of this part of the world, barbarous and unknown to one another, had nothing in common except their quality as human beings—a quality which, greatly suppressed at that time by slavery, hardly differentiated them spiritually from beasts. The Greeks, with their rationalism and vanity, thus came to distinguish two kinds of humanity—one (their own), which was made to command, and the other (which comprised the rest of the world), simply to serve. The result of this principle was that to the Greeks a Gaul or an Iberian meant no more than a Kaffir or an American, nor did the barbarians have any more affinity among themselves than the Greeks had for any of them.

But when this naturally sovereign people had been subjected to the Romans who had been its slaves, and when one whole part of the known world had suffered under the same yoke, a political and civil union gradually developed among all the members of the common Empire. This union was held together by the either quite wise or quite foolish practice of bestowing on the conquered peoples all the rights of the conquerors, and above all by the famous decree of Claudius, which incorporated all the subjects of Rome into the ranks of her citizens.

The political network that thus united all the members into one body was reinforced by civil institutions and laws that determined in an equitable, clear, and precise manner (at least as much as was possible in such a vast empire) the duties and reciprocal rights of the prince and of his subjects and of the citizens among themselves. . . . This . . . greatly slowed down the decline of the Empire and preserved for it a sort of authority even over the barbarians who eventually became the cause of its ruin.

A . . . tie, stronger than the preceding ones, was that of religion, and no one can deny that it is, above all, to Christianity that Europe even today owes the kind of society that has been perpetuated among its members —to the extent that one who has not adopted the sentiment of the others on this point remains a stranger among them. Christianity, so maligned at its birth, served finally as a refuge for its detractors. After having persecuted Christianity so cruelly and so vainly, the Roman Empire found in it the resources that it could no longer find among its own forces. The Empire came to value conversion more than victory, it sent bishops to repair the mistakes of generals, and it triumphed with priests when its soldiers were defeated. It is thus that the Franks, the Goths, the Bourguignons, the Lombards, the Avares, and thousands of others finally recognized the authority of the Empire after having subjugated it, and in appearance at least, received with the law of the Gospel the law of the prince who had had it preached to them. . . .

All these factors together make Europe not just an idealized collection of peoples who have only a name in common, like Asia or Africa, but a real society with its own religion, manners, customs, and even laws, from which no single nation composing it could withdraw without immediately causing problems for the others. When we see, on the other hand, the endless conflicts, violence, usurpations, revolts, wars, and murders that daily lay waste to this respectable abode of the wise, this brilliant haven for the sciences and the arts; when we compare our elegant speeches with our horrifying procedures, the humanity of our maxims with the cruelty of our actions, the gentleness of our religion with the brutality of our prejudices, the wisdom of our politics in theory with its harshness in practice, our benevolent leaders with our miserable people, our moderate governments with our cruel wars — then we hardly know how to reconcile such strange contradictions, and the so-called fraternity of the peoples of Europe seems nothing more than a name of derision to express with irony their mutual hate.

In all this, however, things are only following their natural course. Any society without leaders or without laws, its union formed or maintained by chance, must necessarily degenerate into quarrels or dissension at the first change in circumstance. The ancient union of the peoples of Europe has complicated their interests and their rights in a thousand ways; they overlap at so many points that the slightest movement of some cannot help but trouble the others; their divisions are all the more deadly as their ties are more intimate; and their frequent quarrels have almost the same cruelty as civil wars.

Let us agree then that the relative state of the powers of Europe is properly speaking a state of war, and that all the partial treaties among certain of these powers are but temporary truces rather than true states of peace — either because such treaties commonly have no other guarantee than the contracting parties themselves or because the rights of each of them are never determined in any fundamental way — and thus that these half-stifled rights (or the claims substituted for them between powers that recognize no superior) will infallibly become the source of new wars as soon as different circumstances have given new strengths to the claimants.

International public law, moreover, having never been established or authorized in concert, having no general principles, and varying incessantly according to time and place, is full of contradictory rules that can only be tested by the right of the strongest. With reason having no definite guide and in questionable matters always leaning toward personal self-interest, war thus becomes inevitable even when each side would like to be just. With all good intentions, all that can be done is to settle these kinds of problems by means of arms, or to assuage them by temporary treaties. . . .

Everyone can see that society is formed by common interests; that discord arises out of opposing ones; that since a thousand fortuitous events can change and modify these interests, then once there is a society it is necessary to have a coercive force to organize and coordinate the movements of its members so that the common interests and reciprocal ties are given the solidity they would not be able to have by themselves.

It would be a great error, however, to hope that the violent state of things could ever change simply by the force of circumstances and without the help of art. The European system has precisely the degree of solidity that can maintain it in a perpetual agitation without overthrowing it completely. . . .

Therefore let us not think that such a highly praised equilibrium was established by anyone or that anyone has purposely done anything to preserve it. It is found to exist, and those who do not feel in themselves enough strength to break it apart hide their particular views under the pretext of sustaining it. But whether one thinks about it or not, this equilibrium subsists, and needs nothing but itself to survive, without interference from anyone; and when it disintegrates for a moment on one side, it soon reestablishes itself on the other—to the extent that if the princes whom we accuse of aspiring to universal monarchy really did aspire to it, they would thereby demonstrate more ambition than talent. For how could one envisage such a plan for one moment without immediately perceiving its folly? How can anyone avoid seeing that there is no power in Europe superior enough ever to become its master? Conquerors who have succeeded in overthrowing states have always appeared with unexpected military forces or with strangely armed foreign troops before peoples who were either disarmed or divided or completely lacking in discipline. But where could a European prince, aiming to overthrow all the others, find such an unprecedented force, since the most powerful state is still such a small part of the whole and since the others would be on their guard against such an attack? Could he have more soldiers than all of them? He could not—or would all the sooner be ruined, or his soldiers would be less effective by virtue of their greater number. Could he have troops that were better trained? He would have proportionately fewer of them. Besides, discipline is everywhere pretty much the same, or quickly becomes so. Would he have more money? The sources of funds are common to all, and in any case, money alone has never been the cause of great victories. Could he make a sudden invasion? Famine or fortresses would slow his pace. Would he gain power step by step? He would then give his enemies the means to unite to resist him; his time, his money, and his men would soon disappear. Would he divide the other powers in order to conquer them one by one? The European ethos would make this policy useless, and even the most narrow-minded prince would not give in to this ploy. In sum, because no single one of them could gain exclusive command over resources, the resistance would, in the long run, equal the effort, and time would soon repair the sudden accidents of fortune, if not for each prince in particular, at least for the general constitution.

Shall we now whimsically suppose that two or three powers could agree to subject all the rest? These three powers, whichever they were, could not together make up half of Europe. Moreover, the other half would certainly unite against them, and the aggressors would have to overcome something stronger than themselves. I will add that the views of each one would be too opposed to those of the others and that there would reign too great a jealousy among them for them to be able to form such a plan. I also will add that if they were able to form the plan, to execute it, and to have any kind of success, this success in itself would seed discord among them: It would not be possible for the spoils to be so fairly divided that each one would be equally satisfied with his own share; and the least happy would soon oppose the progress of the others, who, for a similar reason, would quickly become divided among themselves. Indeed, I doubt whether, since the world has existed, there have ever been three or even two great powers well enough united to subjugate others without fighting among themselves over the responsibilities or the profits of war, and without soon providing, by their misunderstandings, additional resources for the weaker powers. Thus, however one looks at it, it is not likely that any prince or league could henceforth change in any considerable or permanent way the present status of things among us.

This is not to say that the Alps, the Rhine, the sea, the Pyrenees, are insurmountable obstacles to ambition, but that these obstacles are fortified by others that reinforce them or that restore states back to the same limits when temporary attempts have been made to transgress them. What provides the real basis of the European system is certainly in part the interplay of negotiations, which almost always ends up in a mutual balance. But the system has another, even more solid support. This is the body of Germanic states placed in the center of Europe, which demands respect from all the others and serves perhaps much more for the maintenance of its neighbors than for that of its own members. A body that is formidable to outsiders on account of its size and its population, it is also useful to everyone else on account of its constitution, which by denying the means and the will to conquer creates an obstruction for conquerors. Despite the defects of this constitution, it is certain that as long as it lasts the equilibrium of Europe will never be broken, that no prince will have to fear being dethroned by another, and that the Treaty of Westphalia will perhaps forever be the basis of the political system among us. Thus the public law that the Germans study with so much care is yet more important than they think and is not only the Germanic public law but in certain respects the public law of all of Europe.

But if the present system is unshakable, it is by the same token all the more violent, for there is among the European powers an action and reaction which, while not dislodging them completely, hold them in a continual agitation. Such efforts are always futile and always recurring, like the currents of the sea that ceaselessly agitate the surface without ever changing its level, and the people are incessantly devastated, without any visible rewards for the sovereigns.

It would be easy for me to deduce the same truth from the individual interests of all the courts of Europe, for I could easily show that these interests coincide in a way that could hold all their forces in mutual respect, except that the ideas of commerce and money have produced a kind of political fanaticism that makes the apparent interests of princes change every day. Since everything now depends on the rather bizarre economic theories that happen to pass through the heads of ministers, it has become impossible to form any firm convictions about princes' true interests. Nevertheless, commerce does tend on a daily basis to move toward an equilibrium: By depriving certain powers of the exclusive advantage that they might gain from it, commerce deprives them at the same time of one of the great means that they have to make others obey them.

If I have insisted on the equal distribution of power that results in Europe from its present situation, it was to point to a consequence that is important for the establishment of any more general association. For, in order to form a solid and durable confederation, it would be necessary to put all the members in such a mutual dependence not only that no one singly would be in a condition to resist all the others, but also that particular associations that might be harmful to the whole would meet in it obstacles sufficient to prevent their execution. Without such mutual dependence the confederation would be useless, and each one while appearing to be subjected, would really remain independent. Now, if these obstacles are such as I have described them above, when at present all the powers are in complete liberty to form leagues and offensive treaties with each other, just imagine what they might be if there were a great armed league, always ready to intervene against those who would like to start to destroy it or resist it. This suffices to show that such an association would not consist simply of futile deliberations that each participant could ignore at will; instead, it would give rise to an effective power capable of forcing ambitious men to keep within the limits of the general treaty.

Three incontestable truths result from this exposition. First, that except for Turkey there reigns among all the peoples of Europe a social bond that is imperfect but tighter than the general and loose ties of humanity; second, that the imperfection of this society makes the condition of those who compose it worse than it would be were there no social structures at all; third, that the original bonds that make this society harmful simultaneously make it easy to perfect: All of its members could draw their happiness from that which at present causes their misery and could change into an eternal peace the state of war that now reigns among them.

Now let us see how this great work, begun by chance, could be achieved by reason, and how, by taking on the force and the solidity of a true body politic, the free and voluntary society that unites all the European states could change into a real Confederation. By giving to this association the perfection it now lacks, it is clear that such an institution would destroy its present abuses, extend its advantages, and force all its members to cooperate for the common good. But for that it is necessary that this Confederation be so general that no considerable power could refuse it; that it have a judiciary tribunal to establish laws and regulations that would be binding on its members; that it have a compulsory and coercive force to constrain each state to submit to the common deliberations, whether by taking action or abstaining from action; finally, that it be firm and durable, to prevent members from seceding from it at will the moment they believe their particular interests to be contrary to the general interest. These are the sure signs that will show whether or not the institution is wise, useful, and sound. . . .

The first question is whether the proposed Confederation would be sure to attain its purpose and would be sufficient to give Europe a solid and perpetual peace.

The second is whether it is in the interest of the sovereigns to establish this confederation and to purchase a continual peace at this price. . . .

Let us consider the motives that cause princes to take up arms. These motives are either to make conquests, or to defend oneself from an invasion, or to weaken a too-powerful neighbor, or to uphold one's rights when those rights have been infringed upon, or to settle a difference that cannot be settled amicably, or, finally, to fulfill the responsibilities of a treaty. There has never been a cause or pretext for war that does not fall under one of these six headings. Now, it is evident that not one of these six motives could exist in the proposed new state of things.

First, any form of invasion would have to be renounced because of the impossibility of its success. Any invader would be sure to be stopped in his tracks by forces much greater than those he could muster alone, and by risking all, he would be powerless to gain anything. An ambitious prince who wishes to gain power in Europe usually does two things. He begins by fortifying himself with good alliances, and then he tries to take his enemy by surprise. But individual alliances will serve no purpose against a more powerful and permanent alliance; and without any real reason for being armed, no prince would be able to do so without being noticed, warned, and punished by the Confederation, which would always be in a state of preparedness.

The same reason that deprives each prince of all hope of invasion relieves him at the same time of all fear of being attacked. And not only would his states be guaranteed by the whole of Europe and made as secure to him as the personal possessions of citizens in a well-regulated nation are, but as much more so than if he were their sole and only protector as Europe as a whole is stronger than he alone.

There is no reason to want to weaken a neighbor from whom one no longer has anything to fear, and there is not even a temptation to do so when one has no hope of succeeding.

Regarding the protection of one's rights, it is first of all necessary to say that an infinite number of quibbles and obscure pretensions and quarrels would be eliminated. . . .

But, within the terms of the Confederation, no one could infringe on my rights by force without incurring the ban of the assembly. Thus it would no longer be by force that I now should defend those rights. The same can be said of insults, damages, reparations, and all the different unforeseen events that can arise between two sovereigns. The same power that must defend their rights must also settle their grievances.

As for the last motive for going to war, the solution offered by the Confederation is right before our eyes. First we can see that, no longer having any aggressor to fear, there would be no longer any need for defensive treaties, and that since one could not devise a treaty that was more solid and more secure than the great Confederation, any others would be useless, illegitimate, and consequently nil.

It would thus be impossible that the Confederation, once established, could let fall a single seed of war between the Confederees, and that the objective of perpetual peace could not be perfectly fulfilled by carrying out the proposed system.

It now remains for us to examine the other question, which has to do with the advantages for the contracting parties, for it is obvious that it would be futile to speak of the public self-interest to the detriment of private self-interest. Proving that peace is in general preferable to war says nothing to someone who believes that he has reasons to prefer war over peace; indeed, showing him the means of establishing a durable peace is only going to arouse his opposition.

Such a person will argue, in effect, that with this plan you are taking away the sovereigns' right to determine justice for themselves — that is to say, their precious right to be unjust when they please. You are taking away their power to grow at the expense of their neighbors; you are making them give up the apparatus of power and of terror with which they love to frighten the world — that glory of conquest from which they derive their honor; finally you are forcing them to become equitable and peaceful. How will they be compensated for such cruel deprivations?

Here I would not dare to reply, as the Abbé de Saint-Pierre does, that the true glory of princes consists in procuring the happiness of their subjects and the well-being of the public; that the whole of their self-interest is subordinate to their reputation and that their reputation among sensible men is measured by how much good they have done for the people; that the institution of a perpetual peace, being the greatest initiative that had ever been undertaken, would be the most capable of covering its author with an everlasting glory; that this same initiative, while being the most advantageous for the people, still would be the most honorable for the sovereigns — the only one, moreover, that is not tainted with blood, rape, tears, and curses; and finally that the most certain means of standing out from the crowd of kings would be to work for the welfare of the public. In the offices of ministers such lofty words may have brought ridicule to the Abbé and his projects, but let us not be mistaken like them about his underlying reasoning. Whatever may be true about the virtues of princes, let us speak only in terms of their own self-interest.

All the powers of Europe have rights or claims relative to one another. However, these rights are inherently unable to be elucidated in any absolute way, both because there is no common or constant rule with which to judge them and because they are often founded on ambivalent or uncertain facts. Nor can the conflicts that they cause ever be completely settled in any permanent way — as much because of the lack of any competent arbiter as because each prince will heedlessly take any chance he can get to revoke the concessions that were forced upon him, either by treaties made by the more powerful or by his defeat in a bitter war. . . .

If every king has not yet renounced the lust for conquest, it seems that the wiser of them are at least beginning to see that wars cost more than they are worth. In this regard, without entering into a thousand distinctions that would lead us too far afield, we can say in general that a prince, who, to extend his frontiers, loses as many former subjects as he acquires new ones, thus becomes weaker through his desire to grow. With a greater territory to defend, he no longer has any defenders. Moreover, we cannot ignore that, in the manner in which war is waged today, it is not in the armies that the greatest fatalities occur. It is there that we may find the most apparent and obvious losses, but at the same time throughout the state the increase in the number of those who will never be born, the rise in taxes, the interruption of commerce, the desertion of the countryside, and the abandonment of agriculture all cause a more serious and irreparable harm than the loss of men who die. Such evils, while perhaps not immediately evident, make themselves known painfully later on, and it is then that people are surprised at being so weak after supposedly making themselves so strong.

What also makes conquest less tempting is that it is now known how to double or triple one's power not only without extending one's territory but sometimes by contracting it, as was done very wisely by the emperor Hadrian. It is clear that men alone constitute the force of kings, and a proposition that follows from what I have just said is that of two states that nourish the same number of inhabitants, the one occupying the least territory is really the more powerful. It is by means of good laws, wise policies, and economic foresight that a judicious sovereign, without leaving anything to chance, can thus add to his strength. The real victories that he will gain over his neighbors will be whatever beneficial institutions he develops in his own states. The number of new subjects born under him are worth as much as the number of enemies that he might have killed.

It would be useless to object here that I am proving too much and that if things were really the way I represent them and each sovereign had a true common interest in maintaining peace, then peace would be established by itself and would last forever without any confederation. This would be to engage in very poor reasoning in the present situation. For although it would be much better for everyone always to be at peace, the common lack of security in this respect makes it so that each one, lacking any assurance of being able to avoid war, tries at least to begin it with an advantage in case the occasion presents itself, and to anticipate his neighbor — who in turn does not miss any favorable occasion to anticipate him. Hence many wars, even offensive wars, result less from the desire to usurp the interests of others than from the unjust precautions that each side takes to make its own interests secure. However worthy a commitment to the public good might be in general, given the objectives that are followed in politics and even in morality, it is certain that these commitments become dangerous to anyone who persists in practicing them with others when no one else practices them with him. . . .

I know that it would not be agreeable to all sovereigns to disband their troops and be completely without armed forces on hand to stifle unexpected uprisings or to push back a sudden invasion; I know also that they would have to furnish a contingent to the Confederation, both to guard the frontiers of Europe and to maintain the Confederative army intended to defend, if need be, the decrees of the assembly. But once these expenses had been paid and the contingencies of war forever done away with, there would remain still more than half the usual military expenses to be divided between the needs of the people and the treasury of the prince. In this way the people would pay much less; the prince, being much richer, would be able to stimulate commerce, agriculture, the arts, and to develop useful institutions that would further increase the people's wealth and his own; and the state would thus have a much more perfect security than that which it could gain from armies and from the whole apparatus of war, which never ceases to weaken it even in times of peace.

One might argue that the countries on the frontiers of Europe would thereby be in a more disadvantageous position and might correspondingly have wars to sustain either with Turkey or with Africa or with the Tartars.

To this I answer (1) that those countries are in the same position today and that consequently it would not be citing a positive disadvantage but simply one less advantage and an inevitable inconvenience that their situation exposes them to; (2) that freed from all uneasiness from the European side, they would be in a much better position to resist an external threat; (3) that getting rid of all the defenses in the interior of Europe and the costs necessary to maintain them would put the Confederation in a position to establish a large number of defenses on the frontiers with no extra burden on the confederees; (4) that these defenses — constructed, maintained, and commissioned at common expense — would similarly provide defenses and savings for the powers at the borders whose states were being guarded; (5) that the armies of the Confederation, distributed within the confines of Europe, would always be ready to repel an aggressor; (6) and, finally, that a body as formidable as the European Republic would discourage foreigners from the desire to attack any of its members — just as the Germanic body, though infinitely less powerful, still is powerful enough to make itself respected by its neighbors and to protect effectively all the princes that compose it.

One might also argue that if Europeans were to have no more wars among themselves, the art of military strategy might fall gradually into oblivion, that troops would lose their courage and their discipline, and that there would be no more generals or soldiers, and Europe would remain at the mercy of the first foreign invader. . . .

Once they are carefully examined, all the so-called inconveniences of the status of confederation can be reduced to nothing. We now ask whether anyone on earth would dare to say as much for the inconveniences that result from the present manner of settling differences between princes by the right of the strongest — that is, from the state of anarchy and war that is necessarily brought on by each sovereign's absolute and mutual independence within the imperfect social context that holds sway among us in Europe. . . .

If we have reasoned well in the exposition of this project, it is demonstrated, first, that the establishment of perpetual peace depends solely on the consent of sovereigns and presents no difficulty other than their resistance; second, that this establishment would be useful to them in every way and that there is no comparison even for them between its inconveniences and its advantages; third, that it is reasonable to suppose that their will accords with their self-interest; finally, that this establishment, once it is developed according to the proposed plan, would be solid and durable and would fulfill its objective perfectly. Doubtless this is not to say that sovereigns will adopt this project (who can speak for the reasoning of others?) but only that if they were to adopt it, they would be acting with respect to their own true interests. For it must be observed that we have not been considering men such as they ought to be — good, generous, disinterested, and loving the public well-being from a humanitarian standpoint — but such as they are — unjust, greedy, and looking to their own self-interest above all else. The only thing that we have assumed about them is that they are both rational enough to perceive what is useful to them and courageous enough to work toward their own happiness. If, despite all this, the project remains unfulfilled, it is not therefore because it is too idealistic; rather, it is because men are insane and because it is a sort of folly to remain wise in the midst of those who are mad. . . .

CRITIQUE OF THE PERPETUAL PEACE PROJECT

As the most worthy cause to which a good man might devote himself, the *Project for Perpetual Peace* must also have been, among all the projects of the Abbé de Saint-Pierre, the one that he thought about the most and the one that he pursued with the greatest obstinancy. For how else could one explain the missionary zeal with which he clung to this project — despite the obvious impossibility of its success, the ridicule that it brought upon him every day, and the hostility that he was made continually to suffer. It seems that this humane soul was so single-mindedly focused on the public good that he measured the efforts that he gave things solely on the basis of their usefulness, without ever letting himself be discouraged by obstacles and without ever thinking about his own personal self-interest.

If ever a moral truth has been demonstrated, it seems to me that it is the general and the specific usefulness of this project. The advantages that would result from its formation both for each prince and for each nation, as well as for Europe as a whole, are immense, clear, and uncontestable. One cannot imagine anything more solid and more precise than the arguments with which the author supports his case. Indeed, so much would the experience allow each individual to gain from the common good, that to realize the European Republic for one day would be enough to make it last forever. However, these same princes who would defend the European Republic with all their might once it existed would now be opposed even to its being set up, and they would invariably prevent it from being established with just as much energy as they would prevent it from being destroyed. The work of the Abbé de Saint-Pierre thus would seem both ineffectual for producing peace and superfluous for maintaining it. Some impatient reader will say that it is therefore nothing but vain speculation. No, it is a solid and sensible book, and it is very important that it exists.

Let us begin by examining the difficulties of those who do not judge arguments with reason but only with events and who have nothing to object to in this project other than that it has not been tried. In effect, they doubtlessly will say, if the advantages are so real, why have the sovereigns of Europe not adopted them already? Why do they neglect their own self-interest, if this self-interest has now been made so clear? Do we see them rejecting all the other ways of increasing their revenues and their power? If this project were as good for that purpose as is claimed, is it plausible that they would be less impressed with it than with those which have failed them so many times before, or that they would prefer a thousand risky chances to one sure gain?

Clearly, all this is plausible unless we pretend that the wisdom of all these sovereigns is equal to their ambition and that the more strongly they desire their own advantages the better they can see them. Instead, the great penalty for excessive *amour propre* is forever to resort to the means that abuse it, and the very heat of the passions is what almost always prevents them from reaching their goal. We must distinguish, then, in politics as well as in morality, real interest from apparent interest. The first is to be found in perpetual peace — that has been demonstrated in the *Project*. The second can be found in the condition of absolute independence that draws sovereigns away from the rule of law in order to submit them to the rule of chance — like a mad sailor who, to show off his knowledge and intimidate his crew, would prefer to drift dangerously among the reefs during a storm than to secure his ship with an anchor. . . .

We must add, in considering the great commercial advantages that would result from a general and perpetual peace, that while they are obviously in themselves certain and incontestable, being common to all they would not be relative advantages to anyone. Since advantage is usually only sensed by virtue of difference, to add to one's relative power one must seek out only exclusive gains.

Ceaselessly deceived by the appearance of things, princes will therefore reject this peace when judging it by their own self-interest. Just think, then, what will happen when they leave such judgments to their ministers, whose interests are always opposed to those of the people and almost always opposed to those of the prince. Ministers need war to make themselves necessary, to precipitate the prince into crises that he cannot get out of without them, and to cause the loss of the state, if it is necessary, rather than the loss of their jobs. They need war to harass the people in the guise of public safety, to find work for their protégés, to make money on the markets, and to form a thousand corrupt monopolies in secret. They need it to satisfy their passions and to push each other out of office. They need it to preoccupy the prince and remove him from the court while dangerous intrigues arise among them. Such resources would all be lost to them if there were a perpetual peace. And the public keeps on demanding why, if the project is possible, it has not been adopted! They fail to see that there is nothing impossible about the project except its adoption. And what will the ministers do to oppose it? What they have always done — they will turn it to ridicule.

Nor is it possible to believe along with the Abbé de Saint-Pierre that, even with the good will which neither princes nor ministers will ever have, it would be easy to find a favorable moment to set this system in motion. For that it would be necessary that the sum of individual interests would not outweigh the common interest, and that each one would believe that he had found in the good of all the greatest good that he could hope for for himself. Now this would require a convergence of wisdom among so many different minds and a convergence of aims among so many different interests that one could hardly hope to get the happy agreement of all these necessary circumstances simply by chance. The only way to make up for the failure of this agreement to come about by chance would be to make it come about by force. Then it would no longer be a question of persuading but of compelling, and then what would be needed is not to write books but to levy troops.

Thus, although the project was very wise, the means of putting it into effect reflect the naiveté of the author. He innocently imagined that all you would need to do is to assemble a committee, propose his articles, have everyone sign them, and that would be it. We must conclude that, as with all the projects of this good man, he could envision quite well the effect of things after they had been established, but he judged with too little sophistication the methods for getting them established in the first place. . . .

We may not say, therefore, that if his system has not been adopted, it is because it was not good; on the contrary, we must say that it was too good to be adopted. For evil and abuse, which so many men profit from, happen by themselves, but whatever is useful to the public must be brought by force — seeing as special interests are almost always opposed to it. Doubtless perpetual peace is at present a project that seems absurd. . . .

We will not see federative leagues establishing themselves except by revolution, and, on this principle, who would dare to say whether this European league is to be desired or to be feared? It would perhaps cause more harm in one moment than it could prevent for centuries to come.

Does Order Exist in World Politics?

Hedley Bull

The late Professor Bull identifies three traditions of thought — Hobbesian (or realist), Kantian (or universalist), and Grotian (or internationalist). Bull's own work is a blend of the Hobbesian and Grotian traditions in that order in world politics rests, in his view, both on the balance of power and agreed-on rules or norms.

Order in world politics may one day take the form of the maintenance of elementary goals of social life in a single world society or great society of all mankind. . . . It cannot be seriously argued, however, that the society of all mankind is already a going concern. In the present phase we are still accustomed to thinking of order in world politics as consisting of domestic order, or order within states, and international order, or order among them.

No one would deny that there exists within some states a high degree of domestic or municipal order. It is, however, often argued that international order does not exist, except as an aspiration, and that the history of international relations consists simply of disorder or strife. To many people the idea of international order suggests not anything that has occurred in the past, but simply a possible or desirable future state of international relations, about which we might speculate or which we might work to bring about. To those who take this view a study of international order suggests simply a design for a future world, in the tradition of Sully, Cruce, St. Pierre and other irenists or peace theorists.

This present study takes as its starting-point the proposition that, on the contrary, order is part of the historical record of international relations; and in particular, that modern states have formed, and continue to form, not only a system of states but also an international society. To establish this proposition I shall begin by showing first that there has always been present, throughout the history of the modern states system, an idea of international society, proclaimed by philosophers and publicists, and present in the rhetoric of the leaders of states. . . .

THE IDEA OF INTERNATIONAL SOCIETY

Throughout the history of the modern states system there have been three competing traditions of thought: the Hobbesian or realist tradition, which views international politics as a state of war; the Kantian or universalist tradition, which sees at work in international politics a potential community of mankind; and the Grotian or internationalist tradition, which views international politics as taking place within an international society.[1] Here I shall state what is essential to the Grotian or internationalist idea of international society, and what divides it from the Hobbesian or realist tradition on the one hand, and from the Kantian or universalist tradition on the other. Each of these traditional patterns of thought embodies a description of the nature of international politics and a set of prescriptions about international conduct.

The Hobbesian tradition describes international relations as a state of war of all against all, an arena of struggle in which each state is pitted against every other. International relations, on the Hobbesian view, represent pure conflict between states and resemble a game that is wholly distributive or zero-sum: the interests of each state exclude the interests of any other. The particular international activity that, on the Hobbesian view, is most typical of international activity as a whole, or best provides the clue to it, is war itself. Thus peace, on the Hobbesian view, is a period of recuperation from the last war and preparation for the next.

The Hobbesian prescription for international conduct is that the state is free to pursue its goals in relation to other states without moral or legal restrictions of any kind. Ideas of morality and law, on this view, are valid only in the context of a society, but international life is beyond the bounds of any society. If any moral or legal goals are to be pursued in international politics, these can only be the moral or legal goals of the state itself. Either it is held (as by Machiavelli) that the state conducts foreign policy in a kind of moral and legal vacuum, or it is held (as by Hegel and his successors) that moral behaviour for the state in foreign policy lies in its own self-assertion. The only rules or principles which, for those in the Hobbesian tradition, may be said to limit or circumscribe the behaviour of states in their relations with one another are rules of prudence or expediency. Thus agreements may be kept if it is expedient to keep them, but may be broken if it is not.

The Kantian or universalist tradition, at the other extreme, takes the essential nature of international politics to lie not in conflict among states, as on the Hobbesian view, but in the transnational social bonds that link the individual human beings who are the subjects or citizens of states. The dominant theme of international relations, on the Kantian view, is only apparently the relationship among states, and is really the relationship among all men in the community of mankind — which exists potentially, even if it does not exist actually, and which when it comes into being will sweep the system of states into limbo.[2]

Within the community of all mankind, on the universalist view, the interests of all men are one and the same; international politics, considered from this perspective, is not a purely distributive or zero-sum game, as the Hobbesians maintain, but a purely cooperative or non-zero-sum game. Conflicts of interest exist among the ruling cliques of states, but this is only at the superficial or transient level of the existing system of states; properly understood, the interests of all peoples are the same. The particular international activity which, on the Kantian view, most typifies international activity as a whole is the horizontal conflict of ideology that cuts across the boundaries of states and divides human society into two camps — the trustees of the immanent community of mankind and those who stand in its way, those who are of the true faith and the heretics, the liberators and the oppressed.

The Kantian or universalist view of international morality is that, in contrast to the Hobbesian conception, there are moral imperatives in the field of international relations limiting the action of states, but that these imperatives enjoin not coexistence and cooperation among states but rather the overthrow of the system of states and its replacement by a cosmopolitan society. The community of mankind, on the Kantian view, is not only the central reality in international politics, in the sense that the forces able to bring it into being are present; it is also the end or object of the highest moral endeavour. The rules that sustain coexistence and social intercourse among states should be ignored if the imperatives of this higher morality require it. Good faith with heretics has no meaning, except in terms of tactical convenience; between the elect and the damned, the liberators and the oppressed, the question of mutual acceptance of rights to sovereignty or independence does not arise.

What has been called the Grotian or internationalist tradition stands between the realist tradition and the universalist tradition. The Grotian tradition describes international politics in terms of a society of states or international society.[3] As against the Hobbesian tradition, the Grotians contend that states are not engaged in simple struggle, like gladiators in an arena, but are limited in their conflicts with one another by common rules and institutions. But as against the Kantian or universalist perspective the Grotians accept the Hobbesian premise that sovereigns or states are the principal reality in international politics; the immediate members of international society are states rather than individual human beings. International politics, in the Grotian understanding, expresses neither complete conflict of interest between states nor complete identity of interest; it resembles a game that is partly distributive but also partly productive. The particular international activity which, on the Grotian view, best typifies international activity as a whole is neither war between states, nor horizontal conflict cutting across the boundaries of states, but trade — or, more generally, economic and social intercourse between one country and another.

The Grotian prescription for international conduct is that all states, in their dealings with one another, are bound by the rules and institutions of the society they form. As against the view of the Hobbesians, states in the Grotian view are bound not only by rules of prudence or expediency but also by imperatives of morality and law. But, as against the view of the universalists, what these imperatives enjoin is not the overthrow of the system of states and its replacement by a universal community of mankind, but rather acceptance of the requirements of coexistence and cooperation in a society of states.

Each of these traditions embodies a great variety of doctrines about international politics, among which there exists only a loose connection. In different periods each pattern of thought appears in a different idiom and in relation to different issues and preoccupations. This is not the place to explore further the connections and distinctions within each tradition. Here we have only to take account of the fact that the Grotian idea of international society has always been present in thought about the states system. . . .

My contention is that the element of a society has always been present, and remains present, in the modern international system, although only as one of the elements in it, whose survival is sometimes precarious. The modern international system in fact reflects all three of the elements singled out, respectively, by the Hobbesian, the Kantian, and the Grotian traditions: the element of war and struggle for power among states, the element of transnational solidarity and conflict, cutting across the divisions among states, and the element of cooperation and regulated intercourse among states. In different historical phases of the states system, in different geographical theatres of its operation, and in the policies of different states and statesmen, one of these three elements may predominate over the others. . . .

NOTES

1. This threefold division derives from Martin Wight. The best published account of it is his "Western Values in International Relations," in *Diplomatic Investigations*, ed. Herbert Butterfield and Martin Wight (London: Allen and Unwin, 1967). The division is further discussed in my "Martin Wight and the Theory of International Relations. The Second Martin Wight Memorial Lecture," *British Journal of International Studies* 2, no. 2 (1976).
2. In Kant's own doctrine there is of course ambivalence as between the universalism of *The Idea of Universal History from a Cosmopolitan Point of View* (1784)

and the position taken up in *Perpetual Peace* (1795), in which Kant accepts the substitute goal of a league of 'republican' states.

3. I have myself used the term 'Grotian' in two senses: (i) as here, to describe the broad doctrine that there is a society of states; (ii) to describe the solidarist form of this doctrine, which united Grotius himself and the twentieth-century neo-Grotians, in opposition to the pluralist conception of international society entertained by Vattel and later positivist writers. See "The Grotian Conception of International Society," in *Diplomatic Investigations*.

Explaining War

Kenneth N. Waltz

In this article excerpted from Man, the State and War, *Professor Waltz provides a causal explanation of war that combines three levels of analysis: individual, state and society, and international system. The permissive cause (providing no obstacle to war) is systemic anarchy; efficient or proximate causes of a given war may also be found at other levels.*

INTRODUCTION

Asking who won a given war, someone has said, is like asking who won the San Francisco earthquake. That in wars there is no victory but only varying degrees of defeat is a proposition that has gained increasing acceptance in the twentieth century. But are wars also akin to earthquakes in being natural occurrences whose control or elimination is beyond the wit of man? Few would admit that they are, yet attempts to eliminate war, however nobly inspired and assiduously pursued, have brought little more than fleeting moments of peace among states. There is an apparent disproportion between effort and product, between desire and result. The peace wish, we are told, runs strong and deep among the Russian people; and we are convinced that the same can be said of Americans.

This condensation originally appeared in John F. Reichart and Steven R. Sturm, eds., *American Defense Policy*, 5th ed. (Baltimore, MD: Johns Hopkins University Press, 1982), pp. 8–18. *From Man, the State and War* by Kenneth N. Waltz, copyright 1954 and 1959, Columbia University Press, New York. Used by permission from the publisher and consent of the author.

From these statements there is some comfort to be derived, but in the light of history and of current events as well it is difficult to believe that the wish will father the condition desired.

Social scientists, realizing from their studies how firmly the present is tied to the past and how intimately the parts of a system depend upon each other, are inclined to be conservative in estimating the possibilities of achieving a radically better world. If one asks whether we can now have peace where in the past there has been war, the answers are most often pessimistic. Perhaps this is the wrong question. And indeed the answers will be somewhat less discouraging if instead the following questions are put: Are there ways of decreasing the incidence of war, of increasing the chances of peace? Can we have peace more often in the future than in the past?

Peace is one among a number of ends simultaneously entertained. The means by which peace can be sought are many. The end is pursued and the means are applied under varying conditions. Even though one may find it hard to believe that there are ways to peace not yet tried by statesmen or advocated by publicists, the very complexity of the problem suggests the possibility of combining activities in different ways in the hope that some combination will lead us closer to the goal. Is one then led to conclude that the wisdom of the statesman lies in trying first one policy and then another, in doing what the moment seems to require? An affirmative reply would suggest that the hope for improvement lies in policy divorced from analysis, in action removed from thought. Yet each attempt to alleviate a condition implies some idea of its causes: to explain how peace can be more readily achieved requires an understanding of the causes of war. It is such an understanding that we shall seek in the following pages.

THE FIRST IMAGE: INTERNATIONAL CONFLICT AND HUMAN BEHAVIOR

There is deceit and cunning and from these wars arise.

CONFUCIUS

According to the first image of international relations, the focus of the important causes of war is found in the nature and behavior of man. Wars result from selfishness, from misdirected aggressive impulses, from stupidity. Other causes are secondary and have to be interpreted in the light of these factors. If these are the primary causes of war, then the elimination of war must come through uplifting and enlightening men or securing their psychic-social readjustment. This estimate of causes and cures has been dominant in the writings of many serious students of human affairs from Confucius to present-day pacifists. It is the leitmotif of many modern behavioral scientists as well.

Prescriptions associated with first-image analyses need not be identical in content, as a few examples will indicate. Henry Wadsworth Longfellow, moved to poetic expression by a visit to the arsenal at Springfield, set down the following thoughts:

> Were half the power that fills the world with terror,
> Were half the wealth bestowed on camps and courts,
> Given to redeem the human mind from error,
> There were no need of arsenals or forts.

Implicit in these lines is the idea that the people will insist that the right policies be adopted if only they know what the right policies are. Their instincts are good, though their present gullibility may prompt them to follow false leaders. By attributing present difficulties to a defect in knowledge, education becomes the remedy for war. The idea is widespread. Beverly Nichols, a pacifist writing in the 1930s, thought that if Norman Angell "could be made educational dictator of the world, war would vanish like the morning mist, in a single generation."[1] In 1920, a conference of Friends, unwilling to rely upon intellectual development alone, called upon the people of the world to replace self-seeking with the spirit of sacrifice, cooperation, and trust.[2] Bertrand Russell, at about the same time and in much the same vein, saw a decline in the possessive instincts as a prerequisite to peace.[3] By others, increasing the chances of peace has been said to require not so much a change in "instincts" as a channeling of energies that are presently expended in the destructive folly of war. If there were something that men would rather do than fight, they would cease to fight altogether. Aristophanes saw the point. If the women of Athens would deny themselves to husbands and lovers, their men would have to choose between the pleasures of the couch and the exhilarating experiences of the battlefield. Aristophanes thought he knew the men, and women, of Athens well enough to make the outcome a foregone conclusion. William James was in the same tradition. War, in his view, is rooted in man's bellicose nature, which is the product of centuries-old tradition. His nature cannot be changed or his drives suppressed, but they can be diverted. As alternatives to military service, James suggests drafting the youth of the world to mine coal and man ships, to build skyscrapers and roads, to wash dishes and clothes. While his estimate of what diversions would be sufficient is at once less realistic and more seriously intended than that of Aristophanes, his remedy is clearly the same in type.[4]

The prescriptions vary, but common to them all is the thought that in order to achieve a more peaceful world men must be changed, whether in their moral-intellectual outlook or in their psychic-social behavior. One may, however, agree with the first-image analysis of causes without admitting the possibility of practicable prescriptions for their removal. Among those who accept a first-image explanation of war there are both optimists and pessimists, those who think the possibilities of progress so great that wars will end before the next generation is dead and those who think that wars will continue to occur though by them we may all die.

THE SECOND IMAGE: INTERNATIONAL CONFLICT AND THE INTERNAL STRUCTURE OF STATES

However conceived in an image of the world, foreign policy is a phase of domestic policy, an inescapable phase.

CHARLES BEARD, *A Foreign Policy for America*

The first image did not exclude the influence of the state, but the role of the state was introduced as a consideration less important than, and to be explained in terms of, human behavior. According to the first image, to say that the state acts is to speak metonymically. We say that the state acts when we mean that the people in it act, just as we say that the pot boils when we mean that the water in it boils. The preceding [section] concentrated on the contents rather than the container; the present [section] alters the balance of emphasis in favor of the latter. To continue the figure: Water running out of a faucet is chemically the same as water in a container, but once the water is in a container, it can be made to "behave" in different ways. It can be turned into steam and used to power an engine, or, if the water is sealed in and heated to extreme temperatures, it can become the instrument of a destructive explosion. Wars would not exist were human nature not what it is, but neither would Sunday schools and brothels, philanthropic organizations and criminal gangs. Since everything is related to human nature, to explain anything one must consider more than human nature. The events to be explained are so many and so varied that human nature cannot possibly be the single determinant.

The attempt to explain everything by psychology meant, in the end, that psychology succeeded in explaining nothing. And adding sociology to the analysis simply substitutes the error of sociologism for the error of psychologism. Where Spinoza, for example, erred by leaving out of his personal estimate of cause all reference to the causal role of social structures, sociologists have, in approaching the problem of war and peace, often erred in omitting all reference to the political framework within which individual and social actions occur. The conclusion is obvious: to understand war and peace political analysis must be used to supplement and order the findings of psychology and sociology. What kind of political analysis is needed? For possible explanations of the occurrence or nonoccurrence of war, one can look to international politics (since war occurs among states), or one can look to the states themselves (since it is in the name of the state that the fighting is actually done). The former approach is postponed [until the next section]; according to the second image, the internal organization of states is the key to understanding war and peace.

One explanation of the second-image type is illustrated as follows. War most often promotes the internal unity of each state involved. The state plagued by internal strife may then, instead of waiting for the accidental attack, seek the war that will bring internal peace. Bodin saw this clearly, for he concludes that "the best way of preserving a state, and guaranteeing it against sedition, rebellion, and civil war is to keep the subjects in amity one with another, and to this end, to find an enemy against whom they can make common cause." And he saw historical evidence that the principle had been applied, especially by the Romans, who "could find no better antidote to civil war, nor one more certain in its effects, than to oppose an enemy to the citizens."[5] Secretary of State William Henry Seward followed this reasoning when, in order to promote unity within the country, he urged upon Lincoln a vigorous foreign policy, which included the possibility of declaring war on Spain and France.[6] Mikhail Skobelev, an influential Russian military officer of the third quarter of the nineteenth century, varied the theme but slightly when he argued that the Russian monarchy was doomed unless it could produce major military successes abroad.[7]

The use of internal defects to explain those external acts of the state that bring war can take many forms. Such explanation may be related to a type of government that is thought to be generically bad. For example, it is often thought that the deprivations imposed by despots upon their subjects produce tensions that may find expression in foreign adventure. Or the explanation may be given in terms of defects in a government not itself considered bad. Thus it has been argued that the restrictions placed upon a government in order to protect the prescribed rights of its citizens act as impediments to the making and executing of foreign policy. These restrictions, laudable in original purpose, may have the unfortunate effect of making difficult or impossible the effective action of that government for the maintenance of peace in the world.[8] And, as a final example, explanation may be made in terms of geographic or economic deprivation or in terms of deprivations too vaguely defined to be labeled at all. Thus a nation may argue that it has not attained its "natural" frontiers, that such frontiers are necessary to its security, that war to extend the state to its deserved compass is justified or even necessary.[9] The possible variations on this theme have been made familiar by the "have-not" arguments so popular in this century. Such arguments have been used both to explain why "deprived" countries undertake war and to urge the satiated to make the compensatory adjustments thought necessary if peace is to be perpetuated.[10]

The examples just given illustrate in abundant variety one part of the second image, the idea that defects in states cause wars among them. But in just what ways should the structure of states be changed? What definition of the "good" state is to serve as a standard? Among those who have taken this approach to international relations there is a great variety of definitions. Karl Marx defines "good" in terms of ownership of the means of production; Immanuel Kant in terms of abstract principles of right; Woodrow Wilson in terms of national self-determination and modern democratic organization. Though each definition singles out different items as crucial, all are united in asserting that if, and only if, substantially all states reform will world peace result. That is, the reform prescribed is considered the sufficient basis for world peace. This, of course, does not exhaust the subject. Marx, for example, believed that states would disappear shortly after they became socialist. The problem of war, if war is defined as violent conflict among states, would then no longer exist. Kant believed that republican states would voluntarily agree to be governed in their dealings by a code of law drawn up by the states themselves. Wilson urged a variety of requisites to peace, such as improved international understanding, collective security and disarmament, a world confederation of states. But history proved to Wilson that one cannot expect the steadfast cooperation of undemocratic states in any such program for peace.

For each of these men, the reform of states in the ways prescribed is taken to be the *sine qua non* of world peace. The examples given could be multiplied. Classical economists as well as socialists, aristocrats and monarchists as well as democrats, empiricists and realists as well as transcendental idealists — all can furnish examples of men who have believed that peace can be had only if a given pattern of internal organization becomes widespread. Is it that democracies spell peace, but we have had wars because there have never been enough democracies of the right kind? Or that the socialist form of government contains within it the guarantee of peace, but so far there have never been any true socialist governments?[11] If either question were answered in the affirmative, then one would have to assess the merits of different prescriptions and try to decide just which one, or which combination, contains the elusive secret formula for peace. The import of our criticism, however, is that no prescription for international relations written entirely in terms of the second image can be valid, that the approach itself is faulty. Our criticisms of the liberals apply to all theories that would rely on the generalization of one pattern of state and society to bring peace to the world.

Bad states lead to war. As previously said, there is a large and important sense in which this is true. The obverse of this statement, that good states mean peace in the world, is an extremely doubtful proposition. The difficulty, endemic with the second image of international relations, is the same in kind as the difficulty encountered in the first image. There the statement that men make the societies, including the international society, in which they live was criticized not simply as being wrong but as being incomplete. One must add that the societies they live in make men. And it is the same in international relations. The actions of states, or, more accurately, of men acting for states, make up the substance of international relations. But the international political environment has much to do with the ways in which states behave. The influence to be assigned to the internal structure of states in attempting to solve the war – peace equation cannot be determined until the significance of the international environment has been reconsidered.

THE THIRD IMAGE: INTERNATIONAL CONFLICT AND INTERNATIONAL ANARCHY

For what can be done against force without force?
CICERO, The Letters to His Friends

With many sovereign states, with no system of law enforceable among them, with each state judging its grievances and ambitions according to the dictates of its own reason or desire — conflict, sometimes leading to war, is bound to occur. To achieve a favorable outcome from such conflict a state has to rely on its own devices, the relative efficiency of which must be its constant concern. This, the idea of the third image, is to be examined [here]. It is not an esoteric idea; it is not a new idea. Thucydides implied it when he wrote that it was "the growth of the Athenian power, which terrified the Lacedaemonians and forced them into war."[12] John Adams implied it when he wrote to the citizens of Petersburg, Virginia, that "a war with France, if just and necessary, might wean us from fond and blind affections, which no Nation ought ever to feel towards another, as our experience in more than one instance abundantly testifies."[13] There is an obvious relation between the concern over relative power position expressed by Thucydides and the admonition of John Adams that love affairs between states are inappropriate and dangerous. This relation is made explicit in Frederick Dunn's statement that "so long as the notion of self-help persists, the aim of maintaining the power position of the nation is paramount to all other considerations."[14]

In anarchy there is no automatic harmony. The three preceding statements reflect this fact. A state will use force to attain its goals if, after assessing the prospects for success, it values those goals more than it values the pleasures of peace. Because each state is the final judge of its own cause, any state may at any time use force to implement its policies. Because any state may at any time use force, all states must constantly be ready either to counter force with force or to pay the cost of weakness. The requirements of state action are, in this view, imposed by the circumstances in which all states exist.

In a manner of speaking, all three images are a part of nature. So fundamental are man, the state, and the state system in any attempt to understand international relations that seldom does an analyst, however wedded to one image, entirely overlook the other two. Still, emphasis on one image may distort one's interpretation of the others. It is, for example, not uncommon to find those inclined to see the world in terms of either the first or the second image countering the oft-made argument that arms breed not war but security, and possibly even peace, by pointing out that the argument is a compound of dishonest myth, to cover the interests of politicians, armament makers, and others, and honest illusion entertained by patriots sincerely interested in the safety of their states. To dispel the illusion, Cobden, to recall one of the many who have argued this way, once pointed out that doubling armaments, if everyone does it, makes no state more secure and, similarly, that none would be endangered if all military establishments were simultaneously reduced by, say, 50 percent.[15] Putting aside the thought that the arithmetic is not necessarily an accurate reflection of what the situation would be, this argument illustrates a supposedly practical application of the first and second images. Whether by educating citizens and leaders of the separate states or by improving the organization of each of them, a condition is sought in which the lesson here adumbrated becomes the basis for the policies of states. The result? —disarmament, and thus economy, together with peace, and thus security, for all states. If some states display a willingness to pare down their military establishments, other states will be able to pursue similar policies. In emphasizing the interdependence of the policies of all states, the argument pays heed to the third image. The optimism is, however, the result of ignoring some inherent difficulties. [Here Waltz takes up Rousseau's view of man in the early state of nature. —*Ed.*]

In the early state of nature, men were sufficiently dispersed to make any pattern of cooperation unnecessary. But finally the combination of increased numbers and the usual natural hazards posed, in a variety of situations, the proposition: cooperate or die. Rousseau illustrates the line of reasoning with the simplest example. The example is worth reproducing, for it is the point of departure for the establishment of government and contains the basis for his explanation of conflict in international relations as well. Assume that five men who have acquired a rudimentary ability to speak and to understand each other happen to come together at a time when all of them suffer from hunger. The hunger of each will be satisfied by the fifth part of a stag, so they "agree" to cooperate in a project to trap one. But also the hunger of any one of them will be satisfied by a hare, so, as a hare comes within reach, one of them grabs it. The defector obtains the means of satisfying his hunger but in doing so permits the stag to escape. His immediate interest prevails over consideration for his fellows.[16]

The story is simple; the implications are tremendous. In cooperative action, even where all agree on the goal and have an equal interest in the project, one cannot rely on others. Spinoza linked conflict causally to man's imperfect reason. Montesquieu and Rousseau counter Spinoza's analysis with the proposition that the sources of conflict are not so much in the minds of men as they are in the nature of social activity. The difficulty is to some extent verbal. Rousseau grants that if we knew how to receive

the true justice that comes from God, "we should need neither government nor laws."[17] This corresponds to Spinoza's proposition that "men in
so far as they live in obedience to reason, necessarily live always in harmony one with another."[18] The idea is a truism. If men were perfect, their
perfection would be reflected in all of their calculations and actions. Each
could rely on the behavior of others, and all decisions would be made on
principles that would preserve a true harmony of interests. Spinoza emphasizes not the difficulties inherent in mediating conflicting interests but
the defectiveness of man's reason that prevents their consistently making
decisions that would be in the interest of each and for the good of all.
Rousseau faces the same problem. He imagines how men must have behaved as they began to depend on one another to meet their daily needs.
As long as each provided for his own wants, there could be no conflict;
whenever the combination of natural obstacles and growth in population
made cooperation necessary, conflict arose. Thus in the stag-hunt example the tension between one man's immediate interest and the general interest of the group is resolved by the unilateral action of the one man. To
the extent that he was motivated by a feeling of hunger, his act is one of
passion. Reason would have told him that his long-run interest depends
on establishing, through experience, the conviction that cooperative action will benefit all of the participants. But reason also tells him that if he
forgoes the hare, the man next to him might leave his post to chase it,
leaving the first man with nothing but food for thought on the folly of being
loyal.

The problem is now posed in more significant terms. If harmony is to
exist in anarchy, not only must I be perfectly rational but I must be able to
assume that everyone else is too. Otherwise there is no basis for rational
calculation. To allow in my calculation for the irrational acts of others can
lead to no determinate solutions, but to attempt to act on a rational calculation without making such an allowance may lead to my own undoing.
The latter argument is reflected in Rousseau's comments on the proposition that "a people of true Christians would form the most perfect society
imaginable." In the first place he points out that such a society "would not
be a society of men." Moreoever, he says, "For the state to be peaceable
and for harmony to be maintained, *all* the citizens *without exception* would
have to be [equally] good Christians; if by ill hap there should be a single
self-seeker or hypocrite . . . he would certainly get the better of his
pious compatriots."[19]

If we define cooperative action as rational and any deviation from it
irrational, we must agree with Spinoza that conflict results from the irrationality of men. But if we examine the requirements of rational action, we
find that even in an example as simple as the stag hunt we have to assume
that the reason of each leads to an identical definition of interest, that each
will draw the same conclusion as to the methods appropriate to meet the
original situation, that all will agree instantly on the action required by
any chance incidents that raise the question of altering the original plan,

and that each can rely completely on the steadfastness of purpose of all the others. Perfectly rational action requires not only the perception that our welfare is tied up with the welfare of others but also a perfect appraisal of details so that we can answer the question: Just *how* in each situation is it tied up with everyone else's? Rousseau agrees with Spinoza in refusing to label the act of the rabbit-snatcher either good or bad; unlike Spinoza, he also refuses to label it either rational or irrational. He has noticed that the difficulty is not only in the actors but also in the situations they face. While by no means ignoring the part that avarice and ambition play in the birth and growth of conflict,[20] Rousseau's analysis makes clear the extent to which conflict appears inevitably in the social affairs of men.

In short, the proposition that irrationality is the cause of all the world's troubles, in the sense that a world of perfectly rational men would know no disagreements and no conflicts, is, as Rousseau implies, as true as it is irrelevant. Since the world cannot be defined in terms of perfection, the very real problem of how to achieve an approximation to harmony in cooperative and competitive activity is always with us and, lacking the possibility of perfection, it is a problem that cannot be solved simply by changing men. Rousseau's conclusion, which is also the heart of his theory of international relations, is accurately though somewhat abstractly summarized in the following statement: That among particularities accidents will occur is not accidental but necessary.[21] And this, in turn, is simply another way of saying that in anarchy there is no automatic harmony.

If anarchy is the problem, then there are only two possible solutions: (1) to impose an effective control on the separate and imperfect states; (2) to remove states from the sphere of the accidental, that is, to define the good state as so perfect that it will no longer be particular. Kant tried to compromise by making states good enough to obey a set of laws to which they have volunteered their assent. Rousseau, whom on this point Kant failed to follow, emphasizes the particular nature of even the good state and, in so doing, makes apparent the futility of the solution Kant suggests.[22] He also makes possible a theory of international relations that in general terms explains the behavior of all states, whether good or bad.[23]

In the stag-hunt example, the will of the rabbit-snatcher was rational and predictable from his own point of view. From the point of view of the rest of the group, it was arbitrary and capricious. So of any individual state, a will perfectly good for itself may provoke the violent resistance of other states.[24] The application of Rousseau's theory to international politics is stated with eloquence and clarity in his commentaries on Saint-Pierre and in a short work entitled *The State of War*. His application bears out the preceding analysis. The states of Europe, he writes, "touch each other at so many points that no one of them can move without giving a jar to all the rest; their variances are all the more deadly, as their ties are more closely woven." They "must inevitably fall into quarrels and dissensions at the first changes that come about." And if we ask why they must "inevitably" clash, Rousseau answers: Because their union is "formed and maintained by nothing better than chance." The nations of Europe are willful units in close juxtaposition with rules neither clear nor enforceable to guide them. The public law of Europe is but "a mass of contradictory rules which nothing but the right of the stronger can reduce to order: so that in the absence of any sure clue to guide her, reason is bound, in every case of doubt, to obey the promptings of self-interest — which in itself would make war inevitable, even if all parties desired to be just." In this condition, it is foolhardy to expect automatic harmony of interest and automatic agreement and acquiescence in rights and duties. In a real sense there is a "union of the nations of Europe," but "the imperfections of this association make the state of those who belong to it worse than it would be if they formed no community at all."[25]

The argument is clear. For individuals the bloodiest stage of history was the period just prior to the establishment of society. At that point they had lost the virtues of the savage without having acquired those of the citizen. The late stage of the state of nature is necessarily a state of war. The nations of Europe are precisely in that stage.[26]

What then is cause: the capricious acts of the separate states or the system within which they exist? Rousseau emphasizes the latter:

> Every one can see that what unites any form of society is community of interests, and what disintegrates [it] is their conflict; that either tendency may be changed or modified by a thousand accidents; and therefore that, as soon as a society is founded, some coercive power must be provided to co-ordinate the actions of its members and give to their common interests and mutual obligations that firmness and consistency which they could never acquire of themselves.[27]

But to emphasize the importance of political structure is not to say that the acts that bring about conflict and lead to the use of force are of no importance. It is the specific acts that are the immediate causes of war,[28] the general structure that permits them to exist and wreak their disasters. To eliminate every vestige of selfishness, perversity, and stupidity in nations would serve to establish perpetual peace, but to try directly to eliminate all the immediate causes of war without altering the structure of the "union of Europe" is utopian.

What alteration of structure is required? The idea that a voluntary federation, such as Kant later proposed, could keep peace among states, Rousseau rejects emphatically. Instead, he says, the remedy for war among states "is to be found only in such a form of federal Government as shall unite nations by bonds similar to those which already unite their individual members, and place the one no less than the other under the authority of the Law."[29] Kant made similar statements only to amend them out of existence once he came to consider the reality of such a federation. Rousseau does not modify his principle, as is made clear in the following quotation, every point of which is a contradiction of Kant's program for the pacific federation:

The Federation [that is to replace the "free and voluntary association which now unites the States of Europe"] must embrace all the important Powers in its membership; it must have a Legislative Body, with powers to pass laws and ordinances binding upon all its members; it must have a coercive force capable of compelling every State to obey its common resolves whether in the way of command or of prohibition; finally, it must be strong and firm enough to make it impossible for any member to withdraw at his own pleasure the moment he conceives his private interest to clash with that of the whole body.[30]

It is easy to poke holes in the solution offered by Rousseau. The most vulnerable point is revealed by the questions: How could the federation enforce its law on the states that comprise it without waging war against them? and How likely is it that the effective force will always be on the side of the federation? To answer these questions Rousseau argues that the states of Europe are in a condition of balance sufficiently fine to prevent any one state or combination of states from prevailing over the others. For this reason, the necessary margin of force will always rest with the federation itself. The best critical consideration of the inherent weakness of a federation of states in which the law of the federation has to be enforced on the states who are its members is contained in the *Federalist Papers*. The arguments are convincing, but they need not be reviewed here. The practical weakness of Rousseau's recommended solution does not obscure the merit of his theoretical analysis of war as a consequence of international anarchy.

CONCLUSION

The third image, like the first two, leads directly to a utopian prescription. In each image a cause is identified in terms of which all others are to be understood. The force of the logical relation between the third image and the world-government prescription is great enough to cause some to argue not only the merits of world government but also the ease with which it can be realized.[31] It is of course true that with world government there would no longer be international wars, though with an ineffective world government there would no doubt be civil wars. It is likewise true, reverting to the first two images, that without the imperfections of the separate states there would not be wars, just as it is true that a society of perfectly rational beings, or of perfect Christians, would never know violent conflict. These statements are, unfortunately, as trivial as they are true. They have the unchallengeable quality of airtight tautologies: perfectly good states or men will not do bad things; within an effective organization highly damaging deviant behavior is not permitted. The near perfection required by concentration upon a single cause accounts for a number of otherwise puzzling facts: the pessimism of St. Augustine, the failure of the behavioral scientists as prescribers for peace, the reliance of many liberals on the forces of history to produce a result not conceivably to be produced by the consciously directed efforts of men, the tendency of socialists to identify a corrupting element every time harmony in socialist action fails to appear. It also helps to explain the often rapid alternation of hope and despair among those who most fully adopt a single-cause approach to this or to almost any other problem. The belief that to make the world better requires changing the factors that operate within a precisely defined realm leads to despair whenever it becomes apparent that changes there, if possible at all, will come slowly and with insufficient force. One is constantly defeated by the double problem of demonstrating how the "necessary changes" can be produced and of substantiating the assertion that the changes described as necessary would be sufficient to accomplish the object in view.

The contrary assertion, that all causes may be interrelated, is an argument against assuming that there is a single cause that can be isolated by analysis and eliminated or controlled by wisely constructed policy. It is also an argument against working with one or several hypotheses without bearing in mind the interrelation of all causes. The prescriptions directly derived from a single image are incomplete because they are based upon partial analyses. The partial quality of each image sets up a tension that drives one toward inclusion of the others. With the first image the direction of change, representing Locke's perspective as against Plato's, is from men to societies and states. The second image catches up both elements. Men make states, *and* states make men; but this is still a limited view. One is led to a search for the more inclusive nexus of causes, for states are shaped by the international environment as are men by both the national and international environments. Most of those whom we have considered in preceding [sections] have not written entirely in terms of one image. That we have thus far been dealing with the consequences arising from differing degrees of emphasis accounts for the complexity of preceding [sections] but now makes somewhat easier the task of suggesting how the images can be interrelated without distorting any one of them.

The First and Second Images in Relation to the Third

It may be true that the Soviet Union poses the greatest threat of war at the present time. It is not true that were the Soviet Union to disappear the remaining states could easily live at peace. We have known wars for centuries; the Soviet Union has existed only for decades. But some states, and perhaps some forms of the state, are more peacefully inclined than others. Would not the multiplication of peacefully inclined states at least warrant the hope that the period between major wars might be extended? By emphasizing the relevance of the framework of action, the third image makes clear the misleading quality of such partial analyses and of the hopes that are often based upon them. The act that by individual moral standards would be applauded may, when performed by a state, be an invitation to the war we seek to avoid. The third image, taken not as a theory of world government but as a theory of the conditioning effects of the state system itself, alerts us to the fact that so far as increasing the chances of peace is concerned there is no such thing as an act good in itself. The pacification of the Hukbalahaps was a clear and direct contribution to the peace and order of the Philippine state. In international politics a partial "solution," such as one major country becoming pacifistic, might be a real contribution to world peace; but it might as easily hasten the coming of another major war.

The third image, as reflected in the writings of Rousseau, is based on an analysis of the consequences arising from the framework of state action. Rousseau's explanation of the origin of war among states is, in broad outline, the final one so long as we operate within a nation–state system. It is a final explanation because it does not hinge on accidental causes— irrationalities in men, defects in states—but upon his theory of the framework within which *any* accident can bring about a war. That state A wants certain things that it can get only by war does not explain war. Such a desire may or may not lead to war. My wanting a million dollars does not cause me to rob a bank, but if it were easier to rob banks, such desires would lead to much more bank robbing. This does not alter the fact that some people will and some will not attempt to rob banks no matter what the law enforcement situation is. We still have to look to motivation and circumstance in order to explain individual acts. Nevertheless one can predict that, other things being equal, a weakening of law enforcement agencies will lead to an increase in crime. From this point of view it is social structure—institutionalized restraints and institutionalized methods of altering and adjusting interests—that counts. And it counts in a way different from the ways usually associated with the word "cause." What causes a man to rob a bank are such things as the desire for money, a disrespect for social proprieties, a certain boldness. But if obstacles to the operation of these causes are built sufficiently high, nine out of ten would-be bank robbers will live their lives peacefully plying their legitimate trades. If the framework is to be called cause at all, it had best be specified that it is a permissive or underlying cause of war.

Applied to international politics this becomes, in words previously used to summarize Rousseau, the proposition that wars occur because there is nothing to prevent them. Rousseau's analysis explains the recurrence of war without explaining any given war. He tells us that war may at any moment occur, and he tells us why this is so. But the structure of the state system does not directly cause state A to attack state B. Whether or not that attack occurs will depend on a number of special circumstances —location, size, power, interest, type of government, past history and tradition—each of which will influence the actions of both states. If they fight against each other it will be for reasons especially defined for the occasion by each of them. These special reasons become the immediate, or efficient, causes of war. These immediate causes of war are contained in the first and second images. States are motivated to attack each other and to defend themselves by the reason and/or passion of the comparatively few who make policies for states and of the many more who influence the few. Some states, by virtue of their internal conditions, are both more proficient in war and more inclined to put their proficiency to the test. Variations in the factors included in the first and second images are important, indeed crucial, in the making and breaking of periods of peace — the immediate causes of every war must be either the acts of individuals or the acts of states.

If every war is preceded by acts that we can identify (or at least try to identify) as cause, then why can we not eliminate wars by modifying individual or state behavior? This is the line of thinking followed by those who say: To end war, improve men; or: To end war, improve states. But in such prescriptions the role of the international environment is easily distorted. How can some of the acting units improve while others continue to follow their old and often predatory ways? The simplistic assumption of many liberals, that history moves relentlessly toward the millennium, is refuted if the international environment makes it difficult almost to the point of impossibility for states to behave in ways that are progressively more moral. Two points are omitted from the prescriptions we considered under the first and second images: (1) If an effect is produced by two or more causes, the effect is not permanently eliminated by removing one of them. If wars occur because men are less than perfectly rational and because states are less than perfectly formed, to improve only states may do little to decrease the number and intensity of wars. The error here is in identifying one cause where two or more may operate. (2) An endeavor launched against one cause to the neglect of others may make the situation worse instead of better. Thus, as the Western democracies became more inclined to peace, Hitler became more belligerent. The increased propensity to peace of some participants in international politics may increase, rather than decrease, the likelihood of war. This illustrates the role of the permissive cause, the international environment. If there were but two loci of cause involved, men and states, we could be sure that the appearance of more peacefully inclined states would, at worst, not damage the cause of world peace. Whether or not a remedy proposed is truly a remedy or actually worse than none at all depends, however, on the content and timing of the acts of all states. This is made clear in the third image.

War may result because state A has something that state B wants. The efficient cause of the war is the desire of state B; the permissive cause is the fact that there is nothing to prevent state B from undertaking the risks of war. In a different circumstance, the interrelation of efficient and permissive causes becomes still closer. State A may fear that if it does not cut state B down a peg now, it may be unable to do so ten years from now. State A becomes the aggressor in the present because it fears what state B may be able to do in the future. The efficient cause of such a war is derived from the cause that we have labeled permissive. In the first case, conflicts arise from disputes born of specific issues. In an age of hydrogen bombs, no single issue may be worth the risk of full-scale war. Settlement, even on bad grounds, is preferable to self-destruction. The use of reason would seem to require the adoption of a doctrine of "non-recourse to force." One whose reason leads him down this path is following the trail blazed by Cobden when in 1849 he pointed out "that it is almost impossible, on looking back for the last hundred years, to tell precisely what any war was about," and thus implied that Englishmen should never have become involved in them.[32] He is falling into the trap that ensnared A. A. Milne when he explained the First World War as a war in which ten million men died because Austria-Hungary sought, unsuccessfully, to avenge the death of one archduke.[33] He is succumbing to the illusion of Sir Edward Grey, who, in the memoirs he wrote some thirty years ago, hoped that the horrors of the First World War would make it possible for nations "to find at least one common ground on which they should come together in confident understanding: an agreement that, in the disputes between them, war must be ruled out as a means of settlement that entails ruin."[34]

It is true that the immediate causes of many wars are trivial. If we focus upon them, the failure to agree to settlement without force appears to be the ultimate folly. But it is not often true that the immediate causes provide sufficient explanation for the wars that have occurred. And if it is not simply particular disputes that produce wars, rational settlement of them cannot eliminate war. For, as Winston Churchill has written, "small matters are only the symptoms of the dangerous disease, and are only important for that reason. Behind them lie the interests, the passions and the destiny of mighty races of men; and long antagonisms express themselves in trifles."[35] Nevertheless Churchill may be justified in hoping that the fear induced by a "balance of terror" will produce a temporary truce. Advancing technology makes war more horrible and presumably increases the desire for peace; the very rapidity of the advance makes for uncertainty in everyone's military planning and destroys the possibility of an accurate estimate of the likely opposing forces. Fear and permanent peace are more difficult to equate. Each major advance in the technology of war has found its prophet ready to proclaim that war is no longer possible: Alfred Nobel and dynamite, for example, or Benjamin Franklin and the lighter-than-air balloon. There may well have been a prophet to proclaim the end of tribal warfare when the spear was invented and another to make a similar prediction when poison was first added to its tip. Unfortunately, these prophets have all been false. The development of atomic and hydrogen weapons may nurture the peace wish of some, the war sentiment of others. In the United States and elsewhere after the Second World War, a muted theme of foreign-policy debate was the necessity of preventive war — drop the bomb quickly before the likely opponent in a future war has time to make one of his own. Even with two or more states equipped with similar weapon systems, a momentary shift in the balance of terror, giving a decisive military advantage temporarily to one state, may tempt it to seize the moment in order to escape from fear. And the temptation would be proportionate to the fear itself. Finally, mutual fear of big weapons may produce, instead of peace, a spate of smaller wars.

The fear of modern weapons, of the danger of destroying the civilizations of the world, is not sufficient to establish the conditions of peace identified in our discussions of the three images of international relations. One can equate fear with world peace only if the peace wish exists in all states and is uniformly expressed in their policies. But peace is the primary goal of few men or states. If it were the primary goal of even a single state, that state could have peace at any time — simply by surrendering. But, as John Foster Dulles so often warned, "Peace can be a cover whereby evil men perpetrate diabolical wrongs."[36] The issue in a given dispute may not be: Who shall gain from it? It may instead be: Who shall dominate the world? In such circumstances, the best course of even reasonable men is difficult to define; their ability always to contrive solutions without force, impossible to assume. If solutions in terms of none of the three images is presently — if ever — possible, then reason can work only within the framework that is suggested by viewing the first and second images in the perspective of the third, a perspective well and simply set forth in the *Federalist Papers*, especially in those written by Hamilton and Jay.

What would happen, Jay asks, if the thirteen states, instead of combining as one state, should form themselves into several confederations? He answers:

> Instead of their being "joined in affection" and free from all apprehension of different "interests," envy and jealousy would soon extinguish confidence and affection, and the partial interests of each confederation, instead of the general interests of all America, would be the only objects of their policy and pursuits. Hence, like most *bordering* nations, they would always be either involved in disputes and war, or live in the constant apprehension of them.[37]

International anarchy, Jay is here saying, is the explanation for international war. But not international anarchy alone. Hamilton adds that to presume a lack of hostile motives among states is to forget that men are "ambitious, vindictive, and rapacious." A monarchical state may go to war because the vanity of its king leads him to seek glory in military victory; a republic may go to war because of the folly of its assembly or because of its commercial interests. That the king may be vain, the assembly foolish, or the commercial interests irreconcilable: none of these is inevitable. However, so many and so varied are the causes of war among states that "to look for a continuation of harmony between a number of independent, unconnected sovereigns in the same neighborhood, would be to disregard the uniform course of human events, and to set at defiance the accumulated experience of the ages."[38]

Jay and Hamilton found in the history of the Western state system confirmation for the conclusion that among separate sovereign states there is constant possibility of war. The third image gives a theoretical basis for the same conclusion. It reveals why, in the absence of tremendous changes in the factors included in the first and second images, war will be perpetually associated with the existence of separate sovereign states. The obvious conclusion of a third-image analysis is that world government is the remedy for world war. The remedy, though it may be unassailable in logic, is unattainable in practice. The third image may provide a utopian approach to world politics. It may also provide a realistic approach, and one that avoids the tendency of some realists to attribute the necessary amorality, or even immorality, of world politics to the inherently bad character of man. If everyone's strategy depends upon everyone else's, then the Hitlers determine in part the action, or better, reaction, of those whose ends are worthy and whose means are fastidious. No matter how good their intentions, policy makers must bear in mind the implications of the third image, which can be stated in summary form as follows: Each state pursues its own interests, however defined, in ways it judges best. Force is a means of achieving the external ends of states because there exists no consistent, reliable process of reconciling the conflicts of interest that inevitably arise among similar units in a condition of anarchy. A foreign policy based on this image of international relations is neither moral nor immoral, but embodies merely a reasoned response to the world about us. The third image describes the framework of world politics, but without the first and second images there can be no knowledge of the forces that determine policy; the first and second images describe the forces in world politics, but without the third image it is impossible to assess their importance or predict their results.

NOTES

1. Beverly Nichols, *Cry Havoc!* (New York: Doubleday, Doran & Co., 1933), p. 164.
2. Margaret E. Hirst, *The Quakers in Peace and War* (London: Swarthmore Press, 1923), pp. 521–25.
3. Bertrand Russell, *Political Ideals* (New York: Century Co., 1917), p. 42. In one way or another the thought recurs in Lord Russell's many writings on international relations.
4. William James, "The Moral Equivalent of War," in *Memories and Studies* (New York: Longmans, Green and Co., 1912), pp. 262–72, 290.
5. Jean Bodin, *Six Books of the Commonwealth*, abridged and trans. M. J. Tooley (Oxford: Basil Blackwell, n.d.), p. 168.
6. "Some Thoughts for the President's Consideration," Apr. 1, 1861, in *Documents of American History*, ed. Henry Steele Commager, 3d ed. (New York: F. S. Crofts & Co., 1946), p. 392.
7. Hans Herzfeld, "Bismarck und die Skobelewespisode," *Historische Zeitschrift* 142 (1930): 279–302.

8. Cf. Robert E. Sherwood, *Roosevelt and Hopkins* (New York: Harper and Brothers, 1948), pp. 67–68, 102, 126, 133–36, 272, and esp. 931; and Secretary of State Hay's statement in Henry Adams, *The Education of Henry Adams* (New York: Book League of America, 1928), p. 374. Note that in this case the fault is one that is thought to decrease the ability of a country to implement a peaceful policy. In the other examples, the defect is thought to increase the propensity of a country to go to war.

9. Cf. Bertrand Russell, who in 1917 wrote: "There can be no good international system until the boundaries of states coincide as nearly as possible with the boundaries of nations" (*Political Ideals*, p. 146).

10. Frank H. Simonds and Brooks Emery, *The Great Powers in World Politics* (New York: American Book Co., 1939), passim; W. S. Thompson, *Danger Spots in World Population* (New York: Alfred A. Knopf, 1930), esp. the Preface and chaps. 1 and 13.

11. Cf. Vladimir Dedijer, "Albania, Soviet Pawn," *Foreign Affairs* 30 (1951): 104: socialism, but not Soviet Union state capitalism, means peace.

12. Thucydides, *History of the Peloponnesian War*, trans. B. Jowett, 2d ed. (London: Oxford University Press, 1900),bk. 1, par. 23.

13. John Adams to the citizens of the town of Petersburg, Virginia, June 6, 1798, reprinted in the program for the visit of William Howard Taft, Petersburg, May 19, 1909.

14. Frederick S. Dunn, *Peaceful Change* (New York: Council on Foreign Relations, 1937), p. 13.

15. Richard Cobden, esp. *Speeches on Peace, Financial Reform, Colonial Reform and Other Subjects Delivered during 1849* (London: James Gilbert, n.d.), p. 135.

16. Jean Jaques Rousseau, *The Social Contract and Discourses*, trans, G.D.H. Cole, Everyman's Library Edition (New York: E. P. Dutton and Co., 1950); see esp. *Inequality*, pp. 234 ff.

17. Ibid., p. 34.

18. Benedict de Spinoza, *The Chief Works of Benedict de Spinoza*, trans. R.H.M. Elwes, 2 vols. (New York: Dover Publications, 1951), *Ethics*, pt. 4, prop. 35, proof.

19. Rousseau, *Social Contract and Discourses*, pp. 135–36 (bk. 4, chap. 8), italics added. The word "equally" is necessary for an accurate rendering of the French text but does not appear in the translation cited.

20. Jean Jacques Rousseau, *A Lasting Peace through the Federation of Europe and the State of War*, trans. C. E. Vaughan (London: Constable and Co., 1917), p. 72.

21. This parallels Hegel's formulation: "It is to what is by nature accidental that accidents happen, and the fate whereby they happen is thus a necessity" [G.W.F.] Hegel, *Philosophy of Right*, trans. T. M. Knox (Oxford: Clarendon Press, 1942), sec. 324].

22. Kant is more willing to admit the force of this criticism than is generally realized.

23. This is not, of course, to say that no differences in state behavior follow from the different constitutions and situations of states. This point raises the question of the relation of the third image to the second, which will be discussed below.

24. Rousseau, *Social Contract and Discourses*, pp. 290–91.

25. Rousseau, *A Lasting Peace*, pp. 46–48, 58–59.

26. Ibid., pp. 38, 46–47. On p. 121, Rousseau distinguishes between the "state of

war," which always exists among states, and war proper, which manifests itself in the settled intention to destroy the enemy state.

27. Ibid., p. 49.
28. In ibid., p. 69, Rousseau presents his exhaustive list of such causes.
29. Ibid., pp. 38–39.
30. Ibid., pp. 59–60.
31. Cf. Karl Popper, *The Open Society and Its Enemies* (Princeton: Princeton University Press, 1950), pp. 158–59; and William Esslinger, *Politics and Science* (New York: Philosophical Library, 1955), passim.
32. Richard Cobden, *Speeches on Questions of Public Policy*, 2 vols., ed. John Bright and James E. Thorold Rogers (London: Macmillan & Co., 1870), 2: 165.
33. A. A. Milne, *Peace and War* (New York: E. P. Dutton & Co., 1934), p. 11.
34. Edward Grey, *Twenty-Five Years*, 2 vols. (New York: Frederick A. Stokes Co., 1925), 2: 285.
35. Winston Churchill, *The World Crisis*, 1911–1914, 4 vols. (New York: Charles Scribner's Sons, 1923–29), 1: 52.
36. "Excerpts from Dulles Address on Peace," Washington, D.C., Apr. 11, 1955, in *New York Times*, Apr. 12, 1955, p. 6.
37. Alexander Hamilton, John Jay, and James Madison, *The Federalist* (New York: Modern Library, 1941), pp. 23–24 (no. 5).
38. Ibid., pp. 27–28 (no. 6); cf. p. 18 (no. 4, Jay) and pp. 34–40 (no. 7, Hamilton).

War and Change in World Politics

Robert Gilpin

Professor Gilpin outlines key factors to explain the rise and decline of states.

During the 1970s and early 1980s a series of dramatic events signaled that international relations were undergoing a significant upheaval. Long-established and seemingly stable sets of relationships and understandings were summarily cast aside. Political leaders, academic observers, and the celebrated "man in the street" were suddenly conscious of the fact that the energy crisis, dramatic events in the Middle East, and tensions in the Communist world were novel developments of a qualitatively different order from those of the preceding decade. These developments and many others in the political, economic, and military realms signaled far-reaching shifts in the international distribution of power, an unleashing of

From Robert Gilpin, *War and Change in World Politics* (1981), pp. 1–15 and 39–44. Reprinted by permission of Cambridge University Press.

new sociopolitical forces, and the global realignment of diplomatic relations. Above all, these events and developments revealed that the relatively stable international system that the world had known since the end of World War II was entering a period of uncertain political changes.

Ours is not the first age in which a sudden concatenation of dramatic events has revealed underlying shifts in military power, economic interest, and political alignments. In the twentieth century, developments of comparable magnitude had already taken place in the decades preceding World War I and World War II. This awareness of the dangers inherent in periods of political instability and rapid change causes profound unease and apprehension. The fear grows that events may get out of hand and the world may once again plunge itself into a global conflagration. Scholars, journalists, and others turn to history for guidance, asking if the current pattern of events resembles the pattern of 1914 and 1939.[1]

These contemporary developments and their dangerous implications raise a number of questions regarding war and change in international relations: How and under what circumstances does change take place at the level of international relations? What are the roles of political, economic, and technological developments in producing change in international systems? Wherein lies the danger of intense military conflict during periods of rapid economic and political upheaval? And, most important of all, are answers that are derived from examination of the past valid for the contemporary world? In other words, to what extent have social, economic, and technological developments such as increasing economic interdependence of nations and the advent of nuclear weapons changed the role of war in the process of international political change? Is there any reason to hope that political change may be more benign in the future than it has been in the past?

The purpose of this book is to explore these issues. In this endeavor we shall seek to develop an understanding of international political change more systematic than the understanding that currently exists. We do not pretend to develop a general theory of international relations that will provide an overarching explanatory statement. Instead, we attempt to provide a framework for thinking about the problem of war and change in world politics. This intellectual framework is intended to be an analytical device that will help to order and explain human experience. It does not constitute a rigorous scientific explanation of political change. The ideas on international political change presented are generalizations based on observations of historical experience rather than a set of hypotheses that have been tested scientifically by historical evidence; they are proposed as a plausible account of how international political change occurs.[2]

To this end we isolate and analyze the more obvious regularities and patterns associated with changes in international systems. However, we make no claim to have discovered the "laws of change" that determine when political change will occur or what course it will take.[3] On the contrary, the position taken here is that major political changes are the consequences of the conjuncture of unique and unpredictable sets of developments. However, the claim is made that it is possible to identify recurrent patterns, common elements, and general tendencies in the major turning points in international history. As the distinguished economist W. Arthur Lewis put it, "The process of social change is much the same today as it was 2,000 years ago. . . . We can tell how change will occur if it occurs; what we cannot foresee is what change is going to occur."[4]

The conception of political change presented in this book, like almost all social science, is not predictive. Even economics is predictive only within a narrow range of issues.[5]

Most of the alleged theories in the field of political science and in the sub-field of international relations are in fact analytical, descriptive constructs; they provide at best a conceptual framework and a set of questions that help us to analyze and explain a type of phenomenon.[6] Thus, Kenneth Waltz, in his stimulating book, *Man, the State and War*, provided an explanation of war in general terms, but not the means for predicting any particular war.[7] In similar fashion, this study seeks to explain in general terms the nature of international political change.

The need for a better understanding of political change, especially international political change, was well set forth by Wilbert Moore in the latest edition of the *International Encyclopedia of the Social Sciences:* "Paradoxically, as the rate of social change has accelerated in the real world of experience, the scientific disciplines dealing with man's actions and products have tended to emphasize orderly interdependence and static continuity."[8]

Moore's judgment concerning the inadequate treatment of political change by social scientists is borne out by analyses of international-relations textbooks and theoretical works. Although there are some recent outstanding exceptions,[9] few of these books have addressed the problem of political change in systematic fashion. As David Easton rightly commented, "students of political life have . . . been prone to forget that the really crucial problems of social research are concerned with the patterns of change."[10]

It is worth noting, as Joseph Schumpeter pointed out, that the natural development of any science is from static analysis to dynamic analysis.[11] Static theory is simpler, and its propositions are easier to prove. Unfortunately, until the statics of a field of inquiry are sufficiently well developed and one has a good grasp of repetitive processes and recurrent phenomena, it is difficult if not impossible to proceed to the study of dynamics. From this perspective, systematic study of international relations is a young field, and much of what passes for dynamics is in reality an effort to understand the statics of interactions of particular international systems: diplomatic bargaining, alliance behavior, crisis management, etc. The question whether or not our current understanding of these static aspects is sufficiently well advanced to aid in the development of a dynamic theory poses a serious challenge to the present enterprise.

A second factor that helps to explain the apparent neglect, until recent years, of the problem of political change is what K. J. Holsti called the decline of "grand theory."[12] The political realism of Hans Morgenthau, the systems theory of Morton Kaplan, and the neofunctionalism of Ernst Haas, as well as numerous other "grand theories," have one element in common: the search for a general theory of international politics. Each in its own way, with varying success, has sought, in the words of Morgenthau, "to reduce the facts of experience to mere specific instances of general propositions."[13] Yet none of these ambitious efforts to understand the issues (war, imperialism, and political change) has gained general acceptance. Instead, "the major preoccupations of theorists during the past decade have been to explore specific problems, to form hypotheses or generalizations explaining limited ranges of phenomena, and particularly, to obtain data to test those hypotheses."[14] In brief, the more recent emphasis on so-called middle-range theory, though valuable in itself, has had the unfortunate consequence of diverting attention away from more general theoretical problems.[15]

A third reason for neglect of the study of political change is the Western bias in the study of international relations. For a profession whose intellectual commitment is the understanding of the interactions of societies, international relations as a discipline is remarkably parochial and ethnocentric. It is essentially a study of the Western state system, and a sizable fraction of the existing literature is devoted to developments since the end of World War II. Thus the profession has emphasized recent developments within that particular state system. Although there are exceptions, the practitioners of this discipline have not been forced to come to terms with the dynamics of this, or any other, state system.[16] As Martin Wight suggested, international relations lacks a tradition of political theorizing. In large measure, of course, this is because of the paucity of reliable secondary studies of non-Western systems.[17] This situation in itself is a formidable obstacle to the development of a theory of international political change.

A fourth reason for neglect of the theoretical problem of political change is the widespread conviction of the futility of the task. Prevalent among historians, this view is also held by many social scientists.[18] The search for "laws of change" is held to be useless because of the uniqueness and complexity of historical events. Thus the search for generalizations or patterns in human affairs is regarded as a hopeless enterprise. Such a position, if taken at face value, denies the very possibility of a science or history of society; yet one should note its admonitions that there are no immutable laws of change and that although repetitive patterns may exist, social change is ultimately contingent on unique sets of historical events.

Finally, the development of a theory of political change has been inhibited by ideology and emotion. In part this is due to a conservative bias in Western social science. Most academic social scientists have a preference for stability or at least a preference for orderly change. The idea of radical changes that threaten accepted values and interests is not an appealing one. This issue is especially acute for the theorist of international political change, who must confront directly the fundamental problem of international relations: war. The inhibiting effect of this dreadful issue has been well put by John Burton in a sweeping indictment of contemporary international-relations scholarship:

> The chief failure of orthodoxy has been in relation to change. The outstanding feature of reality is the dynamic nature of International Relations. No general theory is appropriate which cannot take into consideration the rapidly changing technological, social and political environment in which nations are required to live in peace one with the other. But the only device of fundamental change which is possible in the context of power politics is that of war, for which reason war is recognized as a legitimate instrument of national policy. It is not surprising that International Relations has tended to be discussed in static terms, and that stability has tended to be interpreted in terms of the maintenance of the *status quo*. A dynamic approach to International Relations would immediately confront the analyst with no alternative but to acknowledge war as the only available mechanism for change.[19]

Burton's challenge to orthodox theory of international relations goes to the heart of the present study. In recent years theorists of international relations have tended to stress the moderating and stabilizing influences of contemporary developments on the behavior of states, especially the increasing economic interdependence among nations and the destructiveness of modern weapons. These important developments have encouraged many individuals to believe that peaceful evolution has replaced military conflict as the principal means of adjusting relations among nation-states in the contemporary world. This assumption has been accompanied by a belief that economic and welfare goals have triumphed over the traditional power and security objectives of states. Thus, many believe that the opportunity for peaceful economic intercourse and the constraints imposed by modern destructive warfare have served to decrease the probability of a major war.

In the present study we take a very different stance, a stance based on the assumption that the fundamental nature of international relations has not changed over the millennia. International relations continue to be a recurring struggle for wealth and power among independent actors in a state of anarchy. The classic history of Thucydides is as meaningful a guide to the behavior of states today as when it was written in the fifth century B.C. Yet important changes have taken place. One of the subthemes of this book, in fact, is that modern statecraft and premodern statecraft differ in significant respects, a situation first appreciated by Montesquieu, Edward Gibbon, and other earlier writers on the subject. Nevertheless, we contend that the fundamentals have not been altered. For this reason, the insights of earlier writers and historical experience are considered relevant to an understanding of the ways in which international systems function and change in the contemporary era.

Thus, although there is obviously an important element of truth in the belief that contemporary economic and technological development have altered relations among states, events in Asia, Africa, and the Middle East in the 1970s and early 1980s force us once again to acknowledge the continuing unsolved problem of war and the role of war in the process of international political change. Even more than in the past, in the last decades of the twentieth century we need to understand the relationship of war and change in the international system. Only in this way can we hope to fashion a more peaceful alternative. As E. H. Carr reminded us, this is the basic task of the study of international relations: "To establish methods of peaceful change is . . . the fundamental problem of international morality and of international politics."[20] But if peace were the ultimate goal of statecraft, then the solution to the problem of peaceful change would be easy. Peace may always be had by surrender to the aggressor state. The real task for the peaceful state is to seek a peace that protects and guarantees its vital interests and its concept of international morality.

THE NATURE OF INTERNATIONAL POLITICAL CHANGE

An international system is established for the same reason that any social or political system is created; actors enter social relations and create social structures in order to advance particular sets of political, economic, or other types of interests. Because the interests of some of the actors may conflict with those of other actors, the particular interests that are most favored by these social arrangements tend to reflect the relative powers of the actors involved. That is, although social systems impose restraints on the behavior of all actors, the behaviors rewarded and punished by the system will coincide, at least initially, with the interests of the most powerful members of the social system. Over time, however, the interests of individual actors and the balance of power among the actors do change as a result of economic, technological, and other developments. As a consequence, those actors who benefit most from a change in the social system and who gain the power to effect such change will seek to alter the system in ways that favor their interests. The resulting changed system will reflect the new distribution of power and the interests of its new dominant members. Thus, a precondition for political change lies in a disjuncture between the existing social system and the redistribution of power toward those actors who would benefit most from a change in the system.

This conception of political change is based on the notion that the purpose or social function of any social system, including the international system, may be defined in terms of the benefits that various members derive from its operation.[21]

As in the case with domestic society, the nature of the international system determines whose interests are being served by the functioning of the system. Changes in the system imply changes in the distribution of benefits provided to and costs imposed on individual members of the system. Thus the study of international political change must focus on the international system and especially on the efforts of political actors to change the international system in order to advance their own interests. Whether these interests are security, economic gain, or ideological goals, the achievement of state objectives is dependent on the nature of the international system (i.e., the governance of the system, the rules of the system, the recognition of rights, etc.). As is the case in any social or political system, the process of international political change ultimately reflects the efforts of individuals or groups to transform institutions and systems in order to advance their interests. Because these interests and the powers of groups (or states) change, in time the political system will be changed in ways that will reflect these underlying shifts in interest and power. The elaboration of this approach for the understanding of international political change is the purpose of the subsequent discussion.

A FRAMEWORK FOR UNDERSTANDING INTERNATIONAL POLITICAL CHANGE

The conceptualization of international political change to be presented [here] rests on a set of assumptions regarding the behavior of states:

1. An international system is stable (i.e., in a state of equilibrium) if no state believes it profitable to attempt to change the system.
2. A state will attempt to change the international system if the expected benefits exceed the expected costs (i.e., if there is an expected net gain).
3. A state will seek to change the international system through territorial, political, and economic expansion until the marginal costs of further change are equal to or greater than the marginal benefits.
4. Once an equilibrium between the costs and benefits of further change and expansion is reached, the tendency is for the economic costs of maintaining the status quo to rise faster than the economic capacity to support the status quo.
5. If the disequilibrium in the international system is not resolved, then the system will be changed, and a new equilibrium reflecting the redistribution of power will be established.

Obviously these assumptions are abstractions from a highly complex political reality. They do not describe the actual decision processes of statesmen, but as in the case of economic theory, actors are assumed to behave as if they were guided by such a set of cost/benefit calculations. Moreover, these assumptions are not mutually exclusive; they do overlap. Assumptions 2 and 4 are mirror images of one another, assumption 2 referring to a revisionist state and assumption 4 referring to a status quo state.

On the basis of these assumptions, the conceptualization of international political change to be presented here seeks to comprehend a continuing historical process. Because history has no starts and stops, one must break into the flow of history at a particular point. The following analysis of political change begins with an international system in a state of equilibrium as shown in Figure 1. An international system is in a state of equilibrium if the more powerful states in the system are satisfied with the existing territorial, political, and economic arrangements. Although minor changes and adjustments may take place, an equilibrium condition is one in which no powerful state (or group) believes that a change in the system would yield additional benefits commensurate with the anticipated costs of bringing about a change in the system.[22] Although every state and group in the system could benefit from particular types of change, the costs involved will discourage attempts to seek a change in system. As one writer has put it, "a power equilibrium represents a stable political configuration provided there are no changes in returns to conquest."[23] Under these conditions, where no one has an incentive to change the system, the status quo may be said to be stable.

In the more traditional language of international relations, the international status quo is held to be a legitimate one, at least by the major states in the system. The meaning of legitimacy was defined by Henry Kissinger as follows:

[Legitimacy] implies the acceptance of the framework of the international order by all major powers, at least to the extent that no state is so dissatisfied

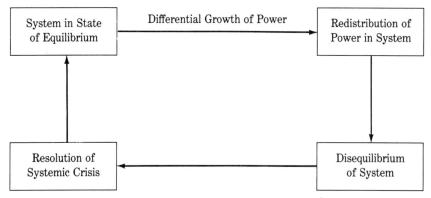

Figure 1. Diagram of international political change

that, like Germany after the Treaty of Versailles, it expresses its dissatisfaction in a revolutionary foreign policy. A legitimate order does not make conflicts impossible, but it limits their scope. Wars may occur, but they will be fought *in the name of* the existing structure and the peace which follows will be justified as a better expression of the "legitimate," general consensus. Diplomacy in the classic sense, the adjustment of differences through negotiations, is possible only in "legitimate international orders."[24]

What this quotation suggests is that an international system or order exists in a condition of homeostatic or dynamic equilibrium. Like any other system, it is not completely at rest; changes at the level of interstate interactions are constantly taking place. In general, however, the conflicts, alliances, and diplomatic interactions among the actors in the system tend to preserve the defining characteristics of the system. Thus, as Kissinger demonstrated, the legitimate order or equilibrium created by the Congress of Vienna (1814) survived limited conflicts and diplomatic maneuvering until it finally collapsed in response to the profound economic, technological, and political upheavals of the latter part of the nineteenth century. This issue of legitimacy will be discussed later.

In every international system there are continual occurrences of political, economic, and technological changes that promise gains or threaten losses for one or another actor. In most cases these potential gains and losses are minor, and only incremental adjustments are necessary in order to take account of them. Such changes take place within the existing international system, producing a condition of homeostatic equilibrium. The relative stability of the system is, in fact, largely determined by its capacity to adjust to the demands of actors affected by changing political and environmental conditions. In every system, therefore, a process of disequilibrium and adjustment is constantly taking place. In the absence of large potential net benefits from change, the system continues to remain in a state of equilibrium.

If the interests and relative powers of the principal states in an international system remained constant over time, or if power relations changed in such a way as to maintain the same relative distribution of power, the system would continue indefinitely in a state of equilibrium. However, both domestic and international developments undermine the stability of the status quo. For example, shifts in domestic coalitions may necessitate redefinition of the "national interest." However, the most destabilizing factor is the tendency in an international system for the powers of member states to change at different rates because of political, economic, and technological developments. In time, the differential growth in power of the various states in the system causes a fundamental redistribution of power in the system.

The concept of power is one of the most troublesome in the field of international relations and, more generally, political science. Many weighty books have analyzed and elaborated the concept. In this book, power refers simply to the military, economic, and technological capabilities of states. This definition obviously leaves out important and intangible elements that affect the outcomes of political actions, such as public morale, qualities of leadership, and situational factors. It also excludes what E. H. Carr called "power over opinion."[25] These psychological and frequently incalculable aspects of power and international relations are more closely associated with the concept of prestige. . . .

As a consequence of the changing interests of individual states, and especially because of the differential growth in power among states, the international system moves from a condition of equilibrium to one of disequilibrium. Disequilibrium is a situation in which economic, political, and technological developments have increased considerably the potential benefits or decreased the potential costs to one or more states of seeking to change the international system. Forestalling one's losses or increasing one's gains becomes an incentive for one or more states to attempt to change the system. Thus there develops a disjuncture between the existing international system and the potential gains to particular states from a change in the international system.

The elements of this systemic disequilibrium are twofold. First, military, technological, or other changes have increased the benefits of territorial conquest or the benefits of changing the international system in other ways. Second, the differential growth in power among the states in the system has altered the cost of changing the system. This transformation of the benefits and/or the costs of changing the system produces an incongruity or disjuncture among the components of the system (Table 1). On the one hand, the hierarchy of prestige, the division of territory, the international division of labor, and the rules of the system remain basically unchanged; they continue to reflect primarily the interests of the existing dominant powers and the relative power distribution that prevailed at the time of the last systemic change. On the other hand, the international distribution of power has undergone a radical transformation that has weakened the foundations of the existing system. It is this disjuncture between the several components of the system and its implica-

TABLE 1   Mechanisms of Control
(Components of System)

Government[a]	Dominance of great power[b]
Authority	Hierarchy of prestige
Property rights	Division of territory
Law	Rules of the system
Domestic economy	International economy

[a]Based on distribution of power among domestic groups, coalitions, classes, etc.

[b]Based on distribution of power among states in the system.

tions for relative gains and losses among the various states in the system that cause international political change.

This disjuncture within the existing international system involving the potential benefits and losses to particular powerful actors from a change in the system leads to a crisis in the international system. Although resolution of a crisis through peaceful adjustment of the systemic disequilibrium is possible, the principal mechanism of change throughout history has been war, or what we shall call hegemonic war (i.e., a war that determines which state or states will be dominant and will govern the system). The peace settlement following such a hegemonic struggle reorders the political, territorial, and other bases of the system. Thus the cycle of change is completed in that hegemonic war and the peace settlement create a new status quo and equilibrium reflecting the redistribution of power in the system and the other components of the system.

NOTES

1. Miles Kahler, "Rumors of War: The 1914 Analogy," *Foreign Affairs* 58 (1979–80), pp. 374–396.
2. However, in principle, these ideas are translatable into specific testable hypotheses. At least we would argue that this is possible for a substantial fraction of them. The carrying out of this task, or part of it, would require another volume.
3. The term "law" . . . is to be interpreted as a general tendency that may be counteracted by other developments. This conception of law is taken from Jean Baechler, *Les Origines du Capitalisme* (Paris: Editions Gallimard, 1971), English edition (Oxford: Basil Blackwell, 1975), p. 52.
4. W. Arthur Lewis, *The Theory of Economic Growth* (New York: Harper & Row, 1970), pp. 17–18.
5. F. S. C. Northrop, *The Logic of the Sciences and the Humanities* (New York: Macmillan, 1947), pp. 243–45.
6. Stanley Hoffmann (ed.), *Contemporary Theory in International Relations* (Englewood Cliffs, N.J.: Prentice Hall, 1960), p. 40.
7. Kenneth N. Waltz, *Man, the State and War* (New York: Columbia University Press, 1959), p. 232.
8. Wilbert E. Moore, "Social Change" in *International Encyclopedia of the Social Sciences*, vol. 14, ed. by David Sills (New York: Crowell Collier and Macmillan, 1968), p. 365.
9. Nazli Choucri and Robert C. North, *Nations in Conflict* (San Francisco: W. H. Freeman, 1975); Robert O. Keohane and Joseph S. Nye, *Power and Interdependence* (Boston: Little, Brown, 1977); Kenneth N. Waltz, *Theory of International Politics* (Reading, MA: Addison-Wesley, 1979).
10. David Easton, *The Political System* (New York: Alfred A. Knopf, 1953), p. 42. It is symptomatic of this continued general neglect that the *Handbook of Political Science* does not contain a section devoted to the problem of political change. Nor does the entry "political change" appear in its cumulative index. See Fred I. Greenstein and Nelson W. Polsby, eds., *Handbook of Political Science* (Reading, Mass.: Addison-Wesley, 1975).

11. Joseph Schumpeter, *History of Economic Analysis* (New York: Oxford University Press, 1954), p. 964.
12. K. J. Holsti, "Retreat from Utopia," *Canadian Journal of Political Science*, Vol. 4 (1971), pp. 165–177.
13. *Ibid.*, p. 167.
14. *Ibid.*, p. 171.
15. Several important books have recently indicated revival of interest in general theory. See Choucri and North, *Nations in Conflict*; Hedley Bull, *The Anarchical Society* (New York: Columbia University Press, 1977); Keohane and Nye, *Power and Interdependence*; Stanley Hoffmann, *Primacy or World Order* (New York: McGraw-Hill, 1978); Ralph Pettman, *State and Class* (London: Croom Helm, 1979); Kenneth N. Waltz, *Theory of International Politics* (Reading, Mass.: Addison-Wesley, 1979). Marxist scholars, of course, never lost interest in "grand theory."
16. Three recent exceptions are Evan Luard, *Types of International Society* (New York: Free Press, 1976); Robert G. Wesson, *The Imperial Order* (Berkeley: University of California Press, 1967); Martin Wight, *Systems of States*, ed. Hedley Bull (Leicester, England: Leicester University Press, 1977).
17. Martin Wight, "Why Is There No International Theory?" in Herbert Butterfield and Martin Wight (eds.), *Diplomatic Investigations* (London: George Allen and Unwin, 1966), pp. 17–34.
18. Albert O. Hirschman, "The Search for Paradigms as a Hindrance to Understanding," *World Politics*, Vol. 22 (1970), pp. 329–43.
19. John Burton, *International Relations: A General Theory* (Cambridge, MA: Cambridge University Press, 1965), pp. 71–72.
20. E. H. Carr, *The Twenty Years' Crisis* (London: Macmillan, 1951).
21. John Harsanyi, "Rational-Choice Models of Political Behavior vs. Functionalist and Conformist Theories," *World Politics*, Vol. 21 (1969), pp. 513–38.
22. R. L. Curry Jr, and L. L. Wade, *A Theory of Political Exchange* (Englewood Cliffs, N.J.: Prentice Hall, 1968), p. 49; and Lance E. Davis and Douglass C. North, *Institutional Change and American Economic Growth* (Cambridge England: Cambridge University Press, 1971), p. 40.
23. Trout Rader, *The Economics of Feudalism* (New York: Gordon and Breach, 1971), p. 50.
24. Henry A. Kissinger, *A World Restored* (Boston: Houghton Mifflin, 1957), pp. 1–2.
25. Carr, *Twenty Years' Crisis*, p. 132.

Chain Gangs and Passed Bucks: Predicting Alliance Patterns in Multipolarity

Thomas J. Christensen and Jack Snyder

The authors argue that contemporary balance-of-power theory has become too parsimonious to yield determinate predictions about state alliance strategies in multipolarity. Kenneth Waltz's theory predicts only that multipolarity predisposes states to either of two opposite errors, which this article characterizes as chain-ganging and buck-passing. To predict which of these two policies will prevail, it is necessary to complicate Waltz's theory by adding a variable from Robert Jervis's theory of the security dilemma: the variable of whether offense or defense is perceived to have the advantage. At least under the checkerboard geographical conditions in Europe before World Wars I and II, perceived offensive advantage bred unconditional alliances, whereas perceived defensive advantage bred free riding on the balancing efforts of others.

Kenneth Waltz's rigorous recasting of traditional balance-of-power theory has provided the intellectual foundation for much of the most fruitful recent work in the fields of international politics and national security.[1] But there is a tension between Waltz's theory and those who apply it in their practical research agendas. Waltz's is a theory of international politics; it addresses properties of the international system, such as the recurrence of war and the recurrent formation of balances of power.[2] Those who have applied Waltz's ideas, however, have normally used them as a theory of foreign policy to make predictions about or prescriptions for the strategic choices of states.[3]

This is a problem because for a particular state in particular circumstances, any foreign policy and its opposite can sometimes be deduced from Waltz's theory. In multipolarity, for example, states are said to be structurally prone to either of two opposite errors that destabilize the balancing system. On the one hand, they may chain themselves unconditionally to reckless allies whose survival is seen to be indispensable to the maintenance of the balance. This, Waltz argues, was the pattern of behavior that led to World War I. On the other hand, they may pass the buck, counting on third parties to bear the costs of stopping a rising hegemon. This was the pattern that preceded World War II.[4]

For Waltz, as a systemic theorist, this is not a crippling problem. He deduces logically that multipolarity is structurally prone to instabilities,

Reprinted from *International Organization* 44, no. 2 (Spring 1990), by permission of the MIT Press, Cambridge, Massachusetts. Copyright 1990 by the World Peace Foundation and the Massachusetts Institute of Technology.

and the two major cases of this century illustrate his theory suitably. But for those who would use Waltz as a theorist of foreign policy, there *is* a problem. To explain, predict, or prescribe alliance strategy in particular circumstances, they need to specify which of the two opposite dangers — chain-ganging or buck-passing — is to be expected in those circumstances. An explanation that can account for any policy and its opposite is no explanation at all. Likewise, a prescription that warns simultaneously against doing too much and doing too little is of less use than one that specifies which of the two errors presents the more pressing danger in particular circumstances.

This does not mean that Waltz's insights about chain-ganging and buck-passing are of no use in a theory of foreign policy. Rather, it means that his ultraparsimonious theory must be cross-fertilized with other theories before it will make determinate predictions at the foreign policy level. Users of Waltz's theory already do this at various levels of explicitness, factoring in military technology, geography, and power variables that go beyond the mere counting of great power poles. In particular, they combine Waltz's insights with the variables stressed in Robert Jervis's version of the security dilemma theory.[5] They also factor in biases affecting how policymakers and soldiers perceive the balance-of-power problem that faces them.[6] By complicating the specification of the state's position in the international system — and in some cases by introducing the role of perception — determinate predictions can be made.[7]

Though a few scholars have de facto been working this way for some time, their method warrants more explicit specification. Toward this end, we will attempt to explain the opposite alliance choices of the European great powers before World Wars I and II, starting with Waltz's theory and adding a minimal number of variables from security dilemma theory and from perceptual theories that are necessary to derive a theoretically determinate and historically accurate account. In a nutshell, we argue that given Europe's multipolar checkerboard geography, the perception of offensive military advantages gave rise to alliance chain-ganging before 1914, whereas the perception of defensive advantages gave rise to buck-passing before 1939. These perceptions of the international conditions constraining strategic choice were, however, misperceptions, rooted in patterns of civil-military relations and the engrained lessons of formative experiences. In the first two sections of the article, we review the theories needed to underpin this interpretation and show how they can be combined in a relatively parsimonious fashion. In subsequent sections, we present short case histories demonstrating the historical plausibility of the interpretation and offer comments on issues for further research.

This exercise should be of practical as well as theoretical and historical interest. Arguably, the world is again becoming more multipolar. Japan has caught up with the Soviet Union in terms of gross national product. Both the United States and the Soviet Union are playing a less dominating global role now than they were when Waltz began to write about the stability of the bipolar balance. As in the periods before World Wars I and II, Germany and Russia may once again be contending for markets and influence in an increasingly heterogeneous, independent, yet vulnerable belt of Eastern European states. Will multipolar alliance patterns make a reappearance? And if so, which pattern — chain-ganging or buck-passing? For which problem should scholars and policymakers begin devising antidotes?

As the new configuration of power emerges, we will need to know not only about its polarity but also about the key security dilemma and perceptual variables that interact with polarity in shaping international alignments. If the potentially unstable condition of multipolarity reemerges, we will need to know how its effects can be mitigated. Since the polarity of the system is generally not subject to conscious manipulation by policymakers, our attention should be especially directed toward the variables that are somewhat more subject to conscious control, variables such as the offense-defense balance of technology and perceptions of it.

CHAIN GANGS AND PASSED BUCKS

Waltz argues that the structure of the international system determines what types of international behavior will be rewarded and punished (the process of selection) and, as a result, what types of foreign policy will seem prudent to actors in the system (the process of socialization). This structure comprises a constant element, anarchy, and a variable element, polarity. The fundamental, invariant structural feature, international anarchy, generally selects and socializes states to form balancing alignments in order to survive in the face of threats from aggressive competitors. However, a variable structural feature, polarity, affects the efficiency of the balancing process.

In multipolarity, two equal and opposite alliance dilemmas impede efficient balancing.[8] The first is the chain gang problem. In multipolarity, the approximate equality of alliance partners leads to a high degree of security interdependence within an alliance. Given the anarchic setting and this relative equality, each state feels its own security is integrally intertwined with the security of its alliance partners. As a result, any nation that marches to war inexorably drags its alliance partners with it. No state can restrain a reckless ally by threatening to sit out the conflict, since the demise of its reckless ally would decisively cripple its own security.[9]

Waltz's entirely apt example of this dilemma is World War I:

> If Austria — Hungary marched, Germany had to follow: the dissolution of the Austro-Hungarian Empire would have left Germany alone in the middle of Europe. If France marched, Russia had to follow; a German victory over France would be a defeat for Russia. And so it was all around the vicious circle. Because the defeat or the defection of a major ally would have shaken the

balance, each state was constrained to adjust its strategy and the use of its forces to the aims and fears of its partners.[10]

In short, as one member of the chain gang stumbles off the precipice, the other must follow. Hyperactive balancing behavior threatens the stability of the system by causing unrestrained warfare that threatens the survival of some of the great powers that form the system's poles.

The second, and opposite, pathology of multipolarity is buck-passing. In the face of a rising threat, balancing alignments fail to form in a timely fashion because some states try to ride free on other states' balancing efforts. They may do this because they wish to avoid bearing unnecessary costs or because they expect their relative position to be strengthened by standing aloof from the mutual bloodletting of the other powers. Waltz illustrates with World War II:

> French Foreign Minister Flandin told British Prime Minister Baldwin that Hitler's military occupation of the Rhineland in 1936 provided the occasion for Britain to take the lead in opposing Germany. As the German threat grew, some British and French leaders could hope that if their countries remained aloof, Russia and Germany would balance each other off or fight to the finish. Uncertainties about who threatens whom, about who will oppose whom, about who will gain or lose from the actions of other states accelerate as the number of states increases.[11]

Barry Posen, in the same vein, shows that the defensive military postures adopted by both Britain and France in the face of German expansion were designed to pass the cost of fighting Germany to other allies.[12] As a result, the balancing process operated inefficiently, giving the aggressor a chance to overturn the balance by eliminating the system's opposing poles through piecemeal aggression.

Waltz argues cogently that neither chain-ganging nor buck-passing dilemmas can arise in bipolarity. Bipolar superpowers do not need to chain themselves to small, reckless allies, since the superpowers are not dependent on allies for their survival. Superpowers also do not pass the buck, since smaller allies cannot possibly confront the opposing superpower alone.[13]

Superficially, it might appear that Waltz's argument about bipolarity suffers from as much underdetermination as his argument about multipolarity does. That is, Waltz appears to associate bipolarity with two equal and opposite stances toward peripheral allies. On the one hand, since the balance of power in bipolarity hinges on the superpowers' internal efforts to generate power capabilities, the loss of peripheral allies is largely irrelevant. Thus, chain gangs need not occur, and the superpower enjoys the luxury of non-involvement in peripheral disputes. On the other hand, each superpower understands that only it has the power to resist encroachments on third parties by the other. Consequently, the buck cannot be passed to others, so superpowers in bipolarity tend to "overreact" to threats in the periphery, Waltz says.[14]

We believe that the tension in this part of Waltz's argument is not difficult to resolve. Since superpowers have no strong incentive to intervene in the periphery, the issue of buck-passing should be irrelevant. The structural logic of limited involvement should override the opposite logic leading to overreaction. Or put somewhat less categorically, bipolar superpowers should practice a policy of limited liability in intervening in defense of peripheral allies. That is, they should incur the costs of intervention only in proportion to the power assets that are at risk. In bipolarity, these assets will always, by definition, be of marginal importance, so superpower interventions in the periphery should be limited. Waltz's policy prescriptions suggest that this is his view.[15]

The behavior of Cold War policymakers has sometimes violated these prescriptions, but we believe that this had more to do with perceptual or domestic political factors than with the structural properties of bipolarity. The structural consequences of bipolarity, unlike those of multipolarity, do lead to a determinate prediction about alliance strategy, even though empirically the behavior of the superpowers sometimes falsifies that prediction. In short, bipolarity is an ameliorator rather than a panacea. It does not entirely rule out overreactions and underreactions caused, for example, by domestic politics or faulty ideas, but bipolarity mitigates the structural causes of such problems.

In creating a theory of international politics, Waltz is interested mainly in showing that a system of two is more stable than a system of many. He therefore evinces no interest in predicting which pathology of multipolarity will appear in particular circumstances. For his purposes, this may be acceptable. Even on Waltz's own terms, however, the failure to specify when chain-ganging and buck-passing will occur is at least mildly troubling. Waltz's argument hinges on the notion that the structure of the system — that is, the number of poles — selects and socializes states to a particular form of behavior. But if chain-ganging and buck-passing, two starkly opposite forms of behavior, are equally selected under multipolar circumstances, how do states become socialized? Arguably, more information about the international setting must be provided in order for Waltz's crucial process of socialization to set states on a determinate path.

This indeterminacy is even more troublesome for Waltz's students, who attempt to adapt Waltz's ideas into a theory of foreign policy. For example, if Posen is to argue that the structural requirements of multipolarity led France to adopt a military strategy designed to pass the buck to Britain, then he must show that other strategies were not equally consistent with the logic of multipolarity. Posen understands this but leaves the solution to the problem only partially expressed.

Why, Posen asks, did states that passed the buck in the 1930s chain gang in the 1910s? In a single paragraph, Posen explains this as a consequence of the different effects of perceived offensive and defensive advantages on security calculations in multipolarity. Perceived offensive advantage before 1914 meant that war was considered cheap. Moreover, allies crucial to maintaining the balance of power were considered highly vulnerable to attack. Thus, states balanced aggressively and unconditionally. By contrast, in the 1930s, perceived defensive advantage led to buck-passing. According to Posen, "Each state had an interest in passing the costs of its own defense to its allies, because these costs [of defensive, attritional war] were high." He adds that "there was a widespread belief in a defensive advantage, so states did not believe that their allies might fold" and that "leaving one's ally a little bit in the lurch was not seen to represent a high risk to the ally's survival or one's own."[16]

Without spelling out the theoretical underpinning behind these arguments, Posen appears to dispense with evidence that falsifies his argument in an unsatisfying, ad hoc manner. By spelling out the underlying logic more explicitly and by combining balance-of-power theory with security dilemma theory, we hope to show that Posen's insight can be used to resolve Waltz's indeterminacy as a theorist of foreign policy. Far from being an ad hoc sleight-of-hand, this is a parsimonious, productive theoretical innovation that has general applicability for scholars working in the realist tradition.

Posen also notes that it was *perceptions* of offensive advantages, driven by the biases of "out-of-control military organizations," which shaped policy through shaping perceptions of systemic incentives before 1914. This introduces still more variables, but parsimony is still not utterly lost. Forces within the state affect alliance behavior and grand strategy, but they do so by affecting perceptions of the international environment. Thus, domestic and perceptual forces can be cleanly plugged into parsimonious international system theories. The next section lays out a framework for doing this.

POLARITY, THE SECURITY DILEMMA, AND PERCEPTION

To turn Waltz's ideas into a theory of foreign policy that accurately explains alliance behavior before World Wars I and II, two complications must be introduced. First, the variable elements of international structure must be broadened to include not only polarity but also the security dilemma variables: technology and geography. Second, perception of the strategic incentives inherent in the systemic structure must be introduced as a potentially autonomous factor.

Waltz approvingly cites Jervis's writings on the security dilemma as support for the notion that states in international anarchy are condemned to behave competitively. Indeed, Waltz's and Jervis's theories are cut from the same cloth, both stressing dilemmas that stem from the requirements of self-help in an anarchical political order. Both agree, moreover, that the intensity of the security dilemma is not constant but instead varies

with the vulnerability of states. Waltz explores the stabilizing consequences of bipolarity, which are due in part to the superpowers' greater
self-sufficiency and consequently lesser vulnerability to the vicissitudes
of international anarchy.[17] Jervis explores the stabilizing consequences of
defensive and deterrent military technologies, as well as geographical
configurations that make conquest more difficult. Both see the same
problem: vulnerability leads to self-help strategies that leave everyone
less secure. Both conceive of the international order similarly: as an anarchy. And both see greater invulnerability as the source of greater stability in international anarchy. There is no reason that their two theories
cannot be combined in order to explore interactions between their
variables.

These interactions include the connection between offensive advantage and chain-ganging and, conversely, the connection between defensive advantage and buck-passing. In multipolarity, the greater the vulnerability of states (that is, the more propitious the technology or
geography for the attacker), the greater is the propensity to align unconditionally and to fight all-out in defense of an ally from the first moment it is
attacked. This happens because the expectation of rapid, easy conquest
leads states to conclude that allies essential to maintaining the balance of
power will be decisively defeated unless they are given immediate and
effective assistance. Conversely, the less the vulnerability of states, the
greater is the tendency to pass the buck. This is due both to the expectation that other states, even singly, will be able to stalemate the aggressor
without assistance and to the expectation that the process of fighting will
be debilitating even for a victorious aggressor. Such an aggressor will
pose a reduced threat to buck-passing onlookers who remain at their full,
pre-war strength. Thus, Jervis's variables provide the determinate predictions that Waltz's theory needs in order to become a theory of foreign
policy.[18]

On theoretical grounds alone, we could be entirely satisfied with this
minor and parsimonious yet productive addendum to Waltz's theory. Unfortunately, for empirical reasons, still further adjustments are needed to
explain alliance dynamics before World Wars I and II. This is because
soldiers' and policymakers' perceptions of offensive and defensive advantages before the two wars were almost exactly wrong. Therefore, we
need to add a perceptual dimension to explain why technological circumstances of defensive advantage were seen as encouraging offensives in 1914, whereas circumstances that were objectively much more
favorable to the attacker in the late 1930s were seen as discouraging
offensives.

In principle, any number of perceptual biases might affect perceptions of the structure of international incentives. In fact, however, two
main hypotheses enjoy the greatest plausibility. The first is that soldiers'
and policymakers' perceptions of international structural incentives, in-

cluding the offense–defense balance, are shaped by their formative experiences, especially the last major war. Thus, since European wars before 1914 had often been short and decisive, most people expected offensives to succeed. But after the experience of 1914–18, most people expected defensives to succeed.[19] The second hypothesis is that uncontrolled militaries favor offensive strategies, and since civilian control over the military was much greater in the 1930s than in the 1910s, the military-fueled "cult of the offensive" no longer dominated strategic perceptions. Instead, a civilian-based "cult of the defensive," aimed at finding strategic excuses for buck-passing, may have had an equal but opposite impact.[20] It is not our main purpose here to argue about the sources of such misperceptions. Rather, we are satisfied to note that either of the above hypotheses is parsimonious and can easily be joined with the Jervis-Waltz international system theory to improve the accuracy of its predictions.

The element of misperception is not as foreign to Waltz's theory as one might first imagine. Indeed, Waltz claims that the basic problem of multipolarity is "miscalculation by some or all of the great powers."[21] In the simpler world of bipolarity, a superpower's responsibilities and vulnerabilities are easier to gauge, and egregious strategic miscalculations are therefore less likely. Of course, Waltz is referring here to random errors of perception and calculation that are inherent in the structural complexity and uncertainty of multipolar conditions; he is not referring to systematic perceptual biases due to cognitive or organizational quirks.

But in explaining the differences between the two multipolar outcomes, Waltz goes much further. For example, he writes that "the keenness of competition between the two camps" led to the chain gang effect in World War I. The "perception of a common threat brought Russia and France together," he adds. "If competing blocs are seen to be closely balanced, and if competition turns on important matters, then to let one's side down risks one's own destruction."[22] Waltz's use of the term "perception" here may have been accidental, but we think not. In purely structural terms, the fate of Austro–Hungarian power in 1914 was not more "important" for the European military balance than was the fate of Czechoslovak power in 1938.[23] There was no structural reason for the competition over it to be less "keen." Consequently, it is entirely appropriate for Waltz to use perceptual language, rather than structural language, in discussing France's and Russia's sense of a common threat.

It is our purpose to make explicit the military and perceptual factors that made competition more keen, alliances tighter, and East European crises seemingly more important in 1914 than in 1938. By doing this, we can account for the differences in multipolar alliance balancing behavior before World Wars I and II and thus rescue Waltz's theory from its predictive indeterminacy. Our proposed theoretical framework is summarized in Figure 1 and discussed in detail below.

The security dilemma

		Perceived defensive advantage (arising from civilian control or defensive lessons of history)	Perceived offensive advantage (arising from military autonomy or offensive lessons of history)
Polarity	Multipolarity	Buck-passing	Chain-ganging
	Bipolarity	Neither buck-passing nor chain-ganging	Neither buck-passing nor chain-ganging

Figure 1. Polarity, the security dilemma, and resulting alliance strategies

ALLIANCE STRATEGIES BEFORE WORLD WARS I AND II

Proposed Explanation for the Differing Alliance Patterns

The two world wars starkly illustrate the consequences of differing assessments of the relative strength of the offensive and the defensive. The strategic situation in these two cases was, in most respects, quite similar: Germany threatened to overturn the balance among the same four leading European powers by establishing its hegemony over Eastern Europe. But because the prevailing perception of the relative strength of offense and defense differed in the two cases, the strategic behavior of the powers in 1938–39 was the opposite of their behavior in 1914.

In 1914, the continental states adhered to essentially unconditional alliances, committing themselves to immediate offensives in full strength to aid their ally with little regard to the circumstances giving rise to the hostilities. In 1938–39, in contrast, the powers tried to pass the buck, luring others to bear the burden of stopping the rise of German hegemony. Stalin said in 1939 that the Soviet Union would not pull others' chestnuts out of the fire, but that is precisely what Russia had done in August 1914 through its premature, ill-fated offensive into East Prussia, an offensive designed to draw German fire away from France during the battle of the Marne.[24]

The aggressors' strategies were also opposite. The originators of the Schlieffen Plan sought to overturn the balance in a single bold stroke, whereas Hitler sought to overturn it through the piecemeal conquest of isolated targets. Finally, the causes of the two wars were essentially opposite. World War I was largely the result of a spiral process in which alliance dynamics magnified the consequences of local disputes, turning them into global issues. World War II, in contrast, has often been considered a deterrence failure in which buck-passing diplomacy by the status quo powers encouraged expansionist powers to risk piecemeal aggression.[25]

Behind these differences in strategic behavior were differing assumptions about the efficacy of strategic offense and defense. In 1914, quick victories that would decisively overturn the military balance were generally thought to be quite feasible. To uphold the balance and to have an effect on the outcome of the fighting, policymakers believed that they had to conclude binding alliances in advance and throw their full weight into the battle at the outset.[26] In the late 1930s, in contrast, policymakers and strategists who had lived through the trench warfare stalemates of 1914–18 believed that conquest was difficult and slow. Consequently, they thought that they could safely stand aside at the outset of a conflict, waiting to intervene only if and when the initial belligerents showed signs of having exhausted themselves.

We contend that given the constant factors of the multipolar checkerboard configuration of power and Germany's aggressive aims, varying perceptions of the offense–defense balance constitute a sufficient explanation for the differing alliance patterns: chain-ganging before World War I and buck-passing before World War II. As we go through the evidence in support of this interpretation, readers may want to keep in mind the following alternative explanations and our reasons for rejecting them.

Alternative Explanations for the Differing Alliance Patterns

Franco–Soviet Ideological Differences.   It is occasionally argued that a balancing alliance failed to form in the 1930s owing to the deep ideological distrust between France and the Soviet Union. This ignores the fact that republican France and autocratic Russia managed to form a tight alliance before World War I, despite their deep ideological differences.[27]

The Creation of Independent States in Eastern Europe.   It is sometimes argued that the creation of independent states in East Europe, especially Poland, hindered Franco–Soviet security cooperation by depriving the Soviet Union of a common frontier with Germany. But after September 1939, Stalin did have a common frontier with Hitler, and he still passed the buck.

The Lesson that Tight Alliances Cause Wars.   It might be argued that tight alliances were shunned owing to the apparent lesson of 1914 that tight alliances cause wars. Even though today's scholars may argue that it was the offensive strategies of 1914 that caused the tight alliances, interwar observers may not have understood this underlying cause.[28] Thus, they may have passed the buck not because perceived defensive advantages made it attractive but, rather, because they wanted to avoid what they thought were reckless alliance strategies. We have uncovered little evidence in favor of this interpretation, but it was not a major focus of our research.

Cost Minimization.   It might be argued that states passed the buck in the 1930s simply because the experience of 1914–18 had radically increased their perceptions of the cost of fighting. This explanation overlaps with our own, since one of the reasons that war was seen as too costly to fight was the expectation that defense dominance would create a slow-moving war of appalling attrition. It differs from our argument, however, in that we see policymakers making essentially strategic decisions driven by the security interests of their states and not by an absolute horror at inordinate bloodshed. Stalin passed the buck even though bloodshed obviously did not trouble him. Moreover, as we argue below, France and Britain passed the buck less than the cost-minimization explanation would lead us to expect.

Germany's Greater Relative Power.   It might be argued that France and Britain adopted defensive buck-passing strategies in the 1930s because they were weaker relative to Germany at that time than they had been in 1914. But defensive buck-passing is the preferred strategy of weak or declining powers only when defense is perceived to have the advantage and thus offers compensation for weakness. When offense is perceived to have the advantage, weak powers compensate through surprise attack, and declining powers compensate through preventive aggression. Logically, Germany's greater power should have made no difference, independent of assessments of offensive and defensive advantage.

Case Study: World War I

Germany: A Strategy for Decisive Victory.   The mainspring driving everyone's strategic calculations in 1914 was the Schlieffen Plan, Germany's strategy for a rapid knockout blow against France and a subsequent campaign against Russia. Whether German war aims were expansionism, self-defense, or "extended deterrence" of Russian pressure on Austria, the German General Staff argued that strategic circumstances dictated that any European war would have to be fought in this way.[29]

To say that this strategy was predicated on an erroneous belief in "offensive advantage" would be too simple. Schlieffen and his collaborators understood that increasing firepower enhanced the tactical advantage of the entrenched defender and that railroad mobility would help a country defend its own territory. However, he also argued that trenches could be outflanked, that railroads would allow a centrally positioned attacker to beat its opponents piecemeal, and that the slowness of Russian mobilization created a "window of opportunity" for implementing such a strategy.

In this sense, Schlieffen saw an offensive advantage for Germany, which he generalized through the maxim that "if one is too weak to attack the whole, one should attack a section."[30]

German strategy was shaped even more strongly by fear of the offensive opportunities open to Germany's opponents. Schlieffen's mentor, the elder Moltke, had concluded that Germany could "extend deterrence" to Austria by mounting a limited attack on Russia in the East and maintaining a positional defense against France in the West. If France balked at attacking stout German defenses in the Saar, the war might be kept localized to Eastern Europe. Schlieffen, however, believed that France would rather easily overrun those defenses if Germany turned the bulk of its army eastward. Consequently, France would have to be disarmed before Germany could turn its attention to Russia.

In short, because Schlieffen and his successors greatly exaggerated France's offensive power and somewhat exaggerated their own, Germany adopted a war plan ensuring that a limited war in Eastern Europe would immediately escalate to a decisive showdown involving all of Europe's great powers. Moreover, the Schlieffen Plan increased Germany's strategic dependency on Austria by weakening German forces facing Russia early in a war. This meant that Germany had to run risks to keep Austria's strategic power intact, making the outbreak of an East European war all the more likely. In general, perceptions of offensive advantages and the adoption of offensive strategies led to unconditional alliances and aggressive balancing behavior.[31]

France: Offensive Advantages and Support for Russia.   When the defender enjoys a net strategic advantage, even a materially inferior power may feel secure. In the years before World War I, however, French authorities exaggerated the advantages of the attacker and thus concluded that a tight alliance with Russia was needed to offset the threat posed by Germany's larger population, army, and material base.

After the 1911 Moroccan crisis, in which Russia had offered only tepid support of France in its confrontation with Germany, the French resolved to tighten their alliance with Russia at all costs.[32] Since active Russian help was seen as essential in parrying the danger from a German offensive, France concluded that the danger of being entrapped in a Russo–German dispute over the Balkans was less worrisome than the danger of being abandoned by Russia in some new Franco–German crisis.[33] Indeed, some French officials concluded that it would be desirable for a war to arise over a Balkan issue, since that would ensure Russia's active participation. France was willing to balance aggressively in order to preclude Russian passivity.

Poincaré, the French President elected in the nationalist upsurge after the Moroccan crisis, was consequently more willing than his predecessors to support Russian efforts to form an alliance of the small Balkan powers against Austria. As it turned out, the Balkan states themselves were more interested in liberating European Turkey. To deter Serbia from excessive territorial aggrandizement as a consequence of the victory over Turkey, Austria mobilized part of its army. As a result, throughout November 1912, Russia and France confronted difficult decisions about what military measures to take in response to Austria's partial mobilization and what to do if Austria attacked Serbia. Though it would be an exaggeration to say that the French actively sought war on this occasion, they seem to have been more keen for the Russians to take military measures than the Russians were themselves.[34]

The Russians did take some precautionary steps, delaying the discharge of a year's cohort of draftees and mobilizing a light security force on the Austro-Hungarian frontier.[35] For the most part, however, the Russians did not think that the situation was especially dangerous and sought to avoid provoking a needless escalation. They believed that Germany was restraining Austria and that Austria's partial mobilization had made a full mobilization against Russia more complicated rather than easier.[36] Russian caution was also based on an emergency review of Russia's material preparedness for war, which concluded that stocks were so low that Russia could not fight.[37]

According to A. J. P. Taylor, the Russians needed to find a scapegoat for their own timidity and "tried again and again to make Poincaré say that he would not support them if they went to war for the sake of Serbia, but Poincaré refused to be caught,"[38] telling the Russian ambassador that "if Russia goes to war, France will also."[39] Even more amazing was an interview in which French Defense Minister Alexandre Millerand took to task the Russian military attaché in Paris for his government's weak response to Austrian military measures. At issue was "the hegemony of Austria throughout the entire Balkan peninsula," Millerand told him. If Russia fails to pick up the challenge, he said, "it is not our fault: we are ready."[40] Similarly, the Russian ambassador reported that French generals saw great advantages in fighting a war in which Austria's strength would be dissipated in a Balkan campaign.[41]

In short, far from buck-passing in the crises of 1912 and 1914, France seems to have been at least as eager to stand up for Russian interests as were the Russians themselves. This contrasts sharply with the extremely tepid support that France offered Russia in the 1909 showdown over Bosnia-Herzegovina.[42] The change in French calculations was primarily due to their belief after the 1911 Moroccan crisis that war between France and Germany was close to inevitable. Thus, abandonment by Russia became a greater risk than entrapment in Russia's quarrels.

Another factor promoting the tightening of the alliance was the rise of the doctrine of *offensive à outrance*, which was accompanied by the presumption that a decisive victory or defeat would be achieved with great speed on the Franco-German front.[43] For this reason, the French felt more dependent on rapid aid from Russia at the earliest possible moment, and they pressed for a premature Russian offensive against East Prussia and offered to pay for the railroads needed to support this maneuver. Greater French faith in their own offensive prospects may also have increased the attractiveness of fighting Germany, especially under circumstances in which Austria's forces would be diverted to the Balkans.[44] In this way, the belief in offensive advantage promoted aggressive balancing behavior.

Russia: Short War Expectations and a Commitment to France. The growing belief that the clash of the French and German offensives would lead to an extremely rapid decision in the West also led to a tightening of Russia's commitment to France. This is an especially interesting case because it helps to refute an alternative explanation for balancing and buck-passing choices — namely, that states seek balancing alliances when they believe that they are the next target on the aggressor's list, but they try to pass the buck when they believe that others will be attacked first.

As late as 1910, the Russian General Staff believed that Germany would direct its main offensive toward Russia if war broke out over a Balkan dispute.[45] Despite seeing themselves as the most immediately threatened power, defense-minded Russian staff officers resisted committing themselves to a tighter French alliance. Though they thought Germany was more likely to attack eastward, they thought that Germany might send the bulk of its forces against France if war arose over some bilateral Franco–German dispute. In that event, they believed that it would be unnecessary and ruinous to agree to a hasty Russian offensive into East Prussia. The Russian attaché in Berlin told his French colleague that Russia's offensive could succeed only after its mobilization was completed and thus would have to lag two weeks behind that of France. Noting that "Napoleon's principle was to act with all his forces united," the Russian insisted that "we should not risk compromising this success by taking the offensive prematurely." The French attaché rebutted that "in the case of two allied armies, such as ours, the true application of the principle would consist not in waiting for the complete concentration of Russian forces, but rather in acting together at the moment when the French and Russian armies could produce simultaneously the maximum effect."[46]

Soon the Russians began to accept the logic of this argument. Even though the Russians came to believe that Germany would almost certainly attack first in the West, this did not reduce their dependency on the French alliance. On the contrary, they now desired a tighter alliance on French terms because they feared that France would be defeated without it. After about 1911, the Russians increasingly accepted the view that the collision of the *offensive à outrance* and the simultaneous German offensive would lead to a rapid decision, one way or the other. Russian planning documents now began to express fears of an immediate rout of the French, leading to a separate peace that would give Germany a free hand in the East.[47] As one military official argued, Russia should mount an early offensive "to prevent Germany from finishing with France or weakening her in order to have the possibility of redeploying forces against us."[48]

In fact, in August 1914, Russia did invade East Prussia hastily, not waiting for the full mobilization of the Russian army or even of the supply trains of the attacking units. One result was that the Germans transferred two army corps to East Prussia from the second echelon of the offensive in the West, perhaps marginally easing France's burden at the battle of the Marne. Another result was the encirclement and destruction of a Russian army of one hundred thousand men at the battle of Tannenberg.

This disaster has often been explained by the assertion that Russian strategy was held in thrall by French financial hegemony. Recent Soviet archival scholarship shows, however, that changes in Russian strategy were not extracted as the price for railroad loans. Rather, the headlong rush to Tannenberg was caused by Russian fears that the clash of offensive strategies would lead to a rapid decision in the West, forcing Russia to act hastily in order to have any chance of influencing the outcome.[49]

In short, Germany's decision to attack France first could have allowed Russia to pass the buck, waiting on developments in the West before committing forces to the fray. Indeed, some Russians advocated a strategy of initially standing aside in order to exploit German weakness after a slow, bloody, Pyrrhic victory over France. Instead, Russia chose to balance aggressively and unconditionally out of the fear that the German offensive might be quick, relatively bloodless, and decisive for the European balance of power.

Britain: Defensive Advantages. Though some British strategists shared Russia's fears of a lightning French defeat, Britain had the English Channel, the British fleet, and the resources of the British Empire to buffer it from the consequences of a shift in the continental military balance. More so than Russia, Britain could afford to wait on developments, seeking accommodation with Germany and Austria up to the very end and limiting Britain's initial liability to an expeditionary force of some four divisions.[50] Moreover, it was not unreasonable for the British to believe that French and Russian power would suffice to contain German expansionism. Consequently, it made sense for Britain to limit its involvement in the attritional campaign in order to emerge from the war as the strongest, least damaged power.

During this period, as in the late 1930s, British policymakers sought to contribute "the smallest amount of money and the smallest number of men with which we may hope, some day, to win the war," through a blockade of the German economy and free riding on French casualties.[51] Lloyd George, for example, anticipated in February 1912 that the German offensive in France would bog down in a stalemate and that modest British efforts would suffice to maintain French morale.[52] Meanwhile, as David French has noted, Britain's own financial strength and expanded military forces would be husbanded "so that Britain would have the strongest army of all the belligerents when the time came to make peace."[53] This approach changed decisively only in 1916, when French resources and morale came near exhaustion and when it seemed likely that Russia would be knocked out of the war if Britain continued its strategy of limited liability.[54]

Thus, in 1914, Britain was the outlier, the country with the most invulnerable defensive position and the country with the most limited, conditional commitment to its allies. While Britain did not entirely pass the buck, it did take advantage of its protected position to pass costs and risks to France and Russia until their collapse seemed imminent.

For each of the major powers before 1914, there was a close connection between the perception of offensive advantage and the adoption of a strategy of aggressive, unconditional balancing. France and Russia tightened their alliance when French strategy became more offensive and when the expectation of a rapid and decisive victory, one way or the other, became more prevalent. Fearing a collapse of the western front, Russia accepted major self-sacrifices to bail France out, despite the temptation offered by the Schlieffen Plan to ride free on French efforts. Britain, in contrast, exploited its special defensive advantages to limit its liability until the strategic situation was clarified in the opening engagements.

Case Study: World War II

Germany: Hitler's Strategy of Piecemeal Expansion. Hitler's strategy in the late 1930s was the opposite of Schlieffen's earlier strategy. Instead of trying to overturn the European balance of power in one bold stroke, Hitler sought to accomplish this in a series of lightning campaigns against diplomatically isolated victims. Especially important in this strategy was the capture of Czechoslovakia's thirty-four divisions and its heavy industrial complex, the Skoda works. Through this piecemeal aggression, Hitler had by 1941 achieved an industrial and raw materials base that would allow him to prosecute a long war against the Soviet Union, despite the British blockade.[55]

A sufficient explanation for the German adoption of this piecemeal strategy of expansion is the buck-passing diplomacy of the other powers. Perhaps if Hitler had been tightly encircled by a Franco–Soviet alliance, he would have sought a Schlieffen-type strategic solution. But the buck-passing of his opponents meant that the easier, piecemeal route was available, so Hitler took it. What was important in this case was not so much German perceptions of the relative advantages of offense and defense but, rather, the perceptions of Germany's opponents on that dimension. Hitler himself was usually optimistic about offensive schemes, though even he expected General Heinz Guderian's blitz through the Ardennes in May 1940 to yield only a limited victory and not the utter collapse of France. Many German generals, steeped in the lessons of World War I, were even more pessimistic about the prospects for armored blitzkrieg breakthroughs.[56] But because those same lessons led Germany's opponents to adopt strategies of passive buck-passing, the Germans never had to face the hard question of whether offense was easy enough to defeat all of Europe in a single campaign, the task that Schlieffen had confronted. Instead, Hitler had only to consider whether offense was feasible enough to lay low one enemy at a time.

The Soviet Union: Stalin's Strategy of Entrapment and Buck-Passing
Two key assumptions shaped Stalin's alliance diplomacy. The first was that France and Britain could hold out for a long time against German attacks, in part owing to the advantages of the defender, even if the Soviet Union offered them no assistance. Even if Germany did defeat France, a victory won through a grueling attritional campaign would be pyrrhic, leaving the free-riding Soviet Union in a strengthened position vis-à-vis the other powers. Khrushchev later reported that Stalin had been not only dismayed but also truly surprised by the collapse of France in 1940. "Couldn't they put up any resistance at all?" complained the stunned dictator to his Politburo colleagues.[57]

Stalin's dismay and surprise were due in part to his overrating of the strength of France and Britain. In his March 1939 speech warning that he would not pull others' chestnuts out of the fire for them, Stalin argued that "the non-aggressive, democratic states are unquestionably stronger . . . both economically and militarily" than Germany and could therefore resist Germany on their own.[58] In part, however, Stalin's reactions were also due to his overrating of the relative strength of the defense. General D. G. Pavlov, whom one historian ironically labels "Stalin's Guderian," returned from the Spanish Civil War and convinced Stalin that massed-armor blitzkrieg offensives were infeasible.[59] Consequently, Stalin overrated not only the defensive strength of France but also that of Poland.[60]

The second assumption behind Stalin's diplomacy was that Germany might get embroiled with the West first if the Soviet Union adopted a stance that was militarily strong but diplomatically nonprovocative. This view was often expressed in terms of the Leninist theory of interimperialist contradictions, which would arise from the uneven growth of the capitalist powers and the consequent need to fight for a redivision of the colonial spoils. As early as 1925, Stalin held the view that if war comes "we shall have to take action, but we shall be the last to do so in order to throw the decisive weight into the scales."[61]

Proceeding from the two assumptions of defensive advantage and interimperialist contradictions, Stalin maneuvered to embroil Germany with the West and to pass to France the costs of checking German revisionism. In this, Stalin was greatly aided by the fact that France had a common border with Germany and alliance commitments to Czechoslovakia and Poland, whereas the Soviet Union did not. At the time of the Munich crisis, for example, Soviet diplomacy tried to lure France to honor the Czech alliance by promising to help Czechoslovakia if France did too. Those who debate whether Stalin's support for "collective security" was sincere in this instance miss the point. If France had agreed to these conditions, a German attack on Czechoslovakia would have triggered a major engagement of French and German forces at the Siegfried line. Meanwhile, even if Rumania allowed the Soviets to send some troops into Slovakia across Rumania's limited rail connections, neutral Poland would have prevented German and Soviet forces from becoming fully engaged. In short, Stalin was pursuing a strategy of limited liability in 1938 as a means to lure France and Germany into an attritional campaign that would debilitate both of them.[62]

Of course, if Germany conquered Poland, Stalin would lose his buffer, making a buck-passing strategy riskier and more difficult to arrange. France and Britain made Stalin's task easier, however, by guaranteeing their support for Poland after Hitler occupied Czechoslovakia. This greatly increased the likelihood that Hitler's next target after Poland would be France rather than the Soviet Union.

Thus, by the end of 1939, the Soviet Union was in a position strikingly analogous to that of Russia at the end of 1913. In the long run, a Russo-German war was likely to occur, but it would almost certainly be preceded by a Franco-German campaign. In both instances, Russia had an incentive to delay the confrontation for two or three years, when its military strength relative to Germany's would peak. Moreover, in both instances, the current military balance favored Germany over France only slightly.

Despite these similar circumstances, imperial Russia chose a strategy of aggressive balancing, whereas Stalin chose buck-passing. This was not due to the ideological antipathy between Soviet Russia and bourgeois France, which was only a little greater than that between reactionary Russia and bourgeois France. Rather, the available evidence suggests that it was due to Stalin's stronger faith in the power of the defense.[63] If Stalin had understood that Germany could conquer France in a month, he probably would have acted just as Russia had in August 1914, mounting a simultaneous offensive regardless of the insufficiently prepared condition of his forces.

France: Defensive Advantages and Buck-Passing. French strategy in 1938–39 was powerfully influenced by the desire to pass the costs of France's defense to Britain and by the perception, based on French experiences in World War I, that offense was much more difficult than defense. However, the French inclination to pass the buck was not all-consuming. In 1939, France might have gambled on offering Hitler a free hand in the East, passing all the costs of French defense to Poland and the Soviet Union. Instead, France agreed to join in a guarantee of Poland, thereby passing only some of the costs of French defense to Britain. Likewise, French confidence in the holding power of the defense was not absolute. If it had been, France could have extended the Maginot line to the English Channel and remained indifferent to the alliance possibilities with Britain, Poland, and the Low Countries.

In fact, French strategy was more complex. The French believed that they would lose if they fought a long war alone against Germany, but they would win a defensive war fought with the assistance of a fully mobilized Britain. French strategy, including both its balancing and buck-passing aspects, was aimed at achieving this end.[64]

This perspective explains the most puzzling aspect of French strategic behavior: France's refusal to fight on extremely favorable terms in September 1938 and its agreement to fight on extremely unfavorable terms a year later. At the time of the Munich crisis, the French potentially had strategic mastery in Europe. To overcome Czechoslovakia's thirty-four crack divisions and formidable frontier fortifications, Hitler planned to use — and would have had to use — the bulk of his army and air force. This would have left France with a seven-to-one advantage in the West. At this time, the Siegfried line (or Westwall) was only 5 percent complete, with recently poured concrete that had not yet set.

By September 1939, the Siegfried line consisted of 11,283 bunkers, in contrast to the 517 of a year before. The German army available for action in the West during the Polish campaign had thirty-five divisions, seven of which were first line, as opposed to only eight divisions in total in 1938. In light of the deficiencies of the French army in offensive operations, these force balances suggest that even an all-out assault on the Siegfried line in September 1939 would not have saved Poland. The weak probes actually carried out by the French were probably the only offensives that were possible under the circumstances.[65]

The French seem to have made no gain, therefore, from declaring war as a result of Hitler's invasion of Poland. They succeeded only in ensuring that they, and not Russia, would be Hitler's next target. Thus, it is ironic that some historians have branded Foreign Minister Georges Bonnet a traitor for allegedly offering Hitler a free hand in the East.[66] Under the circumstances, luring Hitler eastward would seem to have been a vastly superior course to guaranteeing Poland.

The paradoxical reversal in French behavior between September 1938 and September 1939 was due to the change in Britain's attitude. In 1938, Britain offered no help in a war to save Czechoslovakia. By 1939, however, Britain's guarantee to Poland and its decision to increase the size of the British army gave the French reason to expect that if they joined in the British guarantee, Britain would be prepared to deploy a significant expeditionary force in France about six months after the outbreak of war. During this interval, France would be protected by the time needed to occupy Poland and by the winter. Thus, British aid plus defensive advantage would suffice to protect France from Germany at a tolerable price in French lives. In this sense, France's guarantee to Poland was part of a buck-passing strategy predicated on the expectation of defensive advantage.

French perceptions of a qualified defensive advantage played an important role at several stages of decision making. Often, however, assessments of defensive advantage seem to have been less a cause of buck-passing diplomacy than a manipulated rationalization of it. For example, during the Munich crisis, when French Chief of Staff Maurice Gamelin briefed French politicians about the scenario of France attacking the Westwall, he portrayed a bloody campaign with no possibility of rapid results — in short, "a modernized Somme."[67] However, when Gamelin briefed British Prime Minister Neville Chamberlain in September 1938, he argued that a joint Franco–British offensive would surely be successful, owing to the incompletion of German fortifications as well as their lack of trained reservists and raw materials. Alexander Cadogan, a British participant, astutely observed that what the French really had in mind was a "squib offensive (to bring us in) and then retirement on Maginot Line to wait (6 months) for our Kitchener armies."[68] It also smacks of a manipulated double standard that in Gamelin's conversations with French politicians, he depicted the Westwall as a tough nut to crack while predicting a German walkover of the elaborate Czech fortification system.[69]

If the French selectively overrated German defenses, they did not greatly overrate Poland's ability to defend itself. Gamelin understood that Poland would be destroyed, with or without a Franco–British declaration of war. He argued, however, that it would buy France six months, which it did, during which British forces would start to arrive.[70]

Likewise, the French did not greatly overrate their ability to defend themselves behind the Maginot line, even if the line were extended to the sea. Prime Minister Daladier believed that "France could not make war alone against Germany," echoing the views of the French Chiefs of Staff that "France cannot long withstand effectives three times as numerous."[71] Rather than complete the Maginot line, which might encourage Britain to ride free on French defense, French leaders thought it better to leave the invasion routes through Belgium open, thus luring Britain into a joint defense of the Low Countries.[72] But once Britain was entrapped, the French seem to have been overconfident in the efficacy of their defenses.

This selective and partial overrating of the efficacy of defense strongly implies that the desire for buck-passing was driving the estimates of the relative strength of offense and defense, rather than the reverse. Alleged offensive advantages, such as the ease with which the Germans could bomb Paris, were also invoked whenever they served to justify taking no action without British assistance. This raises the question of whether the fear of the high costs of fighting might have been the ultimate force shaping French strategy and not perceptions of defensive advantage per se. This simplification fails, however, to explain the Polish guarantee. If France had been single-mindedly bent on minimizing combat casualties, the best strategy would have been to offer no guarantee to

Poland, hoping that Hitler's ultimate aim was the Ukraine and not France. This might have been risky, jeopardizing Britain's continental commitment if Hitler were to strike France first, but it was not an unreasonable gamble, since France's own estimates were that Hitler's main goals lay in the East.[73]

Instead of gambling on passing the whole costs of the war to the Soviets, France took what it thought was the safer but more costly course of passing part of the costs of fighting to Britain. It was because France overrated the chances of a successful defense with Britain's help that this policy looked superior. Though perceptions of defensive advantage were manipulated in the service of a buck-passing diplomacy, there was also at bottom a real perception that France and Britain together could stalemate Germany, as they had in 1914–18, aided by the inherent advantages of the defender.[74]

Arguably, this left France with the worst of all possible strategies. If France had had more faith in the holding power of the defense, the Maginot line might have been extended to the Channel and the Polish guarantee would have been shunned, even at the loss of British support. That is, France would have tried to pass the buck entirely to Russia, rather than partially to Britain, while preparing to fight successfully on its own if that plan misfired. If, on the other hand, France had had more confidence in offensive operations, supporting Czechoslovakia in 1938 might have looked more attractive. As it was, the British expeditionary force amounted to only four divisions by May 1940, a measure of the illusory success of French buck-passing.[75]

Britain: A Strategy of Limited Liability. Like France, Britain did not count on riding scot-free on inherent defensive advantages and the balancing efforts of other powers. Nonetheless, Britain did count heavily on such advantages to allow it to contribute a minimum to upholding the balance of power as well as the luxury of waiting until the last minute to see what that minimum would be. In short, Britain pursued a strategy of limited liability, based on the defensive advantage provided by the English Channel and on the expectation that a new European war would be a slow-moving rerun of the last one. Chamberlain, both before and after September 1939, thought that French defenses were so strong that Hitler might not even attack them, that Germany would be worn down by a long blockade, and that Hitler's only offensive option would be to try to grab Rumania's oil to help him endure the *Sitzkrieg*.[76]

The Munich crisis is easily explainable in these terms. The specter of a defensive attritional land war, coupled with the fear of a costly air war, gave Britain a strong incentive to make sure that war was absolutely unavoidable before deciding to fight. At the same time, confidence in the Maginot line and the extra cushion provided by Britain's off-shore position gave the British the luxury of waiting until the evidence of Hitler's intentions was all in. As Cadogan remarked after the Munich crisis, "I know that it is said that Mitteleuropa will turn round and rend us. But many things may happen before that."[77]

The puzzling Polish guarantee also seems more sensible when viewed in the light of a strategy of limited liability, anchored on France's apparently formidable defensive military power. Like the French, the British Chiefs of Staff had few illusions that they could take any action to prevent the destruction of Poland. Only the Soviets could stop Hitler in the East, they believed, and then only if Germany attacked the Soviet Union, which was devoid of offensive power.[78] They did believe, however, that Poland might take months to conquer, exacting attrition on German forces and buying time for preparing a defense of the Low Countries.[79] Of course, Polish efforts might have achieved this result without a Franco-British guarantee. Nevertheless, as Brian Bond indicates, "Halifax and Chamberlain feared that the Poles were about to do a deal with Germany which would demolish the hope of a second front in the east."[80]

Another important aim of the guarantee was its effect on France. The British tended to rate the Maginot line and, more generally, France's defensive posture quite highly.[81] The secretary of state for war, Leslie Hore-Belisha, even argued that Britain should announce irrevocably that no expeditionary force would go to the continent under any circumstances, for then France would extend the Maginot line to the sea and give up the game of luring Britain to help defend the invasion corridor across Belgium.[82] This would make both Britain and France more secure — and at France's expense.

The more typical view, however, was that it would harm British security if France mounted a defense on the French borders. Instead, Britain had to induce France to mount a forward defense of the Low Countries to prevent Germany from using them as a base for air attacks on Britain.[83] To make sure that France was willing and able to mount such a forward defense, Britain considered it worthwhile to agree to a limited British commitment to the continent.

Beyond this, after the collapse of Czechoslovak power, there was even a fear that France proper might fold under German pressure. The British Chiefs of Staff, for example, worried that "France might give up the unequal struggle unless supported with the assurance that we should assist them to the utmost."[84] Nonetheless, Britain still held to the assumption of defensive advantage, which implied that a small British force with a primarily moral impact would probably suffice to stiffen French resistance. Defensive advantage would permit Britain the luxury of limiting its initial liability, awaiting further developments to see whether a greater contribution was needed.

Robert Vansittart captured the essence of British thinking:

> We are proceeding on two assumptions both of which I am sure will be falsified: first that France can hold out on two or perhaps three frontiers [German, Italian, and Spanish] with no expeditionary force from us. . . . Secondly we

are assuming that the war, if it comes, will be a long one and we must therefore lay great stress on conserving our [financial] staying power.[85]

Though Vansittart offered this characterization in early 1938, it still captures Britain's basic thinking even after the Polish guarantee. The strategy was still one of limited liability based on the exploitation of defensive advantage and the balancing efforts of others. After April 1939, however, there was a mild upward adjustment in the estimate of the minimal British liability needed to ensure that those balancing forces would operate successfully. In this way, Britain hoped to strike an optimal trade-off between the benefits of riding free and the benefits of balancing aggressively, guaranteeing British security at a minimal cost. If in retrospect the trade-off appears less than optimal to some, that is because the expectation of defensive advantage was too sanguine and not because British deductions from that assumption were faulty.

Finally, the air power element in British liability calculations merits additional attention because it is especially relevant to the choice between strategic deterrence and strategic defense. One of the reasons that Chamberlain appeased Hitler at Munich was his exaggerated estimate of German strategic bombing capabilities and his fear that Britain's own retaliatory capability would not deter attacks on British cities. After the Munich crisis, Chamberlain pushed for a reorientation of British air power expenditures from bombers to fighters. Believing these efforts to be successful, he concluded by mid-1939 that a German air attack on Britain would probably fail. This allowed him to guarantee Poland with less fear of the immediate casualties that this might produce.[86] By analogy, ballistic missile defenses, if they were believed to be highly effective, might encourage future policymakers to be more assertive in their balancing behavior.

Chain-Ganging and Buck-Passing in World Wars I and II

To sum up the findings from the two world wars, in every case perceptions of offensive advantage were associated with chain-ganging — that is, with unconditional balancing behavior. Conversely, perceptions of defensive advantage were associated with buck-passing — that is, with strategies of limited liability. Given a choice, states preferred to pass the costs of balancing to other states or to await developments before making irrevocable commitments. But when offensive advantages were believed to make states extremely vulnerable and wars short, buck-passing strategies were deemed too risky.

This hypothesis is more successful than some obvious competitors. For example, it is not true that states balance when they believe they are an aggressor's next target but pass the buck when they believe they are farther down on the list. If first-line states are seen as vulnerable but willing and able to balance if assisted, second-line states tend to accept the buck.

Likewise, it is not true that buck-passing has been driven strictly by a craven desire to minimize the costs of fighting, regardless of strategic consequences. The French decision to join in guaranteeing Poland was a strategic attempt to ensure the resources needed to stalemate Germany in a costly attritional campaign. If the French had been concerned only with minimizing casualties, but at a greater strategic risk, they would have shunned the British guarantee to Poland and tried instead to embroil Hitler and Stalin. Similarly, Stalin's buck-passing was aimed not at saving the lives of Soviet soldiers per se but, rather, at conserving Soviet power until the decisive moment when the other powers would be exhausted by the first round of fighting.

Finally, the evidence cited above belies the commonly expressed view that appeasers in Britain and France did not calculate strategically at all but were simply reacting to public opinion or inchoate emotion. "Chamberlain was not primarily, if at all, motivated by strategic factors," states a recent historian;[87] likewise, "muddle not machination" is said to have been at the bottom of French policy.[88] Domestic political pressures and other sources of perceptual bias undoubtedly *influenced* strategic calculations. But this is not the same as saying that no calculations were made.

This was the case in 1914 as well as in 1938–39.[89] In 1914, the military had been highly successful in propagating what General Joseph Joffre himself later called a "cult of the offensive," which served military organizational interests. Conversely, in 1938, there existed a civilian "cult of the defensive," headed by B. H. Liddell Hart and others who sought to use any strategic rationalization to avoid a British commitment to fighting a large land war on the European continent. Critics of Liddell Hart have clearly established that the strategy of limited liability came first for him and that only later did he develop his ideas of defensive advantage in armored warfare in order to explain how France could stalemate Germany without the help of a large British expeditionary force.[90]

The point is that strategic calculations were in fact made, if only to sell a policy as plausible, given a certain view of the offense-defense balance. Indeed, policy tended to dovetail with the logic of those arguments. Though these arguments may have sometimes been ex post facto rationalizations rather than root causes, assessments of offensive and defensive advantage were directly tied to grand strategic choices.

These choices had effects on the stability of the system. Strategies of aggressive balancing, based on perceptions of offensive advantage, and passive buck-passing, based on perceptions of defensive advantage, were both destabilizing. These instabilities were triggered by the fact that the underlying strategic assumptions were incorrect. Thus, the European confrontation of July 1914 escalated because of the expectation that states were vulnerable to conquest, but it was prolonged by the fact that they were not. Conversely, Hitler's opponents failed to appreciate that blitzkrieg operations against isolated targets would allow Germany to seize the assets needed to mount a serious bid for European hegemony. By 1941, for example, 40 percent of German steel production came from outside the Reich's 1937 borders.[91]

However, perceptions of defensive advantage need not always lead to this result, even when the aggressor occupies the center of the alliance checkerboard. In the late 1880s, Germany was dissuaded from attacking anyone because each of its opponents looked individually impregnable. However, in the late 1930s, perceptions of defensive advantage were destabilizing because the status quo states saw stronger defensive advantages than did the aggressors. In checkerboard conditions, therefore, the aggressor was not dissuaded from attacking isolated opponents, whereas the status quo states were dissuaded from aiding their allies by attacking the aggressor's rear.

CONCLUSIONS AND ISSUES FOR RESEARCH

Contemporary balance-of-power theory has become too parsimonious to yield determinate predictions about state alliance strategies in multipolarity. Waltz's theory predicts only that multipolarity predisposes states to either of two opposite errors, which we call chain-ganging and buck-passing. To predict which of these two policies will prevail, it is necessary to complicate Waltz's theory by adding a variable from Jervis's theory of the security dilemma: the variable of whether offense or defense is perceived to have the advantage. At least under the checkerboard geographical conditions in Europe before World Wars I and II, perceived offensive advantage bred unconditional alliances, whereas perceived defensive advantage bred free riding on the balancing efforts of others.

The marriage that we propose between Waltz's theory and Jervis's suggests a number of issues for further research as well as a number of applications to current policy analysis. One question of considerable theoretical and policy interest is the source of stability in multipolar periods that lacked major wars. For example, the diplomacy of Bismarck's era managed to avoid the pitfalls of both chain-ganging and buck-passing, despite its multipolar setting. Above, we briefly suggested that this may have been the result of the increasing perception in the 1880s that each of the European powers was individually too well defended to conquer. But Bismarck's limited aims and diplomatic skills may also have been factors. In any event, given the likelihood that the world will become increasingly multipolar, it would be useful to ask what role the offense-defense balance has played in cases in which multipolarity has been managed successfully.

The interaction of polarity and the offense-defense balance might also yield interesting interpretations of regional conflict dynamics outside Europe. The June 1967 Arab – Israeli War might be interpreted as multipolar chain-ganging stemming from perceptions of offensive advantage, whereas the subsequent war of attrition can be seen as Syrian buck-passing stemming from perceptions of a defensive stalemate.[92] Such regional multipolar processes are likely to become a more and more important feature of international politics as the superpowers increasingly withdraw from their overextended positions in the Third World and even in Eastern Europe.

Analytically more difficult are multipolar settings that lack the familiar checkerboard geography which makes one's neighbor an enemy and makes the enemy's neighbor one's friend. Checkerboard balancing hypotheses become decreasingly helpful when sea and air power supplant land power as the dominant factor in the military equation. Insofar as the multipolarity of the twenty-first century is likely to feature the rise of Japan as a major sea and air power, heuristic historical cases of non-checkerboard alliance politics should focus on multipolar naval competition in the Eastern Mediterranean (the nineteenth-century's "Eastern question") or in East Asia.[93]

Nuclear weapons will also have to be factored in to any assessment of multipolar balancing in the future, both because their global reach undermines traditional checkerboard balancing logic and because the nuclear deterrent stalemate is likely to benefit the defender of the status quo.[94] Insofar as nuclear weapons are likely to make each pole individually invulnerable to conquest, a nuclear-armed multipolarity may resemble the stable 1880s more than it will the chain-ganging 1910s or buck-passing 1930s. It cannot be excluded, however, that states with small, vulnerable nuclear arsenals will have to form alliances with larger nuclear powers or with each other to mount a credible deterrent. In that case, the dynamics of chain-ganging and buck-passing may still apply in future nuclear showdowns.

We make no claim to be able to foretell the balancing dynamics of the coming decades. We do claim, however, that realist scholars will have to prepare for this analytic challenge by developing a theory that combines the insights of Waltz's balance-of-power theory and Jervis's security dilemma theory. This is the most parsimonious international system theory that has any hope of explaining and prescribing great power alliance strategies.

NOTES

This article combines the work of two unpublished papers. The theoretical sections are derived from Christensen's "Chained Gangs and Passed Bucks: Waltz and Crisis Management Before the Two World Wars," Columbia University, December 1987. The case study material is based on Snyder's "Offense, Defense and Deterrence in the Twentieth Century," a paper presented at the Conference on the Strategic Defense Initiative, University of Michigan, November 1986. We are grateful to Charles Glaser, Harold Jacobson, Robert Jervis, Stephen Krasner, Helen Milner, David Reppy, Cynthia Roberts, Randall Schweller, Stephen Van Evera, Stephen Walt, Deborah Yarsike, William Zimmerman, and an anonymous reviewer for comments on various earlier drafts. We also thank the Social Science Research Council and the MacArthur Foundation for Christensen's financial support and the Program in International Peace and Security Studies at the University of Michigan for sponsoring Snyder's original paper.

1. Kenneth Waltz, *Theory of International Politics* (Reading, Mass.: Addison-Wesley, 1979).

2. We feel no need to take a position on the epistemological debates surrounding Waltz's theory, spurred in particular by John Ruggie and Robert Cox. We are satisfied to accept Waltz's scheme as what Cox terms a "problem-solving theory." For current purposes, we hope to improve its problem-solving utility rather than to address its deeper epistemological adequacy. See Robert Keohane, ed., *Neorealism and Its Critics* (New York: Columbia University Press, 1986), especially pp. 208 and 214. See also David Dessler, "What's at Stake in the Agent-Structure Debate?" *International Organization* 43 (Summer 1989), pp. 441–74; and John S. Dryzek, Margaret L. Clark, and Garry McKenzie, "Subject and System in International Interaction," *International Organization* 43 (Summer 1989), pp. 475–504.

3. See, for example, Stephen Walt, *The Origins of Alliance* (Ithaca, N.Y.: Cornell University Press, 1987); and Barry Posen, *The Sources of Military Doctrine* (Ithaca, N.Y.: Cornell University Press, 1984). By "theory of foreign policy" we mean a theory whose dependent variable is the behavior of individual states rather than the properties of systems of states. It does not refer to a theory that explains all aspects of a state's foreign policy.

4. Waltz, *Theory of International Politics*, pp. 67 and 165–69.

5. See Robert Jervis, "Cooperation Under the Security Dilemma," *World Politics* 30 (January 1978), pp. 167–214; Stephen Van Evera, "Causes of War," Ph.D. diss., University of California, Berkeley, 1984; Stephen Van Evera, "The Cult of the Offensive and the Origins of the First World War," in Stephen E. Miller, ed., *Military Strategy and the Origins of the First World War* (Princeton, N.J.: Princeton University Press, 1985), pp. 58–107; Stephen Van Evera, "Offense, Defense, and Strategy: When Is Offense Best?" paper presented at the annual meeting of the American Political Science Association, Chicago, 1987. For a work that preceded the publication of Waltz's and Jervis's theories but made many similar points, see George Quester, *Offense and Defense in the International System* (New York: Wiley, 1977), especially chap. 10 on alliance behavior in World War I.

6. In addition to the above-mentioned works by Van Evera, see Posen, *Sources of Military Doctrine*; and Jack Snyder, "Civil-Military Relations and the Cult of the Offensive, 1914 and 1984," in Miller, *Military Strategy*, pp. 139–40. Levy points out that difficulties in measuring offensive and defensive advantage make such judgments problematic for social scientists as well as elusive for policymakers. See Jack S. Levy, "The Offensive/Defensive Balance of Military Technology," *International Studies Quarterly* 28 (June 1984), pp. 219–38.

7. By "determinate predictions" we mean that if all other factors (such as checkerboard geography) are held constant, then knowing the polarity of the system and the perceived offense–defense balance will theoretically suffice

to predict the alliance behavior of states. Of course, in the real world, other factors having some effect on alliance behavior may not be held constant, making our predictions probabilistic rather than strictly "determinate."

8. For related arguments that use the concepts of entrapment and abandonment, see Glenn Snyder, "The Security Dilemma in Alliance Politics," *World Politics* 36 (July 1984), pp. 461–95.
9. Waltz, *Theory of International Politics*, pp. 167–70.
10. Ibid., p. 167.
11. Ibid., p. 165.
12. Posen, *Sources of Military Doctrine*, pp. 232–33.
13. Waltz, *Theory of International Politics*, chaps. 6–9.
14. Ibid., pp. 169 and 171–72.
15. Ibid., chap. 9. This certainly is the view of Waltz's students. See Stephen Walt, "The Case for Finite Containment: Analyzing U.S. Grand Strategy," *International Security* 14 (Summer 1989), pp. 5–49; and Stephen Van Evera, "American Strategic Interests: Why Europe Matters; Why the Third World Doesn't," *Journal of Strategic Studies* 12, 2 (September 1990), pp. 1–51.
16. Posen, *Sources of Military Doctrine*, p. 232. We are grateful to Randall Schweller for helpful comments on this point.
17. This is at least implicit in Waltz's arguments about interdependence in his *Theory of International Politics*, pp. 143–46, juxtaposed to his arguments about the relative invulnerability of the bipolar superpowers, p. 172. Note also Waltz's remarks about firms on p. 135: "More than any other factor, relative size determines the survival of firms. Firms that are large in comparison to most others in their field find many ways of taking care of themselves — of protecting themselves against other large firms."
18. For related discussions, see Posen, *Sources of Military Doctrine*, p. 232; Van Evera, "The Cult of the Offensive," pp. 96–101; Van Evera, "Why Cooperation Failed in 1914," in Kenneth Oye, ed., *Cooperation Under Anarchy* (Princeton, N.J.: Princeton University Press, 1986), especially pp. 83–84; and Walt, *Origins of Alliance*, especially pp. 24–25, fn 31, and pp. 32 and 165–67.
19. For the theory underlying this hypothesis, see Robert Jervis, *Perception and Misperception in International Politics* (Princeton, N.J.: Princeton University Press, 1976), especially chap. 6.
20. See Posen, *Sources of Military Doctrine*; Van Evera, "Causes of War"; Snyder, "Civil-Military Relations"; and Jack Snyder, "International Leverage on Soviet Domestic Change," *World Politics* 41 (October 1989), pp. 1–30. On the cult of the defensive, see John Mearsheimer, *Liddell Hart and the Weight of History* (Ithaca, N.Y.: Cornell University Press, 1988), pp. 107, 111–12, and 128; and Van Evera, "Offense, Defense, and Strategy."
21. Waltz, *Theory of International Politics*, p. 172.
22. Ibid., pp. 165–67.
23. For a detailed description of Czechoslovakia's crucial role in the European balance, see Williamson Murray, *The Change in the European Balance of Power, 1938–1939* (Princeton, N.J.: Princeton University Press, 1984).
24. Stalin's statement of 10 March 1939, cited in Adam Ulam, *Expansion and Coexistence*, 2d ed. (New York: Praeger, 1974), p. 263.
25. This distinction works only as a rough first cut. There were deterrence failure aspects to the 1914 diplomacy. Conversely, even firm, early deterrent threats might not have deterred Hitler's aggression. For a recent corrective along

these lines, see Sean M. Lynn-Jones, "Detente and Deterrence: Anglo-German Relations, 1911–1914," *International Security* 11 (Fall 1986), pp. 121–50. Recent correctives, however, do not negate the main point. Even followers of Fritz Fischer accept that Germany did not want a world war but that it stumbled into it as a result of misguided attempts to ensure German security. For a subtle discussion of these points and a commentary on Fritz Fischer's *German Aims in the First World War* (New York: Norton, 1967) and related works, see Jack S. Levy, "The Role of Crisis Management in the Outbreak of World War I," paper presented at the annual meeting of the International Studies Association, London, 1989, especially pp. 15–16.

26. This argument about World War I, set in a theoretical perspective, is made by Quester in *Offense and Defense*, by Jervis in "Cooperation Under the Security Dilemma," and by Van Evera in "The Cult of the Offensive."

27. Waltz makes this point. See *Theory of International Politics*, p. 125.

28. Van Evera, "The Cult of the Offensive," p. 97. We are grateful to Randall Schweller for raising this issue.

29. For a discussion of the German strategy of 1914 in an alliance context, see Scott Sagan, "1914 Revisited: Allies, Offense, and Instability," *International Security* 11 (Fall 1986), pp. 151–76. See also the dialogue between Scott Sagan and Jack Snyder in "Correspondence: The Origins of Offense and the Consequences of Counterforce," *International Security* 11 (Winter 1986), pp. 187–98. On German strategy more generally, see Gerhard Ritter, *The Schlieffen Plan* (New York: Praeger, 1958); and Jack Snyder, *Ideology of the Offensive: Military Decision-making and the Disasters of 1914* (Ithaca, N.Y.: Cornell University Press, 1984), chaps. 4 and 5.

30. Schlieffen, cited in Snyder, *Ideology of the Offensive*, p. 113.

31. For additional analysis, see Van Evera, "The Cult of the Offensive," especially pp. 96–101.

32. For a perceptive analysis, see A. J. P. Taylor, *The Struggle for Mastery in Europe* (London: Oxford University Press, 1971), pp. 468 and 486.

33. For an analysis of the entrapment–abandonment trade-off in 1914 and in general, see Snyder, "The Security Dilemma in Alliance Politics."

34. Keiger puts this in perspective, arguing that Poincaré was not bellicose. See John Keiger, *France and the Origins of the First World War* (New York: St. Martin's Press, 1983).

35. For what is by far the clearest account of this misunderstood episode, see V. I. Bovykin, *Iz istorii vozniknoveniia pervoi mirovoi voiny: Otnosheniia Rossii i Frantsii v 1912–1914 gg.* (From the history of the origins of the First World War: Relations between Russia and France in 1912–1914) (Moscow: Moskovskii Universitet, 1961), pp. 151–53. See also E. C. Heimreich, *The Diplomacy of the Balkan Wars* (Cambridge, Mass.: Harvard University Press, 1938), p. 216; Louis Garros, "En marge de l'alliance franco-russe, 1902–1914" (A footnote to the Franco-Russian alliance, 1902–1914), *Revue historique de l'armée*, June 1950, p. 33; Frank M. Laney, "The Military Implementation of the Franco-Russian Alliance, 1890–1914," Ph.D. diss., University of Virginia, 1954, p. 390; and Samuel Williamson, "Military Dimensions of Habsburg-Romanov Relations During the Era of the Balkan Wars," in Bela Kiraly and Dimitrije Djordjevic, eds., *East Central European Society and the Balkan Wars* (Boulder, Colo.: Social Science Monographs, 1986), pp. 317–37.

36. See Laney, "The Military Implementation of the Franco-Russian Alliance," p.

402; dispatch by General Marquis de Laguiche, the French military attaché in St. Petersburg, file 7N1478 (6/19 December 1912, 27 November/4 December 1912, and 30 November/13 December 1912) at the French military archive, Chateau de Vincennes; I. V. Bestuzhev, "Bor'ba v Rossii po voprosam vneshnei politiki nakanune pervoi mirovoi voiny, 1910–1914 gg." (The struggle in Russia on questions of foreign policy on the eve of the First World War, 1910–1914), *Istoricheskie zapiski*, vol. 75, 1965, p. 63 ff.; Garros, "En marge de l'alliance franco-russe," p. 36; *Documents diplomatiques français* (DDF), series 3, vol. V, no. 52, p. 65; and "Podgotovka pervoi mirovoi voiny" (Preparations for the First World War), *Voenno-istoricheskii zhurnal*, no. 3, 1939, pp. 132–33.

37. See Bovykin, *Iz istorii vozniknoveniia pervoi mirovoi voiny*, p. 136; and A. A. Manikovskii, *Boevoe snabzhenie russkoi armii, 1914–1918 gg.* (Military supply in the Russian army, 1914–1918) (Moscow: Voennyi Redaktsionnyi Sovet, 1923).

38. This is Taylor's apt characterization of the situation in *Struggle for Mastery in Europe*, p. 494.

39. Poincaré, cited by Taylor in ibid., p. 492.

40. Millerand, cited in A. A. Ignat'ev, *Piatdesiat let v stroiu* (Fifty years of service), vol. 1 (Moscow: Khudozhestvennaia Literatura, 1959), p. 506.

41. Unpublished archival documents, cited in Bovykin, *Iz istorii vozniknoveniia pervoi mirovoi voiny*, pp. 137 and 146 ff.

42. *DDF*, series 2, vol. XII, nos. 51, 55, 74, 86, 87, 90, 100, 113, and 266.

43. For example, in March 1910, Lt. Colonel Pellé, the French attaché in Berlin, wrote to General Jean Jules Brun, the Minister of War, that "both on the German side and on the French, the bulk of the active forces of both countries are planned for deployment in first-line armies [near the frontiers]. The victory or defeat of these armies of the first line will very probably decide the outcome of the campaign" by the twentieth or thirtieth day after mobilization. See *DDF*, series 2, vol. XII, no. 453, p. 691.

44. For some pertinent comments on this matter, see Taylor, *Struggle for Mastery in Europe*, p. 486.

45. See *DDF*, series 2, vol. XII, no. 399, p. 611; and Snyder, *Ideology of the Offensive*, chaps. 6 and 7.

46. Conversation between Colonel Mikhelsson and Lt. Colonel Pellé, reported by Pellé to General Brun in March 1910 and cited in *DDF*, series 2, vol. XII, no. 453, p. 695, and no. 467, p. 717.

47. See Valentin Alekseevich Emets, "O roli russkoi armii v pervyi period mirovoi voiny, 1914–1918 gg." (On the role of the Russian army in the first period of the World War, 1914–1918), *Istoricheskie zapiski*, vol. 77, 1965, p. 64.

48. General N. A. Kliuev, chief of staff of the Warsaw military district, cited by Emets in ibid., p. 64.

49. Valentin Alekseevich Emets, *Ocherki vneshnei politiki rossii v period pervoi mirovoi voiny: Vzaimootnosheniia rossii s soiuznikami po voprosam vedeniia voiny* (Sketches of the foreign policy of Russia during the First World War: Relations of Russia with its allies on questions of the conduct of the war) (Moscow: Nauka, 1977), pp. 47–52.

50. Michael Howard, *The Continental Commitment* (London: Temple Smith, 1972).

51. This is Field Marshal William Robertson's apt characterization of the views of Walter Runciman and Reginald McKenna, cited by David French in *British Strategy and War Aims, 1914–1916* (London: Allen & Unwin, 1986), p. 247.

52. French, ibid., p. 3; for related evidence, see also pp. xii, 106, 118, and 245–46.
53. This is French's characterization of Lord Kitchener's views, cited in ibid., pp. 200–201.
54. French, ibid., pp. xii, 119, and 201.
55. See Murray, *Change in the European Balance of Power*. On the tailoring of German military capability for short campaigns and diplomatic intimidation, see Posen, *Sources of Military Doctrine*, especially p. 200.
56. See John Mearsheimer, *Conventional Deterrence* (Ithaca, N.Y.: Cornell University Press, 1983), chap. 4.
57. Nikita Khrushchev, *Khrushchev Remembers*, vol. 1 (Boston: Little, Brown, 1970), p. 134; see also p. 129. According to Deutscher, "the major premise of Stalin's policy and his major blunder" were that "he expected Britain and France to hold their ground for a long time." See Isaac Deutscher, *Stalin* (New York: Oxford University Press, 1949), p. 441.
58. Stalin, cited in John Erickson, *The Soviet High Command* (New York: St. Martin's Press, 1962), p. 513.
59. See John Erickson, *The Road to Stalingrad*, vol. 1 (New York: Harper & Row, 1975), pp. 8 and 26; and Erickson, *Soviet High Command*, p. 537.
60. See Deutscher, *Stalin*, p. 437. This general predisposition to underestimate the feasibility of blitzkrieg may even have lasted past May 1940 and contributed to the false hope that Hitler would not attack in June 1941. Politburo member Andrei Zhdanov believed in 1940 that "Germany is incapable of fighting on two fronts," and even after the fall of France, he considered that Germany was too "bogged down" by the war with England to attack the Soviet Union. Foreign Minister Vyacheslav Molotov said in June 1941 that "only a fool would attack us." See Gavriel Ra'anan, *International Policy Formation in the USSR* (Hamden, Conn.: Archon, 1983), p. 18. On some new revelations along the same lines, see Y. Perechenev, "Ten Volumes About the War," *Moscow News*, no. 38, 20 September 1987, p. 10, citing K. M. Simonov, "Zametki k biografii G. K. Zhukova" (Notes for the biography of G. K. Zhukov), *Voennoistoricheskii zhurnal*, no. 9, 1987, pp. 49–51. We are grateful to Cindy Roberts for this citation.
61. Stalin, cited in Louis Fischer, *Stalin's Road from Peace to War* (New York: Harper & Row, 1969), p. 304.
62. For insightful analyses of the situation, see Telford Taylor, *Munich* (Garden City, N.Y.: Doubleday, 1979), pp. 452–56; and Barry Posen, "Competing Images of the Soviet Union," *World Politics* 39 (July 1987), pp. 579–604.
63. For this evidence, see footnotes 57 and 59–62 above.
64. In *Sources of Military Doctrine*, chap. 4, Posen describes the French military strategy as driven by the desire to pass the costs of fighting to the British.
65. Murray, *Change in the European Balance of Power*, p. 348.
66. For a review of the complexities of the evidence on this, see Anthony Adamthwaite, *France and the Coming of the Second World War, 1936–1939* (London: Frank Cass, 1977), pp. 269–79.
67. Gamelin, cited in ibid., p. 232.
68. Cadogan, cited in ibid., p. 232. Kitchener had organized the expansion of the British army for deployment in France in World War I.
69. Gamelin, cited in ibid., pp. 232–34.
70. Gamelin's opinion of 23 August 1939, cited in ibid., p. 340. See also ibid., p. 311.
71. Daladier, cited in ibid., pp. 226 and 230.

72. Posen, *Sources of Military Doctrine*, chap. 4.
73. Adamthwaite, *France and the Coming of the Second World War*, pp. 252 and 274.
74. For additional evidence in support of this interpretation, see Eleanor M. Gates, *End of the Affair: The Collapse of the Anglo-French Alliance, 1939–40* (Berkeley: University of California Press, 1981), pp. 57–58.
75. Brian Bond, *British Military Policy Between the Two World Wars* (Oxford: Clarendon, 1980), p. 336.
76. Chamberlain's letters to family members, cited in Maurice Cowling, *The Impact of Hitler* (London: Cambridge University Press, 1975), pp. 355–57. See also Bond, *British Military Power*, p. 253; and N. H. Gibbs, *Grand Strategy*, vol. 1, *Rearmament Policy* (London: Her Majesty's Stationery Office, 1976), pp. 637–38. Bond and Gibbs also note, however, that the notions of defensive advantage held by Chamberlain and Leslie Hore-Belisha were not universally held within British official circles. We are grateful to Randall Schweller for help on this point.
77. David Dilks, ed., *The Diaries of Sir Alexander Cadogan, 1938–1945* (London: Cassell, 1971), p. 119.
78. Murray, *Change in the European Balance of Power*, p. 298.
79. Simon Newman, *March 1939: The British Guarantee to Poland* (Oxford: Clarendon, 1976), pp. 155–56.
80. Bond, *British Military Policy*, p. 306.
81. See, for example, the views of Sir John Simon, Chancellor of the Exchequer, cited in Murray, *Change in the European Balance of Power*, p. 274; and the views of the Chiefs of Staff, cited in Newman, *March 1939*, p. 139. See also Adamthwaite, *France and the Coming of the Second World War*, p. 51.
82. Adamthwaite, *France and the Coming of the Second World War*, p. 71.
83. See Murray, *Change in the European Balance of Power*, pp. 276–77; Dilks, *Diaries of Sir Alexander Cadogan*, p. 139; and Bond, *British Military Policy*, p. 297.
84. British Chiefs of Staff, cited in Adamthwaite, *France and the Coming of the Second World War*, p. 253. See also Dilks, *Diaries of Sir Alexander Cadogan*, p. 166. In *Change in the European Balance of Power*, p. 71, Murray argues, mostly by inference, that the British change on the continental commitment in 1939 was due to the loss of Czechoslovakia's thirty-four divisions from the European military equation. In *British Military Policy*, p. 296, Bond notes that Britain's military attaché in Paris took this view.
85. Vansittart, cited in Murray, *Change in the European Balance of Power*, p. 69.
86. For information on Chamberlain's views, see William R. Rock, *Neville Chamberlain* (New York: Twayne, 1969), p. 180; Cowling, *Impact of Hitler*, p. 395; and Ian Colvin, *The Chamberlain Cabinet* (London: Gollancz, 1971), p. 174. For background on air power policy and perceptions, see Posen, *Sources of Military Doctrine*, chap. 5; and Murray, *Change in the European Balance of Power*, pp. 208 and 251–53.
87. Bond, *British Military Policy*, p. 282.
88. Adamthwaite, *France and the Coming of the Second World War*, p. 320.
89. For a discussion of the events in 1914, see Snyder, *Ideology of the Offensive*. For similar points about 1938–39, see Posen, *Sources of Military Doctrine*. In "Causes of War," Van Evera offers a general theory of this type.
90. See Brian Bond and Martin Alexander, "Liddell Hart and De Gaulle: The Doc-

trine of Limited Liability and Mobile Defense," in Peter Paret, ed., *Makers of Modern Strategy*, 2d ed. (Princeton, N.J.: Princeton University Press, 1986), p. 612; and Mearsheimer, *Liddell Hart and the Weight of History*, pp. 107, 111–12, and 128.

91. Murray, *Change in the European Balance of Power*, p. 13.
92. We thank Stephen Walt for suggesting this possibility. Walt's *Origins of Alliances* applies a variant of balance-of-power theory to Middle Eastern case studies.
93. For background, see C. J. Bartlett, *Great Britain and Sea Power, 1815–1853* (Oxford: Clarendon, 1963).
94. For this argument as applied to the present bipolar setting, see Robert Jervis, *The Meaning of the Nuclear Revolution* (Ithaca, N.Y.: Cornell University Press, 1989).

Theory of World Politics: Structural Realism and Beyond

Robert O. Keohane

The author surveys and critically evaluates the work of some contemporary realists,whom he calls "structural realists."

For over 2000 years, what Hans J. Morgenthau dubbed "Political Realism" has constituted the principal tradition for the analysis of international relations in Europe and its offshoots in the New World (Morgenthau, 1966). Writers of the Italian Renaissance, balance of power theorists, and later adherents of the school of *Machtpolitik* all fit under a loose version of the Realist rubric. Periodic attacks on Realism have taken place; yet the very focus of these critiques seems only to reconfirm the centrality of Realist thinking in the international political thought of the West.[1]

Realism has been criticized frequently during the last few years, and demands for a "new paradigm" have been made. Joseph S. Nye and I called for a "world politics paradigm" a decade ago, and Richard Mansbach and John A. Vasquez have recently proposed a "new paradigm for global politics." In both these works, the new paradigm that was envisaged entailed adopting additional concepts — for instance, "transnational relations," or "issue phases" (Keohane & Nye, 1972, esp. pp. 379–

From *Political Science: The State of the Discipline*, ed. Ada W. Finifter (Washington, D.C.: American Political Science Association, 1983). Reprinted by permission of the APSA.

386; Mansbach & Vasquez, 1981, Chapter 4). Yet for these concepts to be useful as part of a satisfactory general theory of world politics, a theory of state action — which is what Realism purports to provide — is necessary. Understanding the general principles of state action and the practices of governments is a necessary basis for attempts to refine theory or to extend the analysis to non-state actors. Approaches using new concepts may be able to supplement, enrich, or extend a basic theory of state action, but they cannot substitute for it.[2]

The fixation of critics and reformers on the Realist theory of state action reflects the importance of this research tradition. In my view, there is good reason for this. Realism is a necessary component in a coherent analysis of world politics because its focus on power, interests, and rationality is crucial to any understanding of the subject. Thus any approach to international relations has to incorporate, or at least come to grips with, key elements of Realist thinking. Even writers who are concerned principally with international institutions and rules, or analysts in the Marxist tradition, make use of some Realist premises. Since Realism builds on fundamental insights about world politics and state action, progress in the study of international relations requires that we seek to build on this core.

Yet as we shall see, Realism does not provide a satisfactory theory of world politics, if we require of an adequate theory that it provide a set of plausible and testable answers to questions about state behavior under specified conditions. Realism is particularly weak in accounting for change, especially where the sources of that change lie in the world political economy or in the domestic structures of states. Realism, viewed dogmatically as a set of answers, would be worse than useless. As a sophisticated framework of questions and initial hypotheses, however, it is extremely valuable.[3]

Since Realism constitutes the central tradition in the study of world politics, an analysis, like this one, of the current state of the field must evaluate the viability of Realism in the penultimate decade of the twentieth century. Doing this requires constructing a rather elaborate argument of my own, precluding a comprehensive review of the whole literature of international relations. I have therefore selected for discussion a relatively small number of works that fit my theme, ignoring entire areas of research, much of it innovative.[4] Within the sphere of work dealing with Realism and its limitations, I have focused attention on several especially interesting and valuable contributions. My intention is to point out promising lines of research rather than to engage in what Stanley Hoffmann once called a "wrecking operation" (Hoffmann, 1960, p. 171).

Since I have written on the subject of Realism in the past, I owe the reader an explanation of where I think my views have changed, and where I am only restating, in different ways, opinions that I have expressed before. This chapter deals more systematically and more sympathetically with Realism than does my previous work. Yet its fundamental argument is consistent with that of *Power and Interdependence*. In that book Nye and I relied on Realist theory as a basis for our structural models of international regime change (Keohane & Nye, 1977, pp. 42–46). We viewed our structural models as attempts to improve the ability of Realist or neo-Realist analysis to account for international regime change: we saw ourselves as adapting Realism, and attempting to go beyond it, rather than rejecting it.

Admittedly, Chapter 2 of *Power and Interdependence* characterized Realism as a descriptive ideal type rather than a research program in which explanatory theories could be embedded. Realist and Complex Interdependence ideal types were used to help specify the conditions under which overall structure explanations of change would or would not be valid; the term, "Realist," was used to refer to conditions under which states are the dominant actors, hierarchies of issues exist, and force is usable as an instrument of policy (Keohane & Nye, 1977, pp. 23–29). Taken as a full characterization of the Realist tradition this would have been unfair, and it seems to have led readers concerned with our view of Realism to focus excessively on Chapter 2 and too little on the attempt, which draws on what I here call structural realism, to account for regime change (Chapters 3–6).[5]

To provide criteria for the evaluation of theoretical work in international politics—Structural Realism, in particular—I employ the conception of a "scientific research programme" explicated in 1970 by the philosopher of science, Imre Lakatos (1970). Lakatos developed this concept as a tool for the comparative evaluation of scientific theories, and in response to what he regarded as the absence of standards for evaluation in Thomas Kuhn's (1962) notion of a paradigm.[6] Theories are embedded in research programs. These programs contain inviolable assumptions (the "hard core") and initial conditions, defining their scope. For Lakatos, they also include two other very important elements: auxiliary, or observational, hypotheses, and a "positive heuristic," which tells the scientist what sorts of additional hypotheses to entertain and how to go about conducting research. In short, a research program is a set of methodological rules telling us what paths of research to avoid and what paths to follow.

Consider a research program, with a set of observational hypotheses, a "hard core" of irrefutable assumptions, and a set of scope conditions. In the course of research, anomalies are bound to appear sooner or later: predictions of the theory will seem to be falsified. For Lakatos, the reaction of scientists developing the research program is to protect the hard core by constructing auxiliary hypotheses that will explain the anomalies. Yet any research program, good or bad, can invent such auxiliary hypotheses on an *ad hoc* basis. The key test for Lakatos of the value of a research program is whether these auxiliary hypotheses are "progressive," that is, whether their invention leads to the discovery of *new facts* (other than the anomalous facts that they were designed to explain). Progressive research programs display "continuous growth": their auxiliary hypotheses increase our capacity to understand reality (Lakatos, 1970, pp. 116–122, 132–138, 173–180).

Lakatos developed this conception to assess developments in the natural sciences, particularly physics. If we took literally the requirements that he laid down for "progressive" research programs, all actual theories of international politics — and perhaps all conceivable theories —would fail the test. Indeed, it has been argued that much of economics, including oligopoly theory (heavily relied upon by Structural Realists), fails to meet this standard (Latsis, 1976). Nevertheless, Lakatos' conception has the great merit of providing clear and sensible criteria for the evaluation of scientific traditions, and of asking penetrating questions that may help us to see Realism in a revealing light. Lakatos' questions are relevant, even if applying them without modification could lead to premature rejection not only of Realism, but of our whole field, or even the entire discipline of political science.[7]

The stringency of Lakatos' standards suggests that we should supplement this test with a "softer," more interpretive one. That is, how much insight does Realism provide into contemporary world politics?

For this line of evaluation we can draw inspiration from Clifford Geertz's discussion of the role of theory in anthropology. Geertz argues that culture "is not a power, something to which social events, behaviors, institutions, or processes can be causally attributed; it is a context— something within which they can be intelligibly — that is, thickly — described" (1973, p. 14). The role of theory, he claims, is "not to codify abstract regularities but to make thick description possible, not to generalize across cases but to generalize within them" (*ibid.*, p. 26). This conception is the virtual antithesis of the standards erected by Lakatos, and could all too easily serve as a rationalization for the proliferation of atheoretical case studies. Nevertheless, culture as discussed by Geertz has something in common with the international system as discussed by students of world politics. It is difficult to generalize across systems. We are continually bedeviled by the paucity of comparable cases, particularly when making systemic statements — for example, about the operation of balances of power. Much of what students of world politics do, and what Classical Realism in particular aspires to, is to make the actions of states understandable (despite obfuscatory statements by their spokesmen): that is, in Geertz's words, to provide "a context within which they can be intelligibly described." For example, Morgenthau's discussion of the concept of interest defined in terms of power, quoted at length below, reflects this objective more than the goal of arriving at testable generalizations.

This essay is divided into four major sections. The first of these seeks to establish the basis for a dual evaluation of Realism: as a source of interpretive insights into the operation of world politics, and as a scientific research program that enables the investigator to discover new facts. I examine the arguments of Thucydides and Morgenthau to extract the key assumptions of Classical Realism. Then I discuss recent work by Kenneth N. Waltz, whom I regard as the most systematic spokesman for contemporary Structural Realism.

Section II addresses the question of interpretation and puzzle-solving within the Realist tradition. How successful are Realist thinkers in making new contributions to our understanding of world politics? In Section III, I consider the shortcomings of Realism when judged by the standards that Lakatos establishes, or even when evaluated by less rigorous criteria, and begin to ask whether a modified version of Structural Realism could correct some of these faults. Section IV carries this theme further by attempting to outline how a multi-dimensional research program, including a modified structural theory, might be devised; what its limitations would be; and how it could be relevant, in particular, to problems of peaceful change.

The conclusion emphasizes the issue of peaceful change as both a theoretical and a practical problem. Realism raises the question of how peaceful change could be achieved, but does not resolve it. Understanding the conditions under which peaceful change would be facilitated remains, in my view, the most urgent task facing students of world politics.

I. STRUCTURAL REALISM AS RESEARCH PROGRAM

To explicate the research program of Realism, I begin with two classic works, one ancient, the other modern: *The Peloponnesian War*, by Thucydides, and *Politics Among Nations*, by Morgenthau.[8] The three most fundamental Realist assumptions are evident in these books: that the most important actors in world politics are territorially organized entities (city–states or modern states); that state behavior can be explained rationally; and that states seek power and calculate their interests in terms of power, relative to the nature of the international system that they face.

The Peloponnesian War was written in an attempt to explain the causes of the great war of the Fifth Century B.C. between the coalition led by Athens and its adversaries, led by Sparta. Thucydides assumes that to achieve this purpose, he must explain the behavior of the major city–states involved in the conflict. Likewise, Morgenthau assumes that the subject of a science of international politics is the behavior of states. Realism is "state-centric."[9]

Both authors also believed that observers of world politics could understand events by imagining themselves, as rational individuals, in authoritative positions, and reflecting on what they would do if faced with the problems encountered by the actual decision-makers. They both therefore, employ the method of *rational reconstruction*. Thucydides admits that he does not have transcripts of all the major speeches given during the war, but he is undaunted:

It was in all cases difficult to carry [the speeches] word for word in one's memory, so my habit has been to make the speakers say what was in my opinion demanded of them by the various occasions, of course adhering as closely as possible to the general sense of what they really said. (Thucydides, Book I, paragraph 23 [Chapter I, Modern Library edition. p. 14])

Morgenthau argues that in trying to understand foreign policy,

We put ourselves in the position of a statesman who must meet a certain problem of foreign policy under certain circumstances, and we ask ourselves what the rational alternatives are from which a statesman may choose . . . and which of these rational alternatives this particular statesman, acting under these circumstances, is likely to choose. It is the testing of this rational hypothesis against the actual facts and their consequences that gives meaning to the facts of international politics and makes a theory of politics possible. (Morgenthau, 1966, p. 5)

In reconstructing state calculation, Thucydides and Morgenthau both assume that states will act to protect their power positions, perhaps even to the point of seeking to maximize their power. Thucydides seeks to go beneath the surface of events to the power realities that are fundamental to state action:

The real cause [of the war] I consider to be the one which was formally most kept out of sight. The growth in the power of Athens, and the alarm which this inspired in Lacedemon, made war inevitable. (Thucydides, Book I, paragraph 23, Chapter I, Modern Library Edition, p. 15)[10]

Morgenthau is even more blunt: "International politics, like all politics, is a struggle for power" (1966, p. 25, see also Morgenthau, 1946). Political Realism, he argues, understands international politics through the concept of "interest defined as power":

We assume that statesmen think and act in terms of interest defined as power, and the evidence of history bears that assumption out. That assumption allows us to retrace and anticipate, as it were, the steps a statesman—past, present, or future—has taken or will take on the political scene. We look over his shoulder when he writes his dispatches; we listen in on his conversation with other statesmen; we read and anticipate his very thoughts. (1966, p. 5)

The three assumptions just reviewed define the hard core of the Classical Realist research program:

1. The *state-centric assumption:* states are the most important actors in world politics;
2. The *rationality assumption:* world politics can be analyzed as if states were unitary rational actors, carefully calculating costs of alternative courses of action and seeking to maximize their expected utility, although doing so under conditions of uncertainty and without necessarily having sufficient information about alternatives or resources (time or otherwise) to conduct a full review of all possible courses of action;[11]

3. The *power assumption*; states seek power (both the ability to influence others and resources that can be used to exercise influence); and they calculate their interests in terms of power, whether as end or as necessary means to a variety to other ends.

More recently, Kenneth N. Waltz (1959) has attempted to reformulate and systematize Realism on the basis of what he called, in *Man, the State and War*, a "third image" perspective. This form of Realism does not rest on the presumed iniquity of the human race — original sin in one form or another — but on the nature of world politics as an anarchic realm:

> Each state pursues its own interests, however defined, in ways it judges best. Force is a means of achieving the external ends of states because there exists no consistent, reliable process of reconciling the conflicts of interests that inevitably arise among similar units in a condition of anarchy. (p. 238)[12]

Even well-intentioned statesmen find that they must use or threaten force to attain their objectives.

Since the actions of states are conceived of as resulting from the nature of international politics, the paramount theoretical task for Realists is to create a *systemic* explanation of international politics. In a systemic theory, as Waltz explains it, the propositions of the theory specify relationships between certain aspects of the system and actor behavior (1979, pp. 67–73). Waltz's third-image Realism, for instance, draws connections between the distribution of power in a system and the actions of states: small countries will behave differently from large ones, and in a balance of power system, alliances can be expected to shift in response to changes in power relationships. Any theory will, of course, take into account the attributes of actors, as well as features of the system itself. But the key distinguishing characteristic of a systemic theory is that *the internal attributes of actors are given by assumption rather than treated as variables.* Changes in actor behavior, and system outcomes, are explained not on the basis of variations in these actor characteristics, but on the basis of changes in the attributes of the system itself. A good example of such a systemic theory is microeconomic theory in its standard form. It posits the existence of business firms, with given utility functions (such as profit maximization), and attempts to explain their behavior on the basis of environmental factors such as the competitiveness of markets. It is systemic because its propositions about variations in behavior depend on variations in characteristics of the system, not of the units (Waltz, 1979, pp. 89–91, 93–95, 98).

To develop a systemic analysis, abstraction is necessary: one has to avoid being distracted by the details and vagaries of domestic politics and other variables at the level of the acting unit. To reconstruct a systemic research program, therefore, Structural Realists must devise a way to explain state behavior on the basis of systemic characteristics, and to account for outcomes in the same manner. This needs to be a coherent explanation, although it need not tell us everything we would like to know about world politics.

Waltz's formulation of Structural Realism as a systemic theory seeks to do this by developing a concept not explicitly used by Morgenthau or Thucydides: the *structure* of the international system. Two elements of international structure are constants: (1) the international system is anarchic rather than hierarchic, and (2) it is characterized by interaction among units with similar functions. These are such enduring background characteristics that they are constitutive of what we mean by "international politics."[13] The third element of structure, the distribution of capabilities across the states in the system, varies from system to system, and over time. Since it is a variable, this element — the distribution of "power" — takes on particular importance in the theory. The most significant capabilities are those of the most powerful actors. Structures "are defined not by all of the actors that flourish within them but by the major ones" (Waltz, 1979, p. 93).

According to Waltz, structure is the principal determinant of outcomes at the systems level: structure encourages certain actions and discourages others. It may also lead to unintended consequences, as the ability of states to obtain their objectives is constrained by the power of others (1979, pp. 104–111).

For Waltz, understanding the structure of an international system allows us to explain patterns of state behavior, since states determine their interests and strategies on the basis of calculations about their own positions in the system. The link between system structure and actor behavior is forged by the rationality assumption, which enables the theorist to predict that leaders will respond to the incentives and constraints imposed by their environments. Taking rationality as a constant permits one to attribute variations in state behavior to variations in characteristics of the international system. Otherwise, state behavior might have to be accounted for by variations in the calculating ability of states; in that case, the systemic focus of Structural Realism (and much of its explanatory power) would be lost. Thus the rationality assumption — as we will see in examining Waltz's balance of power theory — is essential to the theoretical claims of Structural Realism.[14]

The most parsimonious version of a structural theory would hold that any international system has a single structure of power. In such a conceptualization, power resources are homogeneous and fungible: they can be used to achieve results on any of a variety of issues without significant loss of efficacy.[15] Power in politics becomes like money in economics: "in many respects, power and influence play the same role in international politics as money does in a market economy" (Wolfers, 1962, p. 105).

In its strong form, the Structural Realist research program is similar to that of micro-economics. Both use the rationality assumption to permit inferences about actor behavior to be made from system structure. The

Realist definition of interests in terms of power and position is like the economist's assumption that firms seek to maximize profits: it provides the utility function of the actor. Through these assumptions, actor characteristics become constant rather than variable, and systemic theory becomes possible.[16] The additional assumption of power fungibility simplifies the theory further: on the basis of a *single* characteristic of the international system (overall power capabilities), *multiple* inferences can be drawn about actor behavior and outcomes. "Foreknowledge" — that aspiration of all theory — is thereby attained (Eckstein, 1975, pp. 88–89). As we will see below, pure Structural Realism provides an insufficient basis for explaining state interests and behavior, even when the rationality assumption is accepted; and the fungibility assumption is highly questionable. Yet the Structural Realist research program is an impressive intellectual achievement: an elegant, parsimonious, deductively rigorous instrument for scientific discovery. The anomalies that it generates are more interesting than its own predictions; but as Lakatos emphasizes, it is the exploration of anomalies that moves science forward.

Richard K. Ashley has recently argued that Structural Realism — which he calls "technical realism" — actually represents a regression from the classical Realism of Herz or Morgenthau.[17] In his view, contemporary Realist thinkers have forgotten the importance of subjective self-reflection, and the dialectic between subjectivity and objectivity, which are so important in the writings of "practical," or "classical" Realists such as Thucydides and Morgenthau. Classical Realism for Ashley is interpretive: "a practical tradition of statesmen is the real subject whose language of experience the interpreter tries to make his own" (1981, p. 221). It is self-reflective and non-deterministic. It treats the concept of balance of power as a dialectical relation: not merely as an objective characterization of the international system but also as a collectively recognized orienting scheme for strategic action. Classical Realism encompasses the unity of opposites, and draws interpretive insight from recognizing the dialectical quality of human experience. Thus its proponents understand that the state system is problematic, and that "strategic artistry" is required to keep it in existence (Ashley, 1982, p. 22).

The problem with Classical Realism is that it is difficult to distinguish what Ashley praises as dialectical insight from a refusal to define concepts clearly and consistently, or to develop a systematic set of propositions that could be subjected to empirical tests. Structural Realism seeks to correct these flaws, and thus to construct a more rigorous theoretical framework for the study of world politics, while drawing on the concepts and insights of the older Realism. Structural Realism, as embodied particularly in the work of Waltz, is more systematic and logically more coherent than that of its Classical Realist predecessors. By its own standards, Structural Realism is, in Ashley's words, "a progressive scientific redemption of classical realism" (Ashley, 1982, p. 25). That is, it sees itself, and Classical Realism, as elements of a continuous research tradition.

Ashley complains that this form of Realism objectifies reality, and that in particular it regards the state as unproblematic. This leads, in his view, to some pernicious implications; that the interests expressed by dominant elites must be viewed as legitimate, that economic rationality is the highest form of thought, and that individuals are not responsible for the production of insecurity (1982, pp. 34–41). But Structural Realists need not make any of these claims. It is true that Structural Realism seeks to understand the limits of, and constraints on, human action in world politics. It emphasizes the strength of these constraints, and in that sense could be considered "conservative." But an analysis of constraints, far from implying an acceptance of the *status quo*, should be seen as a precondition to sensible attempts to change the world. To be self-reflective, human action must take place with an understanding of the context within which it occurs. Structural Realists can be criticized, as we will see, for paying insufficient attention to norms, institutions, and change. But this represents less a fault of Structural Realism as such than a failure of some of its advocates to transcend its categories. Structural Realism's focus on systemic constraints does not contradict Classical Realism's concern with action and choice. On the contrary, Classical Realism's emphasis on *praxis* helps us to understand the origins of Structural Realism's search for systematic understanding, and — far from negating the importance of this search — makes it seem all the more important.

I have argued thus far that Structural Realism is at the center of contemporary international relations theory in the United States; that it constitutes an attempt to systematize Classical Realism; and that its degree of success as a theory can be legitimately evaluated in part according to standards such as those laid down by Lakatos, and in part through evaluation of its capacity to generate insightful interpretations of international political behavior. Two distinct tests, each reflecting one aspect of this dualistic evaluative standard, can be devised to evaluate Structural Realism as a research program for international relations:

1. How "fruitful" is the Realist paradigm for puzzle-solving and interpretation of world politics (Toulmin, 1963)? That is, does current work in the Realist tradition make us see issues more clearly, or provide answers to formerly unsolved puzzles? Realism was designed to provide insights into such issues, and if it remains a live tradition, should continue to do so.

2. Does Realism meet the standards of a scientific research program as enunciated by Lakatos? To answer this question, it is important to remind ourselves that the hard core of a research program is irrefutable within the terms of the paradigm. When anomalies arise that appear to challenge Realist assumptions, the task of Realist analysts is to create auxiliary theories that defend them. These theories permit explanation of anomalies consistent with Realist assumptions. For Lakatos, the key question about a research program concerns whether the auxiliary hypotheses of Realism are "progressive." That is, do they generate new insights,

or predict new facts? If not, they are merely exercises in "patching up" gaps or errors on an ad hoc basis, and the research program is degenerative.

Realism cannot be judged fairly on the basis of only one set of standards. Section II addresses the question of fruitfulness by examining works in the central area of Realist theory: the study of conflict, bargaining, and war. Section II then judges Realism by the more difficult test of Lakatos, which (as noted above) is better at asking trenchant questions than at defining a set of standards appropriate to social science. We will see that in one sense, Realism survives these tests, since it still appears as a good starting point for analysis. But it does not emerge either as a comprehensive theory or as a progressive research program in the sense employed by Lakatos. Furthermore, it has difficulty interpreting issues, and linkages among issues, outside of the security sphere: it can even be misleading when applied to these issues without sufficient qualification. It also has little to say about the crucially important question of peaceful change. The achievements of Realism, and the prospect that it can be modified further to make it even more useful, should help students of world politics to avoid unnecessary self-deprecation. Yet they certainly do not justify complacency.

II. PROGRESS WITHIN THE REALIST PARADIGM: THREE ACHIEVEMENTS

The fruitfulness of contemporary Realist analysis is best evaluated by considering some of the finest work in the genre. Poor scholarship can derive from even the best research program; only the most insightful work reveals the strengths as well as the limits of a theoretical approach. In this section I will consider three outstanding examples of works that begin, at least, from Realist concerns and assumptions: Waltz's construction of balance of power theory in *Theory of International Politics* (1979); the attempt by Glenn Snyder and Paul Diesing in *Conflict Among Nations* (1977) to apply formal game-theoretic models of bargaining to sixteen case studies of major-power crises during the seventy-five years between Fashoda and the Yom Kippur "alert crisis" of 1973; and Robert Gilpin's fine recent book, *War and Change in World Politics* (1981). These works are chosen to provide us with one systematic attempt to develop structural Realist theory, one study of bargaining in specific cases, and one effort to understand broad patterns of international political change. Other recent works could have been chosen instead, such as three books on international conflict and crisis published in 1980 or 1981 (Brecher, 1980; Bueno de Mesquita, 1981; Lebow, 1981), or the well-known works by Nazli Choucri and Robert C. North (1975) or by Alexander George and Richard Smoke (1974). But there are limits on what can be done in a single chapter of limited size.

Balance of Power Theory: Waltz

Waltz has explicated balance of power theory as a central element in his Structural Realist synthesis: "If there is any distinctively political theory of international politics, balance of power theory is it" (1979, p. 117). The realization that balances of power periodically form in world politics, is an old one, as are attempts to theorize about it. The puzzle that Waltz addresses is how to "cut through such confusion" as has existed about it: that is, in Kuhn's words, how to "achieve the anticipated in a new way" (1962, p. 36).

Waltz attacks this problem by using the concept of structure, which he has carefully developed earlier in the book, and which he also employs to account for the dreary persistence of patterns of international action (1979, pp. 66–72). Balance of power theory applies to "anarchic" realms, which are formally unorganized and in which, therefore, units have to worry about their survival: "Self-help is necessarily the principle of action in an anarchic order" (p. 111). In Waltz's system, states (which are similar to one another in function) are the relevant actors; they use external as well as internal means to achieve their goals. Relative capabilities are (as we saw above) the variable element of structure; as they change, we expect coalitional patterns or patterns of internal effort to be altered as well. From his assumptions, given the condition for the theory's operation (self-help), Waltz deduces "the expected outcome: namely, the formation of balances of power" (p. 118). His solution to the puzzle that he has set for himself is carefully formulated and ingenious.

Nevertheless, Waltz's theory of the balance of power encounters some difficulties. First, it is difficult for him to state precisely the conditions under which coalitions will change. He only forecasts that balances of power will periodically recur. Indeed, his theory is so general that it hardly meets the difficult tests that he himself establishes for theory. In Chapter 1 we are told that to test a theory, one must "devise a number of distinct and demanding tests" (1979, p. 13). But such tests are not proposed for balance of power theory: "Because only a loosely defined and inconstant condition of balance is predicted, it is difficult to say that any given distribution of power falsifies the theory" (p. 124). Thus rather than applying demanding tests, Waltz advises that we "should seek *confirmation* through observation of difficult cases" (p. 125, emphasis added). In other words, he counsels that we should search through history to find examples that conform to the predictions of the theory: he then proclaims that "these examples tend to confirm the theory" (p. 125). Two pages later, Waltz appears to change his view, admitting that "we can almost always find confirming cases if we look hard." We should correct for this by looking "for instances of states conforming to common international practices even though for internal reasons they would prefer not to" (p. 127). But Waltz is again making an error against which he warns us. He is not examining a universe of cases, in all of which states would prefer not to conform to "international practice," and asking how often they nevertheless do conform. Instead, he is looking only at the latter cases, chosen *because* they are consistent with his theory. Building grand theory that meets Popperian standards of scientific practice is inherently difficult; even the best scholars, such as Waltz, have trouble simultaneously saying what they want to say and abiding by their canons of scientific practice.

Waltz's theory is also ambiguous with respect to the status of three assumptions that are necessary to a strong form of Structural Realism. I have already mentioned the difficult problem of whether a structural theory must (implausibly) assume fungibility of power resources. Since this problem is less serious with respect to balance of power theory than in a broader context, I will not pursue it here, but will return to it in Section III. Yet Waltz is also, in his discussion of balances of power, unclear on the questions of rationality and interests.

Waltz argues that his assumptions do not include the rationality postulate: "The theory says simply that if some do relatively well, others will emulate them or fall by the wayside" (p. 118). This evolutionary principle, however, can hold only for systems with many actors, experiencing such severe pressure on resources that many will disappear over time. Waltz undermines this argument by pointing out later (p. 137) that "the death rate for states is remarkably low." Furthermore, he relies explicitly on the rationality principle to show that bipolar balances must be stable. "Internal balancing," he says, "is more reliable and precise than external balancing. States are less likely to misjudge their relative strengths than they are to misjudge the strength and reliability of opposing coalitions" (p. 168). I conclude that Waltz does rely on the rationality argument, despite his earlier statement to the contrary.

The other ambiguity in Waltz's balance of power theory has to do with the interests, or motivations, of states. Waltz recognizes that any theory of state behavior must ascribe (by assumption) some motivations to states, just as microeconomic theory ascribes motivations to firms. It is not reductionist to do so as long as these motivations are not taken as varying from state to state as a result of their internal characteristics. Waltz specifies such motivations: states "at a minimum, seek their own preservation, and at a maximum, drive for universal domination" (p. 118).

For his balance of power theory to work, Waltz needs to assume that states seek self-preservation, since if at least some major states did not do so, there would be no reason to expect that roughly equivalent coalitions (i.e., "balances of power") would regularly form. The desire for self-preservation makes states that are behind in a struggle for power try harder, according to Waltz, and leads states allied to a potential hegemon to switch coalitions in order to construct balances of power. Neither of these processes on which Waltz relies to maintain a balance — intensified effort by the weaker country in a bipolar system and coalition formation against potentially dominant states in a multipolar system — could operate reliably without this motivation.

The other aspect of Waltz's motivational assumption — that states "at a maximum, drive for universal domination," is reminiscent of the implication of Realists such as Morgenthau that states seek to "maximize power." For a third-image Realist theory such as Waltz's, such an assumption is unnecessary. Waltz's defense of it is that the balance of power depends on the possibility that force may be used. But this possibility is an attribute of the self-help international system, for Waltz, rather than a reflection of the actors' characteristics. That some states seek universal domination is not a necessary condition for force to be used.

This ambiguity in Waltz's analysis points toward a broader ambiguity in Realist thinking: *Balance of power theory is inconsistent with the assumption frequently made by Realists that states "maximize power,"* if power is taken to refer to tangible resources that can be used to induce other actors to do what they would not otherwise do, through the threat or infliction of deprivations.[18] States concerned with self-preservation do not seek to maximize their power when they are not in danger. On the contrary, they recognize a trade-off between aggrandizement and self-preservation; they realize that a relentless search for universal domination may jeopardize their own autonomy. Thus they moderate their efforts when their positions are secure. Conversely, they intensify their efforts when danger arises, which assumes that they were not maximizing them under more benign conditions.

One might have thought that Realists would readily recognize this point, yet they seem drawn against their better judgment to the "power maximization" or "universal domination" hypotheses. In part, this may be due to their anxiety to emphasize the significance of force in world politics. Yet there may be theoretical as well as rhetorical reasons for their ambivalence. The assumption of power maximization makes possible strong inferences about behavior that would be impossible if we assumed only that states "sometimes" or "often" sought to aggrandize themselves. In that case, we would have to ask about competing goals, some of which would be generated by the internal social, political, and economic characteristics of the countries concerned. Taking into account these competing goals relegates Structural Realism to the status of partial, incomplete theory.

Waltz's contribution to the study of world politics is conceptual. He helps us think more clearly about the role of systemic theory, the explanatory power of structural models, and how to account deductively for the recurrent formation of balances of power. He shows that the international system shapes state behavior as well as vice versa. These are major contributions. But Waltz does not point out "new ways of seeing" international relations that point toward major novelties. He reformulates and systematizes Realism, and thus develops what I have called Structural

Realism, consistent with the fundamental assumptions of his classical predecessors.

Game Theory, Structure, and Bargaining: Snyder and Diesing

Game theory has yielded some insights into issues of negotiations, crises, and limited war, most notably in the early work of Thomas Schelling (1960). Snyder and Diesing's contribution to this line of analysis, as they put it, is to "distinguish and analyze nine different kinds of bargaining situations, each one a unique combination of power and interest relations between the bargainers, each therefore having its own dynamics and problems" (1977, pp. 181–182). They employ their game-theoretic formulations of these nine situations, within an explicit structural context, to analyze sixteen historical cases.

This research design is consistent with the hard core of Realism. Attention is concentrated on the behavior of states. In the initial statement of the problem, the rationality assumption, in suitably modest form, is retained: each actor attempts "to maximize expected value across a given set of consistently ordered objectives given the information actually available to the actor or which he could reasonably acquire in the time available for decision" (p. 181). Interests are defined to a considerable extent in terms of power: that is, power factors are built into the game structure. In the game of "Protector," for instance, the more powerful state can afford to "go it alone" without its ally, and thus has an interest in doing so under certain conditions, whereas its weaker partner cannot (pp. 145–147). Faced with the game matrix, states, as rational actors, calculate their interests and act accordingly. The structure of world politics, as Waltz defines it, is reflected in the matrices and becomes the basis for action.

If Structural Realism formed a sufficient basis for the understanding of international crises, we could fill in the entries in the matrices solely on the basis of states' positions in the international system, given our knowledge of the fact that they perform "similar functions," including the need to survive as autonomous entities. Interests would indeed be defined in terms of power. This would make game theory a powerful analytic tool, which could even help us predict certain outcomes. Where the game had no unique solution (because of strategic indeterminacy), complete predictability of outcomes could not be achieved, but our expectations about the range of likely action would have been narrowed.

Yet Snyder and Diesing find that even knowledge of the values and goals of top leaders could not permit them to determine the interests of about half the decision-making units in their cases. In the other cases, one needed to understand intragovernmental politics, even when one ignored the impact of wider domestic political factors (pp. 510–511). The "internal-external interaction" is a key to the understanding of crisis bargaining.

As Snyder and Diesing make their analytical framework more complex and move into detailed investigation of their cases, their focus shifts toward concern with cognition and with the effects on policy of ignorance, misperception, and misinformation. In my view, the most creative and insightful of their chapters use ideas developed largely by Robert Jervis (1976) to analyze information processing and decision-making. These chapters shift the focus of attention away from the systemic-level factors reflected in the game-theoretic matrices, toward problems of perception, personal bias, and group decision-making (Snyder & Diesing, 1977, Chapters IV and V).

Thus Snyder and Diesing begin with the hard core of Realism, but their most important contributions depend on their willingness to depart from these assumptions. They are dissatisfied with their initial game-theoretic classificatory scheme. They prefer to explore information processing and decision-making, without a firm deductive theory on which to base their arguments, rather than merely to elucidate neat logical typologies.

Is the work of Snyder and Diesing a triumph of Realism or a defeat? At this point in the argument, perhaps the most that can be said is that it indicates that work in the Realist tradition, analyzing conflict and bargaining with the concepts of interests and power, continues to be fruitful, but it does not give reason for much confidence that adhering strictly to Realist assumptions will lead to important advances in the field.

Cycles of Hegemony and War: Gilpin

In *War and Change in World Politics*, Gilpin uses Realist assumptions to reinterpret the last 2400 years of Western history. Gilpin assumes that states, as the principal actors in world politics, make cost–benefit calculations about alternative courses of action. For instance, states attempt to change the international system as the expected benefits of so doing exceed the costs. Thus, the rationality assumption is applied explicitly, in a strong form, although it is relaxed toward the end of the book (1981, pp. 77, 202). Furthermore, considerations of power, relative to the structure of the international system, are at the core of the calculations made by Gilpin's states: "the distribution of power among states constitutes the principal form of control in every international system" (p. 29). Thus Gilpin accepts the entire hard core of the classical Realist research program as I have defined it.[19]

Gilpin sees world history as an unending series of cycles: "The conclusion of one hegemonic war is the beginning of another cycle of growth, expansion, and eventual decline" (p. 210). As power is redistributed, power relations become inconsistent with the rules governing the system and, in particular, the hierarchy of prestige: war establishes the new hierarchy of prestige and "thereby determines which states will in effect govern the international system" (p. 33).

The view that the rules of a system, and the hierarchy of prestige, must be consistent with underlying power realities is a fundamental proposition of Realism, which follows from its three core assumptions. If states, as the central actors of international relations, calculate their interests in terms of power, they will seek international rules and institutions that are consistent with these interests by maintaining their power. Waltz's conception of structure helps to systematize this argument, but it is essentially static. What Gilpin adds is a proposed solution to the anomalies (for static Realism) that institutions and rules can become inconsistent with power realities over time, and that hegemonic states eventually decline. If, as Realists argue, "the strong do what they can and the weak suffer what they must" (Thucydides, Book V, paragraph 90 [Chapter XVII, Modern Library edition, p. 331]), why should hegemons ever lose their power? We know that rules do not always reinforce the power of the strong and that hegemons do sometimes lose their hold, but static Realist theory cannot explain this.

In his attempt to explain hegemonic decline, Gilpin formulates a "law of uneven growth":

> According to Realism, the fundamental cause of wars among states and changes in international systems is the uneven growth of power among states. Realist writers from Thucydides and MacKinder to present-day scholars have attributed the dynamics of international relations to the fact that the distribution of power in an international system shifts over a period of time: this shift results in profound changes in the relationships among states and eventually changes in the nature of the international system itself. (p. 94)

This law, however, restates the problem without resolving it. In accounting for this pattern, Gilpin relies on three sets of processes. One has to do with increasing, and then diminishing, marginal returns from empire. As empires grew, "the economic surplus had to increase faster than the cost of war" (p. 115). Yet sooner or later, diminishing returns set in: "the law of diminishing returns has universal applicability and causes the growth of every society to describe an S-shaped curve" (p. 159). Secondly, hegemonic states tend increasingly to consume more and invest less; Gilpin follows the lead of Carlo Cipolla in viewing this as a general pattern in history (Cipolla, 1970). Finally, hegemonic states decline because of a process of diffusion of technology to others. In *U.S. Power and the Multinational Corporation* (1975), Gilpin emphasized this process as contributing first to the decline of Britain, then in the 1970s to that of the United States. In *War and Change* he makes the argument more general:

> Through a process of diffusion to other states, the dominant power loses the advantage on which its political, military, or economic success has been based. Thus, by example, and frequently in more direct fashion, the dominant power helps to create challenging powers. (p. 176)

This third argument is systemic, and, therefore, fully consistent with Waltz's Structural Realism. The other two processes, however, reflect the operation of forces within the society, as well as international forces. A hegemonic power may suffer diminishing returns as a result of the expansion of its defense perimeter and the increased military costs that result (Gilpin, 1981, p. 191; Luttwak, 1976). But whether diminishing returns set in also depends on internal factors such as technological inventiveness of members of the society and the institutions that affect incentives for innovation (North, 1981). The tendency of hegemonic states to consume more and invest less is also, in part, a function of their dominant positions in the world system: they can force costs of adjustment to change onto others, at least for some time. But it would be hard to deny that the character of the society affects popular tastes for luxury, and, therefore, the tradeoffs between guns and butter that are made. Eighteenth-century Saxony and Prussia were different in this regard; so are contemporary America and Japan. In Gilpin's argument as in Snyder and Diesing's, the "external-internal interaction" becomes a crucial factor in explaining state action, and change.

Gilpin explicitly acknowledges his debt to Classical Realism: "In honesty, one must inquire whether or not twentieth-century students of international relations know anything that Thucydides and his fifth-century compatriots did not know about the behavior of states" (p. 227). For Gilpin as for Thucydides, changes in power lead to changes in relations among states: the *real* cause of the Peloponnesian War, for Thucydides, was the rise of the power of Athens and the fear this evoked in the Spartans and their allies. Gilpin has generalized the theory put forward by Thucydides to explain the Peloponnesian War, and has applied it to the whole course of world history:

> Disequilibrium replaces equilibrium, and the world moves toward a new round of hegemonic conflict. It has always been thus and always will be, until men either destroy themselves or learn to develop an effective mechanism of peaceful change. (p. 210)

This Thucydides–Gilpin theory is a systemic theory of change only in a limited sense. It explains the *reaction* to change systematically, in a rationalistic, equilibrium model. Yet at a more fundamental level, it does not account fully for the sources of change. As we saw above, although it is insightful about systemic factors leading to hegemonic decline, it also has to rely on internal processes to explain the observed effects. Furthermore, it does not account well for the rise of hegemons in the first place, or for the fact that certain contenders emerge rather than others.[20] Gilpin's systemic theory does not account for the extraordinary bursts of energy that occasionally catapult particular countries into dominant positions on the world scene. Why were the Athenians, in words that Thucydides attributes to Corinthian envoys to Sparta, "addicted to innovation," whereas the Spartans were allegedly characterized by a "total want of invention" (Thucydides, Book I, paragraph 70 [Chapter III, Modern Library edition, p. 40])? Like other structural theories, Gilpin's theory underpredicts outcomes. It contributes to our understanding but (as its author recognizes) does not explain change.

This is particularly true of peaceful change, which Gilpin identifies as a crucial issue: "The fundamental problem of international relations in the contemporary world is the problem of peaceful adjustment to the consequences of the uneven growth of power among states, just as it was in the past" (p. 230).

Gilpin's book, like much contemporary American work on international politics, is informed and propelled by concern with peaceful change under conditions of declining hegemony. Gilpin sympathetically discusses E. H. Carr's "defense of peaceful change as the solution to the problem of hegemonic war," written just before World War II (Gilpin, p. 206; Carr, 1939/1946). Yet peaceful change does not fit easily into Gilpin's analytical framework, since it falls, by and large, into the category of "interactions change," which does not entail alteration in the overall hierarchy of power and prestige in a system, and Gilpin deliberately avoids focusing on interactions change (p. 44). Yet after one puts down *War and Change*, the question of how institutions and rules can be developed *within* a given international system, to reduce the probability of war and promote peaceful change, looms even larger than it did before.

Thus Gilpin's sophisticated adaptation of Classical Realism turns us away from Realism. Classical Realism, with its philosophical roots in a tragic conception of the human condition, directs our attention in the twentieth century to the existential situation of modern humanity, doomed apparently to recurrent conflict in a world with weapons that could destroy life on our planet. But Realism, whether classical or structural, has little to say about how to deal with that situation since it offers few insights into the international rules and institutions that people invent to reduce risk and uncertainty in world affairs in the hope of ameliorating the security dilemma.[21] Morgenthau put his hopes in diplomacy (1966, Chapter 32). This is a practical art far removed from the abstractions of Structural Realism. But diplomacy takes place within a context of international rules, institutions, and practices, which affect the incentives of the actors (Keohane, 1982). Gilpin realizes this, and his gloomy argument — hardly alleviated by a more optimistic epilogue — helps us to understand their importance, although it does not contribute to an explanation of their creation or demise.

Conclusions

Realism, as developed through a long tradition dating from Thucydides, continues to provide the basis for valuable research in international relations. This point has been made by looking at writers who explicitly draw on the Realist tradition, and it can be reinforced by briefly examining some works of Marxist scholars. If they incorporate elements of Realism despite their general antipathy to its viewpoint, our conclusion that Realism reflects enduring realities of world politics will be reinforced.

For Marxists, the fundamental forces affecting world politics are those of class struggle and uneven development. International history is dynamic and dialectical rather than cyclical. The maneuvers of states, on which Realism focuses, reflect the stages of capitalist development and the contradictions of that development. Nevertheless, in analyzing the surface manifestations of world politics under capitalism, Marxists adopt similar categories to those of Realists. Power is crucial; world systems are periodically dominated by hegemonic powers wielding both economic and military resources.

Lenin defined imperialism differently than do the Realists, but he analyzed its operation in part as a Realist would, arguing that "there can be *no* other conceivable basis under capitalism for the division of spheres of influence, of interests, of colonies, etc. than a calculation of the *strength* of the participants in the division. . . ." (Lenin, 1916/1939, p. 119).

Immanuel Wallerstein provides another example of my point. He goes to some effort to stress that modern world history should be seen as the history of capitalism as a world system. Apart from "relatively minor accidents" provided by geography, peculiarities of history, or luck — which give one country an edge over others at crucial historical junctures — "it is the operations of the world-market forces which accentuate the differences, institutionalize them, and make them impossible to surmount over the long run" (1979, p. 21). Nevertheless, when his attention turns to particular epochs, Wallerstein emphasizes hegemony and the role of military force. Dutch economic hegemony in the seventeenth century was destroyed in quintessential Realist fashion, not by the operation of the world-market system, but by the force of British and French arms (Wallerstein, 1980, pp. 38–39).

The insights of Realism are enduring. They cross ideological lines. Its best contemporary exponents use Realism in insightful ways. Waltz has systematized the basic assumptions of Classical Realism in what I have called Structural Realism. Snyder and Diesing have employed this framework for the analysis of bargaining; Gilpin has used the classical arguments of Thucydides to explore problems of international change. For all of these writers, Realism fruitfully focuses attention on fundamental issues of power, interests, and rationality. But, as we have seen, many of the most interesting questions raised by these authors cannot be answered within the Realist framework.

III. EXPLANATIONS OF OUTCOMES FROM POWER: HYPOTHESES AND ANOMALIES

A Structural Realist theory of interests could be used both for explanation and for prescription. If we could deduce a state's interests from its position in the system, via the rationality assumption, its behavior could be explained on the basis of systemic analysis. Efforts to define the national interest on an a priori basis, however, or to use the concept for prediction and explanation, have been unsuccessful. We saw above that the inability to define interests independently of observed state behavior robbed Snyder and Diesing's game-theoretical matrices of predictive power. More generally, efforts to show that external considerations of power and position play a dominant role in determining the "national interest" have failed. Even an analyst as sympathetic to Realism as Stephen D. Krasner has concluded, in studying American foreign economic policy, that the United States was "capable of defining its own autonomous goals" in a non-logical manner (1978, p. 333). That is, the systemic constraints emphasized by Structural Realism were not binding on the American government during the first thirty years after the Second World War.

Sophisticated contemporary thinkers in the Realist tradition, such as Gilpin, Krasner, and Waltz, understand that interests cannot be derived, simply on the basis of rational calculation, from the external positions of states, and that this is particularly true for great powers, on which, ironically, Structural Realism focuses its principal attentions (Gilpin, 1975; Waltz, 1967). Realist analysis has to retreat to a "fall-back position": that, *given state interests*, whose origins are not predicted by the theory, patterns of outcomes in world politics will be determined by the overall distribution of power among states. This represents a major concession for systemically-oriented analysts, which it is important not to forget. Sensible Realists are highly cognizant of the role of domestic politics and of actor choices within the constraints and incentives provided by the system. Since systemic theory cannot predict state interests, it cannot support deterministic conclusions (Sprout & Sprout, 1971, pp. 73–77). This limitation makes it both less powerful as a theory, and less dangerous as an ideology.[22] Despite its importance, it cannot stand alone.

When realist theorists say that, given interests, patterns of outcomes will be determined by the overall distribution of power among states, they are using "power" to refer to resources that can be used to induce other actors to do what they would not otherwise do, in accordance with the desires of the power-wielder. "Outcomes" refer principally to two sets of patterns: (1) the results of conflicts, diplomatic or military, that take place between states; and (2) changes in the rules and institutions that regulate relations among governments in world politics. This section focuses on conflicts, since they pose the central puzzles that Realism seeks to explain. Section IV and the Conclusion consider explanations of changes in rules and institutions.

Recent quantitative work seems to confirm that power capabilities (measured not only in terms of economic resources but with political variables added) are rather good predictors of the outcomes of wars. Bueno de Mesquita finds, for example, that countries with what he calls positive "expected utility" (a measure that uses composite capabilities but adjusts them for distance, alliance relationships, and uncertainty) won 179 conflicts while losing only 54 between 1816 and 1974, for a success ratio of over 75% (1981, especially p. 151; Organski & Kugler, 1980, Chapter 2).

The question of the fungibility of power poses a more troublesome issue. As I have noted earlier (see footnote 19), Structural Realism is ambiguous on this point; the desire for parsimonious theory impels Realists toward a unitary notion of power as homogeneous and usable for a variety of purposes, but close examination of the complexities of world politics induces caution about such an approach. In his discussion of system structure, for instance, Waltz holds that "the units of an anarchic system are distinguished primarily by their greater or lesser capabilities for performing similar tasks," and that the distribution of capabilities across a system is the principal characteristic differentiating international-political structures from one another (1979, pp. 97, 99). Thus each international political system has one structure. Yet in emphasizing the continued role of military power, Waltz admits that military power is not perfectly fungible: "Differences in strength do matter, *although not for every conceivable purpose*"; "military power no longer brings political control, but then it never did" (1979, pp. 189, 191, emphasis added). This seems to imply that any given international system is likely to have *several* structures, differing by issue-areas and according to the resources that can be used to affect outcomes. Different sets of capabilities will qualify as "power resources" under different conditions. This leads to a much less parsimonious theory and a much more highly differentiated view of the world, in which what Nye and I called "issue-structure" theories play a major role, and in which military force, although still important, is no longer assumed to be at the top of a hierarchy of power resources (Keohane & Nye, 1977, chs. 3 and 6).

The status in a Structural Realist theory of the fungibility assumption affects both its power and the incidence of anomalies. A strong version of Structural Realism that assumed full fungibility of power across issues would predict that when issues arise between great powers and smaller states, the great powers should prevail. This has the advantage of generating a clear prediction and the liability of being wrong much of the time. Certainly it does not fit the American experience of the last two decades. The United States lost a war in Vietnam and was for more than a year unable to secure the return of its diplomats held hostage in Iran. Small allies such as Israel, heavily dependent on the United States, have displayed considerable freedom of action. In the U.S.-Canadian relationship of the 1950s and 1960s, which was virtually free of threats of force, outcomes of conflicts as often favored the Canadian as the American position although this was not true for relations between Australia and the United States (Keohane & Nye, 1977, Chapter 7).

In view of power theory in social science, the existence of these anomalies is not surprising. As James G. March observes, "there appears to be general consensus that either potential power is different from actually exerted power or that actually exerted power is variable." (1966, p. 57) That is, what March calls "basic force models," which rely, like Realist theory, on measurable indices of power, are inadequate tools for either prediction or explanation. They are often valuable in suggesting long-term trends and patterns, but they do not account well for specific outcomes: the more that is demanded of them, the less well they are likely to perform.

Lakatos' discussion of scientific research programs leads us to expect that, when confronted with anomalies, theorists will create auxiliary theories that preserve the credibility of their fundamental assumptions. Thus it is not surprising that Realists committed to the fungibility assumption have devised auxiliary hypotheses to protect its "hard core" against challenge. One of these is what David Baldwin calls the "conversion-process explanation" of unanticipated outcomes:

> The would-be wielder of power is described as lacking in skill and/or the "will" to use his power resources effectively: "The Arabs had the tanks but didn't know how to use them." "The Americans had the bombs but lacked the will to use them." (1979, pp. 163–164)

The conversion-process explanation is a classic auxiliary hypothesis, since it is designed to protect the assumption that power resources are homogeneous and fungible. If we were to accept the conversion-process account, we could continue to believe in a single structure of power, even if outcomes do not favor the "stronger" party. This line of argument encounters serious problems, however, when it tries to account for the discrepancy between anticipated and actual outcomes by the impact of intangible resources (such as intelligence, training, organization, foresight) not recognized until after the fact. The problem with this argument lies in its post hoc quality. It is theoretically degenerate in Lakatos' sense, since it does not add any explanatory power to structural Realist theory, but merely "explains away" uncomfortable facts.

Thus what March says about "force activation models" applies to Structural Realist theories when the conversion-process explanation relies upon sources of power that can be observed only after the events to be explained have taken place:

> If we observe that power exists and is stable and if we observe that sometimes weak people seem to triumph over strong people, we are tempted to rely on an activation hypothesis to explain the discrepancy. But if we then try to use the activation hypothesis to predict the results of social-choice procedures, we discover that the data requirements of 'plausible' activation models are quite substantial. As a result, we retreat to what are essentially degenerate forms of the activation model — retaining some of the form but little of the substance. This puts us back where we started, looking for some device to explain our failures in prediction. (1966, p. 61)

A second auxiliary hypothesis designed to protect the fungibility assumption must be taken more seriously: that discrepancies between power resources and outcomes are explained by an asymmetry of motivation in favor of the objectively weaker party. Following this logic, John Harsanyi has proposed the notion of power "in a schedule sense," describing how various resources can be translated into social power. An actor with intense preferences on an issue may be willing to use more resources to attain a high probability of a favorable result, than an actor with more resources but lower intensity. As a result, outcomes may not accurately reflect underlying power resources (Harsanyi, 1962).

To use this insight progressively rather than in a degenerate way, Realist theory needs to develop indices of intensity of motivation that can be measured independently of the behavior that theorists are trying to explain. Russett, George, and Bueno de Mesquita are among the authors who have attempted, with some success, to do this (Russett, 1963; George *et al.*, 1971; Bueno de Mesquita, 1981). Insofar as motivation is taken simply as a control, allowing us to test the impact of varying power configurations more successfully, Harsanyi's insights can be incorporated into Structural Realist theory. If it became a key variable, however, the effect could be to transform a systemic theory into a decision-making one.

An alternative approach to relying on such auxiliary hypotheses is to relax the fungibility assumption itself. Failures of great powers to control smaller ones could be explained on the basis of independent evidence that in the relevant issue-areas, the states that are weaker on an overall basis have more power resources than their stronger partners, and that the use of power derived from one area of activity to affect outcomes in other areas (through "linkages") is difficult. Thus Saudi Arabia can be expected to have more impact on world energy issues than on questions of strategic arms control; Israel more influence over the creation of a Palestinian state than on the reconstruction of the international financial and debt regime.

Emphasizing the problematic nature of power fungibility might help to create more discriminating power models, but it will not resolve the inherent problems of power models, as identified by March and others. Furthermore, at the limit, to deny fungibility entirely risks a complete disintegration of predictive power. Baldwin comes close to this when he argues that what he calls the "policy-contingency framework" of an influence attempt must be specified before power explanations are employed. If we defined each issue as existing within a unique "policy-contingency framework," no generalizations would be possible. Waltz could reply, if he accepted Baldwin's view of power, that all of world politics should be considered a single policy-contingency framework, characterized by anarchy and self-help.[23] According to this argument, the parsimony gained by assuming the fungibility of power would compensate for the marginal mispredictions of such a theory.

This is a crucial theoretical issue, which should be addressed more explicitly by theorists of world politics. In my view, the dispute cannot be resolved a priori. The degree to which power resources have to be disaggregated in a structural theory depends both on the purposes of the theory and on the degree to which behavior on distinct issues is linked together through the exercise of influence by actors. The larger the domain of a theory, the less accuracy of detail we expect. Since balance of power theory seeks to explain large-scale patterns of state action over long periods of time, we could hardly expect the precision from it that we demand from theories whose domains have been narrowed.

This assertion suggests that grand systemic theory can be very useful as a basis for further theoretical development in international relations, even if the theory is lacking in precision, and it therefore comprises part of my defense of the Realist research program as a foundation on which scholars should build. Yet this argument needs immediate qualification.

Even if a large-scale theory can be developed and appropriately tested, its predictions will be rather gross. To achieve a more finely-tuned understanding of how resources affect behavior in particular situations, one needs to specify the policy-contingency framework more precisely. The domain of theory is narrowed to achieve greater precision. Thus the debate between advocates of parsimony and proponents of contextual subtlety resolves itself into a question of *stages*, rather than an either/or choice. We should seek parsimony first, then add complexity while monitoring the adverse effects that this has on the predictive power of our theory: its ability to make significant inferences on the basis of limited information.

To introduce greater complexity into an initially spare theoretical structure, the conception of an issue-area, developed many years ago by Robert A. Dahl (1961) and adapted for use in international relations by James N. Rosenau (1966), is a useful device. Having tentatively selected an area of activity to investigate, the analyst needs to delineate issue-areas at various levels of aggregation. Initial explanations should seek to account for the main features of behavior at a high level of aggregation — such as the international system as a whole — while subsequent hypotheses are designed to apply only to certain issue-areas.

In some cases, more specific issue-areas are "nested" within larger ones (Aggarwal, 1981; Snidal, 1981). For instance, North Atlantic fisheries issues constitute a sub-set of fisheries issues in general, which comprise part of the whole area of oceans policy, or "law of the sea." In other cases, specific issues may belong to two or more broader issues: the question of passage through straits, for example, involves questions of military security as well as the law of the sea.

Definitions of issue-areas depend on the beliefs of participants, as well as on the purposes of the investigator. In general, however definitions of issue-areas should be made on the basis of empirical judgments about the extent to which governments regard sets of issues as closely interdependent and treat them collectively. Decisions made on one issue must affect others in the issue-area, either through functional links or through regular patterns of bargaining. These relationships of interdependence among issues may change. Some issue-areas, such as international financial relations, have remained fairly closely linked for decades; others, such as oceans, have changed drastically over the past 35 years (Keohane & Nye, 1977, Chapter 4, especially pp. 64–65; Simon, 1969; Haas, 1980).

When a hierarchy of issue-areas has been identified, power-structure models employing more highly aggregated measures of power resources can be compared with models that disaggregate resources by issue-areas. How much accuracy is gained, and how much parsimony lost, by each step in the disaggregation process? In my view, a variegated analysis, which takes some specific "snapshots" by issue-area as well as looking at the broader picture, is superior to either monistic strategy, whether assuming perfect fungibility or none at all.

This approach represents an adaptation of Realism. It preserves the basic emphasis on power resources as a source of outcomes in general, but it unambiguously jettisons the assumption that power is fungible across all of world politics. Disaggregated power models are less parsimonious than more aggregated ones, and they remain open to the objections to power models articulated by March and others. But in one important sense disaggregation is progressive rather than degenerative. Disaggregated models call attention to linkages among issue-areas, and raise the question: under what conditions, and with what effects, will such linkages arise? Current research suggests that understanding linkages systematically, rather than merely describing them on an ad hoc basis, will add significantly to our comprehension of world politics (Oye, 1979, 1983; Stein, 1980; Tollison and Willett, 1979). It would seem worthwhile, in addition, for more empirical work to be done on this subject, since we know so little about when, and how, linkages are made.

Conclusions

Structural Realism is a good starting-point for explaining the outcomes of conflicts, since it directs attention to fundamental questions of interest and power within a logically coherent and parsimonious theoretical framework. Yet the ambitious attempt of Structural Realist theory to deduce national interests from system structure via the rationality postulate has been unsuccessful. Even if interests are taken as given, the attempt to predict outcomes from interests and power leads to ambiguities and incorrect predictions. The auxiliary theory attributing this failure to conversion-processes often entails unfalsifiable tautology rather than genuine explanation. Ambiguity prevails on the question of the fungibility of power: whether there is a single structure of the international system or several. Thus the research program of Realism reveals signs of degeneration. It certainly does not meet Lakatos' tough standards for progressiveness.

More attention to developing independent measures of intensity of motivation, and greater precision about the concept of power and its relationship to the context of action, may help to correct some of these faults. Careful disaggregation of power-resources by issue-area may help to improve the predictive capability of structural models, at the risk of reducing theoretical parsimony. As I argue in the next section, modified structural models, indebted to Realism although perhaps too different to be considered Realist themselves, may be valuable elements in a multi-level framework for understanding world politics.

Yet to some extent the difficulties encountered by Structural Realism reflect the inherent limitations of structural models which will not be corrected by mere modifications or the relaxation of assumptions. Domestic politics and decision-making, Snyder and Diesing's "internal-external interactions," and the workings of international institutions all play a role, along with international political structure, in affecting state behavior and outcomes. Merely to catalog these factors, however, is not to contribute to theory but rather to compound the descriptive anarchy that already afflicts the field, with too many independent variables, exogenously determined, chasing too few cases. As Waltz emphasizes, the role of unit-level forces can only be properly understood if we comprehend the structure of the international system within which they operate.

IV. BEYOND STRUCTURAL REALISM

Structural Realism helps us to understand world politics as in part a systemic phenomenon, and provides us with a logically coherent theory that establishes the context for state action. This theory, because it is relatively simple and clear, can be modified progressively to attain closer correspondence with reality. Realism's focus on interests and power is central to an understanding of how nations deal with each other. Its adherents have understood that a systemic theory of international relations must account for state behavior by examining the constraints and incentives provided by the system; for this purpose to be accomplished, an assumption of rationality (although not of perfect information) must be made. The rationality assumption allows inferences about state behavior to be drawn solely from knowledge of the structure of the system.

Unfortunately, such predictions are often wrong. The concept of power is difficult to measure validly a priori; interests are underspecified by examining the nature of the international system and the position of various states in it; the view of power resources implied by overall structure theories is overaggregated, exaggerating the extent to which power is like money. The problem that students of international politics face is how to construct theories that draw on Realism's strengths without partaking fully of its weaknesses.

To do this we need a multi-dimensional approach to world politics that incorporates several analytical frameworks or research programs. One of these should be that of Structural Realism, which has the virtues of parsimony and clarity, although the range of phenomena that it encompasses is limited. Another, in my view, should be a modified structural research program, which relaxes some of the assumptions of Structural Realism but retains enough of the hard core to generate a priori predictions on the basis of information about the international environment. Finally, we need better theories of domestic politics, decision-making, and information processing, so that the gap between the external and internal environments can be bridged in a systematic way, rather than by simply adding catalogs of exogenously determined foreign policy facts to theoretically more rigorous structural models. That is, we need more attention to the "internal-external interactions" discussed by Snyder and Diesing.

Too much work in this last category is being done for me to review it in detail here. Mention should be made, however, of some highlights. Peter J. Katzenstein, Peter Gourevitch, and others have done pioneering work on the relationship between domestic political structure and political coalitions, on the one hand, and foreign economic policies, on the other (Katzenstein, 1978; Gourevitch, 1978). This line of analysis, which draws heavily on the work of Alexander Gerschenkron (1962) and Barrington Moore (1966), argues that the different domestic structures characteristic of various advanced industrialized countries result from different historical patterns of development; in particular, whether development came early or late, and what the position of the country was in the international political system at the time of its economic development (Kurth, 1979). Thus it attempts to draw connections both between international and domestic levels of analysis, and across historical time. This research does not provide deductive explanatory models, and it does not account systematically for changes in established structures after the formative developmental period, but its concept of domestic structure brings order into the cacophony of domestic political and economic variables that could affect foreign policy, and therefore suggests the possibility of eventual integration of theories relying on international structure with those focusing on domestic structure.

Katzenstein and his associates focus on broad political, economic, and social patterns within countries, and their relationship to the international division of labor and the world political structure. Fruitful analysis can also be done at the more narrowly intragovernmental level, as Snyder and Diesing show. An emphasis on bureaucratic politics was particularly evident in the 1960s and early 1970s, although Robert J. Art has pointed out in detail a number of difficulties, weaknesses, and contradictions in this literature (1973). At the level of the individual decision-maker, insights can be gained by combining theories of cognitive psychology with a rich knowledge of diplomatic history, as in Jervis's work, as long as the investigator understands the systemic and domestic-structural context within which decision-makers operate.[24] This research program has made decided progress, from the simple-minded notions criticized by

Waltz (1959) to the work of Alexander and Juliette George (1964), Alexander George (1980), Ole Holsti (1976), and Jervis (1976).[25]

Despite the importance of this work at the levels of domestic structure, intragovernmental politics, and individual cognition, the rest of my analysis will continue to focus on the concept of international political structure and its relevance to the study of world politics. I will argue that progress could be made by constructing a modified structural research program, retaining some of the parsimony characteristic of Structural Realism and its emphasis on the incentives and constraints of the world system, while adapting it to fit contemporary reality better. Like Realism, this research program would be based on microeconomic theory, particularly oligopoly theory. It would seek to explain actor behavior by specifying a priori utility functions for actors, using the rationality principle as a "trivial animating law" in Popper's sense (Latsis, 1976, p. 21), and deducing behavior from the constraints of the system as modeled in the theory.

Developing such a theory would only be worthwhile if there were something particularly satisfactory both about systemic explanations and about the structural forms of such explanations. I believe that this is the case, for two sets of reasons.

First, systemic theory is important because we must understand the context of action before we can understand the action itself. As Waltz (1979) has emphasized, theories of world politics that fail to incorporate a sophisticated understanding of the operation of the system — that is, how systemic attributes affect behavior — are bad theories. Theoretical analysis of the characteristics of an international system is as important for understanding foreign policy as understanding European history is for understanding the history of Germany.

Second, structural theory is important because it provides an irreplaceable *component* for a thorough analysis of action, by states or non-state actors, in world politics. A good structural theory generates testable implications about behavior on an a priori basis, and, therefore, comes closer than interpretive description to meeting the requirements for scientific knowledge of neo-positivist philosophers of science such as Lakatos. This does not mean, of course, that explanation and rich interpretation — Geertz's "thick description" (1973) — are in any way antithetical to one another. A good analysis of a given problem will include both.[26]

The assumptions of a modified structural research program can be compared to Realist assumptions as follows:

1. The assumption that the principal actors in world politics are states would remain the same, although more emphasis would be placed on non-state actors, intergovernmental organizations, and transnational and transgovernmental relations than is the case in Realist analysis (Keohane & Nye, 1972).

2. The rationality assumption would be retained, since without it, as we have seen, inferences from structure to behavior become impossible without heroic assumptions about evolutionary processes or other forces that compel actors to adapt their behavior to their environments. It should be kept in mind, however, as is made clear by sophisticated Realists, that the rationality postulate only assumes that actors make calculations "so as to maximize expected value across a given set of consistently ordered objectives" (Snyder & Diesing, 1977, p. 81). It does not assume perfect information, consideration of all possible alternatives, or unchanging actor preferences.

3. The assumption that states seek power and calculate their interests accordingly, would be qualified severely. Power and influence would still be regarded as important state interests (as ends or necessary means), but the implication that the search for power constitutes an overriding interest in all cases, or that it always takes the same form, would be rejected. Under different systemic conditions states will define their self-interests differently. For instance, where survival is at stake efforts to maintain autonomy may take precedence over all other activities, but where the environment is relatively benign energies will also be directed to fulfilling other goals. Indeed, over the long run, whether an environment is malign or benign can alter the standard operating procedures and sense of identity of the actors themselves.[27]

In addition, this modified structural approach would explicitly modify the assumption of fungibility lurking behind unitary conceptions of "international structure." It would be assumed that the value of power resources for influencing behavior in world politics depends on the goals sought. Power resources that are well-suited to achieve certain purposes are less effective when used for other objectives. Thus power resources are differentially effective across issue-areas, and the usability of a given set of power resources depends on the "policy-contingency frameworks" within which it must be employed.

This research program would pay much more attention to the roles of institutions and rules than does Structural Realism. Indeed, a structural interpretation of the emergence of international rules and procedures, and of obedience to them by states, is one of the rewards that could be expected from this modified structural research program (Krasner, 1982; Keohane, 1982; Stein, 1982).

This research program would contain a valuable positive heuristic — a set of suggestions about what research should be done and what questions should initially be asked — which would include the following pieces of advice:

1. When trying to explain a set of outcomes in world politics, always consider the hypothesis that the outcomes reflect underlying power resources, without being limited to it;

2. When considering different patterns of outcomes in different relationships, or issue-areas, entertain the hypothesis that power resources are differently distributed in these issue-areas, and investigate ways in which these differences promote or constrain actor attempts to link issue-areas in order to use power-resources from one area to affect results in another;

3. When considering how states define their self-interests, explore the effects of international structure on self-interests, as well as the effects of other international factors and of domestic structure.

Such a modified structural research program could begin to help generate theories that are more discriminating, with respect to the sources of power, than is Structural Realism. It would be less oriented toward reaffirming the orthodox verities of world politics and more inclined to explain variations in patterns of rules and institutions. Its concern with international institutions would facilitate insights into processes of peaceful change. This research program would not solve all of the problems of Realist theory, but it would be a valuable basis for interpreting contemporary world politics.

Yet this form of structural theory still has the weaknesses associated with power analysis. The essential problem is that from a purely systemic point of view, situations of strategic interdependence do not have determinate solutions. No matter how carefully power resources are defined, no power model will be able accurately to predict outcomes under such conditions.[28]

One way to alleviate this problem without moving immediately to the domestic level of analysis (and thus sacrificing the advantages of systemic theory), is to recognize that what it is rational for states to do, and what states' interests are, depend on the institutional context of action as well as on the underlying power realities and state position upon which Realist thought concentrates. Structural approaches should be seen as only a basis for further systemic analysis. They vary the power condition in the system, but they are silent on variations in the frequency of mutual interactions in the system or in the level of information.

The importance of these non-power factors is demonstrated by some recent work on cooperation. In particular, Robert Axelrod has shown that cooperation can emerge among egoists under conditions of strategic interdependence as modelled by the game of prisoners' dilemma. Such a result requires, however, that these egoists expect to continue to interact with each other for the indefinite future, and that these expectations of future interactions be given sufficient weight in their calculations (Axelrod, 1981). This argument reinforces the practical wisdom of diplomats and arms controllers, who assume that state strategies, and the degree of eventual cooperation, will depend significantly on expectations about the future. The "double-cross" strategy, for instance, is more attractive when it is expected to lead to a final, winning move, than when a continuing series of actions and reactions is anticipated.

High levels of uncertainty reduce the confidence with which expectations are held, and may therefore lead governments to discount the future heavily. As Axelrod shows, this can inhibit the evolution of cooperation through reciprocity. It can also reduce the ability of actors to make mutually beneficial agreements at any given time, quite apart from their expectations about whether future interactions will occur. That is, it can lead to a form of "political market failure" (Keohane, 1982).

Information that reduces uncertainty is therefore an important factor in world politics. But information is not a systemic constant. Some international systems are rich in institutions and processes that provide information to governments and other actors; in other systems, information is scarce or of low quality. Given a certain distribution of power (Waltz's "international structure"), variations in information may be important in influencing state behavior. If international institutions can evolve that improve the quality of information and reduce uncertainty, they may profoundly affect international political behavior even in the absence of changes either in international structure (defined in terms of the distribution of power) or in the preference functions of actors.

Taking information seriously at the systemic level could stimulate a new look at theories of information-processing within governments, such as those of Axelrod (1976), George (1980), Jervis (1976), and Holsti (1976). It could also help us, however, to understand a dimension of the concept of complex interdependence (Keohane and Nye, 1977) that has been largely ignored. Complex interdependence can be seen as a condition under which it is not only difficult to use conventional power resources for certain purposes, but under which information levels are relatively high due to the existence of multiple channels of contact among states. If we focus exclusively on questions of power, the most important feature of complex interdependence—almost its only important feature—is the ineffectiveness of military force and the constraints that this implies on fungibility of power across issue-areas. Sensitizing ourselves to the role of information, and information-provision, at the international level brings another aspect of complex interdependence—the presence of multiple channels of contact among societies—back into the picture. Actors behave differently in information-rich environments than in information-poor ones where uncertainty prevails.

This is not a subject that can be explored in depth here.[29] I raise it, however, to clarify the nature of the multi-dimensional network of theories and research programs that I advocate for the study of world politics. We need both spare, logically tight theories, such as Structural Realism, and rich interpretations, such as those of the historically-oriented students of domestic structure and foreign policy. But we also need something in-between: systemic theories that retain some of the parsimony of Structural Realism, but that are able to deal better with differentiations between issue-areas, with institutions, and with change. Such theories could be developed on the basis of variations in power (as in Structural

Realism), but they could also focus on variations in other systemic characteristics, such as levels and quality of information.

CONCLUSION: WORLD POLITICS AND PEACEFUL CHANGE

As Gilpin points out, the problem of peaceful change is fundamental to world politics. Thermonuclear weapons have made it even more urgent than it was in the past. Realism demonstrates that peaceful change is more difficult to achieve in international politics than within well-ordered domestic societies, but it does not offer a theory of peaceful change.[30] Nor is such a theory available from other research traditions. The question remains for us to grapple with: Under what conditions will adaptations to shifts in power, in available technologies, or in fundamental economic relationships take place without severe economic disruption or warfare?

Recent work on "international regimes" has been addressed to this question, which is part of the broader issue of order in world politics (*International Organization*, Spring, 1982). Structural Realist approaches to understanding the origins and maintenance of international regimes are useful (Krasner, 1982), but since they ignore cognitive issues and questions of information, they comprise only part of the story (Haas, 1982).

Realism, furthermore, is better at telling us why we are in such trouble than how to get out of it. It argues that order can be created from anarchy by the exercise of superordinate power: periods of peace follow establishment of dominance in Gilpin's "hegemonic wars." Realism sometimes seems to imply, pessimistically, that order can *only* be created by hegemony. If the latter conclusion were correct, not only would the world economy soon become chaotic (barring a sudden resurgence of American power), but at some time in the foreseeable future, global nuclear war would ensue.

Complacency in the face of this prospect is morally unacceptable. No serious thinker could, therefore, be satisfied with Realism as the correct theory of world politics, even if the scientific status of the theory were stronger than it is. Our concern for humanity requires us to do what Gilpin does in the epilogue to *War and Change* (1981), where he holds out the hope of a "new and more stable international order" in the final decades of the twentieth century, despite his theory's contention that such a benign outcome is highly unlikely. Although Gilpin could be criticized for inconsistency, this would be beside the point: the conditions of terror under which we live compel us to search for a way out of the trap.

The need to find a way out of the trap means that international relations must be a policy science as well as a theoretical activity.[31] We should be seeking to link theory with practice, bringing insights from Structural Realism, modified structural theories, other systemic approaches, and actor-level analyses to bear on contemporary issues in a sophisticated way. This does not mean that the social scientist should adopt the policy-maker's framework, much less his normative values or blinders about the range of available alternatives. On the contrary, independent observers often do their most valuable work when they reject the normative or analytic framework of those in power, and the best theorists may be those who maintain their distance from those at the center of events. Nevertheless, foreign policy and world politics are too important to be left to bureaucrats, generals, and lawyers — or even to journalists and clergymen.

Realism helps us determine the strength of the trap, but does not give us much assistance in seeking to escape. If we are to promote peaceful change, we need to focus not only on basic long-term forces that determine the shape of world politics independently of the actions of particular decision-makers, but also on variables that to some extent can be manipulated by human action. Since international institutions, rules, and patterns of cooperation can affect calculations of interest, and can also be affected incrementally by contemporary political action, they provide a natural focus for scholarly attention as well as policy concern.[32] Unlike Realism, theories that attempt to explain rules, norms, and institutions help us to understand how to create patterns of cooperation that could be essential to our survival. We need to respond to the questions that Realism poses but fails to answer: How can order be created out of anarchy *without* superordinate power; how can peaceful change occur?

To be reminded of the significance of international relations as policy analysis, and the pressing problem of order, is to recall the tradition of Classical Realism. Classical Realism, as epitomized by the work of John Herz (1981), has recognized that no matter how deterministic our theoretical aspirations may be, there remains a human interest in autonomy and self-reflection. As Ashley puts it, the Realism of a thinker such as Herz is committed to an "emancipatory cognitive interest — an interest in securing freedom from unacknowledged constraints, relations of domination, and conditions of distorted communication and understanding that deny humans the capacity to make their future with full will and consciousness" (1981, p. 227).[33] We think about world politics not because it is aesthetically beautiful, because we believe that it is governed by simple, knowable laws, or because it provides rich, easily accessible data for the testing of empirical hypotheses. Were those concerns paramount, we would look elsewhere. We study world politics because we think it will determine the fate of the earth (Schell, 1982). Realism makes us aware of the odds against us. What we need to do now is to understand peaceful change by combining multi-dimensional scholarly analysis with more visionary ways of seeing the future.

NOTES

1. An unfortunate limitation of this chapter is that its scope is restricted to work published in English, principally in the United States. I recognize that this re-

flects the Americanocentrism of scholarship in the United States, and I regret it. But I am not sufficiently well-read in works published elsewhere to comment intelligently on them. For recent discussions of the distinctively American stamp that has been placed on the international relations field see Hoffmann (1977) and Lyons (1982).

2. Nye and I, in effect, conceded this in our later work, which was more cautious about the drawbacks of conventional "state-centric" theory. (See Keohane and Nye, 1977.)

3. For a discussion of "theory as a set of questions," see Hoffmann (1960, pp. 1–12).

4. Bruce Russett has written a parallel essay on "International Interactions and Processes: The Internal vs. External Debate Revisited." Professor Russett discusses the extensive literature on arms control and on dependency, neither of which I consider here.

5. Stanley J. Michalak, Jr. pointed out correctly that our characterization of Realism in *Power and Interdependence* was unfair when taken literally, although he also seems to me to have missed the Realist basis of our structural models. (See Michalak, 1979.)

6. It has often been noted that Kuhn's definition of a paradigm was vague: one sympathetic critic identified 21 distinct meanings of the term in Kuhn's relatively brief book (Masterman, 1970). But Lakatos particularly objected to what he regarded as Kuhn's relativism, which in his view interpreted major changes in science as the result of essentially irrational forces. (See Lakatos, 1970, p. 178.)

7. Lakatos' comments on Marxism and psychology were biting, and a colleague of his reports that he doubted the applicability of the methodology of scientific research programs to the social sciences. (See Latsis, 1976, p. 2.)

8. Robert Jervis and Ann Tickner have both reminded me that Morgenthau and John H. Herz, another major proponent of Realist views in the 1950s, later severely qualified their adherence to what has generally been taken as Realist doctrine. (See Herz, 1981, and Boyle, 1980, p. 218.) I am particularly grateful to Dr. Tickner for obtaining a copy of the relevant pages of the latter article for me.

9. For commentary on this assumption, see Keohane and Nye (1972), and Mansbach, Ferguson, and Lampert (1976). In *Power and Interdependence*, Nye and I were less critical than we had been earlier of the state-centric assumption. In view of the continued importance of governments in world affairs, for many purposes it seems justified on grounds of parsimony. Waltz's rather acerbic critique of our earlier position seems to me essentially correct. (See Waltz, 1979, p. 7.)

10. Emphasis added. Thucydides also follows this "positive heuristic" of looking for underlying power realities in discussions of the Athenian–Corcyrean alliance (Chapter II), the decision of the Lacedemonians to vote that Athens had broken the treaty between them (Chapter III), and Pericles' Funeral Oration (Chapter IV). In the Modern Library edition, the passages in question are on pp. 28, 49–50, and 83.

11. Bruce Bueno de Mesquita (1981, pp. 29–33) has an excellent discussion of the rationality assumption as used in the study of world politics.

12. As Waltz points out, Morgenthau's writings reflect the "first-image" Realist view that the evil inherent in man is at the root of war and conflict.

13. In an illuminating recent review essay, John Gerard Ruggie has criticized Waltz's assumption that the second dimension of structure, referring to the degree of differentiation of units, can be regarded as a constant (undifferentiated units with similar functions) in world politics. Ruggie argues that "when the concept differentiation is properly defined, the second structural level of Waltz's model . . . serves to depict the kind of institutional transformation illustrated by the shift from the medieval to the modern international system." See Ruggie (1983, p. 279).

14. Waltz denies that he relies on the rationality assumption; but I argue in Section II that he requires it for his theory of the balance of power to hold.

15. Sustained earlier critiques of the fungibility assumption can be found in Keohane and Nye (1977, pp. 49–52) and in Baldwin (1979).

16. For a brilliant discussion of this theoretical strategy in micro-economics, see Latsis (1976, especially pp. 16–23).

17. Since the principal purpose of Realist analysis in the hands of Waltz and others is to develop an explanation of international political reality, rather than to offer specific advice to those in power, the label, "technical realism," seems too narrow. It also carries a pejorative intent that I do not share. "Structural Realism" captures the focus on explanation through an examination of the structure of the international system. Capitalization is used to indicate that Realism is a specific school, and that it would be possible to be a Realist — in the sense of examining reality as it really is — without subscribing to Realist assumptions. For a good discussion, see Krasner (1982).

18. This is the commonsense view of power, as discussed, for example, by Arnold Wolfers (1962, p. 103). As indicated in Section III, any such definition conceals a large number of conceptual problems.

19. My reading of Gilpin's argument on pp. 29–34 led me originally to believe that he also accepted the notion that power is fungible, since he argues that hegemonic war creates a hierarchy of prestige in an international system, which is based on the hegemon's "demonstrated ability to enforce its will on other states" (p. 34), and which in turn determines governance of the international system (p. 33). This appears to imply that a single structure of power resources exists, usable for a wide variety of issues. But in letters sent to the author commenting on an earlier draft of this paper, both Gilpin and Waltz explicitly disavowed the assumption that power resources are necessarily fungible. In *War and Change*, Gilpin is very careful to disclaim the notion, which he ascribes to Political Realists but which I have not included in the hard core of Realism, that states seek to maximize their power: "Acquisition of power entails an opportunity cost to a society; some other desired good must be abandoned" (p. 51).

20. A similar issue is posed in Chapter 3 of Part II of *Lineages of the Absolutist State* (1974). Its author, Perry Anderson, addresses the puzzle of why it was Prussia, rather than Bavaria or Saxony, that eventually gained predominance in Germany. Despite his inclinations, Anderson has to rely on a variety of conjunctural, if not accidental, factors to account for the observed result.

21. For a lucid discussion of the security dilemma, see Jervis (1978).

22. The fact that sensitive Realists are aware of the limitations of Realism makes me less worried than Ashley about the policy consequences of Realist analysis.

23. Waltz does not accept Baldwin's (and Dahl's) definition of power in terms of

causality, arguing that "power is one cause among others, from which it cannot be isolated." But this makes it impossible to falsify any power theory; one can always claim that other factors (not specified a priori) were at work. Waltz's discussion of power (1979, pp. 191–192) does not separate power-as-outcome properly from power-as-resources; it does not distinguish between resources that the observer can assess a priori from those only assessable post hoc; it does not relate probabilistic thinking properly to power theory; and it takes refuge in a notion of power as "affecting others more than they affect him," which would result (if taken literally) in the absurdity of attributing maximum power to the person or government that is least responsive to outside stimuli, regardless of its ability to achieve its purposes.

24. Jervis (1976, Chapter 1) has an excellent discussion of levels of analysis and the relationship between perceptual theories and other theories of international relations. Snyder and Diesing discuss similar issues in Chapter VI on "Crises and International Systems" (1977).

25. Waltz commented perceptively in *Man, the State and War* that contributions of behavioral scientists had often been "rendered ineffective by a failure to comprehend the significance of the political framework of international action" (1959, p. 78).

26. Thorough description — what Alexander George has called "process-tracting" — may be necessary to evaluate a structural explanation, since correlations are not reliable where only a small number of comparable cases is involved. (See George, 1979.)

27. I am indebted for this point to a conversation with Hayward Alker.

28. Latsis (1976) discusses the difference between "single-exit" and "multiple-exit" situations in his critique of oligopoly theory. What he calls the research program of "situational determinism" — structural theory, in my terms — works well for single-exit situations, where only one sensible course of action is possible. (The building is burning down and there is only one way out: regardless of my personal characteristics, one can expect that I will leave through that exit.) It does not apply to multiple-exit situations, where more than one plausible choice can be made. (The building is burning, but I have to choose between trying the smoky stairs or jumping into a fireman's net: my choice may depend on deep-seated personal fears.) In foreign policy, the prevalence of multiple-exit situations reinforces the importance of decision-making analysis at the national level.

29. For a more detailed discussion of some aspects of this notion, and for citations to some of the literature in economics on which my thinking is based, see Keohane (1982). Discussions with Vinod Aggarwal have been important in formulating some of the points in the previous two paragraphs.

30. Morgenthau devotes a chapter of *Politics Among Nations* to peaceful change, but after a review of the reasons why legalistic approaches will not succeed, he eschews general statements for descriptions of a number of United Nations actions affecting peace and security. No theory of peaceful change is put forward. In *Politics Among Nations* Morgenthau put whatever faith he had in diplomacy. The chapter on peaceful change is Chapter 26 of the fourth edition (1966).

31. For a suggestive discussion of international relations as policy science, see George and Smoke (1974), Appendix, "Theory for Policy in International Relations," pp. 616–642.

32. Recall Weber's aphorism in "Politics as a Vocation": "Politics is the strong and slow boring of hard boards." Although much of Weber's work analyzed broad historical forces beyond the control of single individuals or groups, he remained acutely aware of "the truth that man would not have attained the possible unless time and again he had reached out for the impossible" (Gerth & Mills, 1958, p. 128). For a visionary, value-laden discourse on future international politics by a scholar "reaching out for the impossible," see North (1976, Chapter 7).

33. Ernst B. Haas, who has studied how political actors learn throughout his distinguished career, makes a similar point in a recent essay, where he espouses a "cognitive-evolutionary view" of change and argues that such a view "cannot settle for a concept of hegemony imposed by the analyst. . . . It makes fewer claims about basic directions, purposes, laws and trends than do other lines of thought. It is agnostic about the finality of social laws" (1982, pp. 242–243). The difference between Haas and me is that he seems to reject structural analysis in favor of an emphasis on cognitive evolution and learning, whereas I believe that modified structural analysis (more modest in its claims than Structural Realism) can provide a context within which analysis of cognition is politically more meaningful.

REFERENCES

Aggarwal, Vinod, *Hanging by a thread: International regime change in the textile apparel system, 1950–1979.* Unpublished doctoral dissertation, Stanford University, 1981.

Anderson, Perry. *Lineages of the Absolutist State.* London: New Left Books, 1974.

Art, Robert J. Bureaucratic Politics and American Foreign Policy: A Critique. *Policy Sciences* 4, 1973, 467–490.

Ashley, Richard K. Political Realism and Human Interest. *International Studies Quarterly* 25, 1981, 204–236.

Ashley, Richard K. Realistic dialectics: Toward a critical theory of world politics. Paper presented at the Annual Meeting of the American Political Science Association, Denver, September 1982.

Axelrod, Robert (Ed.). *The Structure of Decision: The Cognitive Maps of Political Elites.* Princeton, N.J.: Princeton University Press, 1976.

Axelrod, Robert. The Emergence of Cooperation Among Egoists. *American Political Science Review* 25, 1981, 306–318.

Baldwin, David A. Power Analysis and World Politics: New Trends versus Old Tendencies. *World Politics* 31, 1979, 161–194.

Boyle, Francis A. The Irrelevance of International Law: The Schism Between International Law and International Politics. *California Western International Law Journal* 10, 1980.

Brecher, Michael, with Geist, Benjamin. *Decisions in Crisis: Israel 1967–1973.* Berkeley: University of California Press, 1980.

Bueno de Mesquita, Bruce. *The War Trap.* New Haven: Yale Univesity Press, 1981.

Carr, E. H. *The Twenty Years' Crisis, 1919–1939,* 1st ed. London: Macmillan, 1946. (Originally published 1939.)

Choucri, Nazli and North, Robert C. *Nations in Conflict: National Growth and International Violence.* San Francisco: W. H. Freeman & Co., 1975.

Cipolla, Carlo. *The Economic Decline of Empires.* London: Methuen, 1970.

Dahl, Robert A. *Who Governs? Democracy and Power in an American City.* New Haven: Yale University Press, 1961.

Eckstein, Harry. Case Study and Theory in Political Science. In Fred I. Greenstein and Nelson W. Polsby (Eds.), *Handbook of Political Science* (Vol. 7) *Strategies of Inquiry.* Reading, MA: Addison-Wesley, 1975.

Geertz, Clifford. *The Interpretation of Cultures.* New York: Basic Books, 1973.

George, Alexander L. Case Studies and Theory Development: The Method of Structured, Focused Comparison. In Paul Gordon Lauren (Ed.), *Diplomacy: New Approaches in History, Theory and Policy.* New York: Free Press, 1979.

George, Alexander L. *Presidential Decision Making in Foreign Policy: The Effective Use of Information and Advice.* Boulder: Westview, 1980.

George, Alexander L. and George, Juliette. *Woodrow Wilson and Colonel House.* New York: Dover, 1964.

George, Alexander L., Hall, D. K. & Simons, W. E. *The Limits of Coercive Diplomacy.* Boston: Little, Brown, 1971.

George, Alexander L. and Smoke, Richard. *Deterrence in American Foreign Policy.* New York: Columbia University Press, 1974.

Gerschenkron, Alexander. *Economic Backwardness in Historical Perspective.* Cambridge: The Belknap Press of Harvard University Press, 1962.

Gerth, H. H., and Mills, G. Wright. *From Max Weber: Essays in Sociology.* New York: Oxford University Press, 1958.

Gilpin, Robert. *U.S. Power and the Multinational Corporation.* New York: Basic Books, 1975.

Gilpin, Robert. *War and Change in World Politics.* Cambridge: Cambridge University Press, 1981.

Gourevitch, Peter A. The Second Image Reversed: The International Sources of Domestic Politics. *International Organization* 32, 1978, 881–913.

Haas, Ernst B. Why Collaborate? Issue-linkage and International Regimes. *World Politics* 32, 1980, 357–405.

Haas, Ernst B. Words Can Hurt You: Or Who Said What to Whom About Regimes. *International Organization* 36, 1982, 207–244.

Harsanyi, John. Measurement of Social Power, Opportunity Costs, and the Theory of Two-Person Bargaining Games. *Behavioral Sciences* 7, 1962, 67–80.

Herz, John H. Political Realism Revisited. *International Studies Quarterly* 25, 1981, 182–197.

Hoffmann, Stanley. *Contemporary Theory in International Relations.* Englewood Cliffs, N.J.: Prentice Hall, 1960.

Hoffmann, Stanley. An American Social Science: International Relations. *Daedalus,* Summer 1977, 41–60.

Holsti, Ole. Foreign Policy Viewed Cognitively. In Robert Axelrod (Ed.), *The Structure of Decision: The Cognitive Maps of Political Elites.* Princeton, N.J.: Princeton University Press, 1976.

International Organization 36, 1982. Special issue on international regimes edited by Stephen D. Krasner.

Jervis, Robert. *Perception and Misperception in International Politics.* Princeton, N.J.: Princeton University Press, 1976.

Jervis, Robert. Cooperation Under the Security Dilemma. *World Politics* 30, 1978, 167–214.

Katzenstein, Peter J. *Between Power and Plenty: Foreign Economic Policies of Advanced Industrial States.* Madison: University of Wisconsin Press, 1978.

Keohane, Robert O. The Demand for International Regimes. *International Organization* 36, 1982, 325–356.

Keohane, Robert O., and Nye, Joseph (Eds.). *Transnational Relations and World Politics.* Cambridge, MA: Harvard University Press, 1972.

Keohane, Robert O., and Nye, Joseph. *Power and Interdependence: World Politics in Transition.* Boston: Little, Brown, 1977.

Krasner, Stephen D. *Defending the National Interest: Raw Materials Investments and U.S. Foreign Policy.* Princeton: Princeton University Press, 1978.

Krasner, Stephen D. Structural Causes and Regime Consequences: Regimes as Intervening Variables. *International Organization* 36, 1982, 185–206.

Kuhn, Thomas S. *The Structure of Scientific Revolutions.* Chicago: University of Chicago Press, 1962.

Kurth, James R. The Political Consequences of the Product Cycle: Industrial History and Political Outcomes. *International Organization* 33, 1979, 1–34.

Lakatos, Imre. Falsification and the methodology of scientific research programmes. In Imre Lakatos and Alan Musgrave (eds.), *Criticism and the Growth of Knowledge,* Cambridge: Cambridge University Press, 1970.

Latsis, Spiro J. A Research Programme in Economics. In Latsis, ed., *Method and Approval in Economics.* Cambridge: Cambridge University Press, 1976.

Lebow, Richard Ned. *Between Peace and War. The Nature of International Crisis.* Baltimore: Johns Hopkins University Press, 1981.

Lenin, V. I. *Imperialism: The Highest Stage of Capitalism.* New York: International Publishers, 1939. (Originally written 1916.)

Luttwak, Edward. *The Grand Strategy of the Roman Empire—From the First Century A.D. to the Third.* Baltimore: Johns Hopkins University Press, 1976.

Lyons, Gene M. Expanding the Study of International Relations: The French Connection. *World Politics* 35, 1982, 135–149.

Mansbach, Richard, Ferguson, Yale H. and Lampert, Donald E. *The Web of World Politics.* Englewood Cliffs, N.J.: Prentice Hall, 1976.

Mansbach, Richard and Vasquez, John A. *In Search of Theory: A New Paradigm for Global Politics.* New York: Columbia University Press, 1981.

March, James G. The Power of Power. In David Easton (ed.), *Varieties of Political Theory.* Englewood Cliffs, N.J.: Prentice Hall, 1966.

Masterman, Margaret. The Nature of a Paradigm. In Lakatos and Musgrave, eds., *Criticism and the Growth of Knowledge.* Cambridge: Cambridge University Press, 1970.

Michalak, Stanley J., Jr. Theoretical Perspectives for Understanding International Interdependence. *World Politics* 32, 1979, 136–150.

Moore, Barrington, Jr. *Social Origins of Dictatorship and Democracy: Lord and Peasant in the Making of the Modern World.* Boston: Beacon Press, 1966.

Morgenthau, Hans J. *Scientific Man Versus Power Politics.* Chicago: University of Chicago Press, 1946.

Morgenthau, Hans J. *Politics Among Nations,* 4th ed. New York: Knopf, 1966. (Originally published, 1948).

North, Douglass C. *Structure and Change in Economic History.* New York: Norton, 1981.

North, Robert C. *The World That Could Be*. (The Portable Stanford: Stanford Alumni Association.) Palo Alto, CA: Stanford University, 1976.

Organski, A. F. K., and Kugler, Jacek. *The War Ledger*. Chicago: University of Chicago Press, 1980.

Oye, Kenneth A. The Domain of Choice. In Kenneth A. Oye, Donald Rothchild, and Robert J. Lieber (eds.), *Eagle Entangled: U.S. Foreign Policy in a Complex World*. New York: Longman, 1979, pp. 3–33.

Oye, Kenneth A. *Belief Systems, Bargaining and Breakdown: International Political Economy 1929–1934*. Unpublished doctoral dissertation, Harvard University, 1983.

Rosenau, James N. Pre-theories and theories of foreign policy. In R. Barry Farrell (ed.), *Approaches to Comparative and International Politics*. Evanston, IL: Northwestern University Press, 1966.

Ruggie, John Gerard. Continuity and Transformation in the World Polity: Toward a Neo-Realist Synthesis. *World Politics* 35, 1983, 261–285.

Russett, Bruce M. The Calculus of Deterrence. *Journal of Conflict Resolution*, 1963, 97–109.

Schell, Jonathan. *The Fate of the Earth*. New York: Knopf, 1982.

Schelling, Thomas. *The Strategy of Conflict*. New York: Oxford University Press, 1960.

Simon, Herbert A. The Architecture of Complexity. In Simon, ed., *The Sciences of the Artificial*. Cambridge: MIT Press, 1969.

Snidal, Duncan. *Interdependence, Regimes, and International Cooperation*. Unpublished manuscript, University of Chicago, 1981.

Snyder, Glenn H. and Diesing, Paul. *Conflict Among Nations: Bargaining, Decision-Making and System Structure in International Crises*. Princeton, N.J.: Princeton University Press, 1977.

Sprout, Harold and Margaret. *Toward a Politics of the Planet Earth*. New York: Van Nostrand Reinhold, 1971.

Stein, Arthur. The Politics of Linkage. *World Politics* 33, 1980, 62–81.

Stein, Arthur. Coordination and Collaboration: Regimes in an Anarchic World. *International Organization* 36, 1982, 299–324.

Thucydides. *The Peloponnesian War* (John H. Finley, Jr., trans). New York: Modern Library, 1951. (Originally written c. 400 B.C.)

Tollison, Robert D. and Willett, Thomas D. An Economic Theory of Mutually Advantageous Issue Linkage in International Negotiations. *International Organization* 33, 1979, 425–450.

Toulmin, Stephen. *Foresight and Understanding: An Enquiry into the Aims of Science*. New York: Harper Torchbooks, 1963.

Wallerstein, Immanuel. The Rise and Future Demise of the World Capitalist System: Concepts for Comparative Analysis. In Wallerstein, *The Capitalist World Economy*. Cambridge: Cambridge University Press, 1979. (This essay was originally printed in *Comparative Studies in Society and History* 16, 1974.)

Wallerstein, Immanuel. *The Modern World-System II: Mercantilism and the Consolidation of the European World-Economy, 1600–1750*. New York: Academic Press, 1980.

Waltz, Kenneth N. *Man, the State and War*. New York: Columbia University Press, 1959.

Waltz, Kenneth N. *Foreign Policy and Democratic Politics: The American and British Experience*. Boston: Little, Brown, 1967.

Waltz, Kenneth N. *Theory of International Politics*. Reading, MA: Addison-Wesley, 1979, p. 7.

Wolfers, Arnold. *Discord and Collaboration: Essays on International Politics*. Baltimore: Johns Hopkins University Press, 1962.

3

Pluralism: Decision Making, Transnationalism, and Interdependence

MAJOR ACTORS AND ASSUMPTIONS: A SUMMARY

The pluralist image of international relations is based on four key assumptions. First, *nonstate actors* are important entities in world politics. International organizations, for example, may on certain issues be independent actors in their own right. They are more than simply forums within which states compete and cooperate with one another. The staff of a particular international organization may have a great deal of power in terms of agenda setting as well as in providing information which may influence how states define their interests. International organizations may also have an important role in implementing, monitoring, and adjudicating disputes arising from decisions made by constituent states of the organization. Over time, such functions may make the international organization indispensable to member states. Similarly, other nongovernmental, **transnational** organizations such as multinational corporations (MNCs) play important roles in world politics. Nor can one ignore the impact of such nonstate actors as terrorist groups, arms dealers, and guerrilla movements.

Second, for the pluralist *the state is not a unitary actor.* It is composed of competing individuals, interests groups, and bureaucracies. Although it may be convenient for newspapers and governmental representatives to refer to "decisions taken by the United States," it is generally more accurate to speak of a decision made by a particular governmental coalition, bureaucracy, or even perhaps a single individual. The decision is not made by some abstract entity called "the United States" but by some combination of actors within the foreign policy establishment.

Different organizations, for example, may have different perspectives on a particular foreign policy issue. Competition, coalition building, and compromise will eventually result in a decision that is then announced in the name of the United States. Furthermore, this state decision may be the result of lobbying carried out by such nongovernmental actors as multinational corporations, or interest groups, or it may even be influenced by something as amorphous as public opinion. To the pluralist, the state cannot therefore be viewed as a unitary actor because to do so misses the multiplicity of actors comprising the entity termed *the state*, the interactions occurring among these actors, and the role of influences emanating from beyond the territorial boundaries of the state as well as from domestic sources — ideas and values, international and transnational organizations, interest groups, and public opinion.

Third, pluralists *challenge the realist assumption of the state as rational actor*. Given their fragmented view of the state, it is assumed that the clash of interests, bargaining, and need for compromise do not always make for a rational decision-making process. Misperception or bureaucratic politics may dominate decision making, leading to poor decisions that are often *suboptimal* or less than the best in terms of objectives sought. Instead of leading their country, statesmen may be tempted to take their cue from public opinion polls, evincing more concern for their personal standing or power position than for the good of the country as a whole. Pressure resulting from a crisis situation may also make a mockery of the notion of a cool and calculating decision-making process.

Finally, for pluralists the *agenda of international politics is extensive*. Although national security concerns are important, the pluralist is also concerned with a number of economic, social, and ecological issues arising from the growth of **interdependence** among states and societies in the twentieth century. Certain pluralists, for example, emphasize trade, monetary, and energy issues and how these issues have come to be placed high on the international agenda. Other pluralists examine international attempts to deal with the world population problem and famine in parts of the **Third World.** Still others have studied the politics of international pollution and the degradation of the environment. The foreign affairs agendas of states are not exclusively preoccupied with national security issues, narrowly defined in terms of military matters. Economic and social issues can often have a direct bearing on the security and welfare of a particular regime or country. Because this is so, pluralists tend to reject the high versus low politics dichotomy accepted by most realists. Socioeconomic issues are often as important as military concerns.

INTELLECTUAL PRECURSORS AND INFLUENCES

In the case of realism, it was relatively easy to identify its intellectual precursors. At least two of these, Grotius and E. H. Carr, have also had significant impact on scholars associated with the pluralist image. In the case of pluralism, however, the impact of particular theorists has tended to be more indirect. This is because many of these writers have not been observers of international relations per se but have been economists, social scientists, theologians, or political scientists interested in domestic politics. Their one common denominator, however, has been an interest in the individual or group as the unit of analysis, as opposed to the unified state that is the focus of realist writings. Therefore, we have organized the discussion of the intellectual precursors of pluralism around two themes within which individual theorists are mentioned: **liberalism** as a political philosophy and **interest group liberalism** as an approach to the study of domestic politics.

Although some aspects of liberal thought have also influenced realist scholars, we focus here on those aspects of liberalism that lead to rejection of a view of the state as unitary and rational actor. That the state is (or should be) disaggregated into component parts or becomes the battleground for competing interests is a view found in liberalism as well as interest group liberalism. Within the international relations discipline, works on **decision making** and transnationalism best reflect this view of the disaggregated state and the importance of nonstate actors.

Liberalism

Liberalism is a tradition of political thought composed of a set of practical goals and ideals. For classical liberal theorists, the individual is the most important unit of analysis and the claimant of rights. The state is to play a minimal role in a liberal society, principally acting as arbiter in disputes between individuals and ensuring the maintenance of conditions under which individuals can enjoy their rights to the fullest. There are important differences among liberal theorists, but they do agree on the primacy of the individual in political life and on the role of the state as being limited to maintaining a stable political, social, and economic environment within which individuals can interact and pursue their chosen ends. This emphasis on the individual and the limited state is perhaps best exemplified in John Locke's *Second Treatise on Government,* published in England in 1689.[1]

Liberalism as an ideology came to dominate much of the political and economic thought in the eighteenth and nineteenth centuries, particularly in Great Britain and the United States. Liberal concerns for the individual were reinforced by Adam Smith's and David Ricardo's works in economics. They emphasized the important role of the individual entrepreneur who should be relatively unconstrained by a minimalist state — a major theme in early capitalist writings. David Hume's contribution to logic and the philosophy of science similarly stressed the importance of the individual as the unit of analysis. The nineteenth-century essays of such **utilitarians** as Jeremy Bentham viewed people as rational, calculating individuals capable of deciding what was best for themselves without much government interference. Liberalism reigned supreme, virtually unchallenged in the United States and Great Britain until the turn of the century. The spirit of liberalism and its emphasis on the individual pervaded all spheres of life and thought — scientific, political, economic, social, and religious.[2] The industrial revolution, however, eventually resulted in modifications of liberal doctrine, which although retaining an emphasis on the individual now allowed the state to be given a somewhat more activist role in order to mitigate the most harmful effects of unrestrained economic competition.

For liberals the minimal state was a possibility (and necessity) because it was assumed that there was an underlying harmony of interests among individuals.

Just as the competition of the marketplace would produce the best goods, so too would the marketplace of ideas produce sound political sense. It followed that liberals emphasized the positive role played by public opinion in providing guidance to state officials and producing good public policy, including foreign policy. The state, therefore, was not some unitary, solitary actor pursuing its own course independently of the public. To the contrary, it was composed of numerous persons representing a multitude of interests. Nor were decisions the sole province of those individuals acting in the name of the state. Decisions were supposed to be informed by the public opinion and political consensus arising out of the clash of ideas and interests.

This view of the domestic polity was carried over into the international realm. Liberals recognized that war was a defining characteristic of international politics. They also agreed with realists that the state of anarchy that characterized world (as opposed to domestic) politics contributed to suspicion and distrust among states, posing an obstacle to cooperation and peace. But just as it was assumed that there could be a harmony of interests among individuals within a given state, so too did liberal theorists argue that a harmony of interests among states was possible.

It was recognized that war had existed down through the centuries. What, then, had changed to allow for this more optimistic view of interstate relations? Liberals made at least four arguments. First, advocates of what could be termed *commercial liberalism* argued that the expansion of the international economy made it more costly for states to go to war. As economic interdependence increased, there would be a disinclination to cut profitable economic ties.[3] Second, advocates of *democratic liberalism* claimed that the spread of democratic (or, more precisely, republican or representative) political systems meant that questions of war and peace were no longer confined to a small group of political and military elites, as in the past. Instead, leaders would have to be concerned with domestic public opinion that could act as a brake on any moves toward international confrontation and the outbreak of hostilities. Third, *regulatory liberalism* claims that the benefits of international law, accepted "rules of the game," and international organizations would contribute to the peaceful settlement of disputes among states and enhance global cooperation.[4] Finally, it was argued that western civilization had suffered enough from war and that leaders and citizens had learned how costly it was to wage it.

The German, or more precisely East Prussian, philosopher Immanuel Kant (1724–1804) observed that over the years it had become increasingly likely that *reason* would be a substitute for the use of force in world politics. Kant's emphasis on learning seems to have influenced modern works on regional integration and pluralist conceptions of international regimes.[5] Since World War I, liberal thinking has particularly stressed the positive role international law can play in promoting peace and harmony in world politics. Collaborative action by international organizations that represents the consensus of their constituent states works to mitigate the worst aspects of anarchy and to encourage cooperation.[6]

In sum, this brief overview of liberal thought highlights a number of concepts, arguments, and perspectives that directly or indirectly influence the pluralist image of international politics: the importance of the individual and societal **levels of analysis,** the disaggregated and nonunified state broken into its component parts, the intimate connection between international economics and politics, the role of public opinion, the importance of international law and organizations, and the ability of leaders to learn from past historical mistakes and disasters. The latter point is particularly important, injecting a voluntarist strand into thinking about international politics by holding out the prospect of some control over our fate. Current scholars whom we would term pluralist have not been equally influenced by all strands of liberal thought as it has developed over the years. Some have been particularly influenced by the liberal view of the disaggregated state with an emphasis on the *individual* as the unit of analysis. Others have been less influenced by such methodological questions, but more by the optimistic elements of liberalism concerning the possibilities for learning, peaceful change, and potential harmony in the international system.

Interest Group Liberalism

The roots of the pluralist image of international politics also lie in the view held by many scholars of the domestic political order. This is particularly true of American academics who are prone to see international politics through domestic political lenses. Indeed, the pluralist image of international politics held by many American international relations scholars can be understood as a projection of American political processes onto the entire globe. International political processes are not all that different from, and may even be considered an extension of, those conducted within the boundaries of a given state. As a result, pluralists tend to reject the realist distinction between "international" and "domestic" politics. For the pluralist, one is an extension of the other. This perspective is quite evident in much of the literature on decision making and transnationalism that disaggregates the state-as-actor.

The majority (but certainly not all) of authors we would term pluralist are American. Each has either directly or indirectly been influenced by political scientists who are students of the American political system. We use the term interest group liberalism to describe the perspective of these latter individuals.

The connection to the discussion of eighteenth- and nineteenth-century liberal thought is apparent. One critic of interest group liberalism, for example, makes the following observations. First, interest group liberalism assumes the "role of government is one of assuring access to the most effectively organized, and of ratifying the agreements and adjustments worked out among competing leaders and their claims."[7] Secondly, there is a "belief in a natural harmony of group competition." Finally, interest group liberalism defines both "the policy agenda and the public interest . . . in terms of the organized interests in society."[8] All three observations are consistent with the liberal notions of (1) the state as neutral arbiter, (2) the potential for a natural harmony of interest (in this case groups instead of individuals), and (3) public concern for, and participation in, a policy process not restricted to elites.

In the image of politics held by adherents of interest group liberalism, conflict and competition among interest groups play an important role. There is a proliferation of interest groups. Individuals form interest groups in attempts to outmaneuver, end-run, or overwhelm opposing groups or coalitions. Viewed in this way, politics is a game but a game with very real stakes to be won or lost. Authoritative choices (or decisions) are made by government decision makers as the outcome of this process.

David Truman, whose writings are in the school of interest group liberalism, acknowledges his intellectual debt to Arthur F. Bentley, whose 1908 volume *The Process of Government* served as "the principal bench mark for my thinking."[9] Truman observes that "the outstanding characteristic of American politics" is the "multiplicity of co-ordinate or nearly co-ordinate points of access to governmental decisions." He proceeds to describe the conflictual nature of American politics, but comments that "overlapping membership among organized interest groups" provides "the principal balancing force in the politics of a multi-group society such as the United States."[10]

The writings of Harold Lasswell and Robert Dahl are also illustrative of this image of American politics. Dahl describes American politics as a "system in which all the active and legitimate groups in the population can make themselves heard at some crucial stage in the process of decision."[11] Noting that it is a decentralized system, he observes that "decisions are made by endless bargaining." Groups are central to the process. Rather than either majority rule or minority rule, Dahl argues that the term *minorities rule* is the more accurate.[12] Politically active groups — minorities — are the most influential.

Thus, the image of politics that interest group liberals hold is of a fragmented political system, one in which multiple actors compete. The image is shared by most American political scientists even though their views may differ greatly on other conceptual and normative matters. The scholars mentioned are not, of course, creators of this image of American politics. Certainly *The Federalist Papers*, especially the writings of James Madison and later those of the Frenchman Alexis de Tocqueville, expose one to a good dose of this view of American domestic politics.[13]

In sum, what the group is to the interest group liberal, the individual is to the liberal philosopher. What they have in common is agreement on the fragmented nature of the state and society and the potential for harmony to develop out of competition and conflict. The state is not an independent, coherent, autonomous actor separated or aloof from society. Its primary function is as arbiter of conflicting demands and claims, or as an arena for the expression of such interests. Furthermore, the focus of analysis is less on the state and more on the competition among individuals and groups.

DECISION MAKING

If states were the only important actors and all states simply responded to their environment according to the same rational logic, there would be no need to disaggregate the state-as-actor or to consider a multiplicity of domestic and international influences. Although it is possible to chart relations among states (as realists sometimes do) without ever looking "inside" the states, pluralists argue that a complete understanding of the *reasons* for these relations requires analysis of the decision-making process. In this section we first examine some early work on foreign policy decision making, and then we focus on scholarly literature that examines the role of individuals and bureaucracies in the formulation of foreign policy.

One of the first major attempts to develop a systematic decision-making approach to the study of international politics was made in the early 1950s by Richard C. Snyder and his colleagues.[14] Snyder stated that the focus of international relations research should be on the actions, reactions, and interactions of states. For him, the state is specifically its decision makers, and state action "is the action taken by those acting in the name of the state."[15] So far, realists would have little with which to disagree.

Snyder, however, emphasized that his analytical objective was to recreate the world as actual decision makers view it in order to explain behavior. This led him to discuss (1) subjective factors from the standpoint of decision makers — how they define the situation — not from the perspective of the analyst, and (2) potential sources of state action found in the decision makers' setting. The framework hence draws attention to numerous factors at different levels of analysis. Under the heading "internal setting," for example, domestic politics and public opinion are listed as potentially important elements in the formulation and execution of foreign policy. Nongovernmental factors and relations between countries (trade, family ties, shared values, mass media, migration, cultural exchanges) may also be important. Snyder therefore developed a decision-making framework consisting of numerous factors. It was up to the scholar to test them **empirically** by means of case studies. The relative importance of any one factor would vary from case to case.

This work is considered a pioneering effort, particularly given Snyder's claim that the foreign policy process could be studied scientifically. From the standpoint of the current state of the international relations discipline, such a perspective on decision making may seem passé, little more than an inventory of potentially relevant factors. For our purposes, it is important to point out that Snyder argued for the systematic consideration of a number of factors that may influence the decisions of flesh-and-blood policymakers. The framework explicity emphasizes **perception** on the part of decision makers and the role of nongovernmental influences on the foreign policy process. These factors are part of the domestic, international, and decision-making settings within which policymakers operate. Hence, a plurality of factors is given prominence. Despite its innovative nature, Snyder's framework failed to generate more than one major empirical case study.[16] What it did do, however, was to encourage a shift in analytic focus away from the **reified,** abstract state.

The 1960s witnessed a proliferation of studies that identified an almost unending inventory of factors that may influence the foreign policy process. But as James N. Rosenau, a long-time student of foreign policy, stated in 1966:

the dynamics of the processes which culminate in the external behavior of societies remain obscure. To identify factors is not to trace their influence. To uncover processes that affect external behavior is not to explain how and why they are operative under certain circumstances and not under others. To recognize that foreign policy is shaped by internal as well as external factors is not to comprehend how the two intermix or to indicate the conditions under which one predominates the other.[17]

What was missing were attempts to develop general theories of foreign policy — theories that contained testable hypotheses aimed at explaining the external behavior of more than one country. Single case studies were the norm.

Comparative studies — examining the similarities and differences of various decision-making systems — were rare until the late 1960s. Spurred by the comparative analysis of political systems, students of international relations began to generate and test hypotheses concerning the foreign policy behavior of states. Although different levels of analysis and different **variables** were used, what these studies had in common was a commitment to discovering common patterns or processes in the foreign (and most recently defense) policies of states.[18]

The Individual and Small Groups

Scholars engaged in studying decision-making processes from a pluralist perspective emphasize, as we have noted, that entities known as the "United States" or "Canada" do not make decisions; decisions are made by individuals. Similarly, a particular bureaucratic entity termed the "State Department" or "Foreign Office" is composed of individuals. It is, therefore, not surprising that the study of individuals and small groups has been a primary focus of analysis for a number of scholars.

The study of individuals and their role in international relations or foreign policy has drawn heavily on the disciplines of **psychology** and **social psychology**. Some of the work can be termed **psychohistory** and has focused on how life experiences influence an individual's foreign policy behavior and orientation. Other work by such scholars as Alexander George and Ole Holsti has attempted to discern an individual's belief system or **operational code**.[19]

A number of research efforts have drawn on the psychology literature in an attempt to generalize about the circumstances under which certain psychological processes occur. What these approaches have in common is an emphasis on how **cognitive** distortions undermine the realist view of decision making as a rational process. But unlike much of the earlier work, many of these scholars have also studied political science and history in addition to psychology and social psychology. As a result, their insights into the role that perception plays in the foreign policy process or during crisis situations is deserving of further comment.

The work of Robert Jervis, to take one example, starts with some realist assumptions, but then it focuses on individuals and individual perceptions, a more pluralist view.[20] Jervis is concerned less with how emotions affect foreign policy decision making and more with how cognitive factors and a confusing international environment can result in a poor decision even if the individual is relatively unemotional and as intelligent as he or she can be in evaluating alternatives. Furthermore, Jervis takes into account how the **anarchic** nature of international politics contributes to this confusing environment by encouraging cognitive processes that make decision making more difficult. Jervis accepts the realist argument that the anarchic **structure** of the international system breeds suspicion and distrust. The lack of a single **sovereign** or authority makes it a self-help system, and it is not necessarily irrational or a sign of paranoia to be preoccupied with real, potential, or imagined threats.

Jervis devotes a great deal of time to applying psychological concepts to historical events. According to him his propositions are

> generalizations about how decision-makers perceive others' behavior and form judgments about their intentions. These patterns are explained by the general ways in which people draw inferences from ambiguous evidence and, in turn, help explain seemingly incomprehensible policies. They show how, why, and when highly intelligent and conscientious statesmen misperceive their environments in specified ways and reach inappropriate decisions.[21]

Jervis is interested in discerning how a decision maker comprehends a complex world filled with uncertainty. Each decision maker has a particular image of the world that has been shaped by his or her interpretations of historical events. Very often these events (such as wars and revolutions) occurred when the individual was young and impressionable. Lessons learned from history, when combined with personal experiences, contribute to the development of particular expectations and beliefs concerning how the world operates that will have a major impact on the decisions made by policymakers. Once formed, these images of reality are difficult to change. Cognitive consistency is the norm. Information that conflicts with the decision maker's image tends either to be dismissed, ignored, or interpreted in such a manner as to buttress a particular policy preference or course of action.

Jervis emphasizes how the striving for cognitive consistency can have a negative effect on decision-making processes, and other scholars focus on how psychological stress arising out of difficult, emotion-laden situations affects rational calculations. One example of this perspective is the work of Irving L. Janis.[22]

Janis has examined the tendency for social pressure to enforce conformity and consensus in cohesive decision-making groups. He calls this tendency **groupthink,** a "mode of thinking that people engage in when they are deeply involved in a cohesive in-group, when the members' strivings for unanimity override their motivation to realistically appraise alternative courses of action."[23] Indicators of groupthink include limiting discussions to only a few alternative courses of action, failing to reexamine initial decisions and possible courses of action initially rejected, and making little attempt to seek information from outside experts who may challenge a preferred policy. To make his case for the persuasiveness of concurrence seeking within a group and the resultant impact,

Janis examines several foreign policy fiascos, such as the Bay of Pigs invasion in 1961, the military unpreparedness of the United States at Pearl Harbor in 1941, and the American decisions to escalate the Korean and Vietnam wars. He argues that in each case the pressure to conform to group norms interfered with critical, rational thinking.

A number of international relations scholars have been particularly interested in how psychological processes influence decision making during times of crisis — a situation between peace and war. The tendency for individuals to strive for cognitive consistency and for groups to enforce consensus among their members is particularly evident in crisis situations characterized by high stress, surprise, exhausting around-the-clock work schedules, and complex and ambiguous environments. As a result, there is a general erosion of cognitive capabilities. Tolerance for ambiguity is reduced, policy options are restricted, opposing actors and their motives are stereotyped. Compared to noncrisis situations, decisions are based even more on policymakers' predispositions, expectations, biases, and emotional states.[24]

In sum, scholarly work suggests that misperception can play a major role in crisis situations, perhaps contributing to the outbreak of war. Furthermore, it has been argued that not all decision makers operate with the same kind of rationality, making it difficult for leaders to judge what actions may deter an enemy.[25] The cumulative effect of such studies is to undermine the image of decision making as an essentially rational process. Nevertheless, scholars tend at the same time to exhort decision makers "to be more rational."[26]

No one would deny that the study of individuals is important if we wish to improve our understanding of international relations. The important question, however, is how much emphasis should be placed on the individual level of analysis as opposed to other levels. Recall Hans Morgenthau's observation in the previous chapter that in order to understand how a statesman reached a particular decision, we speculate how we would respond in similar circumstances. In other words, by keeping the decision-making environment constant, we could hypothesize that any rational individual would have acted in the same manner. Despite a diversity of backgrounds or temperaments, the structure of the situation encourages decision makers to respond in a similar fashion. What if, however, beliefs and perceptions *do* make a difference and individuals respond to common stimuli or the environment in divergent ways? If so, the individual as a focus of analysis *is* important.

This debate over the relative importance of the individual as opposed to the environment in explaining behavior is common to all the social sciences. It also touches on the matter of **determinism** versus **voluntarism**. If the international system is the key to understanding international relations, then other levels of analysis — individual, organizational, societal, or state — are by definition of less importance. If one accepts a more pluralistic view of international relations, however, then greater consideration and weight are given to the role of the individual. Individuals matter simply because their choices significantly affect the functioning of world politics.

Organizational Process and Bureaucratic Politics

Both the unitary and rational assumptions associated with realism are relaxed from the **organizational process** and **bureaucratic politics** perspectives. Graham Allison's organizational process model of foreign policy decision making, a view of bureaucracy that owes an intellectual debt to the German scholar Max Weber, sees organizational routines and procedures as determining at least some, and influencing other, foreign policy decisions and outcomes.[27] Organizational ethos and world view are also relevant considerations. In an often cited statement, Allison notes that where a given bureaucratic actor "stands" on a given issue is often determined by where he or she "sits"; one's view of alternative courses of action is highly colored by the perspective of the organization to which one belongs. Perceptions of what is the **optimal** or best course of action often vary from one bureaucratic actor to another, reflecting organizational biases that raise serious doubts concerning the rationality of the process as a whole. What assurance is there that optimal choices for the state as a whole will be made? Or is optimality, when achieved, purely accidental?

Allison's bureaucratic politics model of foreign policy decision making involves forming coalitions and countercoalitions among diverse bureaucratic actors in a competitive environment. The focus is on specific individuals in positions at the top of organizations and on the pulling and hauling among them. This is in contrast to the more routine, preprogrammed activity of the organizational process model. Hence, foreign policy decisions at times may be the result of which individual, or which coalition of individuals, can muster the most political power. What may be best for an individual or his bureaucracy in terms of increased prestige and relative standing within the government may lead to less than the best foreign policy for the state as a whole. Parochial personal and bureaucratic interests may reign over any expressed concern for the national interest.

Allison's work does not pose as direct a challenge to the unitary assumption about state behavior as does some of the other literature on decision making. Although multiple actors influenced by diverse organizational and individual interests compete to influence policy choices, in the final analysis these decisions are still made by certain authoritative individuals. Notwithstanding all the competition and airing of alternative views, the state still speaks ultimately with one voice.[28] At the same time, however, the Allison study did at least raise some questions concerning the unitary character of the state in *implementation* of policy. Decisions made were not always carried out as quickly as anticipated or in precisely the same fashion as intended. After all, policy involves both **decisions** and **actions.** Even if the decisions are unitary and the state speaks with one voice (which may not always be the case), if consequent actions are fragmented or otherwise inconsistent, then how unitary is the state after all?

Robert Keohane, Joseph Nye, and others took the pluralist image a major step forward when they argued in their earlier work that the state may not be able to confine these bureaucratic actors.[29] Organizations, whether private or governmental, may well transcend the boundaries of states, forming coalitions with their foreign counterparts. Such transnational actors may even be working at cross-purposes with governmental leaders in their home states who possess the formal authority to make binding decisions. For example, the British Foreign Office may see a given issue similarly to its American State Department counterpart. On the other hand, the British Defence Ministry and the U.S. Defense Department may share a common view contrary to that of both diplomatic organizations. Moreover, nongovernmental interest groups in both countries may also form coalitions supportive of one or another **transgovernmental** coalition.

To what extent, then, do coalitions of bureaucratic actors, multinational corporations, and other transnational actors circumvent the authoritative decision makers of states through formation of such coalitions? An interesting example of a transgovernmental coalition that had a significant, though unpublicized, impact during the October 1962 Cuban missile crisis involved redeployment of Canadian naval units for an "exercise" in the North Atlantic. This decision effectively relieved the U.S. Navy of at least a part of its patrolling responsibilities there, allowing American ships to be redeployed to the Caribbean as part of the naval blockade of Cuba. All of this was apparently established between American and Canadian military officers while the Diefenbaker government was still debating the question of Canadian policy in the crisis. Was this circumvention by the Canadian navy an exception, or is it commonplace for bureaucratic actors to form coalitions across national borders that in effect make policy? Pluralists would argue that it is more commonplace than most realists would suppose.

If it *is* typically the way foreign policy is made, then focus by realists on the state as principal actor would seem to be misdirected. More attention should be given to the entire range of transnational actors and their interactions. On the other hand, if the example used here is indeed an exception, then it is an exception that makes the rule. The state in most cases retains its hard shell, precluding circumvention by transnational bureaucratic actors.

TRANSNATIONALISM

We have referred to transnational actors in the context of foreign policy decision making. We now turn to a lengthier discussion of transnationalism, a phenomenon closely associated with the pluralist image of international relations. Whereas the literature on decision making has generally emphasized political processes within states, the literature on transnationalism emphasizes ties between societies that include much more than state-to-state relations. James Rosenau has offered a useful definition of transnationalism, viewing it as "the processes whereby international relations conducted by governments have been supplemented by relations among private individuals, groups, and societies that can and do have important consequences for the course of events."[80] We begin with the question of what accounts for the increase in transnational ties and actors in the twentieth century.

Modernization

Realists stress the timeless quality of international relations. The insights of Thucydides, for example, are deemed relevant to the modern age of nuclear weapons. The same basic forces are at work, constraining and disposing actors to respond to similar situations in similar fashion. A certain continuity in international affairs is assumed.

Although they do not reject the foregoing assumption, pluralists believe it to be overstated. For them, the nature of international relations has indeed changed over the years. There is a qualitative difference between the world of seventeenth-century diplomacy and its Europe-oriented system and the twentieth-century international system characterized by some 160 states. Modernization describes and explains this fundamental transformation of the international system. **Modernization** can be defined as the social, political, and economic prerequisites for, and consequences of, industrialization and technological development.[31] Proponents of this perspective point to the growth of scientific technology that allows for greater control over nature, the dramatic improvements in transportation and communication, the rise of mass consumption made possible by the industrial revolution, the growth of global ties as a legacy of colonialism, and the extension of European diplomatic and political ideologies throughout the world. National autonomy, the traditional goal of statecraft, has become increasingly difficult as economic activities spill over borders.

The distinction between domestic and foreign policy becomes blurred as domestic policy becomes foreign policy and economic and foreign policies become politicized. For example, protectionist tariff barriers to save jobs and rescue ailing industries are weighed against international consequences to include retaliatory trade or financial measures taken by states adversely affected. Borders become porous as ideas, capital, people, technology, goods, and services move from one geographic point to another.[32] For selfish reasons, states find it in their best interest to cooperate with one another, creating modest yet important international organizations designed to facilitate the flow of mail or more ambitious endeavors aimed at ensuring international peace.

If the invoking image for the realist is that of states as billiard balls colliding with one another, for the pluralist it is a latticework or cobweb image. Instead of visualizing international relations as states and their interactions in an anarchic environment, some scholars argue that a cobweb image depicts a much more complex system composed not simply of states with geographic and political boundaries.[33] Also included would be the interactions and behavior of nonstate actors such as multinational corporations, terrorist groups, international banks, and international organizations such as the European Economic Community (EEC), the Organization of African Unity (OAU), the United Nations, and the North Atlantic Treaty Organization (NATO). The cobweb image would also depict such transactions as migration, tourism, communications, and trade flows. For pluralists, a cobweb image is much more apt in depicting the world than is the billiard ball image with its almost exclusive attention to the interactions of sovereign states. The state-centric model may perhaps have been appropriate in seventeenth- or eighteenth-century Europe, but the modernization process has so transformed societies that pluralists believe an alternative image of the world is required if one is to grasp the nature of world affairs in the twentieth century.

Integration

The impact of modernization on world politics, particularly the use of modern technology in the creation of weapons of mass destruction, is a phenomenon that drew the attention of certain international relations scholars in the period before and after World War II. One such scholar was David Mitrany.[34]

Mitrany was interested in investigating the possibility of how transnational ties might lead to international **integration,** the reduction of extreme nationalism, and hence increase the chances for a stable international peace. How might this come about?

Mitrany argued that by definition modern society has created a myriad of technical problems that can best be resolved by experts as opposed to politicians. This is true within states as well as between states. He believed that the proliferation of common problems logically requires collaborative responses from states. Hence, these essentially nonpolitical problems (economic, social, scientific) should be assigned to nonpolitical experts from the affected countries for resolution.

Mitrany reasoned that successful collaboration in one particular technical field or functional area would lead to further collaboration in other related fields. This process is what he termed **ramification.** Governments would recognize the common benefits to be gained by such cooperative endeavors and so would encourage or allow for a further expansion of collaborative tasks. In effect, Mitrany saw a way to sneak up on the authority of the sovereign state. As states and societies became increasingly integrated due to the expansion of collaboration in technical areas in which all parties gained, the cost of breaking these functional ties would be great and hence give leaders reason to pause before doing so. In particular, Mitrany emphasized how economic unification would contribute to the development of political integration. Hence, as opposed to a tendency among some realists to view international interactions as basically a **zero-sum game** (what one side wins the other loses), Mitrany instead argued that international interactions could be turned into a **variable-** or **positive-sum game** in which all the players could benefit. For Mitrany, this was not an idealistic dream far removed from reality. Rather, he grounded his analysis in what he believed to be a realistic assessment of the likelihood of the need for international cooperation to deal with common problems deriving from a complex and modern world. As international integration based on cooperation in functional, nonpolitical areas developed, the chances for international peace would be enhanced, he felt.

The interest in Mitrany's **functionalist** theory — and integration in general — was spurred by the successful creation of the European Coal and Steel Community (ECSC) in 1952 and the European Economic Community (EEC) or Common Market, in the 1956 Treaty of Rome. The EEC seemed to hold out promise for the eventual political integration of Western Europe. Furthermore, the EEC's initial successes in the realm of economic integration increased interest in the more general question: Under what conditions is integration among states possible? Scholars noted that what was occurring in Western Europe did not match the Hobbesian image of states constantly prepared to go to war, an image that included little faith in the possibility of collaborative behavior among sovereign states. Hence, alternative perspectives were devised to explain international cooperation.

One of the best-known theorists of regional integration, Ernst Haas, defined integration as a *process* "whereby political actors in several distinct national settings are persuaded to shift their loyalties, expectations and political activities toward a new centre, whose institutions possess or demand jurisdiction over the preexisting national states."[35] Haas's conceptual approach to the study of political integration soon acquired the label **neofunctionalism** — an acknowledgment of the intellectual debt owed to Mitrany, but with significant differences. Where Haas parted company with Mitrany was in his rejection of the notion that one could separate technical tasks from politics or welfare from power. For integration to occur, Haas argued that it must be perceived by political elites to be in their self-interest. The assigning of tasks to an international organization — even if this involves a seemingly technical function such as supervising an international mail system — will be attained and sustained only if actors believe their own interests are best served by making a political commitment to an international organization.

What Haas attempted to do, therefore, was to stipulate the conditions and processes whereby individuals find it in their own rational self-interest to collaborate for mutual gain, which results in the potential for a peaceful transformation of international politics. To put it another way, Haas directed his efforts *not* toward understanding conflict among states faced with a security dilemma but toward understanding how states achieve collaborative behavior. In terms of Rousseau's stag hunt fable discussed in Chapter Two, Haas focused on ways to encourage the group to pursue the stag as opposed to assuming individuals will always defect in pursuit of the hare.

Early predictions of progress in regional integration did not occur, at least not to the extent anticipated. That strong nationally oriented leaders would emerge (such as Charles DeGaulle in France) to block transfer of too much authority to regional institutions had not been anticipated. Beyond this strong-leader explanation for the slowing down of regional integration, however, a more fundamental evaluation of integration theory was offered by Haas himself.

Haas described the contemporary period as a "turbulent" one in which there are "confused and clashing perceptions of organizational actors which find themselves in a setting of great social complexity." Moreover,

> the number of actors is very large. Each pursues a variety of objectives which are mutually incompatible; but each is also unsure of the trade-offs between the objectives. Each actor is tied into a network of interdependencies with other actors that are as confused as the first. Yet some of the objectives sought by each cannot be obtained without cooperation from others.[36]

There is also uncertainty or outright confusion on means – ends relations — what the causes of international problems are or what their solutions might be in areas such as the environment, energy, industrial policy, research and development, and technology transfer. Indeed, the approach for dealing with a problem in one area may have negative implications in another. For example, in substituting coal or nuclear power for petroleum as principal sources of energy, there may be a trade-off in terms of an adverse impact on the environment.

Haas argued, therefore, that gaining control over such complexity is emerging as the major political task during the last part of the twentieth century. Significantly, states may be led to seek nonregional solutions to these problems, whatever may be the effect of such solutions on the objectives of regional integration. Haas concluded that his earlier "theory of regional integration ought to be subordinated to a general theory of interdependence."[37]

Moves toward greater integration in Europe have not caused Haas to change his position. Indeed, decisions to establish a single, open market among European Communities (EC) members and to create by the end of the 1990s a European central banking system with a common currency were not so much the result of the neofunctional logic of **spillover.** Rather, these decisions resulted from the recognition by European leaders, prodded by the EC Commission, that European global competitiveness depended upon taking such steps. In short, integration has increased more as a response to external stimuli than to internal processes at work within the EC.[38]

Despite its predictive shortcomings, the literature on integration has provided important insights on the nature of world politics and has contributed to the development of the pluralist image of international relations.

First, the literature on regional integration downplays the state as the unit of analysis. Transactions — economic, social, and technical — have also been the focus of attention as have interest groups, transnational nonstate actors, and public opinion.

Second, the neofunctionalist literature in particular has disaggregated the nation-state, examining such component parts as bureaucracies and elites. The latter are viewed as flesh-and-blood individuals with conflicting perspectives, opinions subject to change, and decision-making power.

Third, integration theorists pose the question of what other forms of political organization — aside from the territorially based nation-state — are possible. How can they be attained?

Finally, integration theorists have analyzed the conditions under which international cooperation is facilitated. The realist emphasis on state competition and international anarchy, it has been argued, provides few clues on this matter, but cooperation is just as much a defining characteristic of international relations as is conflict. Military and security affairs do not monopolize the agenda of international politics. Economic, social, and welfare issues also deserve attention, and integration theorists have addressed these topics.

Interdependence and Regimes

The concept of interdependence is discussed by proponents of all three images of international relations, but the pluralists take it to heart because it captures much of the essence of their view of world politics. Interdependence is to many pluralists what **balance of power** is to realists and what **dependency** is to many globalists. The idea of international interdependence is certainly not new, and its basic notion—that two or more units are dependent on one another—is easy to grasp. In recent years, however, the term has been developed to give it some analytical utility and conceptual content useful for the development of international relations theory. Pluralists have argued that the term provides a more accurate grasp of the current nature of world politics than does the concept of balance of power.

Interdependence means different things to different people. As discussed in Chapter Two, realists tend to see it as the **vulnerability** of one state to another, a view that suggests that interdependence is to be avoided or at least minimized. A common view among pluralists, by contrast, is that interdependence involves "reciprocal effects among countries or among actors in different countries."[39] There is sensitivity in Country B to what is going on in or emanating from Country A. Although there are costs associated with interdependence as **sensitivity,** benefits to either or both parties may outweigh these costs.[40] Thus, interdependence is not necessarily only a matter of country B's vulnerability to Country A. Pluralists do not exclude consideration of interdependence as vulnerability, but instead they focus on the multiple channels that connect societies, including interstate, transgovernmental, and transnational relations. There is a decided absence of hierarchy among issues such that socioeconomic issues may be as or more important than security issues. Moreover, when such complex interdependence exists, military force tends to have less utility in the resolution of conflicts.[41]

To the pluralist, interdependence may have benign implications and may be worth seeking; this is the influence of the liberal view of international relations. Whether the issues are trade, finance, communications, environmental pollution, or transfer of technology, the pluralist sees at least the opportunity for building good relations among the interdependent units. Managing interdependent relations may even involve construction of sets of rules, procedures, and associated institutions or international organizations to govern interactions in these issue areas—so-called **international regimes.** The term *regime* is borrowed from domestic politics where it refers typically to an existing governmental order (democratic, authoritarian, or otherwise) or to a set of rules and institutions established to govern relations among individuals, groups, or classes within a state. In its international context, given the absence of a superordinate or overarching central authority, these rules are voluntarily established by states to provide some degree of order in international relations. Thus, there is a strong Grotian strain in pluralist thought, particularly when talk turns to managing interdependence through the construction of regimes.[42] Compared to realist approaches to international regimes—the theory of hegemonic stability and game theory—pluralist approaches emphasize such factors as the perceptions, beliefs, and values of decision makers; the national and international bureaucratic context within which they work; the role of past experiences in international collaboration; and the influence of scientific knowledge.

There are, after all, costs associated with interdependence that make it very political. Choices have to be made. Given the uneven or **asymmetric** distribution of benefits and costs associated with interdependence, these relations have to be managed if major conflicts are to be avoided. Regimes may be the vehicles for accommodating differences and upgrading the common interest. Consistent with Rousseau's stag hunt fable discussed in Chapter 2, the actors agree to collaborate in hunting the stag rather than serving only narrowly defined, short-term self-interest. Differences arise among actors, but at least a possibility for their peaceful resolution remains.

This is anything but determinist thinking. Voluntarism is central in this mode of thought. Individual statesmen can, if they are willing, shape the world order. They have to deal with power and they understand that political choices have to be made among competing alternatives if international regimes for the management of interdependence are to be maintained in such fields as money, trade, postal service, telecommunication, fishing, and environmental protection. Critical to pluralist work on integration, interdependence, and international regimes, therefore, is the assumption that statesmen and bureaucratic officials can *learn*. While realists tend to take the existence of state interests for granted, pluralists are concerned with how those interests are defined and redefined. In the words of Ernst Haas: "There is no fixed 'national interest' and no 'optimal regime.' "[43] This requires examining not only the interactions among states, but also the manner in which domestic factors, perception, and international norms and organizations influence the formulation and reformulation of those interests.

SYSTEM

Pluralists do not always employ the concept of **system,** although it is common currency in the literature. To the extent that pluralists use the terminology, systems tend to be open.[44] This means that the system is open to both external influences and effective choice by actors within the system. The actors, or component units, of the system can have some effect on outcomes. It is not the system that determines what the actors will do as if the actors were automatons. Or, to put it another way, statesmen impose themselves on events, not the reverse.

There is a good deal of indeterminancy in most pluralist formulations. Outcomes depend on combinations of actors that outmaneuver or overwhelm opposing coalitions. The result is authoritative decisions and actions or, in a word, **policy.** Of course, all this freedom, or indeterminacy, also has its costs. Pluralist theories of politics tend to have less predictive power. One can have a fairly clear understanding of the complexity associated with political processes seen through pluralist lenses without having too much insight as to the outcome that will ultimately be achieved. On the other hand, predictions offered by balance of power theorists in the realist school often are at a very high level of generality that is somewhat removed from day-to-day events.

Pluralists use the term *system* in at least three different ways. First, for some pluralists the international system is merely the sum of the foreign policies of all states. Governmental actions are the principal focus. This is the view accepted by some realists as well. As we have seen, however, pluralists also tend to emphasize the role of specific bureaucracies and pressure groups in the formulation of foreign policy. They have direct impact on the final decision.

Second, other pluralists view the system as the sum of foreign policies plus the activities of nonstate actors. Nonstate actors include multinational corporations, terrorist groups, international banks, and transnational interest groups such as the Red Cross.

Third, certain pluralists include all the foregoing elements in their definition of a system but add all other types of transactions such as ideas, values, communications, trade patterns, and financial flows. This most fully approximates the cobweb image mentioned earlier.[45]

What all these views have in common, however, is a belief in the difficulty (if not impossibility) of insulating the foreign policy process from domestic and international forces. Not only is foreign policy influenced by such factors as public opinion, lobbying, and the policies and performances of allies and foes; it is also influenced by the individual and bureaucratic infighting that occurs within and among most governmental institutions. Government and society in general are penetrated in innumerable ways, making the notion of the impermeable nation-state a myth.[46]

The focus for the pluralist thus tends to be on various parts of the political process and on particular issues. Islands of theory are constructed rather than building such general theory as is offered by realist proponents of balance of power theory.[47] As we have seen, a number of pluralists focus on perception and decision-making processes of small groups. Others have studied regional integration, the impact of domestic and bureaucratic politics on foreign policy, and the roles played by transnational actors in world politics.

Unfortunately for the pluralist, however, these theoretical parts have tended to be nonadditive. To attempt merely to combine islands of theory (referred to by some theorists as **microtheories**) does not necessarily result in a **general theory**. A pluralist does not start with the system and work down to assess its impact on component units, as many realists do. Instead, one creeps up on the system by trying to put its parts together in some coherent fashion, which is not an easy task.[48]

On the other hand, interdependence has been a key concept entertained by theorists seeking to integrate pluralist thought by establishing some common denominator. There have been a number of attempts to measure interdependence as a systemic property or attribute.[49] As one might expect, findings on whether interdependence is rising, declining, or holding relatively constant depend heavily on the analyst's definition of the concept and on its **operationalization** — how it is measured through quantification or even by the use of nonquantitative indicators. Even if agreement were reached on these definitional and measurement problems, there remains considerable disagreement on such questions as whether increasing interdependence is more or less conducive to peace and world prosperity.[50]

Perhaps not surprisingly, the most fruitful issues for the pluralist approach have been the nonsecurity ones — those dealing with social, cultural, economic, technological, and related subjects. This has certainly been the case in **systemic** studies of interdependence and the construction and maintenance of international regimes.

CHANGE

It should be apparent by now that, compared to realists, pluralists place much greater emphasis on the possibilities of change, particularly peaceful change. This is quite evident, as we have noted, in the literature on integration and regimes in which policymakers learn from their experiences in international collaboration. There is also a possibility, but by no means an inevitability, that sovereign state members of international organizations may choose to transfer some authority to these institutions. To the extent that a given state cannot address adequately problems that confront a larger number of states, it may be in the state's interest to effect such transfers of authority. Whether such transfers would be permanent or whether such international institutions would acquire supranational authority that could be exercised over states is not clear. Were either to occur, it would be a fundamental **transformation** of world politics as we now understand it. States, assuming they would continue to exist, would no longer perform the large number of functions they now do. Again, such an outcome is not understood by pluralists as being inevitable or necessarily even desirable. Indeed, the question of alternative futures or alternative world orders continues to be addressed by pluralists of different persuasions.[51] There is, in any event, no single vision of the future that has currency among contemporary pluralists. Where pluralists differ from most realists, however, is that their image of world politics allows for a greater possibility of change. Their states and statesmen are not so constrained by the existing international system and balances of power within that system.

Similarly, much of the work on decision making emphasizes **feedback** processes — actors monitoring responses to actions they have taken so that future policies can be adjusted if necessary. The emphasis on choice in much of the pluralist work reveals a philosophical commitment to voluntarism, a belief that people can control or at least have some impact on their individual and collective destinies. Hence, the international system is viewed as being open and subject to directed change. For pluralists interested in transnational ties and interdependence, understanding the dynamics of system change is one of the most important tasks of scholars. It is not enough to describe particular types of systems (bipolar or multipolar, for example). Instead, efforts need to be directed toward understanding why and how the international system is changing and what this means in terms of war, peace, and stability.[52]

The separate efforts of Ernst Haas and James Rosenau are representative examples of pluralist views of the changing world order. The world is a turbulent one, not just due to the complexity produced by a proliferation of state and nonstate actors, but also due to the different mentalities individuals bring to the issues of the day. Haas focuses on cognitive variables, given the issue complexity he observes in which there is uncertainty and disagreement over both desirable ends to be sought and on the effective means to these ends in public policy deliberations within and across national borders. For his part, Rosenau also looks to the "micro" level, noting, for example, the effect on global processes of an expansion of analytical skills among individuals everywhere. Individual loyalties are also in flux, directed not just toward the traditional state authorities. One cannot understand changes in the "macro" structure of world politics without taking micro-level variables into account. Indeed, bifurcation between "multicentric" and "state-centric" forms or structures in competition with each other now characterizes world politics in an ever more complex, turbulent period.[53]

PLURALISTS AND THEIR CRITICS: AN OVERVIEW

The comments in this section are relatively brief but not because works based on the pluralist image lack their critics. Much of the criticism has already been discussed in Chapter Two and earlier in this chapter, however.

Anarchy

Pluralists generally tend to downplay the role of **anarchy** and the **security dilemma** in explaining international relations. It has been argued by realists, however, that no analysis of world politics is complete unless the anarchical structure of the system is taken into account. How is it possible to assess realistically the possibilities for cooperation and peace between states unless the role of anarchy in creating suspicion and distrust is considered? The realist would contend that if one ignores or reduces the importance of such considerations, thinking can quickly become **utopian** with little relation to reality. In addition, by emphasizing misperception and the role of bureaucratic politics, there is a danger in thinking that all conflicts result from essentially nonrational forces and that somehow better communication would reduce the amount of conflict in the international system. By contrast, realists argue that states often have fundamentally different interests that conflict, and the notions of "slipping into war" and "the war nobody wanted" are overused and misleading.[54]

A pluralist response is that placing so much emphasis on the security dilemma loads the dice against any change from the status quo. To see the world as nothing more than competition and conflict born of mistrust among states is itself a distortion of reality, or even a self-fulfilling prophecy. One's acts, if born of suspicion and distrust, will tend to produce similar responses in others, thus confirming one's initial suspicions.

Furthermore, the history of world politics is a history not only of conflict but also of collaboration. To study instances of when the security dilemma has been overcome is just as important as studying instances when it has contributed to the onset of war. Finally, to argue that misperception, bureaucratic politics, or domestic pressures may contribute to the onset of war is not to argue that states do not have conflicting national interests as well. Historical studies have shown time and again, however, that such factors as misperception are often critical in explaining the outbreak of wars.

Theory Building

Realists have argued that by describing the world in greater and greater detail, descriptive accuracy increases at the expense of developing a **parsimonious** theory of international relations. In other words, theories should be as simple as possible. Understanding increases by moving *away* from the real world, not by moving closer to it. At first, this statement might seem counterintuitive or different from what one might expect. But ambitious theories aim at producing valid generalizations by viewing the forest as a whole, not individual trees. By faithfully cataloguing the complexity of the world, pluralists, according to critics, are in danger of remaining in the realm of merely describing things as opposed to explaining why things happen the way they do.

In response, pluralists claim that before theories of international relations can be constructed, we need an accurate image of international relations. The pluralist image, it is argued, more accurately captures the nature of world politics. Yes, it is admitted, the pluralist image is not as neat and streamlined as the realist image. It consists of a number of different actors and influences that make for complexity, but theories of international relations should aspire to deal with such complexity and not pretend that it doesn't exist. How adequate are theories that fail to deal with and explain many of the changes that have occurred in the nature of world politics over the past century?

Voluntarism

If realists have been criticized for being excessively pessimistic concerning the human condition and the ability of individuals to control international events and forces, pluralists can be criticized for their heavy reliance on the assumption of voluntarism or effective free will. Some pluralist writings leave one with the impression that international harmony can be achieved if only leaders *really* wanted it — that it is a simple matter of human volition, a mere matter of desiring cooperation as opposed to competition. Hence, the transformation of the nature of world politics is seen to be desirable as well as attainable. Either "bad leaders" or "bad governments" stand in the way; if they could be changed or removed, the world would be a better place. Once again the influence of the liberal philosophy is evident, and once again the realist evaluation would be that this view of international change and how it can be achieved ignores constraints placed on *all* leaders and states by the anarchical nature of the international system and the balance of power. Moreover, some realists would argue that people are indeed aggressive with a proclivity toward warlike behavior; it is part of human nature to behave so.

The emphasis on voluntarism is not always acknowledged by pluralist writings. Nor is it necessarily a function of a philosophical commitment to a belief in free will that can influence outcomes. It could also derive from the fact that the focus of analysis for many pluralists happens to be government bureaucracies or individual actors. By studying real individuals within real organizations, world politics takes on a human face.

Pluralists would claim that they are well aware of constraints imposed on the actions of individuals or groups. For example, studies of individual leaders may *not* emphasize voluntarism but, rather, psychological constraints resulting from life experiences. There remains, however, an array of possible options available to decision makers and the ability to make real choices among these competing alternatives. After all, to the pluralist, both opportunities and constraints are associated with foreign policy choice. Too often, history is interpreted as if certain events were inevitable, that a particular war was the result of a number of trends inexorably coming together.

Ethnocentrism

A final criticism of the pluralist school is that many scholars tend to view the world through the lenses of the American political system. If American government and processes are understood to conform to a pluralist image, then the same image is imposed on the rest of the world, where it may bear little relation to reality.[55]

Acknowledging cultural, societal, and other differences, the pluralist who argues that bureaucracies, interest groups, and transnational actors are important to understanding international relations would deny that this image is merely American ethnocentrism imposed on the globe. It is, instead, a fairly accurate description of world politics. The actors and processes studied by pluralists are not confined to the states of the West but are found in and among political systems around the globe.

NOTES

1. John Locke, "An Essay Concerning the True, Original, Extent and End of Civil Government: Second Treatise on Government," in *Social Contract,* introduction by Sir Ernest Barker (London: Oxford University Press, 1962).
2. William Ebenstein, *Great Political Thinkers: Plato to the Present,* 4th ed. (New York: Holt, Rinehart & Winston, 1969) p. 63. Realists have also been influenced by liberalism, particularly by the emphasis on the rational individual pursuing his or her self-interest.
3. A recent work in this tradition is Richard Rosecrance, *The Rise of the Trading State* (New York: Basic Books, 1986).
4. Robert O. Keohane, "International Liberalism Reconsidered," in *The Economic Limits to Modern Politics,* ed. John Dunn (Cambridge, England: Cambridge University Press, 1990), pp. 165–94.
5. Immanuel Kant, *Idea of a Universal History of a Cosmological Plan* (Hanover, NH: The Sociological Press, 1972), and *Perpetual Peace,* trans. Lewis W. Beck (Indianapolis, IN: Bobbs-Merrill, 1957).

6. On the liberal view of international relations, see Kenneth N. Waltz, *Man, the State and War* (New York: Columbia University Press, 1959), pp. 95–123. See also Michael Howard, *War and the Liberal Conscience* (Oxford: Oxford University Press, 1957).

7. Theodore J. Lowi, *The End of Liberalism: Ideology, Policy, and the Crisis of Public Authority* (New York: Norton, 1969), p. 71.

8. Ibid., pp. 48, 71.

9. See David Truman, *The Governmental Process* (New York: Knopf, 1959), p. ix.

10. Ibid., pp. 519, 520.

11. Robert A. Dahl, *A Preface to Democratic Theory* (Chicago: University of Chicago Press, 1963), p. 137. Also see Harold D. Lasswell, *Politics: Who Gets What, When, How* (New York: McGraw-Hill, 1936), pp. 233–50. Reprinted in Dwaine Marvick, ed., *Harold D. Lasswell on Political Sociology* (Chicago: University of Chicago Press, 1977), pp. 108–13.

12. Dahl, *A Preface to Democratic Theory*, p. 128.

13. Alexis de Tocqueville, *Democracy in America*, ed. Phillips Bradley (New York: Vintage Books, 1954).

14. Richard C. Snyder, H. W. Bruck, and Burton Sapin, *Foreign Policy Decision Making: An Approach to the Study of International Politics* (New York: Free Press, 1962). The work was originally published in 1954. Other important early works include: Joseph Frankel, "Towards a Decision-Making Model in Foreign Policy," *Political Studies* 7 (1959): 1–11, and Karl W. Deutsch, "Mass Communications and the Loss of Freedom in National Decision-Making: A Possible Research Approach to Interstate Conflicts," *Journal of Conflict Resolution* 1 (1957): 200–11.

15. Snyder, Bruck, and Sapin, p. 65.

16. Glen D. Paige, *The Korean Decision* (New York: Free Press, 1968).

17. James N. Rosenau, "Pre-Theories and Theories of Foreign Policy," in *The Scientific Study of Foreign Policy*, by James N. Rosenau, 2d ed., rev. and enl. (New York: Nichols, 1980), p. 118.

18. Maurice A. East, Stephen A. Salmore, and Charles F. Hermann, eds., *Why Nations Act: Theoretical Perspectives for Comparative Foreign Policy Studies* (Beverly Hills, CA: Sage Publications, 1978); Patrick J. McGowan and Howard B. Shapiro, *The Comparative Study of Foreign Policy* (Beverly Hills, CA: Sage Publications, 1973); Jonathan Wilkenfeld, Gerald W. Hopple, Paul J. Rossa, and Stephen J. Andriole, *Foreign Policy Behavior: The Interstate Behavior Analysis Model* (Beverly Hills, CA: Sage Publications, 1980); Wolfram F. Hanrieder, ed., *Comparative Foreign Policy: Theoretical Essays* (New York: David McKay, 1971); James N. Rosenau, ed., *Comparing Foreign Policies: Theories, Findings, and Methods* (Beverly Hills, CA: Sage Publications, 1974); and Douglas J. Murray and Paul R. Viotti, eds., *The Defense Policies of Nations: A Comparative Study* (Baltimore, MD: Johns Hopkins University Press, 1982, 1993).

19. H. N. Hirsch, "Clio on the Couch," *World Politics* 32, no. 3 (April 1980): 406–24; Alexander George, "The Operational Code: A Neglected Approach to the Study of Political Leaders and Decision-Making," *International Studies Quarterly* 13, no. 2 (June 1969): 190–220; Robert Axelrod, ed., *The Structure of Decision* (Princeton, NJ: Princeton University Press, 1976); Harvey Starr, "The Kissinger Years: Studying Individuals and Foreign Policy," *International Studies Quarterly* 24, no. 4 (December 1980): 465–96; and Ole Holsti, "The Operational Code Approach to the Study of Political Leaders," *Canadian Journal of Political Science* 3, no. 1 (March 1970): 123–57.

20. Robert Jervis, *Perception and Misperception in International Politics* (Princeton, NJ: Princeton University Press, 1976), p. 29. See also Jervis, *The Logic of Images in International Relations* (Princeton, NJ: Princeton University Press, 1970); "Cooperation Under the Security Dilemma," *World Politics* 30, no. 2 (January 1978): 167 – 214; "Deterrence Theory Revisited," *World Politics* 31, no. 2 (January 1979): 289 – 324.

21. Jervis, *Perception and Misperception*, p. 9.

22. Irving L. Janis, *Victims of Groupthink* (Boston: Houghton Mifflin, 1972). See also Janis and Leon Mann, *Decision Making: A Psychological Analysis of Conflict, Choice, and Commitment* (New York: Free Press, 1977).

23. Janis, *Victims of Groupthink*, p. 9.

24. On crises, see Ole Holsti, *Crisis, Escalation, War* (Montreal and London: McGill-Queen's University Press, 1972); Ole Holsti, "Historians, Social Scientists, and Crisis Management," *Journal of Conflict Resolution* 24, no. 4 (December 1980): 665 – 82; Richard Ned Lebow, *Between Peace and War: The Nature of International Crisis* (Baltimore: Johns Hopkins University Press, 1981). See also Alexander L. George, "Adaptation to Stress in Political Decision Making," *Coping and Adaptation*, ed. G. Coelho, D. Hamburg, and J. Adams (New York: Basic Books, 1974).

25. Alexander L. George and Richard Smoke, *Deterrence in American Foreign Policy: Theory and Practice* (New York: Columbia University Press, 1974), p. 505.

26. Miriam Steiner, "The Search for Order in a Disorderly World: Worldviews and Prescriptive Decision Paradigms," *International Organization* 37, no. 3 (Summer 1983): 373 – 413.

27. See Graham Allison, "Conceptual Models and the Cuban Missile Crisis," *American Political Science Review* 63 (September 1969): 689 – 718. See also Allison, *Essence of Decision* (Boston, MA: Little, Brown, 1971); Graham Allison and Morton H. Halperin, "Bureaucratic Politics: A Paradigm and Some Policy Implications," in *Theory and Policy in International Relations*, ed. Raymond Tanter and Richard H. Ullman (Princeton, NJ: Princeton University Press, 1972), pp. 40 – 79; Halperin with Priscilla Clapp and Arnold Kanter, *Bureaucratic Politics and Foreign Policy* (Washington: The Brookings Institution, 1974). See Weber's classic "Parliament and Government in a Reconstructed Germany," in *Economy and Society*, vol. 2, Appendix 2, ed. Guenther Roth and Claus Wittich (New York: Bedminster Press, 1968), pp. 1381 – 1469.

28. For realist critiques of Allison's work, see Stephen D. Krasner, "Are Bureaucracies Important? (or Allison's Wonderland)," *Foreign Policy* 7 (Summer 1972): 159 – 79; and Robert J. Art, "Bureaucratic Politics and American Foreign Policy: A Critique," *Policy Sciences* 4, no. 4 (December 1973): 467 – 90.

29. See Robert Keohane and Joseph Nye, eds., *Transnational Relations and World Politics* (Cambridge, MA: Harvard University Press, 1972) and their later *Power and Interdependence: World Politics in Transition* (Boston: Little, Brown, 1977). In the latter work an attempt is made to blend pluralist and realist approaches.

30. James N. Rosenau, *The Study of Global Interdependence: Essays on the Transnationalisation of World Affairs* (New York: Nichols, 1980), p. 1.

31. For a detailed treatment of the impact of modernization on international relations that resulted from the global spread of the effect of the industrial revolution, see Edward L. Morse, *Modernization and the Transformation of International Relations* (New York: Free Press, 1976). See also John H. Kautsky, *The Political Consequences*

of Modernization (New York: Wiley, 1972); and C. E. Black, *The Dynamics of Modernization* (New York: Harper & Row, 1966).

32. For a defense of the concept of the "hard shell" of the state, see Stanley Hoffmann's realist perspective in his "Obstinate or Obsolete? The Fate of the Nation-State and the Case of Western Europe," *Daedalus* 3 (Summer 1966): 862–915. See also Samuel P. Huntington's argument that the state retains control over access to its territory by transnational actors in his "Transnational Organizations in World Politics," *World Politics* 26, no. 3 (April 1973): 333–68.

33. See Ernst B. Haas for the latticework metaphor in his "The Study of Regional Integration: Reflections on the Joy and Anguish of Pretheorizing," in *Regional Intergration: Theory and Research*, ed. Leon N. Lindberg and Stuart A. Scheingold (Cambridge, MA: Harvard University Press, 1971) pp. 30–31. For the cobweb image, see Ernst Haas, *Tangle of Hopes: American Commitments and World Order* (Englewood Cliffs, NJ: Prentice-Hall, 1969), Chapter 1; and John W. Burton, *World Society* (Cambridge, England: Cambridge University Press, 1972).

34. See David Mitrany, *A Working Peace System* (Chicago: Quadrangle Books, 1966). See also Mitrany, "The Functional Approach to World Organization," *International Affairs* 24, no. 3 (July 1948): 350–63, and the discussion in Ernst B. Haas, *Beyond the Nation-State* (Stanford, CA: Stanford University Press, 1964), Chapter 1.

35. Ernst B. Haas, *The Uniting of Europe* (Stanford, CA: Stanford University Press, 1958), p. 16. See also the influential work by Karl W. Deutsch and associates, *Political Community and the North Atlantic Area* (Princeton, NJ: Princeton University Press, 1957), p. 5.

36. See Ernst B. Haas, "Turbulent Fields and the Theory of Regional Integration," *International Organization* 30, no. 2 (Spring 1976): 179. This article is a summary of a much more detailed treatment in a monograph by Haas, *The Obsolescence of Regional Integration Theory* (Berkeley: University of California Institute of International Studies, 1975). For antecedents of this argument, see his earlier "Study of Regional Integration."

37. Haas, "Turbulent Fields and Regional Integration," p. 199.

38. Conversation with Ernst Haas, September 1990.

39. Keohane and Nye, *Power and Interdependence*, p. 8.

40. Ibid., p. 9. Alex Inkeles differentiates between "inter-connectedness" or the effect of international transaction flows and "interdependence," which involves some degree of cost for the parties. Alex Inkeles, "The Emerging Social Structure of the World," *World Politics* 27, no. 4 (July 1975): 467–95.

41. See Keohane and Nye, *Power and Interdependence*, pp. 24–29.

42. See Stephen Krasner, ed., *International Regimes*, (Ithaca, NY: Cornell University Press, 1983), p. 57. Oran R. Young, "International Regimes: Problems of Concept Formation," *World Politics* 32, no. 3 (April 1980): 331–56; Ernst Haas, Mary Pat Williams and Don Babai, *Scientists and World Order: The Uses of Technical Knowledge in International Organizations* (Berkeley: University of California Press, 1977); Anthony J. Dolman, *Resources, Regimes, and World Order* (New York: Pergamon Press, 1981); John Gerard Ruggie, "International Organization: A State of the Art on an Art of the State" (Paper presented at the 1985 Annual Meeting of the American Political Science Association, New Orleans, August 29–September 1, 1985).

43. Ernst B. Haas, "Words Can Hurt You: Or Who Said What to Whom About Regimes,"

in Stephen Krasner, ed. *International Regimes*, p. 57. See also Peter M. Haas, ed., "Knowledge, Power and International Policy," special issue of *International Organization* 46, no. 1 (Winter 1992); see also George Modelski's linking of learning and his long cycles theory in "Is World Politics Evolutionary Learning?" *International Organization* 44, no. 1 (Winter 1990): 1–24.

44. See Ernst B. Haas, "On Systems and International Regimes," *World Politics* 27, no. 2 (January 1975): 152–53.

45. One approach to understanding transaction and communications flows in the international system is through the construction of cybernetic models. For example, see Karl W. Deutsch, *The Nerves of Government* (New York: Free Press, 1964).

46. See James N. Rosenau, ed., *Linkage Politics: Essays on the Convergence of National and International Systems* (New York: Free Press, 1969) and an earlier piece by Fred A. Sondermann, "The Linkage between Foreign Policy and International Politics," in *International Politics and Foreign Policy*, ed. James N. Rosenau (New York, Free Press, 1961), pp. 8–17.

47. See Harold Guetzkow, "Long Range Research in International Relations," in *International Politics and Foreign Policy*, ed. James N. Rosenau (New York: Free Press, 1961), pp. 55–56.

48. This evocative idea of creeping up on the nation-state is from Ernst Haas.

49. See Richard Rosecrance and associates, "Whither Interdependence?" *International Organization* 31, no. 3 (Summer 1977): 425–71; Mary Ann Tetreault, "Measuring Interdependence," *International Organization* 34, no. 3 (Summer 1980): 429–43; and rejoinder by Rosecrance and William Gutowitz, followed by Tetreault's response in *International Organization*, 35, no. 3 (Summer 1981): 553–60.

50. For an antidote to the conventional wisdom that the effects of increased interdependence are benign and therefore desirable, see the realist critique of interdependence in Kenneth N. Waltz, "The Myth of National Interdependence," *The International Corporation*, ed. Charles P. Kindleberger (Cambridge, MA: MIT Press, 1970), pp. 205–23.

51. For an example, see Richard A. Falk, *A Study of Future Worlds* (New York: Free Press, 1975).

52. See Ole R. Holsti, Randolph M. Siverson, and Alexander L. George, *Change in the International System* (Boulder, CO: Westview Press, 1980).

53. See Ernst B. Haas, *When Knowledge Is Power* (Berkeley: University of California Press, 1990) and James N. Rosenau, *Turbulence in World Politics* (Princeton, NJ: Princeton University Press, 1990).

54. See Christopher Layne, "1914 Revisited: A Reply to Miles Kahler," *Orbis* 14, no. 4 (Winter 1981): 719–50.

55. Thus, even the making of Soviet foreign policy in the politburo and state apparatus prior to the 1990s was said to involve the same construction of coalitions, end running, and similar tactics observed in American politics. This view was hotly disputed by those who think the analogy between American and Soviet decision-making processes is overdrawn. For example, see the debate between a pluralist and a more unitary conception of high-level Soviet politics during the 1970s in Roman Kolkowicz, "Interest Groups in Soviet Politics: The Case of the Military," *Comparative Politics* 2, no. 3 (April 1970): 445–72; William E. Odom, "The Part Connection," *Problems of Communism* 22, no. 5 (September–October 1973): 12–26; Karen Dawisha, "The Limits of the Bureaucratic Politics Model: Observations on the Soviet Case," *Studies in Comparative Communism* 13, no. 4 (Winter 1980): 300–46; Robert M. Cutler,

"The Formation of Soviet Foreign Policy: Organizational and Cognitive Perspectives," *World Politics* 33, no. 3 (April 1982): 418–36.

SUGGESTED READINGS

Newly added to this edition. Suggested readings from earlier works follow this more recent list.

Aggarwal, Vinod K. *Liberal Protectionism: The International Politics of Organized Textile Trade.* Berkeley: University of California Press, 1985.

Alger, Chadwick F. "The World Relations of Cities." *International Studies Quarterly* 34, 4 (December 1990): 493–518.

Allison, Graham T., Albert Carnesdale, and Joseph S. Nye, Jr. *Hawks, Doves, and Owls: An Agenda for Avoiding Nuclear War.* New York: Norton, 1985.

Apter, David E. *Rethinking Development: Modernization, Dependency, and Postmodern Politics.* Beverly Hills, CA: Sage Publications, 1987.

Barnett, Michael N. and Jack S. Levy. "Domestic Sources of Alliances and Alignments: The Case of Egypt, 1962–73." *International Organization* 45, 3 (Summer 1991): 369–95.

Bremer, Stuart A., ed. *The GLOBUS Model: Computer-Simulation of Worldwide Political and Economic Developments.* Boulder, CO: Westview Press, 1987.

Bremer, Stuart A. and Barry B. Hughes. *Disarmament and Development: A Design for the Future.* Englewood Cliffs, NJ: Prentice Hall, 1990.

Cooper, Richard N. *Economic Policy in an Interdependent World.* Cambridge, MA: MIT Press, 1986.

Cottam, Martha L. *Foreign Policy Decision Making: The Influence of Cognition.* Boulder, CO: Westview Press, 1986.

Cutler, A. Claire. "The 'Grotian Tradition' in International Relations." *Review of International Studies* 17, 1 (January 1991): 41–65.

Donnelly, Jack. "International Human Rights: A Regime Analysis." *International Organization* 40, 3 (Summer 1986): 599–642.

Doyle, Michael. "Liberalism and World Politics." *American Political Science Review* 80, 4 (December 1986): 1151–63.

Gordenker, Leon. *Refugees in International Politics.* New York: Columbia University Press, 1987.

Haggard, Stephan and Beth A. Simmons. "Theories of International Regimes." *International Organization* 41, 3 (Summer 1987): 491–517.

Haas, Ernst B. "Reason and Change in International Life: Justifying a Hypothesis." *Journal of International Affairs.* Summer 1990: 209–40.

———. "War, Interdependence, and Functionalism" in Raimo Vayrynen, ed. *The Quest for Peace.* London: Sage Publications, 1987: 108–26.

———. "What Is Nationalism and Why Should We Study It?" *International Organization* 40, 3 (Summer 1986): 707–44.

———. *When Knowledge Is Power: Three Models of Change in International Organization.* Berkeley: University of California Press, 1990.

———. *Why We Still Need the United Nations: The Collective Management of International Conflict.* Policy Papers in International Affairs No. 26, Berkeley, CA: Institute of International Studies, 1986. Also published in United Nations Institute for Training and Research, The United Nations and the Maintenance of International Peace and Security. Dordrecht, Holland: Martinus Nijhof, 1987.

Haas, Peter M. "Do Regimes Matter? Epistemic Communities and Mediterranean Pollution Control." *International Organization* 43, 3 (Summer 1989): 377–403.

———. ed. "Knowledge, Power and International Policy." Special Issue of *International Organization* 46, 1 (Winter 1992).

Hermann, Charles F. "Changing Course: When Governments Choose to Redirect Foreign Policy." *International Studies Quarterly* 34, 1 (March 1990): 3–21.

Hermann, Charles F., Charles W. Kegley, Jr., and James N. Rosenau, eds. *New Directions in the Study of Foreign Policy*. Boston: Allen & Unwin, 1987.

Hermann, Margaret G. and Charles F. Hermann. "Who Makes Foreign Policy Decisions and How: An Empirical Inquiry." *International Studies Quarterly* 33, 4 (December 1989): 361–87.

Herrmann, Richard. "The Empirical Challenge of the Cognitive Revolution: A Strategy for Drawing Inferences About Perceptions." *International Studies Quarterly* 32, 2 (June 1988): 175–203.

Holsti, Ole R. and James N. Rosenau. "Consensus Lost. Consensus Regained?: Foreign Policy Beliefs of American Leaders, 1976–1980" and "The Foreign Policy Beliefs of American Leaders: Some Further Thoughts on Theory and Method." *International Studies Quarterly* 30, 4 (December 1986): 375–409 and 473–84.

Jervis, Robert, Richard Ned Lebow, and Janice Gross Stein. *Psychology and Deterrence*. Baltimore: Johns Hopkins University Press, 1985.

Jones, R. J. Barry. *Interdependence on Trial: Studies in the Theory and Reality of Contemporary Interdependence*. New York: St. Martin's Press, 1985.

Keohane, Robert O. "International Institutions: Two Approaches." *International Studies Quarterly* 32, 4 (December 1988): 379–96.

Keohane, Robert O. and Joseph S. Nye, Jr. "Power and Interdependence Revisited." *International Organization* 41, 4 (Autumn 1987): 725–53.

Kull, Steven. *Minds at War*. New York: Basic Books, 1988.

Lebow, Richard Ned. *Nuclear Crisis Management: A Dangerous Illusion*. Ithaca, NY: Cornell University Press, 1987.

Levy, Jack S. "An Introduction to Prospect Theory." *Political Psychology* 13, 2 (June 1992): 171–86.

———. "Organizational Routines and the Causes of War." *International Studies Quarterly* 30, 2 (June 1986): 193–222.

Mandel, Robert. *Irrationality in International Confrontation*. New York: Greenwood, 1987.

Milner, Helen. "International Theories of Cooperation Among Nations: Strengths and Weaknesses." *World Politics* 44, 3 (April 1992): 466–96.

Neustadt, Richard E. and Ernest R. May. *Thinking in Time: The Uses of History for Decision Makers*. New York: Free Press, 1986.

Nye, Joseph S., Jr. "Nuclear Learning and U.S.–Soviet Regimes." *International Organization* 41, 3 (Summer 1987): 371–402.

Owen, Wilfred. *Transportation and World Development*. Baltimore: Johns Hopkins University Press, 1987.

Reich, Robert B. *The Work of Nations: Preparing Ourselves for 21st Century Capitalism*. New York: Knopf, 1991.

Rosenau, James N. *Turbulence in World Politics: A Theory of Change and Continuity*. Princeton, NJ: Princeton University Press, 1990.

Snidal, Duncan. "International Cooperation Among Relative Gains Maximizers." *International Studies Quarterly* 35, 4 (December 1991): 387–402.

Vernon, Raymond. *Exploring the Global Economy*. Lanham, MD: University Press of America, 1985.

Walker, R. B. J. and Saul H. Mendlovitz. *Contending Sovereignties: Redefining Political Community*. Boulder, CO: Lynne Rienner Publishers, 1990.

Walt, Stephen M. "Revolution and War." *World Politics* 44, 3 (April 1992): 321–68.

Wittkopf, Eugene R. "Elites and Masses: Another Look at Attitudes Toward America's World Role." *International Studies Quarterly* 31, 2 (June 1987): 131–59.

Weiner, Myron and Samuel P. Huntington, eds. *Understanding Political Development*. Boston: Little, Brown, 1987.

Young, Oran R. "The Politics of International Regime Formation: Managing Resources and the Environment." *International Organization* 43, 3 (Summer 1989): 349–75.

SUGGESTED READINGS FROM THE FIRST EDITION

Allison, Graham. *Essence of Decision: Explaining the Cuban Missile Crisis*. Boston: Little, Brown, 1971.

Allison, Graham, and Morton H. Halperin. "Bureaucratic Politics: A Paradigm and Some Policy Implications." *World Politics* 24, supplement (Spring 1972): 40–79.

Axelrod, Robert. *Framework for a General Theory of Cognition and Choice*. Berkeley, CA: Institute of International Studies, 1972.

————, ed. *Structure of Decision: The Cognitive Maps of Political Elites*. Princeton, NJ: Princeton University Press, 1976.

Baldwin, David A. "Interdependence and Power: A Conceptual Analysis." *International Organization* 34, 4 (Autumn 1980): 471–506.

Banks, Michael, ed. *Conflict in World Society*. New York: St. Martin's Press, 1984.

Bergsten, C. Fred, and Lawrence B. Krause, eds. *World Politics and International Economics*. Washington, DC: Brookings Institution, 1975.

Betts, Richard K. "Analysis, War, and Decision: Why Intelligence Failures Are Inevitable." *World Politics* 31, 1 (October 1978): 61–89.

Brecher, Michael. "Research Findings and Theory-Building on Foreign Policy Behavior." *Sage International Yearbook of Foreign Policy Studies II*. Beverly Hills and London: Sage Publications, 1974.

————. "State Behavior in International Crisis." *Journal of Conflict Resolution* 23 (September 1979): 446–80.

————, ed. *Studies in Crisis Behavior*. New Brunswick, NJ: Transaction Books, 1979.

Brecher, Michael, and Jonathan Wilkenfeld. "Crisis in World Politics." *World Politics* 34, 3 (April 1982): 380–417.

Brown, Lester B. *World Without Borders: The Interdependence of Nations*. New York: Foreign Policy Association, Headline Series, 1972.

Brown, Seyom. *New Forces in World Politics*. Washington, DC: Brookings Institution, 1974.

Burton, John W. *Systems, States, Diplomacy and Rules*. New York: Cambridge University Press, 1968.

————. *World Society*. New York: Cambridge University Press, 1972.

Caldwell, Dan. "Bureaucratic Foreign Policy-Making." *American Behavioral Scientist* 21, 1 (September–October 1977): 87–110.

Cooper, Richard N. *The Economics of Interdependence*. New York: McGraw-Hill, 1968.

De Rivera, Joseph. *The Psychological Dimension of Foreign Policy*. Columbus, OH: C. E. Merrill, 1968.

Deutsch, Karl W. and associates. *Political Community and the North Atlantic Area.* Princeton, NJ: Princeton University Press, 1957.

Etzioni, Amitai. *Political Unification.* New York: Holt, Rinehart & Winston, 1965.

Galtung, Johan. "A Structural Theory of Integration." *Journal of Peace Research* 5 (1968): 375–95.

George, Alexander. "The Operational Code: A Neglected Approach to the Study of Political Leaders and Decision-Making." *International Studies Quarterly* 13, 2 (June 1969): 190–222.

George, Alexander, and Richard Smoke. *Deterrence in American Foreign Policy: Theory and Practice.* New York: Columbia University Press, 1974.

Gourevitch, Peter. "The Second Image Reversed: The International Sources of Domestic Politics." *International Organization* 32, 4 (Autumn, 1978): 881–911.

Guetzkow, Harold, and associates. *Simulation in International Relations: Developments for Research and Teaching.* Englewood Cliffs, NJ: Prentice Hall, 1963.

Haas, Ernst B. *Beyond the Nation-State.* Stanford, CA: Stanford University Press, 1964.

————. "Is There a Hole in the Whole? Knowledge, Technology, Interdependence, and the Construction of International Regimes." *International Organization* 29, 3 (Summer 1975): 827–76.

————. *Tangle of Hopes: American Commitments and World Order.* Englewood Cliffs, NJ: Prentice Hall, 1969.

————. "Turbulent Fields and the Theory of Regional Integration." *International Organization* 30, 2 (Spring 1976): 173–212.

————. "Why Collaborate? Issue-Linkage and International Regimes." *World Politics* 32, 3 (April 1980): 357–405.

Haas, Ernst, B., Mary Pat Williams, and Don Babai. *Scientists and World Order: The Uses of Technical Knowledge in International Organizations.* Berkeley: University of California Press, 1977.

Halperin, Morton H. *Bureaucratic Politics and Foreign Policy.* Washington, DC: Brookings Institution, 1974.

Hermann, Charles F. ed. *International Crises: Insights from Behavioral Research.* New York: Free Press, 1972.

Hermann, Margaret G. "Explaining Foreign Policy Behavior Using the Personal Characteristics of Political Leaders." *International Studies Quarterly* 24, 1 (March 1980): 7–46.

Herz, John. "The Territorial State Revisited: Reflections on the Future of the Nation-State." *Polity* 1, 1 (Fall 1968): 11–34.

Holsti, Kal J. "A New International Politics? Diplomacy in Complex Interdependence." *International Organization* 32, 2 (Spring 1978): 513–30. A review of Nye and Keohane, *Power and Interdependence.*

Holsti, Ole R. *Crisis, Escalation, War.* Montreal: McGill-Queen's University Press, 1972.

Holsti, Ole R., Randolph M. Siverson, and Alexander L. George. *Change in the International System.* Boulder, CO: Westview Press, 1980.

Holsti, Ole R., P. Terrence Hopmann, and John D. Sullivan. *Unity and Disintegration in International Alliances.* New York: Wiley, 1973.

Janis, Irving L. *Victims of Groupthink.* Boston: Houghton Mifflin, 1972.

Janis, Irving L., and Leon Mann. *Decision Making: A Psychological Analysis of Conflict, Choice, and Commitment.* New York: Free Press, 1977.

Jervis, Robert. "Deterrence and Perception." *International Security* 7, 3 (Winter 1982/83): 3–30.

_____. *The Logic of Images in International Relations.* Princeton, NJ: Princeton University Press, 1970.

_____. *Perception and Misperception in International Politics.* Princeton, NJ: Princeton University Press, 1976.

Katzenstein, Peter. "International Interdependence: Some Long-Term Trends and Recent Changes." *International Organization* 29, 4 (Autumn 1975): 1021–34.

Keohane, Robert O. and Joseph S. Nye, Jr. *Power and Interdependence: World Politics in Transition.* Boston: Little, Brown, 1977.

_____. "Transgovernmental Relations and International Organization." *World Politics* 27, 1 (October 1974): 39–62.

_____, eds. *Transnational Relations and World Politics.* Cambridge, MA: Harvard University Press, 1971.

Kinder, Donald R., and Janet A. Weiss. "In Lieu of Rationality: Psychological Perspectives on Foreign Policy Decisionmaking." *Journal of Conflict Resolution* 22 (December 1978): 707–35.

Krasner, Stephen D., ed. *International Regimes.* London and Ithaca, NY: Cornell University Press, 1983.

Lebow, Richard Ned. *Between Peace and War: The Nature of International Crisis.* Baltimore, MD: Johns Hopkins University Press, 1981.

Leonard, H. Jeffrey. "Multinational Corporations and Politics in Developing Countries." *World Politics* 32, 3 (April 1980): 454–83.

Levy, Jack F. "Misperception and the Causes of War." *World Politics* 36, 1 (October 1983): 76–99.

Lindberg, Leon N., and Stuart A. Scheingold, eds. *Regional Integration: Theory and Research.* Cambridge, MA: Harvard University Press, 1971.

McGowan, Patrick J., and Howard B. Shapiro. *The Comparative Study of Foreign Policy.* Beverly Hills, CA: Sage Publications, 1973.

Mansbach, Richard W., Yale H. Ferguson, and Donald F. Lampert. *The Web of World Politics.* Englewood Cliffs, NJ: Prentice Hall, 1976.

Mansbach, Richard W., and John A. Vasquez. *In Search of Theory: A New Paradigm for Global Politics.* New York: Columbia University Press, 1981.

Michalak, Stanley J. "Theoretical Perspectives for Understanding International Interdependence." *World Politics* 32, 1 (October 1979): 136–50. A review of Keohane and Nye, *Power and Interdependence.*

Mitrany, David. *A Working Peace System.* Chicago: Quadrangle Books, 1966.

_____. *The Functional Theory of Politics.* London: St. Martin's Press, 1975.

Modelski, George, ed. *Transnational Corporations and World Order.* San Francisco: W. H. Freeman and Co., 1979.

Morse, Edward L. *Modernization and the Transformation of International Relations.* New York: Free Press, 1976.

_____. "The Politics of Interdependence." *International Organization* 23 (1969): 311–26.

Nau, Henry R. "From Integration to Interdependence: Gains, Losses, and Continuing Gaps." *International Organization* 33, 1 (Winter 1979): 119–47. A review article.

Northedge, F. S. "Transnationalism: The American Illusion." *Millennium* 5 (Spring 1976): 21–27.

Nye, Joseph S. *Peace in Parts: Integration and Conflict in Regional Organization.* Boston, MA: Little, Brown, 1971.

Pirages, Dennis. *The New Context For International Relations: Global Ecopolitics.* North Scituate, MA: Duxbury Press, 1978.

Rosecrance, Richard R., and associates. "Whither Interdependence?" *International Organization* 31, 3 (Summer 1977): 425–72.

Rosecrance, Richard, and Arthur Stein. "Interdependence: Myth or Reality?" *World Politics* 26, 1 (October 1973): 1–27.

Rosenau, James N., ed. *Comparing Foreign Policies: Theories, Findings, and Methods.* Beverly Hills, CA: Sage Publications, 1974.

———, ed. *In Search of Global Patterns.* New York: Free Press, 1976.

———, ed. *International Politics and Foreign Policy,* rev. ed. New York: Free Press, 1969.

———, ed. *Linkage Politics.* New York: Free Press, 1969.

———. "Order and Disorder in the Study of World Politics." In *Globalism Versus Realism: International Relations' Third Debate,* ed. Ray Maghroori and Bennett Ramberg. Boulder, CO: Westview Press, 1982, pp. 1–7.

———. "Pre-Theories and Theories of Foreign Policy." In *The Scientific Study of Foreign Policy,* ed. James N. Rosenau. 2d ed. rev. and enl. New York: Nichols, 1980.

———. "A Pre-Theory Revisited: World Politics in an Era of Cascading Interdependence." *International Studies Quarterly* 28, 3 (September 1984): 245–305.

———. *The Study of Global Interdependence: Essays on the Transnationalisation of World Affairs.* New York: Nichols, 1980.

———. *The Study of Political Adaptation.* London: Frances Pinter, 1981.

Rourke, Francis. *Bureaucracy and Foreign Policy.* Baltimore: Johns Hopkins University Press, 1972.

Ruggie, John Gerard, ed. *The Antinomies of Interdependence.* New York: Columbia University Press, 1983.

Singer, J. David. *Human Behavior and International Politics: Contributions from the Social-Psychological Sciences.* Chicago: Rand McNally, 1965.

Snyder, Glenn H., and Paul Diesing. *Conflict Among Nations: Bargaining, Decision Making, and System Structure in International Crisis.* Princeton, NJ: Princeton University Press, 1977.

Snyder, Jack L. "Rationality at the Brink: The Role of Cognitive Processes in Failures of Deterrence." *World Politics* 30, 3 (April 1978): 345–65.

Snyder, Richard C., H. W. Bruck, and Burton Sapin. *Decisionmaking as an Approach to the Study of International Politics.* Princeton, NJ: Princeton University Press, 1954.

Spero, Joan E. *The Politics of International Economic Relations,* 2d ed. New York: St. Martin's Press, 1981.

Stech, Frank J. *Estimating Intentions in Military and Political Intelligence.* Boulder, CO: Westview Press, 1985.

Steinbruner, John D. *The Cybernetic Theory of Decision: New Dimensions of Political Analysis.* Princeton, NJ: Princeton University Press, 1974.

Strange, Susan. "The Study of Transnational Relations." *International Affairs* 52, 3 (July, 1976): 333–45.

Sylvan, David A., and Steve Chan, eds. *Foreign Policy Decision Making: Perception, Cognition, and Artificial Intelligence.* New York: Praeger, 1984.

Taylor, Philip. *Nonstate Actors in International Politics.* Boulder, CO: Westview Press, 1984.

Vernon, Raymond. *Sovereignty at Bay: The Multinational Spread of U.S. Enterprises.* New York: Basic Books, 1971.

———. "Sovereignty at Bay Ten Years After." *International Organization* 35, 3 (Summer 1981): 517–29.

Ward, Michael Don, ed. *Theories, Models, and Simulations in International Relations.* Boulder, CO: Westview Press, 1985.

Wright, Quincy. *A Study of War.* Chicago: University of Chicago Press, 1964.

Young, Oran R. "International Regimes: Problems of Concept Formation." *World Politics* 32 (April 1980): 331–56.

Young, Robert A., ed. "International Crisis: Progress and Prospects for Applied Forecasting and Management." *International Studies Quarterly* 21, 1 (March 1977). A special issue.

Liberalism and World Politics

Michael W. Doyle

Building on a growing literature in international political science, the author reexamines the traditional liberal claim that governments founded on a respect for individual liberty exercise "restraint" and "peaceful intentions" in their foreign policy. He looks at three distinct theoretical traditions of liberalism, attributable to three theorists: Schumpeter, a democratic capitalist whose explanation of liberal pacifism we often invoke; Machiavelli, a classical republican whose glory is an imperialism we often practice; and Kant, a liberal republican whose theory of internationalism best accounts for what we are. Despite the contradictions of liberal pacifism and liberal imperialism, Professor Doyle finds with Kant and other democratic republicans, that liberalism does leave a coherent legacy on foreign affairs. Liberal states are different. They are indeed peaceful. They are also prone to make war. Liberal states have created a separate peace, as Kant argued they would, and have also discovered liberal reasons for aggression, as he feared they might. The author concludes by arguing that the differences among liberal pacifism, liberal imperialism, and Kant's internationalism are not arbitrary. They are rooted in differing conceptions of the citizen and the state.

Promoting freedom will produce peace, we have often been told. In a speech before the British Parliament in June of 1982, President Reagan proclaimed that governments founded on a respect for individual liberty exercise "restraint" and "peaceful intentions" in their foreign policy. He then announced a "crusade for freedom" and a "campaign for democratic development" (Reagan, June 9, 1982).

In making these claims the president joined a long list of liberal theorists (and propagandists) and echoed an old argument: the aggressive instincts of authoritarian leaders and totalitarian ruling parties make for war. Liberal states, founded on such individual rights as equality before the law, free speech and other civil liberties, private property, and elected representation are fundamentally against war this argument as-

From *American Political Science Review* 80, no. 4 (December 1986).

serts. When the citizens who bear the burdens of war elect their governments, wars become impossible. Furthermore, citizens appreciate that the benefits of trade can be enjoyed only under conditions of peace. Thus the very existence of liberal states, such as the U.S., Japan, and our European allies, makes for peace.

Building on a growing literature in international political science, I reexamine the liberal claim President Reagan reiterated for us. I look at three distinct theoretical traditions of liberalism, attributable to three theorists: Schumpeter, a brilliant explicator of the liberal pacifism the president invoked; Machiavelli, a classical republican whose glory is an imperialism we often practice; and Kant.

Despite the contradictions of liberal pacifism and liberal imperialism, I find, with Kant and other liberal republicans, that liberalism does leave a coherent legacy on foreign affairs. Liberal states are different. They are indeed peaceful, yet they are also prone to make war, as the U.S. and our "freedom fighters" are now doing, not so covertly, against Nicaragua. Liberal states have created a separate peace, as Kant argued they would, and have also discovered liberal reasons for aggression, as he feared they might. I conclude by arguing that the differences among liberal pacifism, liberal imperialism, and Kant's liberal internationalism are not arbitrary but rooted in differing conceptions of the citizen and the state.

LIBERAL PACIFISM

There is no canonical description of liberalism. What we tend to call *liberal* resembles a family portrait of principles and institutions, recognizable by certain characteristics — for example, individual freedom, political participation, private property, and equality of opportunity — that most liberal states share, although none has perfected them all. Joseph Schumpeter clearly fits within this family when he considers the international effects of capitalism and democracy.

Schumpeter's "Sociology of Imperialisms," published in 1919, made a coherent and sustained argument concerning the pacifying (in the sense of nonaggressive) effects of liberal institutions and principles (Schumpeter, 1955; see also Doyle, 1986, pp. 155–59). Unlike some of the earlier liberal theorists who focused on a single feature such as trade (Montesquieu, 1949, vol. 1, bk. 20, chap. 1) or failed to examine critically the arguments they were advancing, Schumpeter saw the interaction of capitalism and democracy as the foundation of liberal pacifism, and he tested his arguments in a sociology of historical imperialisms.

He defines *imperialism* as "an objectless disposition on the part of a state to unlimited forcible expansion" (Schumpeter, 1955, p. 6). Excluding imperialisms that were mere "catchwords" and those that were "objectful" (e.g., defensive imperialism), he traces the roots of objectless imperialism to three sources, each an atavism. Modern imperialism, according to Schumpeter, resulted from the combined impact of a "war machine," warlike instincts, and export monopolism.

Once necessary, the war machine later developed a life of its own and took control of a state's foreign policy: "Created by the wars that required it, the machine now created the wars it required" (Schumpeter, 1955, p. 25). Thus, Schumpeter tells us that the army of ancient Egypt, created to drive the Hyksos out of Egypt, took over the state and pursued militaristic imperialism. Like the later armies of the courts of absolutist Europe, it fought wars for the sake of glory and booty, for the sake of warriors and monarchs — wars *gratia* warriors.

A warlike disposition, elsewhere called "instinctual elements of bloody primitivism," is the natural ideology of a war machine. It also exists independently; the Persians, says Schumpeter (1955, pp. 25–32), were a warrior nation from the outset.

Under modern capitalism, export monopolists, the third source of modern imperialism, push for imperialist expansion as a way to expand their closed markets. The absolute monarchies were the last clear-cut imperialisms. Nineteenth-century imperialisms merely represent the vestiges of the imperialisms created by Louis XIV and Catherine the Great. Thus, the export monopolists are an atavism of the absolute monarchies, for they depend completely on the tariffs imposed by the monarchs and their militaristic successors for revenue (Schumpeter, 1955, pp. 82–83). Without tariffs, monopolies would be eliminated by foreign competition.

Modern (nineteenth century) imperialism, therefore, rests on an atavistic war machine, militaristic attitudes left over from the days of monarchical wars, and export monopolism, which is nothing more than the economic residue of monarchical finance. In the modern era, imperialists gratify their private interests. From the national perspective, their imperialistic wars are objectless.

Schumpeter's theme now emerges. Capitalism and democracy are forces for peace. Indeed, they are antithetical to imperialism. For Schumpeter, the further development of capitalism and democracy means that imperialism will inevitably disappear. He maintains that capitalism produces an unwarlike disposition; its populace is "democratized, individualized, rationalized" (Schumpeter, 1955, p. 68). The people's energies are daily absorbed in production. The disciplines of industry and the market train people in "economic rationalism"; the instability of industrial life necessitates calculation. Capitalism also "individualizes"; "subjective opportunities" replace the "immutable factors" of traditional, hierarchical society. Rational individuals demand democratic governance.

Democratic capitalism leads to peace. As evidence, Schumpeter claims that throughout the capitalist world an opposition has arisen to "war, expansion, cabinet diplomacy"; that contemporary capitalism is associated with peace parties; and that the industrial worker of capitalism is "vigorously anti-imperialist." In addition, he points out that the capitalist world has developed means of preventing war, such as the Hague

Court and that the least feudal, most capitalist society — the United States — has demonstrated the least imperialistic tendencies (Schumpeter, 1955, pp. 95–96). An example of the lack of imperialistic tendencies in the U.S., Schumpeter thought, was our leaving over half of Mexico unconquered in the war of 1846–48.

Schumpeter's explanation for liberal pacifism is quite simple: Only war profiteers and military aristocrats gain from wars. No democracy would pursue a minority interest and tolerate the high costs of imperialism. When free trade prevails, "no class" gains from forcible expansion because

> raw materials and food stuffs are as accessible to each nation as though they were in its own territory. Where the cultural backwardness of a region makes normal economic intercourse dependent on colonization it does not matter, assuming free trade, which of the "civilized" nations undertakes the task of colonization. (Schumpeter, 1955, pp. 75–76)

Schumpeter's arguments are difficult to evaluate. In partial tests of quasi-Schumpeterian propositions, Michael Haas (1974, pp. 464–65) discovered a cluster that associates democracy, development, and sustained modernization with peaceful conditions. However, M. Small and J. D. Singer (1976) have discovered that there is no clearly negative correlation between democracy and war in the period 1816–1965 — the period that would be central to Schumpeter's argument (see also Wilkenfeld, 1968, Wright, 1942, p. 841).

Later in his career, in *Capitalism, Socialism, and Democracy*, Schumpeter (1950, pp. 127–28) acknowledged that "almost purely bourgeois commonwealths were often aggressive when it seemed to pay — like the Athenian or the Venetian commonwealths." Yet he stuck to his pacifistic guns, restating the view that capitalist democracy "steadily tells . . . against the use of military force and for peaceful arrangements, even when the balance of pecuniary advantage is clearly on the side of war which, under modern circumstances, is not in general very likely" (Schumpeter, 1950, p. 128).[1] A recent study by R. J. Rummel (1983) of "libertarianism" and international violence is the closest test Schumpeterian pacifism has received. "Free" states (those enjoying political and economic freedom) were shown to have considerably less conflict at or above the level of economic sanctions than "nonfree" states. The free states, the partly free states (including the democratic socialist countries such as Sweden), and the nonfree states accounted for 24%, 26%, and 61%, respectively, of the international violence during the period examined.

These effects are impressive but not conclusive for the Schumpeterian thesis. The data are limited, in this test, to the period 1976 to 1980. It includes, for example, the Russo-Afghan War, the Vietnamese invasion of Cambodia, China's invasion of Vietnam, and Tanzania's invasion of Uganda but just misses the U.S., quasi-covert intervention in Angola (1975) and our not so covert war against Nicaragua (1981–). More importantly, it excludes the cold war period, with its numerous interventions, and the long history of colonial wars (the Boer War, the Spanish-American War, the Mexican Intervention, etc.) that marked the history of liberal, including democratic capitalist, states (Doyle, 1983b; Chan, 1984; Weede, 1984).

The discrepancy between the warlike history of liberal states and Schumpeter's pacifistic expectations highlights three extreme assumptions. First, his "materialistic monism" leaves little room for noneconomic objectives, whether espoused by states or individuals. Neither glory, nor prestige, nor ideological justification, nor the pure power of ruling shapes policy. These nonmaterial goals leave little room for positive-sum gains, such as the comparative advantages of trade. Second, and relatedly, the same is true for his states. The political life of individuals seems to have been homogenized at the same time as the individuals were "rationalized, individualized, and democratized." Citizens — capitalists and workers, rural and urban — seek material welfare. Schumpeter seems to presume that ruling makes no difference. He also presumes that no one is prepared to take those measures (such as stirring up foreign quarrels to preserve a domestic ruling coalition) that enhance one's political power, despite detrimental effects on mass welfare. Third, like domestic politics, world politics are homogenized. Materially monistic and democratically capitalist, all states evolve toward free trade and liberty together. Countries differently constituted seem to disappear from Schumpeter's analysis. "Civilized" nations govern "culturally backward" *regions*. These assumptions are not shared by Machiavelli's theory of liberalism.

LIBERAL IMPERIALISM

Machiavelli argues, not only that republics are not pacifistic, but that they are the best form of state for imperial expansion. Establishing a republic fit for imperial expansion is, moreover, the best way to guarantee the survival of a state.

Machiavelli's republic is a classical mixed republic. It is not a democracy — which he thought would quickly degenerate into a tyranny — but is characterized by social equality, popular liberty, and political participation (Machiavelli, 1950, bk. 1, chap. 2, p. 112; see also Huliung, 1983, chap. 2; Mansfield, 1970; Pocock, 1975, pp. 198–99; Skinner, 1981, chap. 3). The consuls serve as "kings," the senate as an aristocracy managing the state, and the people in the assembly as the source of strength.

Liberty results from "disunion" — the competition and necessity for compromise required by the division of powers among senate, consuls, and tribunes (the last representing the common people). Liberty also results from the popular veto. The powerful few threaten the rest with tyranny, Machiavelli says, because they seek to dominate. The mass demands not to be dominated, and their veto thus preserves the liberties of the state (Machiavelli, 1950, bk. 1, chap. 5, p. 122). However, since the people and the rulers have different social characters, the people need to be "managed" by the few to avoid having their recklessness overturn or their fecklessness undermine the ability of the state to expand (Machiavelli, 1950, bk. 1, chap. 53, pp. 249–50). Thus the senate and the consuls plan expansion, consult oracles, and employ religion to manage the resources that the energy of the people supplies.

Strength, and then imperial expansion, results from the way liberty encourages increased population and property, which grow when the citizens know their lives and goods are secure from arbitrary seizure. Free citizens equip large armies and provide soldiers who fight for public glory and the common good because these are, in fact, their own (Machiavelli, 1950, bk. 2, chap. 2, pp. 287–90). If you seek the honor of having your state expand, Machiavelli advises, you should organize it as a free and popular republic like Rome, rather than as an aristocratic republic like Sparta or Venice. Expansion thus calls for a free republic.

"Necessity" — political survival — calls for expansion. If a stable aristocratic republic is forced by foreign conflict "to extend her territory, in such a case we shall see her foundations give way and herself quickly brought to ruin"; if, on the other hand, domestic security prevails, "the continued tranquility would enervate her, or provoke internal dissensions, which together, or either of them separately, will apt to prove her ruin" (Machiavelli, 1950, bk. 1, chap. 6, p. 129). Machiavelli therefore believes it is necessary to take the constitution of Rome, rather than that of Sparta or Venice, as our model.

Hence, this belief leads to liberal imperialism. We are lovers of glory, Machiavelli announces. We seek to rule or, at least, to avoid being oppressed. In either case, we want more for ourselves and our states than just material welfare (materialistic monism). Because other states with similar aims thereby threaten us, we prepare ourselves for expansion. Because our fellow citizens threaten us if we do not allow them either to satisfy their ambition or to release their political energies through imperial expansion, we expand.

There is considerable historical evidence for liberal imperialism. Machiavelli's (Polybius's) Rome and Thucydides' Athens both were imperial republics in the Machiavellian sense (Thucydides, 1954, bk. 6). The historical record of numerous U.S. interventions in the postwar period supports Machiavelli's argument (Aron, 1973, chaps. 3–4; Barnet, 1968, chap. 11), but the current record of liberal pacifism, weak as it is, calls some of his insights into question. To the extent that the modern populace actually controls (and thus unbalances) the mixed republic, its diffidence may outweigh elite ("senatorial") aggressiveness.

We can conclude either that (1) liberal pacifism has at least taken over with the further development of capitalist democracy, as Schumpeter predicted it would or that (2) the mixed record of liberalism — pacifism and imperialism — indicates that some liberal states are Schumpeterian democracies while others are Machiavellian republics. Before we accept either conclusion, however, we must consider a third apparent regularity of modern world politics.

LIBERAL INTERNATIONALISM

Modern liberalism carries with it two legacies. They do not affect liberal states separately, according to whether they are pacifistic or imperialistic, but simultaneously.

The first of these legacies is the pacification of foreign relations among liberal states.[2] During the nineteenth century, the United States and Great Britain engaged in nearly continual strife; however, after the Reform Act of 1832 defined actual representation as the formal source of the sovereignty of the British parliament, Britain and the United States negotiated their disputes. They negotiated despite, for example, British grievances during the Civil War against the North's blockade of the South, with which Britain had close economic ties. Despite severe Anglo-French colonial rivalry, liberal France and liberal Britain formed an entente against illiberal Germany before World War I. And from 1914 to 1915, Italy, the liberal member of the Triple Alliance with Germany and Austria, chose not to fulfill its obligations under that treaty to support its allies. Instead, Italy joined in an alliance with Britain and France, which prevented it from having to fight other liberal states and then declared war on Germany and Austria. Despite generations of Anglo-American tension and Britain's wartime restrictions on American trade with Germany, the United States leaned toward Britain and France from 1914 to 1917 before entering World War I on their side.

Beginning in the eighteenth century and slowly growing since then, a zone of peace, which Kant called the "pacific federation" or "pacific union," has begun to be established among liberal societies. More than 40 liberal states currently make up the union. Most are in Europe and North America, but they can be found on every continent, as Table 1 indicates.

Here the predictions of liberal pacifists (and President Reagan) are borne out: liberal states do exercise peaceful restraint, and a separate peace exists among them. This separate peace provides a solid foundation for the United States' crucial alliances with the liberal powers, e.g., the North Atlantic Treaty Organization and our Japanese alliance. This foundation appears to be impervious to the quarrels with our allies that bedeviled the Carter and Reagan administrations. It also offers the promise of a continuing peace among liberal states, and as the number of liberal states increases, it announces the possibility of global peace this side of the grave or world conquest.

Of course, the probability of the outbreak of war in any given year between any two given states is low. The occurrence of a war between any two adjacent states, considered over a long period of time, would be more probable. The apparent absence of war between liberal states, whether adjacent or not, for almost 200 years thus may have significance. Similar claims cannot be made for feudal, fascist, communist, authoritarian, or totalitarian forms of rule (Doyle, 1983a, pp. 222), nor for pluralistic or merely similar societies. More significant perhaps is that when states are forced to decide on which side of an impending world war they will fight, liberal states all wind up on the same side despite the complexity of the paths that take them there. These characteristics do not prove that the peace among liberals is statistically significant nor that liberalism is the sole valid explanation for the peace.[3] They do suggest that we consider the possibility that liberals have indeed established a separate peace — but only among themselves.

Liberalism also carries with it a second legacy: international "imprudence" (Hume, 1963, pp. 346 – 47). Peaceful restraint only seems to work in liberals' relations with other liberals. Liberal states have fought numerous wars with non-liberal states. (For a list of international wars since 1816 see Table 2.)

Many of these wars have been defensive and thus prudent by necessity. Liberal states have been attacked and threatened by nonliberal states that do not exercise any special restraint in their dealings with the liberal states. Authoritarian rulers both stimulate and respond to an international political environment in which conflicts of prestige, interest, and pure fear of what other states might do all lead states toward war. War and conquest have thus characterized the careers of many authoritarian rulers and ruling parties, from Louis XIV and Napoleon to Mussolini's fascists, Hitler's Nazis, and Stalin's communists.

Yet we cannot simply blame warfare on the authoritarians or totalitarians, as many of our more enthusiastic politicians would have us do.[4] Most wars arise out of calculations and miscalculations of interest, misunderstandings, and mutual suspicions, such as those that characterized the origins of World War I. However, aggression by the liberal state has also characterized a large number of wars. Both France and Britain fought expansionist colonial wars throughout the nineteenth century. The United States fought a similar war with Mexico from 1846 to 1848, waged a war of annihilation against the American Indians, and intervened militarily against sovereign states many times before and after World War II. Liberal states invade weak nonliberal states and display striking distrust in dealings with powerful nonliberal states (Doyle, 1983b).

Neither realist (statist) nor Marxist theory accounts well for these two legacies. While they can account for aspects of certain periods of international stability (Aron, 1968, pp. 151 – 54; Russett, 1985), neither the logic of the balance of power nor the logic of international hegemony explains the separate peace maintained for more than 150 years among states sharing one particular form of governance — liberal principles and institutions. Balance-of-power theory expects — indeed is premised upon — flexible

TABLE 1
Liberal Regimes and the Pacific Union, 1700–1982

Period	Period	Period
18th Century	1900–1945 (cont.)	1945– (cont.)
Swiss Cantons[a]	Italy, –1922	Costa Rica, –1948; 1953–
French Republic, 1790–1795	Belgium, –1940	Iceland, 1944–
United States,[a]1776–	Netherlands, –1940	France, 1945–
Total = 3	Argentina, –1943	Denmark, 1945
	France, –1940	Norway, 1945
1800–1850	Chile, –1924, 1932–	Brazil, 1945–1954; 1955–1964
Swiss Confederation	Australia, 1901	Belgium, 1946–
United States	Norway, 1905–1940	Luxemburg, 1946–
France, 1830–1849	New Zealand, 1907–	Netherlands, 1946–
Belgium, 1830–	Colombia, 1910–1949	Italy, 1946–
Great Britain, 1832–	Denmark, 1914–1940	Philippines, 1946–1972
Netherlands, 1848–	Poland, 1917–1935	India, 1947–1975, 1977–
Piedmont, 1848–	Latvia, 1922–1934	Sri Lanka, 1948–1961; 1963–1971; 1978–
Denmark, 1849	Germany, 1918–1932	Ecuador, 1948–1963; 1979–
Total = 8	Austria, 1918–1934	Israel, 1949–
	Estonia, 1919–1934	West Germany, 1949–
1850–1900	Finland, 1919–	Greece, 1950–1967; 1975–
Switzerland	Uruguay, 1919–	Peru, 1950–1962; 1963–1968; 1980–
United States	Costa Rica, 1919–	El Salvador, 1950–1961
Belgium	Czechoslovakia, 1920–1939	Turkey, 1950–1960; 1966–1971
Great Britain	Ireland, 1920–	Japan, 1951–
Netherlands	Mexico, 1928–	Bolivia, 1956–1969; 1982–
Piedmont, –1861	Lebanon, 1944–	Colombia, 1958–
Italy, 1861–	Total = 29	Venezuela, 1959–
Denmark, –1866		Nigeria, 1961–1964; 1979–1984
Sweden, 1864–	1945–[b]	Jamaica, 1962–
Greece, 1864–	Switzerland	
Canada, 1867–		

France, 1871 –
Argentina, 1880 –
Chile, 1891 –
Total = 13

1900–1945
Switzerland
United States
Great Britain
Sweden
Canada
Greece, –1911; 1928–1936

United States
Great Britain
Sweden
Canada
Australia
New Zealand
Finland
Ireland
Mexico
Uruguay, –1973
Chile, –1973
Lebanon, –1975

Trinidad and Tobago, 1962–
Senegal, 1963–
Malaysia, 1963–
Botswana, 1966–
Singapore, 1965–
Portugal, 1976–
Spain, 1978–
Dominican Republic, 1978–
Honduras, 1981–
Papua New Guinea, 1982–
Total = 50

NOTE: I have drawn up this approximate list of "Liberal Regimes" according to the four institutions Kant described as essential: market and private property economies; polities that are externally sovereign; citizens who possess juridical rights; and "republican" (whether republican or parliamentary monarchy), representative government. This latter includes the requirement that the legislative branch have an effective role in public policy and be formally and competitively (either inter- or intra-party) elected. Furthermore, I have taken into account whether male suffrage is wide (i.e., 30%) or, as Kant (*MM* p. 139) would have had it, open by "achievement" to inhabitants of the national or metropolitan territory (e.g., to poll-tax payers or householders). This list of liberal regimes is thus more inclusive than a list of democratic regimes, or polyarchies (Powell, 1982, p. 5). Other conditions taken into account here are that female suffrage is granted within a generation of its being demanded by an extensive female suffrage movement and that representative government is internally sovereign (e.g., including, and especially over military and foreign affairs) as well as stable (in existence for at least three years). Sources for these data are Banks and Overstreet (1983), Gastil (1985), *The Europa Yearbook*, 1985 (1985), Langer (1968), U.K. Foreign and Commonwealth Office (1980), and U.S. Department of State (1981). Finally these lists exclude ancient and medieval "republics," since none appears to fit Kant's commitment to liberal individualism (Holmes, 1979).

[a] There are domestic variations within these liberal regimes: Switzerland was liberal only in certain cantons; the United States was liberal only north of the Mason-Dixon line until 1865, when it became liberal throughout.

[b] Selected list, excludes liberal regimes with populations less than one million. These include all states categorized as "free" by Gastil and those "partly free" (four-fifths or more free) states with a more pronounced capitalist orientation.

TABLE 2   International Wars

British-Maharattan (1817–1818)	Pacific (1879–1883)
Greek (1821–1828)	British-Zulu (1879)
Franco-Spanish (1823)	Franco-Indochinese (1882–1884)
First Anglo-Burmese (1823–1826)	Mahdist (1882–1885)
Javanese (1825–1830)	Sino-French (1884–1885)
Russo-Persian (1826–1828)	Central American (1885)
Russo-Turkish (1828–1829)	Serbo-Bulgarian (1885)
First Polish (1831)	Sino-Japanese (1894–1895)
First Syrian (1831–1832)	Franco-Madagascan (1894–1895)
Texas (1835–1836)	Cuban (1895–1898)
First British-Afghan (1838–1842)	Italo-Ethiopian (1895–1896)
Second Syrian (1839–1940)	First Philippine (1896–1898)
Franco-Algerian (1839–1847)	Greco-Turkish (1897)
Peruvian-Bolivian (1841)	Spanish-American (1898)
First British-Sikh (1845–1846)	Second Philippine (1899–1902)
Mexican-American (1846–1848)	Boer (1899–1902)
Austro-Sardinian (1848–1849)	Boxer Rebellion (1900)
First Schleswig-Holstein (1848–1849)	Ilinden (1903)
Hungarian (1848–1849)	Russo-Japanese (1904–1905)
Second British-Sikh (1848–1849)	Central American (1906)
Roman Republic (1849)	Central American (1907)
La Plata (1851–1852)	Spanish-Moroccan (1909–1910)
First Turco-Montenegran (1852–1853)	Italo-Turkish (1911–1912)
Crimean (1853–1856)	First Balkan (1912–1913)
Anglo-Persian (1856–1857)	Second Balkan (1913)
Sepoy (1857–1859)	World War I (1914–1918)
Second Turco-Montenegran (1858–1859)	Russian Nationalities (1917–1921)
Italian Unification (1859)	Russo-Polish (1919–1920)
Spanish-Moroccan (1859–1860)	Hungarian-Allies (1919)
Italo-Roman (1860)	Greco-Turkish (1919–1922)
Italo-Sicilian (1860–1861)	Riffian (1921–1926)
Franco-Mexican (1862–1867)	Druze (1925–1927)
Ecuadorian-Colombian (1863)	Sino-Soviet (1929)
Second Polish (1863–1864)	Manchurian (1931–1933)
Spanish-Santo Dominican (1863–1865)	Chaco (1932–1935)
Second Schleswig-Holstein (1864)	Italo-Ethiopian (1935–1936)
Lopez (1864–1870)	Sino-Japanese (1937–1941)
Spanish-Chilean (1865–1866)	Russo-Hungarian (1956)
Seven Weeks (1866)	Sinai (1956)
Ten Years (1868–1878)	Tibetan (1956–1959)
Franco-Prussian (1870–1871)	Sino-Indian (1962)

TABLE 2   International Wars (continued)

Dutch-Achinese (1873–1878)	Vietnamese (1965–1975)
Balkan (1875–1877)	Second Kashmir (1965)
Russo-Turkish (1877–1878)	Six Day (1967)
Bosnian (1878)	Israeli-Egyptian (1969–1970)
Second British-Afghan (1878–1880)	Football (1969)
Changkufeng (1938)	Bangladesh (1971)
Nomohan (1939)	Philippine-MNLF (1972–)
World War II (1939–1945)	Yom Kippur (1973)
Russo-Finnish (1939–1940)	Turco-Cypriot (1974)
Franco-Thai (1940–1941)	Ethiopian-Eritrean (1974–)
Indonesian (1945–1946)	Vietnamese-Cambodian (1975–)
Indochinese (1945–1954)	Timor (1975–)
Madagascan (1947–1948)	Saharan (1975–)
First Kashmir (1947–1949)	Ogaden (1976–)
Palestine (1948–1949)	Ugandan-Tanzanian (1978–1979)
Hyderabad (1948)	Sino-Vietnamese (1979)
Korean (1950–1953)	Russo-Afghan (1979–)
Algerian (1954–1962)	Iran-Iraqi (1980–)

NOTE: This table is taken from Melvin Small and J. David Singer (1982, pp. 79–80). This is a partial list of international wars fought between 1816 and 1980. In Appendices A and B, Small and Singer identify a total of 575 wars during this period, but approximately 159 of them appear to be largely domestic, or civil wars.

This list excludes covert interventions, some of which have been directed by liberal regimes against other liberal regimes—for example, the United States' effort to destabilize the Chilean election and Allende's government. Nonetheless, it is significant that such interventions are not pursued publicly as acknowledged policy. The covert destabilization campaign against Chile is recounted by the Senate Select Committee to Study Governmental Operations with Respect to Intelligence Activities (1975, Covert Action in Chile, 1963–73).

Following the argument of this article, this list also excludes civil wars. Civil wars differ from international wars, not in the ferocity of combat, but in the issues that engender them. Two nations that could abide one another as independent neighbors separated by a border might well be the fiercest of enemies if forced to live together in one state, jointly deciding how to raise and spend taxes, choose leaders, and legislate fundamental questions of value. Notwithstanding these differences, no civil wars that I recall upset the argument of liberal pacification.

arrangements of geostrategic rivalry that include preventive war. Hegemonies wax and wane, but the liberal peace holds. Marxist "ultra-imperialists" expect a form of peaceful rivalry among capitalists, but only liberal capitalists maintain peace. Leninists expect liberal capitalists to be aggressive toward nonliberal states, but they also (and especially) expect them to be imperialistic toward fellow liberal capitalists.

Kant's theory of liberal internationalism helps us understand these two legacies. The importance of Immanuel Kant as a theorist of international ethics has been well appreciated (Armstrong, 1931; Friedrich,

1948; Gallie, 1978, chap. 1; Galston, 1975; Hassner, 1972; Hinsley, 1967, chap. 4; Hoffmann, 1965; Waltz, 1962; Williams, 1983), but Kant also has an important analytical theory of international politics. *Perpetual Peace,* written in 1795 (Kant, 1970, pp. 93–130), helps us understand the interactive nature of international relations. Kant tries to teach us methodologically that we can study neither the systemic relations of states nor the varieties of state behavior in isolation from each other. Substantively, he anticipates for us the ever-widening pacification of a liberal pacific union, explains this pacification, and at the same time suggests why liberal states are not pacific in their relations with nonliberal states. Kant argues that perpetual peace will be guaranteed by the ever-widening acceptance of three "definitive articles" of peace. When all nations have accepted the definitive articles in a metaphorical "treaty" of perpetual peace he asks them to sign, perpetual peace will have been established.

The First Definitive Article requires the civil constitution of the state to be republican. By *republican* Kant means a political society that has solved the problem of combining moral autonomy, individualism, and social order. A private property and market-oriented economy partially addressed that dilemma in the private sphere. The public, or political, sphere was more troubling. His answer was a republic that preserved juridical freedom — the legal equality of citizens as subjects — on the basis of a representative government with a separation of powers. Juridical freedom is preserved because the morally autonomous individual is by means of representation a self-legislator making laws that apply to all citizens equally, including himself or herself. Tyranny is avoided because the individual is subject to laws he or she does not also administer (Kant, *PP,* pp. 99–102; Riley, 1985, chap. 5).[5]

Liberal republics will progressively establish peace among themselves by means of the pacific federation, or union (*foedus pacificum*), described in Kant's Second Definitive Article. The pacific union will establish peace within a federation of free states and securely maintain the rights of each state. The world will not have achieved the "perpetual peace" that provides the ultimate guarantor of republican freedom until "a late stage and after many unsuccessful attempts" (Kant, *UH,* p. 47). At that time, all nations will have learned the lessons of peace through right conceptions of the appropriate constitution, great and sad experience, and good will. Only then will individuals enjoy perfect republican rights or the full guarantee of a global and just peace. In the meantime, the "pacific federation" of liberal republics — "an enduring and gradually expanding federation likely to prevent war" — brings within it more and more republics — despite republican collapses, backsliding, and disastrous wars — creating an ever-expanding separate peace (Kant, *PP,* p. 105).[6] Kant emphasizes that

> it can be shown that this idea of federalism, extending gradually to encompass all states and thus leading to perpetual peace, is practicable and has objective reality. For if by good fortune one powerful and enlightened nation

can form a republic (which is by nature inclined to seek peace), this will provide a focal point for federal association among other states. These will join up with the first one, thus securing the freedom of each state in accordance with the idea of international right, and the whole will gradually spread further and further by a series of alliances of this kind. (Kant, *PP*, p. 104)

The pacific union is not a single peace treaty ending one war, a world state, nor a state of nations. Kant finds the first insufficient. The second and third are impossible or potentially tyrannical. National sovereignty precludes reliable subservience to a state of nations; a world state destroys the civic freedom on which the development of human capacities rests (Kant, *UH*, p. 50). Although Kant obliquely refers to various classical interstate confederations and modern diplomatic congresses, he develops no systematic organizational embodiment of this treaty and presumably does not find institutionalization necessary (Riley, 1983, chap. 5; Schwarz, 1962, p. 77). He appears to have in mind a mutual non-aggression pact, perhaps a collective security agreement, and the cosmopolitan law set forth in the Third Definitive Article.[7]

The Third Definitive Article establishes a cosmopolitan law to operate in conjunction with the pacific union. The cosmopolitan law "shall be limited to conditions of universal hospitality." In this Kant calls for the recognition of the "right of a foreigner not to be treated with hostility when he arrives on someone else's territory." This "does not extend beyond those conditions which make it possible for them [foreigners] to attempt to enter into relations [commerce] with the native inhabitants" (Kant, *PP*, p. 106). Hospitality does not require extending to foreigners either the right to citizenship or the right to settlement, unless the foreign visitors would perish if they were expelled. Foreign conquest and plunder also find no justification under this right. Hospitality does appear to include the right of access and the obligation of maintaining the opportunity for citizens to exchange goods and ideas without imposing the obligation to trade (a voluntary act in all cases under liberal constitutions).

Perpetual peace, for Kant, is an epistemology, a condition for ethical action, and, most importantly, an explanation of how the "mechanical process of nature visibly exhibits the purposive plan of producing concord among men, even against their will and indeed by means of their very discord" (Kant, *PP*, p. 108; *UH*, pp. 44–45). Understanding history requires an epistemological foundation, for without a teleology, such as the promise of perpetual peace, the complexity of history would overwhelm human understanding (Kant, *UH*, pp. 51–53). Perpetual peace, however, is not merely a heuristic device with which to interpret history. It is guaranteed, Kant explains in the "First Addition" to *Perpetual Peace* ("On the Guarantee of Perpetual Peace"), to result from men fulfilling their ethical duty or, failing that, from a hidden plan.[8] Peace is an ethical duty because it is only under conditions of peace that all men can treat each other as ends, rather than means to an end (Kant, *UH*, p. 50; Murphy, 1970, chap. 3). In order for this duty to be practical, Kant needs, of course, to show that peace is in fact possible. The widespread sentiment of approbation that he saw aroused by the early success of the French revolutionaries showed him that we can indeed be moved by ethical sentiments with a cosmopolitan reach (Kant, *CF,* pp. 181–82; Yovel, 1980, pp. 153–54). This does not mean, however, that perpetual peace is certain ("prophesiable"). Even the scientifically regular course of the planets could be changed by a wayward comet striking them out of orbit. Human freedom requires that we allow for much greater reversals in the course of history. We must, in fact, anticipate the possibility of backsliding and destructive wars — though these will serve to educate nations to the importance of peace (Kant, *UH,* pp. 47–48).

In the end, however, our guarantee of perpetual peace does not rest on ethical conduct. As Kant emphasizes,

> we now come to the essential question regarding the prospect of perpetual peace. What does nature do in relation to the end which man's own reason prescribes to him as a duty, i.e. how does nature help to promote his *moral purpose?* And how does nature guarantee that what man ought to do by the laws of his freedom (but does not do) will in fact be done through nature's compulsion, without prejudice to the free agency of man? . . . This does not mean that nature imposes on us a *duty* to do it, for duties can only be imposed by practical reason. On the contrary, nature does it herself, whether we are willing or not: *facta volentem ducunt, nolentem tradunt. (PP,* p. 112)

The guarantee thus rests, Kant argues, not on the probable behavior of moral angels, but on that of "devils, so long as they possess understanding" (*PP,* p. 112). In explaining the sources of each of the three definitive articles of the perpetual peace, Kant then tells us how we (as free and intelligent devils) could be motivated by fear, force, and calculated advantage to undertake a course of action whose outcome we could reasonably anticipate to be perpetual peace. Yet while it is possible to conceive of the Kantian road to peace in these terms, Kant himself recognizes and argues that social evolution also makes the conditions of moral behavior less onerous and hence more likely (*CF,* pp. 187–89; Kelly, 1969, pp. 106–13). In tracing the effects of both political and moral development, he builds an account of why liberal states do maintain peace among themselves and of how it will (by implication, has) come about that the pacific union will expand. He also explains how these republics would engage in wars with nonrepublics and therefore suffer the "sad experience" of wars that an ethical policy might have avoided.

The first source of the three definitive articles derives from a political evolution — from a constitutional law. Nature (providence) has seen to it that human beings can live in all the regions where they have been driven to settle by wars. (Kant, who once taught geography, reports on the Lapps, the Samoyeds, the Pescheras.) "Asocial sociability" draws men together to fulfill needs for security and material welfare as it drives them into conflicts over the distribution and control of social products (Kant,

UH, pp. 44-45; *PP*, pp. 110-11). This violent natural evolution tends towards the liberal peace because "asocial sociability" inevitably leads toward republican governments, and republican governments are a source of the liberal peace.

Republican representation and separation of powers are produced because they are the means by which the state is "organized well" to prepare for and meet foreign threats (by unity) and to tame the ambitions of selfish and aggressive individuals (by authority derived from representation, by general laws, and by nondespotic administration) (Kant, *PP*, pp. 112-13). States that are not organized in this fashion fail. Monarchs thus encourage commerce and private property in order to increase national wealth. They cede rights of representation to their subjects in order to strengthen their political support or to obtain willing grants of tax revenue (Hassner, 1972, pp. 583-86).

Kant shows how republics, once established, lead to peaceful relations. He argues that once the aggressive interests of absolutist monarchies are tamed and the habit of respect for individual rights engrained by republican government, wars would appear as the disaster to the people's welfare that he and the other liberals thought them to be. The fundamental reason is this:

> If, as is inevitably the case under this constitution, the consent of the citizens is required to decide whether or not war should be declared, it is very natural that they will have a great hesitation in embarking on so dangerous an enterprise. For this would mean calling down on themselves all the miseries of war, such as doing the fighting themselves, supplying the costs of the war from their own resources, painfully making good the ensuing devastation, and, as the crowning evil, having to take upon themselves a burden of debts which will embitter peace itself and which can never be paid off on account of the constant threat of new wars. But under a constitution where the subject is not a citizen, and which is therefore not republican, it is the simplest thing in the world to go to war. For the head of state is not a fellow citizen, but the owner of the state, and war will not force him to make the slightest sacrifice so far as his banquets, hunts, pleasure palaces and court festivals are concerned. He can thus decide on war, without any significant reason, as a kind of amusement, and unconcernedly leave it to the diplomatic corps (who are always ready for such pruposes) to justify the war for the sake of propriety. (Kant, *PP*, p. 100)

Yet these domestic republican restraints do not end war. If they did, liberal states would not be warlike, which is far from the case. They do introduce republican caution — Kant's "hesitation" — in place of monarchical caprice. Liberal wars are only fought for popular, liberal purposes. The historical liberal legacy is laden with popular wars fought to promote freedom, to protect private property, or to support liberal allies against nonliberal enemies. Kant's position is ambiguous. He regards these wars as unjust and warns liberals of their susceptibility to them (Kant, *PP*, p. 106). At the same time, Kant argues that each nation "can and ought to" demand that its neighboring nations enter into the pacific union of liberal states (*PP,* p. 102). Thus to see how the pacific union removes the occasion of wars among liberal states and not wars between liberal and nonliberal states, we need to shift our attention from constitutional law to international law, Kant's second source.

Complementing the constitutional guarantee of caution, international law adds a second source for the definitive articles: a guarantee of respect. The separation of nations that asocial sociability encourages is reinforced by the development of separate languages and religions. These further guarantee a world of separate states — an essential condition needed to avoid a "global, soul-less despotism." Yet, at the same time, they also morally integrate liberal states: "as culture grows and men gradually move towards greater agreement over their principles, they lead to mutual understanding and peace" (Kant, *PP,* p. 114). As republics emerge (the first source) and as culture progresses, an understanding of the legitimate rights of all citizens and of all republics comes into play; and this, now that caution characterizes policy, sets up the moral foundations for the liberal peace. Correspondingly, international law highlights the importance of Kantian publicity. Domestically, publicity helps ensure that the officials of republics act according to the principles they profess to hold just and according to the interests of the electors they claim to represent. Internationally, free speech and the effective communication of accurate conceptions of the political life of foreign peoples is essential to establishing and preserving the understanding on which the guarantee of respect depends. Domestically just republics, which rest on consent, then presume foreign republics also to be consensual, just, and therefore deserving of accommodation. The experience of cooperation helps engender further cooperative behavior when the consequences of state policy are unclear but (potentially) mutually beneficial. At the same time, liberal states assume that nonliberal states, which do not rest on free consent, are not just. Because nonliberal governments are in a state of aggression with their own people, their foreign relations become for liberal governments deeply suspect. In short, fellow liberals benefit from a presumption of amity; nonliberals suffer from a presumption of enmity. Both presumptions may be accurate; each, however, may also be self-confirming.

Lastly, cosmopolitan law adds material incentives to moral commitments. The cosmopolitan right to hospitality permits the "spirit of commerce" sooner or later to take hold of every nation, thus impelling states to promote peace and to try to avert war. Liberal economic theory holds that these cosmopolitan ties derive from a cooperative international division of labor and free trade according to comparative advantage. Each economy is said to be better off than it would have been under autarky; each thus acquires an incentive to avoid policies that would lead the other to break these economic ties. Because keeping open markets rests upon the assumption that the next set of transactions will also be determined by prices rather than coercion, a sense of mutual security is vital to avoid security-motivated searches for economic autarky. Thus, avoiding a challenge to another liberal state's security or even enhancing each other's security by means of alliance naturally follows economic interdependence.

A further cosmopolitan source of liberal peace is the international market's removal of difficult decisions of production and distribution from the direct sphere of state policy. A foreign state thus does not appear directly responsible for these outcomes, and states can stand aside from, and to some degree above, these contentious market rivalries and be ready to step in to resolve crises. The interdependence of commerce and the international contacts of state officials help create crosscutting transnational ties that serve as lobbies for mutual accommodation. According to modern liberal scholars, international financiers and transnational and transgovernmental organizations create interests in favor of accommodation. Moreover, their variety has ensured that no single conflict sours an entire relationship by setting off a spiral of reciprocated retaliation (Brzezinski and Huntington, 1963, chap. 9; Keohane and Nye, 1977, chap. 7; Neustadt, 1970; Polanyi, 1944, chaps. 1–2). Conversely, a sense of suspicion, such as that characterizing relations between liberal and nonliberal governments, can lead to restrictions on the range of contacts between societies, and this can increase the prospect that a single conflict will determine an entire relationship.

No single constitutional, international, or cosmopolitan source is alone sufficient, but together (and only together) they plausibly connect the characteristics of liberal polities and economies with sustained liberal peace. Alliances founded on mutual strategic interest among liberal and nonliberal states have been broken; economic ties between liberal and nonliberal states have proven fragile; but the political bonds of liberal rights and interests have proven a remarkably firm foundation for mutual nonaggression. A separate peace exists among liberal states.

In their relations with nonliberal states, however, liberal states have not escaped from the insecurity caused by anarchy in the world political system considered as a whole. Moreover, the very constitutional restraint, international respect for individual rights, and shared commercial interests that establish grounds for peace among liberal states establish grounds for additional conflict in relations between liberal and nonliberal societies.

CONCLUSION

Kant's liberal internationalism, Machiavelli's liberal imperialism, and Schumpeter's liberal pacifism rest on fundamentally different views of the nature of the human being, the state, and international relations.[9] Schumpeter's humans are rationalized, individualized, and democratized. They are also homogenized, pursuing material interests "monistically." Because their material interests lie in peaceful trade, they and the democratic state that these fellow citizens control are pacifistic. Machiavelli's citizens are splendidly diverse in their goals but fundamentally unequal in them as well, seeking to rule or fearing being dominated. Extending the rule of the dominant elite or avoiding the political collapse of their state, each calls for imperial expansion.

Kant's citizens, too, are diverse in their goals and individualized and rationalized, but most importantly, they are capable of appreciating the moral equality of all individuals and of treating other individuals as ends rather than as means. The Kantian state thus is governed publicly according to law, as a republic. Kant's is the state that solves the problem of governing individualized equals, whether they are the "rational devils" he says we often find ourselves to be or the ethical agents we can and should become. Republics tell us that

> in order to organize a group of rational beings who together require universal laws for their survival, but of whom each separate individual is secretly inclined to exempt himself from them, the constitution must be so designed so that, although the citizens are opposed to one another in their private attitudes, these opposing views may inhibit one another in such a way that the public conduct of the citizens will be the same as if they did not have such evil attitudes. (Kant, *PP*, p. 113)

Unlike Machiavelli's republics, Kant's republics are capable of achieving peace among themselves because they exercise democratic caution and are capable of appreciating the international rights of foreign republics. These international rights of republics derive from the representation of foreign individuals who are our moral equals. Unlike Schumpeter's capitalist democracies, Kant's republics — including our own — remain in a state of war with nonrepublics. Liberal republics see themselves as threatened by aggression from nonrepublics that are not constrained by representation. Even though wars often cost more than the economic return they generate, liberal republics also are prepared to protect and promote — sometimes forcibly — democracy, private property, and the rights of individuals overseas against nonrepublics, which, because they do not authentically represent the rights of individuals, have no rights to noninterference. These wars may liberate oppressed individuals overseas; they also can generate enormous suffering.

Preserving the legacy of the liberal peace without succumbing to the legacy of liberal imprudence is both a moral and a strategic challenge. The bipolar stability of the international system, and the near certainty of mutual devastation resulting from a nuclear war between the superpowers, have created a "crystal ball effect" that has helped to constrain the tendency toward miscalculation present at the outbreak of so many wars in the past (Carnesale, Doty, Hoffmann, Huntington, Nye, and Sagan, 1983, p. 44; Waltz, 1964). However, this "nuclear peace" appears to be limited to the super-powers. It has not curbed military interventions in the

Third World. Moreover, it is subject to a desperate technological race designed to overcome its constraints and to crises that have pushed even the super-powers to the brink of war. We must still reckon with the war fevers and moods of appeasement that have almost alternately swept liberal democracies.

Yet restraining liberal imprudence, whether aggressive or passive, may not be possible without threatening liberal pacification. Improving the strategic acumen of our foreign policy calls for introducing steadier strategic calculations of the national interest in the long run and more flexible responses to changes in the international political environment. Constraining the indiscriminate meddling of our foreign interventions calls for a deeper appreciation of the "particularism of history, culture, and membership" (Walzer, 1983, p. 5), but both the improvement in strategy and the constraint on intervention seem, in turn, to require an executive freed from the restraints of a representative legislature in the management of foreign policy and a political culture indifferent to the universal rights of individuals. These conditions, in their turn, could break the chain of constitutional guarantees, the respect for representative government, and the web of transnational contact that have sustained the pacific union of liberal states.

Perpetual peace, Kant says, is the end point of the hard journey his republics will take. The promise of perpetual peace, the violent lessons of war, and the experience of a partial peace are proof of the need for and the possibility of world peace. They are also the grounds for moral citizens and statesmen to assume the duty of striving for peace.

NOTES

I would like to thank Marshall Cohen, Amy Gutmann, Ferdinand Hermens, Bonnie Honig, Paschalis Kitromilides, Klaus Knorr, Diana Meyers, Kenneth Oye, Jerome Schneewind, and Richard Ullman for their helpful suggestions. One version of this paper was presented at the American Section of the International Society for Social and Legal Philosophy, Notre Dame, Indiana, November 2–4, 1984, and will appear in *Realism and Morality*, edited by Kenneth Kipnis and Diana Meyers. Another version was presented on March 19, 1986, to the Avoiding Nuclear War Project, Center for Science and International Affairs, The John F. Kennedy School of Government, Harvard University. This essay draws on research assisted by a MacArthur Fellowship in International Security awarded by the Social Science Research Council.

1. He notes that testing this proposition is likely to be very difficult, requiring "detailed historical analysis." However, the bourgeois attitude toward the military, the spirit and manner by which bourgeois societies wage war, and the readiness with which they submit to military rule during a prolonged war are "conclusive in themselves" (Schumpeter, 1950, p. 129).

2. Clarence Streit (1938, pp. 88, 90–92) seems to have been the first to point out (in contemporary foreign relations) the empirical tendency of democracies to maintain peace among themselves, and he made this the foundation of his proposal for a (non-Kantian) federal union of the 15 leading democracies of the 1930s. In a very interesting book, Ferdinand Hermens (1944) explored some of the policy implications of Streit's analysis. D. V. Babst (1972, pp. 55–58) performed a quantitative study of this phenomenon of "democratic peace," and R. J. Rummel (1983) did a similar study of "libertarianism" (in the sense of laissez faire) focusing on the postwar period that drew on an unpublished study (Project No. 48) noted in Appendix 1 of his *Understanding Conflict and War* (1979, p. 386). I use the term *liberal* in a wider, Kantian sense in my discussion of this issue (Doyle, 1983a). In that essay, I survey the period from 1790 to the present and find no war among liberal states.

3. Babst (1972) did make a preliminary test of the significance of the distribution of alliance partners in World War I. He found that the possibility that the actual distribution of alliance partners could have occurred by chance was less than 1% (Babst, 1972, p. 56). However, this assumes that there was an equal possibility that any two nations could have gone to war with each other, and this is a strong assumption. Rummel (1983) has a further discussion of the issue of statistical significance as it applies to his libertarian thesis.

4. There are serious studies showing that Marxist regimes have higher military spending per capita than non-Marxist regimes (Payne, n.d.), but this should not be interpreted as a sign of the inherent aggressiveness of authoritarian or totalitarian governments or of the inherent and global peacefulness of liberal regimes. Marxist regimes, in particular, represent a minority in the current international system; they are strategically encircled, and due to their lack of domestic legitimacy, they might be said to "suffer" the twin burden of needing defenses against both external and internal enemies. Andreski (1980), moreover, argues that (purely) military dictatorships, due to their domestic fragility, have little incentive to engage in foreign military adventures. According to Walter Clemens (1982, pp. 117–18), the United States intervened in the Third World more than twice as often during the period 1946–1976 as the Soviet Union did in 1946–79. Relatedly, Posen and VanEvera (1980, p. 105; 1983, pp. 86–89) found that the United States devoted one quarter and the Soviet Union one tenth of their defense budgets to forces designed for Third World interventions (where responding to perceived threats would presumably have a less than purely defensive character).

5. All citations from Kant are from *Kant's Political Writings* (Kant, 1970), the H. B. Nisbet translation edited by Hans Reiss. The works discussed and the abbreviations by which they are identified in the text are as follows:
PP Perpetual Peace (1795)
UH The Idea for a Universal History with a Cosmopolitan Purpose (1784)
CF The Contest of Faculties (1798)
MM The Metaphysics of Morals (1797)

6. I think Kant meant that the peace would be established among liberal regimes and would expand by ordinary political and legal means as new liberal regimes appeared. By a process of gradual extension the peace would become global and then perpetual; the occasion for wars with nonliberals would disappear as nonliberal regimes disappeared.

7. Kant's *foedus pacificum* is thus neither a *pactum pacis* (a single peace treaty)

nor a *civitas gentium* (a world state). He appears to have anticipated something like a less formally institutionalized League of Nations or United Nations. One could argue that in practice, these two institutions worked for liberal states and only for liberal states, but no specifically liberal "pacific union" was institutionalized. Instead, liberal states have behaved for the past 180 years as if such a Kantian pacific union and treaty of perpetual peace had been signed.

8. In the *Metaphysics of Morals* (the *Rechtslehre*) Kant seems to write as if perpetual peace is only an epistemological device and, while an ethical duty, is empirically merely a "pious hope" (*MM*, pp. 164–75)—though even here he finds that the pacific union is not "impracticable" (*MM*, p. 171). In the *Universal History (UH)*, Kant writes as if the brute force of physical nature drives men toward inevitable peace. Yovel (1980, pp. 168 ff.) argues that from a post-critical (post-*Critique of Judgment*) perspective, *Perpetual Peace* reconciles the two views of history. "Nature" is human-created nature (culture or civilization). Perpetual peace is the "*a priori* of the *a posteriori*"—a critical perspective that then enables us to discern causal, probabilistic patterns in history. Law and the "political technology" of republican constitutionalism are separate from ethical development, but both interdependently lead to perpetual peace—the first through force, fear, and self-interest; the second through progressive enlightenment—and both together lead to perpetual peace through the widening of the circumstances in which engaging in right conduct poses smaller and smaller burdens.

9. For a comparative discussion of the political foundations of Kant's ideas, see Shklar (1984, pp. 232–38).

REFERENCES

Andreski, Stanislav. 1980. On the Peaceful Disposition of Military Dictatorships. *Journal of Strategic Studies,* 3:3–10.

Armstrong, A. C. 1931. Kant's Philosophy of Peace and War. *The Journal of Philosophy,* 28:197–204.

Aron, Raymond. 1966. *Peace and War: A Theory of International Relations.* Richard Howard and Annette Baker Fox, trans. Garden City, NY: Doubleday.

Aron, Raymond. 1974. *The Imperial Republic.* Frank Jellinek, trans. Englewood Cliffs, NJ: Prentice Hall.

Babst, Dean V. 1972. A Force for Peace. *Industrial Research.* 14 (April): 55–58.

Banks, Arthur, and William Overstreet, eds. 1983. *A Political Handbook of the World; 1982–1983.* New York: McGraw Hill.

Barnet, Richard. 1968. *Intervention and Revolution.* Cleveland: World Publishing Co.

Brzezinski, Zbigniew, and Samuel Huntington. 1963. *Political Power: USA/USSR.* New York: Viking Press.

Carnesale, Albert, Paul Doty, Stanley Hoffmann, Samuel Huntington, Joseph Nye, and Scott Sagan. 1983. *Living With Nuclear Weapons.* New York: Bantam.

Chan, Steve. 1984. Mirror, Mirror on the Wall . . .: Are Freer Countries More Pacific? *Journal of Conflict Resolution,* 28:617–48.

Clemens, Walter C. 1982. The Superpowers and the Third World. In Charles Kegley and Pat McGowan, eds., *Foreign Policy: USA/USSR.* Beverly Hills: Sage Publications, pp. 111–35.

Doyle, Michael W. 1983a. Kant, Liberal Legacies, and Foreign Affairs: Part 1. *Philosophy and Public Affairs* 12:205-35.

Doyle, Michael W. 1983b. Kant, Liberal Legacies, and Foreign Affairs: Part 2. *Philosophy and Public Affairs* 12:323-53.

Doyle, Michael W. 1986. *Empires.* Ithaca: Cornell University Press.

The Europa Yearbook for 1985. 1985. 2 vols. London. Europa Publications.

Friedrich, Karl. 1948. *Inevitable Peace.* Cambridge, MA: Harvard University Press.

Gallie, W. B. 1978. *Philosophers of Peace and War.* Cambridge: Cambridge University Press.

Galston, William. 1975. *Kant and the Problem of History.* Chicago: Chicago University Press.

Gastil, Raymond. 1985. The Comparative Survey of Freedom 1985. *Freedom at Issue,* 82:3-16.

Haas, Michael. 1974. *International Conflict.* New York: Bobbs-Merrill.

Hassner, Pierre. 1972. Immanuel Kant. In Leo Strauss and Joseph Cropsey, eds., *History of Political Philosophy.* Chicago: Rand McNally. pp. 554-93.

Hermens, Ferdinand A. 1944. *The Tryants' War and the People's Peace.* Chicago: University of Chicago Press.

Hinsley, F. H. 1967. *Power and the Pursuit of Peace.* Cambridge: Cambridge University Press.

Hoffmann, Stanley. 1965. Rousseau on War and Peace. In Stanley Hoffmann, ed. *The State of War.* New York: Praeger. pp. 45-87.

Holmes, Stephen. 1979. Aristippus in and out of Athens. *American Political Science Review,* 73:113-28.

Huliung, Mark. 1983. *Citizen Machiavelli.* Princeton: Princeton University Press.

Hume, David. 1963. Of the Balance of Power. *Essays: Moral, Political, and Literary.* Oxford: Oxford University Press.

Kant, Immanuel. 1970. *Kant's Political Writings.* Hans Reiss, ed. H. B. Nisbet, trans. Cambridge: Cambridge University Press.

Kelly, George A. 1969. *Idealism, Politics, and History.* Cambridge: Cambridge University Press.

Keohane, Robert, and Joseph Nye. 1977. *Power and Interdependence.* Boston: Little Brown.

Langer, William L., ed. 1968. *The Encyclopedia of World History.* Boston: Houghton Mifflin.

Machiavelli, Niccolo. 1950. *The Prince and the Discourses.* Max Lerner, ed. Luigi Ricci and Christian Detmold, trans. New York: Modern Library.

Mansfield, Harvey C. 1970. Machiavelli's New Regime. *Italian Quarterly,* 13:63-95.

Montesquieu, Charles de. 1949. *Spirit of the Laws.* New York: Hafner. (Originally published in 1748.)

Murphy, Jeffrie, 1970. *Kant: The Philosophy of Right.* New York: St. Martins.

Neustadt, Richard. 1970. *Alliance Politics.* New York: Columbia University Press.

Payne, James L. n.d. Marxism and Militarism. *Polity.* Forthcoming.

Pocock, J. G. A. 1975. *The Machiavellian Moment.* Princeton: Princeton University Press.

Polanyi, Karl. 1944. *The Great Transformation.* Boston: Beacon Press.

Posen, Barry, and Stephen VanEvera. 1980. Overarming and Underwhelming. *Foreign Policy,* 40:99-118.

Posen, Barry, and Stephen VanEvera. 1983. Reagan Administration Defense Policy. In Kenneth Oye, Robert Lieber, and Donald Rothchild, eds., *Eagle Defiant.* Boston: Little Brown. pp. 67–104.

Powell, G. Bingham. 1982. *Contemporary Democracies.* Cambridge, MA: Harvard University Press.

Reagan, Ronald. June 9, 1982. Address to Parliament. *New York Times.*

Riley, Patrick. 1983. *Kant's Political Philosophy.* Totowa, NJ: Rowman and Littlefield.

Rummel, Rudolph J. 1979. *Understanding Conflict and War,* 5 vols. Beverly Hills: Sage Publications.

Rummel, Rudolph J. 1983. Libertarianism and International Violence. *Journal of Conflict Resolution,* 27:27–71.

Russett, Bruce. 1985. The Mysterious Case of Vanishing Hegemony. *International Organization,* 39:207–31.

Schumpeter, Joseph. 1950. *Capitalism, Socialism, and Democracy.* New York: Harper Torchbooks.

Schumpeter, Joseph. 1955. The Sociology of Imperialism. In *Imperialism and Social Classes.* Cleveland: World Publishing Co. (Essay originally published in 1919.)

Schwarz, Wolfgang. 1962. Kant's Philosophy of Law and International Peace. *Philosophy and Phenomenonological Research,* 23:71–80.

Shell, Susan. 1980. *The Rights of Reason.* Toronto: University of Toronto Press.

Shklar, Judith. 1984. *Ordinary Vices.* Cambridge, MA: Harvard University Press.

Skinner, Quentin. 1981. *Machiavelli.* New York: Hill and Wang.

Small, Melvin, and J. David Singer. 1976. The War-Proneness of Democratic Regimes. *The Jerusalem Journal of International Relations,* 1(4):50–69.

Small, Melvin, and J. David Singer. 1982. *Resort to Arms.* Beverly Hills: Sage Publications.

Streit, Clarence. 1938. *Union Now: A Proposal for a Federal Union of the Leading Democracies.* New York: Harpers.

Thucydides. 1954. *The Peloponnesian War.* Rex Warner, ed. and trans. Baltimore: Penguin.

U.K. Foreign and Commonwealth Office. 1980. *A Yearbook of the Commonwealth 1980.* London: HMSO.

U.S. Congress. Senate. Select Committee to Study Governmental Operations with Respect to Intelligence Activities. 1975. *Covert Action in Chile, 1963–74.* 94th Cong., 1st sess., Washington, DC: U.S. Government Printing Office.

U.S. Department of State. 1981. *Country Reports on Human Rights Practices.* Washington, DC: U.S. Government Printing Office.

Waltz, Kenneth. 1962. Kant, Liberalism, and War. *American Political Science Review* 56:331–40.

Waltz, Kenneth. 1964. The Stability of a Bipolar World. *Daedalus,* 93:881–909.

Walzer, Michael. 1983. *Spheres of Justice.* New York: Basic Books.

Weede, Erich. 1984. Democracy and War Involvement. *Journal of Conflict Resolution,* 28:649–64.

Wilkenfeld, Jonathan. 1968. Domestic and Foreign Conflict Behavior of Nations. *Journal of Peace Research,* 5:56–69.

Williams, Howard. 1983. *Kant's Political Philosophy.* Oxford: Basil Blackwell.

Wright, Quincy. 1942. *A Study of History.* Chicago: Chicago University Press.

Yovel, Yirmiahu. 1980. *Kant and the Philosophy of History.* Princeton: Princeton University Press.

Perception and Misperception
in International Politics

Robert Jervis

Professor Jervis discusses the relations among different levels of analysis used by students of international relations. He also makes a case for the importance of understanding individual perception (and misperception) in the study of foreign policy and world politics.

DO PERCEPTIONS MATTER?

Before discussing the causes and consequences of the ways in which decision-makers draw inferences from the world, we must ask a preliminary question: do the decision-makers' perceptions matter? This is an empirical question. Logic permits us to distinguish between the "psychological milieu" (the world as the actor sees it) and the "operational milieu" (the world in which the policy will be carried out) and to argue that policies and decisions must be mediated by statesmen's goals, calculations, and perceptions.[1] But it does not follow from this that we must deal with these intervening variables in order to understand and predict behavior. This is not an uncommon claim:

> One may describe particular events, conditions, and interactions between states without necessarily probing the nature and outcome of the processes through which state action evolves. However, and the qualification is crucial, if one wishes to probe the "why" questions underlying the events, conditions, and interaction patterns which rest upon state action, then decision-making analysis is certainly necessary. We would go so far as to say *that the "why" questions cannot be answered without analysis of decision-making.*[2]

But theory and explanation need not fill in all the links between cause and effect. Indeed, this is impossible. One can always ask for the links between the links. High density theories have no privileged status; they are not automatically illuminating or fruitful.[3] It is true that re-creating a decision-maker's goals, calculations, and perceptions is a satisfying method of explaining his behavior because the scholar, sharing as he does the decision-maker's characteristics of being a thinking, goal-seeking person, can easily say: "If that is the way the statesman saw the situation, it is no wonder that he acted as he did." But the comfort we feel with this form of explanation should not blind us to the fact that, unless there are significant variations in the ways people see the world that affect how they act, we need not explore decision-making in order to explain foreign policy. Most case studies assume that the details presented significantly affected the outcomes. This may not be true, however. "Pleikus are streetcars," McGeorge Bundy said in explaining that the Viet Cong attack on the American installation in February 1965 had affected only the timing of the American bombing of North Vietnam.[4] If you are waiting for one, it will come along. The specifics of the triggering event cannot explain the outcome because so many probable events could have substituted for it. To understand the American policy of bombing the North we should not examine the attack on Pleiku. Had it not occurred, something else would have happened that would have permitted the same response. Logic alone cannot tell us that a similar claim about the decision-making process is invalid: the way people perceive others and make decisions only marginally influences outcomes. So we must seek empirical evidence on the question: do the important explanatory variables in international relations involve decision-making? In terms of perceptions this can be separated into two subsidiary questions: "are important differences in policy preferences traceable to differences in decision-makers' perceptions of their environments?" and "are there important differences between reality and shared or common perceptions?"[5]

These questions raise the familiar level of analysis problem. Although it has been much debated, agreement is lacking not only on the substantive dispute but even on the number of levels. Arnold Wolfers proposes two, Kenneth Waltz three, and James Rosenau five.[6] To fill in the sequence, we will discuss four. One is the level of decision-making, the second is the level of the bureaucracy, the third is that of the nature of the state and the workings of domestic politics, and the fourth focuses on the international environment.[7] Which level one focuses on is not arbitrary and is not a matter of taste — it is the product of beliefs (or often hunches) about the nature of the variables that influence the phenomena that concern one. To restate the first question in terms of the level of analysis problem, we need not adopt a decision-making approach if all states behave the same way in the same objective situation, if all states of the same kind (i.e., with the same internal characteristics and politics) behave the same way in the same objective situation, or if state behavior is determined by bureaucratic routines and interests.

Although the empirical questions are central here, we should also note that the level of analysis problem has important moral implications. When all people would respond the same way to a given situation, it is hard to praise or blame the decision-maker. Thus, those accused of war crimes will argue that their behavior did not differ from others who found themselves in the same circumstances. And the prosecution will charge, as it did against Tojo and his colleagues, that, "These defendants were not automatons; they were not replaceable cogs in a machine. . . . It was theirs to choose whether their nation would lead an honored life . . . or . . . would become a symbol of evil throughout the world. They made their choice. For this choice they must bear the guilt." Similarly, if all nations follow similar courses of action, one cannot argue that some deserve to be branded as immorally aggressive. Thus in 1918 Bethmann-Hollweg rebutted those who blamed Germany for the war by pointing to the "general disposition towards war in the world . . . how else explain the senseless and impassioned zeal which allowed countries like Italy, Rumania and even America, not originally involved in the war, no rest until they too had immersed themselves in the bloodbath?"[8]

The three non-decision-making levels assert the importance of various aspects of the objective situation or the actor's role.[9] They say that if we know enough about the setting—international, national, or bureaucratic—we can explain and predict the actor's behavior. An interesting sidelight is that if other actors believed that the setting is crucial they would not need to scrutinize the details of the state's recent behavior or try to understand the goals and beliefs held by the state's decision-makers.[10] It would be fruitless and pointless to ask what the state's intentions are if its behavior is determined by the situation in which it finds itself. Instead, observers would try to predict how the context will change because this will tell them what the state's response will be. Decision-makers could then freely employ their powers of vicarious identification and simply ask themselves how they would act if they were in the other's shoes. They would not have to worry about the possibility that the other might have values and beliefs that differed from theirs. It is interesting, although not decisive, to note that decision-makers rarely feel confident about using this method. They usually believe both that others may not behave as they would and that the decision-makers within the other state differ among themselves. So they generally seek a great deal of information about the views of each significant person in the other country.

Of course it is unlikely that there is a single answer to the question of which level is most important. Rather than one level containing the variables that are most significant for all problems, the importance of each level may vary from one issue area to another.[11] Furthermore, which level of analysis is the most important may be determined by how rich and detailed an answer we are seeking. The environment may influence the general outline of the state's policy but not its specific responses. Thus it can be argued that, while decision-making analysis is needed to explain why World War I broke out in August 1914, the external situation would have led the states to fight sooner or later. Or the importance of variables at each level may vary with the stages of a decision. For example, domestic politics may dictate that a given event be made the occasion for a change in policy; bargaining within the bureaucracy may explain what options are presented to the national leaders; the decision-maker's predisposition could account for the choice that was made; and the interests and routines of the bureaucracies could explain the way the decision was implemented. And the same variable may have different effects at different stages of the decision-making process — for example, conflicts among subordinates may increase the variety of information and the number of opportunities for decision that the top decision-maker gets, but may simultaneously decrease his ability to see that his decisions are faithfully implemented.

The importance of variables at one level can also vary with the state of variables at other levels. Rosenau suggests that the international environment is more important in determining the policy of small states than it is of large ones and Stanley Hoffmann argues that nuclear weapons and bipolarity have reversed this relationship.[12] More generally, the importance of the other levels decreases if the variables in one level are in extreme states.[13] Thus, maneuvering within the bureaucracy may be more important when the top decision-makers are inexperienced or preoccupied with other matters.[14] And Wolfers argues that states tend to behave the same way when they are faced with extreme danger or extreme opportunity, but that when environmental constraints are less severe there will be differences in behavior that must be explained at the decision-making level. More complex interactions among the levels are also possible. For example, the effect of internal instability on expansionism could vary with the opportunities for success in war. Unstable states may be more prone to aggression than stable ones when the chances of victory are high but might be more cautious than others when their leaders perceive a significant probability of defeat or even of temporary setback. Or the stability of the regime might influence its propensity for aggression, but the nature of the regime (e.g., whether it is democratic or dictatorial) might be more important in explaining how it makes peace.

To deal with all these questions would require another book. Here all I will try to do is to outline the kinds of evidence necessary to establish the validity of simple propositions about the importance of the various levels. In doing so, I will sketch the most extreme arguments for the importance of each level. It is obvious that the questions and arguments could be rephrased in more subtle terms but since I am concerned with the kinds of evidence that the propositions call for the gain in analytical clarity is worth the sacrifice involved in ignoring more complete explanations that combine a multitude of variables at many levels.

The International Environment

To argue that the international environment determines a state's behavior is to assert that all states react similarly to the same objective external situation. Changes in a state's domestic regime, its bureaucratic structure, and the personalities and opinions of its leaders do not lead to changes of policies. Changes in the external situation, however, do alter behavior, even when variables on the other levels remain constant. To test these claims, we would need good measures of all the variables, especially the nature of the objective situation and the state's policies.[15] Even if we had such indicators, we would have to cope with the paucity of the most desired kinds of comparisons. This is easily understood by glancing at the similar issue in the study of individual behavior — the debate over the relative importance of situation and role versus idiosyncratic variables in determining individual behavior.[16] Because so many people of widely differing backgrounds, personalities, and opinions fill the same role and because the same person fills many different roles, we can try to determine the relative impact of situational and idiosyncratic variables by examining how a person's behavior varies as his role changes and how people of widely differing characteristics perform in similar situations.

It is much harder to make the analogous comparisons in international relations. In only a few international systems do we find many cases in which states play, either simultaneously or consecutively, several roles and in which each role is filled by states that are otherwise quite different. This would occur in a long-lasting system where there were frequent changes in the relations among the actors. Thus each state might at one time be a neutral, a "holder of the balance," a state with aggressive designs, a defender faced by a state whose intentions are difficult to determine, and so on. To a limited degree this test is possible in a balance-of-power system. But it is not available for most other systems, for example the one prevailing since World War II. Most nations have not changed roles, and indeed cannot do so because of such permanent factors as size and geography. The United States can never play the role of a second-ranking state caught between two blocs of greater powers. France can never be the leader of one of two dominant blocs. And while the United States and France may have played roles similar to these in the past, the extensive differences in the situation mean that any differences in response that might be found would not show that roles are unimportant.

Compulsion in Extreme Circumstances. It is worthwhile to look at cases of the kind that are supposed to show most strongly the influence of external conditions. If there are differences of behavior here, the argument for not ignoring the other levels of analysis will apply a fortiori to a wider domain of cases. Arnold Wolfers argues that, the greater the external compulsion, the greater the homogeneity of behavior and therefore the less the need to study decision-making. In a well-known passage he says: "Imagine a number of individuals, varying widely in their predispositions, who find themselves inside a house on fire. It would be perfectly realistic to expect that these individuals, with rare exceptions, would feel compelled to run toward the exits. . . . Surely, therefore, for an explanation of the rush for the exits, there is no need to analyze the individual decisions that produced it."[17]

But the case is not as clear as this analogy suggests. If a situation were so compelling that all people would act alike, decision-makers would not hesitate nor feel torn among several alternative policies, nor would there be significant debates within the decision-making elite. In fact, key decisions that are easily reached, such as those involving the Truman Doctrine and Marshall Plan, stand out because they are so rare. For despite the implication of Wolfers' proposition that we know when we are faced by extreme danger, just as we can tell when the house is on fire, in fact this question is often bitterly contested. (To say that once decision-makers perceive the fire they will head for the exits leads us back to decision-making analysis.) For Churchill, the house was burning soon after Hitler took power in Germany; for Chamberlain, this was the case only after March 1939; and for others there never was a fire at all. To some decision-makers, the Soviet Union is a threat to which the United States is compelled to respond. To others the threat passed years ago. Again, to a growing number of scholars it never existed. Similarly, American statesmen saw a much greater threat from communism in both Europe and Southeast Asia than did the leaders of our allies. Decision-makers may even agree that their state's existence is threatened but disagree about the source of the threat. This was true, for example, in the United States around the turn of the nineteenth century, when the Federalists believed France so much a menace that they favored war with her. At the same time, the Republicans believed England an equal menace. (It should be noted that this disagreement was rooted as much in differences in values and interests as in divergent empirical analyses of the situation.)

In extreme cases we can specify with some certainty an indicator of the "fire" that all decision-makers will recognize — for example a large armed attack — and we can be relatively certain that the state will react. But even then the objective situation will not determine all aspects of the state's response. There are apt to be several exits from the burning house. Will the state limit the extent of its involvement? What will its war aims be? While the United States may have had no choice but to declare war on Japan after Pearl Harbor, the major decisions that followed were less compelled and require further explanation. For example: the United States decided not to concentrate its energies on the country that had attacked it but to fight Germany first; the war was to be fought with few considerations for the shape of the postwar world; and no compromise with the enemies would be accepted (had the Japanese realized this would be the case, they almost certainly would not have attacked).

Even if all states and all statesmen responded similarly to similar high threats, we have to explain how the threat arose — i.e., why the adversary was so aggressive. In some cases we may be able to do this by reference to the other's objective situation, for example by focusing on the anarchic nature of the international system and the resulting security dilemma. . . . But when this analysis is insufficient, the state (and later scholars) must examine variables at other levels of analysis to establish some of the most important facts about the objective situation that the state faces.

Finally, one cannot prove that the external environment determines the response by simply showing that the decision-makers believed this to be the cause. It is not enough to say with Kecskemeti that "In tense war situations, the decision-maker is likely to feel that he is acting from necessity rather than from deliberate choice." Nor is it sufficient to cite Holsti's finding that the decision-makers on both sides in July 1914 felt that they had no choice but to make the decision they did, or to show that when "Mr. Acheson was advised not to favor the production of the first thermonuclear bomb, he is reported to have declared that its production was a matter of necessity and not of choice: in other words, that he was experiencing 'compulsion.'"[18] The subjective feeling of determinacy is interesting and may lead decision-makers unnecessarily to restrict their search for alternatives, but it does not show that other decision-makers in the same situation would have felt the same compulsion and acted in the same way. Indeed the theory of cognitive dissonance . . . and other theories of irrational cognitive consistency . . . lead us to expect that decision-makers may avoid psychological conflict by thinking that they had no choice but to act as they did. This also means that, when scholars claim that a situation permitted no policy other than the one that was adopted, it may be that at least part of the reason why the circumstances appear overwhelming in retrospect is that they were claimed to be so by the decision-makers.

These arguments are, of course, far from conclusive. The necessary comparisons have merely been mentioned, not made. But, as we have seen, there are many points at which people can disagree about what the objective situation is or what policies will best cope with it, and there is little evidence for the existence of the homogeneity of behavior that would allow us to ignore everything except the international setting.

Domestic Determinants

Even if all states do not behave similarly in similar situations, the details of decision-making and images may not be significant. Instead, the state may be the appropriate level of analysis — i.e., variations in decision-makers' policies may be accounted for by variations in social and economic structure and domestic politics of the states they are serving. Wilsonian and Marxist theories are examples of this position. Other theories at this level of analysis argue for the importance of a state's geographical position, its traditions, its national style, or the consequences, often unintended, of domestic conflicts. Extreme formulations hold that the state's internal system determines its foreign policy, while weaker versions claim that foreign policies are a product of both domestic politics and international circumstances.

The forms of the assertions correspond to those discussed in the previous section. States with the same critical internal attributes behave the same way in similar situations — and often behave the same way in the face of significant variations in the environment — and this behavior is different from that displayed by other states with different attributes even when the setting is the same. The latter claim denies the overriding importance of the international environment. Thus while Cold War revisionists stress the importance of America's domestic political and economic needs, others replay that American actions were heavily influenced by external constraints and that her behavior was not peculiarly American or perculiarly capitalist but rather was typical of any great power in such a situation.[19] Because we are concerned with examining the importance of decision-making, we will not treat this part of the argument that deals with conflicts between claims for two other levels of analysis.

If states of the same type behave in the same way, then changes in a state's leadership will not produce significant changes in foreign policy, and we need not examine the images, values, and calculations of individual decision-makers. Unfortunately, claims about continuity in a state's foreign policy are notoriously difficult to judge. We might try to see whether we could deduce changes in the identities of the state's decision-makers from the course of its foreign policy. Could we tell when Democrats replaced Republicans or Conservatives replaced Labour governments? Scholars used to agree that Stalin's death led to major foreign policy changes, but now even this is in doubt.[20] Before taking office, decision-makers often claim they will introduce new policies. But these promises are often neglected. Eisenhower's foreign policy more closely resembled that of his predecessor than it did his campaign rhetoric. Gladstone pledged himself to avoid immoral and wasteful imperialism, and, although he successfully extricated Britain from some entanglements, he was eventually drawn into commitments similar to those made by Disraeli. And while in 1937 Clement Atlee said that "the foreign policy of a Government is the reflection of its internal policy," when his party took power the foreign secretary declared that "Revolutions do not change geography, and revolutions do not change geographical needs."[21]

Many arguments about the wisdom of policies can be understood in terms of claims about the autonomy of the decision-making level. Those who praise Bismarck's diplomacy claim that, had he continued in office, he would have been able to maintain German security by avoiding the errors of severing Germany's ties to Russia, being forced to rely on Austria, and recklessly antagonizing several powerful countries. The rejoinder is that the dynamics of German domestic society and of the international system would have destroyed Bismarck's handiwork no matter who was in power. The glittering skill of Bismarck's diplomacy could not alter the underlying forces at work. Debates about the origins of the Cold War must deal with the similar question of whether Roosevelt's death changed American policy. Most traditional accounts argue that F. D. R. was coming to an anti-Soviet position and would have acted much as Truman did. This view is shared by those revisionists who look to the American political and economic system for the roots of foreign policy but is disputed by those who see the Cold War as avoidable. Similarly, those who defend President Kennedy but opposed the war in Vietnam argue that he would not have acted as Johnson did. Those who either favored the war or opposed not only it but also most recent American foreign policies argue that the policies of these — and other — presidents were consistent. While those who supported the war see the determinants as international and those who criticize the general lines of America's postwar policy see the causes as domestic, both argue that few significant differences can be traced to the identity of the president.

These questions are so difficult to resolve partly because the situation facing the new government always differs from that which confronted the old. Kennedy was never forced to choose between defeat in Vietnam and fighting a major war. F. D. R. did not live to see Russia consolidate her hold over East Europe. The questions must then be hypothetical, and the comparisons that underlie our judgments are often strained. This problem can be avoided by using alternative comparisions — by examining the views of members of the elite to see whether they favor the policy that was adopted.[22] Of course disagreement with a policy does not prove that a person would have acted on his views were he in office. His opposition might be rooted in his role in the government, lack of information, freedom from the pressures that accompany holding power, or the belief that opposition is politically expedient. But when these explanations are not satisfactory, internal elite disagreement reveals the limits of the impact of both domestic politics and the international situation.

The Bureaucracy

Even if state behavior cannot be explained by the state's internal politics and external environment, we still may not need to examine the perceptions and calculations of the top decision-makers. The workings of the bureaucracy may determine policy. It is not enough for proponents of this position to show that the state's course of action appears inconsistent and lacks value integration. Such inadequacies can be the product of individual decision-making. As we will show later, normal human behavior often does not fit even a loose definition of rationality. Individuals as well as organizations fail to coordinate their actions and to develop carefully designed strategies. The fact that people must reach decisions in the face of the burdens of multiple goals and highly ambiguous information means that policies are often contradictory, incoherent, and badly suited to the information at hand. Unless we understand this, puzzling state behavior will automatically be seen as the product of either internal bargaining or the autonomous operation of different parts of the government. Thus if we did not know better it would be tempting to argue that the contradictory and erratic behavior displayed by Richard Nixon in Watergate and related matters shows that "Nixon" is not a single individual at all, but rather a title for the set of behaviors that are produced by the interaction of conflicting entities, each pursuing its own narrow interests in ignorance of or indifference to any wider goal of the "general Nixon interest." Similarly, if we were to insist that theories of individual behavior apply only when the actor is following a coherent path guided by his self-interest, we would have to say that Spiro Agnew was an uncoordinated bureaucracy rather than a person because he simultaneously accepted kickbacks and sought the presidency.

Because incoherent policy is insufficient evidence for the importance of bureaucracies, the "pure" theories of this type must make two basic assertions. First, bureaucrats' policy preferences are determined by their positions in the government: "Where you stand is determined by where you sit." The external environment and the nature of the state and domestic politics have only limited and indirect impact on these preferences. Of course if the concept of bureaucratic interest is to be more useful than the concept of national interest, we must be able to specify in advance what the bureaucratic position will be.[23] Even if we cannot do this, it would still be significant if everyone in each unit of the government had the same position on a given issue. If, on the other hand, there is a good deal of disagreement within the organization about the goals to be sought or the means that are appropriate, then we would have to apply decision-making analysis to the bureaucratic level, and so this approach would lose much of its distinctiveness. More importantly, if people in different units share the same policy preferences or if preferences are distributed at random throughout the government, then the first assertion would be undermined.

The second basic claim of theories on this level of analysis is that the state's policies are formed by bureaucratic bargains and routines. Bureaucratic actions either determine the statesman's decision or else implement it in a way that renders the decision largely irrelevant to what is actually done. This point is vital because, even if bureaucrats' policy preferences were linked to their positions within the government, this would be relatively unimportant unless these preferences explain policy outcomes.[24] But we should note at the start that even if this were true we would have to explore the sources of power of parts of the bureaucracy. If we find, for example, that the military often prevails in conflicts with the organization in charge of arms control, this may be because over a period of years the state's leaders have supported the former more than the latter. Sometimes we can go back some years to find a decisive action that set the guidelines for both the policy and the distribution of power within the bureaucracy. In less dramatic cases the relative strengths of interests represent the standing decision of the decision-makers — and often of wider publics — and their choices among competing policies and values.

To the extent that this distribution of power is both important and accounted for by factors outside the bureaucracy, an explanation of specific outcomes in terms of bureaucratic maneuvering will be superficial at best.

Are policy preferences determined by one's role within the government? With the important exception of questions of military hardware and doctrine, the evidence is limited and ambiguous. It is not hard to find examples of units taking consistent and unified stands and political appointees adopting their units' views and thus expressing different opinions depending upon their positions in the government. "General Marshall, while Chief of Staff, opposed the State Department's idea of using aid to promote reforms in the Chinese government. Then, when he became Secretary of State, he defended this very idea against challenges voiced by the new chiefs of staff." In "1910, Winston Churchill, as Home Secretary, led the attack upon the demand of McKenna, First Lord of the Admiralty, for more ships; by 1913 they had exchanged offices and each, with equal conviction, maintained the opposite view." When Samuel Hoare was secretary of state for air, he strongly fought against naval control of the Fleet Air Arm; when he later served as first lord of the Admiralty he took the opposite position. When Théophile Delcassé was the minister of colonies in France before the turn of the century, he supported an expedition to the Nile that would give France a lever to use against Britain. As foreign secretary, he sought to recall the adventure.[25]

But not all policy disagreements are traceable to roles. Organizational perspectives and loyalties are less important when issues are unusual rather than routine, necessitate relatively quick decisions, and involve important and generally shared values. Beliefs about the most important issues of foreign policy — those involving war and peace — are usually unrelated to roles. When we look at the major decisions of American foreign policy — those that set the terms for future debates and established the general framework within which policy was then conducted — it does not seem to be true, at least for the top decision-makers, that "where you sit determines where you stand."

In several important cases what is most striking is the degree of unanimity. In the spring of 1947 there was general agreement within the government that massive aid for Europe was needed. Three years later most officials felt that foreign policy considerations argued for large-scale rearmament, although there was a disagreement — which was not tightly connected with bureaucratic interests — over whether domestic political and economic constraints made such a policy feasible. Once the Korean War removed this opposition, government officials were again in general agreement. In other important cases there are basic disputes, but the key to them is not divergent bureaucratic interests. Doves and hawks on Vietnam were to be found in all parts of the American government. Views on whether to take a hard line toward Japan before World War II, and specifically on the crucial issue of embargoing oil and other vital raw materials, were only loosely related to organizational affiliations. The advice that Truman received at the start of the Berlin blockade and the Korean War and most of the differences that emerged in the discussions during the Cuban missile crisis were not predictable by the participants' roles.

In the missile crisis none of the leading officials espoused views that were linked to his position within the government. The Republican secretary of the treasury was concerned about the effects of a "soft" response on the fortunes of the Democratic party in the coming elections; the secretary of defense at first argued that the missiles did not present a major military threat; the secretary of state did not take a strong position and did not pay special attention to the political consequences of various moves; and the attorney general opposed an air strike. (It should also be noted that his view carried great weight not because of his governmental position or independent political resources, but because he was thought to speak for the president.)

The other claim — that policies can be explained by bureaucratic maneuvering — could be supported in either of two ways. First, it could be shown that different parts of the government carry out, or fail to carry out, policies in ways that are consistent with their preferences and routines rather than with the decisions of the national leaders. But the other possible linkage in the second point — the argument that authoritative decisions can be explained by the interaction of bureaucratic stands — raises difficulties that go deeper than the temporary absence of evidence. To verify this claim we must be able to specify the expected relationship between the variety of bureaucratic positions on the one hand and policy outcomes on the other. It is not enough to show that the outcome can be seen as a compromise among views that have been advocated by various parts of the government. Almost any decision could fit this description. The theory must provide generalizations that tell us more exactly what the outcome will be. If the goals of different parts of the bureaucracy are complementary, then presumably each agency will give up its position on the part of the program it cares least about in order to gain a larger voice on those issues that are more important to it. Presumably the success of an organization in conflicts with others is related to its strength (determined independently of outcomes), although as we noted this raises further questions. Still another likely pattern is that the symbols will be given to one side in a bureaucratic conflict and the substance to the other. But much more detail is needed. Furthermore, these generalizations must not involve the values and beliefs that vary with the identity of the top decision-makers, and they must be able to explain how policies change. The latter task poses great problems since bureaucratic structures and interests often remain constant over periods in which policies shift.

Although the paucity of research on this level makes conclusions especially tentative, it is hard to see how any of the major decisions of American foreign policy in recent years could meet this test. The Marshall

Plan, the establishment of NATO, the crucial decisions in Korea, the re-armament that followed, the decision to integrate West Germany into West Europe, the New Look in defense, American policy in the Suez crisis, Kennedy's attempt to increase conventional forces in Europe, the major decisions to fight and later withdraw from Vietnam, and crucial choices in the Cuban missile crisis cannot be explained as the outcome of intrabureaucratic conflict. That these decisions combined major elements of positions held within the bureaucracy is hardly surprising because different parts of the bureaucracy serve and represent divergent values that the president seeks to further. Thus what seems to be a clash of bureaucratic interests and stands can often be more fruitfully viewed as a clash among values that are widely held in both the society and the decision-makers' own minds. What embarrasses the theories under consideration here is that, while the decisions listed above did embody some of the preferences that had been articulated by parts of the bureaucracy, they did not combine them in a way that can be predicted by rules of bureaucratic politics. Or, to put the argument more exactly, until we have a theory that specifies how policy is formed out of conflicting bureaucratic perspectives and preferences, we cannot tell whether any given outcome can be explained by this level of analysis. As things stand now, there is no way to explore the extent to which bureaucratic factors cause the outcome because we have no ground for claiming that a different constellation of bureaucratic interests and forces would have produced a different result or that the outcome would have been different were there no bureaucracies at all.

PERCEPTIONS, REALITY, AND A TWO-STEP MODEL

Our discussion thus far leads to the conclusion that it is often impossible to explain crucial decisions and policies without reference to the decision-makers' beliefs about the world and their images of others. That is to say, these cognitions are part of the proximate cause of the relevant behavior and other levels of analysis cannot immediately tell us what they will be. And even if we found that people in the same situation — be it international, domestic, or bureaucratic — behave in the same way, it is useful to examine decision-making if there are constant differences between the decision-makers' perceptions and reality. In this case all people might react in the same way to the same situation, but this behavior would puzzle an observer because it was self-defeating, based on incorrect beliefs about the world, or generally lacking in a high degree of rationality.[26] Many of the propositions advanced in here fit in this category: they are generalizations about how decision-makers perceive others' behavior and form judgments about their intentions. These patterns are explained by the general ways in which people draw inferences from ambiguous evidence and, in turn, help explain many seemingly incomprehensible policies. They show how, why, and when highly intelligent and conscientious statesmen misperceive their environments in specified ways and reach inappropriate decisions.

Other propositions deal with cases in which an analysis of decision-making is necessary because people in the same situations behave differently. This is often the case because people differ in their perceptions of the world in general and of other actors in particular. Sometimes it will be useful to ask who, if anyone, was right; but often it will be more fruitful to ask why people differed and how they came to see the world as they did.

The exploration of the images actors hold and the development of the two kinds of propositions discussed above should be seen in the context of a mediated or two-step model.[27] Rather than trying to explain foreign policies as the direct consequence of variables at the three levels of analysis previously discussed, we will examine the actor's perceptions as one of the immediate causes of his behavior. Thus Britain and France felt that their security was endangered by Germany before both world wars. They may have been mistaken in the first case and correct in the second, but both cases can be grouped together in discussing the immediate causes of their responses.

Our understanding of the actor's images and beliefs affects the further question that we ask about that event and the behavior that we expect of the actor in other cases. For example, when it was believed that most American decision-makers had thought that escalation would bring a quick victory in Vietnam, the interesting questions concerned the reasons for the error and the ways by which successive small steps increased the stakes of the conflict. If the decision-makers believed that victory was cheap, it is not surprising that they acted as they did. But by revealing that the decision-makers had a relatively accurate view of the chances of success, the Pentagon Papers and related commentaries have shown that the crucial question is why saving Vietnam was considered important enough to justify the high expected price. This then leads us to look at this and other American actions in terms of beliefs about "domino effects" rather than directing our attention to commitments that develop inadvertently and "quagmires" that trap unwary statesmen. Similarly, the question about Russian behavior raised by the Cuban missile crisis probably is not "What Soviet calculus and risk-taking propensity could explain this bold and dangerous step?" but rather "How could they have so badly misestimated the probable American response?"[28] And previous Soviet behavior can be re-examined to see if it could be explained by similar misperceptions. . . . Actors as well as scholars must engage in these kinds of analyses.

Of course perceptions, and more specifically perceptions of other actors, are not the only decision-making variables that are important. That two actors have the same perceptions does not guarantee that they will adopt the same response. But their responses will often be the same, and, when they are not, it is usually relatively easy to find the causes of the differences. Although people with different images of an adversary may agree on the appropriate response, just as people may favor the same policy for different reasons, this agreement is apt to be short-lived. . . . The roots of many important disputes about policies lie in differing perceptions. And in the frequent cases when the actors do not realize this, they will misunderstand their disagreement and engage in a debate that is unenlightening.

Images, however, are not first causes, and so we will try to find the causes both of common misperceptions and of differences in perceptions. Thus the second step in the model involves relating the images held, if not to reality, then at least to the information available to the actor. How, for example, do statesmen come to develop their images of other actors? What evidence do they pay most attention to? What makes them perceive threat? Under what conditions do they think that the other, although hostile, has only limited objectives? What differentiates legitimate inducements from bribes? What kinds of behavior are most apt to change an established image?

This is not to claim that we will be able to explain nearly all state behavior. Propositions about both the causes and the effects of images can only be probabilistic. There are too many variables at work to claim more. In the cases in which we are interested, decision-makers are faced with a large number of competing values, highly complex situations, and very ambiguous information. The possibilities and reasons for misperceptions and disagreements are legion. For these reasons, generalizations in this area are difficult to develop, exceptions are common, and in many instances the outcomes will be influenced by factors that, from the standpoint of most theories, must be considered accidental. Important perceptual predispositions can be discovered, but often they will not be controlling.

NOTES

1. See especially the following works by Harold and Margaret Sprout: *Man–Milieu Relationship Hypotheses in the Context of International Politics* (Princeton: Center of International Studies, 1956); *The Ecological Perspective on Human Affairs* (Princeton: Princeton University Press, 1965); and *An Ecological Paradigm for the Study of International Politics* (Princeton: Center of International Studies, Princeton University, Research Monograph No. 30, March, 1968).

2. "Decision-Making As an Approach to the Study of International Politics," in Richard Snyder, H. W. Bruck, and Burton Sapin, eds., *Foreign Policy Decision-Making* (New York: Free Press, 1962), p. 33. For a similar argument see Fred Greenstein, "The Impact of Personality on Politics: An Attempt to Clear Away Underbrush," *American Political Science Review* 61 (September 1967), 631–33. This is related to the debate about the significance of developmental sequences. For differing views on this question see Herbert Hyman, *Survey Design and Analysis* (Glencoe, Ill.: Free Press, 1955), pp. 254–63, and Travis

Hirschi and Hanan Selvin, *Delinquency Research* (New York: Free Press, 1967), pp. 82–85. (The latter book [republished in paperback as *Principles of Survey Analysis*] has much broader relevance than its title indicates and is extremely valuable not only for its explanation of the use of survey research data but for its treatment of general questions of theory, causation, and evidence.)

This issue is also related to the broader debate between what Maurice Natanson has called the "Two distinctively opposed philosophic attitudes . . . underlying the social sciences: . . . [the] 'objective' and 'subjective' *Weltanschauungen.*" ("Foreword" in Natanson, ed., *Philosophy of the Social Sciences* [New York: Random House, 1963], p. viii.) This reader is a good introduction to the arguments.

3. Hirschi and Selvin, *Delinquency Research,* p. 38. As Abraham Kaplan puts it, "I would not wish to say that something has been explained only when we have traced the microconnections with their antecedents, or even only when we can believe that such conditions exist." ("Noncausal Explanation," in Daniel Lerner, ed. *Cause and Effect* [New York: Free Press, 1965], p. 146.)

4. Quoted in Townsend Hoopes, *The Limits of Intervention* (New York: McKay, 1969), p. 30.

5. The question of the existence and nature of reality need not be treated here in its profound sense. For our purposes the consensus of later observers usually provides an adequate operational definition of reality.

6. Arnold Wolfers, "The Actors in International Politics," in *Discord and Collaboration* (Baltimore, Md: Johns Hopkins Press, 1962), pp. 3–24; Kenneth Waltz, *Man, the State and War* (New York: Columbia University Press, 1959); James Rosenau, "Pre-Theories and Theories of Foreign Policy," in R. Barry Farrell, ed., *Approaches to Comparative and International Politics* (Evanston, IL: Northwestern University Press, 1966), pp. 29–92.

7. We refer to the international environment rather than the international system because we are not dealing with systems theories. Our concern is with explaining specific foreign policies rather than finding general patterns of interaction.

8. Quoted in Robert Butow, *Tojo and the Coming of the War* (Princeton: Princeton University Press, 1961), p. 506; quoted in Egmont Zechlin, "Cabinet versus Economic Warfare in Germany," in H. W. Koch, ed., *The Origins of the First World War* (London: Macmillan & Co., 1972), p. 165.

9. See K. Holsti, "National Role Conceptions in the Study of Foreign Policy," *International Studies Quarterly* 14 (September 1970), 233–309.

10. It is interesting to note that in interpersonal perception people tend to overestimate the degree to which the other's behavior is determined by his personality and underestimate the impact of the external situation. See, for example, Gustav Ichheiser, *Appearances and Realities* (San Francisco: Jossey-Bass, 1970), pp. 49–59. But when the person explains his own behavior, he will attribute his actions to the requirements of the situation, not to his own predispositions. See Edward Jones and Richard Nisbett, *The Actor and the Observer: Divergent Perceptions of the Causes of Behavior* (New York: General Learning Press, 1971).

11. Two recent articles explore the utility of the concept of issue areas in foreign-policy research, but they are not concerned with the level of analysis problem. See Thomas Brewer, "Issue and Context Variations in Foreign Policy,"

Journal of Conflict Resolution 17 (March 1973), 89–114, and William Zimmerman, "Issue Area and Foreign-Policy Process," *American Political Science Review* 67 (December 1973), 1204–12.

12. James Rosenau, "Pre-Theories and Theories of Foreign Policy," pp. 47–48; Stanley Hoffmann, "Restraints and Choices in American Foreign Policy," *Daedalus* (Fall 1962), 692–94.

13. Most of the propositions in Greenstein, "The Impact of Personality on Politics," about the conditions under which personality is most important can be subsumed under this heading.

14. Thus the famous remark by a cabinet officer that you have to obey the president only when he repeats an order for the third time.

15. An excellent discussion of the evidence on this point derived from quantitative studies is Dina Zinnes, "Some Evidence Relevant to the Man–Milieu Hypothesis," in James Rosenau, Vincent Davis, and Maurice East, eds., *The Analysis of International Politics* (New York: Free Press, 1972), pp. 209–51. But these studies have limited utility for the questions being asked here because they do not provide adequate measures of the similarity of the objective situation and the similarity of the state's responses. This is also true for the growing body of literature that examines these questions using event-scaling techniques. For a study that copes with these problems relatively well and finds that differences in perceptions among decision-makers decrease as tension increases, see Ole Holsti, "Individual Differences in 'Definition of the Situation,'" *Journal of Conflict Resolution* 14 (September 1970), 303–10.

16. For a general discussion, see Herbert Blumer, "Society as Symbolic Interaction," in Arnold Rose, ed., *Human Behavior and Social Processes* (Boston: Houghton Mifflin, 1962), pp. 180–91. For an inventory of findings see Kenneth Terhune, "Personality in Cooperation and Conflict," in Paul Swingle, ed., *The Structure of Conflict* (New York: Academic Press, 1970), pp. 193–234. This subject has received much attention from psychologists in the past few years. For a review of the literature and an excellent argument, see Daryl Bem and Andrea Allen, "On Predicting Some of the People Some of the Time," *Psychological Review* 81 (1974), 506–20.

17. Wolfers, *Discord and Collaboration,* p. 13.

18. Paul Kecskemeti, *Strategic Surrender* (New York: Atheneum, 1964), pp. 19–20; Ole Holsti, "The 1914 Case," *The American Political Science Review* 59 (June 1965), 365–78; Wolfers, *Discord and Collaboration,* p. 14.

19. See, for example, Charles Maier, "Revisionism and the Interpretation of Cold War Origins," *Perspectives in American History* 4 (1970), 313–47; Robert Tucker, *The Radical Left and American Foreign Policy* (Baltimore, MD: Johns Hopkins Press, 1971); James Richardson, "Cold-War Revisionism: A Critique," *World Politics* 24 (July 1972), 579–612; and Ole Holsti, "The Study of International Politics Makes Strange Bedfellows: Theories of the Radical Right and the Radical Left," *American Political Science Review* 68 (March 1974), 217–42. Comparisons with the reactions of European statesmen would also shed light on the question of whether there was anything peculiarly American in the United States' perceptions.

20. Marshall Shulman, *Stalin's Foreign Policy Reappraised* (Cambridge, MA: Harvard University Press, 1963).

21. Michael Gordon, *Conflict and Consensus in Labour's Foreign Policy, 1914–1965* (Stanford, CA: Stanford University Press, 1969), p. 6; M. A. Fitzsimons, *The*

Foreign Policy of the British Labour Government, 1945–1951 (Notre Dame, IN: University of Notre Dame Press, 1953), p. 26.

22. In this group we include potential leaders who could come to power without drastic changes in the state's internal political system. Dissent from those outside this group does not undermine the arguments for the importance of the nature of the state, and, indeed, if such people have been rejected as possible powerholders because of their foreign policy views, this would demonstrate the importance of this level of analysis rather than showing the autonomy of the decision-making level.

23. Most light is shed on this subject by the writings of Philip Selznick. See his *TVA and the Grassroots* (Berkeley, CA and Los Angeles: University of California Press, 1947) and *Leadership in Administration* (Evanston, IL: Row, Peterson, 1957). Also see Morton Halperin, "Why Bureaucrats Play Games," *Foreign Policy,* No. 2 (Spring 1971), 74–88, and *Bureaucratic Politics and Foreign Policy* (Washington: Brookings Institution, 1974), pp. 26–62.

24. During the Second World War the British set up an intelligence section to try to recreate the German perspective. They did well at predicting the positions taken by various parts of the German bureaucracy but could never adequately predict when Hitler would side with a particular faction or impose his own solution. (Donald McLachlan, *Room* 39 [New York: Atheneum, 1968], pp. 252–58.

25. Ernest May, "The Development of Political–Military Consultation in the United States," in Aaron Wildavsky, ed., *The Presidency* (Boston: Little, Brown, 1969), p. 668; Patrick Gordon Walker, *The Cabinet* (New York: Basic Books, 1970), p. 67; W. J. Reader, *Architect of Airpower: The Life of the First Viscount Weir* (London: Collins, 1968), p. 270; Roger Brown, *Fashoda Reconsidered* (Baltimore, MD: Johns Hopkins Press, 1970), pp. 24–32, 85.

26. The knowledge gained by studying how people view the world and process incoming information can lead to the discovery of patterns in state behavior that would not be apparent to an observer who had ignored decision-making. We may be able to say, for example, that two kinds of situations, although not seeming alike to later scholars, will appear to be similar to contemporary decision-makers and will be seen to call for similar responses. Thus, once we have examined a number of cases, detected common deviations, and isolated their causes, we could apply this knowledge to theories that do not call for intensive analysis of decision-making.

27. See Charles Osgood, "Behavior Theory and the Social Sciences," in Roland Young, ed., *Approaches to the Study of Politics* (Evanston, IL: Northwestern University Press, 1958), pp. 217–44. For a recent discussion and application, see Richard Jessor and Shirley Jessor, "The Perceived Environment in Behavioral Science," *American Behavioral Scientist* 16 (July/August 1973), 801–27. In an interesting critique, Robert Gorman asks "Must we look into the perception of the decision-maker at the time the decision was being made by centering our political analysis on the decision-maker himself? Or, should we concentrate on the social organization of which the decision-maker is a part and the social environment in which both the organization and the individual function? If we accept the first choice, then social factors assume a secondary, instrumental purpose. If we choose the second framework, the perceptions of the decision-maker would seem to be *logically* dependent on external rules, and investigation into the nature of individual perception would be absurd. If

we combine the two, as the decision-making theorists seem to have done, we are left with a theory in which each premise is negated by the existence of the other, and the general theory itself is left to flounder in a formalistic but meaningless syncretism." ("On the Inadequacies of Non-Philosophical Political Science: A Critical Analysis of Decision-Making Theory," *International Studies Quarterly* 14 [December 1970], 408.) The use of a two-step model avoids this contradiction.

28. Daniel Ellsberg, "The Quagmire Myth and the Stalemate Machine," in *Papers on the War* (New York: Simon and Schuster, 1972), pp. 42–135; Leslie Gelb, "Vietnam: The System Worked," *Foreign Policy* No. 3 (Summer 1971), 140–67; Klaus Knorr, "Failures in National Intelligence Estimates: The Case of the Cuban Missiles," *World Politics* 16 (April 1967), 455–67. Theodore Draper fails to see the significance of these kinds of questions in explaining the American intervention in the Dominican Republic. ("The Dominican Intervention Reconsidered," *Political Science Quarterly* 86 [March 1971], 26–28.) To take an example from another field, the fact that young people in less politicized homes share fewer of their parents' political views than do those in more highly politicized families is not to be explained by the former group having less desire to adopt their parents' beliefs, but by their lack of knowledge about what their parents believe. (Richard Niemi, *How Family Members Perceive Each Other* [New Haven: Yale University Press, 1974], pp. 200–201.)

Theories of Crisis Decision Making

Ole R. Holsti

The author reviews theoretical work done on crisis decision making, especially the World War I (1914) and the Cuban missile crisis (1962) cases.

In memoirs written some years before he assumed the presidency, Richard Nixon wrote of crises as "mountaintop experiences" in which he often performed at his best: "Only then [in crises] does he discover all the latent strengths he never knew he had and which otherwise would have remained dormant."[1] He added:

It has been my experience that, more often than not, taking a break is actually an escape from the tough, grinding discipline that is absolutely necessary for

From Paul Gordon Lauren, *Diplomacy: New Approaches in History, Theory and Policy* (New York: 1979), by permission.

superior performance. Many times I have found that my best ideas have come when I thought I could not work for another minute and when I literally had to drive myself to finish the task before a deadline. Sleepless nights, to the extent that the body can take them, can stimulate creative mental activity.[2]

Others have appraised the effects of crisis on decision making in a similar vein, suggesting, for example, that "a decision maker may, in a crisis, be able to invent or work out easily and quickly what seems in normal times to both the 'academic' scholar and the layman to be hypothetical, unreal, complex or otherwise difficult."[3] More important, theories of nuclear deterrence presuppose rational and predictable decision processes, even during intense and protracted international crises. They assume that threats and ultimata will enhance calculation, control, and caution while inhibiting recklessness and risk-taking.[4] Deterrence theories, in short, tend to be sanguine about the ability of policy makers to be creative when the situation requires it — and never is that requirement greater than during an intense international crisis.

These observations appear to confirm the conventional wisdom that in crisis decision making necessity is indeed the mother of invention. Is there any reason to question the universal validity of that view? Fortunately, scenarios of inadequate decision making resulting in a nuclear war are thus far limited to novels and movies, but otherwise the evidence is less than totally reassuring. The recollections of those who have experienced intense and protracted crises suggest they may be marked at times by great skill in policy making, and at others by decision processes and outcomes that fail to meet even the most permissive standards of rationality. Some recall the "sense of elation that comes with crises,"[5] whereas others admit to serious shortcomings in their own performance during such situations. Indeed, although the definitive history of the Watergate episode remains to be written, available evidence suggests that Nixon's performance during the culminating crisis of his presidency was at best erratic, certainly falling far short of his own self-diagnosis as described above.

But anecdotes do not provide a sufficient basis for addressing the question: How do policy makers respond to the challenges and demands of crises? Do they tend to approach such situations with high motivation, a keen sense of purpose, extraordinary energy, and an enhanced capacity for creativity? Or, is their capacity for coping with complex problems sometimes impaired, perhaps to the point suggested by Richard Neustadt's phrase, "the paranoid reaction characteristic of crisis behavior"?[6]

This article will address these questions by describing and analyzing several major theories of crisis decision making. It will begin with a discussion of the various definitions of the much abused term, "crisis," and review theoretical models of behavior during crisis. This will be followed by the presentation of several hypotheses concerning some of the effects of intense and protracted crisis on decision making, utilizing recent evidence from several social sciences, especially the field of psychology.

Some of these hypotheses of crisis-induced stress will then be examined in the light of evidence from two classic case studies in diplomatic history: the 1914 crisis leading to the outbreak of World War I and, more briefly, the Cuban missile crisis of 1962. Finally, the conclusion will discuss some of the advantages and disadvantages of interdisciplinary research for psychologists, political scientists, and diplomatic historians.

CRISIS: DEFINITIONS, DESCRIPTIVE THEORIES, AND PRESCRIPTIVE THEORIES

One of the first requirements in establishing any viable body of theory is that of providing workable definitions. In this regard, theories of crisis behavior have been plagued with the fact that "crisis" is a much overused term that has become burdened with a wide range of meanings, some of them quite imprecise. In common usage it is victim of the age of hyperbole, becoming a synonym for virtually every problem of even moderate difficulty. Even in foreign policy research and diplomatic history, diversity is more in evidence than uniformity. As one of the pioneers in crisis research, Charles McClelland, observes:

> So many studies of crisis have been published in the last fifteen years from so many different angles of inquiry that it is more difficult than it once was to be sure about the denotations and connotations of the term. Not only is there a heavy popular usage of the word in ordinary discourse but also there are indications that historical change has brought about an expansion of the variety of situations that are called readily by the crisis name.[7]

In order to resolve this problem, scholars have been working to establish an acceptable definition of a crisis. These efforts fall into two very broad groups. Common to the first is a systematic perspective in which crisis represents a significant change in the quantity, quality, or intensity of interactions among nations. As McClelland describes this approach, it "looks on the whole configuration of parties participating back and forth" and observes changes in the patterns of interaction.[8] Special attention is given to any significant step-level change or turning point. This might be a dramatic increase in the number of border incidents, verbal challenges, or physical threats. After a crisis, the number and type of these exchanges may return to a more "normal" state. Accordingly, one way to identify crises analytically in diplomatic history is through a *post hoc* search for changed interaction patterns between nations.[9]

A second approach to defining a crisis — the decision-making perspective — focuses on the human participants themselves rather than the system. Here, a situation is a crisis when it is so defined by those who are responsible for coping with it. It is thus possible that in a confrontation between nations X and Y, decision makers in the former will believe themselves to be facing a crisis, whereas those in the latter will not. Although differences may be found among those who adopt a decision-making approach to crisis, one definition developed by Charles Hermann has gained a number of adherents: A crisis is a situation characterized by *surprise,* a *high threat* to important values, and *short decision time.*[10] This definition is not without its critics, but most of them tend to disagree only with one or another of the three criteria, usually either surprise,[11] or short decision time.[12] Nevertheless, the Hermann definition offers some important advantages to both theorists and historians, not the least of which is the existence of at least some evidence linking each of the defining criteria with some consequences for decision making.

Most of the extensive literature on crisis extends far beyond this initial problem of definition and concentrates its attention on actual behavior during crisis situations. This proceeds from a wide variety of theoretical and empirical perspectives. It can perhaps be understood best by following the approach of Hermann and Brady, and systematically identifying four rather distinct, descriptive theories.[13]

The first of these is the *organizational response* model. It is directed at decision-making groups and the bureaucratic organizations which may shape and constrain policy choices in crisis. Studies at the level of the decision-making group reveal that the concomitants of crisis — for example, smaller groups or greater cohesion — can have both positive and negative consequences for the quality of decision processes. Leadership skills often determine whether, for example, group cohesion becomes a vehicle for constructive cooperation, or whether it takes on a more pathological form such as "groupthink."[14] Organizational theorists have often regarded crises as occasions in which greater than normal rationality prevails because decisions are made at the top of organizational hierarchies by persons less constrained by narrow parochial views.[15] Moreover, limited time reduces opportunities to adopt bargaining and incremental strategies that may reduce the quality of decisions.[16] But others have shown that not even in crisis situations is decision making free of the organizational processes and bureaucratic politics that may constrain rational choice.[17]

A second approach may be found in the *hostile interaction* model, which examines the antecedents and consequences of interactions among nations in crises, with special attention to the role of perceptions in exacerbating, sustaining, or mitigating the pattern of relations between contending parties. According to this model, those involved in a crisis perceive accurately any hostility directed toward them, and they respond in kind. Thus, crisis is viewed as an occasion that is likely to trigger a "conflict spiral." Stated somewhat differently, this conception of crisis highlights the processes by which hostility breeds more hostility, and it focuses less attention on the means by which such a pattern of interactions may be arrested.[18]

The *cost calculation* model emphasizes the strategic and tactical choices associated with maximizing gains and minimizing losses in crisis management. Crises that pose significant threats to such central goals as national existence are likely to engender greater caution in decision makers, as well as more vigorous efforts to reach peaceful settlements. Conversely, in crises posing threats of lesser magnitude, policy makers will feel less constrained and, therefore, they may be more willing to resort to high-risk strategies and tactics; for example, they may undertake actions that convey irrationality or loss of control in an effort to force concessions from the adversary. Thus, the hostile interaction and cost calculation models differ in some significant ways, especially with respect to the prospects for attenuating escalation in a crisis.[19]

The *individual stress* model focuses upon the impact of crisis-induced stress on certain aspects of cognitive performance that are critical in decision making. Theories and research at the individual level generally emphasize the negative effects of intense and protracted crises on decision processes and outcomes. It should be noted, however, that this model is not merely a variant of a frustration–aggression theory. As will be evident in later sections of this chapter that deal with the individual stress model in much more detail, the probable consequences of intense and protracted stress are by no means confined to or even most clearly manifested by the release of aggressive impulses.

Other theories address themselves to the *consequences* of crisis. These are also marked by diversity. Among those with a systemic perspective, crisis has been viewed both as a prelude to war[20] and as a surrogate for war that offers a means of effectuating needed change.[21] There are also competing views on the consequences of *multiple crises.* The first, suggested by Quincy Wright, among others, states that the more frequent the crises, the greater the likelihood that war will result. "If p_1, p_2, p_3, etc., indicate the probability of war in successive crises in the relations of two states and P indicates the probability of war for n crises, then $P = 1 - (1 - p_1)(1 - p_2)(1 - p_3) \ldots (1 - p_n). \ldots$ Even though p is very small, as n approaches infinity the probability of war approaches certainty."[22] This might be labeled the "actuarial" view of crises. An insurance company typically charges a higher premium for the person who drives thirty thousand miles a year than for one who logs only a quarter of that distance, on the theory that greater exposure to the highways will increase the probability of a claim. The Wright formulation assumes that each crisis can be thought of as a discrete event and that there is little or no learning from [one] episode to another; that is, the participants can be thought of as beginning each time with a "crisis management tabula rasa." Thus, the cumulative probability of crises leading to war increases with each incidence of such an event.

An alternative position denies that decision makers begin with a blank slate at the onset of each crisis. Because the participants learn from their experiences, crises become "routinized." "Outputs received from occurrences and situations in the international environment and from sequences of international interaction are processed by the advanced modernizing social organizations according to their perceived characteristics: if these outputs are recognized as familiar and expected experiences met repeatedly in the remembered past, they will be treated in a highly routine fashion."[23] The participants gain experience in ways of coping with environment and adversaries and, although threats and challenges may continue to characterize relations between parties, uncertainty is reduced. Thus, "repeated exposure to acute crises may reduce the probabilities of an outbreak of general war."[24]

Finally, *prescriptive theories* — that is, theories that emphasize how to achieve one's purposes — of crisis management span an equally broad range. For present purposes, it may be sufficient to identify some basic features of two rather different perspectives. This is done merely for the purpose of illustration, and it should not be construed as an adequate treatment of the various positions or of all aspects of crisis management.

One position holds that the primary task of crisis management is to communicate one's interests and demands as unambiguously as possible, in order to prevent miscalculation on the part of adversaries. With a clear exposition of one's interests, the adversary will either avoid further provocation (ending the crisis) or demonstrate a calculated willingness to escalate the conflict (and thus reveal no interest in resolving it except on one's own terms). Strategies of crisis management include "burning one's bridges" and other forms of seemingly irrational behavior that are intended to convey to adversaries an unambiguous message of one's resolve and commitment.[25]

A rather different theory of crisis management places emphasis not only on protecting one's primary interests, but also on avoiding actions that might drive an opponent into a mutually undesirable process of escalation. Those in the group described in the previous paragraph believe that the primary danger of crisis management is that unwise concessions will mislead a thoroughly rational opponent into making further demands (the "appeasement model"); the opposing view is that an overly rigid policy may lead the adversary, whose rationality is not without limits under circumstances of crisis-induced stress, to strike back in ways that are disadvantageous to both sides.[26]

Perhaps this cursory review of a larger literature is sufficient to establish the point that even if there are fewer than a hundred flowers contending for the attention of those undertaking crisis studies, consensus remains an elusive goal rather than an established condition. Stated somewhat differently, the diplomatic historian who ventures into neighboring disciplines with expectations of finding broad agreement on key concepts that are linked together in well-established theories, and solidly buttressed by empirical evidence, is likely to be somewhat disappointed.

Lest this appraisal paint an overly pessimistic picture, it is also worth pointing to some signs of genuine progress toward the goals of cumulative knowledge. There is a convergence around, and refinements of, certain key terms and definitions (e.g., Hermann's definition of crisis) in the literature. There is also a growing willingness to undertake comparative studies in which a single crisis is viewed from several, rather than from a single, theoretical perspective,[27] or in which two or more crises are examined in a systematic and rigorous comparative manner.[28] Moreover, there is evidence that the crisis literature that has been heavily skewed toward studies of postwar crises involving one or more of the superpowers, is now being significantly broadened by research which includes both pre- and post-1945 cases as well as small- and middle-range powers.[29] Finally, the concept of crisis itself is being subjected to cross-cultural comparisons in order to understand the involvement of more than one decision system in the anticipation, avoidance, control, and termination of international crises.[30] These several developments suggest promising prospects for policy makers, political scientists, and diplomatic historians concerned with crisis behaviors.

CRISIS, STRESS, AND DECISION MAKING: SOME EVIDENCE FROM PSYCHOLOGY

One of the more interesting bodies of theory on crisis behavior is that concentrating upon individual stress. This approach, as indicated previously, focuses upon the impact of crisis-induced stress on certain aspects of cognitive performance that are critical in decision making. In assessing the potential impact of crisis on cognitive performance, it is important to do so against realistic standards. Cognitive limits on rationality include, as suggested by evidence from psychology, limits on the individual's capacity to receive, process, and assimilate information about the situation; an inability to generate the entire set of policy alternatives; fragmentary knowledge about the consequences of each option; and an inability to order preferences for all possible consequences on a single utility scale.[31] Because these constraints exist in all but the most trivial decision-making situations, it is not instructive to assess the impact on crises against a standard of synoptic rationality. A more modest and useful set of criteria might include an individual's ability to do the following:

Identify adequately the objectives to be fulfilled;

Survey the major alternative courses of action;

Estimate the probable costs and risks, as well as the positive consequences, of various alternatives (and, as a corollary, distinguish the possible from the probable);

Search for new information relevant to assessment of the options;

Maintain an open mind to new information, even that which calls into question the validity of preferred courses of action (and as corollaries, discriminate between relevant and irrelevant information, resist premature cognitive closure, and tolerate ambiguity);

Assess the situation from the perspective of other parties;

Resist both defensive procrastination and premature decision;

Make adjustments to meet real changes in the situation (and, as a corollary, distinguish real from apparent changes).[32]

A vast body of theory and evidence suggests that intense and protracted crises tend to erode rather than enhance these cognitive abilities. Figure 1 — a series of hypotheses linking the defining attributes of crisis, first to stress and then to selected aspects of cognitive and decision-making performance — is a variant of the individual stress model described earlier.[33] These propositions are presented not as iron laws but as an alternative to the view that crisis heightens propensities toward rational and calculated decision processes. The remainder of this section summarizes briefly some of the relevant psychological evidence.

An important aspect of crises is that they are characterized by high stress for the individuals and organizations involved. That a severe threat to important values is stress inducing requires little elaboration. The element of surprise is also a contributing factor; there is evidence that unanticipated and novel situations are generally viewed as more threatening.[34] Finally, crises are often marked by almost around-the-clock work schedules, owing to the severity of the situation (high threat), the absence of established routines for dealing with them (surprise), and the absence of extended decision time. Lack of rest and diversion, combined with excessively long working hours, are likely to magnify the stresses in the situation. Moreover, crisis decisions are rarely if ever analogous to the familiar multiple-choice question, in which the full range of options is neatly outlined. The theoretical universe of choices usually exceeds by a substantial margin the number that can or will be considered. Especially in unanticipated situations for which there are no established SOPs (standard operating procedures) or decision rules, it is necessary to search out and perhaps create alternatives. Thus, the decision process itself may be a significant source of stress, arising, for example, from efforts to cope with cognitive constraints on rationality, role factors, small group dynamics, and bureaucratic politics.[35]

Some degree of stress is an integral and necessary precondition for individual or organizational problem solving; in its absence there is no motivation to act. Low levels of stress alert us to the existence of a situation requiring our attention, increase our vigilance and our preparedness to cope with it. Increasing stress to moderate levels may heighten our propensity and ability to find a satisfactory solution to the problem. Indeed, for some elementary tasks a rather high degree of stress may enhance performance, at least for limited periods of time. If the problem is qualitatively simple and performance is measured by quantitative criteria, stress can increase output. Our primary concern, however, is not with the effects of crisis on persons engaged in manual or routine tasks, but with its consequences on the performance of officials in leadership positions

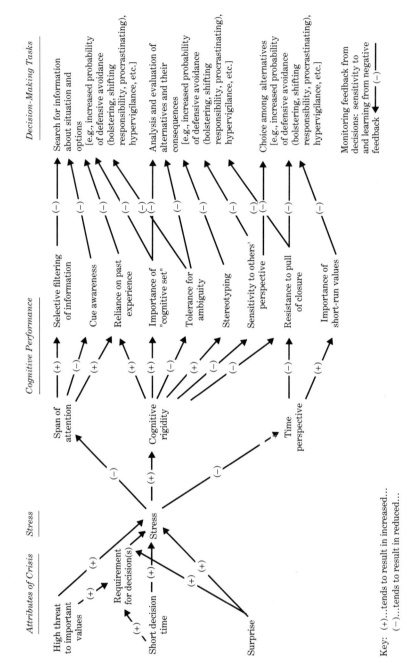

Key: (+)...tends to result in increased...
      (−)...tends to result in reduced...

Figure 3.1 Individual decision making in crisis: some hypotheses

during major international crises. These are nearly always marked by complexity and ambiguity, and they usually demand responses which are judged by qualitative rather than quantitative criteria. It is precisely these qualitative aspects of performance that are most likely to suffer under high stress.[36]

Experimental findings generally indicate a curvilinear relationship, most easily described as an "inverted U," between stress and the performance of individuals and groups. A moderate level of anxiety can be beneficial, but at higher levels it disrupts decision processes.[37] Observational evidence from related field research (e.g., studies of natural disasters, or performance in combat and other dangerous circumstances) also suggests that intense and protracted stress often erodes rather than enhances the ability of individuals to cope with complex problems.[38] To summarize, in situations of high stress, "there is a narrowing of the cognitive organization at the moment; the individual loses broader perspective, he is no longer able to 'see' essential aspects of the situation and his behavior becomes, consequently, less adaptive."[39]

At this point we shall consider in more detail some potential consequences of stress for cognitive rigidity, span of attention, and time perspectives.

Cognitive Rigidity.   Charles Lindblom suggests that "a serious emergency or crisis often transforms a policy analyst's perceptions (and sometimes galvanizes his energies) with the result that he gets a new grasp on his problem."[40] But there is also evidence that the effects of stress on cognitive performance are often less benign. Persons experiencing intense stress tend to suffer increased cognitive rigidity, and erosion of general cognitive abilities, including creativity and the ability to cope with complexity. As a consequence, the range of perceived policy options may be narrow. The decision maker is likely to establish a dominant percept through which to interpret information, and to maintain it tenaciously in the face of information that might seem to call for a reappraisal.[41] Often this percept is a familiar one transferred from previous situations (e.g., "lessons of history"), even though it may be inappropriate for the circumstances at hand,[42] and it is more likely to be characterized by stereotypes than by subtlety as the complexity of the psychological field is reduced.[43] To change one's beliefs and theories each time some discrepant information is received is neither possible nor wise, but it is at least useful to be aware that evidence about an unfolding situation may be consistent with more than a single explanation.[44] A finding of special relevance for crisis decision making is that tolerance for ambiguity is reduced when there is high stress. Under these conditions individuals made decisions before adequate information was available, with the result that they performed much less capably than persons working under normal conditions. The combination of stress and uncertainty leads some persons to feel that "the worst would be better than this."[45] Finally, caricatures of motivational structures may develop: the anxious become more anxious, the energetic become more energetic, the repressors become more repressive, and so on.[46] The effects of stress on perception have been summarized as follows:

> Perceptual behavior is disrupted, becomes less well controlled than under normal conditions, and hence is less adaptive. The major dimensions of perceptual function are affected: selection of percepts from a complex field becomes less adequate and sense is less well differentiated from nonsense; there is maladaptive accentuation in the direction of aggression and escape; untested hypotheses are fixated recklessly.[47]

As a result of these effects of stress, search for information and policy options may be adversely affected in several ways. Other actors and their motives are likely to be stereotyped, for example, and the situation itself may be defined in overly simple, one-dimensional terms — such as, that it is a zero-sum situation, or that everything is related to everything else.[48] The ability to invent nonobvious solutions to complex problems may also be impaired. Finally, complex problems are more likely to be defined by "what is already in" (the decision maker's beliefs, expectations, cognitive and emotional predispositions), and less by the "objective" attributes of the situation.[49]

The inception of a crisis usually results in a sharply increased pace of individual and bureaucratic activity and, concomitantly, an increasing volume of communication. Conversely, information overload in a decision-making situation may itself be a source of serious stress.[50] One way of coping with this phenomenon is to *narrow one's span of attention* to a few aspects of the decision-making task.[51] This may be a functional strategy if it permits the executive to eliminate trivial distractions, filter out irrelevant information, and develop an agenda of priorities. However, a number of costs may offset or even outweigh these benefits.

An experimental study of complex situations revealed that increased information loads resulted in fewer strategic integrated decisions and more unintegrated and simple retaliatory decisions.[52] As the volume of information directed at policy makers rises, the search for information within the communication system will tend to become less thorough, and selectivity in what is read, believed, and retained takes on increasing importance. In ambiguous situations or in circumstances of information overload, one may also be more likely to screen information and to respond in terms of personal predispositions.[53] Unpleasant information and that which does not support preferences and expectations may fall by the wayside, unless it is of such an unambiguous nature that it cannot be disregarded. "All Presidents, at least in modern times," writes Sorensen, "have complained about their reading pile, and few have been able to cope with it. There is a temptation, consequently, to cut out all that is unpleasant."[54] Thus, more communication may in fact result in less useful and valid information being available to policy makers.

Time perspectives are also likely to be affected by high stress. For example, the ability to judge time is impaired in situations which increase anxiety.[55] Thus, there appears to be a two-way relationship between time and stress. On the one hand, short decision time, a defining characteristic of crisis, is likely to increase the stress under which the executive must operate. On the other hand, increasing levels of stress tend to heighten the salience of time and to distort judgements about it. It has been found in "real life" crisis situations, as well as experimentally, that as danger increases there is a significant overestimation of how fast time is passing.[56]

Perceived time pressure may affect decision making in several ways. A number of studies indicate that some time pressure can enhance creativity as well the rate of performance, but most of the evidence suggests that beyond a moderate level it has adverse effects. Because complex tasks requiring feats of memory and inference suffer more from time pressure,[57] its effects on the most important decisions — which are usually marked by complexity — are likely to be particularly harmful. In such situations there is a tendency to fix upon a single approach, to continue using it whether or not it proves effective, and to hang on to familiar solutions, applying them even to problems that may be substantially different.[58]

Experimental research has often shown a curvilinear relationship between time pressure and performance. Under severe time pressure, normal subjects produce errors similar to those committed by schizophrenics. Another study revealed that, although a moderate increase in time pressure can increase the productivity of groups, an increase from low to high pressure has an adverse effect. Increasing the number of decisions required in a given period of time by a factor of five led to a fifteenfold rise in decision errors. There is, in addition, evidence that time pressure increases the propensity to rely upon stereotypes, disrupts both individual and group problem solving, narrows the focus of attention, and impedes the use of available information. Finally, both experimental and historical evidence indicates that high stress tends to result in a shorter time perspective and, as consequence, reduced resistance to premature closure.[59]

When decision time is short, the ability to estimate the range of possible consequences arising from a particular policy choice is likely to be impaired. Both experimental and field research indicate that severe stress is likely to give rise to a single-minded concern for the present and immediate future at the sacrifice of attention to longer range considerations.[60] The uncertainties attending severe crisis make it exceptionally difficult to follow outcomes from a sequence of actions and responses very far into the future. Increasing stress also tends to narrow the focus of attention, thereby further limiting perceptions of time to the more immediate future. During the Korean War, for instance, it was observed that combat troops "cannot exercise complex functions involving the scanning of a large number of factors or long-term foresight because the stress is too massive and time too short for anything but the immediately relevant."[61]

This brief overview of evidence is suggestive rather than exhaustive. Moreover, the emphasis has been on processes rather than on decision outputs and, just as we cannot assume that "good" processes will ensure high-quality decisions, we cannot assume that erratic processes will always result in low-quality decisions. But even if Figure 1 describes only some potential tendencies rather than unvarying responses to crisis, there is sufficient evidence to call into question the universal validity of the premise that we always rise to the occasion in crisis, drawing if necessary upon hidden reservoirs of strength. The evidence cited here suggests that among the more probable casualties of crises and the accompanying high stress are the very abilities that distinguish men from other species: to establish logical links between present actions and future goals; to search effectively for relevant policy options; to create appropriate responses to unexpected events; to communicate complex ideas; to deal effectively with abstractions; to perceive not only blacks and whites, but also to distinguish them from the many subtle shades of gray that fall in between; to distinguish valid analogies from false ones, and sense from nonsense; and, perhaps most important of all, to enter into the frame of references of others. With respect to these precious cognitive abilities, the law of supply and demand seems to operate in a perverse manner; as crisis increases the need for them, it also appears to diminish the supply.

Suggestive as these models and theories of crisis decision making may be, they cannot substitute for evidence from actual foreign policy crisis. Abstract and theoretical work must be examined and analyzed in terms of specific evidence — in this case, evidence from diplomatic history. Toward this end, the next two sections will utilize the "focused comparison" approach[62] — in which case studies aim not at a full historical description but at developing or testing explicit propositions of theoretical or policy relevance — and will explore several very specific aspects of individual stress in crisis decision making from the 1914 and Cuban missile crises.

DECISION MAKING IN THE 1914 CRISIS

The assassination of Archduke Franz Ferdinand on June 28, 1914, set off a chain of events that, within six weeks, brought all of the major powers of Europe into war. Soon after Prince von Bülow asked German Chancellor Bethmann Hollweg how the war had come about. "At last I said to him: 'Well, tell me, at least, how it all happened,' He raised his long, thin arms to heaven and answered in a dull exhausted voice: 'Oh — if I only knew.'" Another colleague wrote that "since the Russian mobilization the Chancellor gave one the impression of a drowning man."[63] Are these merely the self-serving recollections of war criminals or of fools whose incompetence visited upon the world a war of unparalleled devastation? If the answer is an affirmative one, the 1914 case is of little interest to the student of crisis, and the prescription is relatively simple — keep war criminals and fools out of high office.

But perhaps the answer to "how it all happened" is not quite so simple. The proposition to be explored in this section is that the individual stress model may help to explain the disastrous events of 1914. It should be made clear at the outset that what follows is an illustration and not an attempt at a full-scale explanation.[64] It does not deal with the state of military technology, European alliance commitments, the balance of power, contingency plans of foreign and war offices, historical enmities, economic competition, or imperial ambitions and rivalries. All of these were important in 1914 and nothing in the analysis that follows is intended to deny their relevance. Nevertheless, these were also important in 1911, in 1908, and in other years that featured confrontations among the major powers. But, unless we adopt a deterministic view — as is implied, for example, by the popular metaphor of the assassination as a lighted match thrown into a keg of powder — it is appropriate to consider not only the European context in 1914, but also the decision processes. The focus here is on two aspects of Figure 1 — perceptions of time pressure and of policy options.

Perceptions of Time Pressure

To examine the effects of deepening crisis on perceptions of time pressure, techniques of content analysis were employed.[65] All documents written by high-ranking foreign policy officials were coded for evidence of time pressure as a factor in policy decisions. The resulting 167 statements are classified according to date and nation and specific issue (Table 1). Statements of concern about decision time increased steadily (except in the case of Austria–Hungary), not only in absolute frequency, but even in relation to the total number of policy themes. Perceptions of time pressure were also associated with increasing stress, with correlations ranging from .16 to .82.

During the earliest period of the 1914 crisis approximately two-thirds of the references to time focused on the desirability or necessity of early action by Austria–Hungary against Serbia. Count Alexander Hoyos, Chief of the Cabinet of the Austro-Hungarian Foreign Ministry, for example, wrote on July 7 that "from a military standpoint . . . it would be much more favorable to start the war now than later since the balance of power would weigh against us in the future."[66] The view that time was working against the Dual Monarchy was supported, for Germany was exerting considerable pressure on its ally not to postpone a showdown. Gottlieb von Jagow, German Foreign Minister, wrote on July 15: "We are concerned at present with the preeminent political question, perhaps the

TABLE 1 Perception of Time Pressure: The 1914 Crisis

Period	Total Themes	Perceptions of Time Pressure in the Documents of:					Total	% Themes with Time Perceptions
		Austria-Hungary	Germany	Great Britain	France	Russia		
June 27–July 20	1,031	13	9	0	0	0	22	2.1
July 21–28	1,658	3	11	18	13	8	53	3.2
July 29–August 2	1,910	0	35	12	13	3	63	3.3
August 3–4	479	0	14	12	3	0	29	6.1
June 27–August 4	5,078	16	69	42	29	11	167	3.3
Correlation (*gamma*) between stress and perceptions of time pressure		.16	.33	.61	.68	.82		

Period	A	B	C	D	E	Total
June 27–July 20	15	1	0	2	4	22
July 21–28	11	29	10	2	1	53
July 29–August 2	1	8	29	16	9	63
August 3–4	0	0	2	22	5	29
June 27–August 4	27	38	41	42	19	167

Codes for relevance of time:
A—As a factor in Austro-Hungarian action toward Serbia
B—As a factor in localization of conflict between Austria–Hungary and Serbia
C—As a factor in mobilization
D—As a factor in alliance and other political commitments
E—Other

last opportunity of giving the Greater-Serbia menace its death blow under comparatively favorable circumstances."[67] In contrast, the view in London, Paris, and St. Petersburg was initially one of relative lack of concern. There is no evidence that leaders in the capitals of the Entente nations felt themselves under any pressure of time to react to this latest episode of instability in the Balkans.

Time perceptions from July 21 through July 28 focused predominantly on the necessity of delaying the course of events in the Balkans. Once the content of the Austrian ultimatum became known, the forty-eight-hour time limit within which the Serbian government had to draft a reply became an immediate subject of concern. Some European officials recognized that the conflict in the Balkans might well engulf all Europe if existing alliance commitments were honored. Whereas both German and Austro-Hungarian leaders had frequently expressed the desirability of moving swiftly against Serbia, those in London, Paris, St. Petersburg, and Belgrade were especially concerned with the necessity of gaining the time which might be used to work out a peaceful settlement of Vienna's demands on Serbia. Although they were far from united on the details of policy, the single common theme in their proposals was the fear that precipitate action could lead only to war. Typical of diplomatic messages during this period was the assertion that "the immediate danger was that in a few hours Austria might march into Serbia and Russian Slav opinion demand that Russia should march to help Serbia; it would be very desirable to get Austria not to precipitate military action and so to gain more time."[68] By July 29 it was apparent that war between Austria–Hungary and Serbia could not be prevented. At the same time, it was increasingly evident that a chain reaction was in danger of being set off.

As late as August 1 many European leaders continued to express the belief that if time permitted the concert powers to be reconvened, general war might be avoided. British Foreign Secretary Grey wrote, for example: "I still believe that if only a little respite in time can be gained before any Great Power begins war it might be possible to secure peace."[69] By this time, however, the pressure of time had taken a different meaning for many decision makers. A major concern was that one's nation not be caught unprepared for the war which might break out.

The situation, as perceived by leaders in the major capitals of Europe, posed a terrible dilemma. It was widely recognized that more time would be required if a general European war were to be averted; above all, a moratorium on military operations was necessary. It was equally evident that military preparations could become the justification for similar actions by others. The German ambassador in St. Petersburg warned the Russian foreign minister that "the danger of every preparatory military measure lay in the counter measures of the other side."[70] But, increasingly, these considerations were overshadowed by the fear of disastrous consequences if a potential adversary gained even a momentary head start in mobilizing its armed forces. As early as July 24, the French minister of war, apprehensive about the outcome of the crisis in the Balkans, asserted that, for France, "first military precautions could not be delayed."[71] Although no *official* mobilization orders except those of Austria–Hungary and Serbia were issued until July 29, rumors and suspicions of undercover preparations were not wholly without foundation. On July 25 the Russian government decided to set into motion all of the preparations preliminary to mobilization. Despite a badly divided Cabinet, even the British were undertaking a number of important military preparations. Winston Churchill, First Lord of the Admiralty, for example, mobilized the British navy contrary to a decision of the Cabinet.

In the early hours of the morning of July 30, the Kaiser wrote on the margin of a message from the Czar: ". . . the Czar — as is openly admitted by him here — instituted 'mil[itary] measures which have *now come into force*' against Austria and us and as a matter of fact five days ago. Thus it is almost *a week ahead of us.* And these measures are for a *defense* against *Austria,* which is *in no way* attacking him!!! I can not agree to any more mediation, since the Czar who requested it has at the same time secretly mobilized behind my back. It is only a maneuver, in order to hold us back and to increase the start they have already got. My work is at an end!"[72] Later, the Kaiser added, "In view of the colossal war preparations of Russia now discovered, this is all too late, I fear. Begin! Now!"[73] On July 30, German Chancellor Bethmann Hollweg was also concerned with the disadvantages of delay: ". . . the military preparations of our neighbors, especially in the east, will force us to a speedy decision, unless we do not wish to expose ourselves to the danger of surprise."[74]

On the same day René Viviani, French premier, urged Russia to avoid provocative measures that might provide Germany with a pretext for a total or partial mobilization of its own forces. Nevertheless, the Russians decided in favor of general mobilization, German warnings notwithstanding. "In these conditions," according to Foreign Minister Sazonov, "Russia can only hasten its armaments and face the imminence of war and that it counts upon the assistance of its ally France; Russia considers it desirable that England join Russia and France without losing time."[75] In response to what was perceived as a mounting threat against its eastern frontiers, the German Empire proclaimed a "state of threatening danger of war" on July 31, dispatching a twelve-hour ultimatum to Russia demanding a cessation of military preparations along the border. Berlin then ordered mobilization on August 1. "We could not sit back quietly and wait to see whether a more commonsense view would gain the upper hand at Petersburg, while at the same time the Russian mobilization was proceeding at such speed, that, if the worst came, we should be left completely outstripped in a military sense."[76]

The French government simultaneously ordered general mobilization on August 1. General Joffre had earlier argued that "it is absolutely necessary that the government know that from this evening on, any delay of twenty-four hours applied to the calling up of reserves and to the sending of the telegram ordering covering troops will result in a backward movement of our troops, that is to say an initial abandonment of a part of our territory, either 15 or 20 kilometers every day of delay."[77] Although official British naval mobilization was delayed until August 2, many officials in London had advocated such action considerably earlier. Winston Churchill was perhaps the most energetic proponent of early military preparations.[78] Others included Arthur Nicolson, Permanent Under Secretary for Foreign Affairs, who said on July 31: "It seems to me most essential, whatever our future course may be in regard to intervention, that we should at once give orders for mobilization of the army. . . . Mobilization is a precautionary measure—and to my mind essential." Three days later he added that "we ought to mobilize today so that our expeditionary force may be on its way during the next week. Should we waver now we shall rue the day later."[79]

Thus, ten days after the full-scale mobilizations by Serbia and Austria–Hungary on July 25, each of the major European countries had called up its armed forces. As each mobilization was ordered, it was defended as a necessary reaction to a previous decision within the other coalition. And with each mobilization came assurances that it was a defensive measure, although in 1914 a decision to mobilize was commonly regarded as tantamount to an act of war. In the rush to mobilize no one wanted to be beaten to the draw, even though there was sometimes an awareness of the logical end of military measures and countermeasures.

In some cases the escalation of military actions and counteractions was sustained almost by accident, or by the failure to perceive the effects of one's own acts. The mobilization of the Russian Baltic fleet provides a good example. "On 25 July, when the Czar looked over the minutes and resolutions of the Council of Ministers of the 24th, he not only approved them by adding 'agreed,' but, where it was the question of mobilizing the districts of Kiev, Moscow, Odessa and Kazan and the Black Sea fleet, he inserted in his own hand 'and Baltic' without any of his Ministers drawing his attention to the fact that the mobilization of the Baltic fleet constituted an act of hostility toward Germany."[80] Although the Russian Baltic fleet was no match for the powerful German navy, the Kaiser apparently felt genuinely threatened. In response to Bethmann Hollweg's plea that the German fleet be left in Norway, he wrote: "There is a Russian Fleet! In the Baltic there are now five Russian torpedo boat flotillas engaged in practice cruises, which as a whole or in part can be at the Belts within sixteen hours and close them. Port Arthur should be a lesson! My Fleet has orders to sail for Kiel, and to Kiel it is going to sail!"[81]

This inquiry into time pressures associated with the 1914 crisis supports the hypothesis that one reaction to decisional stress is hypervigilance. Concern for time increased as the crisis deepened, and it is also clear that time pressures were related to the central rather than peripheral issues in the crisis. When there was a conflict between the need to delay action in order to seek nonmilitary means of resolving the crisis and the perceived needs of military preparedness, the latter consideration prevailed, in large part because so many officials throughout Europe felt that the costs of falling behind the adversary's timetable would be catastrophic. Many decisions during the crisis were undertaken in great haste, and the processes by which they were made were at times highly erratic. For example, the initial Russian decision for a general mobilization was followed shortly by an order for only a partial callup of forces, and then by another reversal to the original decision. In the meanwhile, when it became clear that the conflict between Serbia and Austria–Hungary might lead to a general European war, a series of highly contradictory messages was dispatched from Berlin to Vienna. Demands for restraint in some of them were offset by a telegram from Moltke stating that Austria–Hungary should immediately mobilize against Russia, and that Germany would soon follow suit.

Policy Options

One way of coping with decision stress is a form of bolstering, attributing to the adversary sole responsibility for choices and outcomes, while absolving oneself, owing to the absence of real alternatives. Data from the 1914 crisis provide some striking support for the proposition that, in a crisis situation, decision makers will tend to perceive the range of their own alternatives to be more restricted than those of their opponents. That is, they will perceive their own decision making to be characterized by *necessity* and *closed* options, whereas those of the adversary are characterized by *open* choices (Table 2).

The 1914 documents are filled with such words as "must," "compelled," "obliged," "unable," "driven," "impossible," and "helpless," but these rarely occur except when the author is referring to the policies of his own nation. To students of strategy the assertions of the Kaiser, the Czar, and others that they were helpless once they had set their military machines into motion may appear to be a "real life" application of the tactics of *commitment,* "a device to leave the last clear chance to decide the outcome with the other party, in a manner that he fully appreciates; it is to relinquish further initiative, having rigged the incentives so that the other party must choose in one's favor."[82] This explanation may be valid for messages that were intended for wide circulation among officials in allied or enemy countries. On the other hand, the most "private" documents — those intended only for circulation within the various foreign offices — do not differ materially from the entire set of documents in respect to the findings reported here. The clearest evidence in support of this assertion is to be found in the Kaiser's marginal notations and in the various minutes of Eyre Crowe, Assistant Under-Secretary of State, in the British Foreign Office.

Even a cursory survey of the diplomatic documents reveals that, with the exception of Austria–Hungary, European leaders consistently per-

TABLE 2   Perceptions of Alternatives (Choice, Necessity, Closed): Top-Ranking Decision Makers During 1914 Crisis

	GERMANY Own Nation	Allies	Opponents
Choice	10	7	25
Necessity	110	20	2
Closed	20	2	0
% Choice	7.1%	24.1%	92.6%

	AUSTRIA–HUNGARY Own Nation	Allies	Opponents
Choice	13	1	1
Necessity	80	2	1
Closed	7	1	0
% Choice	13.0%	25.0%	50.0%

	GREAT BRITAIN Own Nation	Allies	Opponents
Choice	7	21	21
Necessity	20	8	2
Closed	23	2	0
% Choice	14.0%	67.7%	91.3%

	FRANCE Own Nation	Allies	Opponents
Choice	1	6	12
Necessity	13	4	2
Closed	5	2	2
% Choice	5.3%	50.0%	75.0%

	RUSSIA Own Nation	Allies	Opponents
Choice	7	4	6
Necessity	20	3	2
Closed	7	3	0
% Choice	20.6%	40.0%	75.0%

NOTE:

Choice: Decision maker perceives that more than one course of action is open.

Necessity: Decision maker perceives only one possible course of action in a given situation.

Closed: Decision maker perceives that some course of action is not possible.

ceived fewer options open to themselves than to their adversaries. Edward Grey, for example, who took the most active role in seeking mediation, wrote on July 24 that "we can do nothing for moderation unless Germany is prepared *pari passu* to do the same."[83] Until the final hours of the crisis, leaders in Berlin were opposed to mediation of the local conflict, in part because previous conferences called to settle international crises (such as Algeciras in 1906) had, in the eyes of the Kaiser and others, denied them the diplomatic victories to which they were entitled.

According to Bethmann Hollweg, "We cannot mediate in the conflict between Austria and Serbia but possibly later between Austria and Russia."[84] Nor were the Russians inclined to mediation because, in the words of Sazonov, "we have assumed from the beginning a posture which we cannot change."[85]

But the same leaders who expressed varying degrees of inability to cope with the situation in the Balkans tended to perceive more freedom of action for members of the opposing alliance. After the outbreak of war between Serbia and Austria–Hungary, Grey wrote: "The whole idea of mediation or mediating influence was ready to be put into operation by any method that Germany could suggest if mine was not acceptable. In fact, mediation was ready to come into operation by any method that Germany thought possible if only Germany would 'press the button' in the interests of peace."[86]

The tendency to perceive one's own alternatives to be more restricted than those of the adversary is also evident in the reaction to the events leading up to general war. The reaction of German decision makers was typical. On the one hand, they asserted repeatedly that *they* had no choice but to take vigorous military measures against the threat to the east. "Then I must mobilize too! . . . He [Nicholas] expressly stated in his first telegram that he would be presumably forced to take measures that would lead to a European war. Thus he takes the responsibility upon himself."[87] On the other hand, they credited Russia with complete freedom to take the actions necessary to prevent war: "The responsibility for the disaster which is now threatening the whole civilized world will not be laid at my door. In this moment it still lies in your [Nicholas] power to avert it."[88] And Wilhelm, like the Czar, finally asserted that he had lost control of his own military and that only the actions of the adversary could stop further escalation: "On technical grounds my mobilization which had already been proclaimed this afternoon must proceed against two fronts, east and west as prepared. This cannot be countermanded because I am sorry your [George V] telegram came so late."[89] The same theme of a single option open to oneself, coupled with perceptions that the initiative for peace rested with the enemy, is evident in the French and Austrian statements regarding their own mobilizations.

An increasing sense of helplessness and resignation to the irresistible course of events is evident in many of the documents. On the day of the Serbian reply to the Austro-Hungarian ultimatum, Paul Cambon, French ambassador in London, stated that he saw "no way of halting the march of events."[90] In contrast to Edward Grey, who maintained the hope that the European powers would find a way to prevent a general war, Arthur Nicolson asserted on July 29, "I am of the opinion that the resources of diplomacy are, for the present, exhausted."[91] At the same time, in St. Petersburg, Sazonov wrote of the "inevitability of war" while in Berlin, the Kaiser, in one of the most vitriolic of his marginal notes, concluded that "we have proved ourselves helpless."[92]

Significantly contributing to the belief that options were severely restricted was the rigidity of the various mobilization plans. Austria–Hungary and Russia had more than one plan for mobilization, but once any one of them was set in motion, it could be altered only with great effort. The Russians could order either a general mobilization against both Germany and Austria–Hungary, or a partial one directed only at the latter. But, as Russian generals were to argue vehemently during the crucial days at the end of July, a partial mobilization would preclude a general one for months to come, leaving Russia completely at the mercy of Germany. According to General Dobrorolski, "The whole plan of mobilization is worked out ahead to its end in all its detail. When the moment has been chosen, one has only to press the button, and the whole state begins to function automatically with the precision of a clock's mechanism. . . . Once the moment has been fixed, everything is settled; there is no going back; it determines mechanically the beginning of war."[93]

France and Germany each had but a single plan for calling up their armed forces and, in the case of Germany, political leaders were ill informed about the rigidity of mobilization and war plans. The Kaiser's last-minute attempt to reverse the Schlieffen plan — to attack only in the East — shattered Moltke, Chief of the German General Staff, who replied: "That is impossible, Your Majesty. An army of a million cannot be improvised. It would be nothing but a rabble of undisciplined armed men, without a commissariat. . . . It is utterly impossible to advance except according to plan; strong in the west, weak in the east."[94]

Finally, all of the mobilization plans existed only on paper; except for the Russo-Japanese War, no major European power had mobilized since 1878. This fact rendered the plans all the more rigid and made military leaders responsible for carrying them out less likely to accept any last-minute modifications. It may also have added to the widely believed dictum that one did not mobilize for any purpose other than war.

Just as European leaders tended to perceive fewer alternatives open to themselves than to their adversaries, so they regarded their allies to be in a similar position vis-à-vis their enemies. On the one hand, German documents are replete with explanation that Austria was pursuing the only policy open to her and thus Germany could not play a moderating role in Vienna, although only four months earlier Wilhelm had stated that if Vienna gets into a war against the Slavs through "great stupidity," it would "leave us [Germany] quite cold."[95] On the other hand, the Kaiser appealed to England, apparently convinced that the latter could perform the very role which he felt was impossible for Germany — restraining the most belligerent member of the coalition. "Instead of making proposals for conferences, His Majesty the King should order France and Russia, frankly and plainly, at one and the same time — they were HIS ALLIES — to DESIST at once from the mobilization, remain NEUTRAL and await Austria's proposals, which I should immediately transmit as soon as I was informed of them. . . . I could to nothing more direct; it was for him to take hold now and prove the honesty of English love of peace."[96] The assumption of British freedom to determine the policy of her allies, coupled with restrictions on German policy, is nowhere as clear as in one of the Kaiser's marginal notes: "He [Grey] knows perfectly well, that if he were to say one single serious sharp warning word at Paris and Petersburg, and were to warn them to remain neutral, both would become quiet at once. But he takes care not to speak the word, and threatens us instead! Common cur! England *alone* bears the responsibility for peace and war, and not we any longer."[97]

This approach to the problem of allies was not confined to Berlin. Adducing arguments that were strikingly similar to those used by the Kaiser, British leaders denied their ability or willingness to dictate a policy of moderation in Paris or St. Petersburg. Nicolson wrote on July 29: "I do not think that Berlin quite understands that Russia cannot and will not stand quietly by while Austria administers a severe chastisement to Serbia. She does not consider that Serbia deserves it, and she could not, in view of that feeling and of her position in the Slav world, consent to it."[98] Grey assessed the requirements of his French ally in similar terms: "France did not wish to join in the war that seemed about to break out, but she was obliged to join in it, because of her alliance."[99] At the same time, however, he believed that Germany could constrain the cause of her ally: "But none of us could influence Austria in this direction unless Germany would propose and participate in such action in Vienna."[100] On July 28 Nicholas had appealed to his counterpart in Berlin: "To try and avoid such a calamity as a European war, I beg you in the name of our old friendship to do what you can to stop your allies from *going too far.*"[101]

The few attempts made to restrain the militant members of each alliance were either halfhearted or too late. Typical was the advice of Sir Eyre Crowe, who had written on July 25: "The moment has passed when it might have been possible to enlist French support in an effort to hold back Russia. It is clear that France and Russia are decided to accept the challenge thrown to them." He expressed the opinion that it would be both impolitic and dangerous to try to change their minds.[102] Similarly, a last-minute German attempt to hold Austria in check failed. At 2:55 A.M., July 30, Bethmann Hollweg concluded a telegram to Vienna: "Under these circumstances we must urgently and impressively suggest to the consideration of the Vienna Cabinet that acceptance of mediation on the mentioned honorable conditions. The responsibility for the consequences that would otherwise follow would be an uncommonly heavy one both for Austria and for us."[103] A few minutes later, however, Moltke sent a wire to Vienna urging immediate mobilization against Russia promising Germany's full support for such an action — even if it led to general war.[104]

DECISION MAKING DURING THE MISSILE CRISIS[105]

A single U-2 American surveillance plane took off on October 14, 1962, for a reconnaissance flight over Cuba. Immediately upon returning, its high-altitude cameras were unloaded. After intensive study of the developed films, intelligence analysts uncovered unmistakable evidence of two medium-range ballistic missile (MRBM) sites in areas previously photographed and found to be empty. Overflights three days later confirmed these reports and revealed nine sites — 36 launch positions — six for the 1,100-mile MRBM and three for 2,200-mile intermediate-range ballistic missiles (IRBM) in various states of readiness. Thus began the most serious international crisis of the nuclear era, a confrontation during which President Kennedy estimated that the chances of a nuclear war between the United States and the Soviet Union were one in three.

The 1914 and Cuban situations were similar in a number of respects and differed in many others. The similarity of present interest is that both episodes conform to the definition of crisis used here. Despite widespread rumors of Soviet missile installations in Cuba, photographic evidence of their presence was a surprise to virtually all officials in Washington, including the President; the rate of construction on the missile sites made it evident that any decision to prevent their completion could not long be delayed; and, with the exception of Secretary of Defense Robert McNamara, all who joined the American decision group interpreted the Soviet move as a serious threat to national security. As one participant in these discussions put it: "Everyone round the table recognized that we were in a major crisis. We didn't know, that day, if the country would come through it with Washington intact."[106]

The most significant difference between these two events is that the 1914 crisis led to a world war, whereas the Cuban confrontation was resolved without recourse to violence. Thus, the situation that confronted national leaders in the two crises shared a number of attributes (surprise, high threat, short decision time), but the decisions they made led to significantly different results: peaceful settlement versus a world war. In an attempt to explain the different outcomes, the remainder of this section examines several aspects of the decision-making process in 1962, again with special attention to time pressure and the search for and appraisal of alternatives.

Perceptions of Time Pressure

Several sources of time pressure impinged on the President and his advisers during the missile crisis. Initially, there was the need to formulate a policy before the Soviets were alerted by the stepped-up U-2 flights to the fact that their launching installations had been discovered. Conversely, once developments in Cuba became public knowledge, there would be no further time for deliberation and debate on the proper response.

An overriding concern throughout the period was the knowledge that construction on the missile sites was continuing at a rapid pace. The first photographic evidence of construction activities in Cuba indicated that they would be operational within a week to ten days. American officials perceived that their task would become immeasurably more difficult once construction on the launching sites was completed: "For all of us know that, once the missile sites under construction became operational, and capable of responding to any apparent threat or command with a nuclear volley, the President's options would be dramatically changed."[107] Thus, the situation did not compel a reflex-like response — at least, as it was defined by the President. But in relation to the task at hand decision time was indeed short, and all firsthand accounts of decision making during the Cuban crisis, especially that of Robert Kennedy, are replete with indications of time pressure.

Despite the sense of urgency created by these deadlines, the President and his advisers sought to reduce the probability that either side would respond by a "spasm reaction." Efforts were made to delay taking overt actions as long as the situation permitted. Equally important, discussions in Washington revealed a sensitivity for the time pressures under which the adversary was operating. There was a concern that Premier Khrushchev not be rushed into an irrevocable decision; it was agreed among members of the decision group that "we should slow down the escalation of the crisis to give Khrushchev time to consider his next move."[108] Measures designed to increase Soviet decision time included the President's management of the naval quarantine. He ordered American ships to delay intercepting Soviet vessels until the last possible moment, *and had the order transmitted in the clear.* The Soviets, who were certain to intercept the message, would thus learn that they had additional time in which to formulate a response to the blockade. This play also revealed a sophisticated understanding of the social psychology of communication; information from a distrusted source is more likely to be believed if it is obtained through the recipient's own efforts. The Soviet decision on October 25 to slow down the westward progress of their ships in mid-Atlantic can also be interpreted as an effort to lengthen decision time.

A comparison of the 1914 and 1962 crises points to the importance of a subjective rather than an objective definition of decision time. Owing to vast differences in military capabilities, time was objectively of far greater importance in 1962 than in 1914. Hence, Soviet and American leaders were no less aware of time pressures and of the potential costs of delaying action than were their counterparts in 1914. But they also perceived the dangers of acting in haste, and they were successful in mitigating the most severe dangers attending such pressures. They resisted the pressures for premature decisions and took a number of actions which avoided putting their adversaries in a position of having to respond in haste. President Kennedy later acknowledged that the ability to delay a decision after receipt of the photographic evidence of missile sites was crucial to the *content* of American policy: "If we had had to act on Wednesday [October 17], in the first 24 hours, I don't think probably we would have chosen as prudently as we finally did, the quarantine against the use of offensive weapons."[109]

Policy Options

During the missile crisis, the search for alternatives was intimately related to time pressures; in the words of Arthur Schlesinger, "The deadline defined the strategy."[110] Pressures of time notwithstanding, American policy makers made efforts to prevent premature foreclosure of options. McGeorge Bundy noted that upon receiving the first news of the photographic evidence, "his [Kennedy's] first reaction was that we must make sure, and were we making sure, and would there be evidence on which he could decide that this was in fact really the case."[111] As late as October 18, a series of alternatives was being considered pending more accurate information, and while the decision to institute a blockade was being hammered out, open discussion of the alternatives was encouraged. The President recalled that "though at the beginning there was a much sharper division . . . this was very valuable, because the people involved had particular responsibilities of their own."[112] Another participant in the crisis decision group asserted that President Kennedy, aware that discussion of alternatives in the National Security Council would be more frank in his absence, encouraged the group to hold preliminary meetings without him. Thus, the eventual decision was reached by relatively open and frank discussion.

Six alternative responses emerged from the initial discussions between the President's advisers. Ultimately, the choice narrowed down to the blockade and the air strike. Initially, the option of a sudden air strike against the missile sites had strong support among most of the conferees, including that of the President. An informal vote is reported to have revealed an 11–6 majority in favor of the blockade.[113] The United States Air Force could not guarantee, however, that an air strike would be 100 percent effective. The blockade did not necessarily guarantee success; on the other hand, it did not rule out further measures. After much shifting of positions, the blockade option was selected, partly on the reasoning that "the course we finally adopted had the advantage of permitting other steps, if this one was unsuccessful. In other words, we were starting, in a sense, at a minimum place."[114]

The desire to avoid killing Soviet troops also weighed heavily against the air strike option. The blockade shifted the immediate burden of decision concerning the use of violence to Premier Khrushchev and, should the blockade have proved unsuccessful, it did not preclude later employment of a "much more massive action."[115] By adopting the strategy, no irrevocable decisions on the use of violence had been made and multiple options remained for possible future actions by the United States. At the same time, Soviet leaders were given the time and the opportunity to assess their own choices. Thus, unlike several of the key foreign policy officials in the 1914 crisis, those in October 1962 seemed to perceive a close relationship between their own actions and the options of their adversaries. According to Theodore Sorensen, "We discussed what the Soviet reaction would be to any possible move by the United States, what our reaction with them would have to be to that Soviet reaction, and so on, trying to follow each of those roads to their ultimate conclusion."[116]

American decision makers also displayed a sensitivity for the position and perspective of the adversary, trying to insure that a number of options other than total war or total surrender were available to Soviet leaders. An important advantage of the blockade over other strategies was that it appeared to avoid placing Soviet leaders in that situation. An air strike on the missile bases or invasion of the island would have left Soviet leaders only the alternatives of capitulating to the United States or of counterattacking. In that case, the latter might have seemed the less distasteful course. In disagreeing with General Curtis LeMay's optimistic assessment of the likely Soviet response to air raids on the missile installations, the President asserted, "They, no more than we, can let these things go by without doing something."[117] A blockade, on the other hand, gave the Soviet government a choice between turning back the weapons-bearing ships or running the blockade.

By October 26 it seemed clear that, Khrushchev's earlier threats to the contrary notwithstanding, Soviet ships would not challenge the blockade. Despite the advent of negotiations, however, it was far from certain that the Soviet missiles would be removed from Cuba; indeed, there was ample evidence of an accelerated pace of construction on the launching sites in Cuba that, it was then believed, would be completed by October 30. Thus, the question of further steps to be taken in case the blockade proved insufficient to force withdrawal of all offensive missiles again confronted American leaders. Among the options considered were: tightening the blockade to include all commodities other than food and medicine, increased low-level flights over Cuba for purposes of reconnaissance and harassment, action within Cuba, an air strike, and an invasion. In the meanwhile, the President's brother delivered an ultimatum to the Soviet ambassador, and both direct and indirect bargaining resulted in a settlement.[118] Just before "the most serious meeting ever to take place at the White House"[119] was to have started, Premier Khrushchev agreed to withdraw all offensive missiles from Cuba in exchange for President Kennedy's pledge not to invade Cuba.

Time pressure and the search for alternatives are key elements in crisis decision making. Data from 1914 indicates that these factors did in fact vary as crisis-induced stress increased, and these changes apparently had serious consequences for critical policy decisions. A more impressionistic analysis of the Cuban confrontation suggests that the ability of American decision makers to mitigate some of the adverse consequences of crisis contributed to its eventual peaceful resolution. In many respects, President Kennedy's behavior during the Cuban crisis appeared consciously designed to avert repetition of the 1914 disaster. Indeed, he frequently referred to the decision processes leading up to World War I as a source of negative lessons. Having read Barbara Tuchman's *The Guns of August,* for example, the President said: "I am not going to follow a course which will allow anyone to write a comparable book about this time, *The Missiles of October*. If anybody is around to write after this, they are going to understand that we made every effort to find peace and every effort to give our adversary room to move. I am not going to push the Russians an inch beyond what is necessary."[120] Even when discussing the Cuban missile crisis some weeks after its conclusion, he asserted, "Well now, if you look at the history of this century where World War I really came through a series of misjudgments of the intentions of others . . . it's very difficult to always make judgments here about what the effect will be of our decisions on other countries."[121] Yet the ability of American and Soviet leaders to avoid a nuclear Armageddon in October 1962, is not assurance that even great skill in crisis management will always yield a peaceful solution. As President Kennedy said some months later, referring to the missile crisis, "You can't have too many of those."[122]

CONCLUSION

The approach described here suffers from some clear limitations that should be addressed explicitly. Several objections might be raised about the relevance of the individual stress model of crisis decision making.[123] Does it adequately take into account the executive's prior experience in coping with crises? Will not experience, when combined with selective recruitment and promotion, weed out those who cannot stand "the heat in the kitchen" well before they reach top leadership positions? It is true that individuals differ in abilities to cope with crises and stress. The peak, breaking point and slope of the "inverted U" curve may vary not only according to the complexity of the task, but also across individuals. Thus, the point at which increasing stress begins to hamper cognitive performance, and the rate at which it does so, is not the same for all persons. But only the most optimistic will assume that the correlation between the importance of the executive's role and ability to cope with crisis-induced stress approaches unity. Richard Nixon's behavior during the Watergate episode is a grim reminder to the contrary. Perhaps even more sobering is Robert Kennedy's recollection of the Cuban missile crisis: "That kind of [crisis-induced] pressure does strange things to a human being, even to brilliant, self confident, experienced men. For some it brings out characteristics and strengths that perhaps they never knew they had, and for others, the pressure is too overwhelming."[124]

A second possible objection is that, whereas the emphasis here has been on the individual's cognitive performance under conditions of crisis-induced stress, foreign policy leaders rarely need to face crises alone. They can instead draw upon support and resources from both advisory groups and the larger organizations of which they are a part. This point is valid, but on further examination it is not wholly comforting. There is some evidence that during crises advisory groups may be vulnerable to such malfunctions as "groupthink."[125] For various reasons, including perceived needs for secrecy, easier coordination, and the like, decision-making groups tend to become smaller during crises. There may be, moreover, a tendency to consult others less as the pressure of time increases, as well as to rely more heavily upon those who support the prevailing "wisdom."[126] Finally, leaders differ not only in their "executive styles" (note, for example, the strikingly different problem-solving styles exhibited by presidents Coolidge, Franklin Roosevelt, and Nixon), but also in their abilities to employ advisory groups effectively — that is, in ways that may help them to counteract some of the potentially adverse consequences of crisis. Even the same executive may demonstrate great skill during one crisis and equal ineptitude in another instance. John F. Kennedy's use of advisers during the missile crisis and the Bay of Pigs fiasco are illustrative in this respect.

Some more specific limitations can also be identified. Certainly, the two cases are not representative of all crises in any statistical sense. Thus, the results described here should be viewed as illustrative rather than definitive. Moreover, the analysis focused on very limited aspects of crises, to the exclusion of many other potentially fruitful comparisons. The results suggest that the individual stress model identifies some important elements of crises decision making, but the present analysis has not even fully explored the hypotheses identified in Figure 1. In any case, the rather different findings for the 1914 and 1962 crises raise a series of additional questions — about the necessary and sufficient conditions for avoiding decision-making malfunctions — that have barely been touched upon here. The individual stress model focuses on a few aspects of crisis and consciously excludes others. By posing some questions and not others, we have limited the range of answers. Every model or theoretical perspective does so, with some inevitable losses and, it is to be hoped, at least some commensurate gains. The proper question to ask, then, is not whether this approach serves as a complete model for all crises — the answer is unquestionably negative — but whether it directs our attention to important phenomena that might otherwise remain beyond our purview.

Variants of the individual stress model of crisis decision making have been employed in other studies and, not surprisingly, the pattern of findings is mixed. Lentner's study of State Department officials revealed that only about a third of the respondents felt a reduction in perceived alternatives as a result of crisis.[127] In their impressive study of a dozen international crises — including Fashoda (1898), Bosnia (1908–1909), Munich (1938), Iran (1945–1946), and Berlin (1948–1949) — Snyder and Diesing found no evidence of adverse consequences arising from high stress.[128] Yet they did report that misperception, miscalculation, and other cognitive malfunctions were common occurrences during the crises. Because their research was not designed to test for either the existence or consequences of crisis-induced stress, perhaps it is premature to count this study as definitive evidence against the propositions advanced here. On the other hand, drawing on his research on Israeli behavior during the crises of 1956, 1967, and 1970, Brecher found strong support for the hypotheses that time will be perceived as more salient, that decision makers will become more concerned with the immediate rather than the distant future, and that they will perceive the range of alternatives open to themselves to be narrow.[129] The individual stress model also received strong support in a study designed to test the effects of crisis-induced stress on information processing; in this respect, the convergence of findings from historical and experimental research adds an important element of confidence in the validity of the results and the underlying theory.[130]

These mixed results are not surprising, nor should they occasion premature conclusions about lack of significant research progress or the future of this approach for diplomatic history, theory, or even policy. Other studies could be cited in support of and against the individual stress model, but this does not appear to be the more fruitful way of proceeding. Sustained interest in the effects of crisis-induced stress does not depend on finding that *every* crisis from the historical past resulted in substandard decision-making performance, any more than concern for the consequences of smoking must await evidence that all smokers develop lung cancer. The much more interesting and important questions emerge precisely at the point of recognizing that the dangers and opportunities inherent in crises can give rise to various patterns of coping. At that point our attention is directed to a series of further questions — for example, what are the decision-making structures, personal attributes of leaders, strategies of crisis management, and other variables that are associated with more or less successful coping — that have barely been touched upon in this chapter. It is at this point that we can perhaps begin to appreciate the value of interdisciplinary approaches for the study of crises decision making.

NOTES

1. Richard M. Nixon, *Six Crises* (New York: Doubleday, 1962), p. xvi.
2. Ibid., p. 105.
3. Herman Kahn, *On Escalation: Metaphors and Scenarios* (New York: Praeger, 1965), p. 38.
4. The literature on deterrence is enormous. Recent and indispensable are Alexander L. George and Richard Smoke, *Deterrence in American Foreign Policy: Theory and Practice* (New York: Columbia University Press, 1974); and Patrick M. Morgan, *Deterrence: A Conceptual Analysis* (Beverly Hills, CA: Sage Publications, 1977). For more discussion, see Paul Gordon Lauren's chapter in this book [*Diplomacy: New Approaches in History, Theory, and Policy*] on bargaining theories.
5. Chris Argyris, *Some Causes of Organizational Ineffectiveness within the*

Department of State (Washington, D.C.: Center for International Systems Research, Department of State Publication 8180, 1967), p. 42.

6. Richard E. Neustadt, *Alliance Politics* (New York: Columbia University Press, 1970), p. 116.

7. Charles A. McClelland, quoted in Michael Brecher, "Toward a Theory of International Crisis Behavior," *International Studies Quarterly* 21 (March 1977): 40.

8. Charles A. McClelland, quoted in Charles F. Hermann (ed.), *International Crises: Insights from Behavioral Research* (New York: Free Press, 1972), p. 6.

9. See Leo Hazelwood, John Hayes, and James Brownell, Jr., "Planning for Problems in Crisis Management," *International Studies Quarterly* 21 (March 1977): 78.

10. Charles F. Hermann, "Some Consequences of Crisis Which Limit the Viability of Organizations," *Administrative Science Quarterly* 8 (June 1963): 61–82. This definition has achieved moderately wide acceptance among students of foreign policy crises. For further discussions of the term, see Charles F. Hermann, *Crises in Foreign Policy: A Simulation Analysis* (Indianapolis: Bobbs-Merrill, 1969); Charles F. Hermann, "International Crisis as a Situational Variable," in James N. Rosenau (ed.), *International Politics and Foreign Policy* (New York: Free Press, 1969 ed.), pp. 409–421; James A. Robinson, "Crisis: An Appraisal of Concepts and Theories," in Hermann, *International Crises;* Kent Miller and Ira Iscoe, "The Concept of Crisis: Current Status and Mental Health Implications," *Human Organization* 22 (Fall 1963): 195–201; Glenn H. Snyder and Paul Diesing, *Conflict Among Nations: Bargaining, Decision Making and System in International Crises* (Princeton, NJ: Princeton University Press, 1977); Richard W. Parker, "An Examination of Basic and Applied International Crisis Research," *International Studies Quarterly* 21 (March 1977): 225–246; Raymond Tanter, "Crisis Management: A Critical Review of Academic Literature," *Jerusalem Journal of International Relations* 2 (Fall 1975): 71–101; and Richard G. Head, Frisco W. Short, and Robert C. McFarlane, *Crisis Resolution: Presidential Decision Making in the Mayagüez and Korean Confrontations* (Boulder, CO: Westview Press, 1978).

11. Brecher, "Toward a Theory of International Crisis Behavior," pp. 42–44.

12. Snyder and Diesing, *Conflict Among Nations,* pp. 6–21.

13. Charles F. Hermann and Linda P. Brady, "Alternative Models of International Crisis Behavior," in Hermann, *International Crises,* pp. 281–303. For another typology, see Parker, "An Examination of Basic and Applied International Crisis Research."

14. Irving Janis, *Victims of Groupthink: A Psychological Study of Foreign-Policy Decisions and Fiascoes* (Boston: Houghton Mifflin, 1972).

15. Sidney Verba, "Assumptions of Rationality and Non-rationality in Models of the International System," *World Politics* 14 (October 1961): 93–117.

16. H. O. Wilensky, *Organizational Intelligence* (New York: Basic Books, 1967).

17. See Samuel Williamson's chapter in this book [Lauren, *Diplomacy*], as well as Graham T. Allison, "Conceptual Models and the Cuban Missile Crisis," *American Political Science Review* 63 (1969): 689–718; Graham T. Allison, *Essence of Decision: Explaining the Cuban Missile Crisis* (Boston: Little Brown, 1971); Graham T. Allison and Morton H. Halperin, "Bureaucratic Politics: A Paradigm and Some Policy Implications," *World Politics* 24 (1972, special supplement): 40–79; and Leon V. Sigal, "The 'Rational Policy' Model and the

Formosa Straits Crises," *International Studies Quarterly* 14 (June 1970): 121–156.

18. See, for example, Dina A. Zinnes, Joseph L. Zinnes, and Robert D. McClure, "Hostility in Diplomatic Communication: A Study of the 1914 Crisis," in Hermann, *International Crises*, pp. 139–162; and David C. Schwartz, "Decision-Making in Historical and Simulated Crises," in Hermann, *International Crises*, pp. 167–184.

19. See, for example, Snyder and Diesing, *Conflict Among Nations;* Charles A. McClelland, "The Beginning, Duration and Abatement of International Crisis: Comparisons in Two Conflict Arenas," in Hermann, *International Crises*, pp. 83–105; and Glenn H. Snyder, "Crisis Bargaining," in Hermann, *International Crises*, pp. 217–256.

20. Quincy Wright, *A Study of War* (Chicago: University of Chicago Press, 1965), p. 1272; and Lewis F. Richardson, *Statistics of Deadly Quarrels* (Pittsburgh: Boxwood Press, 1960).

21. Charles A. McClelland, "The Acute International Crisis," *World Politics* 14 (October 1961); Kenneth Waltz, "The Stability of a Bipolar World," *Daedalus* 93 (Summer 1964): 883–884; and Coral Bell, *Conventions of Crisis: A Study in Diplomatic Management* (London: Oxford University Press, 1971), pp. 115–116.

22. Wright, *A Study of War*, p. 1272.

23. McClelland, "The Acute International Crisis," p. 199.

24. Ibid., p. 200. However, constant exposure to crises, especially simultaneous crises, may well result in a setting that is not conducive to rational decision making. On this point, see Wilensky, *Organizational Intelligence.*

25. Thomas C. Schelling, *The Strategy of Conflict* (New York: Oxford University Press, 1963) is a classic study. Less subtle and far more ideological are: Robert Strausz-Hupé et al., *Protracted Conflict* (New York: Harper and Brothers, 1959); as well as the many articles published in the journal *Orbis* by William Kintner, Stefan T. Possony, Chester C. Ward, and others.

26. See, for example, Morgan, *Deterrence;* Philip Green, *Deadly Logic* (Columbus, OH: Ohio State University Press, 1966); Barry R. Schneider, "Danger and Opportunity," unpublished Ph.D. dissertation, Columbia University 1972; and Jack L. Snyder, "Rationality at the Brink: The Role of Cognitive Processes in Failures of Deterrence," *World Politics* 30 (April 1978): 345–365. Useful discussions of various views on these issues may be found in Aaron Wildavsky, "Practical Consequences of the Theoretical Study of Defence Policy," *Public Administration Review* 25 (March 1965): 90–103; Snyder and Diesing, *Conflict Among Nations*, pp. 297–310; and Thomas C. Wiegele, "Models of Stress and Disturbances in Elite Political Behaviors: Psychological Variables and Political Decision-Making," in Robert S. Robins (ed.), *Psychopathology and Political Leadership* (New Orleans, LA: Tulane Studies in Political Science, 1977).

27. Allison, *Essence of Decision;* John D. Steinbruner, *The Cybernetic Theory of Decision* (Princeton, NJ: Princeton University Press, 1974); James M. McCormick, "Evaluating Models of Crisis Behavior: Some Evidence from the Middle East," *International Studies Quarterly* 19 (March 1975): 17–45; Raymond Tanter, *Modelling and Managing International Conflicts: The Berlin Crisis* (Beverly Hills, CA: Sage Publications, 1974); Janice Stein and Raymond Tanter, *Crisis Decision Making: Rationality and Israel's Choices;* and R. G.

Trotter, "The Cuban Missile Crisis: An Analysis of Policy Formulation in Terms of Current Decision Making Theory," unpublished Ph.D. dissertation, University of Pennsylvania, 1971.

28. Alexander L. George, David Hall, and William Simons, *The Limits of Coercive Diplomacy* (Boston: Little, Brown, 1971); Head, Short, and McFarlane, *Crisis Resolution;* Richard Smoke, *War: Controlling Escalation* (Cambridge, MA: Harvard University Press, 1977); Thomas Halper, *Foreign Policy Crises: Appearance and Reality in Decision-Making* (Columbus: Merrill, 1971); Holsti, *Crisis, Escalation, War* (Montreal: McGill-Queens University Press, 1972); Glenn D. Paige, "Comparative Case Analysis of Crisis Decisions: Korea and Cuba," in Hermann, *International Crises,* pp. 41–55; Oran Young, *The Politics of Force: Bargaining During International Crises* (Princeton, NJ: Princeton University Press, 1968); Lawrence S. Falkowski, *Presidents, Secretaries of State, and Crises in U.S. Foreign Relations: A Model and Predictive Analysis* (Boulder, CO: Westview Press, 1978); and Phil Williams, *Crisis Management* (New York: Wiley, 1977).

29. Snyder and Diesing, *Conflict Among Nations.* See also the major crisis research project directed by Michael Brecher, most recently described in his "Toward a Theory of International Crisis Behavior."

30. Davis B. Bobrow, Steve Chan, and John A. Kringen, "Understanding How Others Treat Crisis: A Multimethod Approach," *International Studies Quarterly* 21 (March 1977): 199–223. Assessments of how much progress has in fact been made in crisis research vary widely. Compare, in this respect, the optimistic appraisals of Charles A. McClelland, "The Anticipation of International Crises: Prospects for Theory and Research," *International Studies Quarterly* 21 (March 1977): 15–38, and Robert A. Young, "Perspectives on International Crisis: Introduction," *International Studies Quarterly* 21 (March 1977): 3–14; with the much more critical views expressed in James A. Robinson, "Crises: An Appraisal of Concepts and Theories," in Hermann, *International Crises;* and Gerald W. Hopple and Paul J. Rossa, "International Crisis Analysis: An Assessment of Theory and Research," University of Maryland, Cross-National Crisis Indicators Project, Research Report No. 5, April 1978.

31. Herbert Simon, *Organizations* (New York: Wiley, 1958), p. 138.

32. Somewhat different lists appear in Morgan, *Deterrence,* pp. 102–103; and in Irving Janis and Leon Mann, *Decision-Making* (New York: Free Press, 1977).

33. Figure 1 is an expanded version of a diagram that initially appeared in Ole R. Holsti and Alexander L. George, "The Effects of Stress on the Performance of Foreign Policy-Makers," in Cornelius P. Cotter (ed.), *Political Science Annual* (Indianapolis: Bobbs-Merrill, 1975), VI: 284.

34. Sheldon J. Korchin and Seymour Levine, "Anxiety and Verbal Learning," *Journal of Abnormal and Social Psychology* 54 (March 1957): 234–240.

35. For a further elaboration of this point, see Alexander L. George, *Toward A More Soundly Based Foreign Policy: Making Better Use of Information,* Appendix D, vol. 2, *Report of the Commission on the Organization of the Government for the Conduct of Foreign Policy* (Washington, DC: Government Printing Office, 1975), especially pp. 17–53.

36. Alfred Lowe, "Individual Differences in Reaction to Failure: Modes of Coping with Anxiety and Interference Proneness," *Journal of Abnormal and Social Psychology* 62 (May 1961): 303–308; and Sara B. Kiesler, "Stress, Affilia-

tion and Performance," *Journal of Experimental Research in Personality* 1 (December 1966): 227–235.

37. Sheldon J. Korchin et al., "Visual Discrimination and the Decision Process in Anxiety," *AMA Archive of Neurology and Psychiatry* 78 (1957): 424–438; Robert E. Murphy, "Effects of Threat of Shock, Distraction, and Task Design on Performance," *Journal of Experimental Psychology* 58 (August 1959): 134–141; Harold M. Schroeder, Michael J. Driver, and Siegfried Streufert, *Human Information Processing* (New York: Holt, Rinehart and Winston, 1967); and C. R. Anderson, "Coping Behavior as Intervening Mechanisms in the Inverted-U Stress-Performance Relationship," *Journal of Applied Psychology* 60 (February 1976): 30–34.

38. R. R. Grinker and J. P. Spiegel, *Men Under Stress* (New York: McGraw-Hill, 1945); E. Paul Torrance, "A Theory of Leadership and Interpersonal Behavior Under Stress," in Luigi Petrullo and Bernard M. Bass (eds.), *Leadership and Interpersonal Behavior* (New York: Holt, Rinehart, and Winston, 1961), pp. 100–117; George W. Baker and Dwight W. Chapman (eds.), *Man and Society in Disaster* (New York: Basic Books, 1962); and A. D. Baddeley, "Selective Attention and Performance in Dangerous Environments," *British Journal of Psychology* 63 (1972): 537–546.

39. Sheldon J. Korchin, "Anxiety and Cognition," in Constance Sheerer (ed.), *Cognition: Theory, Research, Promise* (New York: Harper & Row, 1964), p. 63.

40. Charles E. Lindblom, *The Policy-Making Process* (Englewood Cliffs, NJ: Prentice Hall, 1968), p. 22.

41. Fredric Bertram Nalven, "Defense Preference and Perceptual Decision-Making," Ph.D. dissertation, Boston University, Boston, 1961, abstracted in Paul Wasserman and Fred S. Silander, *Decision-Making: An Annotated Bibliography,* Supplement, 1958–1963 (Ithaca: Cornell University Press, 1964), p. 78.

42. Melvin Manis, *Cognitive Processes* (Belmont, Calif.: Wadsworth, 1966), pp. 97–102; and F. P. Kilpatrick, "Problems of Perception in Extreme Situations," in Robert R. Evans (ed.), *Readings in Collective Behavior* (Chicago: Rand McNally, 1969), pp. 168, 171. For relevant historical evidence on this point, see Ernest R. May, *"Lessons" of the Past: The Use and Misuse of History in American Foreign Policy* (New York: Oxford University Press, 1973); and Robert Jervis, *Perception and Misperception in International Politics* (Princeton, NJ: Princeton University Press, 1976).

43. Ralph K. White and Ronald Lippitt, *Autocracy and Democracy: An Experimental Inquiry* (New York: Harper and Brothers, 1960), p. 171.

44. Robert Jervis, "Hypotheses on Misperception," *World Politics* 20 (April 1968): 454–479; and Robert Jervis, *Perception and Misperception.*

45. C. D. Smock, "The Influence of Psychological Stress on the 'Intolerance of Ambiguity,'" *Journal of Abnormal and Social Psychology* 50 (March 1955): 177–182.

46. Thomas Milburn, "The Management of Crisis," in Hermann, *International Crisis,* p. 265.

47. Leo Postman and Jerome S. Bruner, "Perception under Stress," *Psychological Review* 55 (1948): 322.

48. Milburn, "The Management of Crisis."

49. Jerome Bruner, cited in Louis C. Gawthrop, *Bureaucratic Behavior in the Executive Branch* (New York: Free Press, 1969), p. 113.

50. James G. Miller, "Information Input Overload and Psychopathology," *American Journal of Psychiatry* 116 (February 1960): 695–704; James G. Miller, "Information Input Overload," *Self Organizing Systems* (1962, n.p.); Harry B. Williams, "Some Functions of Communication in Crisis Behavior," *Human Organization* 16 (Summer 1957): 15–19; Charles F. Hermann, "Some Consequences of Crisis Which Limit the Viability of Organizations"; and Holsti, *Crisis, Escalation, War*, pp. 82–118.
51. Baddeley, "Selective Attention and Performance in Dangerous Environments."
52. George A. Miller, "The Magical Number Seven Plus or Minus Two: Some Limits on our Capacity for Processing Information," *Psychological Review* 63 (March 1956): 81–97.
53. Karl E. Weick, "Processes of Ramification Among Cognitive Links," in Robert P. Abelson et al. (eds.), *Theories of Cognitive Consistency* (Chicago: Rand McNally, 1968), pp. 516–517; and Jerome E. Singer, "Consistency as a Stimulus Processing Mechanism," in the same volume, pp. 337–342.
54. Theodore C. Sorensen, *Decision-Making in the White House* (New York: Columbia University Press, 1964), p. 38.
55. Samuel I. Cohen and A. G. Mezey, "The Effects of Anxiety on Time Judgment and Time Experience in Normal Persons," *Journal of Neurology, Neurosurgery and Psychiatry* 24 (August 1961): 266–268.
56. Harry B. Williams and Jeannette F. Rayner, "Emergency Medical Services in Disaster," *Medical Annals of the District of Columbia* 25 (1956); Jonas Langer, Seymour Wapner, and Heinz Werner, "The Effects of Danger Upon the Experience of Time," *American Journal of Psychology* 74 (March 1961): 94–97. See also John Cohen, "Psychological Time," *Scientific American* (November 1964): 116–124.
57. Jerome Bruner, Jacequeline J. Goodnow, and George A. Austin, *A Study of Thinking* (New York: Wiley, 1956), p. 147.
58. Abraham S. Luchins, "Mechanization in Problem-Solving," *Psychological Monographs* 54 (1942): whole no. 248; Steinbruner, *The Cybernetic Theory of Decision*.
59. George Usdansky and Loren J. Chapman, "Schizophrenic-like Response in Normal Subjects under Time Pressures," *Journal of Abnormal and Social Psychology* 60 (January 1960): 143–146; Pauline N. Pepinsky and William B. Pavlik, "The Effects of Task Complexity and Time Pressure Upon Team Productivity," *Journal of Applied Psychology* 44 (February 1960): 34–38; N. H. Mackworth and J. F. Mackworth, "Visual Search for Successive Decisions," *British Journal of Psychology* 49 (August 1958): 210–221; Herbert G. Birch, "Motivational Factors in Insightful Problem Solving," *Journal of Comparative Psychology* 38 (October 1945): 295–317; Bruner et al., *A Study of Thinking;* Peter Dubno, "Decision Time Characteristics of Leaders and Group Problem Solving Behavior," *Journal of Social Psychology* 59 (April 1963): 259–282; F. E. Horvath, "Psychological Stress: A Review of Definitions and Experimental Research," *General Systems Yearbook* 4 (1959): 203–230; and Donald R. Hoffeld and S. Carolyn Kent, "Decision Time and Information Use in Choice Situations," *Psychological Reports* 12 (February 1963): 68–70.
60. Robert J. Albers, "Anxiety and Time Perspectives," *Dissertation Abstracts* 26 (February 1966): 4848; and James D. Thompson and Robert W. Hawkes, "Disaster, Community Organization, and Administrative Process," in George

Baker and Dwight Chapman (eds.), *Man and Society in Disaster* (New York: Basic Books, 1962).

61. Korchin, "Anxiety and Cognition," p. 63.
62. See the discussion in Alexander L. George's chapter in this book [Lauren, *Diplomacy*]; George and Smoke, *Deterrence in American Foreign Policy,* pp. 94–97; Sidney Verba, "Some Dilemmas in Comparative Research," *World Politics* 20 (October 1967): 111–127; Bruce M. Russett, "International Behavior Research: Case Studies and Cumulation," in Michael Haas and Henry Kariel (eds.), *Approaches to the Study of Political Science* (Scranton, PA: Chandler, 1970); Smoke, *War: Controlling Escalation;* James N. Rosenau, "Moral Fervor, Systematic Analysis, and Scientific Consciousness in Foreign Policy Research," in Austen Ranney (ed.), *Political Science and Public Policy* (Chicago: Markham, 1968); and Glenn D. Paige, *The Korean Decision: June 24–30, 1950* (New York: Free Press, 1968), pp. 3–18. The latter study is also an important contribution to the study of crisis decision making.
63. Prince Bernhard von Bülow, *Memoirs of Prince von Bülow,* 3 vols. (Boston: Little, Brown, 1932), III: 166; and Alfred von Tirpitz, *My Memoirs* (London: Hurst and Blackett, 1919), p. 280.
64. Further discussions of the 1914 crisis may be found in chapters by Robert Jervis and Samuel Williamson in this book. [Lauren, *Diplomacy*]
65. A detailed discussion of the methods of content analysis used with the 1914 data has appeared in Holsti, *Crisis, Escalation, War,* and very briefly in Melvin Small's chapter in this book. [Lauren, *Diplomacy*]
66. Quoted in Luigi Albertini, *Origins of the War of 1914,* 2 vols. (New York: Oxford University Press, 1953), II: 122.
67. Max Montgelas and Walter Schücking (eds.), *Outbreak of the World War, German Documents Collected by Karl Kautsky* (New York: Oxford University Press, 1924), #48. [Hereafter this source will be cited as Germany.]
68. Great Britain, Foreign Office, *British Documents on the Origins of the War, 1898–1914,* 11 vols., ed. G. P. Gooch and Harold Temperely, vol. 11, *Foreign Office Documents June 28th–August 4th, 1914,* collected by J. W. Headlam-Morely (London: His Majesty's Stationery Office, 1926), #99. [Hereafter cited as Great Britain.]
69. Great Britain, #411.
70. Germany, #343.
71. France, Commission de Publication des documents relatifs aux origines de la guerre, 1914, *Documents Diplomatiques Français (1871–1914),* 3rd series, vols. 10, 11 (Paris: Imprimerie nationale, 1936), #32. [Hereafter cited as France.]
72. Germany, #390.
73. Germany, #433.
74. Germany, #451.
75. France, #305.
76. Germany, #529.
77. France, #401.
78. Winston S. Churchill, *The World Crisis, 1911–1914* (New York: Scribner's, 1928), p. 211.
79. Great Britain, #368, 446.
80. Albertini, *Origins of the War in 1914,* II: 558.
81. Germany, #221.

82. Schelling, *The Strategy of Conflict,* pp. 137–138.
83. Great Britain, #103.
84. Germany, #247.
85. Russian, Komissiia po izdaiiu dokumentov epokhi imperializma, *Mezhdunar-odyne otnosheniia v epokhe imperializma;* dokument 12 arkhivov tsarkogo i vremennogo pravitel'stv 1878–1917, gg. 3d series, vols. 4, 5, (Moscow and Leningrad: Gosudarstvennoe sotsial'no-ekonomicheskoe izdatal'stvo, 1931, 1934), #118. [Hereafter cited as Russia.]
86. Great Britain, #263.
87. Germany, #399.
88. Germany, #480.
89. Germany, #575.
90. France, #38.
91. Great Britain, #252.
92. Russia, #221; Germany, #401.
93. Quoted in Sidney B. Fay, *The Origins of the World War* (New York: Macmillan, 1930 ed.), II: 481.
94. Moltke, *Erinnerungen,* quoted in Virginia Cowles, *The Kaiser* (New York: Harper & Row, 1964), pp. 343–346.
95. Quoted in Fay, *The Origins of the World War,* II: 207.
96. Germany, #474.
97. Germany, #368.
98. Great Britain, #264.
99. Great Britain, #447.
100. Great Britain, #99.
101. Russia, #170.
102. Great Britain, #101.
103. Germany, #395.
104. Quoted in Fay, *The Origins of the World War,* II: 509.
105. The literature on the missile crisis is immense, including memoirs of participants, polemics, descriptive accounts, and explicitly comparative or theoretical studies. Of the latter genre, some of the most interesting are George, Hall, and Simons, *The Limits of Coercive Diplomacy;* George and Smoke, *Deterrence in American Foreign Policy;* Allison, *The Essence of Decision;* Roberta Wohlstetter, "Cuba and Pearl Harbor," *Foreign Affairs* 43 (July 1965): 691–707; Snyder and Diesing, *Conflict Among Nations;* Paige, "Comparative Case Analysis of Crisis Decision: Korea and Cuba"; Young, *The Politics of Force;* Snyder, "Rationality at the Brink"; and Albert and Roberta Wohlstetter, *Controlling the Risks in Cuba,* Adelphi Paper No. 17 (London: International Institute for Strategic Studies, 1965).
106. Douglas Dillon, quoted in Elie Abel, *The Missile Crisis* (Philadelphia: Lippincott, 1966), p. 48.
107. Theodore Sorensen, *Decision-Making in the White House* (New York: Columbia University Press, 1963), p. 31.
108. National Broadcasting Company, "Cuba: The Missile Crisis" (mimeo. transcript, February 9, 1964), p. 12.
109. Columbia Broadcasting System, "Conversation with President Kennedy" (mimeo. transcript, December 17, 1963), pp. 2–3.
110. Arthur M. Schlesinger, Jr., *A Thousand Days* (New York: Houghton Mifflin, 1965), p. 804.

111. NBC, "Cuba," p. 14.
112. CBS, "Conversation with President Kennedy," p. 4.
113. Schlesinger, *A Thousand Days,* p. 808.
114. CBS, "Conversation with President Kennedy," p. 4.
115. Ibid.
116. NBC, "Cuba," p. 17.
117. Quoted in Snyder and Diesing, *Conflict Among Nations,* p. 301.
118. The important role of the ultimatum in settlement of the missile crisis is discussed in more detail by George, Hall, and Simons, *The Limits of Coercive Diplomacy.*
119. NBC, "Cuba," p. 42.
120. Robert F. Kennedy, *Thirteen Days* (New York: Norton, 1969), p. 127.
121. CBS, "Conversation with President Kennedy," p. 3.
122. Theodore Sorensen, *Kennedy* (New York: Harper & Row, 1965), p. 726.
123. Interesting alternative explanations for the outcome in 1914, for example, may be found in Bruce M. Russett, "Cause, Surprise, and No Escape," *Journal of Politics* 24 (February 1962): 3–22; and Lancelot L. Farrar, Jr., "The Limits of Choice: July 1914 Reconsidered," *Journal of Conflict Resolution* 16 (March 1972): 1–24. Other approaches to crisis decision making that have not received attention here include those that emphasize aspects of personality; see, for example, Falkowski, *Presidents, Secretaries of State, and Crisis in U.S. Foreign Relations;* James David Barber, *The Presidential Character* (Englewood Cliffs, NJ: Prentice Hall, 1972); and Thomas M. Mongar, "Personality and Decision-Making: John F. Kennedy in Four Crisis Decisions," *Canadian Journal of Political Science* 2 (June 1962): 200–225. The psychobiological effects of crisis are discussed in Wiegele, "Modes of Stress," and in the same author's "Decision Making in an International Crisis: Some Biological Factors," *International Studies Quarterly* 17 (September 1973): 295–335.
124. Robert F. Kennedy, "Thirteen Days: The Story About How the World Almost Ended," *McCall's* (November 1968) p. 148.
125. Janis, *Victims of Groupthink;* and Roland L. Frye and Thomas M. Stritch, "Effects of Timed vs. Non-timed Discussion Upon Measures of Influence and Change in Small Groups," *Journal of Social Psychology* 63 (June 1964): 139–143.
126. Dean G. Pruitt, "Problem Solving in the Department of State" (unpublished paper, Northwestern University, 1961).
127. Howard H. Lentner, "The Concept of Crisis as Viewed by the U.S. Department of State," in Hermann, *International Crisis,* pp. 112–135.
128. Snyder and Diesing, *Conflict Among Nations.*
129. Michael Brecher, "Research Findings and Theory-Building in Foreign Policy Behavior," in Patrick J. McGowan (ed.), *Sage International Yearbook of Foreign Policy Studies* (Beverly Hills: Sage Publications, 1974), II: 71.
130. Peter Suedfield and Philip Tetlock, "Integrative Complexity of Communications in International Crisis," *Journal of Conflict Resolution* 21 (March 1977): 169–186.

Conceptual Models and the Cuban Missile Crisis

Graham T. Allison

The author presents three models of the foreign policy decision-making process. The first (the rational actor model) tends to dominate the realist perspective. The organizational process and bureaucratic politics models, reflecting what we call a pluralist perspective, raise questions concerning the appropriateness of relying exclusively on the rational actor model to explain foreign policy choices.

The Cuban missile crisis is a seminal event. For thirteen days of October 1962, there was a higher probability that more human lives would end suddenly than ever before in history. Had the worst occurred, the death of 100 million Americans, over 100 million Russians, and millions of Europeans as well would make previous natural calamities and inhumanities appear insignificant. Given the probability of disaster — which President Kennedy estimated as "between 1 out of 3 and even" — our escape seems awesome.[1] This event symbolizes a central, if only partially thinkable, fact about our existence. That such consequences could follow from the choices and actions of national governments obliges students of government as well as participants in governance to think hard about these problems.

Improved understanding of this crisis depends in part on more information and more probing analyses of available evidence. To contribute to these efforts is part of the purpose of this study. But here the missile crisis serves primarily as grist for a more general investigation. This study proceeds from the premise that marked improvement in our understanding of such events depends critically on more self-consciousness about what observers bring to the analysis. What each analyst sees and judges to be important is a function not only of the evidence about what happened but also of the "conceptual lenses" through which he looks at the evidence. The principal purpose of this essay is to explore some of the fundamental

Reprinted by permission of the American Political Science Association from *American Political Science Review* 63 (September 1969): 689–718. A longer version of this paper was presented at the Annual Meeting of the American Political Science Association, September, 1968 (reproduced by the Rand Corporation, P–3919). The paper is part of a larger study, *Essence of Decision: Explaining the Cuban Missile Crisis* (Boston: Little, Brown and Co., 1971). For support in various stages of this work I am indebted to the Institute of Politics in the John F. Kennedy School of Government and the Center for International Affairs, both at Harvard University, the Rand Corporation, and the Council on Foreign Relations. For critical stimulation and advice I am especially grateful to Richard E. Neustadt, Thomas C. Schelling, Andrew W. Marshall, and Elisabeth K. Allison.

assumptions and categories employed by analysts in thinking about problems of governmental behavior, especially in foreign and military affairs.

The general argument can be summarized in three propositions:

1. Analysts think about problems of foreign and military policy in terms of largely implicit conceptual models that have significant consequences for the content of their thought.[2]

Though the present product of foreign policy analysis is neither systematic nor powerful, if one carefully examines explanations produced by analysts, a number of fundamental similarities emerge. Explanations produced by particular analysts display quite regular, predictable features. This predictability suggests a substructure. These regularities reflect an analyst's assumptions about the character of puzzles, the categories in which problems should be considered, the types of evidence that are relevant, and the determinants of occurrences. The first proposition is that clusters of such related assumptions constitute basic frames of reference or conceptual models in terms of which analysts both ask and answer the question: What happened? Why did the event happen? What will happen?[3] Such assumptions are central to the activities of explanation and prediction, for in attempting to explain a particular event, the analyst cannot simply describe the full state of the world leading up to that event. The logic of explanation requires that he single out the relevant, important determinants of the occurrence.[4] Moreover, as the logic of prediction underscores, the analyst must summarize the various determinants as they bear on the event in question. Conceptual models both fix the mesh of the nets that the analyst drags through the material in order to explain a particular action or decision and direct him to cast his net in select ponds, at certain depths, in order to catch the fish he is after.

2. Most analysts explain (and predict) the behavior of national governments in terms of various forms of one basic conceptual model, here entitled the Rational Policy Model (Model 1).[5]

In terms of this conceptual model, analysts attempt to understand happenings as the more or less purposive acts of unified national governments. For these analysts, the point of an explanation is to show how the nation or government could have chosen the action in question, given the strategic problem that it faced. For example, in confronting the problem posed by the Soviet installation of missiles in Cuba, rational policy model analysts attempt to show how this was a reasonable act from the point of view of the Soviet Union, given Soviet strategic objectives.

3. Two "alternative" conceptual models, here labeled an Organizational Process Model (Model II) and a Bureaucratic Politics Model (Model III) provide a base for improved explanation and prediction.

Although the standard frame of reference has proved useful for many purposes, there is powerful evidence that it must be supplemented, if not supplanted, by frames of reference which focus upon the large organizations and political actors involved in the policy process. Model I's implication that important events have important causes, i.e., that monoliths perform large actions for big reasons, must be balanced by an appreciation of the facts (a) that monoliths are black boxes covering various gears and levers in a highly differentiated decision-making structure, and (b) that large acts are the consequences of innumerable and often conflicting smaller actions by individuals at various levels of bureaucratic organizations in the service of a variety of only partially compatible conceptions of national goals, organizational goals, and political objectives. Recent developments in the field of organization theory provide the foundation for the second model. According to this organizational process model, what Model I categorizes as "acts" and "choices" are instead *outputs* of large organizations functioning according to certain regular patterns of behavior. Faced with the problem of Soviet missiles in Cuba, a Model II analyst identifies the relevant organizations and displays the patterns of organizational behavior from which this action emerged. The third model focuses on the internal politics of a government. Happenings in foreign affairs are understood, according to the bureaucratic politics model, neither as choices nor as outputs. Instead, what happens is categorized as *outcomes* of various overlapping bargaining games among players arranged hierarchically in the national government. In confronting the problem posed by Soviet missiles in Cuba, a Model III analyst displays the perceptions, motivations, positions, power, and maneuvers of principal players from which the outcome emerged.[6]

A central metaphor illuminates differences among these models. Foreign policy has often been compared to moves, sequences of moves, and games of chess. If one were limited to observations on a screen upon which moves in the chess game were projected without information as to how the pieces came to be moved, he would assume — as Model I does — that an individual chess player was moving the pieces with reference to plans and maneuvers toward the goal of winning the game. But a pattern of moves can be imagined that would lead the serious observer, after watching several games, to consider the hypothesis that the chess player was not a single individual but rather a loose alliance of semi-independent organizations, each of which moved its set of pieces according to standard operating procedures. For example, movement of separate sets of pieces might proceed in turn, each according to a routine, the king's rook, bishop, and their pawns repeatedly attacking the opponent according to a fixed plan. Furthermore, it is conceivable that the pattern of play would suggest to an observer that a number of distinct players, with distinct objectives but shared power over the pieces, were determining the moves as the resultant of collegial bargaining. For example, the black rook's move might contribute to the loss of a black knight with no comparable gain for the black team, but with the black rook becoming the principal guardian of the "palace" on that side of the board.

The space available does not permit full development and support of such a general argument.[7] Rather, the sections that follow simply sketch each conceptual model, articulate it as an analytic paradigm, and apply it to produce an explanation. But each model is applied to the same event: the U.S. blockade of Cuba during the missile crisis. These "alternative explanations" of the same happening illustrate differences among the models — at work.[8] A crisis decision, by a small group of men in the context of ultimate threat, this is a case of the rational policy model *par excellence*. The dimensions and factors that Models II and III uncover in this case are therefore particularly suggestive. The concluding section of this paper suggests how the three models may be related and how they can be extended to generate predictions.

MODEL I: RATIONAL POLICY

Rational Policy Model Illustrated

Where is the pinch of the puzzle raised by the *New York Times* over Soviet deployment of an antiballistic missile system?[9] The question, as the *Times* states it, concerns the Soviet Union's objective in allocating such large sums of money for this weapon system while at the same time seeming to pursue a policy of increasing détente. In former President Johnson's words, "the paradox is that this [Soviet deployment of an antiballistic missile system] should be happening at a time when there is abundant evidence that our mutual antagonism is beginning to ease."[10] This question troubles people primarily because Soviet antiballistic missile deployment, and evidence of Soviet actions towards détente, when juxtaposed in our implicit model, produce a question. With reference to what objective could the Soviet government have rationally chosen the simultaneous pursuit of these two courses of action? This question arises only when the analyst attempts to structure events as purposive choices of consistent actors.

How do analysts attempt to explain the Soviet emplacement of missiles in Cuba? The most widely cited explanation of this occurrence has been produced by two RAND Sovietologists, Arnold Horelick and Myron Rush.[11] They conclude that "the introduction of strategic missiles into Cuba was motivated chiefly by the Soviet leaders' desire to overcome . . . the existing large margin of U.S. strategic superiority."[12] How do they reach this conclusion? In Sherlock Holmes style, they seize several salient characteristics of this action and use these features as criteria against which to test alternative hypotheses about Soviet objectives. For example, the size of the Soviet deployment, and the simultaneous emplacement of more expensive, more visible intermediate range missiles as well as medium range missiles, it is argued, exclude an explanation of the action in terms of Cuban defense — since that objective could have been secured with a much smaller number of medium range missiles alone. Their explanation presents an argument for one objective that permits interpretation of the details of Soviet behavior as a value-maximizing choice.

How do analysts account for the coming of the First World War? According to Hans Morgenthau, "the first World War had its origin exclusively in the fear of a disturbance of the European balance of power."[13] In the period preceding World War I, the Triple Alliance precariously balanced the Triple Entente. If either power combination could gain a decisive advantage in the Balkans, it would achieve a decisive advantage in the balance of power. "It was this fear," Morgenthau asserts, "that motivated Austria in July 1914 to settle its accounts with Serbia once and for all, and that induced Germany to support Austria unconditionally. It was the same fear that brought Russia to the support of Serbia, and France to the support of Russia."[14] How is Morgenthau able to resolve this problem so confidently? By imposing on the data a "rational outline."[15] The value of this method, according to Morgenthau, is that "it provides for rational discipline in action and creates astounding continuity in foreign policy which makes American, British, or Russian foreign policy appear as an intelligent, rational continuum . . . regardless of the different motives, preferences, and intellectual and moral qualities of successive statesmen."[16]

Stanley Hoffmann's essay, "Restraints and Choices in American Foreign Policy" concentrates, characteristically, on "deep forces": the international system, ideology, and national character — which constitute restraints, limits, and blinders.[17] Only secondarily does he consider decisions. But when explaining particular occurrences, though emphasizing relevant constraints, he focuses on the choices of nations. American behavior in Southeast Asia is explained as a reasonable choice of "downgrading this particular alliance (SEATO) in favor of direct U.S. involvement," given the constraint: "one is bound by one's commitments; one is committed by one's mistakes."[18] More frequently, Hoffmann uncovers confusion or contradiction in the nation's choice. For example, U.S. policy towards underdeveloped countries is explained as "schizophrenic."[19] The method employed by Hoffmann in producing these explanations as rational (or irrational) decisions, he terms "imaginative reconstruction."[20]

Deterrence is the cardinal problem of the contemporary strategic literature. Thomas Schelling's *Strategy of Conflict* formulates a number of propositions focused upon the dynamics of deterrence in the nuclear age. One of the major propositions concerns the stability of the balance of terror: in a situation of mutual deterrence, the probability of nuclear war is reduced not by the "balance" (the sheer equality of the situation) but rather by the *stability* of the balance, i.e., the fact that neither opponent in striking first can destroy the other's ability to strike back.[21] How does Schelling support this proposition? Confidence in the contention stems not from an inductive canvass of a large number of previous cases, but rather from two calculations. In a situation of "balance" but vulnerability, there are values for which a rational opponent could choose to strike first, e.g., to destroy enemy capabilities to retaliate. In a "stable balance" where no matter who strikes first, each has an assured capability to retaliate with unacceptable damage, no rational agent could choose such a course of action (since that choice is effectively equivalent to choosing mutual homicide). Whereas most contemporary strategic thinking is driven *implicitly* by the motor upon which this calculation depends, Schelling explicitly recognizes that strategic theory does assume a model. The foundation of a theory of strategy is, he asserts: "the assumption of rational behavior — not just of intelligent behavior, but of behavior motivated by conscious calculation of advantages, calculation that in turn is based on an explicit and internally consistent value system."[22]

What is striking about these examples from the literature of foreign policy and international relations are the similarities among analysts of various styles when they are called upon to produce explanations. Each assumes that what must be explained is an action, i.e., the realization of some purpose or intention. Each assumes that the actor is the national government. Each assumes that the action is chosen as a calculated response to a strategic problem. For each, explanation consists of showing what goal the government was pursuing in committing the act and how this action was a reasonable choice, given the nation's objectives. This set of assumptions characterizes the rational policy model. The assertion that Model I is the standard frame of reference implies no denial of highly visible differences among the interests of Sovietologists, diplomatic historians, international relations theorists, and strategists. Indeed, in most respects, differences among the work of Hans Morgenthau, Stanley Hoffmann, and Thomas Schelling could not be more pointed. Appreciation of the extent to which each relies predominantly on Model I, however, reveals basic similarities among Morgenthau's method of "rational reenactment," Hoffmann's "imaginative reconstruction," and Schelling's "vicarious problem solving;" family resemblances among Morgenthau's "rational statesman," Hoffmann's "roulette player," and Schelling's "game theorist."[23]

Most contemporary analysts (as well as laymen) proceed predominantly — albeit most often implicitly — in terms of this model when attempting to explain happenings in foreign affairs. Indeed, that occurrences in foreign affairs are the *acts* of *nations* seems so fundamental to thinking about such problems that this underlying model has rarely been recognized: to explain an occurrence in foreign policy simply means to show how the government could have rationally chosen that action.[24] These brief examples illustrate five uses of the model. To prove that most analysts think largely in terms of the rational policy model is not possible. In this limited space it is not even possible to illustrate the range of employment of the framework. Rather, my purpose is to convey to the reader a grasp of the model and a challenge: let the reader examine the literature with which he is most familiar and make his judgment. . . .

Variants of the Rational Policy Model

This paradigm exhibits the characteristics of the most refined version of the rational model. The modern literature of strategy employs a model of this sort. Problems and pressures in the "international strategic marketplace" yield probabilities of occurrence. The international actor, which could be any national actor, is simply a value-maximizing mechanism for getting from the strategic problem to the logical solution. But the explanations and predictions produced by most analysts of foreign affairs depend primarily on variants of this "pure" model. The point of each is the same: to place the action within a value-maximizing framework, given certain constraints. Nevertheless, it may be helpful to identify several variants, each of which might be exhibited similarly as a paradigm. The first focuses upon the national actor and his choice in a particular situation, leading analysts to further constrain the goals, alternatives, and consequences considered. Thus, (1) national propensities or personality traits reflected in an "operational code," (2) concern with certain objectives, or (3) special principles of action, narrow the "goals" or "alternatives" or "consequences" of the paradigm. For example, the Soviet deployment of ABMs is sometimes explained by reference to the Soviet's "defense-mindedness." Or a particular Soviet action is explained as an instance of a special rule of action in the Bolshevik operational code.[25] A second, related, cluster of variants focuses on the individual leader or leadership group as the actor whose preference function is maximized and whose personal (or group) characteristics are allowed to modify the alternatives, consequences, and rules of choice. Explanations of the U.S. involvement in Vietnam as a natural consequence of the Kennedy–Johnson Administration's axioms of foreign policy rely on this variant. A third, more complex variant of the basic model recognizes the existence of several actors within a government, for example, Hawks and Doves or military and civilians, but attempts to explain (or predict) an occurrence by reference to the objectives of the victorious actor. Thus, for example, some revisionist histories of the Cold War recognize the forces of light and the forces of darkness within the U.S. government, but explain American actions as a result of goals and perceptions of the victorious forces of darkness.

Each of these forms of the basic paradigm constitutes a formalization of what analysts typically rely upon implicitly. In the transition from implicit conceptual model to explicit paradigm much of the richness of the best employments of this model has been lost. But the purpose in raising loose, implicit conceptual models to an explicit level is to reveal the basic logic of analysts' activity. Perhaps some of the remaining artificiality that surrounds the statement of the paradigm can be erased by noting a number of the standard additions and modifications employed by analysts who proceed *predominantly* within the rational policy model. First, in the course of a document, analysts shift from one variant of the basic model to another, occasionally appropriating in an *ad hoc* fashion aspects of a situation which are logically incompatible with the basic model. Second, in the course of explaining a number of occurrences, analysts sometimes pause over a particular event about which they have a great deal of information and unfold it in such detail that an impression of randomness is created. Third, having employed other assumptions and categories in deriving an explanation or prediction, analysts will present their product in a neat, convincing rational policy model package. (This accommodation is a favorite of members of the intelligence community whose association with the details of a process is considerable, but who feel that by putting an occurrence in a larger rational framework, it will be more comprehensible to their audience.) Fourth, in attempting to offer an explanation — particularly in cases where a prediction derived from the basic model has failed — the notion of a "mistake" is invoked. Thus, the failure in the prediction of a "missile gap" is written off as a Soviet mistake in not taking advantage of their opportunity. Both these and other modifications permit Model I analysts considerably more variety than the paradigm might suggest. But such accommodations are essentially appendages to the basic logic of these analyses.

The U.S. Blockade of Cuba: A First Cut[26]

The U.S. response to the Soviet Union's emplacement of missiles in Cuba must be understood in strategic terms as simple value-maximizing escalation. American nuclear superiority could be counted on to paralyze Soviet nuclear power; Soviet transgression of the nuclear threshold in response to an American use of lower levels of violence would be wildly irrational since it would mean virtual destruction of the Soviet Communist system and Russian nation. American local superiority was overwhelming: it could be initiated at a low level while threatening with high credibility an ascending sequence of steps short of the nuclear threshold. All that was required was for the United States to bring to bear its strategic and local superiority in such a way that American determination to see the missiles removed would be demonstrated, while at the same time allowing Moscow time and room to retreat without humiliation. The naval blockade — euphemistically named a "quarantine" in order to circumvent the niceties of international law — did just that.

The U.S. government's selection of the blockade followed this logic. Apprised of the presence of Soviet missiles in Cuba, the President assembled an Executive Committee (ExCom) of the National Security

Council and directed them to "set aside all other tasks to make a prompt and intense survey of the dangers and all possible courses of action."[27] This group functioned as "fifteen individuals on our own, representing the President and not different departments."[28] As one of the participants recalls, "The remarkable aspect of those meetings was a sense of complete equality."[29] Most of the time during the week that followed was spent canvassing all the possible tracks and weighing the arguments for and against each. Six major categories of action were considered.

1. Do nothing. U.S. vulnerability to Soviet missiles was no new thing. Since the U.S. already lived under the gun of missiles based in Russia, a Soviet capability to strike from Cuba too made little real difference. The real danger stemmed from the possibility of U.S. over-reaction. The U.S. should announce the Soviet action in a calm, casual manner thereby deflating whatever political capital Khrushchev hoped to make of the missiles.

This argument fails on two counts. First, it grossly underestimates the military importance of the Soviet move. Not only would the Soviet Union's missile capability be doubled and the U.S. early warning system outflanked. The Soviet Union would have an opportunity to reverse the strategic balance by further installations, and indeed, in the longer run, to invest in cheaper, shorter-range rather than more expensive longer-range missiles. Second, the political importance of this move was undeniable. The Soviet Union's act challenged the American President's most solemn warning. If the U.S. failed to respond, no American commitment would be credible.

2. Diplomatic pressures. Several forms were considered: an appeal to the U.N. or O.A.S. for an inspection team, a secret approach to Khrushchev, and a direct approach to Khrushchev, perhaps at a summit meeting. The United States would demand that the missiles be removed, but the final settlement might include neutralization of Cuba, U.S. withdrawal from the Guantanamo base, and withdrawal of U.S. Jupiter missiles from Turkey or Italy.

Each form of the diplomatic approach had its own drawbacks. To arraign the Soviet Union before the U.N. Security Council held little promise since the Russians could veto any proposed action. While the diplomats argued, the missiles would become operational. To send a secret emissary to Khrushchev demanding that the missiles be withdrawn would be to pose untenable alternatives. On the one hand, this would invite Khrushchev to seize the diplomatic initiative, perhaps committing himself to strategic retaliation in response to an attack on Cuba. On the other hand, this would tender an ultimatum that no great power could accept. To confront Khrushchev at a summit would guarantee demands for U.S. concessions, and the analogy between U.S. missiles in Turkey and Russian missiles in Cuba could not be erased.

But why not trade U.S. Jupiters in Turkey and Italy, which the President had previously ordered withdrawn, for the missiles in Cuba? The U.S. had chosen to withdraw these missiles in order to replace them with superior, less vulnerable Mediterranean Polaris submarines. But the middle of the crisis was no time for concessions. The offer of such a deal might suggest to the Soviets that the West would yield and thus tempt them to demand more. It would certainly confirm European suspicions about American willingness to sacrifice European interests when the chips were down. Finally, the basic issue should be kept clear. As the President stated in reply to Bertrand Russell, "I think your attention might well be directed to the burglars rather than to those who have caught the burglars."[30]

3. A secret approach to Castro. The crisis provided an opportunity to separate Cuba and Soviet Communism by offering Castro the alternatives, "split or fall." But Soviet troops transported, constructed, guarded, and controlled the missiles. Their removal would thus depend on a Soviet decision.

4. Invasion. The United States could take this occasion not only to remove the missiles but also to rid itself of Castro. A Navy exercise had long been scheduled in which Marines, ferried from Florida in naval vessels, would liberate the imaginary island of Vieques.[31] Why not simply shift the point of disembarkment? (The Pentagon's foresight in planning this operation would be an appropriate antidote to the CIA's Bay of Pigs!)

Preparations were made for an invasion, but as a last resort, American troops would be forced to confront 20,000 Soviets in the first Cold War case of direct contact between the troops of the super powers. Such brinksmanship courted nuclear disaster, practically guaranteeing an equivalent Soviet move against Berlin.

5. Surgical air strike. The missile sites should be removed by a clean, swift conventional attack. This was the effective counter-action which the attempted deception deserved. A surgical strike would remove the missiles and thus eliminate both the danger that the missiles might become operational and the fear that the Soviets would discover the American discovery and act first.

The initial attractiveness of this alternative was dulled by several difficulties. First, could the strike really be "surgical"? The Air Force could not guarantee destruction of all the missiles.[32] Some might be fired during the attack; some might not have been identified. In order to assure destruction of Soviet and Cuban means of retaliating, what was required was not a surgical but rather a massive attack — of at least 500 sorties. Second, a surprise air attack would of course kill Russians at the missile sites. Pressures on the Soviet Union to retaliate would be so strong that an attack on Berlin or Turkey was highly probable. Third, the key problem with this program was that of advance warning. Could the President of the United States, with his memory of Pearl Harbor and his vision of future U.S. responsibility, order a "Pearl Harbor in reverse"? For 175 years, unannounced Sunday morning attacks had been an anathema to our tradition.[33]

6. Blockade. Indirect military action in the form of a blockade became more attractive as the ExCom dissected the other alternatives. An embargo on military shipments to Cuba enforced by a naval blockade was not without flaws, however. Could the U.S. blockade Cuba without inviting Soviet reprisal in Berlin? The likely solution to joint blockades would be the lifting of both blockades, restoring the new *status quo,* and allowing the Soviets additional time to complete the missiles. Second, the possible consequences of the blockade resembled the drawbacks which disqualified the air strike. If Soviet ships did not stop, the United States would be forced to fire the first shot, inviting retaliation. Third, a blockade would deny the traditional freedom of the seas demanded by several of our close allies and might be held illegal, in violation of the U.N. Charter and international law, unless the United States could obtain a two-thirds vote in the O.A.S. Finally, how could a blockade be related to the problem, namely, some 75 missiles on the island of Cuba, approaching operational readiness daily? A blockade offered the Soviets a spectrum of delaying tactics with which to buy time to complete the missile installations. Was a *fait accompli* not required?

In spite of these enormous difficulties the blockade had comparative advantages: (1) It was a middle course between inaction and attack, aggressive enough to communicate firmness of intention, but nevertheless not so precipitous as a strike. (2) It placed on Khrushchev the burden of choice concerning the next step. He could avoid a direct military clash by keeping his ships away. His was the last clear chance. (3) No possible military confrontation could be more acceptable to the U.S. than a naval engagement in the Caribbean. (4) This move permitted the U.S., by flexing its conventional muscle, to exploit the threat of subsequent nonnuclear steps in each of which the U.S. would have significant superiority.

Particular arguments about advantages and disadvantages were powerful. The explanation of the American choice of the blockade lies in a more general principle, however. As President Kennedy stated in drawing the moral of the crisis:

> Above all, while defending our own vital interests, nuclear powers must avert those confrontations which bring an adversary to a choice of either a humiliating retreat or a nuclear war. To adopt that kind of course in the nuclear age would be evidence only of the bankruptcy of our policy—of a collective death wish for the world.[34]

The blockade was the United States' only real option.

MODEL II: ORGANIZATIONAL PROCESS

For some purposes, governmental behavior can be usefully summarized as action chosen by a unitary, rational decisionmaker: centrally controlled, completely informed, and value maximizing. But this simplification must not be allowed to conceal the fact that a "government" consists of a conglomerate of semi-feudal, loosely allied organizations, each with a substantial life of its own. Government leaders do sit formally, and to some extent in fact, on top of this conglomerate. But governments perceive problems through organizational sensors. Governments define alternatives and estimate consequences as organizations process information. Governments act as these organizations enact routines. Government behavior can therefore be understood according to a second conceptual model, less as deliberate choice of leaders and more as *outputs* of large organizations functioning according to standard patterns of behavior.

To be responsive to a broad spectrum of problems, governments consist of large organizations among which primary responsibility for particular areas is divided. Each organization attends to a special set of problems and acts in quasi-independence on these problems. But few important problems fall exclusively within the domain of a single organization. Thus government behavior relevant to any important problem reflects the independent output of several organizations, partially coordinated by government leaders. Government leaders can substantially disturb, but not substantially control, the behavior of these organizations.

To perform complex routines, the behavior of large numbers of individuals must be coordinated. Coordination requires standard operating procedures: rules according to which things are done. Assured capability for reliable performance of action that depends upon the behavior of hundreds of persons requires established "programs." Indeed, if the eleven members of a football team are to perform adequately on any particular down, each player must not "do what he thinks needs to be done" or "do what the quarterback tells him to do." Rather, each player must perform the maneuvers specified by a previously established play which the quarterback has simply called in this situation.

At any given time, a government consists of *existing* organizations, each with a *fixed* set of standard operating procedures and programs. The behavior of these organizations — and consequently of the government — relevant to an issue in any particular instance is, therefore, determined primarily by routines established in these organizations prior to that instance. But organizations do change. Learning occurs gradually, over time. Dramatic organizational change occurs in response to major crises. Both learning and change are influenced by existing organizational capabilities.

Borrowed from studies of organizations, these loosely formulated propositions amount simply to *tendencies*. Each must be hedged by modifiers like "other things being equal" and "under certain conditions." In particular instances, tendencies hold—more or less. In specific situations, the relevant question is: more or less? But this is as it should be. For, on the one hand, "organizations" are no more homogeneous a class than "solids." When scientists tried to generalize about "solids," they achieved similar results. Solids tend to expand when heated, but some do and some don't. More adequate categorization of the various elements now lumped under the rubric "organizations" is thus required. On the other hand, the behavior of particular organizations seems considerably more complex than the behavior of solids. Additional information about a particular organization is required for further specification of the tendency statements. In spite of these two caveats, the characterization of government action as organizational output differs distinctly from Model I. Attempts to understand problems of foreign affairs in terms of this frame of reference should produce quite different explanations. . . . [35]

The U.S. Blockade of Cuba: A Second Cut

Organizational Intelligence. At 7:00 P.M. on October 22, 1962, President Kennedy disclosed the American discovery of the presence of Soviet strategic missiles in Cuba, declared a "strict quarantine on all offensive military equipment under shipment to Cuba," and demanded that "Chairman Khrushchev halt and eliminate this clandestine, reckless, and provocative threat to world peace."[36] This decision was reached at the pinnacle of the U.S. Government after a critical week of deliberation. What initiated that precious week were photographs of Soviet missile sites in Cuba taken on October 14. These pictures might not have been taken until a week later. In that case, the President speculated, "I don't think probably we would have chosen as prudently as we finally did."[37] U.S. leaders might have received this information three weeks earlier— if a U-2 had flown over San Cristobal in the last week of September.[38] What determined the context in which American leaders came to choose the blockade was the discovery of missiles on October 14.

There has been considerable debate over alleged American "intelligence failures" in the Cuban missile crisis.[39] But what both critics and defenders have neglected is the fact that the discovery took place on October 14, rather than three weeks earlier or a week later, as a consequence of the established routines and procedures of the organizations which constitute the U.S. intelligence community. These organizations were neither more nor less successful than they had been the previous month or were to be in the months to follow.[40]

The notorious "September estimate," approved by the United States Intelligence Board (USIB) on September 19, concluded that the Soviet Union would not introduce offensive missiles into Cuba.[41] No U-2 flight was directed over the western end of Cuba (after September 5) before October 4.[42] No U-2 flew over the western end of Cuba until the flight that discovered the Soviet missiles on October 14.[43] Can these "failures" be accounted for in organizational terms?

On September 19 when USIB met to consider the question of Cuba, the "system" contained the following information: (1) shipping intelligence had noted the arrival in Cuba of two large-hatch Soviet lumber ships, which were riding high in the water; (2) refugee reports of countless sightings of missiles, but also a report that Castro's private pilot, after a night of drinking in Havana, had boasted: "We will fight to the death and perhaps we can win because we have everything, including atomic weapons"; (3) a sighting by a CIA agent of the rear profile of a strategic missile; (4) U-2 photos produced by flights of August 29, September 5 and 17 showing the construction of a number of SAM sites and other defensive missiles.[44] Not all of this information was on the desk of the estimators, however. Shipping intelligence experts noted the fact that large-hatch ships were riding high in the water and spelled out the inference: the ships must be carrying "space consuming" cargo.[45] These facts were carefully included in the catalogue of intelligence concerning shipping. For experts sensitive to the Soviets' shortage of ships, however, these facts carried no special signal. The refugee report of Castro's private pilot's remark had been received at Opa Locka, Florida, along with vast reams of inaccurate reports generated by the refugee community. This report and a thousand others had to be checked and compared before being sent to Washington. The two weeks required for initial processing could have been shortened by a large increase in resources, but the yield of this source was already quite marginal. The CIA agent's sighting of the rear profile of a strategic missile had occurred on September 12: transmission time from agent sighting to arrival in Washington typically took 9 to 12 days. Shortening this transmission time would impose severe cost in terms of danger to sub-agents, agents, and communication networks.

On the information available, the intelligence chiefs who predicted that the Soviet Union would not introduce offensive missiles into Cuba made a reasonable and defensible judgment.[46] Moreover, in the light of the fact that these organizations were gathering intelligence not only about Cuba but about potential occurrences in all parts of the world, the informational base available to the estimators involved nothing out of the ordinary. Nor, from an organizational perspective, is there anything startling about the gradual accumulation of evidence that led to the formulation of the hypothesis that the Soviets were installing missiles in Cuba and the decision on October 4 to direct a special flight over western Cuba.

The ten-day delay between that decision and the flight is another organizational story.[47] At the October 4 meeting, the Defense Department took the opportunity to raise an issue important to its concerns. Given the increased danger that a U-2 would be downed, it would be better if the pilot were an officer in uniform rather than a CIA agent. Thus the Air Force should assume responsibility for U-2 flights over Cuba. To the contrary, the CIA argued that this was an intelligence operation and thus within the CIA's jurisdiction. Moreover, CIA U – 2's had been modified in certain ways which gave them advantages over Air Force U – 2's in averting Soviet SAM's. Five days passed while the State Department pressed for less risky alternatives such as drones and the Air Force (in Department of Defense guise) and CIA engaged in territorial disputes. On October 9 a flight plan over San Cristobal was approved by COMOR, but to the CIA's dismay, Air Force pilots rather than CIA agents would take charge of the mission. At this point details become sketchy, but several members of the intelligence community have speculated that an Air Force pilot in an Air Force U – 2 attempted a high altitude overflight on October 9 that "flamed out", i.e., lost power, and thus had to descend in order to restart its engine. A second round between Air Force and CIA followed, as a result of which Air Force pilots were trained to fly CIA U – 2's. A successful overflight took place on October 14.

This ten-day delay constitutes some form of "failure." In the face of well-founded suspicions concerning offensive Soviet missiles in Cuba that posed a critical threat to the United States' most vital interest, squabbling between organizations whose job it is to produce this information seems entirely inappropriate. But for each of these organizations, the question involved the issue: "*Whose* job was it to be?" Moreover, the issue was not simply, which organization would control U – 2 flights over Cuba, but rather the broader issue of ownership of U – 2 intelligence activities — a very long standing territorial dispute. Thus though this delay was in one sense a "failure," it was also a nearly inevitable consequence of two facts: many jobs do not fall neatly into precisely defined organizational jurisdictions; and vigorous organizations are imperialistic.

Organizational Options. Deliberations of leaders in ExCom meetings produced broad outlines of alternatives. Details of these alternatives and blueprints for their implementation had to be specified by the organizations that would perform these tasks. These organizational outputs answered the question: What, specifically, *could* be done?

Discussion in the ExCom quickly narrowed the live options to two: an air strike and a blockade. The choice of the blockade instead of the air strike turned on two points: (1) the argument from morality and tradition that the United States could not perpetrate a "Pearl Harbor in reverse"; (2) the belief that a "surgical" air strike was impossible.[48] Whether the United States *might* strike first was a question not of capability but of morality. Whether the United States *could* perform the surgical strike was a factual question concerning capabilities. The majority of the members of the ExCom, including the President, initially preferred the air strike.[49] What effectively foreclosed this option, however, was the fact that the air strike they wanted could not be chosen with high confidence of success.[50] After having tentatively chosen the course of prudence — given that the surgical air strike was not an option — Kennedy reconsidered. On Sunday morning, October 21, he called the Air Force experts to a special meeting in his living quarters where he probed once more for the option of a *"surgical"* air strike.[51] General Walter C. Sweeny, Commander of Tactical Air Forces, asserted again that the Air Force could guarantee no higher than ninety percent effectiveness in a surgical air strike.[52] That "fact" was false.

The air strike alternative provides a classic case of military estimates. One of the alternatives outlined in the ExCom was named "air strike." Specification of the details of this alternative was delegated to the Air Force. Starting from an existing plan for massive U.S. military action against Cuba (prepared for contingencies like a response to a Soviet Berlin grab), Air Force estimators produced an attack to guarantee success.[53] This plan called for extensive bombardment of all missile sites, storage depots, airports, and in deference to the Navy, the artillery batteries opposite the naval base at Guantanamo.[54] Members of the ExCom repeatedly expressed bewilderment at military estimates of the number of sorties required, likely casualties, and collateral damage. But the "surgical" air strike that the political leaders had in mind was never carefully examined during the first week of the crisis. Rather, this option was simply excluded on the grounds that since the Soviet MRBM's in Cuba were classified "mobile" in U.S. manuals, extensive bombing was required. During the second week of the crisis, careful examination revealed that the missiles were mobile, in the sense that small houses are mobile: that is, they could be moved and reassembled in 6 days. After the missiles were reclassified "movable" and detailed plans for surgical air strikes specified, this action was added to the list of live options for the end of the second week.

Organizational Implementation. ExCom members separated several types of blockade: offensive weapons only, all armaments, and all strategic goods including POL (petroleum, oil and lubricants). But the "details" of the operation were left to the Navy. Before the President announced the blockade on Monday evening, the first stage of the Navy's blueprint was in motion, and a problem loomed on the horizon.[55] The Navy had a detailed plan for the blockade. The President had several less precise but equally determined notions concerning what should be done, when and how. For the Navy the issue was one of effective implementation of the Navy's blockade — without the meddling and interference of political leaders. For the President, the problem was to pace and manage events in such a way that the Soviet leaders would have time to see, think, and blink.

A careful reading of available sources uncovers an instructive incident. On Tuesday, the British Ambassador, Ormsby – Gore, after having attended a briefing on the details of the blockade, suggested to the President that the plan for intercepting Soviet ships far out of reach of Cuban jets did not facilitate Khrushchev's hard decision.[56] Why not make the interception much closer to Cuba and thus give the Russian leader more time? According to the public account and the recollection of a number of individuals involved, Kennedy "agreed immediately, called McNamara, and over emotional Navy protest, issued the appropriate instructions."[57] As Sorensen records, "in a sharp clash with the Navy, he made certain his will prevailed."[58] The Navy's plan for the blockade was thus changed by drawing the blockade much closer to Cuba.

A serious organizational orientation makes one suspicious of this account. More careful examination of the available evidence confirms these suspicions, though alternative accounts must be somewhat speculative. According to the public chronology, a quarantine drawn close to Cuba became effective on Wednesday morning, the first Soviet ship was contacted on Thursday morning, and the first boarding of a ship occurred on Friday. According to the statement by the Department of Defense, boarding of the *Marcula* by a party from the *John R. Pierce* "took place at 7:50 A.M., E.D.T., 180 miles northeast of Nassau."[59] The *Marcula* had been trailed since about 10:30 the previous evening.[60] Simple calculations suggest that the *Pierce* must have been stationed along the Navy's original arc which extended 500 miles out to sea from Cape Magsi, Cuba's eastern most tip.[61] The blockade line was *not* moved as the President ordered, and the accounts report.

What happened is not entirely clear. One can be certain, however, that Soviet ships passed through the line along which American destroyers had posted themselves before the official "first contact" with the Soviet ship. On October 26 a Soviet tanker arrived in Havana and was honored by a dockside rally for "running the blockade." Photographs of this vessel show the name *Vinnitsa* on the side of the vessel in Cyrillic letters.[62] But according to the official U.S. position, the first tanker to pass through the blockade was the *Bucharest*, which was hailed by the Navy on the morning of October 25. Again simple mathematical calculation excludes the possibility of the *Bucharest* and the *Vinnitsa* were the same ship. It seems probable that the Navy's resistance to the President's order that the blockade be drawn in closer to Cuba forced him to allow one or several Soviet ships to pass through the blockade after it was officially operative.[63]

This attempt to leash the Navy's blockade had a price. On Wednesday morning, October 24, what the President had been awaiting occurred. The 18 dry cargo ships heading towards the quarantine stopped dead in the water. This was the occasion of Dean Rusk's remark, "We are eyeball to eyeball and I think the other fellow just blinked."[64] But the Navy had another interpretation. The ships had simply stopped to pick up Soviet submarine escorts. The President became quite concerned lest the Navy — already riled because of Presidential meddling in its affairs — blunder into an incident. Sensing the President's fears, McNamara became suspicious of the Navy's procedures and routines for making the first interception. Calling on the Chief of Naval Operations in the Navy's inner sactum, the Navy Flag Plot, McNamara put his questions harshly.[65] Who would make the first interception? Were Russian-speaking officers on board? How would submarines be dealt with? At one point McNamara asked Anderson what he would do if a Soviet ship's captain refused to answer questions about his cargo. Picking up the Manual of Navy Regulations the Navy man waved it in McNamara's face and shouted, "It's all in there." To which McNamara replied, "I don't give a damn what John Paul Jones would have done; I want to know what you are going to do now."[66] The encounter ended on Anderson's remark: "Now, Mr. Secretary, if you and your Deputy will go back to your office the Navy will run the blockade."[67]

MODEL III: BUREAUCRATIC POLITICS

The leaders who sit on top of organizations are not a monolithic group. Rather, each is, in his own right, a player in a central, competitive game. The name of the game is bureaucratic politics: bargaining along regularized channels among players positioned hierarchically within the government. Government behavior can thus be understood according to the third conceptual model not as organizational outputs, but as outcomes of bargaining games. In contrast with Model I, the bureaucratic politics model sees no unitary actor but rather many actors as players, who focus not on a single strategic issue but on many diverse intra-national problems as well, in terms of no consistent set of strategic objectives but rather according to various conceptions of national, organizational, and personal goals, making government decisions not by rational choice but by the pulling and hauling that is politics.

The apparatus of each national government constitutes a complex arena for the intra-national game. Political leaders at the top of this apparatus plus the men who occupy positions on top of the critical organizations form the circle of central players. Ascendancy to this circle assures some independent standing. The necessary decentralization of decisions required for action on the broad range of foreign policy problems guarantees that each player has considerable discretion. Thus power is shared.

The nature of problems of foreign policy permits fundamental disagreement among reasonable men concerning what ought to be done. Analyses yield conflicting recommendations. Separate responsibilities laid on the shoulders of individual personalities encourage differences in perceptions and priorities. But the issues are of first order importance. What the nation does really matters. A wrong choice could mean irreparable damage. Thus responsible men are obliged to fight for what they are convinced is right.

Men share power. Men differ concerning what must be done. The differences matter. This milieu necessitates that policy be resolved by politics. What the nation does is sometimes the result of the triumph of one group over others. More often, however, different groups pulling in different directions yield a resultant distinct from what anyone intended. What moves the chess pieces is not simply the reasons which support a course of action, nor the routines of organizations which enact an alternative, but the power and skill of proponents and opponents of the action in question.

This characterization captures the thrust of the bureaucratic politics orientation. If problems of foreign policy arose as discreet issues, and decisions were determined one game at a time, this account would suffice. But most "issues," e.g., Vietnam or the proliferation of nuclear weapons, emerge piecemeal, over time, one lump in one context, a second in another. Hundreds of issues compete for players' attention every day. Each player is forced to fix upon his issues for that day, fight them on their own terms, and rush on to the next. Thus the character of emerging issues and the pace at which the game is played converge to yield government "decisions" and "actions" as collages. Choices by one player, outcomes of minor games, outcomes of central games, and "foul-ups" — these pieces, when stuck to the same canvas, constitute government behavior relevant to an issue.

The concept of national security policy as political outcome contradicts both public imagery and academic orthodoxy. Issues vital to national security, it is said, are too important to be settled by political games. They must be "above" politics. To accuse someone of "playing politics with national security" is a most serious charge. What public conviction demands, the academic penchant for intellectual elegance reinforces. Internal politics is messy; moreover, according to prevailing doctrine, politicking lacks intellectual content. As such, it constitutes gossip for journalists rather than a subject for serious investigation. Occasional memoirs, anecdotes in historical accounts, and several detailed case studies to the contrary, most of the literature of foreign policy avoids bureaucratic politics. The gap between academic literature and the experience of participants in government is nowhere wider than at this point. . . .

The U.S. Blockade of Cuba: A Third Cut

The Politics of Discovery. A series of overlapping bargaining games determined both the *date* of discovery of the Soviet missiles and the *impact* on this discovery on the Administration. An explanation of the politics of the discovery is consequently a considerable piece of the explanation of the U.S. blockade.

Cuba was the Kennedy Administration's "political Achilles' heel."[68] The months preceding the crisis were also months before the Congressional elections, and the Republican Senatorial and Congressional Campaign Committee had announced that Cuba would be "the dominant issue of the 1962 campaign."[69] What the administration billed as a "more positive and indirect approach of isolating Castro from developing, democratic Latin America," Senators Keating, Goldwater, Capehart, Thurmond, and others attacked as a "do-nothing" policy.[70] In statements on the floor of the House and Senate, campaign speeches across the country, and interviews and articles carried by national news media, Cuba—particularly the Soviet program of increased arms aid—served as a stick for stirring the domestic political scene.[71]

These attacks drew blood. Prudence demanded a vigorous reaction. The President decided to meet the issue head-on. The Administration mounted a forceful campaign of denial designed to discredit critics' claims. The President himself manned the front line of this offensive, though almost all Administration officials participated. In his news conference on August 19, President Kennedy attacked as "irresponsible" calls for an invasion of Cuba, stressing rather "the totality of our obligations" and promising to "watch what happens in Cuba with the closest attention."[72] On September 4, he issued a strong statement denying any provocative Soviet action in Cuba.[73] On September 13 he lashed out at "loose talk" calling for an invasion of Cuba.[74] The day before the flight of the U-2 which discovered the missiles, he campaigned in Capehart's Indiana against those "self-appointed generals and admirals who want to send someone else's sons to war."[75]

On Sunday, October 14, just as a U-2 was taking the first pictures of Soviet missiles, McGeorge Bundy was asserting:

I *know* that there is no present evidence, and I think that there is no present likelihood that the Cuban government and the Soviet government would, in combination, attempt to install a major offensive capability.[76]

In this campaign to puncture the critics' charges, the Administration discovered that the public needed positive slogans. Thus, Kennedy fell into a tenuous semantic distinction between "offensive" and "defensive" weapons. This distinction originated in his September 4 statement that there was no evidence of "offensive ground to ground missiles" and warned "were it to be otherwise, the gravest issues would arise."[77] His September 13 statement turned on this distinction between "defensive" and "offensive" weapons and announced a firm commitment to action if the Soviet Union attempted to introduce the latter into Cuba.[78] Congressional committees elicited from administration officials testimony which read this distinction and the President's commitment into the *Congressional Record.*[79]

What the President least wanted to hear, the CIA was most hesitant to say plainly. On August 22 John McCone met privately with the President and voiced suspicions that the Soviets were preparing to introduce offensive missiles into Cuba.[80] Kennedy heard this as what it was: the suspicion of a hawk. McCone left Washington for a month's honeymoon on the Riviera. Fretting at Cap Ferrat, he bombarded his deputy, General Marshall

Carter, with telegrams, but Carter, knowing that McCone had informed the President of his suspicions and received a cold reception, was reluctant to distribute these telegrams outside the CIA.[81] On September 9 a U-2 "on loan" to the Chinese Nationalists was downed over mainland China.[82] The Committee on Overhead Reconnaissance (COMOR) convened on September 10 with a sense of urgency.[83] Loss of another U-2 might incite world opinion to demand cancellation of U-2 flights. The President's campaign against those who asserted that the Soviets were acting provocatively in Cuba had begun. To risk downing a U-2 over Cuba was to risk chopping off the limb on which the President was sitting. That meeting decided to shy away from the western end of Cuba (where SAMs were becoming operational) and modify the flight pattern of the U-2s in order to reduce the probability that a U-2 would be lost.[84] USIB's unanimous approval of the September estimate reflects similar sensitivities. On September 13 the President had asserted that there were no Soviet offensive missiles in Cuba and committed his Administration to act if offensive missiles were discovered. Before Congressional committees, Administration officials were denying that there was any evidence whatever of offensive missiles in Cuba. The implications of a National Intelligence estimate which concluded that the Soviets were introducing offensive missiles into Cuba were not lost on the men who constituted America's highest intelligence assembly.

The October 4 COMOR decision to direct a flight over the western end of Cuba in effect "overturned" the September estimate, but without officially raising that issue. The decision represented McCone's victory for which he had lobbied with the President before the September 10 decision, in telegrams before the September 19 estimate, and in person after his return to Washington. Though the politics of the intelligence community is closely guarded, several pieces of the story can be told.[85] By September 27, Colonel Wright and others in DIA believed that the Soviet Union was placing missiles in the San Cristobal area.[86] This area was marked suspicious by the CIA on September 29 and certified top priority on October 3. By October 4 McCone had the evidence required to raise the issue officially. The members of COMOR heard McCone's argument, but were reluctant to make the hard decision he demanded. The significant probability that a U-2 would be downed made overflight of western Cuba a matter of real concern.[87]

The Politics of Issues. The U-2 photographs presented incontrovertible evidence of Soviet offensive missiles in Cuba. This revelation fell upon politicized players in a complex context. As one high official recalled, Khrushchev had caught us "with our pants down." What each of the central participants saw, and what each did to cover both his own and the Administration's nakedness, created the spectrum of issues and answers.

At approximately 9:00 A.M., Tuesday morning, October 16, McGeorge

Bundy went to the President's living quarters with the message: "Mr. President, there is now hard photographic evidence that the Russians have offensive missiles in Cuba."[88] Much has been made of Kennedy's "expression of surprise,"[89] but "surprise" fails to capture the character of his initial reaction. Rather, it was one of startled anger, most adequately conveyed by the exclamation: "He can't do that to *me!*"[90] In terms of the President's attention and priorities at that moment, Khrushchev had chosen the most unhelpful act of all. Kennedy had staked his full Presidential authority on the assertion that the Soviets would not place offensive weapons in Cuba. Moreover, Khrushchev had assured the President through the most direct and personal channels that he was aware of the President's domestic political problem and that nothing would be done to exacerbate this problem. The Chairman had *lied* to the President. Kennedy's initial reaction entailed action. The missiles must be removed.[91] The alternatives of "doing nothing" or "taking a diplomatic approach" could not have been less relevant to *his* problem.

These two tracks — doing nothing and taking a diplomatic approach — were the solutions advocated by two of his principal advisors. For Secretary of Defense McNamara, the missiles raised the spectre of nuclear war. He first framed the issue as a straightforward strategic problem. To understand the issue, one had to grasp two obvious but difficult points. First, the missiles represented an inevitable occurrence: narrowing of the missile gap. It simply happened sooner rather than later. Second, the United States could accept this occurrence since its consequences were minor: "seven-to-one missile 'superiority,' one-to-one missile 'equality,' one-to-seven missile 'inferiority' — the three postures are identical." McNamara's statement of this argument at the first meeting of the ExCom was summed up in the phrase, "a missile is a missile."[92] It makes no great difference," he maintained, "whether you are killed by a missile from the Soviet Union or Cuba."[93] The implication was clear. The United States should not initiate a crisis with the Soviet Union, risking a significant probability of nuclear war over an occurrence which had such small strategic implications.

The perceptions of McGeorge Bundy, the President's Assistant for National Security Affairs, are the most difficult of all to reconstruct. There is no question that he initially argued for a diplomatic track.[94] But was Bundy laboring under his acknowledged burden of responsibility in Cuba I? Or was he playing the role of devil's advocate in order to make the President probe his own initial reaction and consider other options?

The President's brother, Robert Kennedy, saw most clearly the political wall against which Khrushchev had backed the President. But he, like McNamara, saw the prospect of nuclear doom. Was Khrushchev going to force the President to an insane act? At the first meeting of the ExCom, he scribbled a note, "Now I know how Tojo felt when he was planning Pearl Harbor."[95] From the outset he searched for an alternative that would prevent the air strike.

The initial reaction of Theodore Sorensen, the President's Special Counsel and "alter ego," fell somewhere between that of the President and his brother. Like the President, Sorensen felt the poignancy of betrayal. If the President had been the architect of the policy which the missiles punctured, Sorensen was the draftsman. Khrushchev's deceitful move demanded a strong counter-move. But like Robert Kennedy, Sorensen feared lest the shock and disgrace lead to disaster.

To the Joint Chiefs of Staff the issue was clear. *Now* was the time to do the job for which they had prepared contingency plans. Cuba I had been badly done; Cuba II would not be. The missiles provided the *occasion* to deal with the issue: cleansing the Western Hemisphere of Castro's Communism. As the President recalled on the day the crisis ended, "An invasion would have been a mistake — a wrong use of our power. But the military are mad. They wanted to do this. It's lucky for us that we have McNamara over there."[96]

McCone's perceptions flowed from his confirmed prediction. As the Cassandra of the incident, he argued forcefully that the Soviets had installed the missiles in a daring political probe which the United States must meet with force. The time for an air strike was now.[97]

The Politics of Choice. The process by which the blockade emerged is a story of the most subtle and intricate probing, pulling, and hauling; leading, guiding, and spurring. Reconstruction of this process can only be tentative. Initially the President and most of his advisers wanted the clean, surgical air strike. On the first day of the crisis, when informing Stevenson of the missiles, the President mentioned only two alternatives: "I suppose the alternatives are to go in by air and wipe them out, or to take other steps to render them inoperable."[98] At the end of the week a sizeable minority still favored an air strike. As Robert Kennedy recalled: "The fourteen people involved were very significant. . . . If six of them had been President of the U.S., I think that the world might have been blown up."[99] What prevented the air strike was a fortuitous coincidence of a number of factors — the absence of any one of which might have permitted that option to prevail.

First, McNamara's vision of holocaust set him firmly against the air strike. His initial attempt to frame the issue in strategic terms struck Kennedy as particularly inappropriate. Once McNamara realized that the name of the game was a strong response, however, he and his deputy Gilpatric chose the blockade as a fallback. When the Secretary of Defense — whose department had the action, whose reputation in the Cabinet was unequaled, in whom the President demonstrated full confidence — marshalled the arguments for the blockade and refused to be moved, the blockade became a formidable alternative.

Second, Robert Kennedy — the President's closest confidant — was unwilling to see his brother become a "Tojo." His arguments against the air strike on moral grounds struck a chord in the President. Moreover, once his brother had stated these arguments so forcefully, the President could not have chosen his initially preferred course without, in effect, agreeing to become what RFK had condemned.

The President learned of the missiles on Tuesday morning. On Wednesday morning, in order to mask our discovery from the Russians, the President flew to Connecticut to keep a campaign commitment, leaving RFK as the unofficial chairman of the group. By the time the President returned on Wednesday evening, a critical third piece had been added to the picture. McNamara had presented his argument for the blockade. Robert Kennedy and Sorensen had joined McNamara. A powerful coalition of the advisors in whom the President had the greatest confidence, and with whom his style was most compatible, had emerged.

Fourth, the coalition that had formed behind the President's initial preference gave him reason to pause. *Who* supported the air strike — the Chiefs, McCone, Rusk, Nitze, and Acheson — as much as *how* they supported it, counted. Fifth, a piece of inaccurate information, which no one probed, permitted the blockade advocates to fuel (potential) uncertainties in the President's mind. When the President returned to Washington Wednesday evening, RFK and Sorensen met him at the airport. Sorensen gave the President a four-page memorandum outlining the areas of agreement and disagreement. The strongest argument was that the air strike simply could not be surgical.[100] After a day of prodding and questioning, the Air Force had asserted that it could not guarantee the success of a surgical air strike limited to the missiles alone.

Thursday evening, the President convened the ExCom at the White House. He declared his tentative choice of the blockade and directed that preparations be made to put it into effect by Monday morning.[101] Though he raised a question about the possibility of a surgical air strike subsequently, he seems to have accepted the experts' opinion that this was no live option.[102] (Acceptance of this estimate suggests that he may have learned the lesson of the Bay of Pigs — "Never rely on experts" — less well than he supposed.)[103] But this information was incorrect. That no one probed this estimate during the first week of the crisis poses an interesting question for further investigation.

A coalition, including the President, thus emerged from the President's initial decision that something had to be done; McNamara, Robert Kennedy, and Sorensen's resistance to the air strike; incompatibility between the President and the air strike advocates; and an inaccurate piece of information.[104]

CONCLUSION

This essay has obviously bitten off more than it has chewed. For further developments and synthesis of these arguments the reader is referred to the larger study.[105] In spite of the limits of space, however, it would be inappropriate to stop without spelling out several implications of the argument and addressing the questions of relations among the models and extensions of them to activity beyond explanation.

At a minimum, the intended implications of the argument presented here are four. First, formulation of alternative frames of reference and demonstration that different analysts, relying predominantly on different models, produce quite different explanations should encourage the analyst's self-consciousness about the nets he employs. The effect of these "spectacles" in sensitizing him to particular aspects of what is going on — framing the puzzle in one way rather than another, encouraging him to examine the problem in terms of certain categories rather than others, directing him to particular kinds of evidence, and relieving puzzlement by one procedure rather than another — must be recognized and explored.

Second, the argument implies a position on the problem of "the state of the art." While accepting the commonplace characterization of the present condition of foreign policy analysis — personalistic, non-cumulative, and sometimes insightful — this essay rejects both the counsel of despair's justification of this condition as a consequence of the character of the enterprise, and the "new frontiersmen's" demand for a priori theorizing on the frontiers and ad hoc appropriation of "new techniques."[106] What is required as a first step is non-casual examination of the present product: inspection of existing explanations, articulation of the conceptual models employed in producing them, formulation of the propositions relied upon, specification of the logic of the various intellectual enterprises, and reflection on the questions being asked. Though it is difficult to overemphasize the need for more systematic processing of more data, these preliminary matters of formulating questions with clarity and sensitivity to categories and assumptions so that fruitful acquisition of large quantities of data is possible are still a major hurdle in considering most important problems.

Third, the preliminary, partial paradigms presented here provide a basis for serious reexamination of many problems of foreign and military policy. Model II and Model III cuts at problems typically treated in Model I terms can permit significant improvements in explanation and prediction.[107] Full Model II and III analyses require large amounts of information. But even in cases where the information base is severely limited, improvements are possible. Consider the problem of predicting Soviet strategic forces. In the mid-1950s, Model I style calculations led to predictions that the Soviets would rapidly deploy large numbers of long-range bombers. From a Model II perspective, both the frailty of the Air Force within the Soviet military establishment and the budgetary implications of such a buildup, would have led analysts to hedge this prediction. Moreover, Model II would have pointed to a sure, visible indicator of such a buildup: noisy struggles among the Services over major budgetary shifts. In the late 1950s and early 1960s, Model I calculations led to the prediction of immediate, massive Soviet deployment of ICBMs. Again, a

Model II cut would have reduced this number because, in the earlier period, strategic rockets were controlled by the Soviet Ground Forces rather than an independent Service, and in the later period, this would have necessitated massive shifts in budgetary spills. Today, Model I considerations lead many analysts both to recommend that an agreement not to deploy ABMs be a major American objective in upcoming strategic negotiations with the USSR, and to predict success. From a Model II vantage point, the existence of an ongoing Soviet ABM program, the strength of the organization (National Air Defense) that controls ABMs, and the fact that an agreement to stop ABM deployment would force the virtual dismantling of this organization, make a viable agreement of this sort much less likely. A Model III cut suggests that (a) there must be significant differences among perceptions and priorities of Soviet leaders over strategic negotiations, (b) any agreement will affect some players' power bases, and (c) agreements that do not require extensive cuts in the sources of some major players' power will prove easier to negotiate and more viable.

Fourth, the present formulation of paradigms is simply an initial step. As such it leaves a long list of critical questions unanswered. Given any action, an imaginative analyst should always be able to construct some rationale for the government's choice. By imposing, and relaxing, constraints on the parameters of rational choice (as in variants of Model I) analysts can construct a large number of accounts of any act as a rational choice. But does a statement of reasons why a rational actor would choose an action constitute an explanation of the *occurrence* of that action? How can Model I analysis be forced to make more systematic contributions to the question of the determinants of occurrences? Model II's explanation of t in terms of $t - 1$ is explanation. The world is contiguous. But governments sometimes make sharp departures. Can an organizational process model be modified to suggest where change is likely? Attention to organizational change should afford greater understanding of why particular problems and SOPs are maintained by identifiable types of organizations and also how a manager can improve organizational performance. Model III tells a fascinating "story." But its complexity is enormous, the information requirements are often overwhelming, and many of the details of the bargaining may be superfluous. How can such a model be made parsimonious? The three models are obviously not exclusive alternatives. Indeed, the paradigms highlight the partial emphasis of the framework — what each emphasizes and what it leaves out. Each concentrates on one class of variables, in effect, relegating other important factors to a *ceteris parabus* clause. Model I concentrates on "market factors": pressures and incentives created by the "international strategic marketplace." Models II and III focus on the internal mechanism of the government that chooses in this environment. But can these relations be more fully specified? Adequate synthesis would require a typology of decisions and actions, some of which are more amenable to treatment in terms of one model and some to another. Government behavior is but one cluster of factors relevant to occurrences in foreign affairs. Most students of foreign policy adopt this focus (at least when explaining and predicting). Nevertheless, the dimensions of the chess board, the character of the pieces, and the rules of the game—factors considered by international systems theorists—constitute the context in which the pieces are moved. Can the major variables in the full function of determinants of foreign policy outcomes be identified?

Both the outline of a partial, *ad hoc* working synthesis of the models, and a sketch of their uses in activities other than explanation can be suggested by generating predictions in terms of each. Strategic surrender is an important problem of international relations and diplomatic history. War termination is a new, developing area of the strategic literature. Both of these interests lead scholars to address a central question: *Why* do nations surrender *when?* Whether implicit in explanations or more explicit in analysis, diplomatic historians and strategists rely upon propositions which can be turned forward to produce predictions. Thus at the risk of being timely—and in error—the present situation (August, 1968) offers an interesting test case: Why will North Vietnam surrender when?[108]

In a nutshell, analysis according to Model I asserts: nations quit when costs outweigh the benefits. North Vietnam will surrender when she realizes "that continued fighting can only generate additional costs without hope of compensating gains, this expectation being largely the consequence of the previous application of force by the dominant side."[109] U.S. actions can increase or decrease Hanoi's strategic costs. Bombing North Vietnam increases the pain and thus increases the probability of surrender. This proposition and prediction are not without meaning. That—"other things being equal"—nations are more likely to surrender when the strategic cost–benefit balance is negative, is true. Nations rarely surrender when they are winning. The proposition specifies a range within which nations surrender. But over this broad range, the relevant question is: why do nations surrender?

Models II and III focus upon the government machine through which this fact about the international strategic marketplace must be filtered to produce a surrender. These analysts are considerably less sanguine about the possibility of surrender at the *point* that the cost–benefit calculus turns negative. Never in history (i.e., in none of the five cases I have examined) have nations surrendered at that point. Surrender occurs sometime thereafter. *When* depends on process of organizations and politics of players within these governments—as they are affected by the opposing government. Moreover, the effects of the victorious power's action upon the surrendering nation cannot be adequately summarized as increasing or decreasing strategic costs. Imposing additional costs by bombing a nation may increase the probability of surrender. But it also may reduce it. An appreciation of the impact of the acts of one nation upon another thus requires some understanding of the machine which is being influenced. For more precise prediction, Models II and III require considerably more information about the organizations and politics of North Vietnam than is publicly available. On the basis of the limited public information, however, these models can be suggestive.

Model II examines two sub-problems. First, to have lost is not sufficient. The government must know that the strategic cost–benefit calculus is negative. But neither the categories, nor the indicators, of strategic costs and benefits are clear. And the sources of information about both are organizations whose parochial priorities and perceptions do not facilitate accurate information or estimation. Military evaluation of military performance, military estimates of factors like "enemy morale," and military predictions concerning when "the tide will turn" or "the corner will have been turned" are typically distorted. In cases of highly decentralized guerrilla operations, like Vietnam, these problems are exacerbated. Thus strategic costs will be underestimated. Only highly *visible* costs can have direct impact on leaders without being filtered through organizational channels. Second, since organizations define the details of options and execute actions, surrender (and negotiation) is likely to entail considerable bungling in the early stages. No organization can define options or prepare programs for this treasonous act. Thus, early overtures will be uncoordinated with the acts of other organizations, e.g., the fighting forces, creating contradictory "signals" to the victor.

Model III suggests that surrender will not come at the point that strategic costs outweigh benefits, but that it will not wait until the leadership group concludes that the war is lost. Rather the problem is better understood in terms of four additional propositions. First, strong advocates of the war effort, whose careers are closely identified with the war, rarely come to the conclusion that costs outweigh benefits. Second, quite often from the outset of a war, a number of members of the government (particularly those whose responsibility sensitize them to problems other than war, e.g., economic planners or intelligence experts) are convinced that the war effort is futile. Third, surrender is likely to come as the result of a political shift that enhances the effective power of the latter group (and adds swing members to it). Fourth, the course of the war, particularly actions of the victor, can influence the advantages and disadvantages of players in the loser's government. Thus, North Vietnam will surrender not when its leaders have a change of heart, but when Hanoi has a change of leaders (or a change of effective power within the central circle). How U.S. bombing (or pause), threats, promises, or action in the South affect the game in Hanoi is subtle but nonetheless crucial.

That these three models could be applied to the surrender of governments other than North Vietnam should be obvious. But that exercise is left for the reader.

NOTES

1. Theodore Sorensen, *Kennedy* (New York, 1965), p. 705.
2. In attempting to understand problems of foreign affairs, analysts engage in a number of related, but logically separable enterprises: (a) description, (b) explanation, (c) prediction, (d) evaluation, and (e) recommendation. This essay focuses primarily on explanation (and by implication, prediction).
3. In arguing that explanations proceed in terms of implicit conceptual models, this essay makes no claim that foreign policy analysts have developed any satisfactory, empirically tested theory. In this essay, the use of the term "model" without qualifiers should be read "conceptual scheme."
4. For the purpose of this argument we shall accept Carl G. Hempel's characterization of the logic of explanation: an explanation "answers the question, 'Why did the explanadum-phenomenon occur?' by showing that the phenomenon resulted from particular circumstances, specified in C_1, C_2, . . . C_k, in accordance with laws L_1, L_2, . . . L_f. By pointing this out, the argument shows that, given the particular circumstances and the laws in question, the occurrence of the phenomenon was to be expected; and it is in this sense that the explanation enables us to understand why the phenomenon occurred." *Aspects of Scientific Explanation* (New York, 1965), p. 337. While various patterns of explanation can be distinguished (viz., Ernest Nagel, *The Structure of Science: Problems in the Logic of Scientific Explanation,* New York, 1961), satisfactory scientific explanations exhibit this basic logic. Consequently prediction is the converse of explanation.
5. Earlier drafts of this argument have aroused heated arguments concerning proper names for these models. To choose names for ordinary language is to court confusion, as well as familiarity. Perhaps it is best to think of these models as I, II, and III.
6. In strict terms, the "outcomes" which these three models attempt to explain are essentially actions of national governments, i.e., the sum of activities of all individuals employed by a government relevant to an issue. These models focus not on a state of affairs, i.e., a full description of the world, but upon national decision and implementation. This distinction is stated clearly by Harold and Margaret Sprout, "Environmental Factors on the Study of International Politics," in James Rosenau (ed.), *International Politics and Foreign Policy* (Glencoe, Illinois, 1961), p. 116. This restriction excludes explanations offered principally in terms of international systems theories. Nevertheless, this restriction is not severe, since few interesting explanations of occurrences in foreign policy have been produced at that level of analysis. According to David Singer, "The nation state—our primary actor in international relations . . . is clearly the traditional focus among Western students and is the one which dominates all of the texts employed in English-speaking colleges and universities." David Singer, "The Level-of-Analysis Problem in International Relations," Klaus Knorr and Sidney Verba (eds.), *The International System* (Princeton, 1961). Similarly, Richard Brody's review of contemporary trends in the study of international relations finds that "scholars have come increasingly in focus on acts of nations. That is, they all focus on the behavior of nations in some respect. Having an interest in accounting for the behavior of nations in common, the prospects for a common frame of reference are enhanced."
7. For further development and support of these arguments see the author's

larger study, *Essence of Decision: Explaining the Cuban Missile Crisis* (Boston: Little, Brown and Co., 1971). In its abbreviated form, the argument must, at some points, appear overly stark. The limits of space have forced the omission of many reservations and refinements.

8. Each of the three "case snapshots" displays the work of a conceptual model as it is applied to explain the U.S. blockade of Cuba. But these three cuts are primarily exercises in hypothesis generation rather than hypothesis testing. Especially when separated from the larger study, these accounts may be misleading. The sources for these accounts include the full public record plus a large number of interviews with participants in the crisis.
9. *New York Times,* February 18, 1967.
10. Ibid.
11. Arnold Horelick and Myron Rush, *Strategic Power and Soviet Foreign Policy* (Chicago, 1965). Based on A. Horelick, "The Cuban Missile Crisis: An Analysis of Soviet Calculations and Behavior," *World Politics* (April, 1964).
12. Horelick and Rush, *Strategic Power and Soviet Foreign Policy,* p. 154.
13. Hans Morgenthau, *Politics Among Nations* (3rd ed.; New York, 1960), p. 191.
14. Ibid., p. 192.
15. Ibid., p. 5.
16. Ibid., pp. 5-6.
17. Stanley Hoffmann, *Daedalus* (Fall, 1962); reprinted in *The State of War* (New York, 1965).
18. Ibid., p. 171.
19. Ibid., p. 189.
20. Following Robert MacIver; see Stanley Hoffmann, *Contemporary Theory in International Relations* (Englewood Cliffs, NJ, 1960), pp. 178-179.
21. Thomas Schelling, *The Strategy of Conflict* (New York, 1960), p. 232. This proposition was formulated earlier by A. Wohlstetter, "The Delicate Balance of Terror," *Foreign Affairs* (January, 1959).
22. Schelling, *op. cit.,* p. 4.
23. See Hans Morgenthau, *op. cit.,* p. 5; Hoffmann, *Contemporary Theory,* pp. 178-179; Stanley Hoffmann, "Roulette in the Cellar," *The State of War;* Schelling, *op. cit.*
24. The larger study examines several exceptions to this generalization. Sidney Verba's excellent essay "Assumptions of Rationality and Non-Rationality in Models of the International System" is less an exception than it is an approach to a somewhat different problem. Verba focuses upon models of rationality and irrationality of *individual* statements: in Knorr and Verba, *The International System.*
25. See Nathan Leites, *A Study of Bolshevism* (Glencoe, Illinois, 1953).
26. As stated in the introduction, this "case snapshot" presents, without editorial commentary, a Model I analyst's explanation of the U.S. blockade. The purpose is to illustrate a strong, characteristic rational policy model account. This account is (roughly) consistent with prevailing explanations of these events.
27. Theodore Sorensen, *op. cit.,* p. 675.
28. Ibid., p. 679.
29. Ibid., p. 679.
30. Elie Abel, *The Missile Crisis* (New York, 1966), p. 144.
31. Ibid., p. 102.
32. Sorensen, *op. cit.,* p. 684.

33. Ibid., p. 685. Though this was the formulation of the argument, the facts are not strictly accurate. Our tradition against surprise attack was rather younger than 175 years. For example, President Theodore Roosevelt applauded Japan's attack on Russia in 1904.

34. *New York Times,* June, 1963.

35. The influence of organizational studies upon the present literature of foreign affairs is minimal. Specialists in international politics are not students of organization theory. Organization theory has only recently begun to study organizations as decisionmakers and has not yet produced behavioral studies of national security organizations from a decision-making perspective. It seems unlikely, however, that these gaps will remain unfilled much longer. Considerable progress has been made in the study of the business firm as an organization. Scholars have begun applying these insights to government organizations, and interest in an organizational perspective is spreading among institutions and individuals concerned with actual government operations. The "decisionmaking" approach represented by Richard Snyder, R. Bruck, and B. Sapin, *Foreign Policy Decision-Making* (Glencoe, Illinois, 1962), incorporates a number of insights from organization theory.

36. U.S. Department of State, *Bulletin,* XLVII, pp. 715–720.

37. Arthur Schlesinger, *A Thousand Days* (Boston: 1965), p. 803.

38. Theodore Sorensen, *Kennedy,* p. 675.

39. See U.S. Congress, Senate, Committee on Armed Services, Preparedness Investigation Subcommittee, *Interim Report on Cuban Military Build-up,* 88th Congress, 1st Session, 1963, p. 2; Hanson Baldwin, "Growing Risks of Bureaucratic Intelligence," *The Reporter* (August 15, 1963), 48–50; Roberta Wohlstetter, "Cuba and Pearl Harbor," *Foreign Affairs* (July, 1965), 706.

40. U.S. Congress, House of Representatives, Committee on Appropriations, Subcommittee on Department of Defense, Appropriations, *Hearings,* 88th Congress, 1st Session, 1963, 25ff.

41. R. Hilsman, *To Move a Nation* (New York, 1967), pp. 172–173.

42. Department of Defense Appropriations, *Hearings,* p. 67.

43. Ibid., pp. 66–67.

44. For (1) Hilsman, *op. cit.,* p. 186; (2) Abel, *op. cit.,* p. 24; (3) Department of Defense Appropriations, *Hearings,* p. 67; Abel, *op. cit.,* p. 24; (4) Department of Defense Appropriations, *Hearings,* pp. 1–30.

45. The facts here are not entirely clear. This assertion is based on information from (1) "Department of Defense Briefing by the Honorable R. S. McNamara, Secretary of Defense, State Department Auditorium, 5:00 P.M., February 6, 1963," A verbatim transcript of a presentation actually made by General Carroll's assistant, John Hughes; and (2) Hilsman's statement, *op. cit.,* p. 186. But see R. Wohlstetter's interpretation, "Cuba and Pearl Harbor," 700.

46. See Hilsman, *op. cit.,* pp. 172–174.

47. Abel, *op. cit.,* pp. 26 ff; Weintal and Bartlett, *Facing the Brink* (New York, 1967), pp. 62 ff; *Interim Report on Cuban Military Build-up;* J. Daniel and J. Hubbell, *Strike in the West* (New York, 1963), pp. 15 ff.

48. Schlesinger, *op. cit.,* p. 804.

49. Sorensen, *Kennedy,* p. 684.

50. Ibid., pp. 684 ff.

51. Ibid., pp. 694–697.

52. Ibid., p. 697; Abel, *op. cit.,* pp. 100–101.

53. Sorensen, *Kennedy*, p. 669.
54. Hilsman, *op. cit.*, p. 204.
55. See Abel, *op. cit.*, pp. 97 ff.
56. Schlesinger, *op. cit.*, p. 818.
57. Ibid.
58. Sorensen, *Kennedy*, p. 710.
59. *New York Times*, October 27, 1962.
60. Abel, *op. cit.*, p. 171.
61. For the location of the original arc see Abel, *op. cit.*, p. 141.
62. *Facts on File*, Vol. XXII, 1962, p. 376 (New York: Facts on File, Inc., 1962) yearly.
63. This hypothesis would account for the mystery surrounding Kennedy's explosion at the leak of the stopping of the *Bucharest*. See Hilsman, *op. cit.*, p. 45.
64. Abel, *op. cit.*, p. 153.
65. See *ibid.*, pp. 154 ff.
66. Ibid., p. 156.
67. Ibid.
68. Sorensen, *Kennedy*, p. 670.
69. Ibid.
70. Ibid., pp. 670ff.
71. *New York Times*, August, September, 1962.
72. *New York Times*, August 20, 1962.
73. *New York Times*, September 5, 1962.
74. *New York Times*, September 14, 1962.
75. *New York Times*, October 14, 1962.
76. Cited by Abel, *op. cit.*, p. 13.
77. *New York Times*, September 5, 1962.
78. *New York Times*, September 14, 1962.
79. Senate Foreign Relations Committee; Senate Armed Services Committee; House Committee on Appropriations; House Select Committee on Export Control.
80. Abel, *op. cit.*, pp. 17-18. According to McCone, he told Kennedy, "The only construction I can put on the material going into Cuba is that the Russians are preparing to introduce offensive missiles." See also Weintal and Bartlett, *op. cit.*, pp. 60-61.
81. Abel, *op. cit.*, p. 23.
82. *New York Times*, September 10, 1962.
83. See Abel, *op. cit.*, pp. 25-26; and Hilsman, *op. cit.*, p. 174.
84. Department of Defense Appropriation, *Hearings*, 69.
85. A basic, but somewhat contradictory, account of parts of this story emerges in the Department of Defense Appropriations, *Hearings*, 1-70.
86. Department of Defense Appropriations, *Hearings*, 71.
87. The details of the 10 days between the October 4 decision and the October 14 flight must be held in abeyance.
88. Abel, *op. cit.*, p. 44.
89. Ibid., pp. 44f.
90. See Richard Neustadt, "Afterword," *Presidential Power* (New York, 1964).
91. Sorensen, *Kennedy*, p. 676; Schlesinger, *op. cit.*, p. 801.
92. Hilsman, *op. cit.*, p. 195.
93. Ibid.

94. Weintal and Bartlett, *op. cit.*, p. 67; Abel, *op. cit.*, p. 53.
95. Schlesinger, *op. cit.*, p. 803.
96. Ibid., p. 831.
97. Abel, *op. cit.*, p. 186.
98. Ibid., p. 49.
99. Interview, quoted by Ronald Steel, *New York Review of Books*, March 13, 1969, p. 22.
100. Sorensen, *Kennedy*, p. 686.
101. Ibid., p. 691.
102. Ibid., pp. 691–692.
103. Schlesinger, *op. cit.*, p. 296.
104. Space will not permit an account of the path from this coalition to the formal government decision on Saturday and action on Monday.
105. *Essence of Decision.*
106. Thus my position is quite distinct from both poles in the recent "great debate" about international relations. While many "traditionalists" of the sort Kaplan attacks adopt the first posture and many "scientists" of the sort attacked by Bull adopt the second, this third posture is relatively neutral with respect to whatever is in substantive dispute. See Hedley Bull, "International Theory: The Case for a Classical Approach," *World Politics* (April, 1966); and Morton Kaplan, "The New Great Debate: Traditionalism vs. Science in International Relations," *World Politics* (October, 1966).
107. A number of problems are now being examined in these terms both in the Bureaucracy Study Group on Bureaucracy and Policy of the Institute of Politics at Harvard University and at the Rand Corporation.
108. In response to several readers' recommendations, what follows is reproduced *verbatim* from the paper delivered at the September, 1968 Association meetings (Rand P–3919). The decision is heavily indebted to Ernest R. May.
109. Richard Snyder, *Deterrence and Defense* (Princeton, NJ, 1961), p. 11. For a more general presentation of this position see Paul Kecskemeti, *Strategic Surrender* (New York, 1964).

World Society

John W. Burton

Professor Burton contrasts the realist model of the international system with what he terms the cobweb model *— a pluralist image. He argues that the term is descriptively a more accurate image of the world society and that it does a better job in capturing the multitude of political, economic, social, and technological interactions.*

It will be seen that the history of thought about world society includes a steady movement away from relations between states to broader considerations. . . .

"INTERNATIONAL RELATIONS" OR "WORLD SOCIETY"

It is because of the past preoccupation with relations between nations that "International Relations" is the title that is usually given to the discipline concerned with the study of world politics and world society. It is an unfortunate title for our present purposes. States sometimes comprise different national groups, such as English, Irish, Scots and Welsh in the state of the United Kingdom. If we were concerned only with relations among the 150 or so independent political units of today, "inter-state" would be a more appropriate term than "inter-national" relations. The general idea that most of us have of world society is one that is based on maps of the world which emphasize state boundaries, on historical studies which concentrate on relations among governments. We are familiar with a set of national symbols, customs and institutions that make us feel different from peoples in other states. For this reason we think about world affairs as though they were confined to relations between states. But the study of world society is not confined to relations among states or state authorities. There are important religious, language, scientific, commercial and other relationships in addition to a variety of formal non-governmental institutions that are world-wide.

    This is not just a matter of choosing between different words. We are choosing an approach when we choose to speak of world society and not inter-national relations. The study of world society is a much wider study than the relations of units within it. It is, of course, possible and useful to study inter-state trading relations and inter-governmental institutions of

From John W. Burton, *World Society* (Cambridge, England: 1972). Reprinted by permission of Cambridge University Press.

various kinds. It is also possible and useful to make comparative studies of the ways in which different governments behave and how their different institutions function. But these studies based on states cannot give us that understanding we seek of world society, and in particular its processes and trends. Obviously, any separation of domestic politics and world politics is arbitrary and probably misleading. For example, these state studies cannot tell us much about the nature of conflict among communities that originates within states and spills over into world society. The political and social life of people within states, which is always altering with changed thinking and new technologies, influences relations among states. This is clear where there are sudden and fundamental changes such as have taken place this century in Russia and in China. Less dramatic internal political and social changes are altering relations among states year by year. Indeed, it is because this is so that the more powerful states such as the United States of America and the Union of Soviet Socialist Republics endeavour to influence these changes in other states.

State boundaries are significant, but they are just one type of boundary which affects the behaviour of world society. There are local municipal boundaries such as those of the Greater London Council, which include more people than do many states, and in which administrative functions are carried out such as those that occur within small states. At the other end of the scale there are boundaries that include several states, such as those of the European Common Market and the Organization of African Unity. There are also non-geographical boundaries to be taken into account. These are based on functions, for example, the boundaries that separate the work of the World Health Organization from the Food and Agricultural Organization. These cut across geographical or state boundaries. The world geographical map depicting states cannot show these — but they exist and an image of world society is not complete without them.

If states controlled all world activities even to the limited extent that they control the activities of an inter-state institution like the World Health Organization, then one could extend the idea of inter-state relations to include all activities in world society. But there are many transactions in addition to those initiated and regulated by governments within states that cut across state boundaries. Indeed, new ideas and philosophies cut across state boundaries sometimes despite attempts by governments to prevent this happening. There is now one world of science. No state can afford to cut itself off from scientific and technological developments. It is not possible to import just a selection of scientific thoughts. From our own studies we know how knowledge in one subject relates to knowledge in another. Natural science and political thought cannot be separated because the one employs the methodologies and thinking of the other, and developments in the one field lead to developments in the other. Technological inventions change political and social life wherever they occur. The working life of a factory worker in a developed socialist country is little different from the life of a factory worker in another industrialized country. Similarly, administrations and cultures tend to converge with the spread of ideas, and this will occur even more rapidly when television is received as radio is now.

If we employ the term "world society" instead of "international relations," if we approach our study in this global way instead of the more traditional "national" way, we will tend to have a wider focus, to ask questions that are more fundamental and important to civilization, and be able to assess better the relevance of our own national behaviour to the wider world environment. . . .

THE BILLIARD BALL MODEL

Over the ages there have been many models or abstractions used to bring to focus different aspects of world society. At one time, when the fortunes of a nation appeared to fluctuate for no apparent reason, this could be explained by reference to the swing of a pendulum — a simple mechanical device of which everyone was aware. Even today, when conditions responsible for change are not known precisely, we are prepared to refer to a run of unfavourable events as though there were some mysterious influences determining them. In earlier times "fate" seemed to be a sufficient explanation of events.

It is only a few hundred years since it would have been absurd to think of a world society. There was a European society, and going back much further there were Mediterranean and Chinese societies or civilizations. We know how small feudal holdings, almost tribal areas, gradually coming together, led to the establishment of provinces and nation–states. We know of the growth of empires after exploration from Europe, the movement towards independent states, and the increasing relative power of a few main states. As a consequence, we tend to have in mind a world society comprising states, small and large, each pursuing its "national interest." We are aware, too, of international institutions like the United Nations and its agencies, and perhaps we entertain the hope that one day there will be some world body with powers sufficient to regulate the power of states. Some such general notion of a world society of great and small states is in the back of our minds when we read of the events that unfold day by day. We interpret events in the light of this notion. Each event seems to confirm it: Soviet intervention in Czechoslovakia, United States intervention in Latin American countries and in Vietnam, the defence of spheres of influences by both of these great powers with navies, aircraft and forces deployed well outside their territorial boundaries.

This conventional image of a world composed of nation–states which are of different size and power has been termed the *"billiard-ball"* model. Each state is represented by a government and is seen as an entity — a sovereign, independent unit. What takes place within the boundaries of each is not the concern of the others — this is a matter of "domestic jurisdiction," to use the words of the United Nations Charter. The interactions or contacts are like those of different sized billiard balls. Only the hard exteriors touch, and heavier or faster moving ones push others out of the way. The points of contact are governments; it is only governments that are interacting.

This was a model that described conditions when city–states were ruled by feudal lords, when each was independent and virtually isolated from the rest of the world, when negotiation was through leaders, when the main concern was self-defence. It is a model that depicts some of the features of the contemporary world. There are direct diplomatic contacts between governments on many major matters. This same simple model of large and small balls interacting can take into account some of the internal happenings of states that affect relations with others. A new industry in one state affects an industry in another. There are internal political processes in the affected state that might result in tariff protection: the plight of the affected industry is referred to the chamber of manufacturers, to the local member of parliament, to the minister, to the cabinet, and the government might then consult with the government of the other country. The relationship is government to government, and this fits into the idea of world society being composed of sovereign states.

It is this image which leads us to focus our attention on diplomatic relations, on governments as the main actors in world affairs, on their relative power, and on the personal characteristics of their leaders. But with this model in mind our attention is directed away from other relationships. How important are diplomats and governments in the scheme of things? To what extent is the making of policy the free decision of governments, and to what extent do governments reflect the needs and interests of others conducting their own transactions across state boundaries?

Perhaps this general notion was a realistic one many years ago; but there have been some developments in world society, which have become apparent especially since the Second World War, that are forcing us to revise our picture. For example, there is a persistent increase in the number of states, a reduction in the size of political units, and an increase in the size of economic units and the degree of interdependence. The significance of state boundaries is altering as a consequence. There are changing values or priorities in objectives, restrictions on the freedom of action of powerful states, and accentuated racial and class conflict. With education and communication there is an assimilation of ideologies leading to greater similarities between political parties within each state, and between states. These are only some of the main trends. They are interacting and not precisely defined ones. Each one of us could make his own personal list.

On the presence of one trend there will be agreement. Communications of all kinds have become quicker and more frequent between different geographical points. A great many consequences flow from this.

Exchanges are promoted between persons with common and competing interests and objectives. There is a "one world" of science, of ideas, of trade and commerce that is only marginally affected by the barriers of mountains, seas and state boundaries. Values are shared, and objectives never previously entertained are known to be practical. The peasant worker of Asia knows that other people have a higher living standard and work their own land. Peoples who do not govern themselves know that others have revolted and won independence. Asians and Africans know that non-discrimination, equality of opportunity and human dignity are values that can be attained. Communications have brought peoples into contact, and made them aware of possibilities.

Industrial technology is another undisputed influence on world society. Political units or states are not always adequate as industrial units, and specialization has led to the production of aeroplanes and other complex manufactures being spread over many countries. The oil industry knows no state boundaries, and companies make agreements with governments of different ideological outlooks. International or transnational corporations are developing, and they are not responsible to anyone but themselves. The billiard-ball model cannot depict these developments.

Another remarkable change is in values. We now know that people hold some values even higher than material gains: independence, freedom of expression, and a sense of participation in making decisions that affect them. There are psychological and sociological explanations and these we must discuss. We know that values are influencing world society and the policies of states vary greatly. Probably many of these values have always been held: the serf always wanted freedom of expression and freedom from hunger. The significant difference is that now there are opportunities to demand values. Education and communications have made people aware of what is possible, and political institutions and political organizations have helped to make demands effective. The development of the ideal of "welfare state" has had profound effects upon the policies of states, and therefore upon world society. Once a ruler could decide upon a foreign adventure and command the service of princes and their subjects, and raise taxes to fight wars, with few political restraints imposed upon him. In the modern welfare state defence expenditure must compete with expenditure on education and other social services, and welfare generally. Even the most wealthy states find that there are political restraints on the degree to which they can sacrifice welfare needs in order to exercise their military and economic power in other countries. . . .

THE COBWEB MODEL

The conventional map of the world is a physical one: it shows geographical relationships, over which are sometimes drawn political boundaries. It does not tell us much about processes or behaviour. The same proportional space and importance are given to seas and deserts as are given to ports and cities. There do exist diagrammatic maps that tell us where populations are concentrated, where resources are to be found, how many newspapers are read and other information such as this. But even these do not give us much information about behaviour, or more particularly, about transactions and links that exist. We are familiar with maps of the world showing air and shipping routes. What we really need to have, either in map form or conceptually, is an image of world society that shows behaviour by showing these linkages. If we could superimpose on successive sheets of transparent paper air-passenger movements per week, telegraphic flows, ethnic and language relations, movements of scholars, technical advisers, migration, tourism, and all other transactions, we would begin to build up a picture of relationships which would help to explain behaviour in world society far better than traditional maps. Maps were designed to show people how to get from point A to point B. They are useful for this purpose. But they have been used for purposes other than this. They have had the effect of creating in our minds this geographical image of world society. What we need is a map or concept that tells us something about behaviour. The difference is like the difference between a set of photos of a car showing its headlamps and other details, and the type of diagram an electrical engineer would draw showing the wiring links within the electrical system. We cannot understand a car by looking at it. Its processes need to be analysed, and then we can understand it, and remedy any failures.

If we had been brought up with such maps on the wall, if we were not so consciously aware of states whenever we looked at a map of the world, and best of all, if we had never seen an ordinary map of the world, we would think far more in terms of world society and far less in terms of a system of states. We would approach closer to a realistic model of world society.

An easy way to think about this second model is by use of the concept of "system." A system exists when there are relationships or transactions between units of the same set. There is a system of states, and there are also transactions between businessmen, traders, research workers, television stations, drug peddlers, students and others. There are systems or linkages such as those created by amateur radio enthusiasts, by peoples with the same ideological or religious outlooks, by scientists exchanging papers and meeting together, by people behaving in their different ways. It is the total of these which we need to see as a behavioural map of the world. In this model contacts are not only at the boundaries of sovereign states, but between points within each.

We have gone to a great deal of trouble and expense over the years to map rivers and mountains, sea depths and ocean currents; but we have not as yet been sufficiently interested in social and political studies to map the behaviour of men. In most cases we do not even have the basic information required. When we look at the ordinary physical map we have to impose on it our own personal knowledge. For example, we may know where populations are massed, and where there are deserts. We have our own ideas, usually inaccurate, about which populations are friendly, aggressive, backward, developed, black, white, yellow, and perhaps we have a vague idea which are Muslim, Hindu, Christian and Buddhist. We have some idea where different commodities are produced, where trade flows, and which are the most used shipping and air lanes. We rely on our personal knowledge. There are some physical maps which superimpose accurately some of this information for us, and even some diagrammatical "maps" or graphs which show comparative figures, such as percentages of total world wheat produced in various countries. The few maps of this kind that do exist are helpful. They give us a new perspective on the world, and help us to see at a glance what otherwise can be understood only by looking at statistics.

We still have difficulty in conceptualizing world society, first because these "maps" are inadequate, and second because by their nature they are misleading. They are inadequate not only in the sense that data are available which have not been presented in this form, and in the sense that relevant data have never been obtained. They are inadequate in terms of their analytical content. A population figure for a country, even an average population per square mile, does not tell us those things about distribution which would make a glance at a map meaningful. In theory it should be possible to put a dot wherever anyone is; in practice it is possible to do this by taking 10,000 people as a unit. Then we would have the rudimentary basis of a human behavioural map. A next step would be to differentiate between race, language and other differences in more and more detail in a series of superimposed maps. A further step would be to examine relationships between these sets or different groups of people. Take, for example, Malaysia. There are many differents sets: Malays, Chinese, anti-communist and pro-communist Malays and Chinese, traditionally-oriented and religious Muslims and other Malays, Chinese businessmen, and so on. Each of these sets has its own values and interests, and therefore its own external sympathies. Some Chinese look to China, and others to Taiwan, some Malays are nationalist and some look to Indonesia and other Muslim countries for support in any possible confrontation with Chinese. These sets can be represented by interlocking circles: one person can be Chinese by birth, regard himself as a Malay nationalist, a businessman, British educated and oriented and anti-communist. He must be placed in an area in which the circles representing all these sets overlap.

If we considered neighbouring Indonesia in the same way, we would find similar sets. Putting the two alongside each other it would at once become clear that any alliance between the two would be seen as a threat to some sets in each. Chinese, for example, would see such an alliance as a Malayan threat to them. We could reasonably assume, just by looking at these sets, that attempts to establish regional arrangements would lead to increased internal tension and conflict within each political unit. Just by analysing existing data we could come to some important hypotheses about behaviour. We are just beginning to do this—despite the urgent need to solve the problems of world society.

Even though our existing data were fully used in these ways, we would still not have a map of human behaviour. These are data based on state statistics: state populations, state trade, state classifications. We are interested in transactions across state boundaries of which states have little knowledge, and certainly no statistics—the sympathies Jewish people have for one another, the transmission of values attached to participation in decision-making, the way in which people of the same tribe or ethnic group identify with each other across state boundaries, and the flow of ideas. We are also interested in the direction of flow: there are state statistics giving the flow of mail across state boundaries, but not the direction of these flows. . . .

We would begin to get nearer to such a concept of world society if we were to map it without reference to political boundaries, and indeed, without reference to any physical boundaries. We are not particularly concerned with boundaries, except insofar as they affect behaviour by reducing transactions and communications among people. We are concerned with behaviour—boundaries or no boundaries. If we were to start with a clean sheet of paper and plot people in various sets, their transport and communications, we would, in fact, create a map some of which would be recognizable as parts of the physical map of the world. One difference would be that seas and deserts would look the same. We could build on this additional information, perhaps by a series of transparent sheets, and finally superimpose political boundaries.

Communications are a good starting point because they are an important means of transactions or links between people. It is communications or links between units that create systems. A useful map of the world could be drawn by plotting on a blank piece of paper all post offices. In some cases the system links would form clusters recognizable as a country. In others, for example, some areas of the Middle East, it would immediately seem that there were as many or more transactions across boundaries as within. If we could map all movements and communications in world society we would find some ethnic groups communicating across state boundaries as though they did not exist, as for example, between Somalia and Kenya, and between many Western European countries. This would give us a picture of some important aspects of behaviour which a physical map cannot give. Conceptually we could extend this to include all transactions and links, even those we cannot quantify and map, such as ideological sympathies, and the hidden transactions of international corporations and international institutions of all kinds. In practice there are so many direct communications or systems that a world map which represented them would look like a mass of cobwebs superimposed on one another, strands converging at some points more than others, and being concentrated between some points more than between others. The boundaries of states would be hidden from view.

Which is the more representative model of the world — the world of continents, islands and states or the world of transactions? This is not a superficial question. There are two different models or images presented. If we adopt the nation – state one we will use the language of relations between states and their relevant power, and have one set of solutions to problems of conflict and world organization. If we adopt the transactions one we will use a different language to describe world society, and have a different set of solutions to world problems. For example, we will be greatly concerned with political and social conditions within states because it is these which, in this model, determine relationships in world society, including relations between states.

Let us dwell on this a little more. The model we have at the back of our minds determines our interpretation of events, our theories and our policies. For example, the billiard-ball model is a power model — world society is seen to be organized by the relative power of each unit. There are matters of domestic jurisdiction of no concern to others, not even the United Nations. There are legal political entities that have a right to protect themselves and to expect assistance from others, including the United Nations, if they are threatened, even though they have no popular support — no legitimized status. Collective security is the means of preventing "aggression." Economic development is the means to social and political stability.

The model depicting transactions invites a different approach to world problems. The source of conflict between states is in internal politics, in failures by states to adjust to altering conditions, in the struggle of states to preserve their institutions, and in the conflict between states and systems that cut across state boundaries. Conflict cannot be prevented by external coercion, or by great power threats. Communal conflict — race, religious, ideological — invites sympathies across state boundaries and promotes international conflict. The role of authorities is to assist in the making of adjustments to altering conditions so that conflict between interests within the state, and the wider world system, does not occur. Development and stability must rest on internal conditions or political organization, that is, a high degree of participation so that authorities are strongly legitimized. In accordance with this model, a form of world government cannot rest on collective security, and must be based on the transactions inherent in functional organizations that are, by their nature, universal in potential membership. Viable political units can be very small, provided there is a high level of transactions with the wider environment. Communications, and not power, are the main organizing influence in world society.

There is an important practical question raised here. An image of world society that comprises separate state entities, each potentially hostile to others, leads understandably to defensive policies. Is the image a realistic one, or are the conflicts that occur and seem to validate the image merely the consequences of our having this image? An image of world society that depicts transactions, controlled and regulated by local state and international authorities, with a view to securing the maximum benefits from interdependence without loss of security, leads reasonably to integrative policies. Is the image a realistic one, or are the functional arrangements, world corporations and other evidences that seem to validate the image merely the consequence of our having this image? It is possible that the cobweb image is the realistic one, except insofar as lack of confidence has created the one comprising separate and fearful entities. Thus created it becomes part of our perceived reality. . . .

International Interdependence and Integration

Robert O. Keohane and Joseph S. Nye

The authors treat two concepts that are important to the pluralist perspective: interdependence and integration.

During the 1940s and 1950s, and to a considerable extent thereafter, political scientists have tended to describe world politics as a Hobbesian situation in which independent units called nation–states are locked into patterns of fundamental conflict. Some "Realists," such as Morgenthau and Niebuhr, have ascribed international conflict largely to characteristics of human nature. As Morgenthau puts it, "the selfishness of man has limits; his will to power has none."[1] Others have put less stress on human characteristics and more on the nature of the international system as a condition of what Waltz describes as "international anarchy."[2] The existence of powerful and antagonistic states creates a "security dilemma" for statesmen who must "compete for ever more power in order to find more security, an effort which proves self-defeating because complete security remains ultimately unobtainable."[3] Regardless of differences in explanation, however, there has been substantial agreement among many leading analysts about the crucial importance of conflict and war in

Robert Keohane and Joseph S. Nye, Jr., from Fred I. Greenstein and Nelson W. Polsby, *Handbook of Political Science* (Reading, MA: Addison-Wesley, 1975), pp. 363–377, by permission.

the international arena. The title of a volume by a well-known student of the subject, *International Relations: Peace or War?*, summarizes the point.[4]

There was never complete agreement on any particular version of this approach to world politics. Robert W. Tucker, Arnold Wolfers, and I. L. Claude all challenged Morgenthau's analysis, often with devastating effect.[5] Yet global patterns of world politics, particularly during the height of the cold war, seemed to confirm the broad outlines of force- and security-oriented definitions of the subject matter of the field. States were paramount, and their conflicts seemed to threaten not only world peace, but also human existence. International relations was seen essentially as a state of war in the Hobbesian sense:

> For *war* consists not in battle only, or the act of fighting, but in a tract of time wherein the will to contend by battle is sufficiently known; and therefore the notion of *time* is to be considered in the nature of war as it is in the nature of weather. For as the nature of foul weather lies not in a shower or two of rain but in an inclination thereto of many days together, so the nature of war consists not in actual fighting but in the known disposition thereto during all the time there is no assurance to the contrary. All other time is *peace*.[6]

Yet even during the most bitter years of East – West conflict, interstate relations in Western Europe were characterized by unprecedented cooperation, which rapidly went beyond wary diplomatic coexistence — beyond, that is, the traditional "state of war." The European unity movement flourished in the 1950s, first in the European Coal and Steel Community (ECSC), then in the European Economic Community (EEC) or Common Market. Obviously, this change occurred in the context of a bipolar strategic balance and was encouraged both by United States support and Soviet hostility. Nonetheless, the growth of common institutions was spectacular in comparison with previous patterns or developments elsewhere, and despite the absence of supranational government, it would clearly have been misleading to characterize relations in Western Europe as "international anarchy," or to have interpreted those relations in terms of security or possible violent conflict.

The importance of European events, for contemporary world politics as well as for theories of international relations, led several scholars to examine the developments taking place on the continent. In the mid-1950s, the pioneering work of Karl W. Deutsch and his associates[7] and of Ernst B. Haas,[8] focused attention on "regional integration" as an appropriate concept for describing the process that was taking place. As thinking about regional integration developed over the years, it led scholars quite far from the Realists' assumptions about men and states. The movement toward European unity could not be explained as merely a new form of alliance, thus reflecting the hoary principles of the balance of power.[9] It represented a response to opportunity and an expression of hope as much as a response to threat and an expression of fear. To students of European developments, it did not seem helpful to posit war-threatening conflict as the key to understanding the human or international condition. On the contrary, whether there would be progress toward more cooperative association or movement toward intense conflict or dissociation was seen as conditional on a multiplicity of factors. Detailed arguments were therefore developed about the conditions under which the European integration process would persist, speed up, slow down, or reverse itself. The arguments were further elaborated as scholars made efforts to understand regional integration efforts in other parts of the globe such as Latin America and Africa.[10]

The analysis of integration processes tended also to undermine another basic tenet of conventional analysis: that students of world politics should limit their focus to nation–states and their interactions. The "cybernetic" approach pioneered by Deutsch focused largely on transactions among societies and on changes in public attitudes within societies; Haas's "neofunctionalism" stressed the interests of elites and institutions and the extent to which they altered their behavior through learning.[11] Neither took the nation–state as the basic unit of analysis, nor did they rely on traditional notions of "national interest," although both were criticized on this account.[12] Transnational interactions not controlled by central foreign-policy organs of governments were no longer ignored. To the contrary, they were regarded as often being of crucial importance to the integration process.

Students of regional integration eventually developed a complex and ingenious set of notions and distinctions about the processes they were attempting to explain. . . . In the mid-1960s, "integrationists" were a distinct cluster in the matrix of scholars concerned with international relations.[13] Yet the slowdown in European integration during the 1960s, and the failure of the dominant paradigms to explain this adequately, tended to throw doubt on the general validity of "integration theory." At the same time the middling success of regional integration attempts elsewhere produced more evidence about the conditions in which integration would *not* take place than about the process of integration itself. Theoretical progress along the lines of comparative politics was stymied by the infeasibility of testing integration theory in a systematic and comparative manner. To borrow a phrase from the literature, integration theory became "encapsulated."

Despite these difficulties in developing adequate theories, the literature on regional integration is important for the ideas it stimulated about studying world politics. Students of integration raised a number of issues that are highly relevant to understanding the politics of interdependence outside the regional context as well as within. Conversely, analyzing political integration in terms of interdependence may help to place "integration theory" in its proper context: not as a separate and arcane set of notions applicable only to Europe and perhaps a few other areas, but as a highly important part of the literature on world politics — and one which traditionally inclined writers ignore only at their intellectual peril.

Due to the ambiguity of words such as "integration" and "interdependence" as used in the literature, it seems desirable at the outset to define several dimensions of integration and interdependence and to discuss how these relate to one another. . . .

INTERDEPENDENCE AND INTEGRATION

Considerable confusion continues to persist among scholars about the uses of the term "integration." Some scholars define it as a process, others as a terminal condition — the "condition of being integrated" — and still others as a combination of the two. In practice, scholars often use the word interchangeably, so that the reader may have difficulty knowing what is being referred to at any given time. The dictionary definition is of a process or condition of "forming parts into a whole." But what is the relevant whole? And in what units should we measure the process of formation? Galtung stresses the creation of new actors.[14] Deutsch defines integration in terms of turning "previously separate units into components of a coherent system."[15] Elsewhere, however, he stresses the condition of security community.[16] For Haas integration is "a process for the creation of political communities defined in institutional or attitudinal terms," but

> the study of regional integration is concerned with explaining how and why states cease to be wholly sovereign, how and why they voluntarily mingle, merge, and mix with their neighbors so as to lose the factual attributes of sovereignty while acquiring new techniques for resolving conflict between themselves. Regional cooperation, organization, systems, and subsystems may help describe steps on the way; but they should not be confused with the resulting *condition* [italics added.][17]

Some writers interested in comparing regions inquire which region has the higher level of integration have avoided definitions in terms of process or final condition — thus adding a third definition, implicitly, of integration as any level of association ascertained by specified measures.[18]

Since we intend in this chapter to compare the concepts of "integration" and "interdependence," we will define integration in this third way, as any level of association between actors, on one dimension or another. We will then be able to speak not only of various types of integration, such as economic, social, and policy integration, but of various levels of integration as well.

This definition places "integration" on the same analytical level as "interdependence," which is a term not so closely associated with teleological or process-oriented theory. Interdependence has normally been defined simply as a condition. Thus Oran Young uses the concept "interdependence" to refer to the extent to which events occurring in any given part or within any given component unit of a world system affect (either physically or perceptually) events taking place in each of the other parts or component units of the system.[19]

Depending on the type of system involved, it is clear that there can be various types of interdependence, as well as various levels of it. As with integration, relations may take place in a variety of issue-areas and may be more or less intense.

"Integration" and "interdependence" both carry evaluative overtones that have affected the way analysts have used the terms, sometimes with detrimental effects on conceptual clarity. Students of integration have oriented their work heavily toward the analysis of *peaceful* change. Indeed, in Haas's view,

the main reason for studying . . . regional integration . . . is normative: the units and actions provide a living laboratory for observing the peaceful creation of possible new types of human communities at a very high level of organization and of the processes that may lead to such conditions.[20]

This distinguishes it from "previous systematic studies of political unification because it limits itself to noncoercive efforts." Not all scholars share this view. Nonetheless, it does tend to be the prevailing usage.

Similarly, rhetorical uses of "interdependence" frequently carry highly positive and egalitarian overtones. Interdependence is taken to be a characteristic of mutually beneficial relationships. In some cases, however, an interdependent relationship may have such negative consequences that both parties would be quite happy to cease contact with one another entirely, forgoing any benefits that such contact may bring. A tense and rapidly escalating arms race constitutes an example of "negative interdependence" of this type. Yet even within relationships that are beneficial to all parties involved, interdependence may be highly asymmetrical: one actor may depend on another to a much greater extent than applies vice versa. Such asymmetrical relations are quite common in contemporary world politics, particularly between developed and less-developed countries, or between the United States and most other states. Asymmetry is politically important. Being less dependent than other actors in an interdependent system can be an important source of power.

Marxist writers on economic imperialism have been much more aware of this than more traditional analysts.[21] Theorists interested in dependence *(dependencia)* have also stressed asymmetries of interdependent relations, particularly between developed "center" countries and those of the underdeveloped "periphery."[22]

It is important to remember that interdependence by no means implies equality. Interdependent relationships are more or less asymmetrical depending on the characteristics of issue-areas and the attitudes and interests of elites, as well as on the aggregate levels of power of the states involved. Thus we use the term "interdependence" to imply some degree of mutual effect: it is up to the investigator to determine the intensity of a particular relationship and its degree of asymmetry.

Quite apart from the sometime connotations of peace and equality that they carry, both "integration" and "interdependence" are such vague and ill-defined concepts that without further analysis hopeless confusion quickly results. Our first step will therefore be to distinguish types of integration and interdependence that are insofar as possible comparable. We will consider economic integration and interdependence, social integration and interdependence, and policy integration and interdependence. We will also refer to other frequently used notions of integration that can be classified under the broad rubric of "political integration."[23]

Economic Integration and Interdependence

It is important to clarify at the outset that neither economic integration nor interdependence is equivalent to, or perfectly measured by, the volume of economic transactions between the units with which the analyst is concerned. Absolute volumes of transactions in the context of growing world trade and production may mean little; relative volumes (as measured by an index of relative acceptance, or RA)[24] may also lead to interpretive distortions.[25] More significantly, volumes of transactions may not necessarily indicate the extent to which units are affected by events occurring outside (interdependence) or the extent to which a true regional transnational economy is in existence (integration). It is more enlightening in our judgment to define one aspect of economic interdependence, at any rate, as "the *sensitivity* of economic transactions between two or more nations to economic developments within those nations." As Cooper points out,

> this approach means that two countries with much mutual trade would still experience a low degree of interdependence if the value of the trade were not sensitive to price and income developments in the two countries; on the other hand, two countries would be highly interdependent if their transactions were greatly sensitive to economic developments, even if their mutual trade were initially at a low level.[26]

This definition is closer to the intuitive meaning of interdependence than is a definition in terms of transactions volume. Furthermore, it can also be used as a definition of economic integration, consistent with economists' usage.[27] Thus at this level, "integration" and "interdependence" can be regarded as conceptually interchangeable terms. They differ only in the connotation that integration often takes place within an institutional framework.[28]

This definition is superior in our opinion to definitions that rely on the degree of formal suppression of national economic discrimination, as developed in particular by Bela Balassa.[29] Balassa set forth five categories ranging from "free trade area" at the low end of the spectrum to "total economic integration," as depicted in Table 1. These categories, how-

TABLE 1   Balassa's Categories of Economic Integration

	No Tariff or Quotas	Common External Tariffs	Free Flow of Factors	Harmonization of Economic Policies	Unification of Policies, Political Institutions
1. Free trade area	X				
2. Customs union	X	X			
3. Common market	X	X	X		
4. Economic union	X	X	X	X	
5. Total economic integration	X	X	X	X	X

ever, are formal rather than behavioral. They do not measure the extent to which actual flows follow the suppression of formal discriminatory barriers, or the extent to which mutual sensitivity increases as a result. They can be useful in describing policies followed by states, at least on a formal level; but they do not indicate the significance of those politics for economic interdependence or effective levels of economic integration. This is true at the global as well as the regional level. As Cooper argues,

> the integration of the pre-1914 world economy was something of an illusion. While the pre-1914 world was integrated in the sense that government-imposed barriers to the movement of goods, capital and people [i.e., Balassa's indicators of economic integration] were minimal, those imposed by nature were much greater and economic integration was not high in the sense used here: quick responsiveness to differential earning opportunities resulting in a sharp reduction in differences in factor rewards.[30]

Sensitivity is not the only dimension of interdependence. This form of interdependence is created by interaction within a framework that is established and generally taken for granted by the participants. Thus, under the fixed-exchange rate system of the late 1960s, European governments were dependent on (that is, sensitive to) changes in American monetary policy, and the United States was similarly dependent on European decisions to continue to hold dollars without demanding that they be exchanged for gold.

These sensitivities, however, depended on the rules of the system at the time: United States sensitivity to European decisions to continue to hold dollars could be drastically reduced by the simple act of unilaterally changing the rules, refusing any longer to redeem dollars for gold. A further question about interdependence therefore needs to be asked:

Which actors in the system are most and least vulnerable to changes in the rules (as in the monetary system) or to a drastic reduction in the level of transactions in the system?[31] In vulnerability terms, the less dependent actor is not necessarily the one with less sensitivity to changes in transactions taking place within an established structure, but the one that would incur relatively lower costs from the termination or drastic alteration of the relationship.

Vulnerability interdependence has no direct parallel in the various definitions of economic integration. Nevertheless, power relations among a number of actors in a regional grouping or any other set of economic transactions are likely to be strongly affected by the differential costs to them of dissolution.[32] For this reason, vulnerability interdependence is particularly relevant for the analysis of the *structure* of relations in a common market or in an issue-area. In a sense, it asks which actors are the "definers of the *ceteris paribus* clause," or in game-theory terms, which actors can restructure the payoff matrix.[33] Since the relative power of actors is as important within the context of an integration process as elsewhere in politics, careful analysis of patterns of vulnerability interdependence, and asymmetries in those patterns, should be a necessary element of sophisticated explanations of behavior in regional or other economic transactions.

Social Integration and Interdependence

On an analogous basis to that of economic interdependence and levels of economic integration, one can define social interdependence, and levels of social integration, in terms of the sensitivity of societies to changes taking place in other societies. As the present authors have argued elsewhere,

> by facilitating the flow of ideas modern communications have also increased intersocietal sensitivity. Certainly there have been indirect "contagions" of ideas in earlier periods such as the European revolutions of 1848 or Latin American university reforms in 1917. . . . Today, however, television has created a "window on the West" in the living rooms of the elites of the third world. Widely separate elites, whether functionally similar social groups, students, military officers, or racial minorities, become more rapidly aware of each other's activities.[34]

It is clear that such sensitivities can be deliberately fostered or discouraged but rarely completely controlled by governments. Eastern European governments, for example, have not been able to keep younger generations from imitating aspects of Western youth culture. Within Western Europe, younger people tend to be particularly subject to "contagions" from other societies.[35]

Unfortunately, good indicators of social sensitivity have not been developed, and scholars have generally attempted to rely on levels of transactions, either in absolute terms or on a relative basis as expressed by the index of relative acceptance discussed above. Donald Puchala, for instance, has used absolute figures on mail, trade, tourism, and student exchanges, coupled with indices of relative acceptance of trade and mail to demonstrate that the EEC countries have become a distinct transactions network.[36] These data, although they reveal a good deal about transactions, say little about sensitivities.

Sensitivities of societies to one another could be explored, however, by an analysis of the diffusion of innovation in social patterns and of popular opinions and perceptions. Subjects for analysis could range from matters of cultural tastes and clothing styles to issues of labor-union organization, university governance, or social policies of governments. [One] study, for instance, has examined the diffusion of social-security arrangements from one society to another since the 1880s.[37] Some suggestive work has been done on policy diffusion, intranationally as well as cross-nationally, that could provide a base for efforts to explore issues of social integration in this way.[38] By being closely tied intuitively to concepts of interdependence and integration, data on diffusion patterns would be likely to be of greater theoretical value than much of the transactions data that has been gathered so far.

Policy Integration and Interdependence

For political scientists, economic and social integration and interdependence are most interesting when they are perceived and acted upon, or even facilitated, by governments. Students of political integration have therefore concentrated much of their attention on "the evolution over time of a collective decision-making system among nations"[39] or what Nye[40] has elsewhere called "policy integration." This dimension excludes other aspects of political integration such as the construction of common institutions or the development of a sense of community. Instead, it focuses on the extent to which policies are coordinated with one another. Policy interdependence refers to the extent to which decisions taken by actors in one part of a system affect (intentionally or unintentionally) other actors' policy decisions elsewhere in the system. Policy integration can be regarded as an attempt to reduce adverse costs of policy interdependence by deliberately coordinating policy and thus changing the nature of policy interdependence without necessarily reducing its level. This by no means implies that conflict does not exist. Indeed, conflict or the serious threat of conflict may be critical in stimulating attempts at policy integration.

Policy interdependence may be indirect: governmental policies may affect one another without direct contacts between the governments themselves or deliberate attempts by governments to manipulate each other's behavior. Central bank policies toward interest rates in major

Western countries during the 1960s would have affected each other even in the absence of consultation. Changes in Japanese tax policies toward their automobile companies could well affect exports of cars to the United States, and therefore U.S. trade and monetary policy. New antipollution standards for automobiles in California may affect economic policy in Japan. The ineffectiveness of American policy attempts to stop heroin use in the 1960s, and the increases in heroin shipments to the United States during that decade, affected French society and therefore French policies toward narcotics; conversely, the weakness of French law enforcement earlier had contributed to the American problem and to changes in American policy.[41] In all of these cases, we can speak of "indirect policy dependence." The effects of policies can be transmitted through transnational interactions between societies. As government policies extend "downward," deeper into society, and as transnational transactions multiply "horizontally," it can be expected that indirect policy interdependence will continue to increase, particularly among developed, market-economy countries.

Policy interdependence may also be direct. Governments may take action deliberately designed to affect others' policies, may threaten to do so, or may be in such a situation that such actions or threats are continual possibilities. The governments of the United States and the Soviet Union are directly interdependent strategically. Either could destroy the other's society, and leaders of both governments are aware of this situation. The United States, Japan, and Western Europe are interdependent economically. When the United States attempted in 1971 to persuade or force other governments to revalue their currencies, it was taking advantage of the high degree of dependence of other governments on American decisions. Most international negotiations involve the manipulation and management of direct policy interdependencies for national advantage—or sometimes for the advantage of subnational or transnational groups.

Insofar as governments are aware of the processes at work, indirect policy interdependence is likely to lead to direct policy interdependence. Seeing other governments' policies as one source of their troubles, leaders of states are likely to attempt to influence those policies. Possible results short of war include arms races and trade wars, as well as myriads of lesser conflicts. In a situation of high policy interdependence, the threats both to state autonomy and to joint welfare may very well lead to concerted attempts by groups of governments to coordinate policy, as a means to increase welfare *as well as,* on frequent occasions, to regain control of the situation from nongovernmental actors.[42] In the 1960s and early 1970s, for instance, governments faced the problem of coping with private monetary speculation, which threatened the structure of fixed exchange rates to which all governments subscribed. Their collaborations represented attempts to gain control over speculators while preserving what were then perceived as the general benefits of fixed exchange rates.[43]

In a developed and institutionalized system of policy integration, two distinguishing characteristics are present: on the one hand, the expectation that some agreement will eventually be reached; and on the other, a system of decision rules, formal and informal, that determine how the decision will be reached and that legitimize particular nonviolent means of influence while proscribing the use of force. These rules may be more or less institutionalized and may conform more or less closely to typical national democratic procedures. A formal voting scheme, for instance, is not a necessary prerequisite for a high level of policy integration. On the basis of their knowledge of various regional integration schemes, students have sometimes attempted to score them according to the degree to which joint decisions are taken, differentiating by issue-area.[44] Yet policy integration as defined here is by no means limited to the regional context, although the highest levels of it in the contemporary world are found in the European Community. NATO, the International Monetary Fund (IMF), the General Agreement on Tariffs and Trade (GATT), and the Organization for Economic Cooperation and Development (OECD) all represent focal points for varying degrees of policy integration by governments.

One of the most striking features of regional cooperation in Europe has been the way in which policy integration has reinforced economic and social integration, which have then provided new imperatives for further policy integration. This self-reinforcing process is much less evident on the global scale. There, the potential for policy disintegration is more often realized. Nevertheless, whatever the setbacks in particular areas, increased policy interdependence provides continual new opportunities for integrative as well as disintegrative responses. For the national policymaker, it implies decreased efficacy of purely national policies in solving problems, whether these have to do with economic growth, balance of payments equilibrium, maintenance of national control of industry, protection of the environment, or efforts to control the use of harmful narcotics. Insofar as these goals are not shared widely in the world, or measures taken to achieve objectives in one state conflict with measures elsewhere, conflicts over policy are likely to arise. Leaders may in some circumstances attempt to insulate their societies from effects emanating from outside, as in the case of Burma. But where the costs of avoiding policy interdependence appear too high, it may seem more sensible, rather than changing its *level,* to alter its *form:* that is, to institute a joint decision-making procedure. Attempts to develop patterns of policy integration can therefore be regarded as ways to cope with policy interdependence — which may, on occasion, involve increasing it.

Table 2 summarizes the comparisons we have drawn between these principal aspects of interdependence and integration.

TABLE 2   A Summary of Usages: Integration and Interdependence

A. These dimensions of interdependence and integration are defined in virtually interchangeable ways, so that the only difference is in the connotations:
   1. Economic-sensitivity interdependence/economic integration:
   2. Social interdependence/social integration.
B. These dimensions of interdependence and integration are not interchangeable:
   1. Policy integration is one means of coping with the effects of indirect and direct policy interdependence, and may also increase policy interdependence.
   2. Economic interdependence in the sense of "vulnerability interdependence" is not developed explicitly in the intergration literature, although the problem of the extent to which various actors are capable of changing the structure of the situation or "rules of the game" is sometimes discussed.

Institutional and Attitudinal Integration

Two other prominent usages of the term "political integration" deserve brief mention here, although they find no close parallel in the notion of interdependence.

The most common of these usages is that of political integration as "institutional integration," that is, the extent to which common institutions have been developing for a region. Thus one may hear Europeans or Central Americans complain that "economic integration has not led to political integration," by which they usually mean that political institutions have not developed as a result of closer economic ties. Other terms sometimes employed, such as "supranationality," "confederation," and "federation" indicate a similar institutional orientation. Yet institutions are usually sought not for their own sake but for the effects they are likely to have on social and economic conditions, usually through effects on governmental policies. A focus on policy integration therefore concentrates more directly on the critical outcomes that affect people's lives, and the analyst following this approach is less likely than the institutionally oriented observer to be misled into equating the political significance of an integration process with its degree of formal institutionalization.

Another common dimension of political integration, "attitudinal integration," can be defined in terms of the extent to which people share a sense of common identity and/or mutual obligation. This is how theorists of comparative politics tend to use the word "integration,"[45] and it is related to Deutsch's concept of security community as the extent to which a set to people holds reliable expectations of nonviolent relations among themselves. Disputes are rife among theorists about the importance of attitudinal integration for explaining other aspects of the phenomenon, such as institutional or policy integration.[46]

These usages of "political integration," which are often lumped together with joint policy formation, provide one reason for the frequent confusions that surround that term. We saw above that economic integration and interdependence, social integration and interdependence, and policy integration and interdependence, all had something to do with the sensitivities of one unit in a set of events taking place in another, as a result of transactions between them. Institutional integration refers, however, to structures; and attitudinal integration focuses on the compatibility of attitudes at a given time, rather than to sensitivities of attitudes of one set of people to those of another set. These usages of "integration" therefore refer not only to different substantive dimensions of the phenomenon, but to different types of processes as well. This is why they have no exact parallel in usages of the term "interdependence," which always refers to the effects (sensitivity or vulnerability) of patterns of transactions, whether actual or anticipated.

Evaluations of Integration and Interdependence

It should be clear from the foregoing discussion that integration and interdependence are both complex enough concepts that simply evaluating as "good" or "bad" the phenomena to which they refer will be extremely misleading. Their effects on conflict are difficult enough to evaluate. Efforts to increase policy *integration,* in particular, have usually taken place within the context of peaceful relations among states, and may well contribute to the development of such relations, although the patterns of causality are surely mutual. Violent conflicts between states have taken place within regions where integration schemes were in effect — notably, in Central America and East Africa in 1969 and 1972 respectively. Nevertheless, one's overall judgment of the effects of policy integration on peace — regionally or on a broader scope — must, on the evidence available, be positive.[47]

For policy *interdependence,* however, it is difficult indeed to argue persuasively that higher levels of interdependence necessarily promote world concord. Following Rousseau, Waltz has argued the opposite:

> It is hard to get a war going unless the potential participants are somehow closely linked. Interdependent states whose relations remain unregulated must experience conflict and will occasionally fall into violence. If regulation is hard to come by, as it is in the relations of states, then it would seem to follow that a lessening of interdependence is desirable.[48]

Waltz's contention that some degree of interdependence is necessary for conflict is irrefutable, but the conclusion that a lessening of interdependence is desirable does not follow unless we know the relative costs of attaining effective regulation as opposed to those of reducing interdependence. Theories of political integration focus precisely on the question of the attainability of regulation and that a high level of policy interdependence may therefore be tolerable. It would seem that neither the blanket proposition that "interdependence leads to peace," nor the opposite statement, would be well sustained in a systematic, empirical inquiry. Interdependence at some level is obviously a necessary condition for war; but that is quite uninteresting, since it does not tell us anything in particular about thresholds or conditions beyond the minimum requirement. Nevertheless, the proposition that higher levels of policy interdependence do not necessarily imply more peaceful relations seems incontestable.

Quite apart from the effects of integration and interdependence on conflict, it is not true that increases in levels of either are necessarily beneficial. Too often one finds an implicit assumption that integration (and less often interdependence) is a good thing *per se*. This is wrong for a variety of reasons:

1. Where many values are involved, integration and interdependence may enhance some while diminishing others. Many Canadians, for example, argue that increased levels of economic integration and interdependence with the United States have contributed to increased Canadian material welfare but decreased Canadian political and cultural autonomy.[49] In Eastern Europe, a high degree of regional trade has been achieved by forgoing greater welfare gains from trade with the rest of the world.[50]

2. Economic integration and interdependence have distributional effects, and may look different from the periphery than from the center of any unit. What is good for the whole is not necessarily good for each of the parts. The unification of Italy had a deleterious effect upon Southern Italy; the famous gold standard contributed to high levels of economic interdependence in the nineteenth century but accentuated instability in the periphery of the world economy. In the contemporary world, some U.S. workers complain about the effects on their welfare of high levels of interdependence. The British government worries about the effects of British growth rates on monetary union with their partners in the European Community.

3. Social integration and interdependence may introduce changes in societies that are undesired at least by many of the inhabitants. Importation of new patterns of life, whether involving the use of Coca-Cola, automobiles, or drugs, may drastically alter established social patterns and lead to more or less serious problems. Although to some these changes may represent progress, others view them negatively. Mass immigration — for example, into Switzerland during the 1960s — can be viewed as so threatening that special measures are taken to prevent it even at some economic cost.

4. As noted above, policy interdependence may create foci for conflict, although insofar as cleavages tend to be crosscutting, conflicts may be less intense, if more frequent. Yet even if patterns of policy integration

are developed, serious normative problems may arise. Two of the most significant of these are:

a. Costs to democratic control. Insofar as decisions become more responsive to the wishes of external actors within a complex communications network, it may be increasingly difficult for traditional democratic means of internal control to be effective. It may be unclear to domestic interests even how a given decision was made, much less how to influence it effectively.[51]

b. Costs to third parties, and of conflict with third parties. Integration schemes are often designed purposefully to exclude outsiders, or some outsiders, from their benefits. If external interests are hurt, not only may their welfare, and perhaps world welfare, be damaged (for instance, through trade-diversion effects), but retaliation on their part could lead to further costs. The difficult relations between the United States and the European Community in the early years of the 1970s attest to that.

What this discussion suggests is that more explicit attention should be paid in the future to the normatively relevant consequences of regional integration and international interdependence. As Stuart A. Scheingold has argued,

> to date, the students of integration have been mainly describing, analyzing, and measuring the integration process. . . . What has been missing from all this work is some attention to the difference it makes whether or not such regional entities are created.[52]

The literature on integration and interdependence has frequently failed to challenge normative assumptions implying that integration is desirable *per se.* The attempt by students of the subject to correct for this by distinguishing clearly between questions of "more or less" and those of "better or worse" is laudable as far as it goes. But at some point, serious consideration of the normative issues should be reintroduced, on the basis of empirical findings that are as unbiased as possible. "The normative political theory of integration and interdependence" is a topic that could usefully benefit from substantial serious attention. . . .

NOTES

1. Hans J. Morgenthau, *Scientific Man Versus Power Politics* (Chicago: University of Chicago Press, 1946), p. 193.
2. Kenneth N. Waltz, *Man, the State and War* (New York: Columbia University Press, 1959).
3. John Herz, *International Politics in the Atomic Age* (New York: Columbia University Press, 1959).
4. Richard Rosecrance, *International Relations* (New York: McGraw-Hill, 1973).
5. Robert W. Tucker, "Professor Morgenthau's Theory of Political Realism," *American Political Science Review,* vol. 46 (1952), pp. 214–24; Arnold Wolfers,

Discord and Collaboration (Baltimore, MD: Johns Hopkins University Press, 1962); and Inis L. Claude, Jr., *Power and International Relations* (New York: Random House, 1962).

6. Thomas Hobbes, *Leviathan,* first published 1651, Michael Oakeshott, ed. (Oxford: Basil Blackwell, n.d.), Part I, ch. 13, p. 82.

7. Karl W. Deutsch and associates, *Political Community and the North Atlantic Area* (Princeton, NJ: Princeton University Press, 1957).

8. Ernst B. Haas, *The Uniting of Europe* (Stanford, CA: Stanford University Press, 1958).

9. George Liska, *Europe Ascendant* (Baltimore, MD: Johns Hopkins University Press, 1964).

10. A collection of articles by leading scholars is Leon N. Lindberg and Stuart A. Scheingold (eds.), *Regional Integration* (Cambridge, MA: Harvard University Press, 1971). For a critique of that volume, see Roger D. Hansen, "European Integration," *International Organization,* vol. 27 (1973), pp. 225–54.

11. Peter J. Katzenstein, "Hare and Tortoise: The Race Toward Integration," *International Organization,* vol. 25, pp. 290–97.

12. Stanley Hoffmann, *State of War* (New York: Praeger, 1965).

13. Bruce M. Russett, "Methodological and Theoretical Schools in International Relations," in Norman Palmer, ed., *A Design for International Relations Research* (Philadelphia: American Academy of Political and Social Science, 1970).

14. Johan Galtung, "A Structural Theory of Integration," *Journal of Peace Research,* vol. 5 (1968), pp. 375–95.

15. Karl W. Deutsch, *The Analysis of International Relations* (Englewood Cliffs, NJ: Prentice Hall, 1971), p. 158.

16. Deutsch, *Political Community.*

17. Ernst B. Haas, "The Study of Regional Integration" in Lindberg and Scheingold, *Regional Integration,* p. 6.

18. Joseph S. Nye, Jr., "Comparative Regional Integration," *International Organization,* vol. 22 (1968), pp. 855–80.

19. Oran R. Young, "Interdependencies in World Politics," *International Journal,* vol. 24 (1969), pp. 726–50.

20. Haas, "Study of Regional Integration," p. 4.

21. Harry Magdoff, *The Age of Imperialism* (New York: Monthly Review Press, 1969), and Arghiri Emmanuel, *Unequal Exchange* (New York: Monthly Review Press, 1972).

22. Andre Gunder Frank, *Capitalism and Underdevelopment in Latin America* (New York: Monthly Review Press, 1969); Johan Galtung, "A Structural Theory of Imperialism," *Journal of Peace Research,* vol. 8 (1971), pp. 81–117.

23. Joseph S. Nye, *Peace in Parts* (Boston: Little, Brown, 1971).

24. The formula for the index of relative acceptance (RA) is $RA = (A - E)/E$, where A equals actual values of transactions and E equals expected values on a basis of a null model based on the assumption of complete indifference between actors.

25. Richard W. Chadwick, "A Brief Critique of Transaction Data and Analysis" *International Organization,* vol. 26 (1972), pp. 681–85; Hansen, "European Integration"; and Barry B. Hughes, "Transaction Analysis," *International Organization,* vol. 25 (1971).

26. Richard N. Cooper, "Economic Interdependence and Foreign Policies in the Seventies," *World Politics,* vol. 24 (1972), pp. 159–81.

27. Robert D. Tollison and Thomas D. Willett, "International Integration and the Interdependence of Economic Variables," *International Organization*, vol. 27 (1973), pp. 255–72. Cooper does not distinguish between the two terms and appears to regard them as synonyms. The reader who looks up "integration, economic" in Cooper's index is referred to the listing of "interdependence" under "economic policy."

28. Factor price equalization is not the only measure of economic sensitivity, and students of integration have found it important to devise supplementary measurements to take into account nontrade contributions to mutual sensitivity, such as shared services among members of a regional arrangement.

29. Bela Belassa, *The Theory of Economic Integration* (London: Allen & Unwin, 1961).

30. Richard N. Cooper, *The Economics of Interdependence* (New York: McGraw-Hill, 1968), p. 152.

31. Kenneth N. Waltz, "The Myth of National Interdependence," in Charles Kindleberger (ed.), *The International Corporation* (Cambridge, MA: MIT Press, 1970).

32. Leon N. Lindberg, "Decision Making and Integration in the European Community," in *International Political Communities* (Garden City, NY: Anchor Books, 1966).

33. Anthony Lanyi, "Political Aspects of Exchange Rate Systems," in Richard Merritt (ed.), *Communications in International Politics* (Urbana, IL: University of Illinois Press, 1971).

34. Robert O. Keohane and Joseph S. Nye, Jr., *Transnational Relations and World Politics* (Cambridge, MA: Harvard University Press, 1971), p. 376.

35. Anthony Sampson, *Anatomy of Europe* (New York: Harper & Row, 1969), and Ronald Inglehart, "An End to European Integration?" *American Political Science Review*, vol. 61 (1967), pp. 91–105.

36. Donald J. Puchala, "International Transactions and Regional Integration," in Lindberg and Scheingold, *Regional Integration.*

37. David Collier and Richard E. Messick, "Functional Prerequisites Versus Diffusion," unpublished paper presented at the Midwest Political Science Association, Chicago, 1973.

38. Jack L. Walker, "The Diffusion of Innovations Among the American States," *American Political Science Review*, vol. 63 (1969), pp. 880–99; Robert D. Putnam, "Toward Explaining Military Intervention in Latin American Politics," *World Politics*, vol. 20 (1967), pp. 83–110; and Manus Midlarsky, "Mathematical Models of Instability and a Theory of Diffusion," *International Studies Quarterly*, vol. 14 (1970), pp. 60–84.

39. Leon N. Lindberg and Stuart A. Scheingold, *Europe's Would-Be Polity* (Englewood Cliffs, NJ: Prentice Hall, 1970).

40. Nye, *Peace in Parts.*

41. Lester R. Brown, *The Interdependence of Nations* (New York: Foreign Policy Association, 1972).

42. John Ruggie has presented an interesting formal analysis of governmental reactions to interdependence, based on the assumption that joint decision making for the performance of joint tasks implies a sacrifice of governmental autonomy for the sake of benefits from collective action. Yet in situations where governmental autonomy has already been diminished as a result of indirect policy interdependence, coordinative procedures may very well not reduce autonomy further and may even increase it.

43. Lawrence B. Krause (ed.), "Private International Finance" in Keohane and Nye, *Transnational Relations.*

44. Leon N. Lindberg, "The European Community as a Political System," *Journal of Common Market Studies,* vol. 5 (1967), pp. 344–87 and Nye, "Comparative Regional Integration."

45. Claude Ake, *A Theory of Political Integration* (Homewood, IL: Dorsey Press, 1967).

46. For a further discussion, see Nye, *Peace in Parts.*

47. Ibid.

48. Waltz, "The Myth of National Interdependence," p. 205.

49. *International Organization,* Fall 1974.

50. Frederic L. Pryor, *The Communist Foreign Trade System* (Cambridge, MA: MIT Press, 1963).

51. Karl Kaiser, "Transnational Relations As a Threat to the Democratic Process" in Keohane and Nye, *Transnational Relations;* see also Keohane and Nye, "Transgovernmental Relations and International Organization," *World Politics,* vol. 27 (1974), pp. 39–62.

52. Stuart A. Scheingold, "Domestic and International Consequences of Regional Integration" in Lindberg and Scheingold, *Regional Integration,* p. 374.

Realism and Complex Interdependence

Robert O. Keohane and Joseph S. Nye

The authors contrast the realist perspective on international relations with the complex interdependence perspective on world politics associated with the pluralist image.

INTERDEPENDENCE IN WORLD POLITICS

We live in an era of interdependence. This vague phrase expresses a poorly understood but widespread feeling that the very nature of world politics is changing. The power of nations — that age-old touchstone of analysts and statesmen — has become more elusive: "calculations of power are even more delicate and deceptive than in previous ages."[1] Henry Kissinger, though deeply rooted in the classical tradition, has

From Robert O. Keohane and Joseph S. Nye, Jr., *Power and Interdependence: World Politics in Transition* (Boston: Little, Brown, 1977), pp. 3–5, 8–11, 23–37. Reprinted by permission.

stated that "the traditional agenda of international affairs — the balance among major powers, the security of nations — no longer defines our perils or our possibilities. . . . Now we are entering a new era. Old international patterns are crumbling: old slogans are uninstructive; old solutions are unavailing. The world has become interdependent in economics, in communications, in human aspirations."[2]

How profound are the changes? A modernist school sees telecommunications and jet travel as creating a "global village" and believes that burgeoning social and economic transactions are creating a "world without borders."[3] To greater or lesser extent, a number of scholars see our era as one in which the territorial state, which has been dominant in world politics for the four centuries since feudal times ended, is being eclipsed by nonterritorial actors such as multinational corporations, transnational social movements, and international organizations. As one economist put it, "the state is about through as an economic unit."[4]

Traditionalists call these assertions unfounded "globaloney." They point to the continuity in world politics. Military interdependence has always existed, and military power is still important in world politics — witness nuclear deterrence; the Vietnam, Middle East, and India – Pakistan wars, and Soviet influence in Eastern Europe or American influence in the Caribbean. Moreover, as the Soviet Union has shown, authoritarian states can, to a considerable extent, control telecommunications and social transactions that they consider disruptive. Even poor and weak countries have been able to nationalize multinational corporations, and the prevalence of nationalism casts doubt on the proposition that the nation – state is fading away.

Neither the modernists nor the traditionalist have an adequate framework for understanding the politics of global interdependence.[5] Modernists point correctly to the fundamental changes now taking place, but they often assume without sufficient analysis that advances in technology and increases in social and economic transactions will lead to a new world in which states, and their control of force, will no longer be important.[6] Traditionalists are adept at showing flaws in the modernist vision by pointing out how military interdependence continues, but find it very difficult accurately to interpret today's multidimensional economic, social, and ecological interdependence.

Our task . . . is not to argue either the modernist or traditionalist position. Because our era is marked by both continuity and change, this would be fruitless. Rather, our task is to provide a means of distilling and blending the wisdom in both positions by developing a coherent theoretical framework for the political analysis of interdependence. We shall develop several different but potentially complementary models, or intellectual tools, for grasping the reality of interdependence in contemporary world politics. Equally important, we shall attempt to explore the *conditions* under which each model will be most likely to produce accurate predictions and satisfactory explanations. Contemporary world politics is not a seamless web; it is a tapestry of diverse relationships. In such a world, one model cannot explain all situations. The secret of understanding lies in knowing which approach or combination of approaches to use in analyzing a situation. There will never be a substitute for careful analysis of actual situations.

Yet theory is inescapable; all empirical or practical analysis rests on it. Pragmatic policymakers might think that they need pay no more heed to theoretical disputes over the nature of world politics than they pay to medieval scholastic disputes over how many angels can dance on the head of a pin. Academic pens, however, leave marks in the minds of statesmen with profound results for policy. Not only are "practical men who believe themselves to be quite exempt from any intellectual influences" unconscious captives of conceptions created by "some academic scribbler of a few years back," but increasingly the scribblers have been playing a direct role in forming foreign policy.[7] Inappropriate images and ill-conceived perceptions of world politics can lead directly to inappropriate or even disastrous national policies.

Rationale and rationalization, systematic presentation and symbolism, become so intertwined that it is difficult, even for policymakers themselves, to disentangle reality from rhetoric. Traditionally, classical theories of world politics have portrayed a potential "state of war" in which states' behavior was dominated by the constant danger of military conflict. During the Cold War, especially the first decade after World War II, this conception, labeled "political realism" by its proponents, became widely accepted by students and practitioners of international relations in Europe and the United States.[8] During the 1960s, many otherwise keen observers who accepted realist approaches were slow to perceive the development of new issues that did not center on military–security concerns.[9] The same dominant image in the late 1970s or 1980s would be likely to lead to even more unrealistic expectations. Yet to exchange it for an equally simple view — for instance, that military force is obsolete and economic interdependence benign — would condemn one to equally grave, though different, errors. . . .

INTERDEPENDENCE AS AN ANALYTIC CONCEPT

In common parlance, *dependence* means a state of being determined or significantly affected by external forces. *Interdependence,* most simply defined, means *mutual* dependence. Interdependence in world politics refers to situations characterized by reciprocal effects among countries or among actors in different countries.

These effects often result from international transactions — flows of money, goods, people, and messages across international boundaries. Such transactions have increased dramatically since World War II: "Recent decades reveal a general tendency for many forms of human interconnectedness across national boundaries to be doubling every ten years."[10] Yet this interconnectedness is not the same as interdependence. The effects of transactions on interdependence will depend on the constraints, or costs, associated with them. A country that imports all of its oil is likely to be more dependent on a continual flow of petroleum than a country importing furs, jewelry, and perfume (even of equivalent monetary value) will be on uninterrupted access to these luxury goods. Where there are reciprocal (although not necessarily symmetrical) costly effects of transactions, there is interdependence. Where interactions do not have significant costly effects, there is simply interconnectedness. The distinction is vital if we are to understand the *politics* of interdependence.

Costly effects may be imposed directly and intentionally by another actor — as in Soviet-American strategic interdependence, which derives from the mutual threat of nuclear destruction. But some costly effects do not come directly or intentionally from other actors. For example, collective action may be necessary to prevent disaster for an alliance (the members of which are interdependent), for an international economic system (which may face chaos because of the absence of coordination, rather than through the malevolence of any actor), or for an ecological system threatened by a gradual increase of industrial effluents.

We do not limit the term *interdependence* to situations of mutual benefit. Such a definition would assume that the concept is only useful analytically where the modernist view of the world prevails: where threats of military force are few and levels of conflict are low. It would exclude from interdependence cases of mutual dependence, such as the strategic interdependence between the United States and the Soviet Union. Furthermore, it would make it very ambiguous whether relations between industrialized countries and less developed countries should be considered interdependent or not. Their inclusion would depend on an inherently subjective judgment about whether the relationships were "mutually beneficial."

Because we wish to avoid sterile arguments about whether a given set of relationships is characterized by interdependence or not, and because we seek to use the concept of interdependence to integrate rather than further to divide modernist and traditional approaches, we choose a broader definition. Our perspective implies that interdependent relationships will always involve costs, since interdependence restricts autonomy; but it is impossible to specify *a priori* whether the benefits of a relationship will exceed the costs. This will depend on the values of the actors as well as on the nature of the relationship. Nothing guarantees that relationships that we designate as "interdependent" will be characterized by mutual benefit.

Two different perspectives can be adopted for analyzing the costs and benefits of an interdependent relationship. The first focuses on the joint gains or joint losses to the parties involved. The other stresses *rela-*

tive gains and distributional issues. Classical economists adopted the first approach in formulating their powerful insight about comparative advantage: that undistorted international trade will provide overall net benefits. Unfortunately, an exclusive focus on joint gain may obscure the second key issue: how those gains are divided. Many of the crucial political issues of interdependence revolve around the old question of politics, "who gets what?"

It is important to guard against the assumption that measures that increase joint gain from a relationship will somehow be free of distributional conflict. Governments and nongovernmental organizations will strive to increase their shares of gains from transactions, even when they both profit enormously from the relationship. Oil-exporting governments and multinational oil companies, for instance, share an interest in high prices for petroleum; but they have also been in conflict over shares of the profits involved.

We must therefore be cautious about the prospect that rising interdependence is creating a brave new world of cooperation to replace the bad old world of international conflict. As every parent of small children knows, baking a larger pie does not stop disputes over the size of the slices. An optimistic approach would overlook the uses of economic and even ecological interdependence in competitive international politics.

The difference between traditional international politics and the politics of economic and ecological interdependence is *not* the difference between a world of "zero-sum" (where one side's gain is the other side's loss) and "nonzero-sum" games. Military interdependence need not be zero-sum. Indeed, military allies actively seek interdependence to provide enhanced security for all. Even balance of power situations need not be zero-sum. If one side seeks to upset the status quo, then its gain is at the expense of the other. But if most or all participants want a stable status quo, they can jointly gain by preserving the balance of power among them. Conversely, the politics of economic and ecological interdependence involve competition even when large net benefits can be expected from cooperation. There are important continuities, as well as marked differences, between the traditional politics of military security and the politics of economic and ecological interdependence.

We must also be careful not to define interdependence entirely in terms of situations of *evenly balanced* mutual dependence. It is *asymmetries* in dependence that are most likely to provide sources of influence for actors in their dealings with one another. Less dependent actors can often use the interdependent relationship as a source of power in bargaining over an issue and perhaps to affect other issues. At the other extreme from pure symmetry is pure dependence (sometimes disguised by calling the situation interdependence); but it too is rare. Most cases lie between these two extremes. And that is where the heart of the political bargaining process of interdependence lies. . . .

REALISM AND COMPLEX INTERDEPENDENCE

One's assumptions about world politics profoundly affect what one sees and how one constructs theories to explain events. We believe that the assumptions of political realists, whose theories dominated the postwar period, are often an inadequate basis for analyzing the politics of interdependence. The realist assumptions about world politics can be seen as defining an extreme set of conditions or *ideal type*. One could also imagine very different conditions. In this article, we shall construct another ideal type, the opposite of realism. We call it *complex interdependence*. After establishing the differences between realism and complex interdependence, we shall argue that complex interdependence sometimes comes closer to reality than does realism. When it does, traditional explanations of change in international regimes become questionable and the search for new explanatory models becomes more urgent.

For political realists, international politics, like all other politics, is a struggle for power but, unlike domestic politics, a struggle dominated by organized violence. In the words of the most influential postwar textbook, "All history shows that nations active in international politics are continuously preparing for, actively involved in, or recovering from organized violence in the form of war."[11] Three assumptions are integral to the realist vision. First, states as coherent units are the dominant actors in world politics. This is a double assumption: states are predominant; and they act as coherent units. Second, realists assume that force is a usable and effective instrument of policy. Other instruments may also be employed, but using or threatening force is the most effective means of wielding power. Third, partly because of their second assumption, realists assume a hierarchy of issues in world politics, headed by questions of military security: the "high politics" of military security dominates the "low politics" of economic and social affairs.

These realist assumptions define an ideal type of world politics. They allow us to imagine a world in which politics is continually characterized by active or potential conflict among states, with the use of force possible at any time. Each state attempts to defend its territory and interests from real or perceived threats. Political integration among states is slight and lasts only as long as it serves the national interests of the most powerful states. Transnational actors either do not exist or are politically unimportant. Only the adept exercise of force or the threat of force permits states to survive, and only while statesmen succeed in adjusting their interests, as in a well-functioning balance of power, is the system stable.

Each of the realist assumptions can be challenged. If we challenge them all simultaneously, we can imagine a world in which actors other than states participate directly in world politics, in which a clear hierarchy of issues does not exist, and in which force is an ineffective instrument of policy. Under these conditions — which we call the characteristics of complex interdependence — one would expect world politics to be very different than under realist conditions.

We will explore these differences in the next section of this chapter. We do not argue, however, that complex interdependence faithfully reflects world political reality. Quite the contrary: both it and the realist portrait are ideal types. Most situations will fall somewhere between these two extremes. Sometimes, realist assumptions will be accurate, or largely accurate, but frequently complex interdependence will provide a better portrayal of reality. Before one decides what explanatory model to apply to a situation or problem, one will need to understand the degree to which realist or complex interdependence assumptions correspond to the situation.

THE CHARACTERISTICS
OF COMPLEX INTERDEPENDENCE

Complex interdependence has three main characteristics:

1. *Multiple channels* connect societies, including: informal ties between governmental elites as well as formal foreign office arrangements; informal ties among nongovernmental elites (face-to-face and through telecommunications); and transnational organizations (such as multinational banks or corporations). These channels can be summarized as interstate, transgovernmental, and transnational relations. *Interstate* relations are the normal channels assumed by realists. *Transgovernmental* applies when we relax the realist assumption that states act coherently as units; *transnational* applies when we relax the assumption that states are the only units.
2. The agenda of interstate relationships consists of multiple issues that are not arranged in a clear or consistent hierarchy. This *absence of hierarchy among issues* means, among other things, that military security does not consistently dominate the agenda. Many issues arise from what used to be considered domestic policy, and the distinction between domestic and foreign issues becomes blurred. These issues are considered in several government departments (not just foreign offices), and at several levels. Inadequate policy coordination on these issues involves significant costs. Different issues generate different coalitions, both within governments and across them, and involve different degrees of conflict. Politics does not stop at the waters' edge.
3. Military force is not used by governments toward other governments within the region, or on the issues, when complex interdependence prevails. It may, however, be important in these governments' relations with governments outside that region, or on other issues. Military force could, for instance, be irrelevant to resolving disagreements on

economic issues among members of an alliance, yet at the same time be very important for that alliance's political and military relations with a rival bloc. For the former relationships this condition of complex interdependence would be met; for the latter, it would not.

Traditional theories of international politics implicitly or explicitly deny the accuracy of these three assumptions. Traditionalists are therefore tempted also to deny the relevance of criticisms based on the complex interdependence ideal type. We believe, however, that our three conditions are fairly well approximated on some global issues of economic and ecological interdependence and that they come close to characterizing the entire relationship between some countries. One of our purposes here is to prove that contention. . . .

Multiple Channels

A visit to any major airport is a dramatic way to confirm the existence of multiple channels of contact among advanced industrial countries; there is a voluminous literature to prove it.[12] Bureaucrats from different countries deal directly with one another at meetings and on the telephone as well as in writing. Similarly, nongovernmental elites frequently get together in the normal course of business, in organizations such as the Trilateral Commission, and in conferences sponsored by private foundations.

In addition, multinational firms and banks affect both domestic and interstate relations. The limits on private firms, or the closeness of ties between government and business, vary considerably from one society to another; but the participation of large and dynamic organizations, not controlled entirely by governments, has become a normal part of foreign as well as domestic relations.

These actors are important not only because of their activities in pursuit of their own interests, but also because they act as transmission belts, making government policies in various countries more sensitive to one another. As the scope of governments' domestic activities has broadened, and as corporations, banks, and (to a lesser extent) trade unions have made decisions that transcend national boundaries, the domestic policies of different countries impinge on one another more and more. Transnational communications reinforce these effects. Thus, foreign economic policies touch more domestic economic activity than in the past, blurring the lines between domestic and foreign policy and increasing the number of issues relevant to foreign policy. Parallel developments in issues of environmental regulation and control over technology reinforce this trend.

Absence of Hierarchy Among Issues

Foreign affairs agendas — that is, sets of issues relevant to foreign policy with which governments are concerned — have become larger and more diverse. No longer can all issues be subordinated to military security. As Secretary of State Kissinger described the situation in 1975,

> progress in dealing with the traditional agenda is no longer enough. A new and unprecedented kind of issue has emerged. The problems of energy, resources, environment, population, the uses of space and the seas now rank with questions of military security, ideology and territorial rivalry which have traditionally made up the diplomatic agenda.[13]

Kissinger's list, which could be expanded, illustrates how governments' policies, even those previously considered merely domestic, impinge on one another. The extensive consultative arrangements developed by the OECD, as well as the GATT, IMF, and the European Community, indicate how characteristic the overlap of domestic and foreign policy is among developed pluralist countries. The organization within nine major departments of the United States government (Agriculture, Commerce, Defense, Health, Education and Welfare, Interior, Justice, Labor, State, and Treasury) and many other agencies reflects their extensive international commitments. The multiple, overlapping issues that result make a nightmare of governmental organization.[14]

When there are multiple issues on the agenda, many of which threaten the interests of domestic groups but do not clearly threaten the nation as a whole, the problems of formulating a coherent and consistent foreign policy increase. In 1975 energy was a foreign policy problem, but specific remedies, such as a tax on gasoline and automobiles, involved domestic legislation opposed by auto workers and companies alike. As one commentator observed "virtually every time Congress has set a national policy that changed the way people live . . . the action came after a consensus had developed, bit by bit, over the years, that a problem existed and that there was one best way to solve it."[15] Opportunities for delay, for special protection, for inconsistency and incoherence abound when international politics requires aligning the domestic policies of pluralist democratic countries.

Minor Role of Military Force

Political scientists have traditionally emphasized the role of military force in international politics. Force dominates other means of power: *if* there are no constraints on one's choice of instruments (a hypothetical situation that has only been approximated in the two world wars), the state with superior military force will prevail. If the security dilemma for all states were extremely acute, military force, supported by economic and other resources, would clearly be the dominant source of power. Survival is the primary goal of all states, and in the worst situations, force is ultimately necessary to guarantee survival. Thus military force is always a central component of national power.

Yet particularly among industrialized, pluralist countries, the perceived margin of safety has widened: fears of attack in general have declined, and fears of attacks *by one another* are virtually nonexistent. France has abandoned the *tous azimuts* (defense in all directions) strategy that President de Gaulle advocated (it was not taken entirely seriously even at the time). Canada's last war plans for fighting the United States were abandoned half a century ago. Britain and Germany no longer feel threatened by each other. Intense relationships of mutual influence exist between these countries, but in most of them force is irrelevant or unimportant as an instrument of policy.

Moreover, force is often not an appropriate way of achieving other goals (such as economic and ecological welfare) that are becoming more important. It is not impossible to imagine dramatic conflict or revolutionary change in which the use or threat of military force over an economic issue or among advanced industrial countries might become plausible. Then realist assumptions would again be a reliable guide to events. But in most situations, the effects of military force are both costly and uncertain.[16]

Even when the direct use of force is barred among a group of countries, however, military power can still be used politically. Each superpower continues to use the threat of force to deter attacks by the other superpower on itself or its allies; its deterrence ability thus serves an indirect, protective role, which it can use in bargaining on other issues with its allies. This bargaining tool is particularly important for the United States, whose allies are concerned about potential Soviet threats and which has fewer other means of influence over its allies than does the Soviet Union over its Eastern European partners. The United States has, accordingly, taken advantage of the Europeans' (particularly the Germans') desire for its protection and linked the issue of troop levels in Europe to trade and monetary negotiations. Thus, although the first-order effect of deterrent force is essentially negative — to deny effective offensive power to a superpower opponent — a state can use that force positively — to gain political influence.

Thus, even for countries whose relations approximate complex interdependence, two serious qualifications remain: (1) drastic social and political change could cause force again to become an important direct instrument of policy; and (2) even when elites' interests are complementary, a country that uses military force to protect another may have significant political influence over the other country.

In North – South relations, or relations among Third World countries, as well as in East – West relations, force is often important. Military power helps the Soviet Union to dominate Eastern Europe economically as well as politically. The threat of open or covert American military intervention has helped to limit revolutionary changes in the Caribbean, especially in Guatemala in 1954 and in the Dominican Republic in 1965. Secretary of State Kissinger, in January 1975, issued a veiled warning to members of the Organization of Petroleum Exporting Countries (OPEC) that the United States might use force against them "where there is some actual strangulation of the industrialized world."[17]

Even in these rather conflictual situations, however, the recourse to force seems less likely now than at most times during the century before 1945. The destructiveness of nuclear weapons makes any attack against a nuclear power dangerous. Nuclear weapons are mostly used as a deterrent. Threats of nuclear action against much weaker countries may occasionally be efficacious, but they are equally or more likely to solidify relations between one's adversaries. The limited usefulness of conventional force to control socially mobilized populations has been shown by the United States failure in Vietnam as well as by the rapid decline of colonialism in Africa. Furthermore, employing force on one issue against an independent state with which one has a variety of relationships is likely to rupture mutually profitable relations on other issues. In other words, the use of force often has costly effects on nonsecurity goals. And finally, in Western democracies, popular opposition to prolonged military conflicts is very high.[18]

It is clear that these constraints bear unequally on various countries, or on the same countries in different situations. Risks of nuclear escalation affect everyone, but domestic opinion is far less constraining for communist states, or for authoritarian regional powers, than for the United States, Europe, or Japan. Even authoritarian countries may be reluctant to use force to obtain economic objectives when such use might be ineffective and disrupt other relationships. Both the difficulty of controlling socially mobilized populations with foreign troops and the changing technology of weaponry may actually enhance the ability of certain countries, or nonstate groups, to use terrorism as a political weapon without effective fear of reprisal.

The fact that the changing role of force has uneven effects does not make the change less important, but it does make matters more complex. This complexity is compounded by differences in the usability of force among issue areas. When an issue arouses little interest or passion, force may be unthinkable. In such instances, complex interdependence may be a valuable concept for analyzing the political process. But if that issue becomes a matter of life and death—as some people thought oil might become—the use or threat of force could become decisive again. Realist assumptions would then be more relevant.

It is thus important to determine the applicability of realism or of complex interdependence to each situation. Without this determination, further analysis is likely to be confused. Our purpose in developing an alternative to the realist description of world politics is to encourage a differentiated approach that distinguishes among dimensions and areas of world politics — not (as some modernist observers do) to replace one oversimplification with another.

THE POLITICAL PROCESSES
OF COMPLEX INTERDEPENDENCE

The three main characteristics of complex interdependence give rise to distinctive political processes, which translate power resources into power as control of outcomes. As we argued earlier, something is usually lost or added in the translation. Under conditions of complex interdependence the translation will be different than under realist conditions, and our predictions about outcomes will need to be adjusted accordingly.

In the realist world, military security will be the dominant goal of states. It will even affect issues that are not directly involved with military power, or territorial defense. Nonmilitary problems will not only be subordinated to military ones; they will be studied for their politico-military implications. Balance of payments issues, for instance, will be considered at least as much in the light of their implications for world power generally as for their purely financial ramifications. McGeorge Bundy conformed to realist expectations when he argued in 1964 that devaluation of the dollar should be seriously considered if necessary to fight the war in Vietnam.[19] To some extent, so did former Treasury Secretary Henry Fowler when he contended in 1971 that the United States needed a trade surplus of $4 billion to $6 billion in order to lead in Western defense.[20]

In a world of complex interdependence, however, one expects some officials, particularly at lower levels, to emphasize the *variety* of state goals that must be pursued. In the absence of a clear hierarchy of issues, goals will vary by issue, and may not be closely related. Each bureaucracy will pursue its own concerns; and although several agencies may reach compromises on issues that affect them all, they will find that a consistent pattern of policy is difficult to maintain. Moreover, transnational actors will introduce different goals into various groups of issues.

Linkage Strategies

Goals will therefore vary by issue area under complex interdependence, but so will the distribution of power and the typical political processes. Traditional analysis focuses on *the* international system, and leads us to anticipate similar political processes on a variety of issues. Militarily and economically strong states will dominate a variety of organizations and a variety of issues, by linking their own policies on some issues to other states' policies on other issues. By using their overall dominance to prevail on their weak issues, the strongest states will, in the traditional model, ensure a congruence between the overall structure of military and economic power and the pattern of outcomes on any one issue area. Thus world politics can be treated as a seamless web.

Under complex interdependence, such congruence is less likely to occur. As military force is devalued, militarily strong states will find it more difficult to use their overall dominance to control outcomes on issues in which they are weak. And since the distribution of power resources in trade, shipping, or oil, for example, may be quite different, patterns of outcomes and distinctive political processes are likely to vary from one set of issues to another. If force were readily applicable, and military security were the highest foreign policy goal, these variations in the issue structures of power would not matter very much. The linkages drawn from them to military issues would ensure consistent dominance by the overall strongest states. But when military force is largely immobilized, strong states will find that linkage is less effective. They may still attempt such links, but in the absence of a hierarchy of issues, their success will be problematic.

Dominant states may try to secure much the same result by using overall economic power to affect results on other issues. If only economic objectives are at stake, they may succeed: money, after all, is fungible. But economic objectives have political implications, and economic linkage by the strong is limited by domestic, transnational, and transgovernmental actors who resist having their interests traded off. Furthermore, the international actors may be different on different issues, and the international organizations in which negotiations take place are often quite separate. Thus it is difficult, for example, to imagine a militarily or economically strong state linking concessions on monetary policy to reciprocal concessions in oceans policy. On the other hand, poor weak states are not similarly inhibited from linking unrelated issues, partly because their domestic interests are less complex. Linkage of unrelated issues is often a means of extracting concessions or side payments from rich and powerful states. And unlike powerful states whose instrument for linkage (military force) is often too costly to use, the linkage instrument used by poor, weak states — international organization — is available and inexpensive.

Thus as the utility of force declines, and as issues become more equal in importance, the distribution of power within each issue will become more important. If linkages become less effective on the whole, outcomes of political bargaining will increasingly vary by issue area.

The differentiation among issue areas in complex interdependence means that linkages among issues will become more problematic and will tend to reduce rather than reinforce international hierarchy. Linkage strategies, and defense against them, will pose critical strategic choices for states. Should issues be considered separately or as a package? If linkages are to be drawn, which issues should be linked, and on which of the linked issues should concessions be made? How far can one push a linkage before it becomes counterproductive? For instance, should one seek formal agreements or informal, but less politically sensitive, under-standings? The fact that world politics under complex interdependence is not a seamless web leads us to expect that efforts to stitch seams to-gether advantageously, as reflected in linkage strategies, will, very often, determine the shape of the fabric.

The negligible role of force leads us to expect states to rely more on other instruments in order to wield power. For the reasons we have al-ready discussed, less vulnerable states will try to use asymmetrical in-terdependence in particular groups of issues as a source of power; they will also try to use international organizations and transnational actors and flows. States will approach economic interdependence in terms of power as well as its effects on citizens' welfare, although welfare consid-erations will limit their attempts to maximize power. Most economic and ecological interdependence involves the possibility of joint gains, or joint losses. Mutual awareness of potential gains and losses and the danger of worsening each actor's position through overly rigorous struggles over the distribution of the gains can limit the use of asymmetrical inter-dependence.

Agenda Setting

Our second assumption of complex interdependence, the lack of clear hi-erarchy among multiple issues, leads us to expect that the politics of agenda formation and control will become more important. Traditional analyses lead statesmen to focus on politico-military issues and to pay lit-tle attention to the broader politics of agenda formation. Statesmen as-sume that the agenda will be set by shifts in the balance of power, actual or anticipated, and by perceived threats to the security of states. Other issues will only be very important when they seem to affect security and military power. In these cases, agendas will be influenced strongly by considerations of the overall balance of power.

Yet, today, some nonmilitary issues are emphasized in interstate rela-tions at one time, whereas others of seemingly equal importance are ne-glected or quietly handled at a technical level. International monetary politics, problems of commodity terms of trade, oil, food, and multina-tional corporations have all been important during the last decade; but not all have been high on interstate agendas throughout that period.

Traditional analysts of international politics have paid little attention to agenda formation: to how issues come to receive sustained attention by high officials. The traditional orientation toward military and security af-fairs implies that the crucial problems of foreign policy are imposed on states by the actions or threats of other states. These are high politics as opposed to the low politics of economic affairs. Yet, as the complexity of actors and issues in world politics increases, the utility of force declines and the line between domestic policy and foreign policy becomes blurred; as the conditions of complex interdependence are more closely approximated, the politics of agenda formation becomes more subtle and differentiated.

Under complex interdependence we can expect the agenda to be affected by the international and domestic problems created by economic growth and increasing sensitivity interdependence. Discontented domestic groups will politicize issues and force more issues once considered domestic onto the interstate agenda. Shifts in the distribution of power resources within sets of issues will also affect agendas. During the early 1970s the increased power of oil-producing governments over the transnational corporations and the consumer countries dramatically altered the policy agenda. Moreover, agendas for one group of issues may change as a result of linkages from other groups in which power resources are changing; for example, the broader agenda of North–South trade issues changed after the OPEC price rises and the oil embargo of 1973–74. Even if capabilities among states do not change, agendas may be affected by shifts in the importance of transnational actors. The publicity surrounding multinational corporations in the early 1970s, coupled with their rapid growth over the past twenty years, put the regulation of such corporations higher on both the United Nations agenda and national agendas.

Politicization—agitation and controversy over an issue that tend to raise it to the top of the agenda—can have many sources, as we have seen. Governments whose strength is increasing may politicize issues, by linking them to other issues. An international regime that is becoming ineffective or is not serving important issues may cause increasing politicization, as dissatisfied governments press for change. Politicization, however, can also come from below. Domestic groups may become upset enough to raise a dormant issue, or to interfere with interstate bargaining at high levels. In 1974 the American secretary of state's tacit linkage of a Soviet-American trade pact with progress in détente was upset by the success of domestic American groups working through Congress to link a trade agreement with Soviet policies on emigration.

The technical characteristics and institutional setting in which issues are raised will strongly affect politicization patterns. In the United States, congressional attention is an effective instrument of politicization. Generally, we expect transnational economic organizations and transgovernmental networks of bureaucrats to seek to avoid politicization. Domestically based groups (such as trade unions) and domestically oriented bureaucracies will tend to use politicization (particularly congressional attention) against their transnationally mobile competitors. At the international level, we expect states and actors to "shop among forums" and struggle to get issues raised in international organizations that will maximize their advantage by broadening or narrowing the agenda.

Transnational and Transgovernmental Relations

Our third condition of complex interdependence, multiple channels of contact among societies, further blurs the distinction between domestic and international politics. The availability of partners in political coalitions is not necessarily limited by national boundaries as traditional analysis assumes. The nearer a situation is to complex interdependence, the more we expect the outcomes of political bargaining to be affected by transnational relations. Multinational corporations may be significant both as independent actors and as instruments manipulated by governments. The attitudes and policy stands of domestic groups are likely to be affected by communications, organized or not, between them and their counterparts abroad.

Thus the existence of multiple channels of contact leads us to expect limits, beyond those normally found in domestic politics, on the ability of statesmen to calculate the manipulation of interdependence or follow a consistent strategy of linkage. Statesmen must consider differential as well as aggregate effects of interdependence strategies and their likely implications for politicization and agenda control. Transactions among societies — economic and social transactions more than security ones — affect groups differently. Opportunities and costs from increased transnational ties may be greater for certain groups — for instance, American workers in the textile or shoe industries — than for others. Some organizations or groups may interact directly with actors in other societies or with other governments to increase their benefits from a network of interaction. Some actors may therefore be less vulnerable as well as less sensitive to changes elsewhere in the network than are others, and this will affect patterns of political action.

The multiple channels of contact found in complex interdependence are not limited to nongovernmental actors. Contacts between governmental bureaucracies charged with similar tasks may not only alter their perspectives but lead to transgovernmental coalitions on particular policy questions. To improve their chances of success, government agencies attempt to bring actors from other governments into their own decision-making processes as allies. Agencies of powerful states such as the United States have used such coalitions to penetrate weaker governments in such countries as Turkey and Chile. They have also been used to help agencies of other governments penetrate the United States bureaucracy.[21] Transgovernmental politics frequently characterizes Canadian-American relations, often to the advantage of Canadian interests.

The existence of transgovernmental policy networks leads to a different interpretation of one of the standard propositions about international politics — that states act in their own interest. Under complex interdependence, this conventional wisdom begs two important questions: which self and which interest? A government agency may pursue its own interests under the guise of the national interest; and recurrent interactions can change official perceptions of their interests. As a careful study of the politics of United States trade policy has documented, concentrating only on pressures of various interests for decisions leads to an overly mechanistic view of a continuous process and neglects the important role of communications in slowly changing perceptions of self-interest.[22]

The ambiguity of the national interest raises serious problems for the top political leaders of governments. As bureaucracies contact each other directly across national borders (without going through foreign offices), centralized control becomes more difficult. There is less assurance that the state will be united when dealing with foreign governments or that its components will interpret national interests similarly when negotiating with foreigners. The state may prove to be multifaceted, even schizophrenic. National interests will be defined differently on different issues, at different times and by different governmental units. States that are better placed to maintain their coherence (because of a centralized political tradition such as France's) will be better able to manipulate uneven interdependence than fragmented states that at first glance seem to have more resources in an issue area.

Role of International Organizations

Finally, the existence of multiple channels leads one to predict a different and significant role for international organizations in world politics. Realists in the tradition of Hans J. Morgenthau have portrayed a world in which states, acting from self-interest, struggle for "power and peace." Security issues are dominant; war threatens. In such a world, one may assume that international institutions will have a minor role, limited by the rare congruence of such interests. International organizations are then clearly peripheral to world politics. But in a world of multiple issues imperfectly linked, in which coalitions are formed transnationally and transgovernmentally, the potential role of international institutions in political bargaining is greatly increased. In particular, they help set the international agenda, and act as catalysts for coalition-formation and as arenas for political initiatives and linkage by weak states.

Governments must organize themselves to cope with the flow of business generated by international organizations. By defining the salient issues, and deciding which issues can be grouped together, organizations may help to determine governmental priorities and the nature of interdepartmental committees and other arrangements within governments. The 1972 Stockholm Environment Conference strengthened the position of environmental agencies in various governments. The 1974

World Food Conference focused the attention of important parts of the United States government on prevention of food shortages. The September 1975 United Nations special session on proposals for a New International Economic Order generated an intragovernmental debate about policies toward the Third World in general. The International Monetary Fund and the General Agreement on Tariffs and Trade have focused governmental activity on money and trade instead of on private direct investment, which has no comparable international organization.

By bringing officials together, international organizations help to activate potential coalitions in world politics. It is quite obvious that international organizations have been very important in bringing together representatives of less developed countries, most of which do not maintain embassies in one another's capitals. Third World strategies of solidarity among poor countries have been developed in and for a series of international conferences, mostly under the auspices of the United Nations.[23] International organizations also allow agencies of governments, which might not otherwise come into contact, to turn potential or tacit coalitions into explicit transgovernmental coalitions characterized by direct communications. In some cases, international secretariats deliberately promote this process by forming coalitions with groups of governments, or with units of governments, as well as with nongovernmental organizations having similar interests.[24]

International organizations are frequently congenial institutions for weak states. The one-state–one-vote norm of the United Nations system favors coalitions of the small and powerless. Secretariats are often responsive to Third World demands. Furthermore, the substantive norms of most international organizations, as they have developed over the years, stress social and economic equity as well as the equality of states. Past resolutions expressing Third World positions, sometimes agreed to with reservations by industrialized countries, are used to legitimize other demands. These agreements are rarely binding, but up to a point the norms of the institution make opposition look more harshly self-interested and less defensible.

International organizations also allow small and weak states to pursue linkage strategies. In the discussions on a New International Economic Order, Third World states insisted on linking oil price and availability to other questions on which they had traditionally been unable to achieve their objectives. Small and weak states have also followed a strategy of linkage in the series of Law of the Sea conferences sponsored by the United Nations.

Complex interdependence therefore yields different political patterns than does the realist conception of the world. (Table 1 summarizes these differences.) Thus, one would expect traditional theories to fail to explain international regime change in situations of complex interdependence. But, for a situation that approximates realist conditions, traditional theories should be appropriate.

TABLE 1   Political Processes Under Conditions of Realism and
Complex Interdependence

	Realism	Complex Interdependence
Goals of actors	Military security will be the dominant goal.	Goals of states will vary by issue area. Transgovernmental politics will make goals difficult to define. Transnational actors will pursue their own goals.
Instruments of state policy	Military force will be most effective, although economic and other instruments will also be used.	Power resources specific to issue areas will be most relevant. Manipulation of interdependence, international organizations, and transnational actors will be major instruments.
Agenda formation	Potential shifts in the balance of power and security threats will set the agenda in high politics and will strongly influence other agendas.	Agenda will be affected by changes in the distribution of power resources within issue areas; the status of international regimes; changes in the importance of transnational actors; linkages from other issues and politicization as a result of rising sensitivity interdependence.
Linkages of issues	Linkages will reduce differences in outcomes among issue areas and reinforce international hierarchy.	Linkages by strong states will be more difficult to make since force will be ineffective. Linkages by weak states through international organizations will erode rather than reinforce hierarchy.

(continued)

TABLE 1 Political Processes Under Conditions of Realism and
Complex Interdependence (*continued*)

	Realism	Complex Interdependence
Roles of international organizations	Roles are minor, limited by state power and the importance of military force.	Organizations will set agendas, induce coalition-formation, and act as arenas for political action by weak states. Ability to choose the organizational forum for an issue and to mobilize votes will be an important political resource.

NOTES

1. Stanley Hoffmann, "Notes on the Elusiveness of Modern Power," *International Journal* 30: (Spring 1975): 184.
2. "A New National Partnership," speech by Secretary of State Henry A. Kissinger at Los Angeles, January 24, 1975. News release, Department of State, Bureau of Public Affairs, Office of Media Services, p. 1.
3. See, for example, Lester R. Brown, *World Without Borders: The Interdependence of Nations* (New York: Foreign Policy Association, Headline Series, 1972).
4. Charles Kindleberger, *American Business Abroad* (New Haven, CT: Yale University Press, 1969), p. 207.
5. The terms are derived from Stanley Hoffmann, "Choices," *Foreign Policy* 12 (Fall 1973): 6.
6. For instance, see Robert Angell, *Peace on the March: Transnational Participation* (New York: Van Nostrand, 1969).
7. John Maynard Keynes, *The General Theory of Employment, Interest and Money* (London: Macmillan, 1957), p. 383.
8. For the classic contemporary formulation of political realism, see the works of Hans J. Morgenthau, particularly *Politics Among Nations: The Struggle for Power and Peace* (New York: Knopf, 1948 and subsequent editions). See also Morgenthau, "Another 'Great Debate': The National Interest of the United States," *American Political Science Review* 46 (December 1952): 961–88; and Morgenthau, *Scientific Man Versus Power Politics* (Chicago: University of Chicago Press, 1946). A different but equally impressive statement of a "realist" position can be found in E. H. Carr, *The Twenty Years' Crisis, 1919–1939*, 2nd ed. (London: Macmillan, 1946). Carr, however, emphasizes economic sources of power more strongly.
9. In *The Troubled Partnership* (New York: McGraw-Hill for the Council on Foreign Relations, 1965) Henry A. Kissinger discussed alliance problems with hardly a reference to economic issues, although economic issues were beginning seriously to divide the NATO allies.

10. Alex Inkeles, "The Emerging Social Structure of the World," *World Politics* 27 (July 1975): 479.
11. Hans J. Morgenthau, *Politics Among Nations: The Struggle for Power and Peace,* 4th ed. (New York: Knopf, 1967), p. 36.
12. See Inkeles, "The Emerging Social Structure of the World;" Richard Rosecrance and Arthur Stein, "Interdependence: Myth or Reality," *World Politics* 26, no. 1 (October 1973); Peter J. Katzenstein, "International Interdependence: Some Long-Term Trends and Recent Changes," *International Organization* 29, no. 4 (Fall 1975); Edward L. Morse, "Transnational Economic Processes," in Robert O. Keohane and Joseph S. Nye, Jr. (eds.), *Transnational Relations and World Politics* (Cambridge, MA: Harvard University Press, 1972).
13. Henry A. Kissinger, "A New National Partnership," *Department of State Bulletin,* February 17, 1975, p. 199.
14. See the report of the Commission on the Organization of the Government for the Conduct of Foreign Policy (Murphy Commission) (Washington, D.C.: U.S. Government Printing Office, 1975), and the studies prepared for that report. See also Raymond Hopkins, "The International Role of 'Domestic' Bureaucracy," *International Organization* 30, no. 3 (Summer 1976).
15. *New York Times,* May 22, 1975.
16. For a valuable discussion, see Klaus Knorr, *The Power of Nations: The Political Economy of International Relations* (New York: Basic Books, 1975).
17. *Business Week,* January 13, 1975.
18. Stanley Hoffmann, "The Acceptability of Military Force," and Laurence Martin, "The Utility of Military Force," in *Force in Modern Societies: Its Place in International Politics* (Adelphi Paper, International Institute for Strategic Studies, 1973). See also Knorr, *The Power of Nations.*
19. Henry Brandon, *The Retreat of American Power* (New York: Doubleday, 1974), p. 218.
20. *International Implications of the New Economic Policy,* U.S. Congress, House of Representatives, Committee on Foreign Affairs, Subcommittee on Foreign Economic Policy, Hearings, September 16, 1971.
21. For a more detailed discussion, see Robert O. Keohane and Joseph S. Nye, Jr., "Transgovernmental Relations and International Organizations," *World Politics* 27, no. 1 (October 1974): 39–62.
22. Raymond Bauer, Ithiel de Sola Pool, and Lewis Dexter, *American Business and Foreign Policy* (New York: Atherton, 1963), chap. 35, esp. pp. 472–75.
23. Branislav Gosovic and John Gerard Ruggie, "On the Creation of a New International Economic Order: Issue Linkage and the Seventh Special Session of the UN General Assembly," *International Organization* 30, no. 2 (Spring 1976): 309–46.
24. Robert W. Cox, "The Executive Head," *International Organization* 23, no. 2 (Spring 1969): 205–30.

Multilateralism, Knowledge, and Power

Ernst B. Haas

Individuals are not the captives of system structure, but can influence the course of events. According to Haas, "Power is normally used to translate knowledge-informed interests into policy and programs." What these individuals think and the values they hold do matter.

Imagine historians in the twenty-third century busily interpreting the events and documents of international relations in the second half of the twentieth century. They would note, of course, that the world was organized into separate sovereign states and that their number had tripled over the previous half-century. But they would note another curious phenomenon: even though the people who ruled these states seemed to treasure their mutual independence as much as ever, they also built an imposing network of organizations that had the task of managing problems that these states experienced in common. Sometimes these international organizations had the task of transferring wealth from the richer to the poorer states. At other times they were asked to make and monitor rules by which all the states had agreed to live. At still other times the task of these organizations was the prevention of conflict among states. In short, rulers seemed to concede that without institutionalized cooperation among their states, life would be more difficult, dreary, and dangerous. Proof lies in the number and kind of such organizations, which increased at a stupendous rate after 1945.

Our historians would also note a second phenomenon, which gathered force around 1980. Everybody seemed to be disappointed with these organizations. Some of the most powerful states sought to disengage from them. Others demanded more benefits but received fewer. The very idea of moderating the logic of the cohabitation of 160 sovereign units on the same planet with institutionalized cooperation lost its appeal. Did international organizations disappear to give rise to alternative modes of collaboration? Did states examine the reasons for their disappointment and reform the network of international organizations? Did rulers question the very principle of a world order based on sovereign and competing states? Our historians know the eventual outcome. We do not. We can only speculate about the future of international cooperation and wonder whether it will make use of international organizations. I wish to construct concepts that might advance the enterprise of systematic speculation.

THE ARGUMENT SUMMARIZED

Since the speculation is to be systematic, my underlying assumptions require specification. They are as follows: All international organizations are deliberately designed by their founders to "solve problems" that require collaborative action for a solution. No collaboration is conceivable except on the basis of explicit articulated interests. What are the interests? Contrary to lay usage, interests are *not* the opposite of ideals or values. An actor's sense of self-interest includes the desire to hedge against uncertainty, to minimize risk. One cannot have a notion of risk without some experience with choices that turned out to be less than optimal; one's interests are shaped by one's experiences. But one's satisfaction with an experience is a function of what is ideally desired, a function of one's values. Interests cannot be articulated without values. Far from (ideal) values being pitted against (material) interests, interests are unintelligible without a sense of values-to-be-realized. The interests to be realized by collaborative action are an expression of the actors' values.

My speculations concern the future of international organizations, but my assumptions force me to consider the future as a function of the history of collaboration as that history is experienced in the minds of collective actors: national and international bureaucracies. That history is the way "the problem to be solved" was seen at various times by the actors. What the book seeks to explain, then, is *the change in the definition of the problem to be solved by a given organization.* Let us take an example. In 1945 the problem the World Bank was to solve was how most speedily to rebuild war-ravaged Europe. By 1955 the problem the bank was to solve was how most effectively to spur industrial growth in the developing countries. By 1975 the problem to be solved had become the elimination of poverty in the Third World. The task of my book is to explain the change in problem definition, to make clear whether and how the implicit theories held by actors changed.

I shall argue that problems are redefined through one of two complicated processes that I call "adaptation" and "learning." These processes differ in their dependence on new knowledge that may be introduced into decision making:

Adaptation	*Learning*
Behavior changes as actors add new activities (or drop old ones) without examining the implicit theories underlying their programs. Underlying values are not questioned.	Behavior changes as actors question original implicit theories underlying programs and examine their original values.
The ultimate purpose of the organization is not questioned. The emphasis is on altering means of action, not ends. Technical rationality triumphs.	The ultimate purpose is redefined, as means as well as ends are questioned. Substantive rationality triumphs.
New ends (purposes) are added without worrying about their coherence with existing ends. Change is incremental without any attempt at nesting purposes logically.	New nested problem sets are constructed because new ends are devised on the basis of consensual knowledge that has become available, as provided by epistemic communities.

I return to the example of the World Bank. Suppose the bank had been asked to solve problems by simply adding new tasks to old ones, without seeking to justify industrialization as a means toward the eradication of poverty, without explaining infrastructure development projects as a means toward industrial growth, which in turn was eventually seen as a means for eliminating poverty. There was no new theory of economic development, and no cohesive group of experts that "sold" that theory to the bank's management. I call this sequence "change by adaptation." If, conversely, these successive new purposes came about as the result of a systematic pattern of subsuming new means under new ends, legitimated by a new theory of economic development advocated by an epistemic community, then the pattern conforms to what I call "learning."

I argue that adaptation can take place in two different settings, each a distinct model of organizational development. One, labeled "incremental growth," features the successive augmentation of an organization's program as actors add new tasks to older ones without any change in the organization's decision-making dynamics or mode of choosing. The other, labeled "turbulent nongrowth," involves major changes in organizational decision making: ends no longer cohere; internal consensus on both ends and means disintegrates. In contrast, learning is associated with a model of organizational change I call "managed interdependence," in which the reexamination of purposes is brought about by knowledge-mediated decision-making dynamics.

The point of the book is to suggest when and where each model prevails, how a given organization can change from resembling one model to resembling one of the others, and how adaptation can give way to learning and learning to adaptation. Therefore, a set of descriptive variables is introduced to make possible the delineation of key conditions and attributes that vary from model to model. These descriptive variables include the setting in which international organizations operate, the power they have at their disposal, and the modes of behavior typical in their operations.

Description, however, is not enough to permit us to make the judgments we seek. A second set of variables is provided to make possible an evaluation of the variation disclosed by studying the descriptive variables. These evaluative concepts stress the types of knowledge used by the actors in making choices, their political objectives, and the manner in which issues being negotiated are linked into packages. Further evaluations are made about the type of bargaining produced by issue linkage, whether these bargains result in agreement on new ways of conceptualizing the problems to be solved, and whether new problem sets imply institutional changes leading to gains (or losses) in the legitimacy and authority enjoyed by the organization.

I foreshadow some conclusions that will be demonstrated in greater detail later. The World Bank began life in conformity with the incremental-growth model and later developed into the managed-interdependence model. The United Nations' (U.N.) collective-security practices degenerated from incremental growth into the turbulent nongrowth pattern; the U.N. Educational, Scientific, and Cultural Organization (UNESCO) always functioned in conformity with the turbulent nongrowth model. In the World Bank no decline in organizational power occurred. In fact, the president's autonomous ability to lead has increased over the years; merit remains the principle for selecting staff; outside consultants always serve in their personal capacity. Over the years, issue linkage was increasingly informed by technical knowledge and by political objectives of a progressively more complex and interconnected type. As new and more elaborate institutional practices developed, these also became more authoritative in the eyes of the membership, even if they did not become more legitimate as well. The innovations summarized as "peacekeeping" and associated with the special crisis management leadership style of Dag Hammarskjöld suggest that in 1956 U.N. activity relating to collective security conformed to the incremental-growth model, too. But unlike the bank, the United Nations thirty years later has become the victim of turbulent nongrowth. Earlier institutionalization and increases in authority were dissipated, no improvements in technical knowledge informed decision making, political goals became simpler and more immediacy oriented, and the leadership of the secretary-general was all but invisible. Possibly, however, the successes scored by Javier Pérez de Cuéllar in 1988 will reverse this trend. UNESCO, finally, never enjoyed a coherent program informed by consensual knowledge and agreed political objectives; it suffered no decline in institutionalization and power because it had very little of these in the first place. Both authority and legitimacy declined to a nadir in 1986 after decades of internal controversy over the organization's basic mission.

So what? How does the mapping of movement from one model to another help us with the future of international organizations? I want to answer a question that not only incorporates my own uncertainty about that future but also seeks to generalize from the uncertainties against which political actors try to protect themselves. We assume that their attempts are informed by interests that are shaped by implicit theories. States acting on their perceived interests, not scholars writing books, are the architects that will design the international organizations of the future. These interests are informed by the values political leaders seek to defend, not by the ideals of observers. Actors carry in their heads the values that shape the issues contained in their briefing papers. My effort to conceptualize the process of coping with uncertainty is based on this given. Scholarly concern with the question of how we might approach the international organizations of the future relies on understanding how self-conscious actors can learn to design organizations that will give them more satisfaction than the generation of international organizations with which we are familiar. If my demonstration in this book is persuasive, it will give us the tools for saying, "If an organization of type A regularly produces certain outcomes, then this type will (or will not) serve the perceived needs of its members; therefore they will seek to design an organization of type B if they are dissatisfied or will retain type A if they are happy."

Only idealists would presume to prescribe for the future by using their personal values as the definer of suggestions. I am not an idealist. The suggestions for a particular type of organizational learning developed in the final chapter [of my book *When Knowledge Is Power*] are consistent with the nonidealistic line of analysis pursued in the body of the book even though they also project my views as to what ought to be learned.

A TYPOLOGY IS NOT A THEORY

To avoid even the appearance of inflated claims, I maintain that the typological argument I offer falls short of constituting a theory. The demonstrations just made about the World Bank, UNESCO, and the United Nations are not full explanations of what happened to these organizations; nor do they display all the causes for these events. No pretense is made that these partial post hoc explanations provide all the ingredients needed for an informed prediction. Why then offer a typology of models of change?

I want to inquire into only one aspect of organizational life: why and how actors change their explicit or implicit views about what they see as a problem requiring collaborative measures for a solution. The "problem" can be any item on the international agenda. My dependent variable is change in the explicit or implicit view of actors in international organizations about the nature of a "problem." My inquiry, however, depends on my being able (1) to specify the interests and values held by actors and (2) to show how actors redefine interests and perhaps values in response to earlier disappointments. Moreover, I want to determine whether the processes that take place inside international organizations can be credited with the redefinition of interests and values. The idealist takes for granted that such redefining is likely to occur; scholars who stress the predominance of bureaucracies and political forces at the national capitals place the locus of change elsewhere. Granting that important changes in perception are unlikely to occur primarily in Geneva and New York, we must nevertheless hold open the possibility that some of the influences experienced there have a role in the national decision-making process that produces the changes we seek to explore. If that is true, then it also makes sense to observe international organizations in their possible role as innovators. And if international organizations can innovate, then we can inquire whether and when governments look to them as mechanisms for delivering newly desired goods and services. If governments think of international organizations as innovators, finally, we are entitled to ask how they go about redesigning international organizations to improve the solution of a newly redefined set of problems.

In what follows, then, I shall not be testing a theory. I merely experiment with the explanatory power of ideal types of organizations that reflect my conviction that the knowledge actors carry in their heads and project in their international encounters significantly shapes their behavior and expectations. My perspective is more permissive of the workings of volition, of a kind of free will, than is allowed by many popular theories of international politics. If my stance is not "idealist," it is not "structural" either.

The structuralist argues that international collaboration of the multilateral kind is intended to provide a collective good for the parties that bilateral relations could not provide. The provision of that good, in turn, may result in a more harmonious world — though the harmony is likely to be confined to expectations related solely to the good in question. It probably cannot be generalized into the utopia associated with idealism. As for international organizations, they are important in this causal chain only if they are necessary for providing the collective good. International organizations, therefore, are not given a privileged place in the causal chain of the structuralist.

I disagree with this stance because it tends to overstate the constraints on choice and to understate decision makers' continuing enmeshment in past experiences with collaboration mediated by international organizations. Structuralism seeks to discover various deep-seated constraints on the freedom of actors to choose. Although organizations, like any other institutions, can act as constraints, I want to look at them as fora for choosing innovations. Structural constraints may be implicit in the logic of situations, such as the condition of strategic interdependence in anarchic international systems. Belief in the power of such constraints depends on the assumption that actors respond only to *present* incentives and disincentives, that they never try to "climb out" of the system to re-shape opportunities for gain. Strategic interdependence as a permanent constraint is compelling only as long as there is no evidence that some-body works actively toward changing the rules of the game. Modern in-ternational life is replete with such efforts. However, it is equally true that the kinds of constraints on choice that structuralists stress provide the most telling explanation as to why new international organizations are created in the first place. But if we stop our inquiry with this explanation, we never proceed to ask the questions that interest me, questions about the role of changing knowledge in the redefinition of interest.[1]

Unlike structuralists, neorealists, game theorists, and theorists of re-gimes, I am not offering a theory; at best I am offering a probe that might lead to a theory. I am not testing my approach against rival explanations because other approaches are not rivals. Game theory or structural ex-planations do not "fit better" than explanations of change derived from the interplay of knowledge and political objectives, from cognitive and perceptual observations; they "fit differently." Nor is it my purpose to subsume or colonize other theories, or to assert my hegemony over them. Other explanations, given the questions other scholars raise, may be as valid as mine. My effort should be understood as complementary to theirs, not as an approach with unique power. Cognitive explanations coexist, epistemologically speaking, with other approaches to the study of international organizations; they do not supplant them. If I persuade the reader that the history of an organization can be viewed in the context of cognitive variables, then the reader will interpret that history in a novel form, without rendering all other interpretations obsolete. But the success of my claim to novelty still falls short of a real theory.[2]

Nor do the three models around which my interpretations are built constitute a true theory. They remain Weberian ideal types; together they constitute a typology for conceptualizing organizational change, for summing up whether and how adaptation or learning occurs. Yet the models are not just heuristic; they are intended to be "real," albeit not ex-haustive, representations of what took place. They seek to abstract selec-tively (but not arbitrarily) from a historical series of events. The crucial point is this: the notion of causation implicit in these models is as elusive and as nonlinear as in all of Weber's typologies. My approach differs sharply from the more direct ideas of causation embedded in behavioral and in rational-choice approaches to the phenomena studied here be-cause it rejects simple notions of causality.

Basically, I anchor my approach on this bet: the knowledge available about "the problem" at issue influences the way decision makers define the interest at stake in the solution to the problem; political objectives and technical knowledge are combined to arrive at the conception of what constitutes one's interest. But since decision makers are sentient and self-reflective beings, the conceptualization cannot stop here because decision makers take available knowledge into account, including the memory of past efforts to define and solve "the problem." They know that their knowledge is approximate and incomplete. Being aware of the limits of one's knowledge also influences one's choices. Being critical about one's knowledge implies a readiness to reconsider the finality of what one knows and therefore to be willing to redefine the problem.

This point distinguishes my approach from that of theorists of rational choice who are inspired by microeconomics. In the logic of game theory, for instance, what matters is not the history of a perceived preference or the way a utility (interest?) came into being, but the mere fact that at the crucial "choice points," interests are what they are because preferences are as they are stipulated in game theory. It makes sense to speak of shared interests if, at the choice point, the separate interests of the bargainers happen to be sufficiently similar to permit an agreement. In my approach the decision makers are thought to be concerned with causation, with the reasons why a particular definition of their interests matter, as compared with other possible definitions. My analysis must be concerned, therefore, with the question of *why* particular demands are linked into packages, *why* problems are conceived in relatively simple or in very complex ways. Implicit or explicit theories of causation in the actors' minds imply degrees of knowledge, not merely momentarily shared interests. My theory of causation must reflect and accommodate the notions of causation assumed to be in the minds of the decision makers, notions that are true to the insight that there is always another turn of the cognitive screw to be considered.

I reiterate: the typologies that result from this mode of analysis are not truly representative of all of reality. They capture types of behavior, clusters of traits, bundles of results from antecedent regularities in bureaucratic perception that are logically possible, but not necessarily encountered frequently. Many of Weber's typologies, although exhaustive in the sociological and cultural dimensions he wished to represent, nevertheless produced sparsely populated cells. We will find that the managed-interdependence model is rarely encountered in the real world and that learning is far less common than adaptation. But then so is charismatic leadership and the routinization of charisma into bureaucratic practice.

Therefore, we will not follow the mode of demonstration preferred by those who work in the behavioral tradition. We will not seek to cull from our large list of descriptive variables those clusters of traits that most frequently "predict" (or are associated with) either successful adaptation or successful learning. Many of the descriptive variables will be shown to be weakly associated with any pattern, any regularities; some will not vary from type to type. Nevertheless, such variables will not be permitted to "drop out" even though they explain nothing behavioral. They are real because they describe international organizations. They matter in pinpointing what is unique about international organizations, and they may turn up as more powerful in some later analysis or some new set of historical circumstances. Remaining true to a typological commitment demands that the traditional canons of causal theorizing be sacrificed to a less economical procedure that forgoes the search for clusters or straight paths as unique explanations. I am, after all, using systematic speculation and historical reconstruction to anticipate events that have yet to occur.

KNOWLEDGE, POWER, AND INTEREST

My typological approach is anchored on an additional bet, similar to the first one but less moderate: change in human aspirations and human institutions over long periods is caused mostly by the way knowledge about nature and about society is married to political interests and objectives. I am not merely asserting that changes in scientific understanding trigger technological innovations, which are then seized upon by political actors, though this much is certainly true. I am also asserting that as scientific knowledge becomes common knowledge and as technological innovation is linked to institutional tinkering, the very mode of scientific inquiry infects the way political actors think. Science, in short, influences the way politics is done. Science becomes a component of politics because the scientific way of grasping reality is used to define the interests that political actors articulate and defend. The doings of actors can then be described by observers as an exercise of defining and realizing interests informed by changing scientific knowledge about man and nature.

Therefore, it is as unnecessary as it is misleading to juxtapose as rival explanations the following: science to politics, knowledge to power or interest, consensual knowledge to common interests. We do ourselves no good by pretending that scientists have the key for giving us peace and plenty; but we do no better in holding that politicians and capitalists, in defending their immediate interests with superior power, stop creative innovation dead in its tracks. We overestimate the resistance to innovation on the part of politicians and the commitment to change on the part of the purveyors of knowledge if we associate science and knowledge with good, with reform, with disinterested behavior, while saddling political actors with the defense of vested interests. When knowledge becomes consensual, we ought to expect politicians to use it in helping them to define their interests; we should not suppose that knowledge is opposed to interest. Once this juxtaposition is abandoned, it becomes clear that a desire to defend some interests by invoking superior power by no means prevents the defense of others by means of institutional innovations. Superior power is even used to force innovations legitimated by new knowledge, while knowledge-legitimated interest can equally well be used to argue against innovation.

Economists prefer to explain events by stressing the *interests* that motivate actors: coalitions of actors are thought capable of action only if they succeed in defining their *common interests.* Political scientists like to explain events in terms of the *power* to impose preferences on allies and antagonists. Sociologists tend to put the emphasis on *structured* or *institutionalized norms* and to find the origin of such norms in the *hegemonial power* of some group or class. My claim is that these formulations are consistent with the use of knowledge in decision making. My argument is that we need not pit these divergent formulations against each other as explanations of human choice. We are entitled to hold that interests can be (but need not be) informed by available knowledge, and that power is normally used to translate knowledge-informed interests into policy and programs. My concern is to analyze those situations in which interests are so informed and the exercise of power is so motivated, not to deal with all instances of interests, norms, and power as triggers of choice.

I return to the case of the World Bank to illustrate the possible convergence of explanations combining knowledge with interest and power. In the late 1960s the bank changed its basic philosophy of development lending from supporting infrastructure projects that were relatively remote from the direct experiences of poor people — hence the reliance on the theory of trickle-down — to the policy of supporting the advancement of basic human needs, with its implication of much more direct and intrusive intervention in the borrowers' domestic affairs in order to gain access to their poor citizens. Was new knowledge used in motivating the shift? The shift occurred because economists and other development specialists had serious doubts about the adequacy of trickle-down policies and claimed that new techniques were becoming available to help the poor more directly. Was this knowledge generally accepted? This knowledge was generally accepted only by the coalition of donors that dominates the bank; the borrowers frequently opposed the shift and argued that the basic-human needs approach was not in their interest. Was the shift consistent with the interests of the dominant coalition? Indeed it was, because the coalition's common interest in supporting economic development appeared to be implemented more effectively by virtue of the new knowledge.

My account shows how interest informed by knowledge reinforces the explanation of what occurred. What about power? Let us keep in mind that there are at least three different ways of thinking about power in these situations. If the hegemonial power of the capitalist class — as expressed in the instructions issued to the delegates of the donor countries — is considered, then the decision of the bank is an expression of the persuasiveness and influence of that class in foisting a realistic conception of the common interest on the dominant coalition, even though it may also be an instance of false consciousness. Suppose we ignore Gramsci and think of power as the straightforward imposition of the view of the strongest. Even though the United States is the single most powerful member of the bank, its position is not strong enough to enable it to dictate bank policy (in part because the U.S. presidents of the bank often entertained views at variance with opinions within the U.S. government). Power as direct imposition does not explain anything.[3] That leaves a conception of power as the ability of a stable coalition to impose its will simply by virtue of its superior voting strength or as a result of its Gramscian ability to socialize and persuade its opponents into the position the coalition prefers. The new policy, then, is the common interest of the coalition, arrived at by negotiations utilizing knowledge and imposed by threat or verbal guile on the unwilling borrowers. Far from being a rival explanation of what occurred to explanations that rely on interest informed by knowledge, power simply enables us to give a more complete account without having to offer sacrifices at the jealous conceptual altars of any single social science profession.

WHY INTERNATIONAL ORGANIZATIONS ARE IMPORTANT AS INNOVATORS

I am arguing that some, not all, innovations in international life result from the experience of decision makers in international organizations. I am suggesting that we study multilateral processes as agents of change, not that they are the only, or even the most important, such agents. Multilateral processes provide one avenue for the transideological sharing of meanings in human discourse, not the only one. Much more may be going on in bilateral encounters and in informal contacts outside the organizational forum. But since my task is the study of international organizations, I need to stress the role of these entities in mounting innovations without denying the importance of other channels.

Experiences such as the World Bank's permit us to use the history of key international organizations as diagnostic devices for testing when and where knowledge infects multilateral decision making. I want to explore whether international organizations can provide, or have provided, a boundedly rational forum for the mounting of innovations, not a forum for furnishing a collective good determined on the basis of optimization. If we identify the manner of attaining the collective good with pure rational choice, we forget that the choice to be made is not "pure" because it is constrained by what the choosers have already experienced.[4] The game, for them, started some time ago. They are still enmeshed in its consequences and may seek to change the rules if they are unhappy with them. The fact is that the disappointments were, for the most part, associated with policies that were filtered through, and derived much of their legitimacy from, their place on a multilateral agenda. This is true even though such policies usually originated in the politics, the bureaucratics, and the think tanks of the member states. International organizations are part of everybody's experience because they are mediators of policies. They are a part of the international repertory of fora that talk about and authorize innovation. Hence we can study them as agents of innovation.

We can do more. We can also make observations about relative effectiveness in the performance of these organizations and offer suggestions on how to improve effectiveness. In other words, we can contribute to effective innovation on the basis of critical typological study.

My treatment takes for granted that the goals valued by the states that set up organizations are the single most important determinant of later events. Nevertheless, such things as the task environment in which the organization must operate, its choice of core technology to carry out its tasks, and the institutional structure imposed on the staff must influence and probably constrain the attainment of these goals. A concern with institutional innovation must therefore consider environment, structure, and technology along with changing or constant goals.[5]

Must organizations remain the tools their creators have in mind when they set them up — means toward the attainment of some end valued by the creators? Or, alternatively, can international organizations become ends in their own right, become valued as institutions quite apart from the services they were initially expected to perform? If so, what kinds of innovations can or should be designed to bring about such a transition? One might also ask whether effectiveness is good for the survival and prospects of the organization as opposed to the welfare of the world in general; the two outcomes need not be mutually supportive. If they turn out to be contradictory, we might then think of design suggestions to mitigate the contradiction.

Some organizations are hierarchically structured; others are flat. Possibly, each form is optimal for the performance of some task, but not all tasks. Possibly, structure and effective performance are not well matched. If so, our comparative typological study may enable us to offer suggestions on how to adapt structure to effective performance. All organizations select a "core technology" to do their job, and the character of that technology interacts with institutional structure and task environment. It is possible, however, that the technology is not optimal for good performance, or not well integrated with the task environment or the structure. Innovations in design made apparent by historical study may then become appropriate. So can rearrangements in institutional structure, especially when it becomes apparent that better performance requires a different coordinate arrangement among several organizations active in the field. Our first step, then, is the application of organization theory to our study. . . .

In the incremental-growth model, the knowledge available to policymakers does not become more consensual, though it may be growing in scope, and no single epistemic community dominates the flow of knowledge. Politicians in the dominant coalition entertain static and narrowly focused goals; politicians associated with member states outside the dominant coalition, however, are advancing dynamic and expanding goals. Prevalent decision-making styles pit eclectics and/or skeptics against each other. They will link issues tactically for the most part, though some pressure for engaging in fragmented linkages will be in evidence. The modesty of the goals and the relative irrelevance of novel bodies of knowledge result in bargains that are "similar" at the intragovernmental and intracoalitional levels, and only "slightly dissimilar" at the level of intercoalitional encounters. The resulting problem definition is most likely to be a fully decomposable set; we have no reason to expect much intellectual coherence among the constituents of the organization's program, as each item can flourish or founder on its merits without being aided or hindered by other items.

Things work quite differently in the turbulent nongrowth model. Knowledge *among* coalitions is not becoming more consensual; however, *within* some coalitions knowledge applicable to the organization's mandate does command more and more agreement. Some politicians defend static and specific objectives while others advocate dynamic and interconnected ones; the two sets of politicians (and their associated experts) confront each other for control of the dominant coalition. The decision-making style pits skeptics and/or pragmatists against each other. They are able to link issues only in tactical terms, resulting in a bargaining pattern dominated by "dissimilar" styles at all levels. This of course results in a program that is so decomposable as not to merit the label "set" at all. While under conditions of incremental growth, the decomposable program items lack coherence without interfering with each other, under conditions of turbulent nongrowth, the lack of coherence may actually hinder the successful implementation of program items.

Both models of organizational adaptation, then, operate in such a fashion as to give us fully decomposable problem sets, looser and more fragmented than the actors' conceptualization that preceded the change we code. We cannot tell whether the new and more disaggregated set will lead to member-state dissatisfaction: demands for still another reconceptualization of problem sets would depend on whether satisfaction of the members, or its lack, takes the form of an ideologically unified critique.

The managed-interdependence model is the only one capable of inspiring a redefinition of the organization's mandate, giving us nondecomposable, or nearly nondecomposable, sets; but a fully decomposable set may also be produced if the learning pattern suggests this solution as superior to its alternatives. Consensual knowledge, depending on its substantive content, could in principle lead to any of these outcomes.

Our cases of learning to manage interdependence, however, fail to confirm this variety of theoretical possibilities. Mainly, they show that reconceptualization leads to the articulation of nearly nondecomposable sets. The typical sequence of events is as follows. The knowledge being purveyed by experts as relevant to improved organizational performance is becoming more consensual; the objectives of politicians are at the same time expanding and are seen as more tightly interconnected as well. The decision-making style of policymakers will be pragmatic and/or analytic; issue linkage is fragmented, shading into substantive connections among items. Bargaining among members of the same government is likely to become "dissimilar," while intracoalitional negotiations are showing "similar" issue-linkage patterns. Intercoalitional negotiations are becoming "almost similar." This combination of features must result in a problem set that is nested so as to make the disaggregation of the constituent parts very difficult, if not impossible.

True, the increasingly consensual knowledge could also suggest the wisdom of disaggregating issues; the fact that the objectives of politicians are expanding in scope need not imply a tight interconnection among objectives. Decision making would then be consistently pragmatic, and issue linkage would remain fragmented without accretions of substantive linkage. Intercoalitional bargaining would be "dissimilar," or, if "similar" in the sense that only the fragmented style prevails, the substantive differences in positions that the negotiators profess would still militate in favor of decomposability among problems. . . .

None of this amounts to serious advice about deliberately designing organizations that engage in permanent cognitive evolution. In the last analysis, observers and well-wishers of international organizations have very little to offer. There are powerful reasons for the sway of routine, just as there are good reasons for questioning habit. The people responsible for the flawed ways that we call the "crisis of multilateralism" are far from being either fools or knaves. We must admit this, or any attempt to prescribe novel ways of coordinating activities to usher in a more benign world is an act of ultimate hubris. Instead, we ought to look to a master of science fiction for a more playful and permissive view of evolution.

In his novel — set on the planet Solaris, which is dominated by a huge, sentient ocean — Stanislaw Lem describes an imperfect but evolving god. The ocean of Solaris evinces curiosity, cruelty, creativity, and detachment — qualities that baffle the scientists from Earth. The ocean appears to be a god still in his infancy, who plays at being creative and curious without quite knowing why. He is "an evolving god, who develops in the course of time, grows, and keeps increasing in power while remaining aware of his powerlessness." "For this god," says one scientist to another, "the divine condition is a situation without a goal. And understanding that, he despairs. . . . Solaris could be the first phase of the despairing god. Perhaps its intelligence will grow enormously. All the contents of our Solarist libraries could be just a record of his teething troubles . . . and we will have been the baby's toys for a while."[6]

One can think about human progress in similar terms, as an open-ended groping for self-improvement, without a final goal, without a transcendent faith, but with frequent reverses and sporadic self-questioning about the trajectory of change. The very meaning of self-improvement will not stand still. Its content means one utopia for one generation, country, or group; it means quite another one for later generations. Progress is a childlike, groping god, not a purposeful master of the universe. It is difficult to have faith in such a deity. But the lack of faith should not prevent us from asking what makes progress happen.

Progress is a secular god who tolerates the things people, nations, and other large human collectivities do to themselves and to one another. Progress manifests itself more directly and forcefully when such collectivities pause to think about what they do, when they consider doing things differently in the future. Then they engage in what we usually call "learning."

NOTES

1. I call attention to the discovery on the part of Snyder and Diesing that even the situations of crisis they investigated under structuralist assumptions showed a wide variety of actual features with too much variation in behavior and outcome to permit the positing of a small number of structural constraints as determinants. See Glenn Snyder and Paul Diesing, *Conflict Among Nations* (Princeton, NJ: Princeton University Press, 1977), chap. 7. Robert O. Keohane, in *After Hegemony* (Princeton, NJ: Princeton University Press, 1984), concludes that even under microeconomic-structural assumptions the behavior of states in regimes is highly variable and not reliably determined by structuralist assumptions. The case for institutional constraints on behavior is explored and duly qualified by James G. March and Johan P. Olsen in "The New Institutionalism: Organizational Factors in Political Life," *American Political Science Review* 78 (1984): 734–49. My nonstructural epistemological stance is spelled out in greater detail in "Why Collaborate?" *World Politics* 32 (April 1980), and "Words Can Hurt You," *International Organization* 36 (Spring 1982). The present essay is an effort to extend and apply this view to the future of international organizations.

   Theorists and metatheorists customarily differ on how a given writer is to be classified in a field of contending approaches. Even though I reject the labels "idealist" and "liberal" for my theoretical position because of the characteristics I associate with the schools of thought properly so described, I am quite comfortable with being called a "neoidealist," if we follow the description of that stance offered by Charles W. Kegley, Jr., in "Neo-Idealism," *Ethics and International Affairs* 2 (1988): 173–98, although I would be most uncomfortable being identified as a "neoliberal" as defined by Joseph S. Nye, Jr., in "Neorealism and Neoliberalism," *World Politics* 40 (January 1988): 235–51. I am most content, however, to be classed with the nonrationalistic (as he defines them) "reflective" writers elaborated in Robert O. Keohane, "International Institutions: Two Approaches," *International Studies Quarterly* 32 (December 1988).

2. A complete theory would have to offer an explanation of what occurred in an international organization even if the emphasis on changes in the mixture of knowledge and political objective fails. An explanation that stresses changes in available knowledge ought to be able to offer an account of the origin of that knowledge. A claim that issue linkages and bargains that represent different

mixtures of knowledge and political goals explain different modes of organizational development ought to be able to specify the kinds of knowledge and goals most prominent in that history. I am able to specify only *that* a certain mixture was or was not present, not *why* it was present. I am in a position to show only that knowledge was or was not available, not how or why the actors required it.

3. The same lesson emerges from another episode in the history of the World Bank. During the 1980s the U.S. Congress sought to link the authorization of the United States' financial contribution to instructions that no loans should be made to governments that violated a number of congressional preferences in the field of economic policy and the status of human rights. U.S. representatives duly voted against such loans, but in most instances the bank's decision was made in disregard of congressional directives and U.S. votes because the other members of the bank's dominant coalition disagreed with the U.S. definition of interests; the United States' preference did not become the common interest of the coalition. Moreover, the European countries and Japan disputed the U.S. effort to "politicize" the bank's lending policy, arguing that a knowledge of economic development needs makes such efforts illegitimate. The United States' efforts to change the knowledge-informed interests failed.

4. James G. March, one of the theorists of decisions in organizations on whom I rely heavily, clearly explained why this approach is not considered to be in the tradition of pure rational-choice theories. Such theories "portray decision-making as intentional, consequential, and optimizing. That is, they assume that decisions are based on preferences (e.g., wants, needs, values, goals, interests, subjective utilities) and expectations about outcomes associated with different alternative actions. And they assume that the best possible alternative (in terms of its consequences for a decision maker's preferences) is chosen." [James G. March, *Decisions and Organizations* (London: Basil Blackwell, 1988), 1–2]. The decision-making theory of direct concern to me is that which covers decision making "under ambiguity," the opposite of the conditions associated with rational-choice theories derived from microeconomics. The "correctness" of such decisions is always a matter of debate and can never be ascertained in the absence of considerable historical distance from the events. For a telling illustration of the kind of social rationality associated with decisions made in and by organizations, see Ronald Dore's discussion of "relational contracting" in "Goodwill and the Spirit of Market Capitalism," *British Journal of Sociology* 34 (December 1983): 459–82.

5. Gayl D. Ness and Steven Brechin, "Bridging the Gap: International Organizations as Organizations," *International Organization* 42 (Winter 1988), offer a detailed list of suggestions along these lines, on which my treatment draws.

   It is useful to think about the theoretical literature on organizations as being concerned primarily either with decision making or with seeking to explain the persistence of structural forms. The literature on which I rely is essentially the literature on decision making constrained by organizational forms and practices. I am only incidentally interested in the persistence of organizational forms and make no consistent use of the literature in that area, though this theme will make a rather prominent appearance in the final chapter.

6. Stanislaw Lem, *Solaris* (1961; New York: Basic Books, 1971), 205–6.

Turbulent Change

James N. Rosenau

In this article, excerpted from his book Turbulence in World Politics, *Professor Rosenau identifies two competing "worlds"—state-centric and multicentric. He focuses on both micro- and macro-level factors as he explores a world marked by the uncertainties associated with turbulence. Change is being propelled by the dynamics of technology, the emergence of complex issues, the reduced capacity of states to deal effectively with many contemporary problems, and the emergence of "subgroupism" and individuals who are analytically ever more capable and diverse in orientation.*

Doubtless every era seems chaotic to the people who live through it, and the last decades of the twentieth century are no exception. It is as if Spaceship Earth daily encounters squalls, downdrafts, and wind shears as it careens into changing and uncharted realms of experience. Sometimes the turbulence is furiously evident as thunderclouds of war gather or the lightning of a crisis streaks across the global sky; but often the turbulence is of a clear-air kind, the havoc it wreaks unrecognized until after its challenges have been met or its damage done.

In seeking here to account for this turbulence in world politics and the changes that it both reflects and promotes, the analysis will focus on the underlying and enduring dynamics out of which daily events and current issues flow. Some of the dynamics are located at micro levels, where individuals learn and groups cohere; others originate at macro levels, where new technologies are operative and collectivities conflict; and still others derive from clashes between opposing forces at the two levels— between continuity and change, between the pulls of the past and the lures of the future, between the requirements of interdependence and the demands for independence, between centralizing and decentralizing tendencies within and among nations.

While equating the turbulence of world affairs to stormy weather captures well the current human condition, its use here as a metaphor may divert from my larger purpose. The goal in identifying a hitherto unimaginable scheme is to facilitate empirical explanation rather than to provide poetic expression. What is needed is a conception of turbulence that denotes the tensions and changes that ensue when the structures and processes that normally sustain world politics are unsettled and appear to be undergoing rearrangements. Turbulence is thus more than the commotion that accompanies shifts in major variables. Such fluctuations make up the day-to-day life of any system, be it social or meteorological. Just as shifts from cloudiness to showers to sunshine constitute normal weather patterns, so do electoral shifts from right to center to left or industrial shifts from high to moderate to low productivity form standard political and economic patterns, thereby allowing the analysis of such shifts to proceed by treating the system's boundaries as constant and the range within which the variables fluctuate as a measure of underlying stability. When the system's boundaries no longer contain the fluctuations of the variables, however, anomalies arise and irregularities set in as structures waver, new processes evolve, outcomes become transitory, and the system enters a period of prolonged disequilibrium. These are the hallmarks of turbulence. Meteorologically, it appears in the form of hurricanes, tornadoes, tidal waves, droughts, and other "abnormalities" of nature that transform the terrain across which they sweep. Socially, it is manifested in technological breakthroughs, authority crises, consensus breakdowns, revolutionary upheavals, generational conflicts, and other forces that restructure the human landscape in which they erupt.

It follows that uncertainty is a prime characteristic of turbulent politics. While the fluctuations of variables usually adhere to recognizable patterns, regularities disappear when turbulence sets in. At such times, the structures and processes of world politics enter a realm without prior rules or boundaries. Anything may happen, or so it seems, as demands are intensified, tensions exacerbated, relationships transformed, policy-making paralyzed, or outcomes otherwise rendered less certain and the future more obscure.

Closely related to the uncertainties associated with political turbulence is the pace at which it moves. Unlike conventional diplomatic or organizational situations, which evolve in the context of formal procedures, cautious bargaining, and bureaucratic inertia, those beset by turbulent conditions develop rapidly as the repercussions of the various participants' actions cascade through their networks of interdependence. Sustained by the complexity and dynamism of diverse actors whose goals and activities are inextricably linked to each other, and facilitated by technologies that transmit information almost instantaneously, turbulent situations tend to be marked by quick responses, insistent demands, temporary coalitions, and policy reversals, all of which propel the course of events swiftly if erratically along the fault lines of conflict and cooperation.

Viewed in this context, it is not surprising that . . . protests and uprisings [have] followed quickly upon each other in Soviet Armenia, the West Bank, Poland, Burma, and Yugoslavia, or that the same time span was marked by regimes being shaken up in the Soviet Union, Chile, Haiti, and Lebanon. Likewise, and no less conspicuous, [the world has] witnessed cascades of cooperation: within weeks of each other, negotiations to end wars were initiated in Afghanistan, Angola, Central America, Cambodia, the Western Sahara, and the Persian Gulf.[1] The winds of turbulence, in short, can propel postinternational politics in many directions, through the world's diplomatic and legislative chambers, where compromises are reached, no less than through its streets and battlefields, where conflicts are joined.

But how to extend the analysis beyond a suggestive metaphor? How to employ turbulence as a serious and systematic analytic concept that helps to account for the emergence of postinternational politics? . . . [A]n answer is found in the field of organizational theory, where the concept of turbulence is well developed and widely used. In particular, reliance is placed on a model of organizations that identifies turbulence as the condition they face when their environments are marked by high degrees of complexity and dynamism. In this formulation, high complexity is not a synonym for events and trends that are difficult to understand. It refers, rather, to such an inordinate number of actors in the environment, and such an extensive degree of interdependence among them, that the environment is dense (rather than thin) with causal layers. This density is conceived to be so great as to enable any event to give rise to a restless commotion, which reverberates in fast-paced and unexpected ways throughout the environment and its diverse systems. When the dynamism of the environment is also high — i.e., when great variability marks the conduct of its actors — the interdependence of its many parts is bound to be greatly affected by the volatility that accompanies large-scale social transformations.

It could be argued that high complexity and high dynamism are not new to world politics, that global wars, revolutions, and depressions reflect such conditions, and accordingly, that change has always been at work in world politics. In order to differentiate the familiar and commonplace changes from the profound kind of transformations that seem to be occurring today, one other attribute of political turbulence needs to be noted — namely, it involves *parametric* change. Only when the basic parameters of world politics, those boundary constraints that shape and confine the fluctuations of its variables, are engulfed by high complexity and high dynamism is turbulence considered to have set in. Being boundaries, parameters are normally stable. They make possible the continuities of political life, the ability of individual and collective actors to get from one day to the next and from one era to the next. Hence, when the orientations, skills, relationships, and structures that have sustained the parameters of world politics begin to crumble — i.e., when the complexity and the dynamism of the parameters reach a point where the existing rules of conduct no longer serve to constrain behavior and outcomes — the course of events is bound to turn turbulent.

Three dimensions of world politics are conceptualized as its main parameters. One of these operates at the micro level of individuals, one functions at the macro level of collectivities, and the third involves a mix of the two levels. The micro parameter consists of the orientations and skills by which citizens of states and members of nonstate organizations link themselves to the macro world of global politics. I refer to this set of boundary constraints as the *orientational* or *skill* parameter. The macro parameter is here designated the *structural* parameter, and it refers to the constraints embedded in the distribution of power among and within the collectivities of the global system. The mixed parameter is called the *relational* one; it focuses on the nature of the authority relations that prevail between individuals at the micro level and their macro collectivities.

All three of these parameters are judged to be undergoing such a thoroughgoing transformation today as to bring about the first turbulence in world politics since comparable shifts culminated in the Treaty of Westphalia in 1648.[2] At first glance, it doubtless seems excessive to argue that the turbulence of the present era is the first in more than three hundred years. Clearly, the history of most countries is marked by periods of turmoil. As already noted, however, the claim being made here pertains to turbulence in the international system and not to the upheavals experienced within national systems, to the transformation of three specific parametric patterns and not to the commotion that attends the waging of wars or the fluctuation of economies. In the case of the structural parameter, the transformation is marked by a bifurcation in which the state-centric system now coexists with an equally powerful, though more decentralized, multi-centric system. Although these two worlds of world politics have overlapping elements and concerns, their norms, structures, and processes tend to be mutually exclusive, thus giving rise to a set of global arrangements that are new and possibly enduring, as well as extremely complex and dynamic.[3] In the case of the relational parameter, the long-standing pattern whereby compliance with authority tends to be unquestioning and automatic is conceived to have been replaced by a more elaborate set of norms that make the successful exercise of authority much more problematic, thus fostering leadership and followership conflicts within and among state and nonstate collectivities that can fairly be judged as amounting to a series of authority crises which, in both their pervasiveness and their scale, are new and global in scope. Lastly, at the micro level, the analytic skills of individuals have increased to a point where they now play a different and significant role in world politics, a role which has intensified both the processes of structural bifurcation and the breakdown of authority relations.

It is the simultaneity and interaction of these parametric changes that distinguish the present period from the previous three centuries. By virtue of their newly acquired skills, people are more able and ready to question authority, and in turn the new authority relationships have facilitated the development of new, more decentralized global structures. But the causal flows also move from the macro to the micro level as the centralized structures invite the formation of new authority relationships, which then serve to refine further the skills and orientations through which individuals link themselves to their collectivities. Earlier eras have witnessed wars that shifted global structures from multipolar to bipolar foundations and revolutions that undermined the prevailing authority relationships; but not since the seventeenth century have circumstances arisen in which the values of all three of these fundamental parameters underwent reinforcing realignments.

BETWEEN PEACE AND WAR

The turbulent conditions of postinternational politics should not be equated to those of violence. While uncertainty may promote the possibility of armed conflict in world politics, there is no one-to-one relationship between them. Turbulence can prevail within communities, markets, organizations, and alliances without their conflicts bringing on a resort to armed force. To study turbulence is to analyze responses to uncertainty, to the changes wrought by technology and an ever-expanding global interdependence, and war is but one of those responses. What follows, therefore, is only incidentally an analysis of violence in world politics. Indeed, . . . there are good reasons to anticipate that responses involving force will diminish as world politics becomes more turbulent.

In some important respects, in fact, war is free of the uncertainties that accompany turbulence. When war breaks out, adversarial relationships become clear, the goals of policy making self-evident, and the tasks ahead unmistakable. Viewed in this way, turbulence may be more a prewar or postwar condition than a mark of wartime. And of course it is not a characteristic of peacetime, if by the latter is meant stable circumstances in which parameters remain essentially fixed.

In both peace and war, in other words, the day-to-day fluctuations are familiar. They are within the range of variations that have occurred before, that people know how to cope with and adjust to. Under turbulent conditions, on the other hand, even the slightest fluctuation can seem portentous, with each shift confirming that change is the norm, that patterns are fragile, and that expectations can be frustrated.

THE SOURCES OF CHANGE

What are the forces at work toward the end of the twentieth century that drive these parametric transformations? Five seem particularly relevant. One involves the shift from an industrial to a postindustrial order and focuses on the dynamics of technology, particularly on those technologies associated with the microelectronic revolution that have made social, economic, and political distances so much shorter, the movement of ideas, pictures, currencies, and information so much faster, and thus the interdependence of people and events so much greater.[4] A second engine of global change is the emergence of issues — such as atmospheric pollution, terrorism, the drug trade, currency crises, and AIDS — that are the direct products of new technologies or of the world's greater interdependence and are distinguished from traditional political issues by virtue of being transnational rather than national or local in scope. A third dynamic is the reduced capability of states and governments to provide satisfactory solutions to the major issues on their political agendas, partly because the new issues are not wholly within their jurisdiction, partly because the old issues are also increasingly intertwined with significant international components (e.g., agricultural markets and labor productivity), and partly because the compliance of their citizenries can no longer be taken for granted. Fourth, with the weakening of whole systems, subsystems have acquired a correspondingly greater coherence and effectiveness, thereby fostering tendencies toward decentralization (what I call *subgroupism*) at all organizational levels that are in stark contrast to the centralizing tendencies (here regarded as *nation-statism* or *transnationalism*) that marked the early decades of this century and those that preceded it. Finally, there is the feedback of the consequences of all the foregoing for the skills and orientations of the world's adults who comprise the groups, states, and other collectivities that have had to cope with the new issues of interdependence and adjust to the new technologies of the postindustrial order; with their analytic skills enlarged and their orientations toward authority more self-conscious, today's persons-in-the-street are no longer as uninvolved, ignorant, and manipulable with respect to world affairs as were their forebears.

The hypothesized interactions among these five sources of change, and an indication of the historical setting in which they accelerated, are presented diagrammatically in Figure 3.2. This causal model involves more than a simple identification of five prime sources of global turbulence and a presumption that they are highly interactive. One of the five dynamics, the shift in micro capabilities and orientations, is deemed to be more powerful than the other four, so much so as to be a requisite to the expansivity and intensity of the other four. That is, although world politics would not be on a new course today if the microelectronic and other technological revolutions had not occurred, if the new interdependence issues had not arisen, if states and governments had not become weaker, and if subgroupism had not mushroomed, none of these dynamics would have produced parametric change if adults in every country and in all walks of life had remained essentially unskilled and detached with respect to global affairs. To be sure, these shifts in skills and orientations have been hastened and refined by the other dynamics, and in this sense the latter can also be viewed as necessary determinants of the turbulence. Without the micro transformations, however, none of the others could have emerged on a worldwide scale, and in this sense the enlargements of the capacities of citizens is the primary prerequisite for global turbulence.

The analysis, then, is not based on a single-cause model. Nor does it presume that the micro changes preceded the others in time. On the contrary, all of them are seen as being initially responses to the technological upheavals that underlay the ever-growing interdependencies of economic, political, and social life. Once the micro level shifts began, however, alterations in the status of states, governments, and subgroups were bound to follow, as people became receptive to the decentralizing consequences inherent in their growing capacity to locate their own interests more clearly in the flow of events. The subtlety of these interactive processes is perhaps most clearly evident in the links between the expansion of citizen skills and the technologies made available by the microelectronic revolution. If one asks what the advent of instantaneous communications and information retrieval — of satellites bringing pictures of ongoing events into homes everywhere and of computers storing, processing, and disseminating information heretofore unknown and ungatherable — may be doing to individuals as actors on the global stage, the answer seems inescapable that the new technologies have had a profound, if not always desirable, impact upon how individuals perceive, comprehend, judge, enter, avoid, or otherwise interact with the world beyond their workplace and home. For example, the new electronic technologies have so greatly collapsed the time in which organizations and movements can be mobilized that the competence of citizens feeds on itself, in the sense that they can virtually "see" their skills and orientations being cumulated into larger aggregates that have consequence for the course of events. No longer does the translation of commitment into action await word brought by stagecoach that like-minded citizens are banding together or that leaders discern an opportunity for effective participation. Today, events and the words about them are, in effect, simultaneous occurrences. Unlike any prior time in history, therefore, citizens are now able to intrude themselves readily into a situation anywhere in the world, because information about its latest twists and turns is immediately at hand.

Indeed, even if the ensuing analysis exaggerates the extent to which the skills and orientations of citizens have enlarged, the ability to mobilize those skills and orientations is so much greater and speedier than in the past that the practical effect is an expanded capacity for identifying and articulating self-interests and participating effectively in collective action. And if, as seems likely, those who head organizations recognize the effects of this capacity on their leadership circumstances, then their sensitivities to the wishes and demands of their followers will intensify and lend further credence to the perception of citizens as undergoing an expansion and redirection of their skills and orientations.

THE TECHNOLOGICAL DYNAMIC

Given the conception of turbulence as a process of parameter realignment, a further question arises as to the sources of turbulence. Except for the dynamics unleashed by technological innovations, those noted so far are embraced by the three parameters of the global political system and are thus endogenous to it. But there may be exogenous sources in addition to those that derive from technological developments. That is, while turbulence partly feeds on itself, as each parametric alteration gives rise to circumstances that exert pressure for further alterations, political systems are also subject to a broad array of changes originating in the economy and society, all of which are also sufficiently dynamic to spur still further changes once they have been absorbed by the polity.

Following the insightful formulation of Choucri and North, three dynamics are conceived to be especially relevant as exogenous sources of global turbulence.[5] As indicated in Figure 3.2, one is the pressures created by extensive changes in the structure and size of populations in recent decades. A second involves the shifting availability and distribution of natural resources, especially those related to the generation of energy. The third derives from the previously mentioned consequences of technologies in all fields of human endeavor, from information processing to medicine, biogenetics and agriculture.

Since it has also contributed to the shifts in population and natural resources, technology is perhaps the most powerful of the exogenous dynamics. For it is technological developments, those combinations of human ingenuity and material nature, that have transformed the industrial order and brought into being the age of information, the post-industrial society, the technocratic era, the microelectronic revolution — whatever one may wish to call the emergent arrangements by which people move toward goals, satisfy needs, and otherwise conduct their affairs. Technology has expanded the capacity to generate and manipulate information and knowledge even more than the ability to produce material goods, leading to a situation in which the service industries have come to replace the manufacturing industries as the cutting edge of societal life. It is technology too, that has so greatly diminished geographic and social distances through the jet-powered airliner, the computer, the orbiting satellite, and the many other innovations that now move people, ideas, and goods more rapidly and surely across space and time than ever before. It is technology that has profoundly altered the scale on which human affairs take place, allowing more people to do more things in less time and with wider repercussions than could have been imagined in earlier eras. It is technology, in short, that has fostered an interdependence of local, national, and international communities that is far greater than any previously experienced.[6]

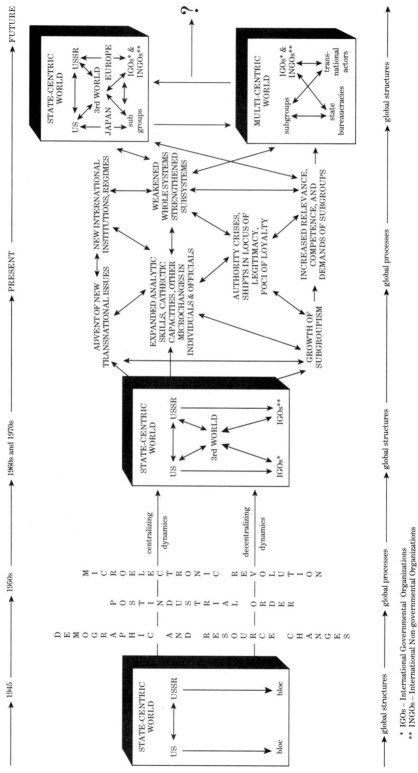

Figure 3.2. Evolution of the two worlds of world politics

* IGOs – International Governmental Organizations
** INGOs – International Non-governmental Organizations

The impact of these technology-driven exogenous dynamics on societies, economies, and polities has been imaginatively and fully recorded by students of national systems. One needs only read the works of Daniel Bell, Peter Drucker, John Naisbitt, and Daniel Yankelovich — to mention a few of the many observers who have focused on the social consequences of modern technology — to appreciate the extraordinary transformations through which the world is passing.[7] They convincingly demonstrate that families, marriages, acquaintanceships, work, unions, businesses, leisure, agriculture, productivity, housing, travel, electoral politics, and every other aspect of life have recently undergone, and still continue to undergo, changes of great magnitude.

Yet somehow, students of global politics have not begun to take account of the transformations at work within societies. While they do not ignore the domestic sources of international relationships when internal conflicts, consensuses, or stalemates predominate, the dynamics of the postindustrial society tend to be taken for granted. That the world is considerably more interdependent is widely recognized, but the ways in which the sources of expanding interdependence sustain or alter the structures and processes of world politics have not been foci of intensive investigation.[8] The prevailing orientation seems, rather, to presume that the basic structures and processes of international politics remain intact even as change swirls through its component parts.

Likewise, students of the postindustrial society have not been especially concerned with the implications of their findings and insights for global politics. While Drucker, for example, does explore these implications for international economics, his analysis is limited to the problems of politically managing the world economy and does not get into the even larger question of management in world politics itself. Similarly, Bell anticipates "that the post-industrial society will involve *more* politics than ever before, for the very reason that choice becomes conscious and the decision-centers more visible,"[9] but his inquiry does not extend beyond the politics of who rules the community and society. The possibility that the global effects of the relatively few postindustrial societies might give rise to worldwide norms and practices that influence the development of preindustrial and industrial societies is not entertained.

AN OVERVIEW

Political turbulence is not so powerful as to sweep away existing institutional arrangements and cultural patterns without resistance. If we are to comprehend the tensions inherent in the clash between the forces that sustain the prevailing order and those that promote transformation, we need to be clear about the concepts of turbulence and change as well as the procedures employed to analyze them. . . .

In sum, by exploring turbulence in world politics we are investigating a major analytic gap that needs to be filled. The gap is that nexus wherein politics on a global scale have been transformed by the diverse dynamics that have taken modern life beyond the rules and arrangements that prevailed throughout the industrial era. The need to fill the gap stems from the premise that it is inconceivable that so many great changes could occur within societies without major consequences for the conduct of affairs among them.

NOTES

1. For an analysis of these developments, see James N. Rosenau, "Interdependence and the Simultaneity Puzzle: Notes on the Outbreak of Peace," in Charles W. Kegley, Jr., ed., *The Long Postwar Peace: The Sources of Great Power Stability* (forthcoming), chapter 15.
2. The Treaty of Westphalia is generally recognized as the beginning of the modern system of nation-states. However, this is not a unanimous view. Wight, for example, argues that the start of the French-Spanish struggle over Italy in 1494 marked the origin of the modern system, noting that "at Westphalia the state system does not come into existence; it comes of age." M. Wight, *Systems of States* (Leicester: Leicester University Press, 1977), p. 152.
3. For reasons indicated in chapter 10, it seems appropriate to treat the state- and multicentric systems as separate "worlds," a formulation not to be confused with the generic label "world politics" that is used throughout to designate structures and processes of global scope. The frequent references to the "two worlds of world politics" (or, occasionally, to the "two-world political universe") are intended to serve as a continual reminder that the global system has structure even though it lacks unity, having entered a period of far-reaching (and possibly irreversible) bifurcation.
4. For a thorough exploration of the diverse dimensions of the microelectronic revolution, see Rob van Tulder and Gerd Junne, *European Multinationals in Core Technologies* (Chichester: John Wiley, 1988).
5. Nazli Choucri and Robert C. North, *Nations in Conflict: National Growth and International Violence* (San Francisco: W. H. Freeman, 1975).
6. For a succinct and cogent discussion of the diverse ways in which new electronic technologies have changed the face of politics at all levels, see Walter B. Wriston, "Technology and Sovereignty," *Foreign Affairs* 67 (Winter 1988/89): 63–75.
7. These authors have each written more than one work on the dynamics of change in the late twentieth century, but their views can be readily grasped in Bell, *Coming of Post-Industrial Society;* Peter Drucker, *Managing in Turbulent Times* (New York: Harper & Row, 1980); John Naisbitt, *Megatrends: Ten New Directions Transforming Our Lives* (New York: Warner Books, 1982); and Daniel Yankelovich, *New Rules: Searching for Self-Fulfillment in A World Turned Upside Down* (New York: Random House, 1981).
8. Exceptions to this generalization can be found in James N. Danziger, "Computing and the Political World," *Computers and the Social Sciences* 2 (1986): 183–200, and Robert Gilpin, "The Computer and World Affairs," in M. L. Dertouzos and J. Moses, eds., *The Computer Age: A Twenty-Year View* (Cambridge, Mass.: MIT Press, 1979), pp. 229–53.
9. Bell, *Coming of Post-Industrial Society,* p. 263 (italics in original).

4

Globalism: Dependency and the Capitalist World-System

MAJOR ACTORS AND ASSUMPTIONS: A SUMMARY

We have seen that realists organize their work around the basic question: How can stability be maintained in an anarchic world? Many pluralists ask how peaceful change can be promoted in a world that is increasingly interdependent politically, militarily, socially, and economically. Our third and final image of international relations, globalism, tends to concentrate on the broad question of why so many **Third World** states in Latin America, Africa, and Asia have been unable to develop. For some globalists this question is part of a larger effort to develop a theory of world capitalist development.

We have avoided the label **Marxism** because there are both Marxists and non-Marxists who work within what we have chosen to call the globalist image. Indeed, some globalists decidedly avoid Marxian modes of analysis. We acknowledge that in adopting the term *globalism* we have appropriated a word sometimes used by pluralists or realists to describe their images of the world. One could, perhaps, find another word as yet unclaimed. But we think globalism is particularly apt for those who see the **capitalist world-system** as their starting point or who focus on **dependency** relations within a global political economy. As already noted in Chapter One, we are not alone in using the term *globalism* in this context.

Globalists are guided by four key assumptions. First, it is necessary to understand the *global context within which states and other entities interact*. Globalists argue that to explain behavior at any and all **levels of analysis** — the individual, bureaucratic, societal, and between states or between societies — one must first understand the overall structure of the global system within which such behavior takes place. As with some realists, globalists believe that the starting point of analysis should be the international system. To a large extent, the behavior of individual actors is explained by a system that provides constraints and opportunities.

Second, globalists stress the importance of *historical analysis* in comprehending the international system. Only by tracing the historical evolution of the system is it possible to understand its current structure. The key historical factor and defining characteristic of the system as a whole is **capitalism.** This particular economic system works to the benefit of some individuals, states, and societies but at the expense of others. Even socialist states must operate within a capitalist world economy that significantly constrains their options. Hence, for globalists the East-West division — even during the height of the Cold War — was not nearly as important as the **North-South** divide and competition among such advanced capitalist states as Germany, Japan, and the United States.

Third, globalists assume that particular *mechanisms of domination* exist that keep Third World states from developing and that contribute to worldwide **uneven development.** To understand these mechanisms requires an examination of dependency relations between the northern industrialized states (Europe and North America) and their poorer neighbors in the southern hemisphere (Africa, Latin America, Asia).

Finally, globalists assume that *economic factors* are absolutely critical in explaining the evolution and functioning of the world capitalist system and the relegation of Third World states to a subordinate position.

The globalist approach would seem to share certain commonalities with the other two perspectives. As noted, globalists and realists both place greater emphasis on the importance of the systems level, or world as a whole, in affecting actors' behavior than do the pluralists. But they differ as to how they characterize the systems level component. Globalists tend to focus on the capitalist mode of production and realists on the distribution of aggregate power. Furthermore, globalists are much more likely than realists to emphasize the intimate connection between the international system and domestic politics — state and society are never viewed as being encapsulated by a metaphorical hard shell.

Globalists and pluralists share at least three commonalities that can be viewed as criticisms of the realist perspective. First, both stress an approach to international relations grounded in **political economy.** The distinction of high politics versus low politics is rejected — if not totally reversed for certain globalists — in terms of the relative importance of economic as compared to political-military factors. For the globalist, various manifestations of political and military power generally reflect the driving force of underlying economic factors. Politics depends on economics; it is not an autonomous realm.

Secondly, both the globalists and pluralists are much more attuned to events, processes, institutions, and actors operating both within and between states; the impermeable billiard ball (the unitary rational actor) is broken down into its component parts. Both approaches tend to range up and down the levels of analysis and focus on a greater variety of actors, but the globalists place a much greater emphasis on the context (i.e., the capitalist nature of the international system) within which these actors operate than do the pluralists.

Third, both the globalists and those pluralists who write in the **transnationalist** tradition emphasize socioeconomic or welfare issues. A number of pluralists have a normative commitment to peaceful change. International relations do not have to be viewed and played as a **zero-sum game** with winners and losers but can be seen as a **positive-sum game** in which the restructuring of interstate relations is achieved through bargaining and compromise, allowing all parties to gain. Although the globalists are also concerned with the welfare of **less developed countries (LDCs)**, they are not so optimistic about the possibility of peaceful change. The hierarchical nature of world politics with South subordinated to North and the economic dictates of the world capitalist system make it unlikely that the northern industrialized states will make any meaningful concessions to the Third World. Change, peaceful or revolutionary, is problematic. In sum, there are major differences between globalists and pluralists.

Although the globalists are primarily concerned with the question of why LDCs cannot develop, answering such a query is difficult. How and why did capitalism develop in Western Europe? How did it expand outward to other continents? As an international phenomenon, how has capitalism changed over the centuries? What are the specific mechanisms of dependency that allow for the maintenance of exploitative relations? What is the relationship between the elites of the wealthy **center** countries (the **First World**) and the elites of the poorer **periphery?** Is it possible for an LDC to break out of a dependent situation? Answers to such questions are addressed in this chapter.

INTELLECTUAL PRECURSORS AND INFLUENCES

Karl Marx

All globalists have been influenced either directly or indirectly by the works of Karl Marx (1818–1883). This is certainly not to suggest that all globalists are Marxists any more than all Marxists accept without qualification the sum total of Marx's efforts. It is simply to acknowledge that they owe an intellectual debt to him in terms of their methods of analysis and certain critical insights into the functioning, development, and expansion of the capitalist mode of production. To appreciate Marx as scholar, one does not have to ascribe to the views of Marx as revolutionary.

Karl Marx's work concerns mankind's historical growth process and movement toward final self-realization and fulfillment in a society he called *communist*. For Marx, history was not so much the story of the rise and fall of particular city-states, empires, and nation-states as it was the story of **class conflict** generated by economic modernization. Having evolved out of a **feudal** system, capitalism reigned supreme in nineteenth century Europe. Marx argued that capitalism —which involves market exchanges, labor as a commodity, and the **means of production** held in private hands — produced particular political, social, and cultural effects. Marx's discussion and analysis of capitalism have influenced globalists in at least three ways.

First, Marx was concerned with exploitation of the many by the few. He may have recognized the historically progressive role played by capitalists (the **prole-**

tarian revolution would not be possible until after the establishment of a capitalist system), but his personal sympathies were with the downtrodden.

Second, according to Marx, capitalism exhibited certain law-like qualities in terms of its development and expansion. He viewed capitalism as part of a world historical process unfolding **dialectically,** an economic system riddled with clashing contradictions or internal tensions that could be resolved only by transformation into a socialist mode of production.

Finally, Marx insisted that a society must be studied in its totality, not piecemeal. An analyst must be aware of how various parts of society were interrelated, including those aspects not so apparent to the casual observer.[1]

This perspective has deeply influenced the globalists, some of whom earlier in their careers had little use for history and were preoccupied almost exclusively with such **units of analysis** as states or individuals. As two leading globalists have argued: "If there is one thing which distinguishes a world-system perspective from any other, it is its insistence that the unit of analysis is a *world*-system defined in terms of *economic* processes and links, and not any units defined in terms of juridical, political, cultural, geographical, or other criteria."[2] Although such units of analysis are not ignored by the globalists, they take on connotations different from those of the realist or pluralist. The state, for example, is not viewed in terms of its being a **sovereign** entity preoccupied with security concerns. Rather, it derives its significance from the role it plays in actively aiding or hindering the capitalist accumulation process. Any one particular stage is not viewed in isolation but in terms of how it fits into the overall global capitalist system.

In sum, Marx has influenced contemporary scholars working within the globalist image by virtue of his emphasis on exploitation, discernible historical patterns of capitalist development and expansion, and the importance of understanding the "big picture" and then asking how individual parts fit into the whole.

Hobson and Imperialism

Marx's observations on capitalism in the nineteenth century have since been modified and generalized to cover the entire globe under various theories of **imperialism**. Imperialism assumes an international, hierarchical division of labor between rich and poor regions of the world, but the relation is not one of mutually beneficial **comparative advantage.** Rather, it is one of exploitation.

Ironically, perhaps one of the most significant theories of imperialism was devised by a non-Marxist, the English economist John A. Hobson (1858–1940). Near the turn of the century Hobson noted that capitalist societies were faced with three basic interrelated problems: overproduction, underconsumption by workers and other classes, and oversavings on the part of capitalists. As the capitalist owners of industry continued to exploit workers and pay the lowest possible wages, profits mounted and goods began to pile up. But who was to purchase the excess goods? Given the low wages, not the mass of the working class, because members of this class did not have sufficient purchasing power. The efficiency of the capitalist mode of production resulted, however, in the relentless production of more and more goods the society was unable to consume.

What could capitalists have done with excess goods and profits, and how could they have resolved the problem of underconsumption? Redistribute wealth? Highly unlikely. Because capitalist European and North American powers were experiencing overproduction and domestic underconsumption, investment opportunities in other developed countries remained limited.

The solution reached by capitalists was to invest in what are now known as Third World countries. The result was imperialism: "the endeavor of the great controllers of industry to broaden the channel for the flow of their surplus wealth by seeking foreign markets and foreign investments to take off the goods and capital they cannot sell or use at home." Hobson argued against "the supposed inevitability of imperial expansion." He stated that it is "not inherent in the nature of things that we should spend our natural resources on militarism, war, and risky, unscrupulous diplomacy, in order to find markets for our goods and surplus capital."[3] Hobson hence rejected the **determinism** so often found in the work of Marxist scholars who write on imperialism.

For Hobson, imperialism did not benefit the home country as a whole. Instead, selected groups such as industrialists, financiers, and the individuals who staffed the colonial empires profited. Furthermore, because the flag followed trade, large military expenditures were required to protect the imperialist system. The drive for capitalist profits by securing overseas territories led to competition and rivalry among European powers. Hence, imperialism was to Hobson a major cause of war, and Hobson suggested that capitalists might indeed profit from such conflicts.

Lenin

V. I. Lenin's (1870–1924) *Imperialism: The Highest Stage of Capitalism* is his most important theoretical work of interest to globalists. Writing in the midst of World War I (1916), Lenin was interested in developing a theory that explained the necessity for capitalist exploitation of lesser developed countries and the causes of war among advanced capitalist states. He drew heavily upon the works of Hobson and the German Social Democrat, Rudolph Hilferding (1877–1941).

From Hobson, Lenin accepted the key argument that underconsumption and overproduction caused capitalists to scramble for foreign markets beyond Europe and to engage in colonialism. From Hilferding, Lenin took the notion that imperialist policies reflected the existence of monopoly and finance capital, or the highest stage of capitalism. In other words, capitalism had developed such that oligopolies and monopolies controlled the key sectors of the economy, squeezing out or taking over smaller firms and milking domestic markets dry. The result was a need to look elsewhere for investment opportunities. This logically entailed the creation of overseas markets. As markets expanded, they required more economic inputs such as raw materials which encouraged the further spread of imperialism to secure such resources.

Marx had seen that rates of profits would decline because of overproduction and underconsumption and that greater misery for the working class would result because more and more people would be out of jobs or receive even less in wages. **Proletarian,** or working-class, consciousness would grow, leading ultimately to revolution in all capitalist countries. For Lenin, imperialism explained why Marx's prediction of proletarian revolution in Europe had failed to come about. Economic contradictions inherent in the capitalist mode of production still existed, but imperialism allowed capitalists a breathing space. Imperialism provided the European working class a taste or small portion of the spoils derived from the exploitation of overseas territories—new markets, cheap labor, and natural resources. By buying off the European working class in the short term, imperialism delayed the inevitable revolution. But an important trade-off was involved. Domestic stability was achieved at the cost of wars among the capitalist powers that resulted from the continual struggle for overseas markets. Once the globe had been effectively divided up, further expansion could come about only at the expense of a capitalist rival.

For Lenin, imperialism was therefore driven by *economic forces,* and it was inevitable that such exploitation and eventual conflict would occur. Hence, he disagreed with Hobson and later theorists (e.g., Joseph Schumpeter) who argued that other factors such as primitive or irrational instincts or an enjoyment of struggle and conquest also played a role in explaining imperialist policies. He also disagreed with writers who argued that imperialism was simply the chosen policy of capitalists and hence was subject to change. Lenin rejected this line of thinking. For him, imperialism was not a matter of choice but inevitability. The capitalists could not save themselves. Imperialism was the direct result of the attainment of monopoly capital. The resulting competition among states, reflecting the domination of capitalist class interests and the differential growth rates of capitalist economies (i.e. **uneven development**), unavoidably led to world wars such as the one being experienced at the time of Lenin's writing.

Although Lenin's theory of imperialism has been subject to a great deal of **empirical** and **conceptual** criticism over the years, Lenin was writing not just as a theorist but also as a revolutionary whose writings were designed to mobilize support for a socialist revolution. He is a prime example of a writer blending theory and practice. In combination with his works on the importance of revolutionary organization, Lenin's *Imperialism* has had a great deal of influence on revolutionaries throughout the Third World.

Strictly as a theorist, Lenin has particularly influenced the globalist literature with his emphasis on the global nature of capitalism and its inherent exploitativeness that primarily benefits the **bourgeoisie** in advanced capitalist states at the expense of poorer countries. Although there is arguably a good deal of determinism in his theory of imperialism, his work as a revolutionary (like that of Marx) reflected considerable voluntarism in practice.[4] The actions of revolutionaries were at the very least to serve as catalysts to the worldwide proletarian revolution whenever the objective conditions of working class exploitation were ripe or had reached their revolutionary stage.[5]

Luxemburg and Revolution vs. Reform

Not to be seduced by the appeal of peaceful, gradual change or reformism, Rosa Luxemburg (1870–1919) expressed deep commitment to revolution as the only effective means of transforming society. She wrote as a critic of Eduard Bernstein's late nineteenth-century German Social Democratic Party politics of **reformism**. She saw reformism as an abandonment of Marxist principles, however helpful such policies might appear to be for the workers in the short run. Luxemburg argued vociferously the necessity for revolution to effect "removal of obstacles that a privileged minority places in the path of social progress."[6] By contrast, she believed that reformism involves compromise with the bourgeoisie, strengthening the hand of the capitalist class: "Only the hammer blow of revolution, that is to say, the conquest of political power by the proletariat," or working class, "can break down this wall" of opposition posed by capitalists to "socialist society."[7] She also described the negative impact of imperialism on colonies.[8]

The issue of whether the kinds of changes anticipated by many globalists can be achieved by reformist tactics or whether they can be achieved only through revolutionary violence remains a matter for dispute. Many globalists are reform-minded, non-Marxists. Globalists who claim to be Marxists are divided. There are reform-minded Marxists in the tradition of Eduard Bernstein who are opposed by those who see revolution as the only effective means to change the existing world order. Even the latter disagree: When will the revolution occur, or when should it occur? Does one wait until objective conditions are ripe, or does one take some affirmative action to move the process along? Are revolutions inevitable, or must they be made? How much is the result of voluntary action, and how much is determined by "historical inevitabilities"? The one point on which these theorists tend to agree is the desirability of change from the present unjust order.[9]

DEPENDENCY THEORISTS

ECLA and UNCTAD Arguments

Some of the more provocative work in the globalist tradition has been produced by Latin Americanists representing various branches of the social sciences. They have come to be known collectively as dependency theorists, and they now include North American and European scholars as well as Latin Americans. Several of these writers were associated in the 1960s with the Economic Commission on Latin America (ECLA) and the United Nations Conference on Trade and Development (UNCTAD). They were concerned with the important problem of explaining why Latin America and other Third World regions were not developing as anticipated. North American social science models had predicted an economic takeoff for LDCs.[10] What had gone wrong? What explained economic stagnation, **balance of payments** difficulties, and deteriorating **terms of**

trade? Why wasn't the North American–Western European experience being repeated?

One response came from mainstream **modernization** writers. This modernization literature attempted to answer these questions by exploring the difficulties of LDCs in moving from "traditional" to "modern" societies. The tradition–modernity dichotomy has been used in one form or another by social scientists as a tool of analysis since the mid-nineteenth century. The ethos and organization of a traditional society, it is argued, are both a cause and an expression of underdevelopment. The cultural values of a traditional society are postulated to be a hindrance to modernization. The LDCs are wedded to their pasts, reflecting a lack of entrepreneurial spirit that was found in European society during the rise of capitalism in the sixteenth century.[11]

This view of development and underdevelopment as the outcomes of internal processes has been criticized on a number of grounds. Two important criticisms are, first, that the modernization writers assume that the tradition–modernity dichotomy is universally applicable. But is the Latin American experience really so similar to the European experience? Are there really no significant historical differences between Africa and the West? Second, the modernization literature usually neglects a state's or society's external environment, particularly international political and economic factors. Instead, modernization writers have tended to focus on state or society, generally ignoring the state's or society's place in the world capitalist order. Is there any society, even in the European historical experience, that is immune to outside influences? Very unlikely, respond the dependency theorists, who place particular emphasis on Latin America's colonial heritage and a historical legacy of exploitation.

The focus of the ECLA and UNCTAD economists was initially quite narrow. They examined the unequal terms of trade between LDCs that exported raw materials and northern industrialized countries that exported finished manufactured goods. They questioned the supposed benefits of free trade. The ECLA at one point favored the diversification of exports, advising that LDCs produce goods instead of importing them. This policy did not result in the anticipated amount of success and in fact increased the influence of foreign multinational corporations brought in to facilitate domestic production.

Did all countries fail to experience economic growth? No, some economies did grow, but growth tended to occur in an LDC only when the developed countries had a need for a particular raw material or agricultural product. Because many LDCs are dependent on only a few of these commodities for their foreign exchange earnings, a drastic decline in the demand for one of them (perhaps caused by a recession in North America) would have a calamitous impact on a LDC's economy. Or, alternatively, a bumper crop in several LDCs heavily dependent on one particular export (such as coffee or sugar) would also cause prices to fall.

The volatility of prices for minerals and agricultural products and the generally downward tendency of those prices contrast sharply with more stable and gradually increasing prices for manufactured items produced by industrial countries. Thus, the terms of trade are thought to be stacked against those Third World states that export farm products or natural resources.

Radical Critiques

Writers in ECLA and UNCTAD (e.g., Argentine economist Raul Prebisch), although critical of the more conservative views of development, nevertheless tended to restrict their analyses to economic dimensions and to cast their arguments in terms of nationalism and the need for state-guided capitalism.[12] Other writers, however, more boldly emphasized political and social factors within the context of a capitalist economic system that bind Latin America to North America. Development, it was argued, is not autonomous. If it occurs at all, it is reflexive — subject to the vagaries and ups and downs of the world's advanced economies. Choices for Latin American countries are restricted or constrained as a result of the dictates of capitalism but also due to supporting political, social, and cultural relations. The result is a structure of domination. This multifaceted web of dependency reinforces unequal exchange between the northern and southern parts of the hemisphere. Opportunities for LDCs are few and far between because LDCs are allocated a subordinate role in world capitalism.

That various states and societies produce those things of which they are relatively the most efficient producers or sell those items in which they have a comparative advantage is seen by dependency theorists as a "one-way advantage." Economic exploitation of LDCs by the industrialized states is not an accident or simply an additional means by which these states enrich themselves. Rather, economic exploitation is an integral part of the capitalist system and is required to keep it functioning.

The result is a situation of dependency, succinctly defined as a "situation in which a certain number of countries have their economy conditioned by the development and expansion of another . . . , placing the dependent countries in a backward position exploited by the dominant countries."[13] The modernization experience of a particular society should not be seen in isolation, "but as part of the development of an internationalist capitalist system, whose dynamic has a determining influence on the local processes." As a result, underdevelopment is not "a moment in the evolution of a society which has been economically, politically and culturally autonomous and isolated."[14] Instead, Latin American and other Third World countries are attempting to develop under historical conditions quite different from those of the northern industrialized states.

Some globalists use Marxist terminology and Leninist insights to explain this situation of dependency. More important than relations between states are transnational class coalitions linking elites in industrially developed countries (the center) with their counterparts in the South (or periphery). This version of class analysis emphasizes how transnational ties within the global bourgeois or capitalist class work to the disadvantage of workers and peasants in the periphery. The multinational corporation (MNC) and international banks, therefore, are viewed from a much different perspective than that of the realist or pluralist. To the pluralist, MNCs and international banks appear merely as other, potentially benign, actors. To the realist, they tend to be of secondary importance because of the emphasis on the state-as-actor. To the globalist, however, they are central players in establishing and maintaining dependency relations. To globalists of Marxist persuasion, MNCs and banks are agents *par excellence* of the international bourgeoisie. They represent two of the critical means by which Third World states are maintained in their subordinate position within the world capitalist economy.

Domestic Forces

Dependency theorists deal not only with external factors (such as foreign states, multinational corporations, international banks, multilateral lending institutions, foreign control of technology, and an international bourgeoisie). They also deal increasingly with internal constraints on development (such as patterns of land tenure, social structures, class alliances, and the role of the state). These internal factors tend to reinforce instruments of foreign domination. It is argued, for example, that the inability to break out of a dependent situation is often strengthened by citizens of a Latin American country who accrue selfish benefits at the expense of the country as a whole. This so-called **comprador class,** or national bourgeoisie, aids in the exploitation of its own society. Allied with foreign capitalists, its self-serving policies encourage the expansion of social and economic inequality, which may take the form of an ever-widening rural-urban gap. Although limited development may occur in a few urban centers, the countryside stagnates and is viewed only as a provider of cheap labor and raw materials. These exploiters, therefore, have more in common with the elites of the center countries than they do with their fellow citizens of the periphery.

Such arguments are rather sweeping in scope. The importance of internal dimensions, however, will vary depending on the particular country under examination. Class coalitions, for example, will differ and may relate to external actors in a variety of ways. As two noted dependency theorists have stated:

> We conceive the relationship between external and internal forces as forming a complex whole whose structural links are not based on mere external forms of exploitation and coercion, but are rooted in coincidence of interests between local dominant classes and international ones.[15]

In some cases this "coincidence of interests" might even involve portions of the working class.

As a result of the interplay of external and internal factors, the nature of the development or underdevelopment of a society will vary. Changes in the international economy will affect LDCs in different ways. Dependency theorists, therefore, do not claim that economic stagnation in LDCs is always and inevitably the norm. They argue, however, that development benefits some at the expense of others, increases social inequalities, and leads to greater foreign control over Third World economies.

THE CAPITALIST WORLD-SYSTEM

The dependency theorists pointed the way for scholars who write from what is known as the capitalist world-system perspective. This perspective is truly globalist and differs from dependency in two ways.

First, advocates of the capitalist world-system perspective not only are concerned with the lack of Third World development but also wish to understand the economic, political, and social development of regions throughout the *entire* world. Developed and underdeveloped states, winners and losers, are all examined in attempts to explain the global existence of uneven development.

Second, the goal is to understand the fate of various parts of the world at various times in history within the larger context of a developing world political economy. Latin America, for example, is not unique. Its experience is an integral part of the capitalist world-system. Third World underdevelopment and exploitation are central to maintaining the present structure of dominance in the capitalist world-system. The first priority, therefore, is to understand this global system from a historical perspective. Only then can the fates of particular societies or regions of the globe be understood.

The writings of Immanuel Wallerstein represent the most ambitious of the globalist work and have been the catalyst for an extensive amount of subsequent research. In attempting to understand the origins and dynamics of the modern world economy and the existence of worldwide uneven development, he aspires to no less than a historically based theory of global development, which he terms *world-system theory*.[16]

Wallerstein begins by analyzing the emergence of capitalism in Europe, tracing its development into a capitalist world-system that contains a **core**, a **periphery**, and a **semi-periphery**. The core areas historically have engaged in the most advanced economic activities: banking, manufacturing, technologically advanced agriculture, and ship building. The periphery has provided raw materials such as minerals and timber to fuel the core's economic expansion. Unskilled labor is repressed, and the peripheral countries are denied advanced technology in those areas that might make them more competitive with core states. The semi-periphery is involved in a mix of production activities, some associated with core areas and others with peripheral areas. The semi-periphery also serves a number of other functions such as being an outlet for investment when wages in core economies become too high. Over time, particular regions of the world may gravitate between core, peripheral, and semi-peripheral status.

Class structure varies in each zone depending on how the dominant class relates to the world economy. Contrary to the liberal economic notion of specialization based on comparative advantage, this division of labor *requires* as well as *increases* inequality between regions. States in the periphery are weak in that they are unable to control their fates, whereas states in the core are economically, politically, and militarily dominant. The basic function of the state is to ensure the continuation of the capitalist mode of production.

Wallerstein's explanatory goals are breathtaking in scope, and his debt to

Marx and other globalist intellectual precursors is evident. He deals with such topics as the cause of war among states and factors leading to the rise and fall of core powers. These issues are discussed in the context of the creation and expansion of capitalism as a historical world system. The focus is first and foremost on economic processes and how they in turn influence political and security considerations.

System

Wallerstein and other globalists insist that in order to understand the development of global economic, political, and social processes, we must keep our eye on the development of capitalism. Capitalism is a system-wide, or global, phenomenon. We should not concentrate on individual states and national economies and then extrapolate from their experiences. Instead, we should examine capitalism as an integrated, historically expanding system that transcends any particular political or geographic boundaries. By first understanding capitalism as a truly integrated world-system, we then can better understand the fate of particular countries. This emphasis on the system as the key to understanding may sound familiar. It should; some realists also claim that to develop a true theory of international relations, one must give precedence to the system as opposed to focusing on individual states. Do globalists operating from the world-system perspective in fact share the realist view as to what constitutes the international system? There are some interesting parallels, particularly if one closely examines Wallerstein's work.

First, some realists acknowledge that Wallerstein is attempting to develop a systems level theory, although he emphasizes economic factors over political variables.[17]

Second, Wallerstein explicitly recognizes the importance of **anarchy**, a concept of critical importance to many realist writers. Recall that anarchy simply refers to the absence of a superordinate or central political authority. Wallerstein notes that "the absence of a single political authority makes it impossible for anyone to legislate the general will of the world-system and hence to curtail the capitalist mode of production."[18] Anarchy, therefore, is defined in political terms for both Wallerstein, who notes the absence of a single world empire, and those realists who discuss the importance of the absence of any central authority in the world.

The implications of anarchy for the realist and globalist are quite different, however, as evidenced by the latter part of the quotation: "to curtail the capitalist mode of production." For the realist, anarchy leads one to examine international political stability, war, and balance-of-power politics involving major states. For the globalist, the economic ramifications of political anarchy are paramount. The political anarchy of the interstate system facilitates the development and expansion of world capitalism because no single state can control the *entire* world economy. The result is an economic division of labor involving a core, a periphery, and a semi-periphery that is the focal point of globalist analysis. Political anarchy becomes a backdrop for an extensive analysis of capitalist dynamics.

Finally, Wallerstein addresses the issue of the international distribution of capabilities or power. Once again, it would appear that Wallerstein has much in common with the realists. The following quotation is illustrative:

> Of course, we shall find on closer inspection that there are periods where one state is relatively quite powerful and other periods where power is more diffuse and contested, permitting weaker states broader ranges of action. We can talk then of the relative tightness or looseness of the world-system as an important variable and seek to analyze why this dimension tends to be cyclical in nature, as it seems to have been for several hundred years.[19]

There is, however, a major difference in how realists and Wallerstein use this notion of a distribution of capabilities.

For Wallerstein, *the very existence* of a particular distribution of power or capabilities cannot be explained without reference to the underlying *economic* order. In other words, he would argue that realists spend a great deal of time talking about the balance of power but that they fail to appreciate that there are important economic processes at work that are critical in accounting for the particular distribution of capabilities or balance of power in the first place!

In sum, despite sharing a similar systems vocabulary, the use and relative importance of these concepts is quite different. For a globalist such as Wallerstein, merely focusing on the distribution of capabilities among states is insufficient if one wishes to comprehend fully the nature of the world-system. The international system has always been comprised of weak and strong political units. Differential power alone is not the defining characteristic of the system. Once again, what is critical for the Wallersteinian globalist is the fact that the key aspect of the system is its capitalist nature, the existence of global class relations, and the various functions states and societies perform in the world economy. Capitalism has been the defining attribute of the international system since the sixteenth century. It is capitalism that helps to account for a core, a periphery, and a semi-periphery. It is capitalism that provides the critical environment in which states and classes operate by constraining, shaping, and channeling behavior. Some states and classes are rewarded. Others are doomed to play subordinate roles in a worldwide division of labor determined by the dictates of capitalism. So, although states and politics are certainly important to the globalist, they must be analyzed in the context of the capitalist world-system.

Political, Economic, and Social Factors

As noted in Chapter One, realists understand the importance of economic factors, but they focus on power, the balance of power, and political explanations of international relations. Pluralists interested in transnationalism emphasize political, economic, and social factors, depending on the issue. And globalists tend to stress economic factors as underlying or driving politics.

These are generalizations, and as with all generalizations, they are subject to qualification. All globalists emphasize economic factors in their conceptions of the world-system, but the degree of their emphasis varies. There even has been recent debate as to whether the capitalist mode of production has been overemphasized. At one extreme, there is Wallerstein, who is claimed by critics to have reduced the derivation and operation of the state system to economics. Other globalists, although accepting the logic of the capitalist world-system approach, stress the interdependence of political and economic **variables.** Christopher Chase-Dunn, for example, argues that "the capitalist mode of production exhibits a single logic in which both political-military power" and exploitative economic processes "play an integrated role."[20] Patrick McGowan states that "distinctions between economic and political processes represent false dichotomies. . . . Accumulation, imperialism, and conflict can be considered part of a single dynamic whereby a hegemonic core state in an increasingly competitive world-system attempts to ensure its own stability, prosperity, and primacy."[21] Political processes, however, are still basically derivative of the world capitalist mode of production, or they are placed in the context of economic structures and processes. Chase-Dunn, for example, develops the argument that "both the attempts and the failures of imperium can be understood as responses to the pressures of uneven development in the world-economy. . . . The interstate system is dependent on the institutions and opportunities presented by the world market for its survival."[22]

Johan Galtung goes one step further in his perspective on imperialism, which has had a major impact on globalists.[23] In examining the mechanisms of imperialism that cause and perpetuate the tremendous inequality within and among nations, Galtung parts company with Marx and Lenin in that for him imperialism is not simply an economic relation arising out of capitalism. Imperialism is a structural relation of dominance defined in political, economic, military, cultural, and communication terms. These types of imperialism have to be seen in their totality. It is not enough for international relations scholars to be preoccupied with only political and military factors, or economists to restrict their focus to economic factors. The entire structure of dominance has to be comprehended.

Equally important, Galtung argues that one must look *inside* societies to understand the effects of interactions *among* them. Imperialism means, for example, that elites in center nations dominate and collaborate with elites in periphery nations to the disadvantage of the majority of people in the latter. This would be a political effect of imperialism. Economic effects would include the production of only a few commodities by a periphery state, and trade being concentrated with a particular center state. Equal emphasis, however, is given to other forms of imperialism.

CHANGE

Many international relations scholars are interested in understanding system change. A common distinction is between changes *of* the system and lesser changes *within* an existing system that retains its basic characteristic. For globalists, changes within the world-system appear to fall into three categories. First, there are changes in the actors' positions within the world capitalist economy. As

Wallerstein states: "There is constant and patterned movement between groups of economic actors as to who shall occupy various positions in the hierarchy of production, profit, and consumption."[24] The Dutch empire of the seventeenth century, for example, gave way to British domination, and eventually the United States rose to prominence in the twentieth century. Despite different core powers, however, the hierarchical nature of the system remains the same.

Second, some scholars identify phases or cycles of capitalist growth and contraction that affect all societies. A period of relative social stability and economic stagnation precedes twenty or thirty years of rapid economic growth. This is then followed by another two or three decades of economic decline, followed again by expansion. Overproduction, a key factor discussed by Hobson, is central to the interplay of economic, social, and political forces.[25]

Third, there is what has been termed a *structural transformation* of the system. This term refers to the historical and geographical expansion of the capitalist world-system, incorporating new areas of the globe and nonintegrated sectors of the world economy.[26] Although the term *transformation* is used, these changes could still be viewed as changes within the system because the capitalist mode of production, although perhaps changing its character, is still capitalist. In sum, the globalist view of the capitalist world-system is hardly static. The world-system is dynamic, reflecting a myriad of activities and changes.[27]

But what about changes *of* the capitalist system? World-system theorists point to one major historical occurrence: the transformation of feudalism into capitalism in sixteenth-century Europe. What are the chances of going beyond capitalism? Globalists are ambivalent on this point. Wallerstein may entitle one article "The Rise and Future Demise of the World Capitalist System," but he also refers to "The Limited Possibilities of Transformation within the Capitalist World Order." Similarly, in the early 1980s, a number of theorists discussed how Eastern European and socialist states might succumb to the powerful forces of the capitalist world-system.[28]

Other globalists point to possible transformational processes that might make significant system change possible. Such non-Marxist scholars as Hayward Alker and Johan Galtung, for example, downplay the notion of constraints that supposedly limit the evolution of alternative world orders. Alker sees change occurring through the dialectical clash of world forces and different visions of world futures. These contradictory world-order contenders (capitalist power balancing, Soviet socialism, collective self-reliance, and corporatist authoritarianism) make system transformation possible. For his part, Galtung sees the international system as open and subject to change. He even speculates on the decline not only of the nation-state but also of multinational corporations and even any world government that may be constructed in the distant future.[29]

What role does human volition play in system change? At one extreme there are scholars who apparently see large-scale historical processes as relatively immune from the actions of human beings. A strong dose of determinism seems to be reflected in their work. They are challenged by critics who downplay constraints. Some of these critics call for revolutions to end capitalist exploitation. They argue that despite the "particularity" of Latin America or other Third

World regions that is emphasized by dependency theorists, these areas remain consistent with the patterns of capitalist development discussed by Marx. The "subordinated classes," they claim, have been neglected by some globalists in favor of a focus on exchange relations among societies. Such critics state that class contradictions and the intensification of class conflict still make possible the type of worker revolution discussed by Marx. Hence, these authors have taken the more voluntarist position in a long-standing Marxist debate on the potential for revolution in the Third World — that revolutionaries can help produce world-system change.[30]

Some world-system theorists take an intermediate position. Powerful "structures of domination" are acknowledged, but so also is the permanent struggle among classes. As Henrique Cardoso states of dependency theory: "Instead of accepting the existence of a determined course in history, there is a return to conceiving of it as an open-ended process. Thus, if structures delimit the range of oscillation, the actions of humans, as well as their imagination, revive and transfigure these structures and may even replace them with others that are not predetermined."[31] Similarly, Terence Hopkins and Immanuel Wallerstein argue that the study of the capitalist world economy is the "theoretical side of the practical work of transforming the modern world-system into the socialist world-order that modern social change has made at once politically necessary and historically possible."[32] In this formulation, there is room for human political will to effect transformation. Thus, if one accepts globalists at their word (and some critics do not), globalist theory is not determinist. It allows for (and even requires) political action.

GLOBALISTS AND THEIR CRITICS: AN OVERVIEW

The globalist literature has been subject to a great deal of criticism by specialists in international relations and comparative politics. Much of the criticism is harsh, particularly of dependency theorists and Immanuel Wallerstein's ambitious work. Much of this criticism also perhaps reflects ideological biases. We first discuss some of the more telling critiques and then present rebuttals from globalists.

The Question of Causality

Some critics question whether dependency creates economic and social backwardness (as globalists claim), or whether it is economic and social backwardness that leads to a situation of dependency. In short, there is no agreement on causality — whether dependency is the *cause* of backwardness or whether it is the *effect* of this condition.

Reliance on Economics

Critics have argued that some globalists have reduced the operation of the international system down to the process of capital accumulation and related dynamics. What of other, noneconomic explanations of imperialism and relations among states? Are not political and strategic motives equally or even more important? For example, how can one account for nineteenth-century European states scrambling for economically low-value pieces of terrain such as present-day Chad or lifeless Pacific atolls? What was the economic motive? If the competitive interstate system is derived from the capitalist mode of production, how does one explain similar competitive behavior among political units in precapitalist eras before the fifteenth century? For example, recall Thucydides' discussion of the Peloponnesian War that lends support to the validity of such notions as anarchy and the security dilemma. This suggests the autonomy of the political realm and a distinctly political dynamic involving competition among sovereign units well before the emergence of a capitalist world-system.

The economic variable, critics claim, cannot carry the very great explanatory weight assigned to it. Insights generated from the contemplation of international relations over the centuries should not be ignored. Realists, for example, would argue that if anything it is the international political-security system that largely determines the international economic system, not the other way around.

System Dominance

Despite globalist references to internal factors, critics claim that there is an excessive globalist reliance on international factors in explaining poverty and dependence in the periphery and that domestic variables are downplayed. The cruder dependency work, it is argued, is too sweeping in its claims, blaming virtually every Third World political, economic, and social problem on the northern industrialized states. Lack of economic growth, social unrest, and repressive governments are all laid at the doorstep of the richer capitalist countries.

Theoretical Rigidity

The criticism of economics and system dominance as bases for causality logically leads to the following: It is claimed that individual cases are examined solely in terms of general theoretical constructs such as "dependency" or "capitalist world-system." A society's experiences are reduced to or explained in terms of one or two concepts. Major political, economic, and social changes all supposedly fall under the general explanatory logic of a term such as *dependency*. Furthermore, rather than modifying the theories or concepts in light of empirical evidence (often supposedly lacking) or questions raised by case studies, it is claimed that case studies are used by globalists only when they appear to provide evidence to support the line of argument. There is no tension between theory and findings, little questioning of the framework, and an unwillingness to consider alternative hypotheses. Such criticisms, however, could just as easily be leveled at work associated with both the realist and pluralist images.

Accounting for Anomalies

It is also argued that the globalists are unable to account for Third World countries that have been relatively economically successful: Venezuela, Brazil, Singapore, South Korea. In addition there is the greatest success story of any non-European, non-North American country: Japan. What is it about these countries that has allowed them to escape abject poverty? Nor are they examples of autonomous development. In fact, they seem to have benefited greatly from international ties.

In response, it should be noted that no theory can be expected to explain everything. The virtue of good theorizing is that it points out and accounts for commonalities, what particular cases have in common. Anomalies are expected and do not detract from the utility of the theory if it can adequately be explained why a unique case does not fit the general pattern.

Critics comment, however, that globalists such as Wallerstein and the dependency theorists simply group all anomalies under the concept of the semi-periphery, a theoretically and empirically poorly defined concept. Furthermore, what of the insights of authors who argue that there are certain advantages to backwardness when a state is trying to catch up economically with more advanced states? What of the work by scholars who emphasize the importance of different types of state structures, political and social coalitions, and shifting alliances in accounting for the differential modernization success of various countries?[33] Such literature is ignored, it is argued, because the globalist perspective refuses to give due consideration to domestic factors that are not the result of capitalist dynamics.

Defining Alternatives and Science as Ideology

It is argued that some globalists have done a poor job in defining reasonable alternative world futures, let alone strategies, for LDCs to pursue. What is meant, for example, by the call for autonomous development? Is such a goal feasible? How is it to be achieved? What would a world socialist system entail? Would redistributive policies of a world government be combined with political repression and the abuse of power?

Critics also charge that value preferences infuse the globalist work. Globalists, however, are not apologetic for their normative commitment to fundamental changes in the relations between the North and the South. As one noted writer has stated, in analyses of dependency relations "there is no presumption of scientific neutrality." Such works are considered to be "more true because they assume that, by discerning which are the historical agents capable of propelling a process of transformation . . . , these analyses thus grasp the meaning of historical movement and help to negate a given order of domination."[34]

Critics of the dependency literature in particular believe that much of the work seeks less to explain underdevelopment than to unite Third World nationalists and socialists against the West by providing a politically attractive doctrine packaged in social science terms that blames all LDC problems on outside powers. By diverting attention from domestic sources of underdevelopment that have little to do with external factors, the dependency theorists, it is claimed, actually help to perpetuate the very problem they seek to resolve.

Responses

Why has the globalist literature—when it has not been totally ignored—received such a great deal of criticism? Is it simply because it is deserving of such critical scrutiny? Three comments are in order.

First, it is not surprising that most of the criticism comes from scholars working within mainstream North American social science. The vocabulary of the globalist literature is alien to many of these scholars. Analyses based on Marxian insights and categories are still generally viewed with distrust in North American universities and often dismissed out of hand. And although some of the globalist work is characterized as being ideological, globalists have similarly surmised that the attacks on them are based less on dispassionate critiques and more on the value preferences of the reviewer. Ideological biases are wrapped in the cloak of supposedly objective criticisms.

Second, it was pointed out that a number of critics charge that the dependency literature in particular has been insufficiently empirical, failing to marshal evidence based on the dictates of scientific behavioralism. Where's the data, they ask? In fact, it is claimed that the empirical testing of selective hypotheses from the dependency literature indicates that these hypotheses do not hold up.

Dependency theorists respond that such a charge is based on the assumption that the behavioralist methods are the only means to comprehend reality. In point of fact, critics argue, there are alternative **epistemological** premises or assumptions from which one can start that question the value of formal hypothesis testing with its often exclusive focus on what can be measured, counted, and added. As one dependency theorist notes:

> The divergence is not merely methodological-formal. It is, rather, at the very heart of studies of dependency. If these studies do in fact have any power of attraction at all, it is not merely because they propose a methodology to substitute for a previously existing paradigm or because they open up a new set of themes. It is principally because they do this from a *radically critical* viewpoint.[35]

Furthermore, many of these supposed empirical tests of dependency hypotheses completely ignore location and timing—the spatial and temporal context in which development occurs. They are, in other words, nonhistorical empirical tests of globalist hypotheses. Empirical tests cognizant of the historical context, by contrast, are said to support dependency propositions.[36] In addition, much of the world-system literature has actually been conspicuously empirical in a number of cross-national studies.[37]

Finally, some of the more insightful criticisms of the globalist literature are not based on antipathy toward the work but are meant to strengthen it by pointing out its weaknesses.[38]

To conclude, judging by the international relations textbooks currently on the market, it is apparent that the globalist perspective is not considered mainstream. Realist and pluralist writers dominate the literature, but this certainly does not mean that the globalist image of international relations is unimportant or undeserving of the student's attention. Its contribution to increased understanding of the world around us should not be seen only as a function of its degree of popularity with professors and textbook publishers. By providing a very different, challenging, and provocative perspective on world politics, it is worthy of attention. After all, as Thomas Kuhn has noted, dominant scientific paradigms of one particular period have a tendency to decay. What is at one time considered to be heretical or at the fringes of "normal science" may one day itself become the prevailing orthodoxy.[39] At a minimum, the globalist perspective should encourage the student of international relations to analyze critically the realist and pluralist images and the assumptions on which they are based. At the maximum, globalist writers have provided challenging hypotheses concerning the dynamics and development of the international system.

NOTES

1. As Robert L. Heilbroner states, "The entire contribution of Marxism to social thought rests ultimately on its effort to penetrate the veil of appearances to discover the hidden essence of things, the web of relations that is the real ground of reality and not the surface manifestations that are its facade." *Marxism: For and Against* (New York: Norton, 1980), p. 49.
2. Terence K. Hopkins, Immanuel Wallerstein and associates, "Patterns of Development of the Modern World-System," in *World-System Analysis: Theory and Methodology*, ed. Hopkins, Wallerstein, and associates (Beverly Hills, CA: Sage Publications, 1982), p. 72.
3. John A. Hobson, *Imperialism: A Study* (Ann Arbor: University of Michigan Press, 1965), pp. 85–86.
4. For example, see Lenin's "What Is to Be Done?" in *The Lenin Anthology*, ed. Robert C. Tucker (New York: Norton, 1975), pp. 12–114.
5. Others who would later write in this tradition would argue that revolutionaries play more of a role than mere catalysts. They can actually create the conditions for revolution; the "subjective" can create the "objective." This is most explicit in the writings, for example, of Che Guevara, although one also finds shades of it in Mao Zedong's writings on guerrilla warfare. As Karl Marx argued, "Men make their own history, but they do not make it just as they please; they do not make it under circumstances chosen by themselves, but under circumstances directly found, given, and transmitted from the past. The tradition of all dead generations weighs heavily like a nightmare on the brain of the living." "The Eighteenth Brumaire of Louis Bonaparte" in *The Marx-Engels Reader*, ed. Robert C. Tucker (New York: Norton, 1972), p. 436.
6. Rosa Luxemburg, *Reform or Revolution* (New York: Pathfinder Press, 1970, 1973), p. 72. The original publication was in German in 1898 and 1899.
7. Ibid, p. 29.
8. Rosa Luxemburg, *The Accumulation of Capital* (New Haven, CT: Yale University Press, 1951).
9. For important early discussions, see Leon Trotsky, *The Russian Revolution* (New York: Doubleday, 1959); N. I. Bukharin, *Imperialism and World Economy* (New

York: International Publishers, 1929); and Eduard Bernstein, *Evolutionary Social-ism* (New York: B. W. Huebsch, 1911).

10. W. W. Rostow, *The Process of Economic Growth*, 2d ed. (New York: Norton, 1962).

11. The classic statement is found in Max Weber, *The Protestant Ethic and the Spirit of Capitalism* (New York: Scribner's, 1958).

12. Raul Prebisch, *Towards a Dynamic Development Policy for Latin America* (New York: United Nations, 1963).

13. Theotonio dos Santos, "La crisis del desarrollo y las relaciones de dependencia en America Latina," in *La Dependencia politico-economica de America Latina*, ed. H. Jaguaribe et al. (Mexico, 1970), p. 180, as cited in J. Samuel Valenzuela and Ar-turo Valenzuela, "Modernization and Dependency: Alternative Perspectives in the Study of Latin American Underdevelopment," *Comparative Politics* 10, 4 (July 1978): 544.

14. Osvaldo Sunkel, "Big Business and Dependencia: A Latin American View," *Foreign Affairs* 50, 3 (1972): 519–20.

15. Fernando Henrique Cardoso and Enzo Faletto, *Dependency and Development in Latin America* (Berkeley: University of California Press, 1979), p. xvi. See also three works by Samir Amin, *Imperialism and Unequal Development* (New York: Monthly Review Press, 1977); *Neo-Colonialism in West Africa* (New York: Monthly Review Press, 1974); and *Accumulation on a World Scale: A Critique of the Theory of Un-derdevelopment* (New York: Monthly Review Press, 1974). See also Walter Rodney, *How Europe Underdeveloped Africa* (London: Bogle-l'Ouverture, 1973); Arghiri Emmanuel, *Unequal Exchange* (New York: Monthly Review Press, 1972); A. G. Frank, *World Accumulation, 1492–1789* (New York: Monthly Review Press, 1978).

16. Immanuel Wallerstein, *The Modern World-System I: Capitalist Agriculture and the Origins of the European World-Economy in the Sixteenth Century* (New York: Aca-demic Press, 1974); and *The Modern World-System II: Mercantilism and the Con-solidation of the European World-Economy, 1600–1750* (New York: Academic Press, 1980). For a discussion of the non-Marxist elements upon which Wallerstein's work is based, see Robert Brenner, "The Origins of Capitalist Development: A Criti-que of Neo-Smithian Marxism," *New Left Review* 104 (July–August 1977): 25–92.

17. Kenneth N. Waltz, *Theory of International Politics* (Reading, MA: Addison-Wesley, 1979), p. 38.

18. Immanuel Wallerstein, *The Capitalist World-Economy* (Cambridge: Cambridge University Press, 1979), p. 69.

19. Ibid., p. 25.

20. Christopher Chase-Dunn, "Interstate System and Capitalist World-Economy: One Logic or Two?" in *World System Structure: Continuity and Change*, ed. W. Ladd Hollist and James N. Rosenau (Beverly Hills, CA: Sage Publications, 1981), p. 31

21. Patrick J. McGowan with Bohdan Kordan, "Imperialism in World-System Perspec-tive: Britain 1870–1914," in *World System Structure*, ed. Hollist and Rosenau, p. 78.

22. Chase-Dunn, "Interstate System and Capitalist World-Economy," pp. 50–51.

23. Johan Galtung, "A Structural Theory of Imperialism," *Journal of Peace Research* 2 (1971): 81–98.

24. Wallerstein, *Capitalist World-Economy*, p. 67.

25. Hopkins and Wallerstein, "Structural Transformations of the World-Economy," in *World-System Analysis*, pp. 121–122. For a discussion of cycles, see also Waller-stein, *Modern World-System II*, Chapter 1.

26. Ibid., p. 123.

27. For the argument that a new version of capitalism is emerging, see Robert J. S. Ross and Kent Trachte, "The Theory of Global Capitalism and Change in the World System: The New Leviathan." Paper presented at the annual meeting of the International Studies Association, March 1985, Washington, DC.

28. Immanuel Wallerstein, "The Rise and Future Demise of the World Capitalist System," *Comparative Studies in Society and History* 16, no. 4 (September 1974): 387–415, and his "Dependence in an Interdependent World: The Limited Possibilities of Transformation Within the Capitalist World Economy," *African Studies Review* 18, no. 1 (April 1974): 1–26. Christopher Chase-Dunn, ed., *Socialist States in the World-System* (Beverly Hills, CA: Sage Publications, 1982).

29. Hayward R. Alker, Jr., "Dialectical Foundations of Global Disparities," in *World System Structure*, ed. Hollist and Rosenau, pp. 80–109; Johan Galtung, "Global Processes and the World in the 1980s," in *World System Structure*, ed. Hollist and Rosenau, pp. 110–138. Chase-Dunn (also in Hollist and Rosenau, p. 43) states that transformation might involve the dissolution of states, the elimination of economic exchanges between national territories, or the creation of a world state.

30. Augustin Cueva, "A Summary of Problems and Perspectives of Dependency Theory," *Latin American Perspectives* 3, 4 (Fall 1976): 12–16. On the need to build a revolutionary party, see Raul A. Fernandez and Jose F. Ocampo, "The Latin American Revolution: A Theory of Imperialism, Not Dependence," *Latin American Perspectives* 1 (Spring 1974): 30–61.

31. Fernando Henrique Cardoso, "The Consumption of Dependency Theory in the United States," *Latin American Research Review* 12, 3 (1977): 10–11.

32. Hopkins and Wallerstein, *World-System Analysis*, p. 8.

33. See, for example, Alexander Gerschenkron, *Economic Backwardness in Historical Perspective* (New York: Praeger, 1965); Barrington Moore, *Social Origins of Dictatorship and Democracy* (Boston: Beacon Press, 1966); Theda Skocpol, *States and Social Revolutions* (New York: Cambridge University Press, 1979).

34. Henrique Cardoso, "The Consumption of Dependency Theory," p. 16. See also the comments by James A. Caporaso, "Introduction," *International Organization* 32, 1 (Winter 1978): 2–3. A special issue on dependence and dependency.

35. Ibid.

36. David Sylvan and associates, "The Peripheral Economies: Penetration and Economic Distortion," in *Contending Approaches to World System Analysis*, ed. William R. Thompson (Beverly Hills, CA: Sage Publications, 1983) pp. 79–111. See also Raymond Duvall et al., "A Formal Model of Dependencia Theory: Structure and Measurement," in *From National Development to Global Community*, ed. Richard Merritt and Bruce Russett (London: George Allen & Unwin, 1981), pp. 312–50.

37. See John W. Meyer and Michael T. Hannan, eds., *National Development and the World System: Educational, Economic, and Political Change, 1950–1970* (Chicago: University of Chicago Press, 1979); Albert Bergesen, ed., *Studies of the Modern World-System* (New York: Academic Press, 1980); Richard Rubinson, "The World Economy and the Distribution of Income Within States: A Cross-National Study," *American Sociological Review* 41 (1976): 638–59; and Christopher Chase-Dunn, "The Effects of International Economic Dependence on Development and Inequality: A Cross-National Study," *American Sociological Review* 40 (1975): 720–38.

38. See, for example, Theda Skocpol, "Wallerstein's World Capitalist System: A Theoretical and Historical Critique," *American Journal of Sociology* 82, 5 (March 1977): 1075–91.

39. Thomas S. Kuhn, *The Structure of Scientific Revolutions* (Chicago: University of Chicago Press, 1970).

SUGGESTED READINGS

Newly added to this edition. Suggested readings from earlier works follow this more recent list.

Abu-Lughod, Janet. *Before European Hegemony: The World System A.D. 1250–1350.* New York: Oxford University Press, 1989.

Ayoob, Mohammed. "The Security Problematic of the Third World." *World Politics* 43, 2 (January 1991): 257–83.

Boswell, Terry and Immanuel Wallerstein, eds. *Revolution in the World-System.* Westport, CT: Greenwood, 1989.

Chase-Dunn, Christopher. *Global Formation: Structures of the World Economy.* Oxford: Blackwell, 1989.

Chase-Dunn, Christopher and Thomas D. Hall, eds. *Core-Periphery Relations in Precapitalist Worlds.* Boulder, CO: Westview Press, 1991.

Cox, Robert W. *Power, Production, and World Order.* New York: Columbia University Press, 1987.

Denemark, Robert A. "The Brenner-Wallerstein Debate." *International Studies Quarterly* 32, 1 (March 1988): 47–65.

Elster, Jon. *Making Sense of Marx.* Cambridge, England: Cambridge University Press, 1985.

Frank, Andre Gunder. "A Plea for World System History." *Journal of World History* II,1 (Winter 1991).

———. "A Theoretical Introduction to 5,000 Years of World System History." *Review* XIII,2. Binghamton, New York (Spring 1990): 155–248.

———. "The Thirteenth Century World System: A Review Essay." *Journal of World History* I,2 (Autumn 1990): 249–56.

Gill, Stephen R. and David Law. "Global Hegemony and the Structural Power of Capital." *International Studies Quarterly* 33,4 (December 1989): 475–99.

Gills, Barry K. and Andre Gunder Frank. "The Cumulation of Accumulation: Theses and Research Agenda for 5000 Years of World System History." *Dialectical Anthropology* 15,1. New York/Amsterdam (July 1990): 19–42.

Heilbroner, Robert L. *The Nature and Logic of Capitalism.* New York: Norton, 1985.

Holl, Otmar, ed. *Small States in Europe and Dependence.* Boulder, CO: Westview Press, 1985.

Hollist, W. Ladd and F. Lamond Tullis. *An International Political Economy.* Boulder, CO: Westview Press, 1985.

Jowitt, Ken. "After Leninism: The New World Disorder." *Journal of Democracy* 2,1 (Winter 1991): 11–20.

Klink, Frank F. "Rationalizing Core-Periphery Relations: The Analytical Foundations of Structural Inequality in World Politics." *International Studies Quarterly* 34,2 (June 1990): 183–209.

Mazrui, Ali A. *Cultural Forces in World Politics.* Portsmouth, NH: Heinemann, 1990.

Mommsen, Wolfgang J. and Jurgen Osterhammel, eds. *Imperialism and After: Continuities and Discontinuities.* London: Allen & Unwin, 1986.

Parenti, Michael. *The Sword and the Dollar: Imperialism, Revolution, and the Arms Race.* New York: St. Martin's, 1988.

Pater, Cheryl. *The World Bank: A Critical Analysis.* New York: Monthly Review Press, 1982.

Pfister, Ulrich and Christian Suter. "International Financial Relations as Part of the World-System." *International Studies Quarterly* 31,3 (September 1987): 239–72.

Rowlands, Michael, Mogens Larsen, and Kristian Krisitansen, eds. *Centre and Periphery in the Ancient World.* Cambridge, England: Cambridge University Press, 1987.

Schaeffer, Robert K. and Immanuel Wallerstein, eds. *War in the World-System.* Westport, CT: Greenwood, 1989.

Shannon, Thomas Richard. *An Introduction to the World-System Perspective.* Boulder, CO.: Westview Press, 1989.

Smith, Joan, Jane Collins, et al., eds. *Racism, Sexism, and the World-System.* Westport, CT: Greenwood, 1988.

Tetreault, Mary Ann and Charles Frederick Abel, eds. *Dependency Theory and the Return of High Politics.* Westport, Conn.: Greenwood Press, 1986.

Wallerstein, Immanuel. *Geopolitics and Geoculture: Essays on the Changing World-System.* New York: Cambridge University Press, 1991.

——. "Systeme Mondiale contre Systeme-Monde." *Sociologie et Societe* XXII,2 (October 1990).

SUGGESTED READINGS FROM THE FIRST EDITION

Alker, Hayward R. "The Dialectical Foundations of Global Disparities." *International Studies Quarterly* 25, 1 (March 1981): 69–98.

Alker, Hayward R., and Thomas J. Biersteker. "The Dialectics of World Order: Notes for a Future Archeologist of International Savoir Faire." *International Studies Quarterly* 28 (1984): 121–42.

Amin, Samir. *Accumulation on a World Scale.* New York: Monthly Review Press, 1978.

——, ed. *Dynamics of Global Crisis.* New York: Monthly Review Press, 1982.

——. *Imperialism and Unequal Development.* New York: Monthly Review Press, 1977.

——. *Neo-Colonialism in West Africa.* New York: Monthly Review Press, 1976.

——. *Unequal Development: An Essay on the Social Formations of Peripheral Capitalism.* New York: Monthly Review Press, 1977.

Andrews, Bruce. "The Political Economy of World Capitalism: Theory and Practice." *International Organization* 36, 1 (Winter 1982): 135–63. A review essay.

Bergesen, Albert, ed. *Crises in the World-System.* Beverly Hills, CA: Sage Publications, 1983.

——, ed. *Studies of the Modern World-System.* New York: Academic Press, 1980.

H. Bernstein, ed. *Underdevelopment and Development: The Third World Today.* London: Penguin, 1976.

Bodenheimer, Susanne. "Dependency and Imperialism: The Roots of Latin American Underdevelopment." *Politics and Society* 1, 3 (May 1971): 327–57.

Bornschier, Volker. "Multinational Corporations and Economic Growth." *Journal of Development Economics* 7 (June 1980): 191–210.

Brenner, Robert. "The Origins of Capitalist Development: A Critique of Neo-Smithian Marxism." *New Left Review* 104 (July–August 1977): 25–92.

Caporaso, James A. "Dependence, Dependency, and Power in the Global System: A

Structural and Behavioral Analysis." *International Organization* 32, 1 (Winter 1978): 13–44.

———. "Dependency Theory: Continuities and Discontinuities in Development Studies." *International Organization* 34, 4 (Autumn 1980): 605–28. A review essay.

Cardoso, Fernando Henrique. "Associated-Dependent Development: Theoretical and Practical Implications." In *Authoritarian Brazil*, edited by Alfred Stepan. New Haven, CT: Yale University Press, 1973.

———. "Dependency and Development in Latin America." *New Left Review* 74 (July–August 1972): 83–95.

———. "Imperialism and Dependency in Latin America." In *Structures of Dependency*, edited by Frank Bonilla and Robert Girling. Stanford, CA: Stanford Institute of Political Studies, 1973.

Casanova, Pablo Gonzalez. "The Economic Development of Mexico." *Scientific American* 243, 3 (September 1980): 192–204.

Chase-Dunn, Christopher. "Comparative Research on World-System Characteristics." *International Studies Quarterly* 23, 4 (December 1979): 601–23.

———. "The Effects of International Economic Dependence on Development and Inequality: A Cross-National Study." *American Sociological Review* 40 (1975): 720–38.

Chase-Dunn, Christopher, and Richard Rubinson. "Toward a Structural Perspective on the World-System." *Politics and Society* 7, 4 (1977): 453–76.

Chilcote, Ronald H., ed. *Dependency and Marxism: Toward a Resolution of the Debate*. Boulder, CO: Westview Press, 1982.

———. "Dependency: A Critical Synthesis of the Literature." *Latin American Perspectives* 1 (Spring 1974): 4–29.

Chilcote, Robert H., and Dale L. Johnson, eds. *Theories of Development: Mode of Production or Dependency?* Beverly Hills, CA: Sage Publications, 1983.

Cockcroft, James D., Andre Gunder Frank, and Dale L. Johnson, eds. *Dependence and Underdevelopment in Latin America*. New York: Anchor, 1972.

Cocks, Peter. "Towards a Marxist Theory of European Integration." *International Organization* 34, 1 (Winter 1980): 1–40.

Cohen, Benjamin J. *The Question of Imperialism*. New York: Basic Books, 1973.

dos Santos, Theotonio. *Imperialismo y dependencia*. Mexico City: Ediciones Era, 1978.

———. "The Structure of Dependence." *American Economic Review* 60, 2 (May 1970): 231–36.

Duvall, Raymond and associates, "A Formal Model of Dependencia Theory: Structure and Measurement." In *From National Development to Global Community*, edited by Richard Merritt and Bruce Russett. London and Boston: Allen & Unwin, 1981.

Emmanuel, Arghiri. *Unequal Exchange*, New York: Monthly Review Press, 1972.

Evans, Peter. *Dependent Development: The Alliance of Multinational, State, and Local Capital in Brazil*. Princeton, NJ: Princeton University Press, 1979.

Foster-Carter, Aidan. "Neo-Marxist Approaches to Development and Underdevelopment." In *Sociology and Development*, edited by Emmanuel de Kadt and Gavin Williams. London: Tavistock Press, 1974.

Frank, Andre Gunder. *Capitalism and Underdevelopment in Latin America*. London: Penguin, 1971.

———. *Crisis: In the Third World*. New York: Holmes and Meier, 1981.

———. *Crisis: In the World Economy*. New York: Holmes and Meier, 1980.

———. *Critique and Anti-Critique: Essays on Dependence and Reformism*. New York: Praeger, 1983.

———. *Latin America: Underdevelopment or Revolution*. New York: Monthly Review Press, 1969.

————. *World Accumulation, 1492–1789.* New York: Monthly Review Press, 1978.

Friedman, Edward, ed. *Ascent and Decline in the World-System.* Beverly Hills, CA: Sage Publications, 1982.

Galtung, Johan. "A Structural Theory of Imperialism." *Journal of Peace Research* 2 (1971): 81–98.

————. *Peace and World Structure.* Atlantic Highlands, NJ: Humanities Press, 1980.

————. *Peace Problems: Some Case Studies.* Atlantic Highlands, NJ: Humanities Press, 1980.

Goldfrank, Walter L., ed. *The World-System of Capitalism: Past and Present.* Beverly Hills, CA: Sage Publications, 1979.

Hollist, W. Ladd, and James N. Rosenau, eds. *World System Structure: Continuity and Change.* Beverly Hills, CA: Sage Publications, 1981.

Hopkins, Terence K., and Immanuel Wallerstein, eds. *Processes of the World-System.* Beverly Hills, CA: Sage Publications, 1980.

Hopkins, Terence K., Immanuel Wallerstein, and associates. *World-System Analysis: Theory and Methodology.* Beverly Hills, CA: Sage Publications, 1982.

Hymer, Stephen. "The Multinational Corporation and the Law of Uneven Development." In *Economics and World Order,* edited by Jagdish Bhagwati. New York: Macmillan, 1972.

Janowitz, Morris. "A Sociological Perspective on Wallerstein." *American Journal of Sociology* 82, 5 (March 1977): 1090–1102.

Kaplan, Barbara Hockey, ed. *Social Change in the Capitalist World Economy.* Beverly Hills, CA: Sage Publications, 1978.

Kolko, Gabriel. *The Politics of War.* New York: Vintage Books, 1968.

Kolko, Joyce, and Gabriel Kolko. *The Limits of Power.* New York: Harper & Row, 1972.

Laclau, Ernesto. *Politics and Ideology in Marxist Theory.* London and New York: New Left Books and Schocken Books, 1977.

Leys, Colin. *Underdevelopment in Kenya: The Political Economy of Neo-Colonialism, 1964–71.* Berkeley: University of California Press, 1975.

McGowan, Patrick, and Stephen G. Walker. "Radical and Conventional Models of U.S. Foreign Economic Policymaking." *World Politics* 33, 3 (April 1981): 347–82.

Meyer, John W., and Michael T. Hannan, eds. *National Development and the World System: Educational, Economic, and Political Change, 1950–1970.* Chicago: University of Chicago Press, 1979.

Muñoz, Heraldo, ed. *From Dependency to Development.* Boulder, CO: Westview Press, 1981.

O'Brien, Philip. "A Critique of Latin American Theories of Dependency." In *Beyond the Sociology of Development,* edited by Ivar Oxaal, Tony Barnett, and David Booth. London: Routledge and Kegan Paul, 1975.

Political Economy of the World-System, annual. Beverly Hills, CA: Sage Publications, 1978, 1979, 1980.

Prebisch, Raul. *Towards a Dynamic Development Policy for Latin America.* New York: United Nations, 1963.

Rodney, Walter. *How Europe Underdeveloped Africa.* London: Bogle-l'Ouverture, 1973.

Rubinson, Richard. *Dynamics of World Development.* Beverly Hills, CA: Sage Publications, 1981.

————. "The World Economy and the Distribution of Income Within States: A Cross-National Study." *American Sociology Review* 41 (1976): 638–59.

Skocpol, Theda. "Wallerstein's World Capitalist System: A Theoretical and Historical Critique." *American Journal of Sociology* 82, 5 (March 1977): 1075–90.

Seers, Dudley, ed. *Dependency Theory: A Critical Assessment.* London: Frances Pinter, 1981.

Seers, Dudley, et al. *Underdeveloped Europe: Studies in Core-Periphery Relations.* Atlantic Highlands, NJ: Humanities Press, 1979.

Semmel, Bernard, ed. *Marxism and the Science of War.* New York: Oxford University Press, 1981.

Smith, Tony. "The Underdevelopment of Development Literature: The Case of Dependency Theory." *World Politics* 31, 2 (January 1979): 247–88.

Sunkel, Osvaldo. "National Development Policy and External Dependence in Latin America." *Journal of Development Studies* 61 (1969): 23–48.

Sylvan, David J. "The Newest Mercantilism." *International Organization* 35, 2 (Spring 1981): 375–93. A review essay.

Taylor, John G. *From Modernisation to Modes of Production: A Critique of the Sociologies of Development and Underdevelopment.* London: Macmillan, 1979.

Thompson, William R. *Contending Approaches in World System Analysis.* London and Beverly Hills, CA: Sage Publications, 1983.

Wallerstein, Immanuel. *The Capitalist World-Economy.* Cambridge: Cambridge University Press, 1979.

———. *Historical Capitalism.* London: Verso, 1983.

———. *The Modern World-System* I. New York: Academic Press, 1974.

———. *The Modern World-System* II. New York: Academic Press, 1980.

———. *The Politics of the World-Economy.* New York: Cambridge University Press, 1984.

Wallerstein, Immanuel, and Peter C. W. Gutkind, eds. *Political Economy of Contemporary Africa.* 2d ed. Beverly Hills, CA: Sage Publications, 1985.

———. "The Rise and Future Demise of the World Capitalist System." *Comparative Studies in Society and History* 16, 4 (September 1974): 387–415.

Zolberg, Aristide R. "Origins of the Modern World System: A Missing Link." *World Politics* 33, 2 (January 1981): 253–81. A review of Wallerstein, *The Modern World-System.*

The Economic Taproot of Imperialism

J. A. Hobson

John Hobson discusses the economic taproot, or driving force, of imperialism. A high rate of savings and the power of production outstrip consumption. Industrialists and manufacturers therefore seek foreign sources of investment and markets in Third World countries to solve these problems.

No mere array of facts and figures adduced to illustrate the economic nature of the new imperialism will suffice to dispel the popular delusion that the use of national force to secure new markets by annexing fresh tracts of territory is a sound and a necessary policy for an advanced industrial country like Great Britain. It has indeed been proved that recent annexations of tropical countries, procured at great expense, have furnished poor and precarious markets, that our aggregate trade with our colonial possessions is virtually stationary, and that our most profitable and progressive trade is with rival industrial nations, whose territories we have no desire to annex, whose markets we cannot force, and whose active antagonism we are provoking by our expansive policy.

But these arguments are not conclusive. It is open to Imperialists to argue thus: "We must have markets for our growing manufactures, we must have new outlets for the investment of our surplus capital and for the energies of the adventurous surplus of our population: such expansion is a necessity of life to a nation with our great and growing powers of production. An ever larger share of our population is devoted to the manufactures and commerce of towns, and is thus dependent for life and work upon food and raw materials from foreign lands. In order to buy and pay for these things we must sell our goods abroad. During the first three-quarters of the nineteenth century we could do so without difficulty by a natural expansion of commerce with continental nations and our colonies, all of which were far behind us in the main arts of manufacture and the carrying trades. So long as England held a virtual monopoly of the world markets for certain important classes of manufactured goods, Imperialism was unnecessary. After 1870 this manufacturing and trading suprem-

From John A. Hobson, *Imperialism.* Reprinted by permission of George Allen & Unwin.

States, and Belgium, advanced with great rapidity, and while they have acy was greatly impaired: other nations, especially Germany, the United not crushed or even stayed the increase of our external trade, their competition made it more and more difficult to dispose of the full surplus of our manufactures at a profit. The encroachments made by these nations upon our old markets, even in our own possessions, made it most urgent that we should take energetic means to secure new markets. These new markets had to lie in hitherto undeveloped countries, chiefly in the tropics, where vast populations lived capable of growing economic needs which our manufacturers and merchants could supply. Our rivals were seizing and annexing territories for similar purposes, and when they had annexed them closed them to our trade. The diplomacy and the arms of Great Britain had to be used in order to compel the owners of the new markets to deal with us: and experience showed that the safest means of securing and developing such markets is by establishing 'protectorates' or by annexation. The value in 1905 of these markets must not be taken as a final test of the economy of such a policy; the process of educating civilized needs which we can supply is of necessity a gradual one, and the cost of such Imperialism must be regarded as a capital outlay, the fruits of which posterity would reap. The new markets might not be large, but they formed serviceable outlets for the overflow of our great textile and metal industries, and, when the vast Asiatic and African populations of the interior were reached, a rapid expansion of trade was expected to result.

"Far larger and more important is the pressure of capital for external fields of investment. Moreover, while the manufacturer and trader are well content to trade with foreign nations, the tendency for investors to work towards the political annexation of countries which contain their more speculative investments is very powerful. Of the fact of this pressure of capital there can be no question. Large savings are made which cannot find any profitable investment in this country; they must find employment elsewhere, and it is to the advantage of the nation that they should be employed as largely as possible in lands where they can be utilized in opening up markets for British trade and employment for British enterprise.

"However costly, however perilous, this process of imperial expansion may be, it is necessary to the continued existence and progress of our nation[1]; if we abandoned it we must be content to leave the development of the world to other nations, who will everywhere cut into our trade, and even impair our means of securing the food and raw materials we require to support our population. Imperialism is thus seen to be, not a choice, but a necessity."

The practical force of this economic argument in politics is strikingly illustrated by the later history of the United States. Here is a country which suddenly broke through a conservative policy, strongly held by both political parties, bound up with every popular instinct and tradition, and flung itself into a rapid imperial career for which it possessed neither the material nor the moral equipment, risking the principles and practices of liberty and equality by the establishment of militarism and the forcible subjugation of peoples which it could not safely admit to the condition of American citizenship.

Was this a mere wild freak of spread-eaglism, a burst of political ambition on the part of a nation coming to a sudden realization of its destiny? Not at all. The spirit of adventure, the American "mission of civilization," were as forces making for Imperialism, clearly subordinate to the driving force of the economic factor. The dramatic character of the change is due to the unprecedented rapidity of the industrial revolution in the United States from the eighties onwards. During that period the United States, with her unrivalled natural resources, her immense resources of skilled and unskilled labour, and her genius for invention and organization, developed the best equipped and most productive manufacturing economy the world has yet seen. Fostered by rigid protective tariffs, her metal, textile, tool, clothing, furniture, and other manufactures shot up in a single generation from infancy to full maturity, and, having passed through a period of intense competition, attained, under the able control of great trust-makers, a power of production greater than has been attained in the most advanced industrial countries of Europe.

An era of cut-throat competition, followed by a rapid process of amalgamation, threw an enormous quantity of wealth into the hands of a small number of captains of industry. No luxury of living to which this class could attain kept pace with its rise of income, and a process of automatic saving set in upon an unprecedented scale. The investment of these savings in other industries helped to bring these under the same concentrative forces. Thus a great increase of savings seeking profitable investment is synchronous with a stricter economy of the use of existing capital. No doubt the rapid growth of a population, accustomed to a high and an always ascending standard of comfort, absorbs in the satisfaction of its wants a large quantity of new capital. But the actual rate of saving, conjoined with a more economical application of forms of existing capital, exceeded considerably the rise of the national consumption of manufactures. The power of production far outstripped the actual rate of consumption, and, contrary to the older economic theory, was unable to force a corresponding increase of consumption by lowering prices.

This is no mere theory. The history of any of the numerous trusts or combinations in the United States sets out the facts with complete distinctness. In the free competition of manufactures preceding combination the chronic condition is one of "over-production," in the sense that all the mills or factories can only be kept at work by cutting prices down towards a point where the weaker competitors are forced to close down, because they cannot sell their goods at a price which covers the true cost of production. The first result of the successful formation of a trust or combine is to close down the worse equipped or worse placed mills, and supply the entire market from the better equipped and better placed ones.

This course may or may not be attended by a rise of price and some restriction of consumption: in some cases trusts take most of their profits by raising prices, in other cases by reducing the costs of production through employing only the best mills and stopping the waste of competition.

For the present argument it matters not which course is taken; the point is that this concentration of industry in "trusts," "combines," etc. at once limits the quantity of capital which can be effectively employed and increases the share of profits out of which fresh savings and fresh capital will spring. It is quite evident that a trust which is motivated by cut-throat competition, due to an excess of capital, cannot normally find inside the "trusted" industry employment for that portion of the profits which the trust-makers desire to save and to invest. New inventions and other economies of production or distribution within the trade may absorb some of the new capital, but there are rigid limits to this absorption. The trust-maker in oil or sugar must find other investments for his savings: if he is early in the application of the combination principles to his trade, he will naturally apply his surplus capital to establish similar combinations in other industries, economising capital still further, and rendering it ever harder for ordinary saving men to find investments for their savings.

Indeed, the conditions alike of cut-throat competition and of combination attest the congestion of capital in the manufacturing industries which have entered the machine economy. We are not here concerned with any theoretic question as to the possibility of producing by modern machine methods more goods than can find a market. It is sufficient to point out that the manufacturing power of a country like the United States would grow so fast as to exceed the demands of the home market. No one acquainted with trade will deny a fact which all American economists assert, that this is the condition which the United States reached at the end of the century, so far, as the more developed industries are concerned. Her manufactures were saturated with capital and could absorb no more. One after another they sought refuge from the waste of competition in "combines" which secure a measure of profitable peace by restricting the quantity of operative capital. Industrial and financial princes in oil, steel, sugar, railroads, banking, etc. were faced with the dilemma of either spending more than they knew how to spend, or forcing markets outside the home area. Two economic courses were open to them, both leading towards an abandonment of the political isolation of the past and the adoption of imperialist methods in the future. Instead of shutting down inferior mills and rigidly restricting output to correspond with profitable sales in the home markets, they might employ their full productive power, applying their savings to increase their business capital, and, while still regulating output and prices for the home market, may "hustle" for foreign markets, dumping down their surplus goods at prices which would not be possible save for the profitable nature of their home market. So likewise they might employ their savings in seeking investments outside their country, first repaying the capital borrowed from Great Britain and other countries for the early development of their railroads, mines and manufactures, and afterwards becoming themselves a creditor class to foreign countries.

It was this sudden demand for foreign markets for manufactures and for investments which was avowedly responsible for the adoption of Imperialism as a political policy and practice by the Republican party to which the great industrial and financial chiefs belonged, and which belonged to them. The adventurous enthusiasm of President Theodore Roosevelt and his "manifest destiny" and "mission of civilization" party must not deceive us. It was Messrs. Rockefeller, Pierpont Morgan, and their associates who needed Imperialism and who fastened it upon the shoulders of the great Republic of the West. They needed Imperialism because they desired to use the public resources of their country to find profitable employment for their capital which otherwise would be superfluous.

It is not indeed necessary to own a country in order to do trade with it or to invest capital in it, and doubtless the United States could find some vent for their surplus goods, and capital in European countries. But these countries were for the most part able to make provision for themselves; most of them erected tariffs against manufacturing imports, and even Great Britain was urged to defend herself by reverting to Protection. The big American manufacturers and financiers were compelled to look to China and the Pacific and to South America for their most profitable chances; Protectionists by principle and practice, they would insist upon getting as close a monopoly of these markets as they can secure, and the competition of Germany, England, and other trading nations would drive them to the establishment of special political relations with the markets they most prize. Cuba, the Philippines, and Hawaii were but the *hors d'oeuvre* to whet an appetite for an ampler banquet. Moreover, the powerful hold upon politics which these industrial and financial magnates possessed formed a separate stimulus, which, as we have shown, was operative in Great Britain and elsewhere; the public expenditure in pursuit of an imperial career would be a separate immense source of profit to these men, as financiers negotiating loans, shipbuilders and owners handling subsidies, contractors and manufacturers of armaments and other imperialist appliances.

The suddenness of this political revolution is due to the rapid manifestation of the need. In the last years of the nineteenth century the United States nearly trebled the value of its manufacturing export trade and it was to be expected that, if the rate of progress of those years continued, within a decade it would overtake our more slowly advancing export trade, and stand first in the list of manufacture-exporting nations.[2]

This was the avowed ambition, and no idle one, of the keenest business men of America; and with the natural resources, the labour and the administrative talents at their dis~ ~sal, it was quite likely they would achieve their object.[3] The stronger and more direct control over politics exercised in America by business men enabled them to drive more quickly and more straightly along the line of their economic interests than in Great Britain. American Imperialism was the natural product of the economic pressure of a sudden advance of capitalism which could not find occupation at home and needed foreign markets for goods and for investments.

The same needs existed in European countries, and, as is admitted, drove Governments along the same path. Over-production in the sense of an excessive manufacturing plant, and surplus capital which could not find sound investments within the country, forced Great Britain, Germany, Holland, and France to place larger and larger portions of their economic resources outside the area of their present political domain, and then stimulate a policy of political expansion so as to take in the new areas. The economic sources of this movement are laid bare by periodic trade-depressions due to an inability of producers to find adequate and profitable markets for what they can produce. The Majority Report of the Commission upon the Depression of Trade in 1885 put the matter in a nutshell. "That, owing to the nature of the times, the demand for our commodities does not increase at the same rate as formerly; that our capacity for production is consequently in excess of our requirements, and could be considerably increased at short notice; that this is due partly to the competition of the capital which is being steadily accumulated in the country." The Minority Report straightly imputed the condition of affairs to "over-production." Germany was in the early 1900's suffering severely from what is called a glut of capital and of manufacturing power; she had to have new markets; her Consuls all over the world were "hustling" for trade; trading settlements were forced upon Asia Minor; in East and West Africa, in China and elsewhere the German Empire was impelled to a policy of colonization and protectorates as outlets for German commercial energy.

Every improvement of methods of production, every concentration of ownership and control, seems to accentuate the tendency. As one nation after another enters the machine economy and adopts advanced indus-

TABLE 1   Export Trade of United States, 1890–1900

Year	Agriculture	Manufactures	Miscellaneous
	£	£	£
1890	125,756,000	31,435,000	13,019,000
1891	146,617,000	33,720,000	11,731,000
1892	142,508,000	30,479,000	11,660,000
1893	123,810,000	35,484,000	11,653,000
1894	114,737,000	35,557,000	11,168,000
1895	104,143,000	40,230,000	12,174,000
1896	132,992,000	50,738,000	13,639,000
1897	146,059,000	55,923,000	13,984,000
1898	170,383,000	61,585,000	14,743,000
1899	156,427,000	76,157,000	18,002,000
1900	180,931,000	88,281,000	21,389,000

trial methods, it becomes more difficult for its manufacturers, merchants, and financiers to dispose profitably of their economic resources, and they are tempted more and more to use their Governments in order to secure for their particular use some distant undeveloped country by annexation and protection.

The process, we may be told, is inevitable, and so it seems upon a superficial inspection. Everywhere appear excessive powers of production, excessive capital in search of investment. It is admitted by all business men that the growth of the powers of production in their country exceeds the growth in consumption, that more goods can be produced than can be sold at a profit, and that more capital exists than can find remunerative investment.

It is this economic condition of affairs that forms the taproot of Imperialism. If the consuming public in this country raised its standard of consumption to keep pace with every rise of productive powers, there could be no excess of goods or capital clamorous to use Imperialism in order to find markets: foreign trade would indeed exist, but there would be no difficulty in exchanging a small surplus of our manufactures for the food and raw material we annually absorbed, and all the savings that we made could find employment, if we chose, in home industries.

There is nothing inherently irrational in such a supposition. Whatever is, or can be, produced, can be consumed, for a claim upon it, as rent, profit, or wages, forms part of the real income of some member of the community, and he can consume it, or else exchange it for some other consumable with some one else who will consume it. With everything that is produced a consuming power is born. If then there are goods which cannot get consumed, or which cannot even get produced because it is evident they cannot get consumed, and if there is a quantity of capital and labour which cannot get full employment because its products cannot get consumed, or which cannot even get produced because it is evident they cannot get consumed, the only possible explanation of this paradox is the refusal of owners of consuming power to apply that power in effective demand for commodities.

It is, of course, possible that an excess of producing power might exist in particular industries by misdirection, being engaged in certain manufactures, whereas it ought to have been engaged in agriculture or some other use. But no one can seriously contend that such misdirection explains the recurrent gluts and consequent depressions of modern industry, or that, when over-production is manifest in the leading manufactures, ample avenues are open for the surplus capital and labour in other industries. The general character of the excess of producing power is proved by the existence at such times of large bank stocks of idle money seeking any sort of profitable investment and finding none.

The root questions underlying the phenomena are clearly these: "Why is it that consumption fails to keep pace automatically in a community with power of production?" "Why does under-consumption or over-saving occur?" For it is evident that the consuming power, which, if exercised, would keep tense the reins of production, is in part withheld, or in other words is "saved" and stored up for investment. All saving for investment does not imply slackness of production; quite the contrary. Saving is economically justified, from the social standpoint, when the capital in which it takes material shape finds full employment in helping to produce commodities which, when produced, will be consumed. It is saving in excess of this amount that causes mischief, taking shape in surplus capital which is not needed to assist current consumption, and which either lies idle, or tries to oust existing capital from its employment, or else seeks speculative use abroad under the protection of the Government.

But it may be asked, "Why should there be any tendency to oversaving? Why should the owners of consuming power withhold a larger quantity for savings than can be serviceably employed?" Another way of putting the same question is this. "Why should not the pressure of present wants keep pace with every possibility of satisfying them?" The answer to these pertinent questions carries us to the broadest issue of the distribution of wealth. If a tendency to distribute income or consuming power according to needs were operative, it is evident that consumption would rise with every rise of producing power, for human needs are illimitable, and there could be no excess of saving. But it is quite otherwise in a state of economic society where distribution has no fixed relation to needs, but is determined by other conditions which assign to some people a consuming power vastly in excess of needs or possible uses, while others are destitute of consuming power enough to satisfy even the full demands of physical efficiency. The following illustration may serve to make the issue clear. "The volume of production has been constantly rising owing to the development of modern machinery. There are two main channels to carry off these products — one channel carrying off the product destined to be consumed by the workers, and the other channel carrying off the remainder to the rich. The workers' channel is in rock-bound banks that cannot enlarge, owing to the competitive wage system preventing wages rising *pro rata* with increased efficiency. Wages are based upon cost of living, and not upon efficiency of labour. The miner in the poor mine gets the same wages per day as the miner in the adjoining rich mine. The owner of the rich mine gets the advantage — not his labourer. The channel which conveys the goods destined to supply the rich is itself divided into two streams. One stream carries off what the rich 'spend' on themselves for the necessities and luxuries of life. The other is simply an 'overflow' stream carrying off their 'savings.' The channel for spending, i.e. the amount wasted by the rich in luxuries, may broaden somewhat, but owing to the small number of those rich enough to indulge in whims it can never be greatly enlarged, and at any rate it bears such a small proportion to the other channel that in no event can much hope of avoiding a flood of capital be hoped for from this division. The rich will never be so ingenious as to spend enough to prevent over-production. The great safety overflow channel which has been continuously more and more widened and deepened to carry off the ever-increasing flood of new capital is that division of the stream which carried the savings of the rich, and this is not only suddenly found to be incapable of further enlargement, but actually seems to be in the process of being dammed up."[4]

Though this presentation over-accentuates the cleavage between rich and poor and over-states the weakness of the workers, it gives forcible and sound expression to a most important and ill-recognised economic truth. The "over-flow" stream of savings is of course fed not exclusively from the surplus income of "the rich"; the professional and industrial middle classes, and to some slight extent the workers, contribute. But the "flooding" is distinctly due to the automatic saving of the surplus income of rich men. This is of course particularly true of America, where multi-millionaires rise quickly and find themselves in possession of incomes far exceeding the demands of any craving that is known to them. To make the metaphor complete, the overflow stream must be represented as re-entering the stream of production and seeking to empty there all the "savings" that it carries. Where competition remains free, the result is a chronic congestion of productive power and of production, forcing down home prices, wasting large sums in advertising and in pushing for orders, and periodically causing a crisis followed by a collapse, during which quantities of capital and labour lie unemployed and unremunerated. The prime object of the trust or other combine is to remedy this waste and loss by substituting regulation of output for reckless over-production. In achieving this it actually narrows or even dams up the old channels of investment, limiting the overflow stream to the exact amount required to maintain the normal current of output. But this rigid limitation of trade, though required for the separate economy of each trust, does not suit the trust-maker, who is driven to compensate for strictly regulated industry at home by cutting new foreign channels as outlets for his productive power and his excessive savings. Thus we reach the conclusion that Imperialism is the endeavour of the great controllers of industry to broaden the channel for the flow of their surplus wealth by seeking foreign markets and foreign investments to take off the goods and capital they cannot sell or use at home.

The fallacy of the supposed inevitably of imperial expansion as a necessary outlet for progressive industry is now manifest. It is not industrial progress that demands the opening up of new markets and areas of investment, but mal-distribution of consuming power which prevents the absorption of commodities and capital within the country. The over-saving which is the economic root of Imperialism is found by analysis to consist of rents, monopoly profits, and other unearned or excessive elements of income, which, not being earned by labour of head or hand have no legitimate *raison d'être*. Having no natural relation to effort of production, they impel their recipients to no corresponding satisfaction of consumption: they form a surplus wealth, which, having no proper place in the normal economy of production and consumption, tends to accumulate as excessive savings. Let any turn in the tide of politico-economic forces divert from these owners their excess of income and make it flow, either to the workers in higher wages, or to the community in taxes, so that it will be spent instead of being saved, serving in either of these ways to swell the tide of consumption — there will be no need to fight for foreign markets or foreign areas of investment.

Many have carried their analysis so far as to realise the absurdity of spending half our financial resources in fighting to secure foreign markets at times when hungry mouths, ill-clad backs, ill-furnished houses indicate countless unsatisfied material wants among our own population. If we may take the careful statistics of Mr. Rowntree[5] for our guide, we shall be aware that more than one-fourth of the population of our towns is living at a standard which is below bare physical efficiency. If, by some economic readjustment, the products which flow from the surplus saving of the rich to swell the overflow streams could be diverted so as to raise the incomes and the standard of consumption of this inefficient fourth, there would be no need for pushful Imperialism, and the cause of social reform would have won its greatest victory.

It is not inherent in the nature of things that we should spend our natural resources on militarism, war, and risky, unscrupulous diplomacy, in order to find markets for our goods and surplus capital. An intelligent progressive community, based upon substantial equality of economic and educational opportunities, will raise its standard of consumption to correspond with every increased power of production, and can find full employment for an unlimited quantity of capital and labour within the limits of the country which it occupies. Where the distribution of incomes is such as to enable all classes of the nation to convert their felt wants into an effective demand for commodities, there can be no over-production, no under-employment of capital and labour, and no necessity to fight for markets.

The most convincing condemnation of the current economy is conveyed in the difficulty which producers everywhere experience in finding consumers for their products: a fact attested by the prodigious growth of classes of agents and middlemen, the multiplication of every sort of advertising, and the general increase of the distributive classes. Under a sound economy the pressure would be reversed: the growing wants of progressive societies would be a constant stimulus to the inventive and operative energies of producers, and would form a constant strain upon the powers of production. The simultaneous excess of all the factors of production, attested by frequently recurring periods of trade depression, is a most dramatic exhibition of the false economy of distribution. It does not imply a mere miscalculation in the application of productive power, or a brief temporary excess of that power; it manifests in an acute form an economic waste which is chronic and general throughout the advanced industrial nations, a waste contained in the divorcement of the desire to consume and the power to consume.

If the apportionment of income were such as to evoke no excessive saving, full constant employment for capital and labour would be furnished at home. This, of course, does not imply that there would be no foreign trade. Goods that could not be produced at home, or produced as well or as cheaply, would still be purchased by ordinary process of international exchange, but here again the pressure would be the wholesome pressure of the consumer anxious to buy abroad what he could not buy at home, not the blind eagerness of the producer to use every force or trick of trade or politics to find markets for his "surplus" goods.

The struggle for markets, the greater eagerness of producers to sell than of consumers to buy, is the crowning proof of a false economy of distribution. Imperialism is the fruit of this false economy; "social reform" is its remedy. The primary purpose of "social reform," using the term in its economic signification, is to raise the wholesome standard of private and public consumption for a nation, so as to enable the nation to live up to its highest standard of production. Even those social reformers who aim directly at abolishing or reducing some bad form of consumption, as in the Temperance movement, generally recognise the necessity of substituting some better form of current consumption which is more educative and stimulative of other tastes, and will assist to raise the general standard of consumption.

There is no necessity to open up new foreign markets; the home markets are capable of indefinite expansion. Whatever is produced in England can be consumed in England, provided that the "income" or power to demand commodities, is properly distributed. This only appears untrue because of the unnatural and unwholesome specialisation to which this country has been subjected, based upon a bad distribution of economic resources, which has induced an overgrowth of certain manufacturing trades for the express purpose of effecting foreign sales. If the industrial revolution had taken place in an England founded upon equal access by all classes to land, education and legislation, specialisation in manufactures would not have gone so far (though more intellligent progress would have been made, by reason of a widening of the area of selection of inventive and organising talents); foreign trade would have been less important, though more steady; the standard of life for all portions of the population would have been high, and the present rate of national consumption would probably have given full, constant, remunerative employment to a far larger quantity of private and public capital than is now employed.[6] For the over-saving or wider consumption that is traced to excessive incomes of the rich is a suicidal economy, even from the exclusive standpoint of capital; for consumption alone vitalises capital and makes it capable of yielding profits. An economy that assigns to the "possessing" classes an excess of consuming power which they cannot use, and cannot convert into really serviceable capital, is a dog-in-the-manger policy. The social reforms which deprive the possessing classes of their surplus will not, therefore, inflict upon them the real injury they dread; they can only use this surplus by forcing on their country a wrecking policy of Imperialism. The only safety of nations lies in removing the unearned increments of income from the possessing classes, and adding them to the wage-income of the working classes or to the public income, in order that they may be spent in raising the standard of consumption.

Social reform bifurcates, according as reformers seek to achieve this end by raising wages or by increasing public taxation and expenditure. These courses are not essentially contradictory, but are rather complementary. Working-class movements aim, either by private cooperation or by political pressure on legislative and administrative government, at increasing the proportion of the national income which accrues to labour in the form of wages, pensions, compensation for injuries, etc. State Socialism aims at getting for the direct use of the whole society an increased share of the "social values" which arise from the closely and essentially cooperative work of an industrial society, taxing property and incomes so as to draw into the public exchequer for public expenditure the "unearned elements" of income, leaving to individual producers those incomes which are necessary to induce them to apply in the best way their economic energies, and to private enterprises those businesses which do not breed monopoly, and which the public need not or cannot undertake. These are not, indeed, the sole or perhaps the best avowed objects of social reform movements. But for the purposes of this analysis they form the kernel.

Trade Unionism and Socialism are thus the natural enemies of Imperialism, for they take away from the "imperialist" classes the surplus incomes which form the economic stimulus of Imperialism.

This does not pretend to be a final statement of the full relations of these forces. When we come to political analysis we shall perceive that the tendency of Imperialism is to crush Trade Unionism and to "nibble" at or parasitically exploit State Socialism. But, confining ourselves for the present to the narrowly economic setting, Trade Unionism and State Socialism may be regarded as complementary forces arrayed against Imperialism, in as far as, by diverting to working-class or public expenditure elements of income which would otherwise be surplus savings, they raise the general standard of home consumption and abate the pressure for foreign markets. Of course, if the increase of working-class income were wholly or chiefly "saved," not spent, or if the taxation of unearned incomes were utilised for the relief of other taxes borne by the possessing classes, no such result as we have described would follow. There is, however, no reason to anticipate this result from trade-union or socialistic measures. Though no sufficient natural stimulus exists to force the well-to-do classes to spend in further luxuries the surplus incomes which they save, every working-class family is subject to powerful stimuli of economic needs, and a reasonably governed State would regard as its prime duty the relief of the present poverty of public life by new forms of socially useful expenditure.

But we are not here concerned with what belongs to the practical issues of political and economic policy. It is the economic theory for which we claim acceptance—a theory which, if accurate, dispels the delusion that expansion of foreign trade, and therefore of empire, is a necessity of national life.

Regarded from the standpoint of economy of energy, the same "choice of life" confronts the nation as the individual. An individual may expend all his energy in acquiring external possessions, adding field to field, barn to barn, factory to factory—may "spread himself" over the widest area of property, amassing material wealth which is in some sense "himself" as containing the impress of his power and interest. He does this by specialising upon the lower acquisitive plane of interest at the cost of neglecting the cultivation of the higher qualities and interests of his nature. The antagonism is not indeed absolute. Aristotle has said, "We must first secure a livelihood and then practise virtue." Hence the pursuit of material property as a reasonable basis of physical comfort would be held true economy by the wisest men; but the absorption of time, energy, and interest upon such quantitative expansion at the necessary cost of starving the higher tastes and faculties is condemned as false economy. The same issue comes up in the business life of the individual; it is the question of intensive *versus* extensive cultivation. A rude or ignorant farmer, where land is plentiful, is apt to spread his capital and labour over a large area, taking in new tracts and cultivating them poorly. A skilled, scientific farmer will study a smaller patch of land, cultivate it thoroughly, and utilise its diverse properties, adapting it to the special needs of his most remunerative markets. The same is true of other businesses; even where the economy of large-scale production is greatest there exists some limit beyond which the wise business man will not go, aware that in doing so he will risk by enfeebled management what he seems to gain by mechanical economies of production and market.

Everywhere the issue of quantitative *versus* qualitative growth comes up. This is the entire issue of empire. A people limited in number and energy and in the land they occupy have the choice of improving to the utmost the political and economic management of their own land, confining themselves to such accessions of territory as are justified by the most economical disposition of a growing population; or they may proceed, like the slovenly farmer, to spread their power and energy over the whole earth, tempted by the speculative value or the quick profits of some new market, or else by mere greed of territorial acquisition, and ignoring the political and economic wastes and risks involved by this imperial career. It must be clearly understood that this is essentially a choice of alternatives; a full simultaneous application of intensive and extensive cultivation is impossible. A nation may either, following the example of Denmark or Switzerland, put brains into agriculture, develop a finely varied system of public education, general and technical, apply the ripest science to its special manufacturing industries, and so support in progressive comfort and character a considerable population upon a strictly limited area; or it may, like Great Britain, neglect its agriculture, allowing its lands to go out of cultivation and its population to grow up in towns, fall behind other nations in its methods of education and in the capacity of adapting to its uses the latest scientific knowledge, in order that it may squander its pecuniary and military resources in forcing bad markets and finding speculative fields of investment in distant corners of the earth, adding millions of square miles and of unassimilable population to the area of the Empire.

The driving forces of class interest which stimulate and support this false economy we have explained. No remedy will serve which permits the future operation of these forces. It is idle to attack Imperialism or Militarism as political expedients or policies unless the axe is laid at the economic root of the tree, and the classes for whose interest Imperialism works are shorn of the surplus revenues which seek this outlet.

NOTES

1. "And why, indeed, are wars undertaken, if not to conquer colonies which permit the employment of fresh capital, to acquire commercial monopolies, or to obtain the exclusive use of certain highways of commerce?" (Loria, *Economic Foundations of Society,* p. 267).
2. Post-war conditions, with the immense opportunities afforded for export of American goods and capital brought a pause and a temporary withdrawal from imperialist policy.
3. "We hold now three of the winning cards in the game for commercial greatness, to wit—iron, steel and coal. We have long been the granary of the world, we now aspire to be its workshop, then we want to be its clearinghouse." (The President of the American Bankers' Association at Denver, 1898).
4. *The Significance of the Trust,* by H. G. Wilshire.
5. *Poverty: A Study of Town Life.*
6. The classical economists of England, forbidden by their theories of parsimony and of the growth of capital to entertain the notion of an indefinite expansion of home markets by reason of a constantly rising standard of national comfort, were early driven to countenance a doctrine of the necessity of finding external markets for the investment of capital. So J. S. Mill: "The expansion of capital would soon reach its ultimate boundary if the boundary itself did not continually open and leave more space" (*Political Economy*). And before him Ricardo (in a letter to Malthus): "If with every accumulation of capital we could take a piece of fresh fertile land to our island, profits would never fall."

Imperialism: The Highest Stage of Capitalism

V. I. Lenin

Lenin explains the scramble for colonies by capitalist states. His intellectual debt to Hobson is obvious.

IMPERIALISM AS A SPECIAL STAGE OF CAPITALISM

Imperialism emerged as the development and direct continuation of the fundamental attributes of capitalism in general. But capitalism only became capitalist imperialism at a definite and very high stage of its development, when certain of its fundamental attributes began to be transformed into their opposites, when the features of a period of transition from capitalism to a higher social and economic system began to take shape and reveal themselves all along the line. Economically, the main thing in this process is the substitution of capitalist monopolies for capitalist free competition. Free competition is the fundamental attribute of capitalism, and of commodity production generally. Monopoly is exactly the opposite of free competition; but we have seen the latter being transformed into monopoly before our very eyes, creating large-scale industry and eliminating small industry, replacing large-scale industry by still larger-scale industry, finally leading to such a concentration of production and capital that monopoly has been and is the result: cartels, syndicates and trusts, and merging with them, the capital of a dozen or so banks manipulating thousands of millions. At the same time monopoly, which has grown out of free competition, does not abolish the latter, but exists over it and alongside of it, and thereby give rise to a number of very acute, intense antagonisms, friction and conflicts. Monopoly is the transition from capitalism to a higher system.

If it were necessary to give the briefest possible definition of imperialism we should have to say that imperialism is the monopoly stage of capitalism. Such a definition would include what is most important, for on the one hand, finance capital is the bank capital of a few big monopolist banks, merged with the capital of the monopolist combines of manufacturers; and, on the other hand, the division of the world is the transition from a colonial policy which has extended without hindrance to territories unoccupied by any capitalist power, to a colonial policy of monopolistic possession of the territory of the world which has been completely divided up.

But very brief definitions, although convenient, for they sum up the main points, are nevertheless inadequate, because very important features of the phenomenon that has to be defined have to be especially reduced. And so, without forgetting the conditional and relative value of all definitions, which can never include all the concatenations of a phenomenon in its complete development, we must give a definition of imperialism that will embrace the following five essential features:

1. The concentration of production and capital developed to such a high stage that it created monopolies which play a decisive role in economic life.
2. The merging of bank capital with industrial capital, and the creation, on the basis of this "finance capital," of a "financial oligarchy."
3. The export of capital, which has become extremely important, as distinguished from the export of commodities.
4. The formation of international capitalist monopolies which share the world among themselves.
5. The territorial division of the whole world among the greatest capitalist powers is completed.

Imperialism is capitalism in that stage of development in which the dominance of monopolies and finance capital has established itself; in which the export of capital has acquired pronounced importance; in which the division of the world among the international trusts has begun; in which the division of all territories of the globe among the great capitalist powers has been completed. . . .

In this matter of defining imperialism, however, we have to enter into controversy, primarily, with K. Kautsky, the principal Marxian theoretician of the epoch of the so-called Second International — that is, of the twenty-five years between 1889 and 1914.

Kautsky, in 1915 and even in November 1914, very emphatically attacked the fundamental ideas expressed in our definition of imperialism. Kautsky said that imperialism must not be regarded as a "phase" or stage of economy, but as a policy; a definite policy "preferred" by finance capital; that imperialism cannot be "identified" with "contemporary capitalism"; that if imperialism is to be understood to mean "all the phenomena of contemporary capitalism" — cartels, protection, the domination of the financiers and colonial policy — then the question as to whether imperialism is necessary to capitalism becomes reduced to the "flattest tautology"; because, in that case, "imperialism is naturally a vital necessity for capitalism" and so on. The best way to present Kautsky's ideas is to quote his own definition of imperialism, which is diametrically opposed to the substance of the ideas which we have set forth. . . .

Kautsky's definition is as follows:

Imperialism is a product of highly developed industrial capitalism. It consists in the striving of every industrialist capitalist nation to bring under its control and to annex increasingly big *agrarian* (Kautsky's italics) regions irrespective of what nations inhabit those regions. . . .

Imperialism is a striving for annexations—this is what the *political* part of Kautsky's definition amounts to. It is correct, but very incomplete, for politically, imperialism is, in general, a striving towards violence and reaction. For the moment, however, we are interested in the *economic* aspect of the question, which Kautsky *himself* introduced into *his* definition. The inaccuracy of Kautsky's definition is strikingly obvious. The characteristic feature of imperialism is not industrial capital, *but* finance capital. It is not an accident that in France it was precisely the extraordinarily rapid development of *finance* capital, and the weakening of industrial capital, that, from 1880 onwards, gave rise to the extreme extension of annexationist (colonial) policy. The characteristic feature of imperialism is precisely that it strives to annex *not only* agricultural regions, but even highly industrialized regions (German appetite for Belgium; French appetite for Lorraine), because 1) the fact that the world is already divided up obliges those contemplating a *new* division to reach out for *any kind* of territory, and 2) because an essential feature of imperialism is the rivalry between a number of great powers in the striving for hegemony, *i.e.,* for the conquest of territory, not so much directly for themselves as to weaken the adversary and undermine *his* hegemony (Belgium is chiefly necessary to Germany as a base for operations against England; England needs Bagdad as a base for operations against Germany, etc.). . . .

Kautsky's definition is not only wrong and un-Marxian. It serves as a basis for a whole system of view which run counter to Marxian theory and Marxian practice all along the line. . . . The fact of the matter is that Kautsky detaches the politics of imperialism from its economics, speaks of annexations as being a policy "preferred" by finance capital, and opposes to it another bourgeois policy which, he alleges, is possible on this very basis of finance capital. According to his argument, monopolies in economics are compatible with non-monopolistic, non-violent non-annexationist methods in politics. According to his argument, the territorial division of the world, which was completed precisely during the period of finance capital, and which constitutes the basis of the present peculiar forms of rivalry between the biggest capitalist states, is compatible with a non-imperialist policy. The result is a slurring-over and a blunting of the most profound contradictions of the latest stage of capitalism, instead of an exposure of their depth; the result is bourgeois reformism instead of Marxism. . . .

Kautsky writes: "from the purely economic point of view it is not impossible that capitalism will yet go through a new phase, that of the extension of the policy of cartels to foreign policy, the phase of ultra-imperialism," *i.e.,* of a super-imperialism, a union of world imperialisms and not struggles among imperialisms; a phase when wars shall cease under capitalism, a phase of "the joint exploitation of the world by internationally combined finance capital."

Is "ultra-imperialism" possible "from the purely economic point of view" or is it ultra-nonsense? . . .

Compare . . . the vast diversity of economic and political conditions, the extreme disparity in the rate of development of the various countries, etc., and the violent struggles of the imperialist states, with Kautsky's silly little fable about "peaceful" ultra-imperialism. Is this not the reactionary attempt of a frightened philistine to hide from stern reality? Are not the international cartels which Kautsky imagines are the embryos of "ultra-imperialism" . . . an example of the division and the *re-division* of the world, the transition from peaceful division to non-peaceful division and vice versa? Is not American and other finance capital, which divided the whole world peacefully, with Germany's participation for example, in the international rail syndicate, or in the international mercantile shipping trust, now engaged in *re-dividing* the world on the basis of a new relation of forces, which has been changed by methods *by no means* peaceful?

Finance capital and the trusts are increasing instead of diminishing the difference in the rate of development of the various parts of world economy. When the relation of forces is changed, how else, *under capitalism,* can the solution of contradictions be found, except by resorting to violence . . . ?

Capitalism is growing with the greatest rapidity in the colonies and in overseas countries. Among the latter, *new* imperialist powers are emerging (e.g., Japan). The struggle of world imperialism is becoming more acute.

It is well known that the development of productive forces in Germany, and especially the development of the coal and iron industries, has been much more rapid during this period than in England — not to mention France and Russia. In 1892, Germany produced 4,900,000 tons of pig iron and Great Britain produced 6,800,000 tons; in 1912, Germany produced 17,600,000 tons and Great Britain 9,000,000 tons. Germany, therefore, had an overwhelming superiority over England in this respect. We ask, is there *under capitalism* any means of removing the disparity between the development of productive forces and the accumulation of capital on the one side, and the division of colonies and "spheres of influence" for finance capital on the other side — other than by resorting to war? . . .

The imperialism of the beginning of the twentieth century completed the division of the world among a handful of states, each of which today exploits (i.e., draws super-profits from) a part of the world only a little smaller than that which England exploited in 1858. Each of them, by means of trusts, cartels, finance capital, and debtor and creditor relations, occupies a monopoly position in the world market. Each of them enjoys to some degree a colonial monopoly. (We have seen that out of the total of 75,000,000 sq. km. which comprise the *whole* colonial world, 65,000,000 sq. km., or 86 per cent, belong to six great powers; 61,000,000 sq. km., or 81 per cent, belong to three powers.) . . .

Embryonic imperialism has grown into a dominant system; capitalist monopolies occupy first place in economics and politics; the division of the world has been completed. On the other hand, instead of an undisputed monopoly by Great Britain, we see a few imperialist powers contending for the right to share in this monopoly, and this struggle is characteristic of the whole period of the beginning of the twentieth century. . . .

THE CRITIQUE OF IMPERIALISM

By the critique of imperialism, in the broad sense of the term, we mean the attitude toward imperialist policy of the different classes of society as part of their general ideology.

The enormous dimensions of finance capital concentrated in a few hands and creating an extremely extensive and close network of ties and relationships which subordinate not only the small and medium, but also even the very small capitalists and small masters, on the one hand, and the intense struggle waged against other national state groups of financiers for the division of the world and domination over other countries, on the other hand, cause the wholesale transition of the possessing classes to the side of imperialism. The signs of the times are a "general" enthusiasm regarding its prospects, a passionate defence of imperialism and every possible embellishment of its real nature. . . .

Bourgeois scholars and publicists usually come out in defence of imperialism in a somewhat veiled form, and obscure its complete domination and its profound roots; they strive to concentrate attention on partial and secondary details and do their very best to distract attention from the main issue by means of ridiculous schemes for "reform," such as police supervision of the trusts and banks, etc. Less frequently, cynical and frank imperialists speak out and are bold enough to admit the absurdity of the idea of reforming the fundamental features of imperialism. . . .

The question as to whether it is possible to reform the basis of imperialism, whether to go forward to the accentuation and deepening of the antagonisms which it engenders, or backwards, towards allaying these antagonisms, is a fundamental question in the critique of imperialism. As a consequence of the fact that the political features of imperialism are reaction all along the line, and increased national oppression, resulting from the oppression of the financial oligarchy and the elimination of free competition, a petty-bourgeois-democratic opposition has been rising against imperialism in almost all imperialist countries since the beginning of the twentieth century. . . .

In the United States, the imperialist war waged against Spain in 1898 stirred up the opposition of the "anti-imperialists," the last of the Mohicans of bourgeois democracy. They declared this war to be "criminal"; they denounced the annexation of foreign territories as being a violation of the Constitution, and denounced the "Jingo treachery" by means of which Aguinaldo, leader of the native Filipinos, was deceived (the Americans promised him the independence of his country, but later they landed troops and annexed it). They quoted the words of Lincoln:

> When the white man governs himself, that is self-government; but when he governs himself and also governs another man, that is more than self-government—that is despotism.

But while all this criticism shrank from recognizing the indissoluble bond between imperialism and the trusts, and, therefore, between imperialism and the very foundations of capitalism; while it shrank from joining up with the forces engendered by large-scale capitalism and its development—it remained a "pious wish."

. . . Here is an example of Kautsky's economic criticism of imperialism. He takes the statistics of the British export and import trade with Egypt for 1872 and 1912. These statistics show that this export and import trade has developed more slowly than British foreign trade as a whole. From this Kautsky concludes that:

> We have no reason to suppose that British trade with Egypt would have been less developed simply as a result of the mere operation of economic factors, without military occupation. . . . The urge of the present-day states to expand . . . can be best promoted, not by the violent methods of imperialism, but by peaceful democracy.

. . . Kautsky departed from Marxism by advocating what is, in the period of finance capital, a "reactionary ideal," "peaceful democracy," "the mere operation of economic factors," for *objectively* this ideal drags us back from monopoly capitalism to the non-monopolist stage, and is a reformist swindle.

Trade with Egypt (or with any other colony or semi-colony) "would have grown more" *without* military occupation, without imperialism, and without finance capital. What does this mean? That capitalism would develop more rapidly if free competition were not restricted by monopolies in general, by the "connections" or the yoke (*i.e.,* also the monopoly of finance capital, or by the monopolist possession of colonies by certain countries?

Kautsky's argument can have no other meaning; and *this* "meaning" is meaningless. But suppose, for the sake of argument, free competition, without any sort of monopoly, *would* develop capitalism and trade more rapidly. Is it not a fact that the more rapidly trade and capitalism develop, the greater is the concentration of production and capital which *give rise* to monopoly? And monopolies have already come into being — precisely *out of* free competition! Even if monopolies have now begun to retard progress, it is not an argument in favor of free competition, which has become impossible since it gave rise to monopoly.

Whichever way one turns Kautsky's argument, one will find nothing in it except reaction and bourgeois reformism.

Even if we modify this argument and say . . . that the trade of the British colonies with the mother country is now developing more slowly than their trade with other countries, it does not save Kautsky; for it is *also* monopoly and imperialism that is beating Great Britain, only it is the monopoly and imperialism of another country (America, Germany). It is known that the cartels have given rise to a new and peculiar form of protective tariffs, *i.e.,* goods suitable for export are protected (Engels noted this in Vol. III of *Capital*). It is known, too, that the cartels and finance capital have a system peculiar to themselves, that of "exporting goods at cutrate prices," or "dumping," as the English call it; within a given country the cartel sells its goods at a high price fixed by monopoly; abroad it sells them at a much lower price to undercut the competitor, to enlarge its own production to the utmost, etc. If Germany's trade with the British colonies is developing more rapidly than that of Great Britain with the same colonies, it only proves that German imperialism is younger, stronger and better organized than British imperialism, is superior to it. But this by no means proves the "superiority" of free trade, for it is not free trade fighting against protection and colonial dependence, but two rival imperialisms, two monopolies, two groups of finance capital that are fighting. The superiority of German imperialism over British imperialism is stronger than the wall of colonial frontiers or of protective tariffs. To use this as an argument in favor of free trade and "peaceful democracy" is banal, is to forget the essential features and qualities of imperialism, to substitute petty-bourgeois reformism for Marxism. . . .

Kautsky's theoretical critique of imperialism has nothing in common with Marxism and serves no other purpose than as a preamble to propaganda for peace and unity with the opportunists and the social-chauvinists, precisely for the reason that it evades and obscures the very profound and radical contradictions between monopoly and free competition that exist side by side with it, between the gigantic "operations" (and gigantic profits) of finance capital and "honest" trade in the free market, the contradictions between cartels and trusts, on the one hand and non-cartelised industry, on the other, etc.

The notorious theory of "ultra-imperialism," invented by Kautsky, is equally reactionary. . . .

Cannot the present imperialist policy be supplanted by a new, ultra-imperialist policy, which will introduce the common exploitation of the world by internationally united finance capital in place of the mutual rivalries of national finance capital? Such a new phase of capitalism is at any rate conceivable. Can it be achieved? Sufficient premises are still lacking to enable us to answer this question.

   . . . The only objective, i.e., real, social significance Kautsky's "theory" can have, is that of a most reactionary method of consoling the masses with hopes of permanent peace being possible under capitalism, distracting their attention from the sharp antagonisms and acute problems of the present era, and directing it towards illusory prospects of an imaginary "ultra-imperialism" of the future. Deception of the masses — there is nothing but this in Kautsky's "Marxian" theory.

Indeed, it is enough to compare well-known and indisputable facts to become convinced of the utter falsity of the prospect which Kautsky tries to conjure up before the German workers (and the workers of all lands). Let us consider India, Indo-China and China. It is known that these three Colonial and semi-colonial countries, inhabited by six to seven hundred million human beings, are subjected to the exploitation of the finance capital of several imperialist states: Great Britain, France, Japan, the U.S.A., etc. We will assume that these imperialist countries form alliances against one another in order to protect and extend their possessions, their interests and their "spheres of influence" in these Asiatic states; these alliances will be "inter-imperialist" or "ultra-imperialist" alliances. We will assume that all the imperialist countries conclude an alliance for the "peaceful" division of these parts of Asia; this alliance would be an alliance of "internationally united finance capital." As a matter of fact, alliances of this kind have been made in the twentieth century, notably with regard to China. We ask, is it "conceivable," assuming that the capitalist system remains intact — and this is precisely the assumption that Kautsky does make — that such alliances would be more than temporary, that they would eliminate friction, conflicts and struggle in all and every possible form?

This question need only be stated clearly enough to make it impossible for any other reply to be given than that in the negative; for there can be no other conceivable basis under capitalism for the division of spheres of influence, of interests, of colonies, etc., than a calculation of the strength of the participants in the division, their general economic, financial, military strength, etc. And the strength of these participants in the division does not change to an equal degree, for under capitalism the development of different undertakings, trusts, branches of industry, or countries cannot be even. Half a century ago, Germany was a miserable, insignificant country, as far as its capitalist strength was concerned, compared with the strength of England at that time. Japan was similarly insignificant compared with Russia. Is it "conceivable" that in ten or twenty years' time the relative strength of the imperialist powers will have remained unchanged? Absolutely inconceivable.

Therefore, in the realities of the capitalist system . . . no matter what form they may assume, whether of one imperialist coalition against another, or of a general alliance embracing *all* the imperialist powers, are *inevitably* nothing more than a "truce" in periods between wars. Peaceful alliances prepare the ground for wars, and in their turn grow out of wars; the one is the condition for the other, giving rise to alternating forms of peaceful and nonpeaceful struggle out of *one and the same* basis of imperialist connections and the relations between world economics and world politics. . . .

Kautsky's toning down of the deepest contradictions of imperialism, which inevitably becomes the embellishment of imperialism, leaves its traces in this writer's criticism of the political features of imperialism. Imperialism is the epoch of finance capital and of monopolies, which introduce everywhere the striving for domination, not for freedom. The result of these tendencies is reaction all along the line, whatever the political system, and an extreme intensification of existing antagonisms in this domain also. Particularly acute becomes the yoke of national oppression and the striving for annexations, i.e., the violation of national independence (for annexation is nothing but the violation of the right of nations to self-determination). Hilferding justly draws attention to the connection between imperialism and the growth of national oppression.

> In the newly opened up countries themselves, [he writes] the capitalism imported into them intensifies contradictions and excites the constantly growing resistance against the intruders of the peoples who are awakening to national consciousness. This resistance can easily become transformed into dangerous measures directed against foreign capital. The old social relations become completely revolutionized. The age-long agrarian incrustation of "nations without a history" is blasted away, and they are drawn into the capitalist whirlpool. Capitalism itself gradually procures for the vanquished the means and resources for the emancipation and they set out to achieve the same goal which once seemed highest to the European nations: the creation of a united national state as a means to economic and cultural freedom. This movement for national independence threatens European capital just in its most valuable and most promising fields of exploitation, and European capital can maintain its domination only by continually increasing its means of exerting violence.

To this must be added that it is not only in newly opened up countries, but also in the old, that imperialism is leading to annexation, to increased national oppression, and, consequently, also to increasing resistance. . . . Let us suppose that a Japanese is condemning the annexation of the Philippine Islands by the Americans. Will many believe that he is doing so because he has a horror of annexations as such, and not because he himself has a desire to annex the Philippines? And shall we not be constrained to admit that the "fight" the Japanese are waging against annexations can be regarded as being sincere and politically honest only if he fights against the annexation of Korea by Japan, and urges freedom for Korea to secede from Japan?[1]

Kautsky's theoretical analysis of imperialism, as well as his economic and political criticism of imperialism, are permeated *through and through* with a spirit, absolutely irreconcilable with Marxism, of obscuring and glossing over the most profound contradictions of imperialism. . . .

THE PLACE OF IMPERIALISM IN HISTORY

We have seen that the economic quintessence of imperialism is monopoly capitalism. This very fact determines its place in history, for monopoly that grew up on the basis of free competition, and precisely out of free competition, is the transition from the capitalist system to a higher social-economic order. We must take special note of the four principal manifestations of monopoly capitalism, which are characteristic of the epoch under review.

Firstly, monopoly arose out of the concentration of production at a very advanced stage of development. This refers to the monopolist capitalist combines, cartels, syndicates and trusts. We have seen the important part that these play in modern economic life. At the beginning of the twentieth century, monopolies acquired complete supremacy in the advanced countries. And although the first steps towards the formation of the cartels were first taken by countries enjoying the protection of high tariffs (Germany, America), Great Britain, with her system of free trade, was not far behind in revealing the same basic phenomenon, namely, the birth of monopoly out of the concentration of production.

Secondly, monopolies have accelerated the capture of the most important sources of raw materials, especially for the coal and iron industries, which are the basic and mostly highly cartelised industries in capitalist society. The monopoly of the most important sources of raw materials has enormously increased the power of big capital, and has sharpened the antagonism between cartelised and non-cartelised industry.

Thirdly, monopoly has sprung from the banks. The banks have developed from modest intermediary enterprises into the monopolists of finance capital. Some three or five of the biggest banks in each of the foremost capitalist countries have achieved the "personal union" of industrial and bank capital, and have concentrated in their hands the disposal of thousands upon thousands of millions which form the greater part of the capital and income of entire countries. A financial oligarchy, which throws a close net of relations of dependence over all the economic and political institutions of contemporary bourgeois society without exception — such is the most striking manifestation of this monopoly.

Fourthly, monopoly has grown out of colonial policy. To the numerous "old" motives of colonial policy, finance capital has added the struggle for the sources of raw materials, for the export of capital, for "spheres of influence," *i.e.,* for spheres for profitable deals, concessions, monopolist profits and so on; and finally, for economic territory in general. When the colonies of the European powers in Africa, for instance, comprised only one-tenth of that territory (as was the case in 1876), colonial policy was able to develop by methods other than those of monopoly — by the "free grabbing" of territories, so to speak. But when nine-tenths of Africa had been seized (approximately by 1900), when the whole world had been divided up, there was inevitably ushered in a period of colonial monopoly and, consequently, a period of particularly intense struggle for the division and the redivision of the world.

The extent to which monopolist capital has intensified all the contradictions of capitalism is generally known. It is sufficient to mention the high cost of living and the oppression of the cartels. This intensification of contradictions constitutes the most powerful driving force of the transitional period of history, which began from the time of the definite victory of world finance capital.

Monopolies, oligarchy, the striving for domination instead of striving for liberty, the exploitation of an increasing number of small or weak nations by an extremely small group of the richest or most powerful nations —all these have given birth to those distinctive characteristics of imperialism which compel us to define it as parasitic or decaying capitalism. More and more prominently there emerges, as one of the tendencies of imperialism, the creation of the "bond-holding" (rentier) state, the usurer state, in which the bourgeoisie lives on the proceeds of capital exports and by "clipping coupons." It would be a mistake to believe that this tendency to decay precludes the possibility of the rapid growth of capitalism. It does not. In the epoch of imperialism, certain branches of industry, certain strata of the bourgeoisie and certain countries betray, to a more or less degree, one or other of these tendencies. On the whole, capitalism is growing far more rapidly than before. But this growth is not only becoming more and more uneven in general; its unevenness also manifests itself, in particular, in the decay of the countries which are richer in capital (such as England). . . .

NOTE

1. [This] pamphlet . . . was written in Zurich in the spring of 1916 . . . with an eye to the tsarist censorship. . . .
   "In order to show, in a guise acceptable to the censors, how shamefully the capitalists and the social-chauvinist deserters (whom Kautsky opposes with so much inconsistency) lie on the question of annexations, in order to show with what cynicism they *screen* the annexations of *their* capitalists, I was forced to quote as an example — Japan! The careful reader will easily substitute Russia for Japan, and Finland, Poland, Courland, the Ukraine, Khiva, Bokhara, Estonia or other regions peopled by non-Great Russians, for Korea." — quoted from Lenin's "Preface to the Russian Edition," written in Petrograd, April 26, 1917.

Patterns and Perspectives of the Capitalist World-Economy

Immanuel Wallerstein

Professor Wallerstein outlines key concepts and propositions associated with the capitalist world-system.

1. THE NATURE OF THE WORLD-ECONOMY

1.1. The concept world-economy (*économie-monde* in French) should be distinguished from that of world economy (*économie mondiale*) or international economy. The latter concept presumes there are a series of separate "economies" which are "national" in scope, and that under certain circumstances these "national economies" trade with each other, the sum of these (limited) contacts being called the international economy. Those who use this latter concept argue that the limited contacts have been expanding in the 20th century. It is thus asserted that the world has become "one world" in a sense it wasn't prior to the 20th century.

By contrast, the concept "world-economy" assumes that there exists an "economy" wherever (and if but only if) there is an ongoing extensive and relatively complete social division of labor with an integrated set of production processes which relate to each other through a "market" which has been "instituted" or "created" in some complex way. Using such a concept, the world-economy is not new in the 20th century, nor is it a coming together of "national economies," none of the latter constituting complete divisions of labor. Rather, a world-economy, capitalist in form, has been in existence in at least part of the globe since the 16th century. Today, the entire globe is operating within the framework of this singular social division of labor we are calling the capitalist world-economy.

1.2. The capitalist world-economy has, and has had since its coming into existence, boundaries far larger than that of any political unit. Indeed, it seems to be one of the basic defining features of a capitalist world-economy that there exists no political entity with ultimate authority in all its zones.

Reprinted with permission of Immanuel Wallerstein and *Contemporary Marxism,* No. 9 San Francisco: Synthesis Publications, 1984. Originally prepared for Seminar on Culture and Thought in the Transformation of the World (third international seminar of the United Nations University Project on Socio-Cultural Development Alternatives in a Changing World), held in Algiers, 13–17 December 1981.

Rather, the political superstructure of the capitalist world-economy is an interstate system within which and through which political structures called "sovereign states" are legitimized and constrained. Far from meaning the total autonomy of decision-making, the term "sovereignty" in reality implies a formal autonomy combined with real limitations on this autonomy, which are implemented both via the explicit and implicit rules of the interstate system and via the power of other states in the interstate system. No state in the interstate system, even the single most powerful one at any given time, is totally autonomous — but obviously some enjoy far greater autonomy than others.

1.3. The world-economy is a complex of cultures — in the sense of languages, religions, ideologies — but this complex is not haphazard. There exists a *Weltanschauung* of imperium, albeit one with several variants, and there exist cultures of resistance to this imperium.

1.4. The major social institutions of the capitalist world-economy — the states, the classes, the "peoples," and the households — are all shaped (even created) by the ongoing workings of the world-economy. None of them are primordial, in the sense of permanent, pre-existing relatively fixed structures to which the working of the capitalist world economy are exogenous.

1.5. The capitalist world-economy is a *historical* social system. It came into existence, and its genesis must be explained. Its existence is defined by certain patterns — both cyclical rhythms and secular trends — which must be explicated. It is highly probable that it will one day go out of existence (become transformed into another type of historical social system), and we can therefore assess the historical alternatives that are before us.

2. THE PATTERNS OF THE WORLD-ECONOMY

All historical structures constantly evolve. However, the use of any concept is a capturing in fixed form of some continuing pattern. We could not discern the world, interpret it, or consciously change it unless we used concepts, with all the limitations that any reification, however slight, implies.

2.1. The world-economy has a capitalist mode of production. This is an empirical statement. Although there have been other world-economies (as defined above) known in history, the modern one of which we are speaking is the only one which has survived over a long period of time without either disintegrating or being transformed into a world-empire (with a singular political structure). This modern one has had a capitalist mode of production — that is, its economy has been dominated by those who operate on the primacy of endless accumulation, such entrepreneurs (or controllers of production units) driving from the arena those who seek to operate on other premises. Since only one world-economy has survived over a long period of time, and since this one has been capitalist in form, we may suspect that the two phenomena are theoretically linked: that a world-economy to survive must have a capitalist mode of production, and inversely that capitalism cannot be the mode of production except in a system that has the form of a world-economy (a division of labor more extensive than any one political entity).

2.2. The capitalist world-economy has operated via a social relationship called capital/labor, in which the surplus created by direct producers has been appropriated by others either at the point of production or at the most immediate market place, in either case by virtue of the fact that the appropriators control the "capital" and that their "rights" to the surplus are legally guaranteed. The extractors of surplus-value may in many cases be individuals, but they have tended increasingly to be collective entities (private or state corporations).

2.3. Once surplus-value has been extracted, it has yet to be "distributed" among a network of beneficiaries. The exchange processes of the "market" are one mode through which this redistribution occurs, in particular, the structure of the world-economy permits an unequal exchange of goods and services (primarily trans-state), such that much of the surplus-value extracted in the peripheral zones of the world-economy is transferred to the core zones.

2.4. The exchange of products containing unequal amounts of social labor we may call the core/periphery relationship. This is pervasive, continuing, and constant. There tend to be geographical localizations of productive activities such that core-like production activities and periphery-like production activities tend each to be spatially grouped together. We can thus, for shorthand purposes, refer to some states as core states and others as peripheral states.

2.5. Insofar as some states function as loci of mixed kinds of production activities (some core-like, some periphery-like), we can speak of such states as semi-peripheral. There always exist semi-peripheral zones.

2.6. While the pattern of a spatial hierarchy of production processes within the capitalist world-economy is a constant, the position of any given state is not, since there have been regular partial relocations of core-like and periphery-like economic activities.

2.7. Since what makes a production process core-like or periphery-like is the degree to which it incorporates labor-value, is mechanized, and is highly profitable, and all these characteristics shift over time for any given product because of "product cycles," it follows that no product is inherently core-like or periphery-like, but has that characteristic for a given time. Nonetheless, there are always some products which are core-like and others which are periphery-like at any given time.

2.8. Because the imperatives of accumulation operate via the individual decisions of entrepreneurs, each seeking to maximize his profit — the so-called anarchy of production — there is an inherent tendency to the expansion of absolute volume of production in the world-economy. Profit can, however, only be realized if there is effective demand for the global product. World effective demand, however, is a function of the sum of political arrangements in the various states (the result of prior class struggles), which determine the real distribution of the global surplus. These arrangements are stable for intermediate periods of time. Consequently, world supply expands at a steady rate while world demand remains relatively fixed for intermediate periods. Such a system must result, and historically has resulted, in recurring bottlenecks for accumulation, which are translated into periods of economic stagnation. The A-phases of expansion and the B-phases of stagnation seem to have occurred historically in cycles of 40–55 years (sometimes called "Kondratieff cycles").

2.9. Each period of stagnation has created pressures to restructure the network of production processes and the social relations that underlie them in ways that would overcome bottlenecks to accumulation. Among the mechanisms that have operated to renew expansion are:

a. reduction of production costs of former core-like products by further mechanization and/or relocation of these activities in lower-wage zones;
b. creation of new core-like activities ("innovation"), which promise high initial rates of profit, thus encouraging new loci of investment;
c. an intensified class struggle both within the core states and between groups located in different states such that there may occur at the end of the process some political redistribution of world surplus to workers in core zones (often by means of fully proletarianizing hitherto semi-proletarian households) and to bourgeois in semi-peripheral and peripheral zones, thereby augmenting world effective demand;
d. expansion of the outer boundaries of the world-economy, thereby creating new pools of direct producers who can be involved in world production as semi-proletarianized workers receiving wages below the cost of reproduction.

2.10. States in which core-like activities occur develop relatively strong state apparatuses which can advance the interests of their bourgeoisies, less by protection (a mechanism of the medium-strong seeking to be stronger) than by preventing other states from erecting political barriers to the profitability of these activities. In general, states seek to shape the world market in ways that will advance the interests of some enterpreneurs against that of others.

2.11. There seem to be cycles as well, within the interstate system. On three separate occasions, one state has been able to achieve what may be called a hegemonic position in the world-economy: the United Provinces, 1620–1650; the United Kingdom, 1815–1873; the United States, 1945–1967. When producers located within a given state can undersell producers located in other core states in the latter's "home market," they can over time transform this production advantage into one in the commercial arena and then into one in the financial arena. The combined advantages may be said to constitute hegemony and are selected as well in a political-military advantage in the interstate system. Such hegemonies are relatively short-lived, since the production advantages cannot be sustained indefinitely and mechanisms of the balance of power intrude to reduce the political advantage of the single most powerful state.

2.12. The core states in general, and the hegemonic state when one exists in particular, seek to reinforce the advantages of their producers and to legitimize their role in the interstate system by imposing their cultural dominance on the world. To some extent, this occurs in the easily visible form of language, religion, and mores, but more importantly this occurs in the form of seeking to impose modes of thought and analysis, including in particular the paradigms that inform philosophy and the sciences/social sciences.

3. THE SECULAR TRENDS OF THE WORLD-ECONOMY

The patterns of the world-economy may be at first glance cyclical in form, but they are not perfectly cyclical. The world-economy has a historical development which is structural and can be analyzed in terms of its secular trends.

3.1. The drive to accumulate leads to the constant deepening of the capitalist development. The search to reduce long-term costs of production leads to a steady increase in the degree to which production is mechanized. The search for the least expensive source of factors of production (including as an expense delays in time in acquiring access) leads to a steady increase in the degree to which these factors (land, labor, and goods) are commodified. The desire to reduce barriers to the process of accumulation leads to a steady increase in the degree to which economic transactions are contractualized. It is important to recognize two things about these processes of mechanization, commodification, and contractualization.

3.1.1. While there are regular increases in the world-economy taken as a whole of the degree of mechanization, commodification, and contractualization, the pattern is not linear but stepwise, each significant advance leading to overall expansion, and each overall stagnation leading to a restructuring of the world-economy such that there is further advance.

3.1.2. The capitalist development of the world-economy at the world level is far from complete in the 20th century. These processes are still in full operation.

3.2 The recurring stagnations of the world-economy, which have led to the regular restructuring of this world-economy, have involved as part of restructuring the expansion of the "outer" boundaries of the world-economy, a process which, however, has been nearly completed as of now. This expansion, which was central to world history of the past several hundred years, gradually eliminated from the globe other kinds of historical social systems, creating the historically unique situation of there being, for all effects and purposes, a single social division of labor on the earth.

3.3. The steady but still incomplete commodification of labor, side by side with the now largely completed expansion of the outer boundaries of the world-economy, accounts for the shape of two of the major institutional structures of the capitalist world-economy: the classes and the households.

3.3.1. The commodification of labor ultimately means a structure in which direct producers have no access to the means of production except by selling their labor-power on a market; that is, they become proletarians. Although the percentage of direct producers who are full-lifetime proletarians has been growing worldwide over time, nonetheless, even today such proletarians are still probably no more than half of the world's work force.

3.3.2 The commodification of land and capital ultimately means a structure in which controllers of land or capital (including "human capital") have no access to the maintenance and reproduction of land and capital except by pursuing an active policy of maximizing the accumulation of capital; that is, they become bourgeois. In the 20th century, there are very few who control land or capital — directly (individually) or indirectly (collectively) — who are not bourgeois, that is, persons whose economic raison d'être is the accumulation of capital.

3.3.3. Hence, we have a situation in which *a part but not all* of the direct producers are (full-lifetime) proletarians (the other part we may designate as "semi-proletarians"), but *most* of the controllers of land and capital are bourgeois.

3.3.4. The creation of two large worldwide classes has led to the molding of appropriate household structures as the member-units of these classes. We mean by household the unit which, over a longish (30–50 year) period, pools the income of all its members, from whatever source and in whatever form is this income.

3.3.5. The "semi-proletarian" household, so extensive in peripheral zones in the world-economy, permits the wage-employment of some of its members for parts of their lives at wages below the proportionate cost of reproduction by pooling this wage-income with that received from subsistence, petty commodity, rental, and transfer income. This is what is meant by "super-exploitation" (since in this case the employer of the wage-laborer is receiving not merely the surplus-value created by the wage-laborer, but that which other members of the household are creating).

3.3.6. The proletarian household, tending to receive wage-income approximating the real costs of reproduction (no less but also not much more) tends to move in the direction of more "nucleated" households, sloughing off *affines* and others not defined as pulling their full weight.

3.3.7. The bourgeois household, seeking to maximize the use of capital, the direct control of which tends to increase by age, and utilizing the family structure as the primary mechanism of avoiding social redistribution, tends to take the form of extended, multilocal households.

3.4 The steady (now largely completed) expansion of the outer boundaries of the world-economy, combined with the continuing competition among bourgeois for advantage in the capitalist world-economy, accounts for the shape of the other two major institutional structures of the capitalist world-economy: the states and the peoples.

3.4.1. The drive of bourgeois for competitive advantage has led to increasing definition ("power") of the states as political structures and increasing emphasis on their constraint by the interstate system. This push for a "strong" state (strong vis-à-vis both other internal loci of power and vis-à-vis other states and external nonstate forces) has been greatest and therefore most efficacious in those states with core-like production activities. The strong state has been the principal mechanism by which the bourgeois controlling these core-like production activities have been able a) to limit and moderate the economic demands of their national work forces, b) to shape the world market so as to compete effectively with bourgeoisies located in other states, and c) to incorporate new zones into the world-economy, thus constantly re-creating new centers of peripheral production activities.

3.4.2. The increasing definition of state structures has led to the shaping, reshaping, creation, destruction, and revival of "peoples." To the extent that these "peoples" are defined by themselves (and by others) as controlling or having the "moral" right to control state structures, these "peoples" become "nations." To the extent that they are not defined as having the right to control a state structure, these people become "minorities" or "ethnic groups." Defining given states as nation–states is an aid in strengthening the state. Such a definition requires emphasizing one "people" and de-emphasizing, even destroying (conceptually or literally), others. This is particularly important for semi-peripheral states seeking to transform their structural role in the world-economy. Various groups have interests supporting and opposing any particular nation–state definition. "Nationalism" is a mechanism both of imperium/integration and of resistance/liberation. The peoples are not haphazardly defined but neither are they simple and unfixed derivations from a historical past. They are solidarity groupings whose boundaries are a matter of constant social transmittal/redefinition.

3.5. As the classes come to be defined vis-à-vis the developing division of labor in the world-economy and the peoples come to be defined vis-à-vis the increasing rationalized interstate system, the locational concentration of various oppressed groups gives rise over time to anti-systemic movements. These movements have organized in two main forms around two main themes: the social movement around "class" and the national movement around "nation" or people.

3.5.1. The seriously anti-systemic (or revolutionary) forms of such movements first emerged in *organized* form in the 19th century. Their general objective, human equality, was by definition incompatible with the functioning of the capitalist world-economy, a hierarchical system based on uneven development, unequal exchange, and the appropriation of surplus-value. However, the political structure of the capitalist world-economy — the fact that it was not a single unit but a series of sovereign states — pressed the movements to seek the transformation of the world-system via the achievement of political power within separate states. The organization of these anti-systemic movements at the state level had contradictory effects.

3.5.2. Organization at the state level for the social movement was ideologically confusing from the beginning, as it counterposed the logical and ideological necessity of worldwide struggle (proletarian internationalism) against the immediate political need of achieving power within one state. Either the social movement resisted "nationalism" and was rendered inefficacious or it utilized nationalism and then faced ambiguously the so-called "national question" — that is, the "nationalisms" of the "minorities" within the boundaries of the state. Whatever the tactic of a given social movement, the achievement of partial or total state power involved power in a structure constrained by the interstate system, hence unable by itself to transform the system entirely (that is, to withdraw totally from the capitalist world-economy).

3.5.3. Organization at the state level created dilemmas for the national movements as well. The smaller the zone within which the national movement defined itself, the easier the access to state power but the less consequential. Hence, all national movements have oscillated in terms of the unit of definition, and the various "pan-" movements have had limited success. But defeats of "pan-" movements have tended to dilute the anti-systemic thrust of particular national movements.

3.5.4. In general, both social and national movements have had a difficult time reconciling long-run anti-systemic objectives and short-run "developmentalist" or "catching-up" objectives, which tend to reinforce rather than undermine the world-system. Nonetheless, the collective momentum of the social and national movements over time has been anti-systemic in effect, despite the "reformism" or "revisionism" of the various movements taken separately. Furthermore, the collective momentum of these movements has been such as to confound increasingly the social and national movements, which has in fact been a source of additional strength.

3.6. The unfolding of the institutional structures of the world-system — the classes, the states, the peoples, the households — has been reflected in the cultural mosaic of the world-system, whose pattern has been increasingly that of the tension between imperium and resistance.

3.6.1. As the axial division of labor became more pronounced and more unequal, the need to facilitate its operation through the allocation of work forces and the justification of inequality led to an ideology of racism that became the central organizing cultural theme of the world bourgeoisie. The existence of superior groups (whether in particular instances these groups were defined as Caucasians or Anglosaxons or other variants on this theme) became a method of simple *triage* in job and income allocation.

3.6.2. Whereas racism has served as a mechanism of worldwide control of direct producers, the bourgeoisie of strong core states (and particularly of the hegemonic power) sought also to direct the activities of the bourgeois of other states and various middle strata worldwide into channels that would maximize the close integration of production processes and the smooth operation of the interstate system such that the accumulation of capital was facilitated. This required the creation of a world bourgeois cultural framework that could be grafted onto "national" variations. This was particularly important in terms of science and technology, but quite important too in the realm of political ideas and of the social sciences.

3.6.3. The concept of a neutral "universal" culture to which the cadres of the world division of labor would be "assimilated" (the passive tense being important here) hence came to serve as one of the pillars of the world-system as it historically evolved. The exaltation of progress, and later of "modernization," summarized this set of ideas, which served less as true norms of social action than as status-symbols of obeisance and of participation in the world's upper strata.

3.6.4. Resistance to this cultural assimilationism was to be found among competitive bourgeois in semi-peripheral and nonhegemonic core states and took the form of asserting the autonomy of "national" traditions and/or antipathy to structural generalizations in the domain of ideas. It also took the form of reinforcing alternative world linguistic groupings to the hegemonic one (in practice, of English).

3.6.5. More fundamental cultural resistance on the part of anti-systemic movements has come slowly to take the form of positing civilizational alternatives to dominant cultural forms. In particular, it has counterdistinguished civilizations (plural) to civilization (singular and imperial).

4. THE SYSTEM IN CRISIS

4.1. A system that has cyclical patterns has recurring downturns, whatever we wish to call them. We have argued the regularity of world economic stagnations as one of the patterns of the capitalist world-economy. But insofar as there are also mechanisms that regularly bring these stagnations to an end and relaunch world economic expansion, we cannot count these cyclical downturns as crises, however much they are perceived as such by the individuals living through them.

4.2. Rather, a "crisis" is a situation in which the restitutive mechanisms of the system are no longer functioning well, and therefore the system will either be transformed fundamentally or disintegrate. It is in this sense that we could talk for example of the "crisis of feudalism" in Europe in the period 1300–1450, a crisis whose resolution was the historic emergence of a capitalist world-economy located in that particular geographic arena. We may say that this capitalist world-economy in turn entered into a long "crisis" of a comparable nature in the 20th century, a crisis in the midst of which we are living.

4.3. The causes of the crisis are internal to the system, the result of the contradictions built into the process.

4.3.1. One of the mechanisms whereby the world-economy has overcome its downturn phases has been the expansion of the outer boundaries of the world-economy, but this is a process which has inbuilt limits which are nearly reached.

4.3.2. Another of the mechanisms whereby the world-economy has overcome its downturn phases has been the expansion of world effective demand, in part through proletarianization of the direct producers, in part by redistribution of the surplus among the world bourgeoisie.

4.3.2.1. Proletarianization is also a process that has inbuilt limits. While they have hardly yet been reached, the process has been speeding up, and one can foresee it reaching its asymptote within the coming century.

4.3.2.2. Redistribution of the surplus among the bourgeoisie is itself the result of bourgeoisification, which has entailed an increase of the total percentage of the world population who are bourgeois. If one distinguishes between the small group of bourgeois who control most of the fixed capital and the much larger group of bourgeois who control principally human capital, the growth and social concentration of the latter group have resulted in their acquisition of considerable political power in core states. They have been able, as the price of their political support for the world-system as a system, to ensure that an increasing proportion of the appropriated surplus will be redistributed to them, reducing over the long run the rate of profit to the holders of fixed capital.

4.4. Increasing proletarianization and the increasing constraint on individual mobility because of the degree to which definitions of peoples have been linked to position in the world-economy have led to the rise of the anti-systemic movements. These movements have a cumulative effect which may be said to draw a logarithmic curve. We have entered into the phase of acute escalation.

4.5. The fact that we are in a systemic crisis and have been in one at least since the Russian Revolution — which was its symbolic detonator and has always been seen as such — does not mean that the capitalist development of the world-economy has come to an end. Quite the contrary. It is as vigorous as ever, perhaps more so. This is indeed the prime cause of the crisis. The very vigor of capitalist development has been and will continue to be the main factor that exacerbates the contradictions of the system.

4.6. It is therefore not the case that the crisis will be imminently resolved. A crisis of a system is a long, slow, difficult process, and for it to play itself out over a 150-year period is scarcely surprising, We have little perspective on it as we are amidst it, and we therefore tend to exaggerate each minor fork in the road. There is some constructive value in being overly optimistic in a short run, but the negative side of such exaggeration is the disillusionments it breeds. A crisis is best navigated by a cool, long-run strategy. It cannot however be totally planned, as the crisis itself gives rise to new possibilities of human action.

5. PROSPECTIVES

There are three different logics which are playing themselves out in the present world crisis. The outcome will be the result of their interaction.

5.1. There is the logic of socialism.

5.1.1. The capitalist development of the world-economy itself moves toward the socialization of the productive process. There is an *organizational* (as opposed to a political) imperative in which the full achievement of capitalist relations of production — through its emphasis on the increase of relative surplus-value and the maximum efficiency (free flow) of the factors of production — pushes toward a fully planned single productive organizational network in the world-economy.

5.1.2. Furthermore, the political logic of the appropriation of surplus by the few leads to the growth of the anti-systemic movements and therefore toward the spread of socialist values among the world's direct producers.

5.1.3. Finally, the structure of the world-economy (multiple states within the division of labor) has created the possibility of socialist political movements coming to power in individual states, seeking to "construct socialism." Despite the fact that their continued location in the capitalist world-economy and the interstate system seriously constrains the kinds of transformations they can effectuate within boundaries of a given state, their attempts to approximate in various ways a socialist order create additional institutional pressures on the world-system to move in the direction of socialism.

5.2. There is also the logic of domination.

5.2.1. Insofar as the powerful have, by definition, more power than the mass of the world population, and insofar as the process of transformation is slow and contradictory, it creates much opportunity for the ruling strata (the world bourgeoisie) to invent modes of continuity of power and privilege. The adoption of new social roles and new ideological clothing may be a route for existing dominant strata to perpetuate themselves in a new system. It is certainly the logic of domination that dominant groups seek to survive even a "crisis." As the landowning hero of de Lampedusa's *Il Gattopardo* says: "We must change everything in order that everything remain the same."

5.2.2. In the process of the world bourgeoisie seeking to retain their power, they may engage in policies which lead to a nuclear world war. This could bring about a demise of the present system in a manner that would destroy much of the forces of production and thereby make a socialist world order far less structurally feasible.

5.5. There is a logic of the civilizational project.

5.3.1. While the capitalist world-economy has been the first and only social system that has managed to eliminate from the earth all contemporaneous social systems, this has been historically true only for a very recent period of time. We could regard it as simply the conquest by Western Europeans of the globe. In this case, in the long run of history, the political and technological supremacy of the West constitutes a short interval and, from the perspective of alternative "civilizational" centers, might be thought of as a transitory and aberrant interlude. There is thus a drive for a restituted civilizational balance, which the very process of capitalist development of the world-economy makes more urgent and more realizable.

5.3.2. How a restituted civilizational balance fits in, however, with world socialism on the one hand and the drive of world ruling strata to survive on the other is not at all clear.

5.4. We live facing real historical alternatives. It is clear that the capitalist world-economy cannot survive, and that as a historical social system it is in the process of being superseded. The forces at play are also clear, as are the secular trends. We can struggle for our preferences. We can analyze probabilities. But we cannot foretell, because we cannot yet know for certain how the conjuncture of forces at play will constrain the directions of change and even less can we know what new possibilities of human liberation they will afford. The only thing of which we may be certain is that our present activity will be a major factor in the outcome of the crisis.

FREEZING THE NORTH-SOUTH BLOC(K) AFTER THE EAST-WEST THAW

Craig N. Murphy

Professor Murphy applies Antonio Gramsci's concept of "historical bloc" in a contemporary, globalist perspective on "North-South" politics. Seen in the context of a capitalist world-system, global development is portrayed as a superstructure central to present-day patterns of North-South relations.

In their forecast for the new decade the editors of the venerable third world news magazine *West Africa* insisted:

> One legacy of the ending of super-power conflict would thus seem to be that the agenda for the next decade will much more be one of North-South than of East-West. With the possible fusion of the First and Second Worlds, the third world now moves to center stage.

The editors supported their claim with three bits of evidence from the news in late January 1990: Willy Brandt's decision to try to restart negotiations on reforming international monetary and financial institutions; the announcement of the broad reform agenda that an increasingly reinvigorated United Nations would take up in 1990; and, most significantly, the creation of a new focus of third world power to coordinate action within all international organizations and conferences: the Group of 15, a club of nonaligned states centered on those governing the bulk of the third world's population yet balanced to represent the diversity of opinion within the much larger group.[1]

The same issue of *West Africa* also reported a quite different view: The eminent historian of pan-Africanism, Tony Martin, pressed to comment on events in Europe by those attending his Du Bois Memorial Lectures in Accra, stated that the disintegration of the Communist bloc would mean a further consolidation of white racism against blacks as Western Europe aided Eastern Europe's development. North-South relations would not be at the center of the world agenda of the 1990s. Africans could only make strides if they put autonomy and unity at the center of their own agendas.[2]

That same month Africans heard a third assessment: Pope John Paul II arrived in Cape Verde at the beginning of a tour of Sahelian nations to highlight Africa's needs at a time when the privileged nations of the world were all too focused on the needs of the more-advantaged people of Eastern Europe.[3] The Pope's message was that choices were involved:

From *Socialist Review*, v. 20, no. 3 (July-September 1990): 25-46. Reprinted by permission.

Northerners need not limit their generosity to others like themselves. A positive transformation of North–South relations *could* be made in the 1990s.

Of the three, Martin's assessment will likely prove to be the most prescient. Even the evidence that leads the editors of *West Africa* to their rosier conclusion really should point us toward a bleaker view of the prospects of North–South relations in the 1990s. The recent changes in international institutions after more than a decade of crisis point to the consolidation of North–South relations that are less generous and less conducive to the real development of the third world than those which existed before the crisis.

Still, there is also something to be learned from John Paul's speech, and not just from its text, but also from its ironic context. Text and context share a single message. The text emphasizes the opportunities inherent in crisis, the possibilities for choice. The ironic context of the Pope's speech provides a clue to what reasonable choices might be. At a moment when many were consigning socialism to history's rubbish bin, Poland's most-celebrated anticommunist chose to make his commentary on the liberation of Eastern Europe as the guest of an incontrovertibly successful, Marxist-oriented, democratic socialist: Aristedes Marie Pereira, president of a nation whose transformation since its independence in 1975 has been profound.

One of Europe's first colonies, as well as one of its last, Cape Verde suffered 500 years of grinding exploitation and periodic devastation by drought and famine. Its history epitomizes all of the hypocritical horrors of Europe's five centuries of world supremacy; what was sinful and hidden at home in Europe became "necessary" and commonplace in the colony. (Pereira himself is one of the many children of a Catholic priest, a connection that the otherwise chummy Pope failed to note.)

This fractured society could still nurture the political movement organized by Pereira's comrade-in-arms, Amilcar Cabral, which defeated the Portuguese colonial army in Guinea-Bissau. The army returned to Portugal to overthrow Europe's last fascist state and, as consequence, to end European colonialism in Africa. Since then, Cape Verdeans have had fifteen years to undo some of the damage of centuries. Forests have been replanted on land that colonialism made a moonscape. Famine has become a memory, even though rains have failed in at least half the years since independence. Life expectancy has reached North American levels. Given Cape Verde's unusual success in dealing with Africa's four-fold crises of the 1980s (debt, drought, environmental degradation, and political decay), the leaders of the "most seriously affected" states turned to Pereira as their leader and representative in international forums, even though his country remains the most remote (ideologically as well as physically) from the rest.[4]

Third world governments that make the kind of choices that Cape Verde's has made will continue to find some small opportunities for transformation even after the warming of the East–West relations—opportunities in the as yet incomplete reconstruction of North–South international institutions (as emphasized by *West Africa*'s editors), as well as the greater opportunities available to those third world governments that pursue Martin's preferred strategy of unity and autonomy, even if they lead small and deeply dependent states like Cape Verde.

I reach these conclusions using a framework centered on Gramsci's concept, "historical bloc," to help understand both the changes in East–West relations of the moment, and the significant changes in North–South relations over the last fifteen years. My argument focuses on the crisis in North–South relations which predates the current changes in East–West relations.

THE NORTH–SOUTH HISTORICAL BLOC(K)

Many who study the third world have come to employ frameworks that posit a unitary world economy, whether it is the structural economics of "core" and "periphery" developed by Raul Prebisch, the various political economies and sociologies of "dependency," the self-styled "revolutionary internationalist" theory advanced by Nigel Harris and Michael Kidron,[5] or the "world-systems" theory of Immanuel Wallerstein. These frameworks have special appeal, and remain significant, particularly because they were developed by progressive third world intellectuals as a means of making sense of their own practical experience. Argentine government economist, Raul Presisch, experimented with "neoclassical" orthodoxy and then Keynesianism before coming to his own synthesis.[6] Similarly, colonial government agronomist Amilcar Cabral, to whom Wallerstein acknowledges a special debt, started with a simple comparative approach, treating countries as separate social formations, before he came to see the capitalist world-system as a single class-driven society.

The case for general adoption of such frameworks has been strengthened in recent months by their unusual capacity to anticipate and make sense of the recent events in Eastern Europe. Nearly a decade ago, at the beginning of the "second cold war" (marked by the Soviet intervention in Afghanistan and the start of the United States' recent military buildup), Wallerstein pooh-poohed the widespread notion that the East–West conflict would remain the fundamental divide in world politics; he argued, instead, that the struggle for supremacy among Germany, Japan, and the United States would soon come to the fore.[7] That conclusion seemed strange when it first appeared, in the month that Reagan was elected president. Now it looks almost prophetic. Even more prophetic is the decade-old work of world-system's sociologist Christopher Chase-Dunn and his colleagues on "socialist states" in the capitalist world-system.[8] They argued that what was fundamentally different about the Soviet Union and its Eastern European satellites was not their attempts to create fundamentally new, post-capitalist social formations, but their relative position within the singular modern social formation of world capitalism. These states occupied a "semi-peripheral" position, which gave them opportunities for autonomous development that the "peripheral" states of the third world did not have. Nevertheless, if the opportunity for moving from semi-peripheral to "core" status were to arise, Eastern European societies might be pushed back into the main world market, and "socialism" might, in retrospect, be seen as "the transitional system between capitalism and capitalism."

However, despite the prescience of some world-systems thinkers, their framework may not be sufficient to deal with the question of what effect the current changes in East–West relations are likely to have on North–South relations. After all, from 1945 until (at least) 1990 the East–West division meant something more than a division between a large, relatively autonomous economic region and the rest of world society. It represented a division between two complex, international social systems with autonomous economic bases as well as separate political and ideological superstructures. In contrast, the North–South division, remained, for the most part, a division *within* a single complex international social system, a system defined by a single interdependent economy and by a host of superstructures, international institutions linking the South to the North, from the US Trusteeship Council, to the World Bank, to UNCTAD.

Antonio Gramsci's concept of a "historical bloc" can help us capture these distinctions. In the post-war period, the Soviet Union, its Eastern European satellites, and its most-dependent third world countries (perhaps only Cuba) can be thought of as constituting one "historical bloc." The wealthy capitalist OECD states along with most of the dependent third world constituted another.[9]

Gramsci's concept proves useful because he developed it, in large part, to help understand another situation in which the territorial and social boundaries of societies were shifting and the boundaries of juridical states did not necessarily correspond to the most meaningful boundaries between social systems: the history of Italian state-building from the early Renaissance through the Italian imperialism of his own day.[10] Any conceptual framework that made it difficult to see that the boundaries of social systems are not, themselves, contestable and often contested, would not have served Gramsci's purposes. Similarly, in an era when one group of national societies appears to be attempting to rejoin the capitalist core and when observers as disparate as Martin and John Paul see the exclusion of another group of national societies from some larger (but still not "global") world society as a likely consequence of this attempt, we also need such a framework.

Gramsci also developed his concept to overcome some of the misunderstandings arising from use of the traditional, rigid Marxist architectural metaphor for society with its contingent political and cultural "superstructures" resting upon a determining foundation or "base." Gramsci recognizes the reciprocal determination between base and superstructure. All ideas, all culture, all politics, all public laws are not simply functions of economic interests and the powers granted to people by their roles in production. Moreover, no economic system can fully develop—not even the contradictions within its inner logic can fully develop—outside of a conducive political and cultural environment. A historical bloc is, "the dialectical unity of base and superstructure, theory and practice, of intellectuals and masses (and not, as it is sometimes mistakenly asserted, simply an alliance of social forces),"[11] which makes such development impossible.

It is easiest to understand Gramsci's central notion by recognizing that it, like the older superstructure-base distinction, was developed through metaphor, using analogies to articulate something that had not been recognized in quite the same way before. Thus, Gramsci's work suggests a whole series of ways in which specific aspects of social life are "like" a *blocco*. In one sense a historical bloc *is* an alliance—a "bloc"— the alliance of social forces whose aspirations are fulfilled within a particular social order. In that sense, the postwar "North–South bloc" could be identified as being the alliance among three groups: the "Atlantic" or "Trilateral" ruling class;[12] some of the subordinate classes within the OECD states;[13] and the rising governing class, the "organizational bourgeoisie," in dependent third world states, a class made up of those who occupy positions at the top of both public and private hierarchies.[14]

But a historical bloc is always much more than just an alliance. "*Blocco*" in Italian can also be translated as "block" in English, and Gramsci plays on many of the meanings of that word as well. Consider just one: A historical bloc(k) is a social order that must be looked at in different ways, whose different faces must be examined the way we might examine a block of marble, a child's building block, or a Rubik's cube. Only when we have looked at all of the faces of a historical bloc(k)—its economic face, its political face, its cultural and ideological face, etc.— and have begun to understand the ways that they are internally connected one to another can we begin to understand what makes the characteristic form of its social development possible.

An alternative way to make the same point is to treat Gramsci's notion of a historical bloc(k) as an architectural metaphor per se, just like the base-superstructure metaphor that it was designed to supersede. A historical bloc(k) is like a building of a specific kind, a complex urban multiuse "block" where all different kinds of life go on, perhaps one of those massive seven or eight story blocks of shops and flats centered around a large courtyard built near the center of so many European cities in the boom years before the first world war, the years when Gramsci first arrived in Turin from the Sardinian countryside. The depth of the foundation, the base, establishes "limits of the possible"[15] for what is above. (No more than seven or eight floors can be built on unreinforced foundations of concrete and stone.) No doubt Gramsci—the "theorist of the superstructure"—would also mention that height is just as constrained by the construction of the walls. (Bricks or stone cannot take you as high as iron or steel.)

To remain functional, the whole "structure of the superstructure"—the building above ground—has to have a coherent form. Likewise, Gramsci characterizes the *polity* or, "State in the wider organic sense,"[16] as consisting of both coercive structures—"the state proper"—like the walls of a building, and enabling structures—political and social space, "civil society"—like the rooms and halls of a building and its doors and windows.

Others have found different ways to describe the social unities that Gramsci calls "historical blocs." David M. Gordon and his colleagues call the historical superstructures "social structures of accumulation."[17] Alain Lipietz and other Regulation School theorists write of the unity of an "industrial paradigm" and "macroeconomic structure" as a "regime of accumulation," a conception similar to, but somewhat broader than Gramsci's conception of the economic base.[18] The Regulation School scholars investigate regimes of accumulation along with their superstructures, which they call modes of regulation, "the totality of institutional forms and implicit norms that assure the consistency of behaviors and expectations within the framework of the regime"[19] Together, a regime of accumulation and mode of regulation constitute a historical bloc(k) within which a characteristic "mode of development" becomes possible, "founded on an industrial paradigm, stabilizing itself in a regime of accumulation, and guaranteed by a mode of regulation."[20]

Both groups of scholars have concentrated their attention on the "Northern" aspects of the historical bloc(k) in which capitalism developed from the end of the World War II through the 1970s. They emphasize the so-called Fordism of lead sectors in the OECD economies, where both profits and markets for goods are reciprocally assured by high wages and all economies of scale in manufacturing, thus establishing economies of mass-consumption and capital-intensive mass production. They highlight the role of the welfare state in helping maintain that system, as well as the role played by postwar intergovernmental economic institutions—the International Monetary Fund (IMF) as well as the regular cooperation among treasury ministries and central banks organized through the Bank for International Settlements in shielding first world states from short-term fiscal pressures that could make Keynesian policies untenable. I want to focus, instead, on the North–South links in the same historical bloc(k)—the economic as well as superstructural connections linked the first world to the dependent third world.

Perhaps most significantly, in the postwar world, the South has been a place where an industrial regime of high wages, economies of scale in manufacturing, mass-consumption, and capital-intensive mass-production has *not* been encouraged. Quite the contrary, the institutions of "international civil society" (both the formal intergovernmental institutions, such as the World Bank, and the regular patterns of cooperative "bilateral" relations bilateral aid, bilateral investment incentives, etc.) have encouraged third world economies to remain directed toward the ends identified by the classic writings on imperialism: third world economies have been encouraged to maintain significant low-wage sectors providing primary commodities used in the industrial economies of the North. At least until the mid-1970s, Northern investment in third world manufacturing did little to transform local economies fundamentally, let alone to transform the traditional relations between core and periphery. In fact, arguably, the postwar years proved John A. Hobson's prescription and prediction in *Imperialism:* In a world in which the wages of labor in the core were allowed (or forced) to remain high, the relative importance of the periphery as an outlet for Northern investment capital has declined.

Certainly the direct control of the North over the South, which Hobson argued was designed to serve that investment, has diminished. For those willing to accept *ex post facto* functionalist explanations for social institutions, the fact that the periphery may have become *increasingly* peripheral to the reproduction of core capitalism in the postwar period would be sufficient explanation for the most striking consequences of North–South relations in the postwar period: decolonization. Direct coercive political control of the South by the North (the argument might go) was no longer necessary.

The actual history of decolonization is a bit more complex. As is usually the case, both national governments and conscious change-oriented social movements appeared as central actors on the world stage. And, as is often the case, formal intergovernmental organizations were more than just settings in which these actors performed; they influenced the action itself. Three elements of the decolonization story stand out. First is the mid-century emergence of mass movements for local autonomy throughout the colonial world. As one of the most perceptive analysts of North–South relations throughout the century, C.L.R. James, always argued, even in countries where decolonization appeared to be the nonviolent transfer of authority from Europeans to a Europeanized native elite, mass movements both forced the hands of the colonial governments and, initially, provided the native elite with legitimacy. Second is the role of formal international institutions encouraging decolonization, which the United Nations inherited from the League of Nations, a role which was constantly strengthened as the percentage of newly independent states within the United Nations grew. The support that the international institutions provided to nationalist movements—an international forum in which to speak and promotion of the presumption that colonialism was a thing of the past—may seem minor, but successful nationalist leaders almost all argue that it was critical. Third, there is the role of the competition between the two new postwar superpowers, both less involved with overseas empires than the Belgians, British, Dutch, or French had been before the war, and both with their own reasons for wanting to appear the champion of self-determination.

Of course, US involvement in most third world countries continued after decolonization in a way Soviet involvement did not. For most of the postwar period the US government stood at the center of the network of institutions in international civil society — bilateral and multilateral, public and private — which provide development assistance to the governments of the South. This "development system" was an innovation of the postwar period, and an increasingly significant one. "Development" has become the most important item on the agendas of every one of the postwar global intergovernmental organizations, including agencies like the IMF, the International Telecommunications Union, the communication satellite agency (INTELSAT), and the World Intellectual Property Organization, which were originally established to deal with issues that were almost exclusively of interest to industrial countries.

We could try to "derive" the development system as a "necessary superstructure" of global capitalism in a number of ways: even "Fordist" capitalism has an expansionary logic and development regimes are therefore necessary to encourage rational private investment toward that end; or, "development" replaces colonialism at a lower cost, propping up regimes that continue the flow of necessary resources into the capitalist core; or, "development" preserves the international financial system from the impact of the inevitable fiscal crises of weak states in the periphery; or, "development" at one time discouraged third world governments from allying with the Soviet Union or China or from attempting their own experiments at autonomous development. In fact, each of these arguments has been used at one time or another by significant policymakers in the North to justify their commitment to the whole development system of designing projects, transferring funds and "experts," building roads, schools, hospitals, etc., and (occasionally) even evaluating results in terms of macroeconomic growth rates and changes in indicators of quality of life in the "developing" countries. Again, one group of key social actors was made up of the national governments of the North, governments pursuing a variety of different aims with the same means.

But the development system was not built by Northern governments alone. Southern governments and the intergovernmental development organizations themselves have played key roles. Inside governments in the south and among development professionals (whether operating within aid bureaucracies in donor countries, in international organizations, and/or in the field), the self-justifications of those involved in constructing and maintaining the development system sound a bit different. They sound populist, as A. F. Robertson concludes in his study of the entire system from donors to intergovernmental intermediaries to recipients.[21] In the South and among development professionals the justifications one hears are also often recognized as a bit contradictory by those who offer them: "Development" — a professionalized, hierarchical, top-down process, whose centers of power lie (literally) half a world away from its clients — is designed to give "the people" some of what they want: longer lives, better health, more chances for their children.

Northern and southern justifications of the development system converge if we consider it a non-coercive superstructure of the North–South bloc(k) which helps cement the alliance between the subordinate third world organizational bourgeoisie and dominant ruling class in the North. Even by strengthening the third world state and by providing "populist" benefits, "development" helps maintain the position of the most privileged groups within third world societies, groups who are more often vitally linked to the state and thus to its success than the most privileged groups in the North are.

If the development system can be considered a key non-coercive superstructure of the North–South bloc(k), encompassing some of the most significant institutions of North–South civil society, then overt and covert military intervention by the North (most frequently by the US, but also, significantly, by France) might be considered the key coercive institution of North–South "political society." Again, looking backward, it appears as if intervention "functionally" served to stop third world regimes from attempting autonomous development outside the North–South bloc, whether or not such an attempt involved choosing to ally with an alternative power center (especially the Soviet Union). But the actual logic by which that pattern emerged was, again, a bit more confusing than a retrospective rational reconstruction might suggest.

Again, both national governments and social movements were the key actors on the world stage, even though formal intergovernmental organizations provided more than just a setting. The United States and the Soviet Union (not to mention France, Britain, and China) found themselves taking opposite sides in a host of locally-emerging protracted social conflicts in the third world for a variety of reasons, ranging from a desire to demonstrate "resolve" in a nuclear world where direct military confrontation was unthinkable, to an honest desire to aid local supporters of "international socialism" or the values of the "free world." Of course, the postwar world was one in which there were international institutions designed to manage and reduce violent confrontations between sovereign states, UN peacekeeping activities, the World Court, etc. Those institutions worked to a much greater extent than many recognize, but they only worked well when the states in violent conflict were both allies of the same superpower; the international institutions helped manage the violent conflicts between the less-developed allies of the United States, e.g., between Greece and Turkey in Cyprus and between Egypt and Israel after Sadat changed superpower partners. The international institutions did not stop superpower violence against members of their own blocs. Nor did they stop the boundary wars between the blocs.

CRISES IN THE NORTH–SOUTH BLOC(K)

Gramsci's ultimate purpose in developing the concept of a historical bloc(k) was to emphasize that only within such a coherent ensemble of coercive and enabling institutions, linked to a particular base of technologies and relations of production, could the "normal" development of society occur; only in such an ensemble can the inner logic of capitalism identified by Marx unfold. Such bloc(k)s become the framework for history, a framework within which people's normal lives occur, like the Parisian apartment block George Perec uses to frame the many stories in his novel of the late-industrial age, *Life: A User's Manual.*

In the postwar North–South historical bloc(k) a kind of normal life went on in the North. Capitalist development and capital accumulation continued, especially in the separate Northern nation-states, each like a separate luxury apartment linked to others by "enabling" institutions (the GATT, IMF, OECD, and European Community) which were as significant to "normal" life as halls, stairs, elevators, dumbwaiters, and garbage-chutes are to those who live in any block of expensive flats.

Normal life continued in the servants' apartments of the third world as well. To a great extent, C. L. R. James's harsh assessment is accurate, "Colonialism is alive and will continue to be alive until another *positive doctrine* takes its place"[22] Still, decolonization meant that the servants could buy their flats. Some (Singapore, South Korea, Taiwan) were able to fix them up quite well, though Nigel Harris argues that this was only because local capitalists there had an unusually clear understanding of the few opportunities offered by the expansionary logic of Fordist capitalism and their societies were small enough that integration into the "global manufacturing system" could bring general prosperity. However, even those living in states without these advantages, those living in the humbler units of the third world, saw the material quality of their life improve until sometime in the 1970s.

The same cannot be said for the 1980s, especially in Africa and much of Latin America. When commentators on Africa call the current problems "the crisis" they have in mind a complex of social problems of the base (ecological degradation, famine) and superstructures (debt, political decay) which reflect a crisis of the North–South historical bloc(k). When a society is in crisis, when a historical bloc(k) is crumbling or partially deserted (like a house in a city under siege) or when it no longer can support the dynamic life within it (like a flat that a family has outgrown) patterns of normal life cannot return until the bloc(k) is rebuilt, reclaimed, or other structures found.

Those who argue that there has been a crisis in world capitalism for fifteen, twenty, or more years, and who focus more on the wealthy capitalist states are apt to concentrate on contradictions within the industrial regime or the fiscal crises of governments in the first world, which first appeared in the early 1970s and were made acute by the "cascading monetarism" of the early 1980s as state after state in the industrial world (except, initially, the United States) had to cut back on government expenditures in order to stem the outflow capital attracted by high US interest rates.[23] Yet, as Samir Amin argues, because the "normal" development of capitalism has not been bounded within individual nation-states or even within the whole of the "advanced" capitalist world, "any crisis of the capitalist system will be a crisis of the international division of labor and thus, especially, a North–South crisis."[24] Moreover, it will not be "merely" an economic crisis, but rather a crisis of the entire social order linking North and South.[25] The African and Latin American crises and the crisis of Fordism are one in the same.

The connections become particularly evident when we consider the concurrent crises in the institutions of international civil society that link North and South. The postwar system of intergovernmental organizations has been in a state of ongoing crisis and decay for twenty years, at least since the unilateral US decision to end the IMF's fixed exchange rate regime in 1971, a decision designed to support a national (rather than multilateral) attack on the "stagflation" that first became acute in the Nixon administration.

The consequences of that decision have been manifold. In the North, the most significant result has been the institutionalization of a floating exchange rate system that does not provide the same multilateral support for expansive government economic policies, and, hence, for the welfare state, as the old regime did. In the South, the most important consequence has been the resulting shift in the agenda of the IMF itself. No longer serving the role as protector of the fixed-exchange rate system and, hence, the macroeconomic policies of the industrialized countries with hard currencies, the IMF's dominant role has become enforcer of "sound" government policies in the third world, as lender of last resort to poorer countries with soft currencies.

While the IMF's role in North–South relations has increased since 1971 (and, especially, since the beginning of the third world debt crisis of the 1980s), the 1971 decision otherwise contributed to the spiralling decay of the North–South aspects of the postwar international organization system. Fears about the stability of the dollar contributed to OPEC's unprecedented unity in the 1970s, and, thus, to the petroleum alliance's ability to raise and maintain oil prices. OPEC's power, and its willingness to use that power to promote the third world's proposals for reforming international economic organizations, shaped the agenda of the United Nations system in the 1970s. The third world's call for a "New International Economic Order," based on fundamentally different international monetary, financial, trade, and intellectual property institutions, not only offered a new vision of North–South relations, it helped undermine the institutions of the old order simply because of opposition it engendered in the North.

Ronald Reagan came into office in 1981 the sworn enemy of the third world alliance and of the entire United Nations system. He inherited a strong weapon to use against OPEC: the high interest rates engineered by the Federal Reserve System at the end of the Carter administration, a policy designed to "squeeze" inflation out of the stagnant economy. That meant engineering a sharp recession in the US economy, which, given the defensive macroeconomic policies that other industrial states had to follow in a world of floating exchange rates, meant a worldwide recession, one significant enough to cause a great deal of energy "conservation" as Northern factories closed and production fell. At the same time the policy contributed to the third world debt crisis, and to the willingness of debt-ridden third world oil producers to break OPEC pricing and production norms.[26]

Reagan's first, surprising, targets in the United Nations system were the institutions that third world partisans had long claimed were the strongest institutions of neocolonialism, the IMF and the World Bank. Ultimately the administration relented after exhaustive interagency studies proved that those agencies, on balance, worked to force *laissez faire* policies on the third world. But Reagan's policy of non-support for other international organizations involved in North–South relations continued. From 1985 onward the United States, which normally would provide about a quarter of the UN system's finances, stopped paying much of its assessment, plunging the central organs of the United Nations (which support peacekeeping operations) as well as the Specialized Agencies (with their "development" programs) into a financial crisis at the moment that the human costs of third world debt and IMF-World Bank *laissez faire* "structural adjustment" policies were becoming the most acute.

RECONSTRUCTION AHEAD

By contributing to the demise of the third world challenge to postwar North–South relations and by privileging institutions of international civil society that encourage market discipline on third world development policies, the Reagan administration began to confront the challenge of reconstructing the North–South historical bloc(k). To construct a historical bloc(k), a social movement (a party, faction, government, etc.) must figure out how to piece together not only an alliance of social groups, but also the ideas that will motivate that alliance, the political institutions that will both dominate its opponents and help keep the bloc(k) together, and the institutions of production, distribution, and consumption which will mediate the relations of the dominant and the dominated with their physical environment — the economic institutions on which the social order will rest. Breaking the power of OPEC helped reestablish, at least temporarily, the North–South energy system on which postwar prosperity in the industrial countries relied. Transforming the system of intergovernmental organizations involved with "development" not only represented a triumph of the particularly laissez faire ideology that Reagan represented, it provided a fairly low-cost way to dominate opponents in the reemerging North–South order by transforming their interest. The policies imposed upon debtor countries diminished the capacity of members of the third world organizational bourgeoisie to rely upon positions in *public* hierarchies for their power, at the same time as the policies imposed upon debtor countries further privileged positions at the top of hierarchies in the *private* economies of the third world.

Still, the puzzle is far from being solved. In fact, it is not even clear that it is a *single* puzzle that is being solved. Intellectuals, political parties, business leaders, and governments in the North all seem to be working on at least two puzzles at a time. We may end up with three North–South systems, one centered on western Europe, one on the United States, and one on Japan, or with four, with one centered on Moscow. Or we could end up with two bloc(k)s or one. But no matter which order emerges, most signs point to a continuation of the pattern of the early 1980s. The position of the dependent third world in new bloc(k) or bloc(k)s will be subordinate, probably even more subordinate than in the postwar North–South bloc(k).

Responses to the thaw in East–West relations already point in that direction, at the same time that they suggest that the most likely outcome will be a unitary world capitalist order, still centered on the OECD, but with the dominant US, Japanese, and European centers playing slightly different roles. Eastern Europe will probably be integrated back in to this order, while China will likely remain out of it, as may India and its dependencies.

One consequence of the East–West thaw has been a strengthening of the role of United Nations in dealing with violent protracted social conflicts that spill across third world boundaries. Superficially, it may appear that we are back to the system envisioned at Yalta, with the two superpowers presiding over a system of relatively universal international conflict management. The United Nations has taken on or is planning new peacekeeping roles in Afghanistan, Angola, Indochina, and Iraq–Iran. The agency has also played key roles in ending the wars in Namibia and Nicaragua. In the last case the United Nation's role as an observer and guarantor of elections in a long-independent state was unprecedented.

However, looked at more closely, these innovations do not involve a return to the sort of cooperative policing of the world by the wartime victors envisioned in the UN Charter. It would be more accurate to argue that the UN's expanded role in conflict management is a continuation of the postwar pattern of successful multilateral intervention in conflicts between or within states that are dependencies of *one* of the dominant superpowers. Now, however, *only* one of the superpowers may be relevant. The UN's new successes have been cases where the Soviet Union or its military allies have withdrawn from conflicts, or else cases where both parties in the conflict have come to rely upon the United States. There have been no signs of an increased effectiveness of the United Nations in managing conflicts where the superpowers are, themselves, directly responsible for the violence, which, in a world where Soviet involvement in the third world is declining, may just mean that the United States and, to a lesser extent, France will be the only Northern states continuing their policies of actively policing the South. In fact, the United States may end up "specializing" in building the coercive links of the North-South bloc(k), while Japan specializes in building North–South economic links, and the European Community specializes in "Keynesian" assistance to Eastern Europe. The coercive institutions of the old North–South bloc(k) have, if anything, been strengthened by the thaw in East–West relations.

The coercive institutions also may be called on to play a more significant role in maintaining the North–South order because the cooperative institutions of the North–South bloc(k) are likely to be weakened by improving East–West relations, further than they have already been weakened by the Reagan-era attacks on the UN system. The development system can no longer be supported by the threat that third world states will join the Soviet camp. After all, most of the Warsaw Pact appears to be trying to join the Western bloc(k). Even more significantly, to the extent to which "development" really aimed at, and succeeded at, bringing other regions into the OECD world of mass production and mass consumption market economies, Eastern Europe, in all likelihood, will become the focus of that effort. West German ideas for economic union with the East already envision the largest international economic transfers, the largest "aid effort" since the Marshall Plan. Moreover, given the differing degrees to which all the governments of the industrial states have experienced fiscal crises, and given their different international debt positions, it is likely that for the foreseeable future only Germany and Japan will be in the position to be major providers of development assistance. The likely primary target of Germany's generosity is clear. Japan will also be tempted to make a special effort in Eastern Europe, as a way to obtain privileges in the European market. Alternatively, the Japanese may look to developing a Pacific sphere, focusing on the increasingly aid-needy United States. In any event, the funds for new "Marshall Plans" for Africa or Latin America, called for a decade ago by the Brandt Commission and the conveners of the Cancún summit, are unlikely to materialize.

What, then, is the basis for the hope expressed by *West Africa's* editors and evidenced by Willy Brandt's return to North–South issues as well as by the formation of the Group of 15? There has been a shift in US policy toward intergovernmental organizations in recent months, marked by a renewed (proclaimed) willingness to pay and a fundamentally new willingness to discuss *negotiating* major reforms in postwar international economic institutions. But it would be incorrect to suggest that this represents a willingness to entertain the proposals advanced in the third world program for a New International Economic Order, or even an interest in returning to the aggressive "poverty elimination" development goals of Robert McNamara's World Bank in the 1970s. It represents, instead, a recognition that the third world debt crisis, while eased,[27] is not yet over and that the "structural adjustments" urged upon third world debtors have most often failed, on their own terms, leaving states in balance of payments difficulties and searching for more funds from the IMF or other sources. Moreover, even the intellectual leaders of the Reagan revolution have come to recognize that their attack on UN-system economic institutions has undermined their ability to regulate economic relations among industrialized capitalists states, especially in the new industrial sectors which are likely to be the major engines of economic growth. The authors in a recent collection on international regulation (introduced by Jeane J. Kirkpatrick) constantly reiterate that international regulation through the UN system is probably essential; what matters is who designs it.[28] The authors want the third world's role minimized, arguing that effective negotiations suffer when too many people, with too little fundamental interest in the issues at stake are at the table. However, under those terms it would be hard to argue that a representative bloc designed like the Group of 15 should not take part, which is one of the primary incentives for forming the group at this time.

But the Group of 15 should not expect that they will get much from those negotiations. The best that can be hoped for is a negotiated end to some of the most destructive of the "structural adjustment" requirements placed on third world states. Throughout the 1980s, many Keynesians argued that policies aimed at diminishing the third world state and orienting all debtor economies toward exports would not work. Experience has proved them right and it is conceivable that Northern governments could be convinced to let the international economic institutions adopt policies of "adjustment with a human face" in order to protect the IMF and World Bank's deeper purpose, maintaining international freedom for capital. "Adjustment with a human face" simply means that debtor governments would be given greater credit, greater opportunity for surviving a debt crisis without gutting the state, in exchange for maintaining those programs that support "human resource development" health care, primary education, sanitation, etc. Some consider social programs of this kind the most important "development" policies for the least developed states, those with great poverty, great dependence, and no absolute advantages in the world trade system. But, of course, it is only in a limited number of third world states, like socialist Cape Verde, that the current governments, after a decade of "structural adjustment," have made such commitments in the first place.

If the larger states in the third world were governed by movements like Cape Verde's ruling party, the possibilities might be more dramatic. To illustrate why, let me go back for a moment to the different ways that world-system's theory and my interpretation of the postwar historical bloc(k)s treat the Soviet Union and its sphere. The world-system's theorists emphasize *the choices that were open* to the dominant social forces in the Soviet Union in this century; because of its "semiperipheral" location in the world economy (with characteristics of both the core and the periphery) governments had choices not available to those in the third world. Given the size of the Soviet economy, one reasonable choice that could be made at the end of the World War II was a choice for *autonomy*, for separation from the rest of the world economy.[29] It was a reasonable choice because the size of the Soviet economy assured that all known economies of scale could still be achieved in the new industries that state planners could envision as part of an effort to develop the forces of production. (And this remained true for about twenty years.) Other, smaller, semiperipheral states did not have that option. In most, as in South Korea or Taiwan, the governing parties chose to try to fight their way into the core. Other, larger, semiperipheral states, such as Brazil, may have had the same options as the Soviet Union, but they chose differently.

In thinking about historical bloc(k)s I emphasize the *choices that were actually made* by dominant social forces. In the case of the Soviet Union, the choice meant that the governing party had to figure out the whole puzzle of forming a historical bloc(k) in the "communist" world, piecing together not only an alliance of other social groups, but also the ideas to motivate that alliance, the political institutions to dominate its opponents, and the economic institutions on which the social order rested.

Today, other large semiperipheral states have the same options that the Soviet Union faced in 1945. Arguably, it is an option still open to Brazil. Should political developments occur rapidly in South Africa, it is just as conceivable that the Southern African economic region could reasonably entertain the option of autonomous development. Perhaps even more significantly, it is an option open to India, one peripheral state that really did break most of its bonds of dependency after decolonization and successfully manipulated the opportunities available to it through the development system. India has become the center of its own regional international system, which perhaps could even be thought of as a separate, and, at the moment, less-crisis ridden world historical bloc(k) than the North–South or Eastern bloc(k)s.[30] A similar argument could be made about China.

China's next path is difficult to guess. The internal politics of India hardly suggest that social movements advocating continued autonomy are likely to gain power in the near future. If anything, India's dominant capitalist class may be developing its own imperialist ambitions. In Southern Africa the progressive political forces in every country remain sympathetic to autonomous socialist development; in fact, Nelson Mandela seems to be the only major international leader who remembers why policies of nationalization were so fundamental to the revolutionary program not only of the Bolsheviks, but of most African and Asian liberation movements. Yet, the key compromises that may be needed to assure a transition to majority rule may include continued close involvement in the North–South economy, involvement beyond the exchange of precious commodities for capital equipment. In Brazil a government of the left sympathetic to autonomous development may be a bit more likely, but it is not probable.

Which takes us back to the image of Aristedes Pereira and the Pope in tiny Cape Verde. As the North–South bloc(k) forms again, the choices that are likely to be made may leave us with only a few small, isolated third world places as sites of deep social transformation and beacons into a truly post-colonial world.

NOTES

1. "North-South and G-15," *West Africa* no. 3780 (5–11 February 1990), p. 163.
2. "Du Bois Memorial Lectures," *West Africa*, p. 196.
3. "Pope Tours Sahel," *West Africa*, p. 199.
4. After all, foreign observers almost always credit the govermment's "pragmatic socialism" as key to Cape Verde's transformation (even if many observers, including the Pope, emphasize only the first part of the equation). On Cape Verde's history, success, and the wide support it has received in the international development community see Basil Davidson, *The Fortunate Isles: A Study in African Transformation* (Trenton, NJ: Africa World Press, 1989); Davidson, "Country Profile: Cape Verde," *The New Internationalist*, no. 203 (January 1990), p. 32; "The Right to Food," *The New Internationalist*, no. 179 (January 1988), p. 15; Craig N. Murphy, "Learning the National Interest in Africa: Focus on Cape Verde," *TransAfrica Forum*, 4 (Winter 1987), pp. 49–63.
5.. Nigel Harris, *The End of the Third World: Newly Industrializing Countries and the Decline of an Ideology* (Harmondsworth: Penguin, 1987): Michael Kidron, *Western Capitalism Since the War* (London: Weidenfeld and Nicholson, 1968).
6. Fernando Cardoso, "The Originality of a Copy: CEPAL and the Idea of Development," *CEPAL Review*, no. 2, (1977), pp. 7–40. Raul Predisch, "Five Stages in My Thinking on Development," in Gerald M. Meier and Dudley Seers, eds. *Pioneers In Development* (New York: Oxford University Press for the World Bank, 1984).
7. Immanuel Wallerstein, "Friends as Foes," *Foreign Policy*, no. 40 (Fall 1980): 119–31.
8. Christopher Chase-Dunn, ed., *Socialist States in the World System* (Beverly Hills: Sage Publications, 1982).
9. I would argue that since the 1950s China has formed a third historical bloc and that more recently India and its dependencies have formed a fourth.
10. See the final section of Enrico Augelli and Craig N. Murphy, "Gramsci and International Relations: A General Perspective with Examples from US Policy in the Reagan Era," in *Gramsci and World Politics*, Stephen Gill, ed. (New York: Columbia University Press, forthcoming).
11. This is Forgacs' short definition, not Gramsci's own words. It is, I believe, an accurate reflection of Gramsci's views. David Forgacs, *An Antonio Gramsci Reader* (New York: Shocken Books, 1989), p. 424.
12. See Kees van de Piji, *The Making of an Atlantic Ruling Class* (London: Verso, 1984).
13. The debate over which subordinate classes in which advanced capitalist countries have been part of the "Western" or North–South historical bloc and at what times has general significance, but is not central to the argument

here. See Enrico Augelli and Craig N. Murphy, *America's Quest for Supremacy and the Third World* (London: Pinter Publishers, 1988), p. 140.

14. See Irving L. Markovitz, *Power and Class in Africa* (Englewood Cliffs, NJ: Prentice Hall, 1977) and Markovitz, ed., *Studies in Power and Class in Africa* (New York: Oxford University Press, 1987).

15. Fernand Braudel's phrase corresponds to Gramsci's understanding of the economy as limiting what we can reasonably aspire for and thus "determining" things "in the last instance" (as the Althusserians would have it).

16. See the selections from Gramsci's *Prison Notebooks* in Forgacs, *An Antonio Gramsci Reader*, pp. 234–35; and Augelli and Murphy, *America's Quest for Supremacy and the Third World*, p. 130.

17. David M. Gordon, "Stages of Accumulation and Long Economic Cycles," in eds. *Processes of the World-System*, Terence K. Hopkins and Immanuel Wallerstein, eds. (Beverly Hills: Sage Publications, 1980); David M. Gordon, "The Global Economy: New Edifice, or Crumbling Foundation?" *New Left Review* 169 (March/April), pp. 24–64; David M. Gordon, Richard Edwards, and Michael Reich, *Segmented Work, Divided Workers: The Historical Transformation of Labor in the United States*, (New York: Cambridge University Press, 1982).

18. Alain Lipietz, *Mirages and Miracles: The Crises of Global Fordism*. London: Verso, 1986); Alain Lipietz, "Building an Alternative Movement in France," *Rethinking Marxism*, vol. 1, no. 3, pp. 80–99.

19. Lipietz, *Mirage and Miracles*, p. 83.

20. Lipietz, *Mirages and Miracles*.

21. A.F. Robertson, *People and the State: An Anthropology of Planned Development* (Cambridge: Cambridge University Press, 1984).

22. James, *Nkrumah and the Ghana Revolution*, p. 28.

23. See, most recently, Alain Lipietz, "The Debt Problem, European Integration, and the New Phase of World Crisis," *New Left Review* 178 (November/December 1989), pp. 37–50.

24. Samir Amin, "The Crisis: The Third World, North–South and East–West," in Emmanuel Hansen, ed., *Africa: Perspectives on Peace and Development* (London: Zed Books, Ltd. for the United Nations University, 1987), p. 28.

25. I generally agree with Gordon's assessment in "The Global Economy: New Edifice of Crumbling Foundations?" that we have not yet witnessed a significant transformation of the international division of labor and, thus, that "We are still experiencing the decay of the old order and not yet the inauguration of a new." Nonetheless, in terms of both the social relations linking North and South and those within the parts of the South something more than simply "decay" has occurred.

26. See Augelli and Murphy, *America's Quest for Supremacy*, ch. 6.

27. That is to say, eased as far as the interests of the North are concerned; the crisis is much less likely to cause chaos in the international financial markets than it once was.

28. See *United States Participation in the Multilateral Development Banks in the 1980s* (Washington: US Department of the Treasury, February 1982); and National Advisory Council on International Monetary and Financial Policies, *Special Report to the President and Congress on the Proposed Increases in the Resources of the International Monetary Fund* (Washington: US Department of the Treasury, March 1983).

29. See the contributors to Gerald K. Helleiner, ed., *Africa and the International Monetary Fund* (Washington: International Monetary Fund, 1987) especially John Loxley, "Alternative Approaches to Stabilization in Africa."
30. India and its dependencies, with nearly a quarter of the world's population, make up a social system of the same order of magnitude as the Soviet bloc, China, or the North–South system of the OECD states and the more-dependent third world. On the sources of India's decision to pursue increasing autonomy see J. Ann Tickner, *Self-Reliance versus Power Politics: The American and Indian Experience in Building Nation States* (New York: Columbia University Press, 1987).

5

Normative Considerations and International Relations Theory

In recent years, textbooks on international relations have been conspicuous for the absence of much discussion of **normative** or value considerations.[1] This is a rather strange turn of events in that the intellectual traditions underlying realism, pluralism, and globalism are a blend of normative (what *should* be the case?) and **empirical** questions (what *is* the case?). For writers as divergent as Machiavelli, Kant, Carr, Madison, or Marx it was inconceivable to discuss politics without at least some attention to the relation between facts and values. The two were thought by them to be inseparable.

In this chapter, we raise some of the issues and value considerations central to an understanding of normative international relations theory. When, if ever, is war just, and what is just conduct in war? Is the global distribution of wealth equitable, and if not, what authoritative steps should be taken to alter the status quo? On what moral bases should statesmen make foreign policy choices? It is not our intention here to delve deeply into such complex questions, an enterprise well beyond the scope of this effort. Over the centuries, many international relations theorists have grappled with value questions, and we want to alert the reader to some of the most critical of these.

Second, we also want to recognize normative international relations theory building as a legitimate enterprise worthy of more scholarly efforts than has been the case in recent years. As discussed in Chapter One, normative theory differs fundamentally from empirical theory. Propositions in normative theory that deal with what *ought* to be are not subject to the formal empirical tests of hypotheses about what *is*, which is the realm of empirical theory. This fact does not make normative theory any less important, however. Choices among competing alternatives made by policymakers are informed not just by knowledge of what *is* or could be but also by a rationale for what *ought* to be. Developing the basis for such value choices is the domain of normative theory.

Finally, value orientations are present even among empirical theorists in all three international relations images we identify. *What* is studied and *how* it is studied are preferences that vary from theorist to theorist across all three images. True, empirical theorists try to minimize the effect of individual value bias through objective testing of hypotheses, but personal values cannot be filtered out completely. We have recognized these value preferences in previous chapters, but we find it useful to identify them explicitly in this chapter as well.

MORAL CHOICE: ALTERNATIVE CRITERIA

Various criteria exist for providing guidance as to what constitutes **moral** choice in international relations. The **relativist** position — that values are not universal in character but are specific to a particular culture, situation, or set of circumstances — holds that such universal criteria cannot be devised or discerned. This relativist view is rejected by those who hold to **Kantian, utilitarian**, and **social contract** bases for moral choice. If what is *right* is so variable as potentially to mean so many different things to the relativist, then does it really mean anything?

Relativist thinking is, therefore, a rejection of the universalist tradition in Western thought that has its roots in ancient Stoic and Roman writings. For example, the Roman orator Cicero (106 – 43 B.C.) states that "true law is right reason in agreement with nature; it is of universal application, unchanging and everlasting." He asserts: "Justice is one; it binds all society, and is based on one law." Indeed, he observes: "Justice does not exist at all if it does not exist in Nature."[2]

This universalism was the basis for the idea of a law common to the nations of the Roman empire. That values transcend a single community or state, thus having truly global reach *and* that they are revealed in scripture or can be discovered as part of natural law by use of right reason would be central to the thought of Augustine, Aquinas, and other religious writers of the Middle Ages. As discussed in Chapter Two, Grotius and others would provide a secular basis for international law — whether based on general principles, customary international practice, the writings of jurists, or treaties or conventions voluntarily undertaken by states. The important point, however, is that values exist that are applicable to all leaders and their states.

Immanuel Kant (1724 – 1804), whose work has already been mentioned in Chapter Three, is best known for his writings on ethics and reason, but he also addressed war and peace in international society. According to Kant, the individual has free will to choose the correct moral course, clearly a **voluntarist** position. Individual behavior is not predetermined, but the individual is obligated, nevertheless, to follow the moral law that is discoverable through the proper exercise of reason. What this means is that the individual is to treat other human beings as ends worthy in themselves, not just as means. Moreover, the correct prescription for moral conduct is knowable by the individual and amounts to those precepts that have universally binding character.[3]

It is this universal dimension in Kantian ethics that is also the basis for his thinking on international relations. The Kantian ideal was a cosmopolitan international society of individuals, states, or other actors following ethical principles and aiming toward perfection. In other words, "right reason" is to be used to discern obligations stemming from a universal law that transcends the laws made by individual states. This was to be the path toward "perpetual peace" — a world free of war. A federation of peaceful states could (but would not necessarily) come to be established as a response to the very real security needs of states.

By contrast to Kantian ethics, the writings of Jeremy Bentham (1748–1832), John Stuart Mill (1806–1873), and others focus on attaining the greatest good for the greatest number as the principal criterion of utilitarian thought. A "society is rightly ordered," according to utilitarians, if "its major institutions are arranged so as to achieve the greatest net balance of satisfaction."[4] In principle, utilitarian and Kantian criteria may provide a philosophical basis for international law because the application of these criteria transcends the boundaries of any given state or society. In practice, however, given the present division of the world into separate, sovereign states with very different perspectives on global issues, it is not clear that either Kantian or utilitarian ethics *can*, as a practical matter, be the basis for constructing some radically new and just world order.

Yet another approach to finding a guide to right behavior is that of the social contract: that individuals may voluntarily agree to bind or obligate themselves to some set of principles. In Rousseau's stag hunt discussed in Chapter Two, the hunters in a state of nature can be understood as maximizing individual, short-term self-interest by going for the hare. In a Hobbesian world of no sovereign authority to compel collaboration or to force the honoring of contracts, no other outcome can be expected. On the other hand, by making assumptions different from Hobbes about human beings in a hypothetical state of nature, there is at least the possibility that the hunters may agree to upgrade their common interest by collaborating to hunt the stag. Such agreement is a social contract in its most primitive form. Binding obligations are made as a voluntary, positive act.

Building on this approach as a means to finding justice, for example, John Rawls asks what would be considered fair if individuals were in a state of nature and none knew in advance what one's place in society, class position, or social status would be. Behind this common "veil of ignorance" about outcomes, what principles of **distributive justice** would these hypothetically free agents choose?

One principle taken from Rawls's analysis is that "all social values — liberty and opportunity, income and wealth, and the bases of self-respect — are to be distributed equally unless an unequal distribution of any, or all, of these values is to everyone's advantage."[5] Beyond that, socioeconomic inequality is admissible only if it benefits everyone in society and if there is an equal opportunity for everyone to acquire those positions associated with unequal rewards. Whether one extends such propositions as the basis for global justice for individuals or for states as if they were individuals is not altogether clear. Rawls himself makes no such claim. Indeed, he formulates a "conception of justice for the basic structure of society" and observes that "the conditions for the law of nations may require different principles arrived at in a somewhat different way."[6] Nevertheless, Rawls's notion of justice could conceivably provide the philosophical basis for the demands of poor Third World countries for a new international economic order designed to reduce the gap between **North** and **South**.

If social contract theory cannot be applied to states as if they were persons, it cannot be a source of moral or legal obligations among states. If one allows it, however, to be applied to states (as if they were individual persons) social contract becomes a basis for a **positivist** interpretation of international law. Among positivists, international law and the obligation to follow other international rules or norms stem not from natural law or religious notions but from affirmative actions taken by states. Kantian, utilitarian, or other principles may be part of the calculus of deciding which rules are to be made binding, but it is the voluntary contract, or choice, made by states in the form of a treaty, convention, or customary practice (so routine in performance as to amount to an implicit contract) that creates the obligation. That there is no higher authority to enforce obligations undertaken by states makes them no less binding in principle.

Values, therefore, are not new to the study of international relations. They may be addressed in terms of "right reason" to discern obligations stemming from some natural law. Alternatively, they may conform more closely to a positivist approach to constructing international law—that treaties, for example, are binding (*pacta sunt servanda*) and that such obligations *ought* to be kept. The Kantian perspective in particular contrasts sharply with the views of Machiavelli and Hobbes described in Chapter Two. Although values and value choices certainly are present in classic realism, power and the balance of power have clearly been the more important considerations in this tradition. It is, however, incorrect to view power and values as if they were mutually exclusive approaches to international politics. As E. H. Carr noted:

> The utopian who dreams that it is possible to eliminate self-assertion from politics and to base a political system on morality alone is just as wide of the mark as the realist who believes that altruism is an illusion and that all political action is self-seeking.[7]

In short, international politics involves a blend of values and power, utopianism and realism. Such a perspective can be found in virtually all the intellectual precursors discussed in this book. There is disagreement, however, as to the relative importance of values and power, and which values should be pursued.[8]

THE PROBLEM OF JUSTICE AND WAR

One fairly well developed area that stands as an exception to our general observation of the paucity of normative international relations theory is that which deals with the morality of war itself (*jus ad bellum*) and the ethical constraints within any given war (*jus in bello*). Scholars have pondered the subject, building on a tradition in Western thought extending to the writings of St. Augustine (354–430 A.D.) and before. Contrary to the absolute pacifism of early Christians, Augustine drew from the work of Cicero and addressed war as something that was to be avoided but that was sometimes necessary: "It is the wrong-doing of the opposing party which compels the wise man to wage wars."[9] The corpus of just war theory grew with additions made by Aquinas, Suarez, Vitoria, and other political philosophers of the medieval period. That we can develop a theory of just war through the exercise of right reason and right conduct are philosophical assumptions underlying normative theory on armed conflict.

Perhaps not surprisingly, given their preoccupation with national security issues, much contemporary thinking on just war has occurred primarily among realists. Not all realists would accept the Machiavellian characterization of war as something useful for acquiring or maintaining rule and that, if postponed, might work only to the advantage of the enemy. A Machiavellian principle underscored by Clausewitz is that war is decidedly not a legitimate end in itself but is merely a means used to achieve essentially political purposes. That war should not be waged without "legitimate" purpose — that it should at least be subordinate to the political objective or serve some national interest — can be understood as a limited but nevertheless moral statement in itself.

Defense against provoked aggression is generally conceded (except by absolute pacifists) to be a legitimate political objective justifying war. Nevertheless, in just-war thinking, war is a last resort to be undertaken only if there appears to be some chance of success. The death and destruction wrought by war are to be minimized, consistent with achieving legitimate military purposes. Indeed, there can be no positive moral content in war unless legitimate political objectives and military purposes are served. Following conventional military logic, the purpose in any war is to destroy or substantially weaken an enemy's war-making capability. Military necessity, so defined, however, does not justify the use of means disproportionate to the ends sought or the use of weapons that are indiscriminate or that cause needless human suffering. Moreover, the lives of noncombatants are to be spared.[10]

Realists of Grotian persuasion identify rules or laws that constrain states, statesmen, and soldiers in the exercise of their war powers. Beginning with the Hague Conventions in the late nineteenth and early twentieth centuries, a large body of treaties and conventions based largely on earlier just-war thinking has come into force, providing the basis for the contemporary law of war. There are difficulties, however, beyond the usual problem of no international enforcement authority and the problems of defining aggression and dealing with insurgencies, in which the legitimacy of the parties is in question. Quite apart from such concerns, however, the focus on limits in just-war theory and international law are seen by some theorists to be impractical in an age dominated by weapons of mass destruction. Moreover, some theorists question whether just war theory can be used to legitimate deterrence doctrines that argue that in order to maintain peace one must threaten devastation on a global scale.[11]

ALTERNATIVE IMAGES AND FOREIGN POLICY CHOICE

The relative emphasis placed on *order, justice, freedom, and change* — values that are part of foreign policymaking and that have a direct bearing on international politics — varies widely among realists, pluralists, and globalists. Realist concern with power and the balance of power is closely related to value commitments of statesmen who see order as essential to national security. If they are committed further to the avoidance of war, they may see their task as one of managing conflict and seeking to maximize accomplishment of state objectives, however constrained by states comprising the balance. Following Machiavelli, the realist sees national security or the national interest — at a minimum, survival in an anarchic world — as the *raison d'état* justifying state policy.

Justice and freedom may also be valued by realists, particularly those of Grotian persuasion, but even they must first confront the realities of power among states. Some states rise in power relative to others, and other states decline. Power and the balance of power persist, nevertheless. Changes in international politics occur within the international system or among states, but the anarchic nature of the international system (or of international politics) remains as a constant condition. Fundamental change of the international system that would alter the anarchy of sovereign states remains a possibility, but to most realists this seems unlikely to occur any time soon. Moreover, consistent with liberal thought that, as discussed in Chapter Three, has also had major impact on the pluralist school, there is a preference among many realists for a world order in which states are "free" — that is, not constrained by any superior authority. There is, then, a conservative value bias among realists that leads most of them to view schemes for new world orders as so much wishful thinking, products of utopian thought and divorced from reality.

To some extent, the value bias among pluralists is also conservative, if not to the same degree. To pluralists, change tends to be evolutionary and incremental. If change is to be willed, then *reformist*, not *revolutionary*, measures are the appropriate ones. Pluralist theories, given the fragmentation of states and proliferation of actors that are their starting point, focus on the formation of coalitions and countercoalitions, whether within a state or across national borders. This is hardly the environment for radical changes that would require greater societal unity or at least a strong and unitary leadership. Faction against faction, governmental department against governmental department — the Madisonian formula underlying the American Constitution — is not the means to sweeping change. There are simply too many obstacles (or potential obstacles in the form of opposing groups or factions) to make change easy to come by.

Although for different theoretical reasons and to a different degree, pluralists therefore share with realists a conservative bias and a predisposition toward order as a desired value. Many pluralists, however, place greater emphasis on democratic notions of *freedom* and *justice* for individuals, groups, and societies than they do on order within and among states, although all three are desired values. Richard Falk, for example, identifies four values to be maximized as part of his World Order Models Project: "minimization of collective violence; maximization of economic well-being; maximization of social and political justice; and maximization of ecological quality."[12] To minimize collective violence, order remains important to Falk, but his focus quickly shifts to social and welfare issues that need to be addressed as part of the world order. The pluralism in Falk's approach is evident in his characterization of it as "a transnational social movement dedicated to global reform."[13]

Justice, especially *distributive* justice, is a central concern not only to a number of pluralists but also to many globalists. Rawls presents a non-Marxist formulation that supports the normative preferences of both pluralists like Falk and those globalists who focus on inequalities in the distribution of wealth between the industrial countries of the North and the less-developed countries of the South. Globalists of Marxist persuasion do not need Rawls, of course, given their own long-standing moral concern with exploitative class relations and associated prescriptions for overturning what they see as the existing, unjust world order.

To many globalists, reformism and incremental change are merely prescriptions for maintaining the status quo. If justice is to be served, what may be needed is revolutionary change that sweeps out an unjust world order and replaces it with one that allows for an equitable distribution of wealth and resources. Whether understood as exploitation of peasants and workers by an international **bourgeoisie** or as domination by highly industrial core states and societies over poor, industrially underdeveloped peripheral states, the answer is always the same: justice requires change. Order, peace, and individual freedom will only be established after fundamental (or revolutionary) change of the existing order has been effected.

RATIONALITY AND FOREIGN POLICY CHOICE

Foreign policy choice is the domain in which values apply directly. On the basis of some set of criteria, decision makers choose authoritatively among competing alternatives. The rational model, often a critical element in realist thinking, amounts to policymakers' ordering of alternatives, making decisions, and taking actions to achieve the most *efficient* outcome in terms of ends sought. This process is not value free. First, determining the objective or ends to be sought obviously involves value choices.[14] Second, the idea that the means chosen to achieve these goals should be the most efficient, the best, or even just "good enough" is itself a value underlying the decision-making calculus. Finally, even if statesmen can reach a consensus on what general values should be pursued internationally, there may be honest disagreement as to how these values are to be defined and implemented. A good example of this problem involves human rights.

Notwithstanding a Universal Declaration of Human Rights in 1948 and a number of human rights conventions since then, it often has been difficult to forge a consensus among governments on which criteria should apply in approaching questions of human rights: which rights are to be protected, the relative importance or weight of different values when they conflict, and whose rights — individuals, groups, classes, states — take precedence. As Ernst Haas comments: "Rights come in various hues and stripes."[15] Indeed, the Jeffersonian tradition in American politics predisposes U.S. decisionmakers to emphasize political and civil rights of individuals. As a consequence, economic, social, and cultural rights of groups and classes that receive greater emphasis in many other countries tend to be downgraded or ignored by makers of American foreign policy. Rights claimed by other states to be due them as *sovereign* entities also receive less American emphasis when prerogatives exercised by them are seen as infringing on individual rights.[16]

In sum, contrary to what one might first presume, the rational model of foreign policy decisionmaking is by no means a value-free apoproach, particularly given the wide range of values pursued by statesmen and different views as to how a particular value should be defined and implemented. As has been discussed in Chapters One and Three, many pluralists challenge whether foreign policy decision making can ever conform to a rational model when the actors involved are various organizations and small groups of individuals and when decisions are typically the outcome of bargaining, compromise, "end-running," or related tactics. Each separate actor may act rationally to achieve its own goals and values, but this is not the same thing as assuming that statesmen act rationally to achieve the goals or interests of the entire state and society. Similarly, some globalists may question the rationality of a decision-making or foreign policy process that, from their point of view, is dominated by narrow class interests. Whatever may be the rationality of individuals, institutions, or classes in maximizing or serving their own values or interests, the outcome for the whole may be suboptimal or less than the best.

VALUES, CHOICES, AND THEORY

Normative theory is relevant to each of the images and associated empirical theories we discuss in this book to the extent that one finds allowance for the exercise of human will within them. How much can statesmen affect the course of events? If those statesmen are driven internally, consistent with some psychological theories, or if they are severely constrained by their external environment, then normative theory plays a reduced, if any, role in their decision making. On the other hand, if human beings do have some degree of control over their affairs, including international relations, and if empirical theories take this effect of the will into account and exclude determinist "inevitabilities," then why has the normative part been as neglected in international relations theory as it has been in recent years?

A central argument made in this book is that the image and set of assumptions one holds concerning international relations do affect interpretations — the sense one makes of facts and the causal explanations or predictions one offers. Realists evaluate what they see in a manner that is different from those persons holding what we have labeled pluralist and globalist images of international relations. Nor are these three images necessarily the last word. Other competing images may emerge and in time supersede the three discussed in this volume.

Although it is important to come to an understanding of biases or perspectives associated with any particular image of international relations, we are by no means making the argument that knowledge of international relations is a function only of prior assumptions, preferences, or values. Reality will not so easily be subordinated to myth, however deeply held or sacred these myths may seem. When what we see as facts contradicts the image we hold, then it is the image that should be altered or even overturned to accommodate new information.[17] Our knowledge of international relations is imperfect and various biases color our vision, but facts have a way of breaking down our preconceptions when these preconceptions are fallacious. Scientific skepticism about claims to truth forces testing of various propositions or hypotheses with historical or other empirical data. Whether in the natural or social realms, scientific progress that enhances our knowledge of the world is painfully slow, but it is persistent.

NOTES

1. One can draw a distinction between normative and value considerations, perhaps seeing values as just one part of normative theory. Indeed, one can see that some normative considerations are nonmoral ones, as when an artist uses the terms *ought* and *right* in an esthetic context that does not have the moral content usually associated with these words. For our purposes, however, we use the terms *normative, moral,* and *value* interchangeably.
2. See, for example, Cicero, "'The Republic' and 'The Laws'" in William Ebenstein, *Great Political Thinkers*, 4th ed. (New York: Holt, Rinehart and Winston, 1969), pp. 136–38.
3. According to Kant, one should exercise free will and act according to the "categorical imperative" whereby one acts "according to the maxim which you can at the same time will to be a universal law." Moreover, one should "treat humanity, in your own person, and in the person of everyone else as an end as well as a means, never merely as a means." The literature on Kant is vast, and no attempt is made to summarize it here. We are particularly drawn, however, to the late Hannah Arendt's *Lectures on Kant's Political Philosophy* (Chicago: University of Chicago Press, 1982). There are numerous translations of what is perhaps Kant's most important contribution to the international relations literature, his *Perpetual Peace.*
4. See John Rawls, *A Theory of Justice* (Cambridge, MA: Harvard University Press, 1971), p. 22.
5. Ibid., p. 62.
6. Ibid., p. 8.
7. E. H. Carr, *The Twenty Years' Crisis, 1919–1939* (New York: Harper & Row, 1964), p. 97.
8. Part of an effort to revive and develop normative international relations theory is a relatively recent study by Charles R. Beitz. See his *Political Theory and International Relations* (Princeton, NJ: Princeton University Press, 1979).
9. See, for example, St. Augustine, "The City of God" in Ebenstein, *Great Political Thinkers*, pp. 181–84.
10. Noncombatancy, particularly if "innocents" are involved, may be construed as conveying an absolute immunity. As a practical matter, however, attacks in war on what are understood to be legitimate military targets are usually accompanied by some collateral death and destruction. Following the logic of just war, however, such effects should always be minimized.
11. See, for example, Louis René Beres, *Mimicking Sisyphus: America's Countervailing Nuclear Strategy* (Lexington, MA: Lexington Books, 1983).
12. See Richard A. Falk, *A Study of Future Worlds* (New York: Free Press, 1975), pp. 11–30.

13. Richard A. Falk, *The End of World Order: Essays on Normative International Relations* (New York: Holmes and Meier, 1983), p. 53.

14. For an excellent summary of theories of rational choice, see Anthony Heath, *Rational Choice and Social Exchange: A Critique of Exchange Theory* (London: Cambridge University Press, 1976). See also Mancur Olson, *The Logic of Collective Action: Public Goods and the Theory of Groups* (Cambridge, MA: Harvard University Press, 1971), and William Riker, *The Theory of Political Coalitions* (New Haven, CT: Yale University Press, 1962).

15. See Ernst B. Haas, *Global Evangelism Rides Again: How to Protect Human Rights Without Really Trying* (Berkeley, CA: Institute of International Studies, 1978), pp. 1–23.

16. Thus, sovereign state jurisdiction exercised by the USSR over its citizens clashed with what was claimed by the U.S. government to be a fundamental human right of those Jews wishing to emigrate to the West.

17. Thomas Kuhn, for example, did not argue that one paradigm was as good as another. To the contrary, it was when anomalies accumulated to the point at which the empirical validity of a perspective was undermined that an alternative paradigm, one better able to account for such anomalies, would emerge. See Kuhn's *The Structure of Scientific Revolutions,* 2d ed. (Chicago: University of Chicago Press, 1970).

SUGGESTED READINGS

Newly added to this edition. Suggested readings from earlier works follow this more recent list.

Bok, Sissela. *A Strategy for Peace: Human Values and the Threat of War.* New York: Pantheon, 1989.

Booth, Ken. *Law, Force and Diplomacy at Sea.* London: Allen & Unwin, 1985.

Booth, William James. *Interpreting the World: Kant's Philosophy of History and Politics.* Toronto: University of Toronto Press, 1986.

Boyle, Francis A. *World Politics and International Law.* Durham, NC: Duke University Press, 1985.

Brilmayer, Lea. *Justifying International Acts.* Ithaca, NY: Cornell University Press, 1989.

Coate, Roger A. and Jerel A. Rosati, eds. *The Power of Human Needs in World Society.* Boulder, CO: Lynn Rienner, 1988.

Donnelly, Jack. *Universal Human Rights in Theory and Practice.* Ithaca, NY: Cornell University Press, 1989.

Fain, Haskell. *Normative Politics and the Community of Nations.* Philadelphia: Temple University Press, 1987.

Falk, Richard. *The Promise of World Order.* Philadelphia: Temple University Press, 1987.

―――. *Reviving the World Court.* Charlottesville: University Press of Virginia, 1986.

Finnis, John, Joseph M. Boyle, Jr., and Germain Grisez. *Nuclear Deterrence, Morality, and Realism.* New York: Oxford University Press, 1987.

Fisher, David. *Morality and the Bomb: An Ethical Assessment of Nuclear Deterrence.* New York: St. Martin's Press, 1985.

Frost, Mervyn. *Towards a Normative Theory of International Relations.* Cambridge, England: Cambridge University Press, 1986.

Green, L. C. *Essays on the Modern Law of War.* New York: Transnational Publishers, 1985.

Henkin, Louis *et al., Right v. Might: International Law and the Use of Force.* New York: Council on Foreign Relations, 1989.

Hoffmann, Stanley. *The Political Ethics of International Relations.* New York: Carnegie Council on Ethics and International Affairs, 1988.

Holmes, Robert L. *On War and Morality.* Princeton, NJ: Princeton University Press, 1989.

Hughes, Barry B. *World Futures: A Critical Analysis of Alternatives.* Baltimore: The Johns Hopkins University Press, 1985.

Jackson, Robert H. *Quasi-States: Sovereignty, International Relations and the Third World.* New York: Cambridge University Press, 1991.

Kavka, Gregory S. *Moral Paradoxes of Nuclear Deterrence.* New York: Cambridge University Press, 1987.

Kegley, Charles W. "Neo-Idealism: A Practical Matter." *Ethics and International Affairs* 2 (1988): 173–97.

Kegley, Charles W., Jr. and Gregory A. Raymond. *When Trust Breaks Down: Alliance Norms and World Politics.* Columbia: University of South Carolina Press, 1990.

Kim, Samuel S. *The Quest for a Just World Order.* Boulder, CO: Westview Press, 1984.

Kratochwil, Friedrich V. *Rules, Norms, and Decisions: On the Conditions of Practical and Legal Reasoning in International Relations and Domestic Affairs.* Cambridge, England: Cambridge University Press, 1989.

Kreml, William P. and Charles W. Kegley Jr. "Must the Quest be Elusive? Restoring Ethics to Theory Building in International Relations." *Alternatives* 15 (1990): 155–75.

McGovern, Arthur F. *Liberation Theology and Its Critics: Toward an Assessment.* Maryknoll, N.Y.: Orbis, 1989.

Myers, Robert J., ed. *Ethics and International Affairs.* New York: Carnegie Council on Ethics and International Affairs, 1987.

Nadelman, Ethan A. "Global Prohibition Regimes: The Evolution of Norms in International Society." *International Organization* 44,4 (Autumn 1990): 479–526.

Novak, Michael, ed. *Liberation Theology and the Liberal Society.* Washington, DC: American Enterprise Institute, 1987.

Nye, Joseph S., Jr. *Nuclear Ethics.* New York: Free Press, 1986.

O'Brien, William V. and John Langan. *The Nuclear Dilemma and the Just War Tradition.* Lexington, MA: D.C. Heath, 1986.

Onuf, Nicholas Greenwood. *World of Our Making: Rules and Rule in Social Theory and International Relations.* Columbia: University of South Carolina Press, 1989.

Osgood, Robert E. *The Nuclear Dilemma in American Strategic Thought.* Boulder, CO: Westview Press, 1988.

Planas, Ricardo. *Liberation Theology: The Political Expression of Religion.* Kansas City: Sheed & Ward, 1986.

Pottenger, John R. *The Political Theory of Liberation Theology: Toward a Reconvergence of Social Values and Social Science.* Albany: State University of New York Press, 1989.

Russell, Greg. *Hans J. Morgenthau and the Ethics of American Statecraft.* Baton Rouge: Louisiana State University Press, 1990.

Sigmund, Paul E. *Liberation Theology at the Crossroads: Democracy or Revolution?* New York: Oxford University Press, 1990.

Smoke, Richard and Willis Harman. *Paths to Peace: Exploring the Feasibility of Sustainable Peace.* Boulder, CO: Westview Press, 1987.

Stone, Julius. *Visions of World Order: Between State Power and Human Justice*. Baltimore: The Johns Hopkins University Press, 1984.

Suganami, Hidemi. *The Domestic Analogy and World Order Proposals*. New York: Cambridge University Press, 1989.

Thompson, Kenneth W., ed. *Ethics and International Relations*. New Brunswick, NJ: Transaction Books, 1985.

Turner, Stephen P. and Regis A. Factor. *Max Weber and the Dispute over Reason and Value: A Study in Philosophy, Ethics, and Politics*. London: Routledge & Kegan Paul, 1984.

Walden, George. *The Shoeblack and the Sovereign: Reflections on Ethics and Foreign Policy*. New York: St. Martin's, 1988.

Warren, Mark. "Max Weber's Liberalism for a Nietzchean World." *American Political Science Review* 82,1 (March 1988): 31–50.

Waltz, Kenneth N. "Kant, Liberalism, and War." *American Political Science Review* LVI (June 1962): 331–40.

Williams, Howard. *Kant's Political Philosophy*. Oxford, England: Oxford University Press, 1983.

Wooley, Wesley T. *Alternative to Anarchy*. Bloomington University Press, 1988.

SUGGESTED READINGS FROM THE FIRST EDITION

Ajami, Fouad. "The Global Logic of the Neoconservatives." *World Politics* 30, 3 (April 1978): 450–468. A review of Tucker, *The Inequality of Nations*.

Arendt, Hannah. *Lectures on Kant's Political Philosophy*. Edited by Ronald Beiner. Chicago: University of Chicago Press, 1982.

———. *On Violence*. New York: Harcourt, Brace and World, 1970.

Aron, Raymond. *Peace and War: A Theory of International Relations*. Translated by Richard Howard and Annette Baker Fox. New York: Doubleday, 1966 and Praeger Publishers, 1968. See especially Chapters 20 and 21.

Aron, Raymond, and associates. *Scientists in Search of Their Conscience*. Edited by Anthony R. Michaelis and Hugh Harvey. Berlin and New York: Springer-Verlag, 1973.

Ashley, Richard K. "Political Realism and Human Interests." *International Studies Quarterly* 25,2 (June 1981): 204–36.

Beitz, Charles R. "Bounded Morality: Justice and the State in World Poltics." *International Organization* 33,3 (Summer 1979): 405–24. A review essay on Walzer, *Just and Unjust Wars* and Brown and Shue, *Food Policy*.

———. "Economic Rights and Distributive Justice in Developing Societies." *World Politics* 33,3 (1981): 321–46.

———. "Justice and International Relations." *Philosophy and Public Affairs* 4, 4 (Summer 1975).

———. *Political Theory and International Relations*. Princeton, NJ: Princeton University Press, 1979.

Bindschedler-Robert, Denise. *A Reconsideration of the Law of Armed Conflicts*. New York: Carnegie Endowment for International Peace, 1971.

Bondurant, Joan V. *Conquest of Violence: The Gandhian Philosophy of Conduct*. Berkeley: University of California Press, 1971.

Brierly, J. L. *The Law of Nations: An Introduction to the International Law of Peace*. 6th ed. Edited by Sir Humphrey Waldock. New York and Oxford: Oxford University Press, 1963.

Brown, Peter G. and Henry Shue, eds. *Food Policy: The Responsibility of the United States in the Life and Death Choices.* New York: Free Press, 1977.

Bull, Hedley. "Recapturing the Just War for Political Theory." *World Politics* 31, 4 (July 1979): 588–99. A review of Walzer, *Just and Unjust Wars.*

Burton, John W. *Dear Survivors.* London: Frances Pinter; Boulder, CO: Westview Press, 1982.

———. *Deviance, Terrorism and War.* New York: St. Martin's Press, 1979.

Carr, E. H. *The Twenty Years' Crisis, 1919–1939.* New York: Harper & Row, 1964.

Cohen, Raymond. *International Politics: The Rules of the Game.* New York: Longman, 1981.

Deutsch, Karl W., and Stanley Hoffmann, eds. *The Relevance of International Law.* Cambridge, MA: Schankman, 1968.

Donnelly, Jack. "Human Rights and Foreign Policy." *World Politics* 34, 4 (July 1982): 574–95.

Falk, Richard A. *A Study of Future Worlds.* New York: Free Press, 1975.

———. *The End of World Order: Essays on Normative International Relations.* New York: Holmes and Meier, 1983.

———. *This Endangered Planet: Prospects and Proposals for Human Survival.* New York: Random House, 1971.

———. "The World Order Models Project and Its Critics." *International Organization* 32,2 (Spring 1978): 531–45.

Farer, Tom J. "The Greening of the Globe: A Preliminary Appraisal of the World Order Models Project (WOMP)." *International Organization* 31, 1 (Winter 1977): 129–47.

Friedrich, Carl Joachim. *Inevitable Peace.* Cambridge, MA: Harvard University Press, 1948.

Gallie, W. B. *Philosophers of Peace and War: Kant, Clausewitz, Marx, Engels, and Tolstoy.* Cambridge, England: Cambridge University Press, 1978.

Haas, Ernst B. *Global Evangelism Rides Again: How to Protect Human Rights Without Really Trying.* Berkeley: University of California Institute of International Studies, 1978.

———. *Human Rights and International Action: The Case of Freedom of Association.* Stanford, CA: Stanford University Press, 1970.

Herz, John H. *The Nation-State and the Crisis of World Politics.* New York: David McKay, 1976.

———. "Political Realism Revisited." *International Studies Quarterly* 25, 2 (June 1981): 182–97.

Hoffmann, Stanley, *Duties Beyond Borders: On the Limits and Possibilities of Ethical International Politics.* Syracuse, NY: Syracuse University Press, 1981.

Jacobson, Harold K. "The Global System and the Realization of Human Dignity and Justice." *International Studies Quarterly.* 26, 3 (September 1982): 315–32.

Johansen, Robert C. "Human Rights in the 1980s: Revolutionary Growth or Unanticipated Erosion." *World Politics* 35, 2 (January 1983): 286–314. A review essay.

Johnson, James Turner. *Can Modern War Be Just?* New Haven, CT: Yale University Press, 1984.

———. *Just War Tradition and the Restraint of War: A Moral and Historical Inquiry.* Princeton, NJ: Princeton University Press, 1981.

Jones, Christopher D. "Just Wars and Limited Wars: Restraints on the Use of the Soviet Armed Forces," *World Politics* 28, 1 (October 1975): 44–68.

Kaplan, Morton A., ed. *Strategic Thinking and Its Moral Implications.* Chicago: University of Chicago Press, 1973.

Kennan, George F. "Morality and Foreign Policy." *Foreign Affairs* 64, 2 (Winter 1985– 1986): 205–18.

Lefever, Ernest S. *Ethics and World Politics.* Baltimore: Johns Hopkins University Press, 1972.

Mendlovitz, Saul, ed. *On the Creation of a Just World Order,* New York: Free Press, 1975.

Mill, John Stuart. *Utilitarianism.* New York: E. P. Dutton, 1951. Originally published in 1861.

Niebuhr, Reinhold. *Christian Realism and Political Problems.* New York: Scribners, 1953.

O'Brien, William V. *The Conduct of Just and Limited War.* New York: Praeger, 1981.

Orwin, Clifford. "The Just and the Advantageous in Thucydides." *The American Political Science Review* 78, 2 (June 1984): 485–94.

Osgood, Robert E. *Ideals and Self-interest in American Foreign Relations.* Chicago: University of Chicago Press, 1953.

Osgood, Robert E., and Robert W. Tucker. *Force, Order, and Justice.* Baltimore: Johns Hopkins University Press, 1967.

Pettmann, Ralph. *Moral Claims in World Affairs.* New York: St. Martin's Press, 1979.

Ramsey, Paul. *The Just War: Force and Political Responsibility.* New York: University Press of America, 1968, 1983.

Rapoport, Anatol. *Strategy and Conscience.* New York: Schocken Books, 1964, 1969.

Rawls, John. *A Theory of Justice.* Cambridge, MA: Harvard University Press, 1971.

Reilly, Robert R., James V. Schall and associates. *Justice and War in the Nuclear Age.* New York: University Press of America, 1983.

Rummel, R. J. *Understanding Conflict and War:* Vol. V, *The Just Peace.* Beverly Hills, CA: Sage Publications, 1981.

Sandel, Michael J. *Liberalism and the Limits of Justice.* Cambridge: Cambridge University Press, 1982.

Singer, J. David. "The Responsibilities of Competence in the Global Village." *International Studies Quarterly* 29, 3 (September 1985): 245–62.

Steiner, Miriam. "Human Nature and Truth as World Order Issues." *International Organization* 34, 3 (Summer 1980): 335–53.

Stone, Julius. "Approaches to the Notion of International Justice." In *The Future of the International Legal Order,* eds. Richard A. Falk and Cyril E. Black. Vol. I. Princeton, NJ: Princeton University Press, 1969.

Tucker, Robert W. *The Inequality of Nations.* New York: Basic Books, 1976.

Wakin, Malham M., ed. *War, Morality, and the Military Profession.* Boulder, CO: Westview Press, 1979.

Walzer, Michael. *Just and Unjust Wars: A Moral Argument with Historical Illustrations.* New York: Basic Books, 1977.

Wasserstrom, Richard A. *War and Morality.* Belmont, CA: Wadsworth, 1970.

Wolfers, Arnold. "Statesmanship and Moral Choice." *World Politics* (1949): 175–95.

Young, Oran R. "Anarchy and Social Choice: Reflections on the International Polity." *World Politics* 30, 2 (January 1978), 241–63.

War, Peace, and the Law of Nations

Hugo Grotius

The "father of international law," focusing on the problem of war and peace, develops the idea of law among nations. The Grotian view of international relations is one of states constrained by mutually agreed-upon rules or law to govern their interactions with one another in both war and peace. That international relations ought to be governed by law is a classic statement in normative political theory.

The municipal law of Rome and of other states has been treated by many, who have undertaken to elucidate it by means of commentaries or to reduce it to a convenient digest. That body of law, however, which is concerned with the mutual relations among states or rulers of states, whether derived from nature, or established by divine ordinances, or having its origin in custom and tacit agreement, few have touched upon. Up to the present time no one has treated it in a comprehensive and systematic manner; yet the welfare of mankind demands that this task be accomplished.

Cicero justly characterized as of surpassing worth a knowledge of treaties of alliance, conventions, and understandings of peoples, kings and foreign nations — a knowledge, in short, of the whole law of war and peace. And to this knowledge Euripides gives the preference over an understanding of things divine and human, for he represents Theoclymenus as being thus addressed:

> For you, who know the fate of men and gods,
> What is, what shall be, shameful world it be
> To know not what is just.

Such a work is all the more necessary because in our day, as in former times, there is no lack of men who view this branch of law with contempt

From Hugo Grotius, *Prolegomena to the Law of War and Peace*, trans. Francis W. Kelsey. (New York: Liberal Arts Press, 1957). Published with the permission of the Carnegie Endowment for International Peace.

as having no reality outside of an empty name. On the lips of men quite generally is the saying of Euphemus, which Thucydides quotes, that in the case of a king or imperial city nothing is unjust which is expedient. Of like implication is the statement that for those whom fortune favors might makes right, and that the administration of a state cannot be carried on without injustice.

Furthermore, the controversies which arise between peoples or kings generally have Mars as their arbiter. That war is irreconcilable with all law is a view held not alone by the ignorant populace; expressions are often let slip by well-informed and thoughtful men which lend countenance to such a view. Nothing is more common than the assertion of antagonism between law and arms. Thus Ennius says:

> Not on grounds of right is battle joined,
> But rather with the sword do men
> Seek to enforce their claims.

Horace, too describes the savage temper of Achilles in this wise:

> Laws, he declares, were not for him ordained;
> By dint of arms he claims all for himself.

Another poet depicts another military leader as commencing war with the words:

> Here peace and violated laws I leave behind.

Antigonus when advanced in years ridiculed a man who brought to him a treatise on justice when he was engaged in besieging cities that did not belong to him. Marius declared that the din of arms made it impossible for him to hear the voice of the laws. Even Pompey, whose expression of countenance was so mild dared to say: "When I am in arms, am I to think of laws?"

Among Christian writers a similar thought finds frequent expression. A single quotation from Tertullian may serve in place of many: "Deception, harshness, and injustice are the regular business of battles." They who so think will no doubt wish to confront us with this passage in Comedy:

> These things uncertain should you, by reason's aid,
> Try to make certain, no more would you gain
> Than if you tried by reason to go mad.

Since our discussion concerning law will have been undertaken in vain if there is no law, in order to open the way for a favorable reception of our work and at the same time to fortify it against attacks, this very serious error must be briefly refuted. In order that we may not be obliged to deal with a crowd of opponents, let us assign to them a pleader. And whom should we choose in preference to Carneades?[1] For he had attained to so perfect a mastery of the peculiar tenet of his Academy that he was able to devote the power of his eloquence to the service of falsehood not less readily than to that of truth.

Carneades, then, having undertaken to hold a brief against justice, in particular against that phase of justice with which we are concerned, was able to muster no argument stronger than this, that, for reasons of expediency, men imposed upon themselves laws, which vary according to customs, and among the same peoples often undergo changes as times change; moreover, that there is no law of nature, because all creatures, men as well as animals, are impelled by nature toward ends advantageous to themselves; that, consequently, there is no justice, or, if such there be, it is supreme folly, since one does violence to his own interests if he consults the advantage of others.

What the philosopher [Horace] here says, and the poet reaffirms in verse,

And just from unjust Nature cannot know,

must not for one moment be admitted. Man is, to be sure, an animal, but an animal of a superior kind, much farther removed from all other animals than the different kinds of animals are from one another; evidence on this point may be found in the many traits peculiar to the human species. But among the traits characteristic of man is an impelling desire for society, that is, for the social life — not of any and every sort, but peaceful, and organized according to the measure of his intelligence, with those who are of his own kind; this social trend the Stoics called "sociableness." Stated as a universal truth, therefore, the assertion that every animal is impelled by nature to seek only its own good cannot be conceded. . . .

This maintenance of the social order, which we have roughly sketched, and which is consonant with human intelligence, is the source of law properly so called. To this sphere of law belong the abstaining from that which is another's, the restoration to another of anything of his which we may have, together with any gain which we may have received from it; the obligation to fulfill promises, the making good of a loss incurred through our fault, and the inflicting of penalties upon men according to their deserts.

From this signification of the word "law" there has flowed another and more extended meaning. Since over other animals man has the advantage of possessing not only a strong bent toward social life, of which we have spoken, but also a power of discrimination which enables him to decide what things are agreeable or harmful (as to both things present and things to come), and what can lead to either alternative, in such things it is meet for the nature of man, within the limitations of human intelligence, to follow the direction of a well-tempered judgment, being neither led astray by fear or the allurement of immediate pleasure, nor carried away by rash impulse. Whatever is clearly at variance with such judgment is understood to be contrary also to the law of nature, that is, to the nature of man. . . .

Herein, then, is another source of law besides the source in nature, that is, the free will of God, to which beyond all cavil our reason tells us we must render obedience. But the law of nature of which we have spoken, comprising alike that which relates to the social life of man and that which is so called in a larger sense, proceeding as it does from the essential traits implanted in man, can nevertheless rightly be attributed to God because of his having willed that such traits exist in us. In this sense, too, Chrysippus and the Stoics used to say that the origin of law should be sought in no other source than Jupiter himself; and from the name Jupiter the Latin word for law (*ius*) was probably derived. . . .

Again, since it is a rule of the law of nature to abide by pacts (for it was necessary that among men there be some method of obligating themselves one to another, and no other natural method can be imagined), out of this source the bodies of municipal law have arisen. For those who had associated themselves with some group, or had subjected themselves to a man or to men, had either expressly promised, or from the nature of the transaction must be understood impliedly to have promised, that they would conform to that which should have been determined, in the one case by the majority, in the other by those upon whom authority had been conferred.

What is said, therefore, in accordance with the view not only of Carneades but also of others, that

Expediency is, as it were, the mother
Of what is just and fair.

is not true, if we wish to speak accurately. For the very nature of man, which even if we had no lack of anything would lead us into the mutual relations of society, is the mother of the law of nature. But the mother of municipal law is that obligation which arises from mutual consent; and since this obligation derives its force from the law of nature, nature may be considered, so to say, the great-grandmother of municipal law.

The law of nature nevertheless has the reinforcement of expediency; for the author of nature willed that as individuals we should be weak, and should lack many things needed in order to live properly, to the end that we might be the more constrained to cultivate the social life. But expediency afforded an opportunity also for municipal law, since that kind of association of which we have spoken, and subjection to authority, have their roots in expediency. From this it follows that those who prescribe laws for others in so doing are accustomed to have or ought to have some advantage in view.

But just as the laws of each state have in view the advantage of that state, so by mutual consent it has become possible that certain laws should originate as between all states, or a great many states; and it is apparent that the laws thus originating had in view the advantage, not of particular states, but of the great society of states. And this is what is called the law of nations, whenever we distinguish that term from the law of nature.

This division of law Carneades passed over altogether. For he divided all law into the law of nature and the law of particular countries. Nevertheless if undertaking to treat of the body of law which is maintained between states — for he added a statement in regard to war and things acquired by means of war — he would surely have been obliged to make mention of this law. . . .

But, not to repeat what I have said, that law is not founded on expediency alone, there is no state so powerful that it may not at some time need the help of others outside itself, either for purposes of trade, or even to ward off the forces of many foreign nations united against it. In consequence we see that even the most powerful peoples and sovereigns seek alliances, which are quite devoid of significance according to the point of view of those who confine law within the boundaries of states. Most true is the saying that all things are uncertain the moment men depart from law.

If no association of men can be maintained without law, as Aristotle showed . . . also that association which binds together the human race, or binds many nations together, has need of law; this was perceived by him who said that shameful deeds ought not to be committed even for the sake of one's country. Aristotle takes sharply to task those who, while unwilling to allow anyone to exercise authority over themselves except in accordance with law, yet are quite indifferent as to whether foreigners are treated according to law or not. . . .

Least of all should that be admitted which some people imagine, that in war all laws are in abeyance. On the contrary war ought not to be undertaken except for the enforcement of rights; when once undertaken, it should be carried on only within the bounds of law and good faith. Demosthenes well said that war is directed against those who cannot be held in check by judicial processes. For judgments are efficacious against those who feel that they are too weak to resist; against those who are equally strong, or think that they are, wars are undertaken. But in order that wars may be justified, they must be carried on with not less scrupulousness than judicial processes are wont to be.

Let the laws be silent, then, in the midst of arms, but only the laws of the state, those that the courts are concerned with, that are adapted only to a state of peace; not those other laws, which are of perpetual validity and suited to all times. It was exceedingly well said by Dio of Prusa, that between enemies written laws, that is, laws of particular states, are not in force, but that unwritten laws are in force, that is, those which nature prescribes, or the agreement of nations has established. This is set forth by that ancient formula of the Romans: "I think that those things ought to be sought by means of a war that is blameless and righteous."

The ancient Romans, as Varro noted, were slow in undertaking war, and permitted themselves no license in that matter, because they held the view that a war ought not to be waged except when free from reproach. Camillus said that wars should be carried on justly no less than bravely; Scipio Africanus, that the Roman people commenced and ended wars justly. In another passage you may read: "War has its laws no less than peace." Still another writer admires Fabricius as a great man who maintained his probity in war—a thing most difficult—and believed that even in relation to an enemy there is such a thing as wrongdoing.

The historians in many a passage reveal how great in war is the influence of the consciousness that one has justice on his side; they often attribute victory chiefly to this cause. Hence the proverbs that a soldier's strength is broken or increased by his cause; that he who has taken up arms unjustly rarely comes back in safety; that hope is the comrade of a good cause; and others of the same purport.

No one ought to be disturbed, furthermore, by the successful outcome of unjust enterprises. For it is enough that the fairness of the cause exerts a certain influence, even a strong influence upon actions, although the effect of that influence, as happens in human affairs, is often nullified by the interference of other causes. Even for winning friendships, of which for many reasons nations as well as individuals have need, a reputation for having undertaken war not rashly nor unjustly, and of having waged it in a manner above reproach, is exceedingly efficacious. No one readily allies himself with those in whom he believes that there is only a slight regard for law, for the right, and for good faith.

Fully convinced, by the considerations which I have advanced, that there is a common law among nations, which is valid alike for war and in war, I have had many and weighty reasons for undertaking to write upon this subject. Throughout the Christian world I observed a lack of restraint in relation to war, such as even barbarous races should be ashamed of; I observed that men rush to arms for slight causes, or no cause at all, and that when arms have once been taken up there is no longer any respect for law, divine or human; it is as if, in accordance with a general decree, frenzy had openly been let loose for the committing of all crimes.

Confronted with such utter ruthlessness, many men who are the very furthest from being bad man, have come to the point of forbidding all use of arms to the Christian, whose rule of conduct above everything else comprises the duty of loving all men. To this opinion sometimes John Ferus and my fellow countryman Erasmus seem to incline, men who have the utmost devotion to peace in both Church and State; but their purpose, as I take it, is, when things have gone in one direction, to force them in the opposite direction, as we are accustomed to do, that they may come back to a true middle ground. But the very effort of pressing too hard in the opposite direction is often so far from being helpful that it does harm, because in such arguments the detection of what is extreme is easy, and results in weakening the influence of other statements which are well within the bounds of truth. For both extremes therefore a remedy must be found, that men may not believe either that nothing is allowable, or that everything is.

At the same time through devotion to study in private life I have wished — as the only course now open to me, undeservedly forced out from my native land, which had been graced by so many of my labors — to contribute somewhat to the philosophy of the law, which previously, in public service, I practiced with the utmost degree of probity of which I was capable. Many heretofore have purposed to give to this subject a well-ordered presentation; no one has succeeded. And in fact such a result cannot be accomplished unless — a point which until now has not been sufficiently kept in view — those elements which come from positive law are properly separated from those which arise from nature. For the principles of the law of nature, since they are always the same, can easily be brought into a systematic form; but the elements of positive law, since they often undergo change and are different in different places, are outside the domain of systematic treatment, just as other notions of particular things are. . . .

In order to prove the existence of this law of nature, I have, furthermore, availed myself of the testimony of philosophers, historians, poets; finally also of orators. Not that confidence is to be reposed in them without discrimination, for they were accustomed to serve the interests of their sect, their subject, or their cause. But when many at different times and in different places affirm the same thing as certain, that ought to be referred to a universal cause; and this cause, in the lines of inquiry which we are following, must be either a correct conclusion drawn from the principles of nature, or common consent. The former points to the law of nature, the latter to the law of nations.

The distinction between these kinds of law is not to be drawn from the testimonies themselves (for writers everywhere confuse the terms law of nature and law of nations), but from the character of the matter. For whatever cannot be deduced from certain principles by a sure process of reasoning, and yet is clearly observed everywhere, must have its origin in the free will of man.

These two kinds of law, therefore, I have always particularly sought to distinguish from each other and from municipal law. . . .

In my work as a whole I have, above all else, aimed at three things: to make the reasons for my conclusions as evident as possible; to set forth in a definite order the matters which needed to be treated; and to distinguish clearly between things which seemed to be the same and were not.

I have refrained from discussing topics which belong to another subject, such as those that teach what may be advantageous in practice. For such topics have their own special field, that of politics, which Aristotle rightly treats by itself, without introducing extraneous matter into it. Bodin, on the contrary, mixed up politics with the body of law with which we are concerned. In some places nevertheless I have made mention of that which is expedient, but only in passing, and in order to distinguish it more clearly from what is lawful.

If anyone thinks that I have had in view any controversies of our own times, either those that have arisen or those which can be foreseen as likely to arise, he will do me an injustice. With all truthfulness I aver that, just as mathematicians treat their figures as abstracted from bodies, so in treating law I have withdrawn my mind from every particular fact. . . .

I beg and adjure all those into whose hands this work shall come, that they assume toward me the same liberty which I have assumed in passing upon the opinions and writings of others. They who shall find me in error will not be more quick to advise me than I to avail myself of their advice.

And now if anything has here been said by me inconsistent with piety, with good morals, with Holy Writ, with the concord of the Christian Church, or with any aspect of truth, let it be as if unsaid.

NOTE

1. 214(?)–129 B.C., Greek skeptic philosopher and founder of the New or Third Academy in Athens.

Morality, Politics, and Perpetual Peace

Immanuel Kant

In this essay Kant presents an argument for politics compatible with moral principle within a state and among states. He rejects classic notions that in politics might makes right or that one must compromise ethics for prudential reasons.

Taken objectively, morality is in itself practical, being the totality of unconditionally mandatory laws according to which we ought to act. It would obviously be absurd, after granting authority to the concept of duty, to pretend that we cannot do our duty, for in that case this concept would itself drop out of morality (*ultra posse nemo obligatur*). Consequently, there can be no conflict of politics, as a practical doctrine of right, with ethics, as a theoretical doctrine of right. That is to say, there is

From Immanuel Kant, *Perpetual Peace*, ed. Lewis White Beck (Indianapolis and New York: Bobbs-Merrill Company, 1957), pp. 35–46. Reprinted by permission.

no conflict of practice with theory, unless by ethics we mean a general doctrine of prudence, which would be the same as a theory of the maxims for choosing the most fitting means to accomplish the purposes of self-interest. But to give this meaning to ethics is equivalent to denying that there is any such thing at all.

Politics says, "Be ye wise as serpents"; morality adds, as a limiting condition. "and guileless as doves." If these two injunctions are incompatible in a single command, then politics and morality are really in conflict; but if these two qualities ought always to be united, the thought of contrariety is absurd, and the question as to how the conflict between morals and politics is to be resolved cannot even be posed as a problem. Although the proposition, "Honesty is the best policy," implies a theory which practice unfortunately often refutes, the equally theoretical "Honesty is better than any policy" is beyond refutation and is indeed the indispensable condition of policy.

The tutelary divinity of morality yields not to Jupiter, for this tutelary divinity of force still is subject to destiny. That is, reason is not yet sufficiently enlightened to survey the entire series of predetermining causes, and such vision would be necessary for one to be able to foresee with certainty the happy or unhappy effects which follow human actions by the mechanism of nature (though we know enough to have hope that they will accord with our wishes). But what we have to do in order to remain in the path of duty (according to rules of wisdom) reason instructs us by her rules, and her teaching suffices for attaining the ultimate end.

Now the practical man, to whom morality is mere theory even though he concedes that it can and should be followed, ruthlessly renounces our fond hope [that it will be followed]. He does so because he pretends to have seen in advance that man, by his nature, will never will what is required for realizing the goal of perpetual peace. Certainly the will of each individual to live under a juridical constitution according to principles of freedom (i.e., the distributive unity of the will of all) is not sufficient to this end. That all together should will this condition (i.e., the collective unity of the united will)—the solution to this troublous problem—is also required. Thus a whole of civil society is formed. But since a uniting cause must supervene upon the variety of particular volitions in order to produce a common will from them, establishing this whole is something no one individual in the group can perform; hence in the practical execution of this idea we can count on nothing but force to establish the juridical condition, on the compulsion of which public law will later be established. We can scarcely hope to find in the legislator a moral intention sufficient to induce him to commit to the general will the establishment of a legal constitution after he has formed the nation from a horde of savages; therefore, we cannot but expect (in practice) to find in execution wide deviations from this idea (in theory).

It will then be said that he who once has power in his hands will not allow the people to prescribe laws for him; a state which once is able to stand under no external laws will not submit to the decision of other states how it should seek its rights against them; and one continent, which feels itself superior to another, even though the other does not interfere with it, will not neglect to increase its power by robbery or even conquest. Thus all theoretical plans of civil and international laws and laws of world citizenship vanish into empty and impractical ideas, while practice based on empirical principles of human nature, not blushing to draw its maxims from the usages of the world, can alone hope to find a sure ground for its political edifice.

If there is no freedom and no morality based on freedom, and everything which occurs or can occur happens by the mere mechanism of nature, certainly politics (which is the art of using this mechanism for ruling men) is the whole of practical wisdom, and the concept of right is an empty thought. But if we find it necessary to connect the latter with politics, and even to raise it to a limiting condition thereon, the possibility of their being united must be conceded. I can easily conceive of a moral politician, i.e., one who so chooses political principles that they are consistent with those of morality; but I cannot conceive of a political moralist, one who forges a morality in such a way that it conforms to the statesman's advantage.

When a remediable defect is found in the constitution of the state or in its relations to others, the principle of the moral politician will be that it is a duty, especially of the rulers of the state, to inquire how it can be remedied as soon as possible in a way conforming to natural law as a model presented by reason; this he will do even if it costs self-sacrifice. But it would be absurd to demand that every defect be immediately and impetuously changed, since the disruption of the bonds of a civil society or a union of world citizens before a better constitution is ready to take its place is against all politics agreeing with morality. But it can be demanded that at least the maxim of the necessity of such a change should be taken to heart by those in power, so that they may continuously approach the goal of the constitution that is best under laws of right. A state may exercise a republican rule, even though by its present constitution it has a despotic sovereignty, until gradually the people becomes susceptible to the influence simply of the idea of the authority of law (as if it possessed physical power) and thus is found fit to be its own legislator (as its own legislation is originally established on law). If a violent revolution, engendered by a bad constitution, introduces by illegal means a more legal constitution, to lead the people back to the earlier constitution would not be permitted; but, while the revolution lasted, each person who openly or covertly shared in it would have justly incurred the punishment due to those who rebel. As to the external relations of states, a state cannot be expected to renounce its constitution even though it is a despotic one (which has the advantage of being stronger in relation to foreign enemies) so long as it is exposed to the danger of being swallowed up by other states. Thus even in the case of the intention to improve the constitution, postponement to a more propitious time may be permitted.[1]

It may be that despotizing moralists, in practice blundering, often violate rules of political prudence through measures they adopt or propose too precipitately; but experience will gradually retrieve them from their infringement of nature and lead them on to a better course. But the moralizing politician, by glossing over principles of politics which are opposed to the right with the pretext that human nature is not capable of the good as reason prescribes it, only makes reform impossible and perpetuates the violation of law.

Instead of possessing the *practical science* they boast of, these politicians have only *practices*; they flatter the power which is then ruling so as not to be remiss in their private advantage, and they sacrifice the nation and, possibly, the whole world. This is the way of all professional lawyers (not legislators) when they go into politics. Their task is not to reason too nicely about the legislation but to execute the momentary commands on the statute books; consequently, the legal constitution in force at any time is to them the best, but when it is amended from above, this amendment always seems best, too. Thus everything is preserved in its accustomed mechanical order. Their adroitness in fitting into all circumstances gives them the illusion of being able to judge constitutional principles according to concepts of right (not empirically, but a priori). They make a great show of understanding *men* (which is certainly something to be expected of them, since they have to deal with so many) without understanding *man* and what can be made of him, for they lack the higher point of view of anthropological observation which is needed for this. If with these ideas they go into civil and international law, as reason prescribes it, they take this step in a spirit of chicanery, for they still follow their accustomed mechanical routine of despotically imposed coercive laws in a field where only concepts of reason can establish a legal compulsion according to the principles of freedom, under which alone a just and durable constitution is possible. In this field the pretended practical man thinks he can solve the problem of establishing such a constitution without the rational idea but solely from the experience he has had with what was previously the most lasting constitution — a constitution which in many cases was opposed to the right.

The maxims which he makes use of (though he does not divulge them) are, roughly speaking, the following sophisms:

1. *Fac et excusa.* Seize every favourable opportunity for usurping the right of the state over its own people or over a neighboring people; the justification will be easier and more elegant *ex post facto*, and the power can be more easily glossed over, especially when the supreme power in the state is also the legislative authority which must be obeyed without argument. It is much more difficult to do the violence when one has first to

wait upon the consideration of convincing arguments and to meet them with counterarguments. Boldness itself gives the appearance of inner conviction of the legitimacy of the deed, and the god of success is afterward the best advocate.

2. *Si fecisti, nega.* What you have committed, deny that it was your fault — for instance, that you have brought your people to despair and hence to rebellion. Rather assert that it was due to the obstinacy of your subjects; or, if you have conquered a neighboring nation, say that the fault lies in the nature of man, who, if not met by force, can be counted on to make use of it to conquer you.

3. *Divide et impera.* That is, if there are certain privileged persons in your nation who have chosen you as their chief (*primus inter pares*), set them at variance with one another and embroil them with the people. Show the latter visions of greater freedom, and all will soon depend on your untrammeled will. Or if it is foreign states that concern you, it is a pretty safe means to sow discord among them so that, by seeming to protect the weaker, you can conquer them one after another.

Certainly no one is now the dupe of these political maxims, for they are already universally known. Nor are they blushed at, as if their injustice were too glaring, for great powers blush only at the judgment of other great powers but not at that of the common masses. It is not that they are ashamed of revealing such principles (for all of them are in the same boat with respect to the morality of their maxims); they are ashamed only when these maxims fail, for they still have political honor which cannot be disputed — and this honor is the aggrandizement of their power by whatever means.[2]

All these twistings and turnings of an immoral doctrine of prudence in leading men from their natural state of war to a state of peace prove at least that men in both their private and their public relationships cannot reject the concept of right or trust themselves openly to establish politics merely on the artifices of prudence. Thus they do not refuse obedience to the concept of public law, which is especially manifest in international law; on the contrary, they give all due honor to it, even when they are inventing a hundred pretenses and subterfuges to escape from it in practice, imputing its authority, as the source and union of all laws, to crafty force.

Let us put an end to this sophism, if not to the injustice it protects, and force the false representatives of power to confess that they do not plead in favor of the right but in favor of might. This is revealed in the imperious tone they assume as if they themselves could command the right. Let us remove the delusion by which they and others are duped, and discover the supreme principle from which the intention to perpetual peace stems. Let us show that everything evil which stands in its way derives from the fact that the political moralist begins where the moral politician would correctly leave off, and that, since he thus subordinates principles to the end (putting the cart before the horse), he vitiates his own purpose of bringing politics into agreement with morality.

To make practical philosophy self-consistent, it is necessary, first, to decide the question: In problems of practical reason, must we begin from its material principles, i.e., the end as the object of choice? Or should we begin from the formal principles of pure reason, i.e., from the principle which is concerned solely with freedom in outer relations and which reads, "So act that you can will that your maxim could become a universal law regardless of the end"?

Without doubt it is the latter which has precedence, for as a principle of law it has unconditional necessity. On the other hand, the former is obligatory only if we presuppose the empirical conditions of the proposed end, i.e., its practicability. Thus if this end (in this case, perpetual peace) is a duty, it must be derived from the formal principle of the maxims of external actions. The first principle, that of the political moralist, pertaining to civil and international law and the law of world citizenship, is merely a problem of technique (*problema technicum*); the second, as the problem of the moral politician to whom it is an ethical problem (*problema morale*), is far removed from the other in its method of leading toward perpetual peace, which is wished not merely as a material good but also as a condition issuing from an acknowledgment of duty.

For the solution of the former, the problem of political prudence, much knowledge of nature is required so that its mechanism may be employed toward the desired end; yet all this is uncertain in its results for perpetual peace, with whatever sphere of public law we are concerned. It is uncertain, for example, whether the people are better kept in obedience and maintained in prosperity by severity or by the charm of distinctions which flatter their vanity, by the power of one or the union of various chiefs, or perhaps merely by a serving nobility or by the power of the people. History furnishes us with contradictory examples from all governments (with the exception of the truly republican, which can alone appeal to the mind of a moral politician). Still more uncertain is an international law allegedly erected on the statutes of ministries. It is, in fact, a word without meaning, resting as it does on compacts which, in the very act of being concluded, contain secret reservations for their violation.

On the other hand, the solution of the second problem, that of political wisdom, presses itself upon us, as it were; it is clear to everyone and puts to shame all affectation. It leads directly to the end, but, remembering discretion, it does not precipitately hasten to do so by force; rather, it continuously approaches it under the conditions offered by favorable circumstances.

Then it may be said, "Seek ye first the kingdom of pure practical reason and its righteousness, and your end (the blessing of perpetual peace) will necessarily follow." For it is the peculiarity of morals, especially with respect to its principles of public law and hence in relation to a politics known a priori, that the less it makes conduct depend on the proposed end, i.e., the intended material or moral advantage, the more it agrees with it in general. This is because it is the universal will given a priori (in a nation or in the relations among different nations) which determines the law among men, and if practice consistently follows it, this will can also, by the mechanism of nature, cause the desired result and make the concept of law effective. So, for instance, it is a principle of moral politics that a people should unite into a state according to juridical concepts of freedom and equality, and this principle is based not on prudence but on duty. Political moralists may argue as much as they wish about the natural mechanism of a mass of men forming a society, assuming a mechanism which would weaken those principles and vitiate their end; or they may seek to prove their assertions by examples of poorly organized constitutions of ancient and modern times (for instance, of democracies without representative systems). They deserve no hearing, particularly as such a pernicious theory may itself occasion the evil which it prophesies, throwing human beings into one class with all other living machines, differing from them only in their consciousness that they are not free, which makes them, in their own judgment, the most miserable of all beings in the world.

The true but somewhat boastful sentence which has become proverbial, *Fiat iustitia, pereat mundus* ("Let justice reign even if all the rascals in the world should perish from it"), is a stout principle of right which cuts asunder the whole tissue of artifice or force. But it should not be misunderstood as a permission to use one's own right with extreme rigor (which would conflict with ethical duty); it should be understood as the obligation of those in power not to limit or to extend anyone's right through sympathy or disfavor. This requires, first, an internal constitution of the state erected on pure principles of right, and, second, a convention of the state with other near or distant states (analogous to a universal state) for the legal settlement of their differences. This implies only that political maxims must not be derived from the welfare or happiness which a single state expects from obedience to them, and thus not from the end which one of them proposes for itself. That is, they must not be deduced from volition as the supreme yet empirical principle of political wisdom, but rather from the pure concept of the duty of right, from the *ought* whose principle is given a priori by pure reason, regardless of what the physical consequences may be. The world will by no means perish by a diminution in the number of evil men. Moral evil has the . . . property of being opposed to and destructive of its own purposes (especially in the relationships between evil men); thus it gives place to the moral principle of the good, though only through a slow progress.

Thus objectively, or in theory, there is no conflict between morals and politics. Subjectively, however, in the selfish propensity of men (which should not be called "practice," as this would imply that it rested on rational maxims), this conflict will always remain. Indeed, it should remain, because it serves as a whetstone of virtue, whose true courage (by the principle, *tu ne cede malis, sed contra audentior ito*)[3] in the present case does not so much consist in defying with strong resolve evils and sacrifices which must be undertaken along with the conflict, but rather in detecting and conquering the crafty and far more dangerously deceitful and treasonable principle of evil in ourselves, which puts forward the weakness of human nature as justification for every transgression.

In fact, the political moralist may say: The ruler and people, or nation and nation, do each other no injustice when by violence or fraud they make war on each other, although they do commit injustice in general in that they refuse to respect the concept of right, which alone could establish perpetual peace. For since the one does transgress his duty against the other, who is likewise lawlessly disposed toward him, each gets what he deserves when they destroy each other. But enough of the race still remains to let this game continue into the remotest ages in order that posterity, some day, might take these perpetrators as a warning example. Hence providence is justified in the history of the world, for the moral principle in man is never extinguished, while with advancing civilization reason grows pragmatically in its capacity to realize ideas of law. But at the same time the culpability for the transgressions also grows. If we assume that humanity never will or can be improved, the only thing which a theodicy seems unable to justify is creation itself, the fact that a race of such corrupt beings ever was on earth. But the point of view necessary for such an assumption is far too high for us, and we cannot theoretically support our philosophical concepts of the supreme power which is inscrutable to us.

To such dubious consequences we are inevitably driven if we do not assume that pure principles of right have objective reality, i.e., that they may be applied, and that the people in a state and, further, states themselves in their mutual relations should act according to them, whatever objections empirical politics may raise. Thus true politics can never take a step without rendering homage to morality. Though politics by itself is a difficult art, its union with morality is no art at all, for this union cuts the knot which politics could not untie when they were in conflict. The rights of men must be held sacred, however much sacrifice it may cost the ruling power. One cannot compromise here and seek the middle course of a pragmatic conditional law between the morally right and the expedient. All politics must bend its knee before the right. But by this it can hope slowly to reach the stage where it will shine with an immortal glory.

NOTES

1. These are permissive laws of reason. Public law laden with injustice must be allowed to stand, either until everything is of itself ripe for complete reform or until this maturity has been brought about by peaceable means; for a legal constitution, even though it be right to only a low degree, is better than none at all, the anarchic condition which would result from precipitate reform. Political wisdom, therefore, will make it a duty to introduce reforms which accord

with the ideal of public law. But even when nature herself produces revolutions, political wisdom will not employ them to legitimize still greater oppression. On the contrary, it will use them as a call of nature for fundamental reforms to produce a lawful constitution founded upon principles of freedom, for only such a constitution is durable.

2. Even if we doubt a certain wickedness in the nature of men who live together in a state, and instead plausibly cite lack of civilization, which is not yet sufficiently advanced, i.e., regard barbarism as the cause of those antilawful manifestations of their character, this viciousness is clearly and incontestably shown in the foreign relations of states. Within each state it is veiled by the compulsion of civil laws, because the inclination to violence between the citizens is fettered by the stronger power of the government. This relationship not only gives a moral veneer (*causae non causae*) to the whole but actually facilitates the development of the moral disposition to a direct respect for the law by placing a barrier against the outbreak of unlawful inclinations. Each person believes that he himself would hold the concept of law sacred and faithfully follow it provided he were sure that he could expect the same from others, and the government does in part assure him of this. Thereby a great step (though not yet a moral step) is taken toward morality, which is attachment to this concept of duty for its own sake and without regard to hope of a similar response from others. But since each one with his own good opinion of himself presupposes a malicious disposition on the part of all the others, they all pronounce the judgment that they in fact are all worth very little. We shall not discuss how this comes about, though it cannot be blamed on the nature of man as a free being. But since even respect for the concept of right (which man cannot absolutely refuse to respect) solemnly sanctions the theory that he has the capacity of conforming to it, everyone sees that he, for his part, must act according to it, however others may act.

3. "Yield not to evils, but go against the stronger" (*Aeneid* VI. 95).

The Nature of Politics

E. H. Carr

The late E. H. Carr argues that the practice and study of politics require an appreciation of realism as well as utopianism, power as well as morality.

Man has always lived in groups. The smallest kind of human group, the family, has clearly been necessary for the maintenance of the species. But so far as is known, men have always from the most primitive times formed semi-permanent groups larger than the single family; and one of the functions of such a group has been to regulate relations between its members. Politics deals with the behavior of men in such organised permanent or semi-permanent groups. All attempts to deduce the nature of society from the supposed behavior of man in isolation are purely theoretical, since there is no reason to assume that such a man ever existed. Aristotle laid the foundation of all sound thinking about politics when he declared that man was by nature a political animal.

Man in society reacts to his fellow men in two opposite ways. Sometimes he displays egoism, or the will to assert himself at the expense of others. At other times he displays sociability, or the desire to cooperate with others, to enter into reciprocal relations of good-will and friendship with them, and even to subordinate himself to them. In every society these two qualities can be seen at work. No society can exist unless a substantial proportion of its members exhibits in some degree the desire for cooperation and mutual good-will. But in every society some sanction is required to produce the measure of solidarity requisite for its maintenance; and this sanction is applied by a controlling group or individual acting in the name of the society. Membership of most societies is voluntary, and the only ultimate sanction which can be applied is expulsion. But the peculiarity of political society, which in the modern world takes the form of the state, is that membership is compulsory. The state, like other societies, must be based on some sense of common interests and obligations among its members. But coercion is regularly exercised by a governing group to enforce loyalty and obedience; and this coercion inevitably means that the governors control the governed and "exploit" them for their own purposes.[1]

The dual character of political society is therefore strongly marked. Professor Laski tells us that "every state is built upon the consciences of men."[2] On the other hand, anthropology, as well as much recent history, teaches that "war seems to be the main agency in producing the state"; and Professor Laski himself, in another passage, declares that "our civilisation is held together by fear rather than by good-will."[3] There is no contradiction between these apparently opposite views. When Tom Paine, in the *Rights of Man*, tries to confront Burke with the dilemma that "governments arise either *out* of the people or *over* the people," the answer is that they do both. Coercion and conscience, enmity and good-will, self-assertion and self-subordination, are present in every political society. The state is built up out of these two conflicting aspects of human nature. Utopia and reality, the ideal and the institution, morality and power, are from the outset inextricably blended in it. In the making of the United States, as a modern American writer has said, "Hamilton stood for strength, wealth, and power, Jefferson, for the American dream"; and both the power and the dream were necessary ingredients.[4]

If this be correct, we can draw one important conclusion. The utopian who dreams that it is possible to eliminate self-assertion from politics and to base a political system on morality alone is just as wide of the mark as the realist who believes that altruism is an illusion and that all political action is based on self-seeking. These errors have both left their mark on popular terminology. The phrase "power politics" is often used in an invidious sense, as if the element of power or self-assertion in politics were something abnormal and susceptible of elimination from a healthy political life. Conversely, there is a disposition, even among some writers who are not strictly speaking realists, to treat politics as the science of power and self-assertion and exclude from it by definition actions inspired by the moral consciousness. Professor Catlin describes the *homo politicus* as one who "seeks to bring into conformity with his own will the wills of others, so that he may the better attain his own ends."[5] Such terminological implications are misleading. Politics cannot be divorced from power. But the *homo politicus* who pursues nothing but power is as unreal a myth as the *homo economicus* who pursues nothing but gain. Political action must be based on a coordination of morality and power.

This truth is of practical as well as theoretical importance. It is as fatal in politics to ignore power as it is to ignore morality. The fate of China in the nineteenth century is an illustration of what happens to a country which is content to believe in the moral superiority of its own civilisation and to despise the ways of power. The Liberal Government of Great Britain nearly came to grief in the spring of 1914 because it sought to pursue an Irish policy based on moral authority unsupported (or rather, directly opposed) by effective military power. In Germany, the Frankfort Assembly of 1848 is the classic example of the impotence of ideas divorced from power; and the Weimar Republic broke down because many of the policies it pursued — in fact, nearly all of them except its opposition to the communists — were unsupported, or actively opposed, by effective military power.[6] The utopian, who believes that democracy is not based on force, refuses to look these unwelcome facts in the face.

On the other hand, the realist, who believes that, if you look after the power, the moral authority will look after itself, is equally in error. The most recent form of this doctrine is embodied in the much-quoted phrase: "The function of force is to give moral ideas time to take root." Internationally, this argument was used in 1919 by those who, unable to defend the Versailles Treaty on moral grounds, maintained that this initial act of power would pave the way for subsequent moral appeasement. Experience has done little to confirm this comfortable belief. The same fallacy is implicit in the once popular view that the aim of British policy should be "to rebuild the League of Nations, to make it capable of holding a political aggressor in restraint by armed power, and thereafter to labour faithfully for the mitigation of just and real grievances."[7] Once the enemy has been crushed or the "aggressor" restrained by force, the "thereafter" fails to arrive. The illusion that priority can be given to power and that morality will follow, is just as dangerous as the illusion that priority can be given to moral authority and that power will follow.

Before proceeding, however, to consider the respective roles of power and morality in politics, we must take some note of the views of those who, though far from being realists, identify politics with power and believe that moral concepts must be altogether excluded from its scope. There is, according to this view, an essential antinomy between politics and morality; and the moral man as such will therefore have nothing to do with politics. This thesis has many attractions, and reappears at different periods of history and in different contexts. It takes at least three forms.

1. Its simplest form is the doctrine of non-resistance. The moral man recognises the existence of political power as an evil, but regards the use of power to resist power as a still greater evil. This is the basis of such doctrines of non-resistance as those of Jesus or of Gandhi, or of modern pacifism. It amounts, in brief, to a boycott of politics.

2. The second form of the antithesis between politics and morality is anarchism. The state, as the principal organ of political power, is "the most flagrant, most cynical and most complete negation of humanity."[8] The anarchist will use power to overthrow the state. This revolutionary power is, however, not thought of as political power, but as the spontaneous revolt of the outraged individual conscience. It does not seek to create a new political society to take the place of the old one, but a moral society from which power, and consequently politics, are completely eliminated. "The principles of the Sermon on the Mount," an English divine recently remarked, would mean "sudden death to civilised society."[9] The anarchist sets out to destroy "civilised society" in the name of the Sermon on the Mount.

3. A third school of thought starts from the same premise of the essential antithesis between morality and politics, but arrives at a totally different conclusion. The injunction of Jesus to "render unto Caesar the things that are Caesar's, and unto God the things that are God's," implies the

coexistence of two separate spheres: the political and the moral. But the moral man is under an obligation to assist — or at any rate not to obstruct — the politician in the discharge of his non-moral functions. "Let every soul be subject to the higher powers. The powers that be are ordained of God." We thus recognise politics as necessary but non-moral. This tradition, which remained dormant throughout the Middle Ages, when the ecclesiastical and the secular authority was theoretically one, was revived by Luther in order to effect his compromise between reformed church and state. Luther "turned on the peasants of his day in holy horror when they attempted to transmute the 'spiritual' kingdom into an 'earthly' one by suggesting that the principles of the gospel had social significance."[10] The division of functions between Caesar and God is implicit in the very conception of an "established" church. But the tradition has been more persistent and more effective in Lutheran Germany than anywhere else. "We do not consult Jesus," wrote a German liberal nineteenth-century pastor, "when we are concerned with things which belong to the domain of the construction of the state and political economy"[11] and Bernhardi declared that "Christian morality is personal and social, and in its nature cannot be political."[12] The same attitude is inherent in the modern theology of Karl Barth, which insists that political and social evils are the necessary product of man's sinful nature and that human effort to eradicate them is therefore futile; and the doctrine that Christian morality has nothing to do with politics is vigorously upheld by the Nazi régime. This view is basically different from that of the realist who makes morality a function of politics. But in the field of politics it tends to become indistinguishable from realism.

The theory of the divorce between the spheres of politics and morality is superficially attractive, if only because it evades the insoluble problem of finding a moral justification for the use of force.[13] But it is not ultimately satisfying. Both non-resistance and anarchism are counsels of despair, which appear to find widespread acceptance only where men feel hopeless of achieving anything by political action; and the attempt to keep God and Caesar in watertight compartments runs too much athwart the deep-seated desire of the human mind to reduce its view of the world to some kind of moral order. We are not in the long run satisfied to believe that what is politically good is morally bad; and since we can neither moralise power nor expel power from politics, we are faced with a dilemma which cannot be completely resolved.[14] The planes of utopia and of reality never coincide. The ideal cannot be institutionalised, nor the institution idealised. "Politics," writes Dr. Niebuhr, "will, to the end of history, be an area where conscience and power meet, where the ethical and coercive factors of human life will interpenetrate and work out their tentative and uneasy compromises."[15] The compromises, like solutions of other human problems, will remain uneasy and tentative. But it is an essential part of any compromise that both factors shall be taken into account.

We have now therefore to analyse the part played in international politics by these two cardinal factors: power and morality.

NOTES

1. "Everywhere do I perceive a certain conspiracy of the rich men seeking their own advantage under the name and pretext of the commonwealth" (More, *Utopia*). "The exploitation of one part of society by another is common to all past centuries." (*Communist Manifesto*)
2. *A Defence of Liberty against Tyrants* (*Vindiciae contra Tyrannos*), ed. Laski, Introd. p. 55.
3. Linton, *The Study of Man*, p. 240; Laski, *A Grammar of Politics*, p. 20.
4. J. Truslow Adams, *The Epic of America*, p. 112. The idea that the state has a moral foundation in the consent of its citizens as well as a power foundation was propounded by Locke and Rousseau and popularised by the American and French revolutions. Two recent expressions of the idea may be quoted. The Czecho-Slovak declaration of independence of October 18, 1918, described Austria-Hungary as "a state which has no justification for its existence, and which, since it refuses to accept the fundamental basis of modern world-organisation [i.e. self-determination], is only an artificial and unmoral construction." In February 1938, Hitler told Schuschnigg, the then Austrian Chancellor, that "a régime lacking every kind of legality and which in reality ruled only by force, must in the long run come into continually increasing conflict with public opinion" (speech in the Reichstag of March 17, 1938). Hitler maintained that the two pillars of the state are "force" and "popularity." (*Mein Kampf*, p. 579)
5. Catlin, *The Science and Method of Politics*, p. 309.
6. It is significant that the word *Realpolitik* was coined in the once famous treatise of von Rochau, *Grundsätze der Realpolitik* published in 1853, which was largely inspired by the lessons of Frankfort. The inspiration which Hitler's *Realpolitik* has derived from the lessons of the Weimar Republic is obvious.
7. Winston Churchill, *Arms and the Covenant*, p. 368. The argument that power is a necessary motive force for the remedy of "just" grievances is further developed on pp. 209–216.
8. Bakunin, *Œuvres*, i. p. 150; cf. vi. p. 17: "If there is a devil in all human history, it is this principle of command and authority."
9. The Dean of St. Paul's, quoted in a leading article in *The Times*, August 2, 1937.
10. R. Niebuhr, *Moral Man and Immoral Society*, p. 77.
11. Quoted in W. F. Bruck, *Social and Economic History of Germany*, p. 65.
12. Bernhardi, *Germany and the Next War* (Engl. transl.), p. 29.
13. "Force in the right place," as Mr. Maxton once said in the House of Commons, is a meaningless conception, "because the right place for me is exactly where I want to use it, and for him also, and for everyone else." (House of Commons, November 7, 1933: *Official Record*, col. 130). Force in politics is always the instrument of some kind of group interest.

14. Acton was fond of saying that "great men are almost always bad men," and quotes Walpole's dictum that "no great country was ever saved by good men" (*History of Freedom*, p. 219). Rosebery showed more acuteness when he remarked that "there is one question which English people ask about great men: Was he 'a good man'?" (*Napoleon: The Last Phase*, p. 364)
15. R. Niebuhr, *Moral Man and Immoral Society*, p. 4.

6

Conclusion

We conclude with several observations concerning the current state of scholarly thinking about international relations. A constant lament among scholars and students is that the field consists of a confusing array of competing perspectives and conceptual approaches. Professors have trouble deciding which theories to emphasize from this intellectual smorgasbord in a ten-to fifteen-week class, and students have to wrestle with the problem of coming to terms with vast amounts of material for upcoming exams. The basic question we pose is whether the field is becoming less fragmented — whether there are indications of movement toward a greater degree of consensus on how to approach the study of international phenomena. One could argue that this is not a burning issue, and in fact a multiplicity of interests, methods, paradigms, concepts, and value preferences is actually beneficial and should be applauded. Greater unity, it is feared, could result in uniformity and the intellectual tyranny of a dominant paradigm or school of thought. Hence, eclecticism is to be encouraged, and any signs of uniformity regarded with suspicion.

No one would argue against diversity per se — it is the lifeblood of scientific enquiry. Seemingly unrelated research may some day come together to help explain a significant aspect of international relations. The concern, however, is whether diversity might more appropriately be described as parochialism. Scholars at times engage in narrowly focused research programs that ignore alternative conceptual approaches, develop specialized jargon that unintentionally serves to confuse and mystify the uninitiated, and unduly restrict their course syllabus to literature that reinforces their own value and theoretical preferences. It is to overcome parochialism, encourage communication among scholars, and stimulate the growth of cumulative knowledge on such important issues as war and peace that has led scholars to search for common threads that may serve to bring a greater degree of unity to the field, not some desire to stifle alternative perspectives or create some sort of paradigmatic Leviathan. Are there any indications of increasing unity or coherence in the study of international relations?

We will examine this question in three areas: underlying images, theory building, and normative concerns.

UNDERLYING IMAGES

By simply positing the existence of three basic images that influence theory building, we have in effect argued that a certain degree of coherence already exists in the study of international relations. A logical follow-up question is whether it is possible to combine elements of the three perspectives to provide a more comprehensive and integrated approach to the study of international politics that draws on the strengths of all three images. Simply combining all the actors and assumptions would result in a conceptual grab bag with contradictory elements. But what about a more careful selection of certain insights and assumptions? This could possibly result in creative and fruitful theory building.

To date, calls for such a synthesis have involved combining elements of realism and pluralism. Two scholars whose earlier work is associated with pluralism, Robert Keohane and John Ruggie, have indicated why such a synthesis is desirable and how it might be achieved.[1] Both argue that in attempting to construct a theory of international relations, one must begin with the realist emphasis on power and the state. Structural analyses of international politics that stress the importance of the system provide the critical context, they argue, in which pluralist insights and actors are to be analyzed. By itself, realism is inadequate in explaining recent patterns of interaction and changes in the world political economy. The same is true of pluralism. Realist systemic theory, however, provides a necessary "first cut," or context, within which international regimes, transnational actors, the political structure of states, bureaucratic politics, and the perceptions of decision makers are examined. Some of the best work in the pluralist image, it is noted, takes explicit account of the international system within which such actors and domestic institutions operate.

What of the globalists? Can their work perhaps also be combined with elements of the other two perspectives? There appears to be some common ground. First, as noted in Chapter Four, pluralists and globalists have a common interest in political economy, transnational actors and processes, and welfare issues. It was argued, however, that they deal with these topics in fundamentally different ways.

Second, and more important, globalists very often focus on hegemonic states or groups of states that reflect the distribution of power during a particular historical epoch. This is also characteristic of many realist analyses. Some globalists, however, might contend that this use of state-centered analysis is an exception and that a focus on broader patterns of social, economic, and political domination tends to be the norm. Nevertheless, a number of observers have noted an affinity between realist and globalist discussions of hegemony when it comes to explaining particular international events and outcomes.[2]

Third, it should be recalled that both the realist and the globalist images of world politics have proponents of structural, systemic analysis such as Immanuel

Wallerstein and Kenneth Waltz. The former, however, emphasizes economic structures and processes, whereas the latter emphasizes political, military, and economic components of power and capabilities.

Finally, John Ruggie has made the interesting observation that modern political relations as exemplified by the nation-state (the realist preoccupation) as well as modern modes of capitalist production (a concern for many globalists) are both derived from the same historical factors: the redefinition of property rights toward the end of the medieval era, which occurred simultaneously with the emergence of the principle of sovereignty as a legitimation for the interstate order.[3] If realism (emphasizing political factors) and globalism (emphasizing economic factors) are both derived from similar roots, is it possible that they may be at least partially reconciled?

Our expectations should remain suitably modest. A problem that is difficult to overcome concerns the basic incommensurability of the three images.[4] First, the topics addressed are often incommensurable. Realists may examine balances of power, pluralists decision-making processes, and globalists patterns of domination. Different topics may require not only the use of different levels of analysis but also conflicting assumptions. Second, meanings are often incommensurable, the same term being defined in different ways by different theorists. The concept of imperialism is a good example. Morgenthau defined it as "a reversal of the power relations between two or more nations," and Lenin defined it as "the highest stage of capitalism."[5] Finally, there is the problem of competing normative prescriptions often embedded in alternative images and theories. At the extreme, this might mean the adoption of a particular research program designed to produce results consistent with the expectations of a private or public funding agency. More commonly, the relative attractiveness of a realist or globalist explanation of imperialism, for example, may be based on a student's personal value preferences than on critical scholarly scrutiny.

THEORY BUILDING

In Chapter One we noted that we did not find the traditionalist – behavioralist debate of the late 1960s on the issue of appropriate methodology to be of overwhelming importance. In the 1990s, scholars still have not reached a consensus on the relative merits of quantitative vrsus nonquantitative research, in-depth single-case studies versus an examination of multiple cases, or inductive as opposed to deductive approaches to theory building. Each still has its advocates and practitioners. Furthermore, in recent years **critical theory** perspectives have challenged not only mainstream methodological approaches, but also have raised basic issues concerning the **ontology** and **epistemology** underlying most of the international relations literature.[6] As a result, periodic reviews of the literature characterize the field with such terms as "disarray," "chaotic," and "fragmented." It is therefore best to discuss recent trends in theory building efforts as opposed to signs of any growing consensus.

First, pure empiricism in the form of mere correlation of variables is in general disrepute. Studies involving bivariate and multivariate relations flourished in the 1960s, and it was assumed that various patterns in and of themselves told us something significant about international relations. Such studies have been criticized for simply seeking out that which is easily quantifiable, ignoring the larger context within which states interact, and failing to relate the empirical efforts to more general theoretical constructs or research programs. This supposedly hampered the goal of cumulative research.

Second, there is a heightened awareness of the need to take into account the structure of the international system when engaged in theorizing. According to Kenneth Waltz's influential formulation, the existence of anarchy and various distributions of capabilities constrain and influence states and other actors to behave in certain ways. Simply examining state interactions is insufficient. In recent years a number of scholars interested in alliance formation, theories of foreign policy, and military doctrine have worked to link the structure of the international system to state-societal variables.[7]

Third, and in part as a response to the influence of neorealist writings, there is a growing interest in understanding the historical development of such important concepts as "anarchy," "sovereignty," and "structure," particularly for those scholars interested in investigating the potential for transforming international relations. This is part of a larger trend: a renewed interest in the political thought of writers dating back to Thucydides, and the manner in which the works of these scholars have influenced contemporary international relations theorizing.[8]

Finally, there has been greater emphasis on theoretical rigor, which requires explicitly stating one's theoretical assumptions, delineating causal links, and noting the types of evidence to be used in testing propositions and hypotheses. This may all seem commonsensical and basic to any theoretical effort. In fact, very often work fails to meet such standards of theoretical rigor.[9]

NORMATIVE CONCERNS

Some scholars of international relations are quite explicit about their normative concerns. J. David Singer, for example, states, "Specialists in world affairs have a special responsibility to not only teach and conduct high-quality research, but to address the major problems confronting the global village. . . . The human condition is, on balance, morally unacceptable. Too many of our fellows continue to die prematurely from war, terrorism, assassination, poverty, starvation, disease, and even more of them suffer untold misery, pain, and degradation en route to the grave."[10] Few scholars would disagree that the ultimate goal of research should be to contribute to the storehouse of knowledge in an effort to ameliorate if not eliminate the scourge of war and poverty. The road may be difficult, the degree of commitment may vary, but few persons would probably care to admit even to themselves that they had no interest in furthering our understanding of the problems faced by the global community. The choice of a particular research topic may reflect a normative concern, but we believe that there is also a general consensus in the discipline that the final product should be the result of a good-faith effort to avoid allowing personal values to affect directly the construction of models, gathering of data, empirical testing of hypotheses and propositions, and interpretation of results. A normative commitment to improving our understanding of global problems does not sanction conducting biased research. Indeed, biased research could very well hinder the amelioration of the very problems of concern to a scholar.

Finally, as we noted in Chapter Five, some scholars are concerned with developing normative theories. Although both empirical and normative theorists may be motivated by such similar concerns as the devastation wrought by war, they operate in different domains. Normative theorists hope to provide the logical or philosophical bases for value choices facing decision makers and others by addressing such questions as "when is war justified?" or "Do wealthier states and societies have obligations to assist their less-fortunate counterparts in the third world?" We consider work in both domains to be important. In this regard, we applaud a recent upsurge in interest in normative international relations theory while, at the same time, we call for continued efforts to develop better empirical theory.

NOTES

1. See Keohane's "Theory of World Politics" in this volume and John Gerard Ruggie, "Continuity and Transformation in the World Polity: Toward a Neorealist Synthesis," *World Politics* 35, 2 (January 1983):261–85. See also Robert O. Keohane, *After Hegemony: Cooperation and Discord in the World Political Economy* (Princeton, NJ: Princeton University Press, 1984); Joseph S. Nye, Jr., "Neorealism and Neoliberalism, "*World Politics* 40, no. 2 (January 1988):235–41.
2. See, for example, Robert Brenner, "The Origins of Capitalist Development: A Critique of Neo-Smithian Marxism," *New Left Review* 104 (July-August 1977):25–92; David J. Sylvan, "The Newest Mercantilism," *International Organization* 35, 2 (Spring 1981):375–93. As Keohane notes, the globalist Fred Block and the realist Robert Gilpin "both emphasize the role of U.S. hegemony in creating order after the Second World War and the disturbing effects of the erosion of American power." Keohane, After Hegemony, p. 42.
3. Ruggie, "Continuity and Transformation," p. 281. As he argues: "Despite its defects, Waltz's model is powerful and elegant. And, as I have suggested, its defects can be compensated for in a suitably amended and augmented neo-realist formulation. Such a formulation would also go some way toward subsuming the major competing systemic theories." P. 285.
4. The following discussion is based on Stephen D. Krasner, "Toward Understanding in International Relations," *International Studies Quarterly* 29, 2 (June 1985): 138–140.
5. Krasner uses the imperialism example to illustrate the problem of competing normative prescriptions, but it is just as relevant to the problem of incommensurability in meaning.
6. Jim George and David Campbell, "Patterns of Dissent and the Celebration of Difference: Critical Social Theory and International Relations," *International Studies Quarterly* 34, no. 3 (September 1990):269–93.
7. Kenneth N. Waltz, *Theory of International Politics* (Reading, MA: Addison-Wesley,

1979). Waltz is repeatedly criticized for his explanatory emphasis on the structure of the international system. He, in turn, repeatedly states that he is interested in constructing a theory of international politics, not a theory of the foreign policy behavior of states. Waltz is all too aware of the importance of the state-societal units and levels of analysis when it comes to the development of theories of foreign policy. As he stated in 1967 in his book on American and British foreign policy: "The principal purpose of the book remains . . . to determine the ways in which the internal politics of democracies affect their external policies." *Foreign Policy and Democratic Politics: The American and British Experience* (Boston: Little, Brown, 1967), p. 17.

In terms of linking levels of analysis, it is fair to ask "So what's new?" In 1969, James Rosenau called for "systematic conceptual exploration of the flow of influence across the changing boundaries of national and international systems." The difference between then and now, however, is the consideration of the concept of system structure. James N. Rosenau, "Introduction: Political Science in a Shrinking World" in *Linkage Politics: Essays on the Convergence of National and International Systems*, James N. Rosenau, ed. (New York: Free Press, 1969), p. 3.

8. Helen Milner, "The Assumption of Anarchy in International Relations Theory: A Critique," *Review of International Studies* 17, no. 1 (January 1991): 67–85; R.B.J. Walker and Saul H. Mendlovitz, eds., *Contending Sovereignties: Redefining Political Community* (Boulder, CO.: Lynne Rienner, 1990); Nicholas Greenwood Onuf, "Sovereignty: Outline of a Conceptual History," *Alternatives* 16, no. 4 (Fall 1991): 425–46; John Gerard Ruggie, "International Structure and International Transformation: Space, Time, and Method," in *Global Changes and Theoretical Challenges: Approaches to World Politics for the 1990s*, eds. Ernst-Otto Czempiel and James N. Rosenau (Lexington, Mass.: Lexington Books, 1989), 21–35; Richard Ned Lebow and Barry S. Strauss, eds., *Hegemonic Rivalry: From Thucydides to the Nuclear Age* (Boulder, CO.: Westview Press, 1991); Mark V. Kauppi and Paul R. Viotti, *The Global Philosophers: World Politics in Western Thought* (New York: Macmillan/ Lexington, 1992).

9. For a discussion covering these and other points, see the articles by Bruce Bueno de Mesquita, Robert Jervis, and Stephen Krasner in *International Studies Quarterly* 29, 2 (June 1985).

10. J. David Singer, "The Responsibilities of Competence in the Global Village," *International Studies Quarterly* 29, 3 (September 1985): 245, 259.

Glossary

abstraction. A general idea, principle, or concept without physical or tangible quality. International relations theorists sometimes write of systems, the balance of power, and equilibrium — examples of abstractions that may be useful to the theorist who wishes to explain or account for political or other phenomena.

action. A movement or physical act, as when the state or its decisionmakers take some concrete step in a given situation. An action is the practical expression of policy. See also **policy, interaction.**

actor. A participant or player. The state is considered by realists to be the principal actor in international relations; other nonstate actors include transnational actors such as multinational corporations and banks. See also **rational, unitary, transnational,** and **transgovernmental** actors.

aggregation. The bringing together of parts into a single whole, as when the state is understood to be a *unitary* actor. Pluralists tend to see the state not as a single, unitary whole but as many parts, thus disaggregating or breaking the state apart into its component institutions, groups, and individual persons.

amoral. Morally neutral; without moral content. See also **moral.**

anarchic. See **anarchy.**

anarchy. The absence of political authority. International politics or the international system are said to be anarchic in that there is no central or superordinate authority over states.

anthropology. The scientific study of humankind, including its physical, social, and cultural origins and development.

appeasement. The policy of allowing another state to have what it wants — an attempt to avoid aggression by that state; for an example, see **learning.**

assumption. A premise or statement taken to be true without empirical or factual proof. The theorist typically makes assumptions as the starting point in developing a given theory. For example, some balance-of-power theorists make assumptions about the state as principal, unitary, and rational actor.

asymmetry, asymmetric. Not symmetrical; lacking precise correspondence or relation between or among components. An interdependence relation is said to be asymmetric if Party A is more dependent on Party B than Party B is on Party A.

autarky. An independent posture of self-sufficiency without dependence on other actors. Autarky occurs when a state attempts as a matter of policy to exist in economic isolation from other states.

authority. A legitimate right to direct or command and to make, decide, and enforce rules. The term *authority* has a moral or legal quality and, as such, can be distinguished from control by brute force or by coercion. See also **power.**

autonomous development. See **development.**

balance of payments. Accounting concept by which the international economic transactions (inflows and outflows) of states and their corporate and private elements are tracked. Balance of payments includes export and import of goods and services (balance of trade), capital investment and other "invisible" or financial flows, and gold or other financial reserve transactions. "Balance" is achieved when gold or other financial reserves flow in or out to cover differences in the other accounts as when a country exporting more than it imports receives foreign currency that it can hold as a financial reserve.

balance of power. A key concept among realists that refers to a condition of equilibrium among states. Realists differ on whether the equilibrium or balance among states is (a) created by statesmen or (b) occurs quite apart from the will of statesmen as an inherent characteristic of international politics. Balance-of-power considerations may be used by decision makers as justification for a given foreign policy. Some critics have noted that the multiple definitions or meanings of balance of power diminish its utility as a concept in international relations theory.

behavior. The actions and interactions among units; the behavior of policymakers or of states. **Behavioralism** refers to a way to study politics or other social phenomena that focuses on the actions and interactions among units by using scientific methods of observation to include quantification of variables whenever possible. A practitioner of *behavioralism* is often referred to as a *behavioralist*. *Behaviorism* refers to the ideas held by those behavioral scientists who consider only observed behavior as relevant to the scientific enterprise and who reject what they consider to be metaphysical notions of "mind" or "consciousness."

behavioralism. See **behavior.**

bipolar, bipolarity. The condition of having two poles as when the distribution of power or capabilities in international politics is said to be *bipolar*. Some theorists consider the contemporary international political system to have had a bipolar *structure*—the United States and the former Soviet Union. Others consider it to be multipolar or to conform to some other characterization. See also **structure.**

bourgeoisie. The capitalist (and, at the time of its emergence, the "middle") class. The class defined in Marxian terms by its relation to the means of production—its ownership of capital, including factories and other machinery of production in a capitalist economic mode. A member of this class is sometimes referred to as a *bourgeois.*

bureaucracy. The administrative arm of government staffed primarily by appointed, nonelected officials. A given governmental agency may be referred to as a bureaucracy, whereas the generic category of such agencies may be referred to as the bureaucracy. An individual member of a bureaucracy or administrator is sometimes referred to as a *bureaucrat.* Bureaucracy, bureaucrat, and bureaucratic are words sometimes used to convey negative connotations about government, but most academic usage is merely descriptive of the governmental administrative function.

bureaucratic politics. The formulation of policy is a function of the competition among opposing individuals who represent diverse governmental institutions. Coalitions and counter-coalitions typically form as a part of the process of bureaucratic politics. See also **organizational process.**

capitalism. An economic system or mode of production that emphasizes private ownership of the means of production and a free market. One who owns the means of production is a capitalist, or *bourgeois.* See also **bourgeoisie.**

capitalist world-system. An approach to international relations that emphasizes the impact of the worldwide spread of capitalism; a focus on class and economic relations and the division of the world into a core, periphery, and semi-periphery. See also **core, periphery, semi-periphery, class.**

causality. B occurs on account of A, which precedes it in time. A produces or is responsible for the subsequent occurrence of B. In this sequence, A is the *cause* and B is the *effect*. Some causes have multiple effects, as when A causes B, C, and D. Some effects have multiple causes, as when effect T is caused by Q, R, and S. Some causes may be *necessary*, but not *sufficient* to produce a given effect, as when A is necessary to cause D but will not do so unless B or C is also present (thus, A and B or A and C are *necessary and sufficient* causes of D). Some causes are sufficient in themselves to produce a given effect, as when the presence of A always produces B. An *efficient* cause is the factor immediately responsible for a given effect, whereas a *permissive* cause may refer to an underlying condition that allows a certain effect to be produced (Kenneth Waltz, for example, argues that international anarchy is the permissive cause of — the absence of any obstacle to — war whereas other factors proximate to a particular situation, such as misperception in a crisis, are among the efficient causes of a given war). Some theorists reject causality as an abstract or metaphysical notion: One can observe B as coming after or following A in terms of time, but that does not prove that A is a "cause" of B.

causal modeling. The depiction, such as by a computer simulation or diagram, of sequential relations among two or more variables and how they result in a particular event, action, or outcome, including the relative importance or "weight" of each variable in producing a particular outcome. Causal models depict cause – effect relations, as in a model of an arms race that hypothesizes a causal connection between the decision of the former Soviet Union to increase the level of its military expenditure and an increase in the later military expenditure of the United States in an action – reaction sequence. The Soviet Union's actions, it may be hypothesized, caused the United States to react in a similar fashion, resulting in an overall increase in the amount of money devoted to military expenditures and producing, in turn, similar reaction by the Soviet Union — in effect, an arms race spiral.

center. The term used especially by many dependency theorists to refer to First World or the industrialized countries in the global political economy — Japan and the countries in Europe and North America. Also sometimes used to refer to the elites or dominant classes. See also **core** and **periphery**.

city-state. A political entity composed of a city and its surrounding territory as in the city-states of ancient Greece (Sparta, Athens, Corinth, etc.) or Renaissance Italy (Florence, Venice, Padua, etc.)

class. A stratum of society with an identifiable characteristic or set of characteristics that differentiate it from another stratum. In Marxian usage, the term is defined by relations to the means of production. Under capitalism the *bourgeoisie* is defined by its ownership of capital (not only money but, significantly, the factories and machinery that are the means of production), and the *proletariat*, or working class, is defined by its labor. Under feudalism, the *aristocracy* is defined by its ownership of land, and the *serfs*, or peasants, by their labor.

class conflict. A concept associated with Marxism that emphasizes the inevitable clash of interests between strata, or classes, defined in terms of their relations to the means of production (i.e., how goods are produced). Marx, for example, analyzed the conflict between the *bourgeoisie* (owners of capital, especially factories and machinery of production) and the *proletariat*, or workers, who were being exploited by the bourgeoisie. Marx argued that eventually exploitation would reach the point at which a proletarian revolution would occur and the power of the bourgeoisie would be broken. See **proletarian revolution, Marxism**.

coalition. A combination or alliance of individuals, factions, or states, including both temporary and more enduring groupings of actors around a common interest or purpose.

cognition. The process by which human beings come to know or acquire knowledge through perception, reasoning, and (some would say) intuition. The term *cognitive* refers to this process.

cognitive dissonance. A concept developed by Leon Festinger wherein human beings tend not to perceive what is contrary to their preconceived or previously held perspectives. To avoid cognitive dissonance, individuals either (a) unconsciously screen out information or evidence that contradicts what they already believe to be true, or (b) interpret such discordant information in such a way as to support their preconceptions.

collective goods theory. Relates to the allocation of, and payment for, goods that, once provided, cannot easily be denied to others and whose use does not deny their use to others. Providing national security or international security through alliances has been described by some theorists as collective goods. Collective goods are referred to by some as public goods. See also **public choice theory.**

colonialism. See **imperalism.**

communism. A mode of production in Marxist thought that is to be achieved after the passing of capitalism and a socialist transition period. Communism is a classless society in which each person produces according to his or her ability and receives or consumes according to need. In Marxist thought, given the absence of classes, the state as an instrument of class domination ceases to exist.

communist. An individual committed to the eventual attainment of communism, particularly through revolutionary means that would lead to the overthrow of capitalism.

comparative advantage. The concept that holds that countries specialize in the production of those goods and services which they produce most efficiently. In a free trade environment there would be, according to theory, a global specialization or division of labor with aggregate productivity maximized. As critics point out, however, free trade theory does not address such matters as equity in the distribution of wealth. Some dependency theorists see free trade theory as the vehicle by which Third World countries are kept in a status of dependency and precluded from development.

complex interdependence. A term developed by Robert Keohane and Joseph Nye that refers to the multiple transnational channels that connect societies, including interstate, transgovernmental, and transnational relations. The resulting relations are extremely complex, with economic interests assuming far greater importance than in classic realism. See also **interdependence.**

comprador class. A term referring originally to the stratum of native businessmen in various Asian countries (including China) who served as local agents for foreign, colonial business interests. In contemporary usage, it refers to the aggregate of business elites in a Third World country or countries who maintain close links with their counterparts in the industrial countries of the First World. Particularly in Marxist usage, the term is used to explain relations of exploitation by the bourgoisie of Third World workers and peasants.

compromise. Reaching accommodation or settlement between or among parties. A process typically involving give-and-take and concessions by one or more of the parties.

concept. An idea of a general or abstract nature; sometimes referred to as a *construct*. Such concepts as *power, interdependence, order, justice,* and *peace* are used in the construction of international relations theories.

conceptual. See **conceptualization.**

conceptualization. The process of creating general ideas or concepts.

condition. A set of circumstances or state of being. An underlying condition of international politics, for example, is the absence of a single or central source of authority. When a given population has established a sense of community, this can be described as a condition.

conflict. Disagreement; the opposition or clash of units. Conflicts may be nonviolent or at varying degrees or levels of violence. Some theorists see the management of conflicts that cannot be resolved as being central to maintaining peace. Conflict of interest among states or other actors is a widely used concept.

constant. A factor that does not vary. See **variable**.

constitutionalism. The liberal idea that individual freedom is served by constraining the power or authority of government and setting formal limits, whether written or unwritten.

construct. Used synonymously with *concept*. A construct can be understood as an abstraction created or put together often out of simpler elements. See **concept**.

core. A term used synonymously with *center*; a reference to the industrialized countries in the global political economy. The term is also sometimes used to refer to the elites or dominant classes. See also **center** and **periphery**.

correlation. An association between two, or among more than two, variables, of such a nature that a change in one seems to be tied or related to a change in another. A correlation among variables does not necessarily mean that they are causally linked. See also **causality, variable**.

cost. A loss as opposed to a benefit; something paid as opposed to something received. The concept is central to game theory, including coalition and alliance formation. Costs may be distributed asymmetrically or unevenly among the actors in interdependence relations.

counterintuitive. Against, or contrary to, what is thought to be true. See **intuition, intuitive**.

critical theory. Associated with Jurgen Habermas and the "Frankfurt School" in Germany that offered a theory of social reality based on the dialectic of knowledge and power, arguing that theory must be connected to practice. This also entailed a critique of positivist–empiricist approaches to knowledge, with critical theorists claiming all knowledge is historical and political in nature. Current "dissidents" in the field of international relations have also drawn, among others, from Antonio Gramsci's own version of critical theory, Ludwig Wittgenstein's work on linguistics and hermeneutics, and the post-structuralist perspective of such writers as Michel Foucault. Critical theory challenges the stated and unstated assumptions and alleged objectivity of mainstream social science. Ideologies that represent particular interests, while masquerading as "theories," are especially suspect. Such theories are depicted deceptively as if they were objective portrayals of sociopolitical time and space. Critical theorists reject the pretense to objective knowledge—the logical positivism of the "Vienna Circle" advanced in the interwar period and followed by many social scientists in subsequent decades. The rigid division between normative and empirical theory is illusory. Moreover, what we think we know really is a function of language and sociopolitical context. Critical theory calls for interpretive understanding of time and space, an insight drawn originally from Max Weber's work in social science methodology.

decision. Making a choice among often competing alternatives or options; making a judgment or drawing a conclusion. A *rational* decision-making process is one in which alternative means to achieve certain objectives are evaluated and the option or options best (or at least satisfactorily) leading to the attainment of these objectives are selected. See also **policy**, which can be understood as being composed of both *decisions* and *actions*.

decision making. See **decision**.

dependency. A situation in which the economies of Third World countries are conditioned by and subordinate to the economic development, expansion, and contraction of the economies of advanced capitalist states. It is a situation of exploitation and is examined in a historical context. Domestic constraints and structures (such as land tenure patterns) are also critical in inhibiting balanced economic development.

dependent variable. The thing that is to be explained or accounted for. Some theorists have tried to explain, or find the causes of, war, which is their dependent variable. See also **variable, independent variable.**

description. A verbal statement that provides an understanding or meaning. Description is often differentiated from *explanation* or *prediction*, which are understood to be *theoretical* tasks. Thus, *theory* is considered to be different from mere *description*. From this perspective, description is a necessary but pretheoretical task.

détente. An easing or relaxation of tensions as when the relations between the superpowers are said to be less tense. The Cold War was said to have given way in the late 1960s and 1970s to a period of détente.

determinism, deterministic. A philosophical view that what we observe inevitably occurs as the consequence of factors over which human beings have no volition or control. Most social theorists who accept the characterization or who can be labeled as *determinists* do not reject totally the role of human will, as the strict definition of determinism would imply, but they do allow much less freedom of action for individuals to affect outcomes than those theorists labeled as *voluntarists*. The determinism–voluntarism issue among social science theorists has its analog in theological disputes over determinism or predestination on the one hand and free will on the other. See also **voluntarism.**

deterrence. Psychological effect on an opponent that results in a decision not to take some act such as attacking or starting a war. Deterrence is thought to be achieved either through fear of retaliatory punishment or through rational calculation that taking this action will not succeed in achieving intended objectives or that the costs of doing so will be too high.

development. The process associated with the industrialization of societies. *Modernization* is a term sometimes used synonymously with *development*, but some theorists differentiate between the two. For some, *modernization* refers to societal values and processes that undergo major changes from preindustrial traditional society, including the effects of industrialization, whereas *development* refers to the building of societal or governmental administrative infrastructure more capable of coping with increasing demands brought on by the modernization process. *Autonomous* development occurs in isolation, or independent of what is going on outside of a given country, a circumstance more difficult to achieve in the contemporary period than may have been true in the nineteenth century. *Reflexive* development, when and if it occurs, is responsive to external economic conditions and may well be dependent on them.

diachronic. Refers to a study over a period of time; sometimes referred to as a *longitudinal* study, as in a study of the causes of war between 1815 and 1945. See also **synchronic.**

dialectic, dialectical. A form of reasoning or argument that juxtaposes contradictory ideas with the goal of resolving the contradiction and thus moving closer to the truth. The term is associated with the ancient Greek philosophers, the German philosopher Hegel, and Karl Marx. Marx substituted materially based class conflict and the contradictions between means and modes of production for the clash of ideas. Whereas Hegel argued that the dialectical clash of ideas moved history forward, Marx focused on the importance of material forces. See also **class conflict, proletarian revolution, Marxism, means of production, modes of production.**

diffuse. Dispersed widely; not concentrated or narrowly focused. When a state is said to be a functionally diffuse actor, it performs a multitude of functions. The opposite of functionally diffuse is to be functionally specific or more narrowly focused.

diplomacy. The process or art of communication among states and their statesmen in international relations; negotiation, including positive inducements or persuasive tactics, compromise, threats, or other measures understood to be part (or tools) of diplomacy. Diplomacy is the state's political or policy element in the conduct of its foreign relations. The terms *diplomat* and *diplomatic* have a positive connotation, referring in common parlance to peaceful, nonwarlike approaches. As a technical term, *diplomacy* includes the threat or imposition of punishment or sanctions as tactics that may be employed by the diplomat in addition to (or in place of) more positive inducements.

disaggregation. See **aggregation**.

distributive justice. The question of the rightness of (or moral criteria associated with) the allocation of scarce resources, particularly material or economic resources. The rightness of a particular distribution of wealth or profit could be subject to normative standards of distributive justice. See also **justice, normative**.

dyad, dyadic. As between two units. See **interdependence**.

East. During the Cold War years, *East* referred to the Soviet Union and other Marxist-Leninist countries, mainly those in Eastern Europe. A more traditional meaning is the Orient or countries of Asia. Variants are the Far East (the countries of East Asia, including China, Japan, and the Koreas), the Middle East (originally referring to such south Asian countries as India and Pakistan, but now more commonly used to refer to Egypt, Israel, Jordan, Syria, Saudia Arabia, and neighboring countries), and the Near East (originally referring to countries in North Africa and Arabia; now more commonly referred to as the Middle East). See also **East–West**.

East–West. During the Cold War years, *East–West* referred to conflict between capitalist, industrial democracies of the First World or West (including West Europe, North America, and paradoxically even Japan) and the Marxist-Leninist countries of the Second World, or East (including the former USSR and other Marxist-Leninist countries, mainly those in Eastern Europe, but sometimes including China, particularly in the Maoist years). The more traditional meaning of East–West refers to Europe and the Americas as "West" and Asia as "East"—the meaning in Kipling's observation that East is East and West is West and never the twain shall meet. See also **East** and **West**.

EC. See **European Communities**.

econometrics. Quantitative techniques used in economic analysis.

efficient cause. See **causality**.

elite. The upper stratum or strata of a society.

empirical, empirically. Factual or known through observation. Propositions or hypotheses may be subject to empirical or factual test to determine whether observed "facts" are consistent with what is predicted.

endogenous factor. See **system**.

epistemology. Refers to the study of how one knows or how one acquires knowledge.

equilibrium. When various elements of a system are in balance. When disturbed, some systems are said to have an inherent tendency to restore this balance or equilibrium. For example, when a state or group of states upset the balance of power, other states respond in opposition, restoring the balance.

ethnocentrism. An inward-looking tendency or favorable disposition toward the people or nation with which one identifies, particularly when it is seen as superior to others.

European Communities (EC). Refers to European collaborative activity or international organization in several issue areas—the European Coal and Steel Community (ECSC), The European Economic Community (EEC), and the European Atomic Energy Community (EURATOM).

exogenous factor. See **system.**

explanation. See **theory.**

factor analysis. A quantitative technique by which the analyst tries to identify underlying and related elements or factors (usually as part of a causal explanation of some observed phenomenon or phenomena).

federalism. See **world federalism.**

feedback. A concept in systems theory and communication theory (or cybernetics) by which responses to decisions or actions taken are returned by affected elements to the sender or taker of these decisions or actions, thus allowing for corrective actions.

feudal, feudalism. A system of political, social, and economic organization that existed in Europe from approximately the ninth to approximately the fifteenth centuries. Reciprocal rights and duties were expected between the lord and his vassals—for example, protection of the vassal by the lord in return for the vassal's giving up a percentage of his crops. Feudalism is viewed in Marxist usage as a mode of production dominant in the Middle Ages and that preceded capitalism. See also **modes of production.**

First World. See **Third World.**

force. Usually refers to efforts undertaken by states in an attempt to compel others to take a certain course of action or to cease an action. The term usually means the use of armed or military force.

foreign policy. Refers to external affairs, particularly to decisions and actions taken by states in their dealings with other states or such "external" actors as international organizations, multinational corporations, and other transnational actors.

functionalism, functionalist. A focus on purposes or tasks, particularly those performed by organizations. Some theorists have explained the growth of organizations, particularly international organizations, as a response to an increase in the number of purposes or tasks demanding attention. *Neofunctionalism* as a theory of regional integration emphasizes the political calculation and payoff to elites who agree to collaborate in the performance of certain tasks. See also **integration, spillover.**

functionally diffuse. See **diffuse.**

fungibility. The condition that exists when one element or unit has no unique identity and can easily be exchanged or replaced by another of like nature. Money is said to be fungible (for example, funds in a national budget can easily be shifted from one account to another when cuts are made in one area of the budget to fund increases in another). Whether the power of states, like money, is fungible and can readily be transferred from one issue area to another is a point of some dispute among international relations theorists.

game theory. A decision-making approach based on the assumption of actor rationality in a situation of competition. Each actor tries to maximize gains or minimize losses under conditions of uncertainty and incomplete information, which requires each actor to rank order preferences, estimate probabilities, and try to discern what the other actor is going to do. In a two-person *zero-sum* game, what one actor wins the other loses; if A wins 5, B loses 5, and the sum is zero. In a two-person, *non-zero-sum* or *variable sum* game, gains and losses are not necessarily equal; it is possible that both sides may gain. This is sometimes referred to as a *positive-sum* game. In some games, both parties can lose, and by different amounts or to a different degree. So-called *n-person* games include more than two actors or sides. Game theory has contributed to the development of models of deterrence and arms race spirals, but it is also the basis for work concerning the question of how collaboration among competitive states in an anarchic world can be achieved: The central problem is that the rational decision for an individual actor such as a state may be to "defect" and go it alone as opposed to taking a chance on collaboration with another state actor. Dealing with this problem is a central concern of much of the literature on international regimes, regional integration, and conflict resolution. See also **anarchy, rational, theory.**

general theory. See **theory.**

globalism, globalist. As used in this volume, *globalism* refers to an image of politics different from *realism* and *pluralism.* Globalism focuses on the importance of economy, especially capitalist relations of dominance or exploitation, to understanding world politics. The globalist image is influenced by Marxist analyses of exploitative relations, although not all globalists are Marxists. Dependency theory, whether understood in Marxist or non-Marxist terms, is categorized here as part of the globalist image. Also included is the view that international relations are best understood if one sees them as occurring within a capitalist world-system. See also **image.**

government. The lawmaking, judicial, administrative, and enforcement apparatus of a state.

Grotian. Refers to the influence of Hugo Grotius, seventeenth-century Dutch scholar usually identified as the father of international law. The Grotian view is that international relations, although lacking central authority, can be subject to rules or norms, some of which have the binding character of law, that are expressly or tacitly agreed to by states.

groupthink. According to Irving Janis: a "mode of thinking that people engage in when they are deeply involved in a cohesive in-group, when the members' strivings for unanimity override their motivation to realistically appraise alternative courses of action." Indicators of groupthink include social pressure to enforce conformity, limiting discussion to a few alternatives, failing to reexamine initial decisions, and making little attempt to seek information from outside experts who may challenge a preferred policy.

hegemony, hegemon. Relations of dominance as when a major power exercises hegemony over countries within its sphere of influence. A state exercising hegemony is sometimes referred to as a *hegemon.* An alternative characterization reflecting preeminent position for a state, but not necessarily implying dominance, is to refer to it as a leader exercising leadership of other states within its sphere. The difference between hegemony and leadership is often a subtle distinction and perhaps more a matter of nuance or connotation intended by the user of the terms. See also **hegemonic stability.**

hegemonic stability. The view that stability in international relations stems from the presence of hegemony or dominance. The absence of hegemony or hegemons would imply a lack of order in the relations among states whether in commercial activities (trade, the exchange of money, and investment), social issues, or security concerns. See also **hegemony.**

heuristic. Refers to the illustrative value of some device or schematic presentation. Such a presentation is not intended as an actual or precise, empirically verified representation of relations among variables in a model, but it is useful for gaining a better understanding of some concept or set of concepts under investigation.

high politics. Refers to matters of security, particularly the strategic interests of states. Realists have tended traditionally to draw a distinction between such high political concerns and those dealing with socioeconomic or welfare issues of lesser interest to statesmen — the so-called *low politics.*

Hobbesian (or Hobbist). Deriving from the influence of Thomas Hobbes, seventeenth-century English philosopher, who characterized anarchic politics — the absence of a sovereign or central authority — as producing grave threat to individual security. The absence of central authority in international relations in this Hobbesian view poses a security threat to all states to which they may respond internally by strengthening their power positions, or externally by forming alliances. International security in the Hobbesian view rests, therefore, more on power and the balance of power than on law and other rules or norms.

hypothesis, hypotheses (plural). A proposition usually relating two or more variables (such as "Arms races cause wars") but subject to empirical or factual test. In one view, hypotheses may be verified or confirmed to the extent that tests do not show the hypothesis to be false. Repeated tests, including *replication* of earlier work, increase confidence in the correctness of the original hypothesis, although it is always subject to being shown to be false in subsequent tests and thus can never be confirmed with 100 percent certainty. A *null* hypothesis, the starting point, is a proposition in which no relation between or among variables is specified (as in "There is no relation between arms races and the onset of war") in contrast to a *working* hypothesis in which such a relation is specified. If one's empirical tests show no relation, then the null hypothesis is retained and the working hypothesis is rejected.

idealist. One who sees such values or human preferences as justice or a desire for world peace as potentially decisive and capable of overcoming obstacles to their realization. Referred to by critics as utopian, in that the idealist does not understand the realities that constrain human choice. An idealist considers ideas as having important causal effects as opposed to others who see power or material factors as being the determinants of political outcomes.

ideal (pure) type. A concept developed by the German sociologist Max Weber to describe an extreme, or pure, case that is not found in this form anywhere but that serves as an analytical benchmark useful in comparing real-world cases. Strictly defined, ideal types for democracy or modern and traditional societies are constructed by theorists even though the actual cases they examine are, at best, only approximations of the conditions they specify.

ideology. A belief system or set of ideas or values usually held as a matter of conviction. Ideological views are usually not subjected to the same standards of empirical test as are theories and associated hypotheses. Marxism–Leninism as ideology offers not only explanation and prediction of world politics but also a means for interpreting social relations.

idiographic. A detailed study of a particular case or event. See also **nomothetic.**

IGO. An abbreviation used to designate international, governmental organizations in which membership is composed of states — for example, the United Nations and its affiliated agencies. See also **INGO.**

image. As used in this book, an image refers to a general perspective of international relations and world politics that consists of certain assumptions about actors and processes. See also **realism, pluralism, globalism.**

imperalism. In its classic meaning, a position or policy of preeminence or dominance with respect to foreign elements, as in the Roman, Ottoman, or British empires. Imperialism in earlier centuries involved the establishment of colonies, which led to so-called *colonialism*. Although most of these colonies have become formally independent states, the relations of economic, social, cultural, and even political dominance by the former colonial power remain — so-called *neocolonialism*. Some theorists also contend that contemporary imperialism involves economic and other forms of exploitation or dominance by multinational corporations in less developed countries. Marxist theories of imperialism tend to emphasize the economic dynamics of capitalism and associated class relations.

incrementalism. A step-by-step rather than a comprehensive, all-encompassing, sweeping approach. In an incremental decision-making process, decisions are often deferred until information on which to base a choice has been maximized (or until not making a decision would foreclose certain options and thus, in effect, be a decision in itself).

independent variable. A factor used to explain some outcome. See also **variable, dependent variable.**

indeterminacy. The degree to which an outcome cannot be predicted with a reasonable degree of confidence or is subject to seemingly random influences. There may be a great deal of indeterminacy in voluntarist theories that maximize the effect of human choice or volition. See also **determinism, voluntarism.**

indeterminate solution. Refers to problems in which the outcome cannot be predicted with much, if any, confidence, as when the influence of variables appears to have random effect. See also **indeterminacy.**

INGO. An abbreviation used to designate international, nongovernmental organizations, those in which membership is composed of private individuals and groups, but usually *not* states or their governments. Examples are the International Red Cross and the World Council of Churches. See also **IGO.**

integration. The coming together of separate states or other political units under a common authority. Integration may occur as an international or regional phenomenon with varying degrees of authority given to institutions established to deal with common issues or problems facing member states. Integration can be viewed either as *process* or as *outcome* that reflects and encourages cooperation among states operating under conditions of international anarchy (i.e., lack of common government). Research on integration has tended to focus on the assignment of economic and social tasks to regional or international authorities. Earlier theories of regional integration saw political union as a possible outcome of collaboration in economic or social issues. See also **functionalism, ramification, spillover.**

interaction. An exchange between two, or among more than two, units as in the *interactions* of states, groups, classes, or individuals. By contrast, *actions* do not refer to the back-and-forth of an exchange but to steps or measures taken by a state, group, class, individual, or other unit. See also **action.**

interdependence, interdependent. A relation or relations between two (a *dyadic* relation) or among more than two units in which one is *sensitive* or *vulnerable* to the decisions or actions of the other or others. The flow of capital or money to or from one country may respond to (or be *sensitive* to) changes in the interest rates in other countries — so-called *sensitivity interdependence.* To the extent that one unit may be adversely affected by decisions or actions of another, it is said to be *vulnerable* to the other unit or units, as when State A depends on State B as the principal source of its oil supply and thus is vulnerable or would be adversely affected by its cutoff. To many theorists, such *vulnerability interdependence* is to be minimized or avoided altogether. Interdependence may be *symmetric* (affecting both or all sides equally), but it is more likely to be *asymmetric* (with effects varying from actor to actor). State A may be more dependent on a supply of oil from State B than State B is on the security of its investments in State A. See also **complex interdependence, balance of power.**

interest. That which is of importance to a unit (state, class, group, or individual), usually including, as a minimum, its survival. *National* interest refers to matters of importance to a state. Some theorists have found the concept of national interest to be too vague; they prefer to substitute the notion that states do formulate certain objectives that can be identified more easily. Others view the national interest as little more than what leaders say it is.

interest group liberalism. An approach to politics that emphasizes competing groups or institutions. Not only is interest group liberalism thought to be an accurate description of democratic politics, particularly in the United States, but it is also thought by many to be the way politics *should* be conducted. See also **liberalism**.

international. Specifically, relations between or among states. More loosely, it is a reference to matters outside a state, which has led to the synonymous usage by many persons of the terms *international politics* and *world politics*.

International Court of Justice. Located in the Hague; a principal organ of the United Nations. See **international law**.

international law. A body of rules considered to be binding on states and other actors even though there is no central enforcement authority to assure compliance. Sources of international law include treaties or covenants made by states, customary practice, generally accepted principles, and the writings of jurists. International courts such as the International Court of Justice interpret international law and apply it to individual cases brought by states. National courts and enforcement systems (those of individual states) are the primary mechanisms for dealing with international law. International law (particularly that based on treaty commitments) may have precedence over domestic laws that conflict with such international obligations.

international organization. An institution composed of states as members (for example, the United Nations [UN], European Communities [EC], and the North Atlantic Treaty Organization [NATO]. More broadly, the term refers to patterns of behavior or structures and actors that cross or go beyond national frontiers.

international politics. The *political* focus is on choices made by actors with authority to do so on issues external to states or that cross the frontiers or boundaries of state jurisdiction. *International politics* is often used synonymously with *world politics* or *international relations*, although these terms do have separate, more precise meanings. See also **international relations**.

international regimes. See **regime**.

international relations. The total of political, social, economic, cultural, and other interactions among states (and even nonstate) actors. *International politics* can be understood to be a part (or subset) of international relations, although the terms *international relations*, *world politics*, and *international politics* are often used synonymously. See also **international politics**.

intuition, intuitive. That which is held, assumed, or seems to be true *a priori* (beforehand). The term refers to a view that usually has not been subject to formal or empirical test but merely seems to make sense. See also **counterintuitive**.

jus ad bellum. See **just war**.

jus in bello. See **just war**.

justice. In common usage, that which is right, fair, or equitable for (or pertaining to relations among) individuals, groups, classes, states, or other units. See also **distributive justice, just war**.

just war. Normative theory referring to conditions under which (1) states rightfully go to war (*jus ad bellum*) with just cause, as in self-defense in response to aggression, when the decision to go to war is made by legitimate authority in the state, as a last resort after exhausting peaceful remedies, *and* with some reasonable hope of achieving legitimate objectives; (2) states exercise right conduct in war (*jus in bello*) when the means employed are proportional to the ends sought, when noncombatants are spared, when weapons or other means that are immoral in themselves are not used (typically those that are indiscriminate or cause needless suffering), *and* when actions are taken with a *right intention* to accomplish legitimate military objectives and to minimize collateral death and destruction. Many of these principles of just war are part of the body of international law and thus are legally binding on states and their agents.

Kantian. Deriving from the influence of Immanuel Kant, eighteenth-century East Prussian philosopher whose ethical writings emphasized certain *categorical imperatives* as being universal, morally binding norms such as the obligation to treat other human beings as ends important in themselves and not merely as means. In normative international relations theory, the Kantian preference was for a cosmopolitan world society, perhaps a world federation based on universal values in which perpetual peace would be maintained.

law. In domestic and international politics, the term refers to authoritative rules that are binding on those subordinate to them. In the natural sciences, the term refers to a general statement that specifies some regularity, as in Newton's second law of motion that force is equal to the time derivative of momentum: $F = d(mv)/dt = m(dv/dt) = ma$. Such specificity of relations among variables and constants has been elusive in the social sciences, and theorists have had to be content with identifying tendencies and generating what are at best "lawlike" statements.

LDC. Abbreviation for *less*-developed country. In some usages, LDC refers to *lesser*-developed country. See also **Third World, South.**

learning. Inferences or lessons drawn from the experiences of states (and statesmen) that guide future policy choices. For example, correctly or incorrectly (the inference is disputed by some), statesmen "learned" that appeasement of aggressors does not make such states less aggressive but may actually whet their appetites for more aggressive behavior (the case usually cited is appeasement of Hitler's Germany in 1938 when diplomats, meeting in Munich and wishing to avoid war, allowed the Germans to annex that portion of western Czechoslovakia inhabited primarily by Germanic peoples). Statesmen may "learn" the benefits of international collaboration as opposed to going it alone, an inference that might lead them to create new and expand existing international organizations.

legitimacy. The implication of the existence of *right*, as when a government is said to have, or to have been granted, a right to govern based on such criteria as its popular acceptance, the legal or constitutional processes that brought it to, or maintains it in, a position of authority, traditional grounds as in the divine right of kings, or the charismatic quality of its leadership that commands a following and thus contributes to its popular acceptance. See also **authority.**

less-developed country, lesser-developed country (LDC). A country in Latin America, Africa, Asia, or the Pacific that is in the early stages of industrialization or that has not yet industrialized to the extent that Japan and countries in Europe and North America have. See also **North–South.**

levels of analysis. Individuals, groups, state, and society, or international system as separate points of focus. Such levels help scholars to be systematic in their approach to understanding international relations. In explaining a phenomenon such as war, for example, the theorist may identify possible causes as being some characteristic or characteristics of the international system, states and their societies, groups or individuals. In accounting for or explaining such a phenomenon, one may look both within a unit such as a state, as well as how the unit relates to its external environment, which are different levels of analysis. In current usage, "unit level" factors such as state, society, interest groups, bureaucracies, and individuals are contrasted to structural factors operating at the system level. See **structure, system.**

Leviathan. The biblical beast of gargantuan proportions used as a metaphor by Thomas Hobbes to refer to the state — the supreme authority that provides order and security to individuals living under its sway; also the title of Hobbes's classic work. See also **Hobbesian.**

liberalism. Political philosophy with origins in the seventeenth and eighteenth centuries that emphasizes individual liberty to be achieved through a minimal state. A *laissez-faire* government, one that provides for law and order (sometimes referred to as a "night watchman" state) but otherwise constrained or not granted authority to infringe on the rights of individuals, is said to be a liberal government. In both domestic and international economy, this classic liberalism implies commitment to free market principles without government intervention, including free trade policies and unconstrained commercial activities both at home and abroad. In contemporary American political usage, influenced by President Franklin Roosevelt and those who have followed him, *liberalism* usually means enhancing individual rights and well-being through government action or government programs—a substantial departure from the *laissez-faire* of classic liberalism. See also **interest group liberalism.**

linkage. Coupling among units or issues as in ties that cross state boundaries and thus link internationally or transnationally the domestic elements (corporations, groups, individuals, etc.) of various states. In another sense, various policies may be tied to one another in such a way that international trade policy is affected by changes in international monetary policy (linkages sometimes referred to as "policy interdependence"). The term *linkage* has also been used to describe foreign policy connections, as when a government ties negotiations with another government in one field (such as progress in arms control) to behavior by that government in another field (such as demonstration that it will not intervene in the affairs of some third state).

longitudinal. See **diachronic.**

low politics. See **high politics.**

Machiavellian, Machiavellianism, Machiavellism. Deriving from the influence of Niccolo Machiavelli, the sixteenth-century Florentine political philosopher. In its perjorative meaning, the term refers to unprincipled behavior by statesmen or other state agents who aim to achieve certain objectives deemed to be in the state's interest. In this view, the ends of the state (its survival and its continuing security) may justify means or actions taken for these purposes, even though the same means might otherwise be considered immoral or illegal.

macrotheory. See **theory.**

Madisonian. Deriving from the influence of James Madison, often referred to as the "father of the U.S. Constitution." Madison's ideas (along with those of such other Federalists as Alexander Hamilton and John Jay) on the separation of powers among various branches of government and the division of powers between central and state governments were central to framing the U.S. Constitution.

Marxism. A body of thought inspired by the German Karl Marx. It emphasizes the *dialectical* unfolding of historical states. It stresses the importance of economic and material forces and *class analysis*. It predicts that contradictions inherent in each historical epoch eventually lead to the rise of a new dominant class. The era of capitalism, according to Marx, is dominated by the *bourgeoisie* and will give way to a *proletarian*, or working class, revolution and an era of *socialism* in which the workers own the *means of production* and move toward a classless, *communist* society in which the state, historically a tool of the dominant class, will wither away. A number of contemporary theorists have drawn on Marxian insights and categories of analysis—an influence most evident in work on *dependency* and the *capitalist world-system.* See also **dialectic, means of production, proletarian revolution, class, capitalist world-system, bourgeoisie, socialism.**

means of production. A concept particularly associated with Marxist analyses that refers to factors essential to the production of goods—combinations of land, labor, and capital. Classes are defined in Marxian terms as relations to the means of production: The feudal aristocracy owned land, the bourgeoisie own capital (including factories and machines), and the proletariat is defined by its labor. See also **class, modes of production.**

methodology. The approach one takes to an academic study; modes of research and analysis, as in the use of historical case and comparative case studies, or the use of statistics as in formal hypothesis testing or causal modeling of variables. See also **causal modeling.**

microtheory. See **theory.**

minimum winning coalition. The smallest number of actors needed to agree to a policy or course of action in order to put it into effect. See also **game theory.**

MNC. See **multinational corporation.**

modernization. See **development.**

modes of production. The organization of the economy for the production of goods, as in such historical epochs identified by Marx as slavery, feudalism, and capitalism. According to Marx, as technology has advanced, the mode of production has also changed —feudalism being a more productive mode than slavery and capitalism being more productive than feudalism.

monopoly. Occurs when a firm has solitary or complete control of a market. Marx noted an increasing concentration of capital or a tendency toward monopoly in advanced capitalism.

moral. Principles of right and wrong in one's behavior.

multinational corporation (MNC). A firm usually with headquarters in one country but with production facilities in more than one country. Because they operate across national borders, MNCs are among those units referred to as transnational actors. See also **transnational.**

multipolar, multipolarity. A distribution of power in the international system with more than two centers or "poles," such as a world in which there are five principal or major powers.

nation. A group of people with a common identity. A nation coterminous with state boundaries is referred to as a *nation-state,* although in common language the terms *nation, state,* and *nation-state* are used synonymously. It is possible for there to be a nation without a single state — for example, a *no   te nation* such as the Palestinian and Kurdish peoples in the Middle East. Some states such as India contain more than one nation and are usually referred to as multinational states.

nation-state. See **nation.**

national interest. See **interest.**

national security. Issues dealing with the survival, welfare, and protection of a state.

national self-determination. The view that a people with a common identity have the right to be independent from outside control, as in establishing a state for such a national group. National self-determination has been an important rallying cry for Third World countries that have demanded an end to colonial rule.

NATO. The North Atlantic Treaty Organization; a mutual defense organization founded in 1949 by the United States, Canada, and Western European countries. There are currently sixteen members.

natural law, universal law. A philosophical view dating back to at least the times of the ancient Greeks that posits there are laws inherent in nature that transcend any laws made by mere mortals. All leaders and all forms of government, it is argued, are bound by these laws, and they should not be violated. Some scholars have dealt with natural law as a means to develop a body of international law to govern the relations among states.

neocolonialism. See **imperialism.**

neofunctionalism. See **functionalism, spillover.**

neorealism. A label applied to those realists who are interested in explaining state behavior under conditions of anarchy and who emphasize the importance of the structure of the international system and how this influences and constrains state behavior. The term may also have negative connotations in the eyes of some critics who claim that the neorealists have neglected the importance of values and norms as stressed by earlier realists such as Hans Morgenthau and E. H. Carr. Neorealists deny the validity of such charges, and some even reject the neorealist label. See also **structure, structural determinist.**

NIC. Newly industrializing country.

nomothetic. Related to finding general or universal laws as in the study of numerous, different cases over time. See also **idiographic.**

nonstate actors. International actors other than governments, such as multinational corporations, international banks, terrorist groups, and the Red Cross. Pluralists with a transnationalist perspective on international relations emphasize the importance of such nonstate actors. See also **transnational.**

non-zero-sum. See **game theory.**

normative, norm. A principle of right action; a standard to guide behavior, as in norms or obligations governing the conduct of war, transit on the high seas, diplomacy, trade and commerce. Normative judgments are often equated to value judgments and the idea of what *ought* to be; some norms may have the binding character of international law.

North. See **North–South.**

North–South. Terms meant to distinguish between the advanced industrialized states of the northern hemisphere and the poorer states of the southern hemisphere. The South is also referred to as the Third World. Some authors include the former Soviet Union and Eastern Europe as part of the North, but most others restrict the definition to Western Europe, Japan, and North America. Debate and discussion revolve around the question of how the North–South economic gap can be bridged and what, if any, obligation the North has toward the South.

n-person game. See **game theory.**

oligopoly. An economic market in which a few firms control the production (or distribution) of certain goods or services. Marx and Lenin argued that capitalism tended to move toward greater concentration of capital, resulting in oligopolies.

ontology. Philosophical term referring to the study of existence or being or, in Kant's terms, "the more general properties of things." Thus, dialectical materialism as universal law or set of laws with historical implications for humanity is an example of a materialist ontology central to Marxist thought.

operationalize, operationalization. See **variable.**

operational code. The world view or belief system of foreign policy elites. The path-breaking work was by Nathan Leites on the Bolsheviks and was later developed by Alexander George and others.

optimal. In the context of decision making, the best possible outcome.

organizational process. A model developed by Graham Allison to distinguish *bureaucratic politics* from organizational process—the institutional perspectives, routines, standard procedures, and processes of particular bureaucracies.

pacta sunt servanda. Latin for "treaties are binding"; the idea that treaties or formal covenants are legally binding even in the absence of a central authority to enforce adherence to them.

paradigm. A pattern, model, or perspective that helps one organize and guide research.

A paradigm may include key assumptions about the world and the best way to go about understanding it. The concept was central in Thomas Kuhn's influential *The Structure of Scientific Revolutions* (1962) and has since been applied to the social sciences. According to Kuhn, a scientific era is characterized by a dominant paradigm that represents "normal science"; the majority of scholars work within this paradigm, often accepting the assumptions of the paradigm in an unquestioning manner. These assumptions have an impact on how research is conducted and the resultant scholarly work.

parsimonious theory. A theory that contains only a few elements yet can explain or predict a wide variety of phenomena. See also **theory, hypothesis.**

partial theory. See **theory.**

peace. A wide variety of definitions exist, including the absence of war; a situation of security, order, or stability; harmonious relations among states. For some theorists, it means worldwide collaboration to solve common global problems.

perception, perceptual. Awareness of the world through the medium of the senses. In international relations, the literature on deterrence and crisis situations, for example, often deals with the importance of perception and misperception.

periphery. The less-developed countries or areas of Asia, Latin America, and Africa. In the dependency literature, the periphery is dominated by the *center*, which consists of the economically and politically dominant countries of the world (usually viewed as North America, Western Europe, and Japan). The literature on the capitalist world-system has applied the concept of periphery back to the origins of capitalism in Europe. The periphery plays a subordinate but important role in a worldwide capitalist division of labor by providing raw materials and cheap labor. As capitalism expanded, countries that at one time were part of the center slipped into peripheral or semiperipheral status. See also **semiperiphery, core,** and **center.**

permissive cause. See **causality.**

phenomenology. A philosophical term with various complex meanings, one of which is the classification and description of phenomena, including identification of the formal structures of phenomena as part of an attempt to establish their scientific foundations.

phenomenon, phenomena (plural). An observed or observable occurrence.

pluralism, pluralist. As used in this book, pluralism refers to an image of international relations that assumes that nonstate actors are important entities in international relations. The state is not necessarily a rational and unitary actor but is composed of a multitude of competing bureaucracies, individuals, and groups. The agenda of world politics is extensive and goes well beyond security concerns. Much of the work on decision making and transnationalism falls within the pluralist image as the result of a focus on a multiplicity of factors and actors. See also **image.**

policy. A decision or a course of action chosen from alternatives.

politburo. The supreme policy and decision-making body of the former Soviet Union and other Marxist-Leninist states; an organ of the Communist Party.

political economy. There are at least two major ways in which this term is used in international relations research: (1) the view that politics and economics are inextricably linked, leading one to study the interrelations of political and economic variables, and (2) the use of economic models of rationality to explain political actions. For example, some theorists use economic models of rationality in order to determine under what conditions international collaboration can be achieved among states.

politics, political. Numerous definitions have been offered including the processes that determine who gets what, when, and how (Harold Lasswell), the authoritative allocation of values (David Easton), or simply authoritative choice.

polity. In common usage, a political system such as the American polity or the Canadian polity. In the original Aristotelian usage, the term referred to an ideal form of government.

positive-sum game. See **game theory.**

positivist. The view that laws stem only from the actions of those having the political authority to make them rather than being the derivation of divine or natural law. In science, the view that knowledge comes from empirical testing of propositions or hypotheses against evidence or facts.

power. Capabilities, or the relative capabilities, of actors such as states. The ability to control or influence outcomes or the actions of others. Central to realist works on international relations. For more detailed discussion, see the text.

prediction. See **theory.**

proletarian. See **proletarian revolution, proletariat.**

proletarian revolution. A Marxist concept referring to the rising up of the working class, or proletariat, and the overthrow of the capitalist system dominated by the bourgeoisie who own capital—the factors, industries, and banks. The revolution is, theoretically, the result of contradictions internal to the nature of capitalism.

proletariat. A Marxist concept referring to a particular class or stratum of people, in this case the working class. The proletariat is usually viewed as being in opposition to the bourgeois class, which owns the means of production. See also **Marxism, means of production.**

prophecy. See **self-fulfilling prophecy.**

psychohistory. The study of historically significant individuals through the analysis of what is known about their personality and psychological development.

psychology. The study of the mind and its impact on behavior. See also **social psychology.**

public choice theory. The use of economic methods to analyze what are essentially political problems (issues involving choices or decisions by political authorities). See also **collective goods theory.**

pure type. See **ideal type.**

ramification. A concept developed by David Mitrany in his work on functionalist integration: Successful collaboration by states in one particular technical area would encourage the expansion of collaboration into other areas. Mitrany hypothesized that if states became increasingly integrated in a number of technical or functional areas, the cost of breaking these ties (such as by going to war) would be high enough to prevent such actions from occurring in the first place. See also **functionalism, spillover.**

rational. To act rationally requires a rank ordering of preferred goals, consideration of all feasible alternatives to attain those goals in the light of existing capabilities, and consideration of the costs and benefits associated with using particular methods to attain particular goals. The assumption is often made in international relations research that actors do indeed act rationally. The assumption is made in order to develop hypotheses and to produce insights on world politics. See **decision, action, policy.**

rationality. See **rational.**

realism, realist. A perspective on international relations that focuses on the state as unitary and rational actor and on the actions and interactions of states. Realists attempt to understand patterns of conflict and collaboration under conditions of anarchy or lack of common government. Security issues are usually the most important for realists. *National interest* or objectives, *power*, and *balance of power* are key concepts for most realists. See also **image.**

Realpolitik. A German term referring to power politics. It emphasizes policies based more on practical power considerations and less on moral or ethical considerations. The attainment and maintenance of state security in a hostile world through power or balance-of-power politics is viewed as the primary goal of leaders.

reductionism. An analytic approach leading to oversimplification and incompleteness of explanation. In some usages, the term refers to explanations that look only within a unit, such as state or individual, ignoring the environment within which the unit is immersed and the interaction of that unit with elements in its environment. Reducing the explanation of some phenomenon such as war among states to something deep within the human psyche (as being, for example, at the level of synapses between nerve endings) is an extreme example of *reductio ad absurdum* — explanation reduced to an absurd degree of oversimplification and incompleteness — as if one could explain the recurrence of war among states purely in neurological terms. Similarly, theorists who have tried to explain revolution solely in social or social-psychological terms, ignoring economic, political, and other factors, have been criticized for reductionism.

reformism. The idea that revolution or the violent overthrow of an existing capitalist political-economic order is not necessary, but that change can occur incrementally and nonviolently. The possibility of evolving toward socialism by peaceful means such as parliamentary methods or the creation of trade unions is a tenet of reformism. The issue of reformism is one reason the socialist movement split in the late nineteenth and early twentieth centuries. V. I. Lenin and Rosa Luxemburg argued that the reformist policies of Karl Kautsky, Eduard Bernstein, and others were wrong. Lenin believed that capitalism could not be reformed to benefit the working class, that a revolution was required. See **proletarian revolution.**

regime, international regime. In its domestic context, an existing governmental or constitutional order defined in terms of sets of rules and institutions established to govern relations among individuals, groups, or classes within a state. In its international context, the term is defined as voluntarily agreed-upon sets of principles, norms, rules, and procedures around which actor expectations converge in a given area of international relations. The literature on international regimes blossomed in the 1970s. Scholars argued that international collaboration was obviously not restricted to formal international organizations such as the United Nations — cooperation was necessary in monetary and trade areas, telecommunications, air traffic control, and a whole host of areas of greater and lesser importance.

reified, reification. Giving a concrete reality to what is in fact an abstract concept of analysis. For example, some critics claim that realists have reified the state, attributing to it human characteristics such as rationality, or treating the state as if it operated in the international arena like an actual human being. The concept of system, used by some realist, pluralist, and globalist theorists, has also been criticized on similar grounds.

relativist, relativism. A view that what is true varies from individual to individual, group to group, and context to context. See **natural law.**

satisficing. A less-than-optimal choice that does not completely maximize the values or goals one is pursuing but is good enough; work on decision making shows that people often choose the first viable option that is minimally acceptable.

Second World. See **Third World.**

security dilemma. A term coined by John Herz: In an anarchic international system, State A may sincerely increase its level of defense spending only for defensive purposes and self-preservation, but it is rational for other states to assume the worst and impute aggressive intentions to State A. They therefore also increase their level of arms, leading State A to feel insecure and contemplate a further increase in military spending.

Hence, by initially trying to enhance its own security, State A sets in motion a process that results ironically in its feeling less secure. In another usage, the term merely refers to the security problem faced by all states in a world without central authority or lack of common government among states. See also **anarchy, self-help.**

self-fulfilling prophecy. To predict a particular outcome and then choose policies or actions that help to bring about the predicted outcome even though this is not the intended effect. For example, predicting that State B will increase support for a war of national liberation against an ally of State A, State A provides its ally with more military assistance to combat rebels, resulting in State B's feeling it is necessary to increase its support for the guerrillas. State A's prophecy that State B will increase support for the guerrillas hence becomes self-fulfilling.

self-help. In the international arena, there is no superordinate authority, world government, or "Leviathan" to ensure order or to see that all parties to an agreement keep their end of a bargain. Each state must look after its own security and not assume the help of other states. See also **anarchy.**

semi-periphery. As used by capitalist world-system theorists (see Chapter 4), term refers to those countries or regions that occupy an intermediate position between core and peripheral areas. The semi-pheriphery is engaged in a mix of activities, some associated with the core and some with the periphery. It serves as an outlet for investment when wages, and thus the cost of production, in core areas become too high. The semi-periphery may at one time have been a core or peripheral area, or it may be moving into either status. See also **bourgeoisie, class conflict.**

sensitivity interdependence. See **interdependence.**

social contract. A philosophical idea used by theorists such as Thomas Hobbes, John Locke, and Jean-Jacques Rousseau to justify their preference for a particular type of political order. Living in an imaginary "state of nature" — a condition without any social or political structure — individuals contract with one another to create a political community or society governed by certain rules. For Hobbes, the social contract resulted in the establishment of a sovereign or central authority who is given the task of maintaining order. In international relations, however, no such sovereign exists. See also **self-help, security dilemma.**

socialism. Ownership of the means of production and distribution of goods by the society or the people as a whole (the public) rather than by private individuals. In a more limited form of socialism, only major industries and utilities are publicly owned. In some usages, socialism refers not only to public ownership of the means of production; it also includes public welfare programs and government acts in the name of the people in carrying out these programs. In Marxist thought, socialism is a stage or mode of production between capitalism and communism.

social psychology. The study of the mental processes of individuals and how they relate to their environment, especially to other individuals and groups. Behavior is explained by the interaction of individual and environment, not solely by elements within an individual's psyche.

sociology. The study of society, particularly social groups and classes and relations among them.

South. See **North–South.**

sovereign, sovereignty. The supreme, independent, and final authority. The attribute of a state that refers to its right to exercise complete jurisdiction over its own territory. In international relations, states as sovereign units have a right to be independent or autonomous with respect to other states. States may differ in their power, but as sovereign entities all are legal equals.

spillover. In the regional integration literature, a concept referring to a process whereby successful collaboration by states in one technical area leads to the realization by state authorities that it is in their rational self-interest to expand collaboration into related fields. Thus, progress in reducing barriers to trade may depend on, and lead to, further progress in rules facilitating the exchange of money among states. As used by Ernst Haas, the term refers to a process whereby states upgrade or collaborate in issue areas of common interest, similar to the concept of ramification. See also **ramification.**

state. A legal entity composed of territory, a population, and an administration or government. It possesses sovereignty and recognition by other states. See also **government, sovereignty.**

structural. See **structure.**

structural determinist. One who believes that the structure of the international system largely determines the behavior of individual states and that there is very little effective choice for leaders of states. The term is usually used in a negative or critical sense against realists, neorealists, and some Marxists. Few, if any, theorists would admit to complete structural determinism in their theories, but some do assign greater weight to structure as a determinant of the behavior of states and other actors. See also **system, structure, neorealism, realism, Marxism.**

structure. The arrangement of parts of a whole, as in the structure of the international system being defined in terms of the distribution of capabilities or power among states. The international system structure, following this usage, may be bipolar, multipolar, or unipolar. Some theorists look for underlying structure associated with the anarchy of the system — the lack of central authority. For others, structure refers to observed patterns of behavior as among states, although still others contend that such a definition confuses underlying *structure* with *behavior*, or the interactions of states — concepts that are, and should be, kept analytically separate. Some theorists of dependency and the capitalist world-system use the term *structure* to describe relations or mechanisms of dominance, dependence, and exploitation. *Note:* One can also apply the term "structure" to the state–society level of analysis — such as the Federalist structure of the United States — and deduce expected behavior on the part of actors. See also **system, behavior, bipolar, multipolar, structural determinist.**

suboptimal. See **optimal.**

supranational. Beyond or above the state. For example, a world government would be a supranational authority that governs the relations among states.

synchronic. Refers to a study of phenomena at a given point in time as opposed to over a period of time. See also **diachronic.**

synthesis. Putting together parts to make a whole.

system. A set of interrelated parts or an arrangement of units connected in such a way as to form a unity or whole; an abstract concept used by many theorists to bring order to their work. The use of the term varies. For example, some theorists see the *international* system as being composed of states and other actors, whereas some authors see world capitalism as a system composed of classes with conflicting interests. Some systems are said to be *open* to external influences, whereas others are *closed* systems. Factors external to a system that may affect it are *exogenous*, whereas those internal to the system are often referred to as *endogenous* factors. Some systems are said to have certain inherent qualities or attributes, such as a tendency toward balance or equilibrium, although not all systems theorists assign such automaticity to systems. Some theorists use systems merely as toxonomies, or frameworks, for organizing research and analysis.

systemic. See **system.**

taxonomy, taxonomies. A classification as in a categorization of states as democratic, socialist, or fascist.

teleology, teleological. That phenomena are to be explained by the purposes they serve. In systems theory, for example, it is teleological to argue that the need for a system to return to some natural state of equilibrium causes units within the system to behave the way they do. It may be that unit interactions within a system have a tendency to produce equilibrium, but it is teleological in effect to reverse the causal flow and argue that this systemic purpose (equilibrium) somehow causes the behavior of actors within the system to occur so as to achieve this result. Similarly, some functionalist theories have been criticized to the extent that they are also teleological.

terms of trade. The ratio of a country's average export prices to its average import prices, especially regarding merchandise trade. When import prices rise faster than export prices, the terms of trade worsen. This is said to be the case for most less-developed countries since the 1950s; the prices of raw materials have generally lagged behind the prices of imported manufactured goods from developed countries.

theory. A set of interrelated propositions that aims to *explain* or *predict* phenomena, thereby attempting to make the world more intelligible. *Explanation* involves accounting for, or understanding causes of, such phenomena as war, arms races, and regional integration. In a loose sense, *prediction* amounts merely to forecasting, but in a strict sense it implies explanation sufficient to anticipate outcomes, given the presence of certain variables or conditions (for example, theories that would predict war as the outcome of arms races). *General* theories attempt a comprehensive or complete explanation of some phenomenon, whereas *partial* theories are often understood as initial steps or attempts to explain narrower aspects of the phenomenon under investigation. There are considerable differences about the use of the terms *microtheory* and *macrotheory*. Most theorists use the term *microtheory* to refer to partial theories and *macrotheory* to refer to grand theory that would, for example, explain all of international relations. For a more extensive discussion, see the text. See also **parsimonious theory, hypothesis.**

Third World. The economically less-developed (or underdeveloped) states of Asia, Africa, and Latin America. The *First World* includes the more industrially developed states in North America, Western Europe, Japan, Australia, and New Zealand; the *Second World* consists of the few remaining Marxist-Leninist countries. Some theorists have identified the poorest of the less-developed countries as constituting a *Fourth World*. See also **North–South, East, West,** and **East–West.**

traditionalism. A mode of thinking about international relations that emphasizes the studying of such disciplines as diplomatic history, international law, and philosophy in an attempt to develop better insights. Traditionalists tend to be skeptical of behavioralist approaches that are confined to strict scientific standards that include formal hypothesis testing and, usually, the use of statistical analysis. See also **behavior, methodology.**

transformation, system transformation. A *fundamental* change in the system, as in a shift from a multipolar to a bipolar world or vice versa. The creation of a world government to replace an anarchic system of sovereign states would be such a system transformation. In a domestic context, the overthrow of the bourgeoisie by the proletariat would be considered a transformation of the political, social, and economic order.

transgovernmental. Relations involving links, ties, or even coalitions among bureaucratic or other official actors of different states. To the extent that these are effective, they may be a means for bypassing central government authorities in each state, although some theorists consider such circumvention of authority more an exception to the usual pattern in which the state remains unitary and speaks with one voice. See also **transnational.**

transnational, transnationalism. Interactions and coalitions across state boundaries that involve such diverse nongovernmental actors as multinational corporations and banks, church groups, and terrorist networks. In some usages, transnationalism includes both nongovernmental as well as *transgovernmental* links. The term *transnational* is used both to label the actor (for example, a transnational actor) or a pattern of behavior (for example, an international organization that acts *transnationally*— operates across state borders). Theorists focusing on transnationalism often deemphasize the state as primary and unitary actor. See also **transgovernmental.**

uneven development. A concept used by Marxists and other theorists that emphasizes capitalism's unequal spread of global economic benefits. In Lenin's *Imperialism*, for example, he argued that the increasing concentration of capital in advanced capitalist states led to monopolies and cartels that sought foreign investments once national markets were exhausted. This spread of capitalism inevitably resulted in the exploitation of colonies. In the present period, uneven development continues to characterize not only individual national economies but the capitalist world as a whole. Both domestically and internationally, benefits accrue to the few.

unitary. Undivided, whole. In many realist analyses, states are viewed as unitary actors.

units of analysis. That which is being studied, such as a state.

utilitarians, utilitarianism. A doctrine developed in the nineteenth century that postulated that the greatest happiness of the greatest number should be the aim of all action. The term can also mean a belief that the value of anything is determined solely by its utility. Utilitarian thinking as applied to theory building tends to emphasize a rational decision-making process in which actors seek to maximize benefit or minimize cost.

utopian. See **idealist.**

values. Refers to the way things *ought* to be quite apart from the way things *are*. Political values would include preferences with respect to liberty, equality, order, and so on. A value is an estimate made of the worth or goodness of a goal or action. Also refers to measures as in numerical values. See also **normative.**

variable. A characteristic of an object or class of objects that may take on different values. The variable may be quantitative (such as height) or qualitative (such as marital status). In international relations research, for example, the class of objects may be states and the variable military power. Researchers wish to *operationalize* a variable, which means finding a way to measure the variable. Military power may be operationalized, for example, by using such indicators as number of nuclear weapons, amount of the gross national product devoted to military expenditures, or number of persons under arms. A *dependent variable* is simply what one is trying to explain, such as the frequency and intensity of war since 1800. *Independent variables* are factors that may help to explain or predict the dependent variable.

variable sum game. See **game theory.**

voluntarism, voluntarist. A philosophical position that reality is created by human will; that humans can affect, if not control, their destinies. In international relations, it generally means that decision makers have effective choice and are able to influence outcomes. As used in this volume, voluntarism is in opposition to the philosophical idea of determinism. See also **determinism.**

vulnerability interdependence. See **interdependence.**

war. To engage in hostilities and military operations, usually for some political purpose. War among states is *interstate* war; war between opposing parties within a state is *civil* war; war involving irregulars and unconventional tactics is *guerrilla* war. The explanation of war is traditionally the primary concern of scholars of international relations.

welfare issues. Socioeconomic and other issues associated with improving the living conditions and standards of people.

West. Generally, the countries of North America, Western Europe, and, paradoxically, Japan because of its level of industrial development and its links to other advanced capitalist states. See **East–West.**

world federalism. The goal of individuals favoring a world government that would have authority in certain areas over constituent states.

world politics. See **international relations.**

zero-sum game. See **game theory.**

INDEX

Order, in world politics, 119–122
Organizational process model
  crisis decision making, 307
  Cuban missile crisis, 343, 353–359
  and decision making, 238–239
Organski, A.F.K, 45

P

Pacifism, liberal pacifism, 263–266
Paine, Tom, 563
Pan movements, 508
Pavlov, D.G., 170
Peace
  and democratic capitalism, 264–265
  peaceful change, 218–219
Pearl Harbor, 237, 291
Peloponnesian War, The (Thucydides),
  37–39, 190, 203
Perceptions, and study of international
  relations, 286–300
Perpetual Peace (Kant), 274, 275
Pluralism
  anarchy in, 248–249
  basic assumptions in, 7–8, 228–229
  change in, 247–248
  compared to globalism, 450–451
  decision making in, 233–239
  ethnocentrism in, 250
  intellectual roots of, 229–233
  interdependence in, 229
  state in, 228–229
  system in, 245–247
  theory building in, 249
  transnationalism in, 239–245
  voluntarism in, 249–250
Poland, 163
Policy integration, and interdependence,
  392–394, 397
Political change, 144–152
  framework for understanding, 148–152
  nature of, 147–148
  neglect of study of, 144–145
Political economy, 13
  and globalism, 450
Political integration, 395–396
Politics
  high and low politics, 7
  and morality, 553–560, 564–565
  nature of, 562–566
  power politics, 563
Politics Among Nations (Morgenthau),
  190
Posen, Barry, 157, 158–159
Positivist view, 66

Power, 7
  definitions of, 44, 206
  measurement of, 44–45
  realism perspective, 44–45
  in structural realism, 206–211
Prebisch, Raul, 457, 515
Prince, The (Machiavelli), 39, 61, 91–94
Process of Government, The (Bentley), 233
Proletarian, 454
  proletarian revolution, 451–452
  semi-proletarian, 506
Public choice theory, 13
Public goods theory, 13
Puchala, Donald, 392

R

Rational policy model, Cuban missile
  crisis, 343, 345–352
Rational reconstruction method, 190
Rawls, John, 534, 538
Reagan, Ronald, 262–263, 523–524
Realism, 35–36
  balance of power in, 50–55, 64
  basic assumptions in, 5–7, 11, 187–189
  change in, 59–61, 64–65, 201–204
  criticisms of, 62, 65–66, 194–195
  intellectual roots of, 37–43
  interdependence in, 55–58, 406–407
  Melian dialogue, 84–90
  neorealism, 66
  power in, 44–45
  state in, 63–64
  structural. *See* Structural realism
  system in, 45–55, 62–63
  use of term, 61–62
Realpolitik, 39
Reformism, 455
Relativist position, moral choice, 533
Republic, Machiavellian, 266–267
Revolution, versus reform, 455
Ricardo, David, 230
Rights of Man (Paine), 563
Rosenau, James N., 2, 23, 210, 234, 247,
  287, 289, 438
Rousseau, Jean Jacques, 49, 50, 98, 130,
  132, 133–134, 136
Rummel, Rudolph J., 47, 265
Rush, Myron, 345
Russell, Bertrand, 125
Russett, Bruce, 11

S

Schelling, Thomas, 200, 346–347
Schlieffen Plan, 162, 164–165

Schumpeter, Joseph, 144, 263–266
Second Treatise on Government (Locke), 230
Security dilemma, 48, 159–161
  and alliance strategies, 162–164
  pluralist perspective, 248
Self-help situation, 48, 197
Seward, William Henry, 127
Singer, J. David, 3, 45, 53, 54, 265
Skobelev, Mikhail, 127
Small, M., 265
Smith, Adam, 230
Smoke, Richard, 196
Snyder, Glenn, 196, 200–201, 205
Snyder, Jack, 154
Snyder, Richard C., 234
Social contract, 41
  and moral choice, 533
Social integration, and interdependence, 391–392, 397
Socialism, 487
Social reform, 486–487
  purpose of, 486
"Sociology of Imperialisms" (Schumpeter), 263
Sovereignty, 41
  use of term, 502
Soviet Union, 54, 135, 163, 170–171
Stalin, Joseph, 170–171
States
  globalist view, 9–11
  pluralist perspective, 7–8, 228–229
  realist view, 5–6
  structure of, and war, 126–129
Strategy of Conflict (Schelling), 346–347
Structural realism, 52, 189
  balance of power in, 197–199
  and game theory, 200–201
  and historical cycles, 201–205
  and international systems, 192–195
  power in, 206–211
  as research program, 190–196
  usefulness of study of, 212–219
Structural transformation, 463
Study of War, A (Wright), 3
Subgroupism, 443
System
  as anarchy, 47–50
  and balance of power, 53–55
  and determinism, 63–64
  as distribution of capabilities, 50–53
  as interactions, 47
  pluralist perspective, 245–247
  realism perspective, 45–55
  stability and balance of power, 53–55

use of term, 46, 245–246, 380

T

Taylor, A.J.P., 166
Technological factors, change, 443, 445, 447
Terms of trade, 455
Theory
  creative theorizing, pre-conditions for, 24–33
  and international relations, 3–5
  meanings of, 3–4
  normative theory, 5
  parsimonious theory, 249
  pluralist perspective, 249
Theory of International Politics (Waltz), 196
Third World, 229, 410, 423, 450, 453, 459, 466, 527
Thucydides, 43, 50, 59, 84, 146, 203
  as realist, 37–39, 189, 190–191
Tocqueville, Alexis de, 233
Traditionalists, 2
Transformation, structural, 463
Transgovernmental coalitions, 239
Transnationalism, 443
  and globalism, 450–451
  and integration, 241–243
  and interdependence, 243–245
  and modernization, 239–240
  pluralist perspective, 239–245
Transnational organizations, 35
Treaty of Rome, 241
Truman, David, 233
Truman Doctrine, 291
Tucker, Robert W., 385
Twenty Years' Crisis (Carr), 42–43

U

Uneven global development, 450
Unionism, 487
United Nations Conference on Trade and Development, 455, 456, 457
United States, 45, 54–55
U.S. Power and the Multinational Corporation (Gilpin), 202–203
Units of analysis, 5, 452
Universalist, 119, 121
Utopianism, 43

V

Values
  of foreign policy making, 536–540

and integration and interdependence, 397
moral choice, 533–535
and world society, 379
Vansittart, Robert, 175, 176
Variables, 47, 235
independent and dependent, 58, 62
Variable-sum game, 241
Vasquez, John A., 186
Vietnam War, 237
Voluntarism, 237
and balance of power, 51, 52
pluralist perspective, 249–250
Vulnerability, and interdependence, 55–56

W

Wallerstein, Immanuel, 205, 459–461, 464, 501, 515
Waltz, Kenneth, 3, 11, 13, 51, 52, 53, 54, 123, 144, 154–162, 190, 192–193, 196, 207, 287, 396
War, 103–105
and historical cycles, 201–205
and human behavior, 124–126
and imperialism, 264
and international anarchy, 129–134
international wars, listing of, 272–273
morality of, 535–536
state of war, meaning of, 104–105, 108
and structure of states, 126–129
and tight alliances, 163–164
and uncertainty, 442
War and Change in World Politics (Gilpin), 59, 196, 201, 202, 204, 218
War Trap, The (de Mesquita), 3
Weber, Max, 2, 238

Welfare state, 379
Wight, Martin, 145
Wilson, Woodrow, 128
Wolfers, Arnold, 289, 290, 385
World Bank, 423–426, 431, 432
World-economy
nature of, 501–502
patterns of, 502–505
secular trends of, 505–509
as system in crisis, 509–512
use of term, 501
World Event/Interaction Survey project, 47
World society
billiard ball model, 377–379
cobweb model, 379–384
use of term, 377
and values, 379
World War I
alliance patterns in, 164–169
chain-ganging and buck-passing in, 176–178
crisis decision making in 1914 crisis, 316–326
origins of, 346
World War II
alliance patterns in, 169–176
chain-ganging and buck-passing in, 176–178
Wright, Quincy, 3, 308

Y

Yankelovich, Daniel, 447
Young, Oran, 387

Z

Zero-sum game, 241, 405, 451